KJV

Standard
LESSON COMMENTARY®

2008–2009

International Sunday School Lessons

Edited by
Ronald L. Nickelson

Published by
Standard Publishing
Jonathan Underwood, Senior Editor

Fifty-sixth Annual Volume

In This Volume

Artist
TITLE PAGES: James E. Seward
Cover design by DesignTeam
Lessons based on International Sunday School Lessons © 2006 by the Lesson Committee.

CD-ROM AVAILABLE

The *Standard Lesson Commentary*® is available separately in an electronic format. This compact disk contains the full text of the King James *Standard Lesson Commentary*® and *The NIV Standard Lesson Commentary*®, a variety of preparation resources powered by the Libronix Digital Library System, and a collection of presentation helps that can be projected or reproduced as handouts. Order #06009.

System Requirements: Windows Vista/XP/2000; Pentium 133 MHz processor (300MHz recommended), 64 Meg RAM (128 recommended); 60 Meg Available Hard Drive Space; 2x or better CD-ROM drive.

Index of Printed Texts, 2008–2009

The printed texts for 2008–2009 are arranged here in the order in which they appear in the Bible. Opposite each reference is the number of the page on which it appears in this volume.

Cumulative Index

A cumulative index for the Scripture passages used in the STANDARD LESSON COMMENTARY
for the years September 2004–August 2009 is provided below.

Fall Quarter 2008

The New Testament Community
(New Testament Survey)

Special Features

Lessons

Unit 1: Birth of a New Community

Unit 2: Growth of the New Community

Unit 3: Challenges in the New Community

About These Lessons

God's plan to bring the church into existence took centuries to implement. Growing the church has been His main project for centuries since. He will not allow His church to be defeated by challenges along the way! This quarter's lessons will show us the heart of God in all these areas.

Sep 7
Sep 14
Sep 21
Sep 28
Oct 5
Oct 12
Oct 19
Oct 26
Nov 2
Nov 9
Nov 16
Nov 23
Nov 30

A New Year's Resolution

THE ANCIENT JEWS observed the beginning of a new year twice annually in the forms of a "religious new year" and a "civil new year." Perhaps you have not thought about it, but most churches also recognize the arrival of a new year twice annually: our "civil year" begins on January 1, while our "curriculum year" begins with the first Sunday in September. So—happy New Year!

The arrival of this new year offers us a natural time for personal reflection, to examine our thinking about things. Our level of commitment to Bible study is one area all of us should review. There is no more important book to study! Yet how does the amount of time we spend reading the Bible compare with, say, reading the newspaper?

Bible study is demanding, but "worth it." Two useful tools that will help you get the most from your studies are the commentary that you are now reading and the *Standard Full Color Bible*. Use them together as you keep this New Year's resolution: "I will study my Bible with diligence this year."
—R. L. N.

International Sunday School Lesson Cycle
September 2004–August 2010

YEAR	FALL QUARTER (Sep., Oct., Nov.)	WINTER QUARTER (Dec., Jan., Feb.)	SPRING QUARTER (Mar., Apr., May)	SUMMER QUARTER (June, July, Aug.)
2004-2005	The God of Continuing Creation (Bible Survey)	Called to Be God's People (Bible Survey)	God's Project: Effective Christians (Romans, Galatians)	Jesus' Life, Ministry, and Teaching (Matthew, Mark, Luke)
2005-2006	"You Will Be My Witnesses" (Acts)	God's Commitment—Our Response (Isaiah; 1 & 2 Timothy)	Living in and as God's Creation (Psalms, Job, Ecclesiastes, Proverbs)	Called to Be a Christian Community (1 & 2 Corinthians)
2006-2007	God's Living Covenant (Old Testament Survey)	Jesus Christ: A Portrait of God (John, Philippians, Colossians, Hebrews, 1 John)	Our Community Now and in God's Future (1 John, Revelation)	Committed to Doing Right (Various Prophets, 2 Kings, 2 Chronicles)
2007-2008	God Creates (Genesis)	God's Call to the Christian Community (Luke)	God, the People, and the Covenant (1 & 2 Chronicles, Daniel, Haggai, Nehemiah)	Images of Christ (Hebrews, Gospels, James)
2008-2009	The New Testament Community (New Testament Survey)	Human Commitment (Character Studies)	Christ and Creation (Ezekiel, Luke, Acts, Ephesians)	Call Sealed with Promise (Exodus, Leviticus, Numbers, Deuteronomy)
2009-2010	Covenant Communities (Joshua, Judges, Ezra, Nehemiah, Mark, 1 & 2 Peter)	Christ the Fulfillment (Matthew)	Teachings on Community (Jonah, Ruth, New Testament)	Christian Commitment in Today's World (1 & 2 Thessalonians, Philippians)

"Creation" "Call" "Covenant" "Christ" "Community" "Commitment"

Our New Community

by Mark S. Krause

ARE YOU A "romantic" when it comes to the church? The term *romantic* came into use in the eighteenth century in relation to the rise of interest in classical studies. As Europe experienced a revival in the love of learning, many thinkers longed for the wisdom of the ancient world, the Roman world. They were categorized as *romantics*. Elements of romanticism were seen in art, literature, and especially in music. In this sense, we may define *romantic* as idealizing the heroic, the long ago, and the far away.

Now let's reconsider our question: Are you a romantic when it comes to the church? Was it always better in the past? What was it like to "do church" back in the days of the apostles?

Sometimes we forget that the early church was made up of people like us. They had different levels of commitment, integrity, and ability. Yet the first-century church had the guiding influence of men trained by Jesus to carry on His work—the apostles. The romanticist tendency in us may wish we could consult these heroic individuals concerning our church issues, but they are long ago and far away.

Yet their influence survives in the writings left to us in the pages of the New Testament. Here we may learn what the early church was like and how it negotiated the many crises and conflicts that it faced. This quarter's lessons will look at the new community of believers as found in the New Testament church.

Unit 1: September
Birth of a New Community

We will begin by exploring the birth of this new community as portrayed in the Gospels. Some Christians contend that the Gospels do not really apply to the church, since they describe events that happened before the birth of the church on the Day of Pentecost. Yet all of the Gospels were written many years *after* Pentecost for the benefit of the early church.

While we may not see the full manifestation of the new community (the church) in the Gospels, we can learn much by tracing the divine intentions of Jesus and the group of followers He was preparing. This unit's lessons focus primarily on the Gospel of Matthew.

Lesson 1 begins this series by looking at the work of the forerunner of Jesus, namely John the Baptist. John preached a message of repentance. He understood his task to be to prepare Israel for the Messiah by turning the people's hearts back to God. We do not look to John to provide answers for the general functioning of the modern church, but his bottom-line call for repentance will never be outdated.

The birth of Jesus as portrayed in Matthew is the focus of **Lesson 2**. We are used to seeing such a lesson at Christmastime, so its presence here may surprise us. Yet this lesson is important at this point because it reminds us that the mighty church of today had the humblest of beginnings. The key figures, namely Joseph and Mary, were not famous, well educated, or wealthy. They were simple people of faith whom God used for His glorious purposes.

The most comprehensive summary of Jesus' teachings is found in Matthew's "Sermon on the Mount." **Lesson 3** will examine the core message of this sermon, including the famous Beatitudes.

In this lesson, we begin to understand Jesus' introduction of the kingdom of Heaven into the human realm. Jesus intends that believers live by a set of values different from that of the world. When we live out those heavenly values, we will be blessed in our relationship to God and in the service we offer to Him.

Lesson 4 is the final lesson taken from Matthew. It deals with a seeming paradox in the teachings of Jesus: great leaders must be great servants. This principle of servant-leadership is often forgotten in the modern, hard-driving church. The concept is almost absent from modern culture. But it certainly deserves our renewed attention.

Unit 2: October
Growth of the New Community

Next, we will examine how the community grew and developed as we look at passages from the book of Acts. Acts is unique in the New Testament in tracing the historical development of the new community after the resurrection and ascension of Jesus. Some have proposed that "Acts of the Apostles," which traditionally has been the longer designation of this book, be changed to "Acts of the Holy Spirit." The Spirit is indeed the key figure in this book.

Lesson 5 introduces us to the Holy Spirit's work in bringing the new community (the church) into existence. The book of Acts depicts this as an empowerment and a unifying factor at this crucial point in time. As we will see, the power of the Holy Spirit is still available (and necessary) to the church today.

Some organizational growing pains of the new community are sketched in **Lesson 6.** The apostles found themselves confronted with the need to do a certain important ministry that nonetheless was a distraction from their main task. Even Jesus' handpicked associates, the apostles, couldn't do everything!

Delegation was the key. Here we will learn principles of delegation, shared responsibility, and selection of leaders. These principles still apply to the church today.

Lesson 7 does not focus on the community itself, but on an individual named Saul. Saul started out as a murderous enemy of the church. Under authority of the Jewish leaders, Saul persecuted Christians.

However, Saul (renamed Paul) eventually became a towering figure of influence for the church of then and now. How he got to that position provides insight into God's role in providing key leaders for the first-century church.

Our unit of lessons from the book of Acts concludes with an investigation of how the new community began to fulfill its mandate to evangelize all peoples. **Lesson 8** looks at the first strategic missionary activity in the history of the church. That effort involved a team sponsored by the church of Antioch.

Unit 3: November
Challenges in the New Community

Our third unit focuses on understanding how the early community dealt with the conflicts and struggles that were part of its growing pains. These final lessons come from Paul's epistles.

Diversity is a familiar topic in today's world. Much of the modern discussion centers on how to achieve greater diversity. But certain congregations of the first century already *were* diverse. What they needed was unity in their diversity. **Lesson 9** finds a church that was called to come to terms with a variety of spiritual gifts present within its community. That was the church in Corinth. Understanding diversity of gifts from God's perspective is a key requirement for a church to function according to God's plan, both then and now.

From a historical perspective, **Lesson 10** deals with a fascinating incident: Paul confronting Peter over an issue of hypocrisy. Our imperfect churches will always have varying levels of hypocrisy and attempts at self-righteousness. In this lesson,

we will learn why a certain hypocrisy was so damaging that Paul, the relative newcomer, was willing to risk everything to correct it.

Lesson 11 studies the benefits of a strife-free community. The primary blessing is the great joy that comes from having mutual support and a common purpose. Paul's letter to the Philippian church gives a taste of this joy yet today.

As the apostles of Christ aged and began to die, the need for a new generation of leaders became apparent. People should not be thrust into leadership roles without preparation. **Lesson 12** looks at some of the principles used by the apostle Paul for selecting and training church leaders.

Service for the church is not all fun and games. Sometimes it exacts a heavy emotional toll as we suffer hardships and share in the sufferings of others. The final lesson of this quarter, **Lesson 13,** reminds us that we are all weak without the grace of God and the support of our brothers and sisters in Christ.

Changed Times,
Unchanged Principles

Times certainly have changed, and the world of the apostles is markedly different from the world of the twenty-first century. Yet the foundational principles of how the church is to understand itself have remained constant.

This means that we can all use a touch of that romanticism that we mentioned at the outset. That touch will involve our longing to know of the early days of the new community more fully. Their struggles and victories are ours.

Answers to Quarterly Quiz
on page 8

Lesson 1—1. Judea. 2. false, he called them vipers. **Lesson 2**—1. in a dream. 2. false, they went by night. **Lesson 3**—1. true, the "poor in spirit" and those "persecuted for righteousness' sake." 2. works. **Lesson 4**—1. of James and John. 2. ransom. **Lesson 5**—1. false, they heard a sound like a mighty rushing wind. 2. Joel. **Lesson 6**—1. widows. 2. prayer. **Lesson 7**—1. true. 2. a vision. **Lesson 8**—1. deputy (also acceptable: proconsul or governor). 2. blinded. **Lesson 9**—1. peace. 2. deacons. **Lesson 10**—1. James, Cephas, John. 2. false, Peter refused to eat with the Gentiles. **Lesson 11**—1. belly. 2. true. **Lesson 12**—1. a good soldier. 2. equipped. **Lesson 13**—1. true. 2. grace.

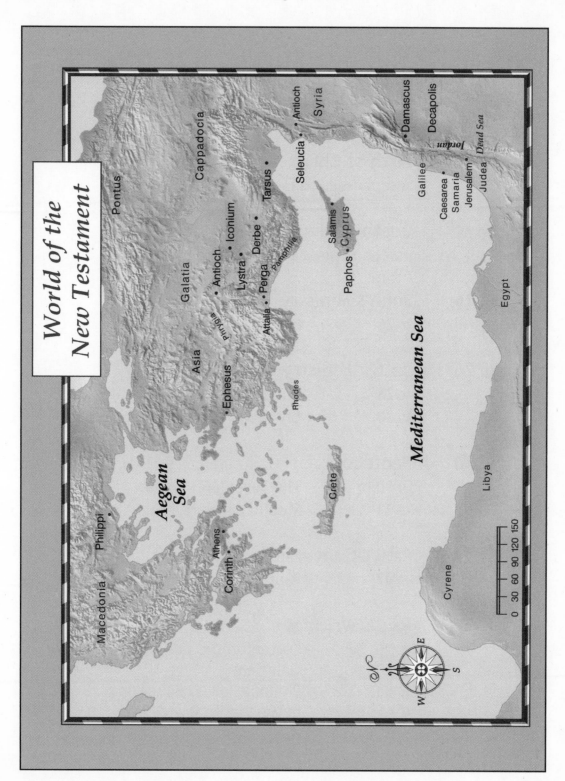

World of the New Testament

New Testament Survey 5 BC to AD 67

5 BC	**Birth of Christ**	
	Joseph flees to Egypt with Mary and Jesus	
4 BC	**Death of Herod**	
	Joseph returns to Nazareth with Mary and Jesus	
AD 26	**John's Ministry**	
	AD 26	Baptism of Jesus
AD 26	**Jesus' Ministry**	
	AD 28	The Sermon on the Mount
	AD 30	Crucifixion and Resurrection
AD 30	**Pentecost**	
	AD 30 or 31	The Seven are chosen
	AD 32	Stephen is martyred
AD 34	**Paul's Conversion**	
	AD 47	Paul's missionary journeys begin
AD 56-57	**Paul's writings**	
	AD 56, 57	Letters to the Corinthians
	AD 58	Galatians
	AD 63	Philippians and Ephesians
	AD 65, 67	Letters to Timothy

"Let Us Reason Together"

Using Study Groups in Teaching

by James Riley Estep, Jr.

CHRISTIAN EDUCATORS often advocate the use of small groups as a teaching method for adults. However, the effectiveness of this method sometimes falls short. This occurs when small group discussions become mere time-fillers or serve as little more than opportunities for fellowship over coffee. To maximize the learning potential of small groups, we can make them *study groups*.

What makes a *small group* a *study group*? In study groups, adult learners are asked to do more than merely reflect on personal experience or share perspective. Rather, a study group processes *content*. While group members may on occasion share in a personal way, that will be primarily a means of introducing the subject of the content to be learned. This approach maximizes the learning potential of this teaching method.

What are the benefits of study groups? In the lecture method, the instructor "stands and delivers." It is a static method of teaching, since the teacher often does not plan for engagement or dialogue. The use of study groups is more dynamic. Not only does such a method *require* dialogue between the teacher and the learners, the learners themselves also will be engaged in dialogue among themselves. Thus the class is not only taught by the teacher, but also forms what may be thought of as minicommunities of learning that are centered on studying the biblical text. Thus everyone is involved in learning God's truth actively.

What is your role as teacher in preparing to use study groups? The use of study groups requires you to prepare in four ways. First, you as the teacher must be prepared both to talk and to be silent! You may have a ready answer to a question posed to the class (or posed by someone in the class), but you will need to harness your enthusiasm to share that answer until your learners have had adequate opportunity to discuss it among themselves.

Second, you as a teacher often will need more intellectual preparation for study groups than for the lecture method because of the near certainty of alternative answers or even (gasp!) wrong answers. You will find it helpful to think through in advance possible responses to the study group questions provided in the lesson plan.

Third, you as the teacher often will have to begin your lesson preparation earlier in the week. This is because the study group method can require handouts, overhead transparencies or PowerPoint® slides, or objects and games.

Fourth, a vital part of your preparation will be to arrive early in your classroom since you may need to make physical changes in the seating arrangements to fit the study group method. Also, with more teaching materials to use more time may be needed to set things up (example: getting your computer ready for a PowerPoint® presentation). Preparation for the use of study groups often requires more work than does the lecture method.

What about presentation? Five practices make for the effective use of study groups. First, allow students adequate time to share with one another. Let them know how many minutes they have to discuss an item; then give a one-minute warning that "time is almost up." Second, make an intentional decision when you form groups whether or not you want to keep couples together. Groups of odd numbers (three, five, etc.) allow for "unattached" students to feel like they fit in. Groups larger than eight usually don't work well.

Third, roam around while your students are in their groups. This lets you hear what directions the discussions are taking and redirect if needed. Fourth, write student responses on the board when that time comes. This conveys the fact that you as teacher value their responses. It also ensures that you are hearing them accurately. It also allows students to remember what has been said.

Fifth, try to affirm every answer. Rarely will a response be so off track that it deserves an outright *No!* Instead, affirm what is right in the answer, and then provide the correction. "I see your point, but . . ." or "Well, that would be true if . . ." will encourage discussion and dialogue without the fear of being slapped down for a "wrong" response.

No fear! Teachers of adults may avoid using small groups out of fear—fear of losing focus, fear of allowing personal interests to take over, fear that the Bible study will degenerate into a "what it means to me" outcome. But designing your *small groups* to be *study groups* will help your students benefit from a focused investigation of the content and proper application of Scripture. Try it!

Quarterly Quiz

The questions on this page may be used in several ways: as a pretest at the beginning of the quarter; as a review at the end of the quarter; or as a review after each lesson. The questions are based on the Scripture text of each lesson (King James Version). ***The answers are on page 4.***

Lesson 1

1. John the Baptist preached in a region referred to as the wilderness of _____. *Matthew 3:1*
2. John called some Jews a family of poisonous spiders. T/F. *Matthew 3:7*

Lesson 2

1. How did the angel of the Lord appear to Joseph? (sudden physical appearance, in a vision, in a dream?) *Matthew 1:20*
2. Joseph, Mary, and baby Jesus rose early in the morning to flee to Egypt according to the Lord's command. T/F. *Matthew 2:14*

Lesson 3

1. In the Beatitudes, two groups are promised "the kingdom of heaven." T/F. *Matthew 5:3-10*
2. The command to "let your light so shine," refers to our good _____. *Matthew 5:16*

Lesson 4

1. Whose mother asked Jesus that her sons be allowed to sit at His side in the new kingdom? (of James and John; of some famous priests; of the children He blessed?) *Matthew 20:20*
2. Jesus came to give His life as a _____ for many. *Matthew 20:28*

Lesson 5

1. On Pentecost, the apostles experienced the physical force of a strong wind before they began to speak in other languages. T/F. *Acts 2:2*
2. In Peter's sermon on the Day of Pentecost, his main Scripture text was from the Old Testament book of _____. *Acts 2:16*

Lesson 6

1. In Acts 6, the neglect of which group caused dissension in the church? (the orphans, the unsaved, certain widows?) *Acts 6:1*
2. The apostles appointed seven men to serve tables so that the apostles could devote themselves to the ministry of the Word and _____. *Acts 6:4*

Lesson 7

1. Saul was commissioned by the high priest to go to Damascus and arrest both men and women who were disciples of Jesus. T/F. *Acts 9:2*

2. How did Ananias know how to find Saul in Damascus? (he heard the news in the synagogue, he had a vision, through a friend?) *Acts 9:10*

Lesson 8

1. Sergius Paulus was the _____ of Cyprus. *Acts 13:4, 7*
2. What happened to the sorcerer Elymas as a result of his opposition to Paul? (struck dead, converted to Christianity, blinded?) *Acts 13:11*

Lesson 9

1. Paul called believers to maintain the unity of the Spirit in the bond of _____. *Ephesians 4:3*
2. Which is not part of the list of people given by God to perfect the saints? (deacons, prophets, evangelists?) *Ephesians 4:11, 12*

Lesson 10

1. Which three did Paul identify as the pillars of the church in Jerusalem? (Barnabas, Peter, Silas; James, Cephas, John; Peter, Paul, Mary?) *Galatians 2:9*
2. Paul corrected Peter in Antioch because Peter required the Gentiles to be circumcised. T/F. *Galatians 2:12*

Lesson 11

1. In the third chapter of Philippians, Paul condemned those whose god is their _____. *Philippians 3:19*
2. Paul found it necessary to ask two believers to quit fighting. T/F. *Philippians 4:2*

Lesson 12

1. Paul asked Timothy to endure hardship in the manner of what? (an athlete in training, a slave for the Lord, a good soldier?) *2 Timothy 2:3*
2. Paul stated that all Scripture is useful to help believers be _____ for every good work. *2 Timothy 3:16, 17*

Lesson 13

1. In 2 Corinthians, Paul said he had been in three shipwrecks as a part of his travels for the gospel. T/F. *2 Corinthians 11:25*
2. God told Paul that His _____ was sufficient for him. *2 Corinthians 12:9*

Community of Repentance

September 7
Lesson 1

DEVOTIONAL READING: 1 Peter 2:1-10.

BACKGROUND SCRIPTURE: Mark 1:1-8; Matthew 3:1-12.

PRINTED TEXT: Mark 1:1-8; Matthew 3:1-3, 7-9.

Mark 1:1-8

1 The beginning of the gospel of Jesus Christ, the Son of God.

2 As it is written in the prophets, Behold, I send my messenger before thy face, which shall prepare thy way before thee.

3 The voice of one crying in the wilderness, Prepare ye the way of the Lord, make his paths straight.

4 John did baptize in the wilderness, and preach the baptism of repentance for the remission of sins.

5 And there went out unto him all the land of Judea, and they of Jerusalem, and were all baptized of him in the river of Jordan, confessing their sins.

6 And John was clothed with camel's hair, and with a girdle of a skin about his loins; and he did eat locusts and wild honey;

7 And preached, saying, There cometh one mightier than I after me, the latchet of whose shoes I am not worthy to stoop down and unloose.

8 I indeed have baptized you with water: but he shall baptize you with the Holy Ghost.

Matthew 3:1-3, 7-9

1 In those days came John the Baptist, preaching in the wilderness of Judea,

2 And saying, Repent ye: for the kingdom of heaven is at hand.

3 For this is he that was spoken of by the prophet Isaiah, saying, The voice of one crying in the wilderness, Prepare ye the way of the Lord, make his paths straight.

. . . .

7 But when he saw many of the Pharisees and Sadducees come to his baptism, he said unto them, O generation of vipers, who hath warned you to flee from the wrath to come?

8 Bring forth therefore fruits meet for repentance:

9 And think not to say within yourselves, We have Abraham to our father: for I say unto you, that God is able of these stones to raise up children unto Abraham.

GOLDEN TEXT: Repent ye: for the kingdom of heaven is at hand.—Matthew 3:2.

The New Testament Community
Unit 1: Birth of a New Community
(Lessons 1–4)

Lesson Aims

After participating in this lesson, each student will be able to:

1. Summarize the content of John the Baptist's preaching.

2. Explain the meaning of repentance.

3. Write a song, poem, prayer, or other expression of repentance.

Lesson Outline

INTRODUCTION

    A. Repent!

    B. Lesson Background

I. PROPHECY OF REPENTANCE (Mark 1:1-3)

    A. Person (vv. 1, 2)

    B. Preparation (v. 3)

II. NEED FOR REPENTANCE (Mark 1:4-6)

    A. Message (v. 4)

    B. Response (v. 5)

        Starting Over

    C. Messenger (v. 6)

III. OBJECT OF REPENTANCE (Mark 1:7, 8)

    A. Messiah's Worthiness (v. 7)

    B. Messiah's Action (v. 8)

IV. CALL FOR REPENTANCE (Matthew 3:1-3, 7-9)

    A. Time for Repentance (vv. 1-3)

    B. Fruit of Repentance (vv. 7-9)

        "Mistakes Were Made"

CONCLUSION

    A. "It's Time to Get Ready!"

    B. Repentance Means Change

    C. Prayer

    D. Thought to Remember

Introduction

A. Repent!

The ancient city of Nineveh must have been astonished to have a whale-bleached Jew stand on the city streets and proclaim, "Repent or perish!" Fortunately for them, they listened to the warning and escaped destruction (see Jonah 1:2; 3:5-10).

It is hard to imagine a prophet finding similar success in any modern city. If someone stands on the sidewalks of New York or London and shouts a message of doom, he will be ignored or hustled off to a psychiatric ward. Trying to get an entire community to repent is a tough job assignment.

John the Baptist had such an assignment. He was sent to warn the Jewish people to repent so that they would be ready for the coming of the Messiah. God wanted the people to whom Jesus would be sent to be a community of repentance.

B. Lesson Background

For over 400 years the Jewish nation had not heard a word from God. During that time they suffered oppression under the Greeks, the Syrians, and the Romans, but there was no word from God. At one point they rose up and tried to win their freedom during the time of the Maccabees, but there was still no word from God.

Malachi was the last prophet who had spoken for God. He promised another messenger (Malachi 3:1). In the closing verse of the Old Testament, the Lord called for changed hearts: "Lest I come and smite the earth with a curse" (Malachi 4:6). Then there was silence . . . for 400 years.

Suddenly, loudly, outlandishly, the silence was broken. The rabbis in the cities and the peasants in the villages began to hear reports of a man in the desert who claimed to speak for God. The message he brought for the people of God was always the same: *Repent! Prepare the way for the Lord!*

I. Prophecy of Repentance (Mark 1:1-3)

God loves His people. In spite of their sins and backsliding, God repeatedly has sent messengers to summon His people to repentance. As prophesied by Isaiah, John the Baptist issues a great call for repentance by God's community. The people are to prepare for the arrival of the Lord: God's own Son is coming to redeem the world.

A. Person (vv. 1, 2)

1. The beginning of the gospel of Jesus Christ, the Son of God.

Just as the story of creation opens "In the beginning" (Genesis 1:1), the story of Jesus' ministry in the Gospel of Mark also starts at *the beginning*. What Mark proceeds to write is more than just a biography; it is a *gospel*. It has the historical facts of a biography, but it is also like a sermon—a message intended to create repentance and faith.

Our modern word *gospel* comes from the Old English *god-spel*, which means "good talk" or "good tale." The original Greek word used by Mark literally means "good news." Mark's good news is full of action, moving quickly from one exciting event to another.

This is the story *of Jesus Christ, the Son of God*. The name *Jesus* means "Yahweh is salvation." Just as that name implies, He has come from Heaven to bring forgiveness and eternal salvation. *Christ* means the "Anointed One," the one chosen for an important office. Mark will tell us, then, how God's own Son is being sent as God's chosen instrument of salvation for humanity.

2. As it is written in the prophets, Behold, I send my messenger before thy face, which shall prepare thy way before thee.

God had long ago prepared for the sending of His Son. He told Adam and Eve that one would come who would bruise the serpent's head (Genesis 3:15). He assured faithful Abraham that his descendant would bless "all families of the earth" (Genesis 12:3). He pledged that King David would have a descendant who would have an everlasting kingdom (2 Samuel 7:12, 13). He foretold through many of *the prophets* that the Messiah was coming.

The quotation in this verse is taken from Malachi 3:1 (also quoted in Luke 7:27), where the Lord promises to send a *messenger* before He comes (compare Exodus 23:20). In fulfillment of this prophecy, the messenger is John the Baptist.

B. Preparation (v. 3)

3. The voice of one crying in the wilderness, Prepare ye the way of the Lord, make his paths straight.

The next part of Mark's quotation of prophecy comes from Isaiah 40:3. Isaiah, sometimes called "the gospel prophet," wrote much about the coming Messiah (example: Isaiah 53). He wrote words of encouragement to the Hebrew nation that later (from Isaiah's perspective) would be held in captivity in Babylon. They could be sure that God had not forgotten them and would give them deliverance. In a greater sense, his words become encour-

---

How to Say It

BABYLON. *Bab*-uh-lun.
BETHLEHEM. *Beth*-lih-hem.
JONAH. *Jo*-nuh.
JUDEA. Joo-*dee*-uh.
MACCABEES. *Mack*-uh-bees.
MALACHI. *Mal*-uh-kye.
NAAMAN. *Nay*-uh-mun.
NAZARETH. *Naz*-uh-reth.
NINEVEH. *Nin*-uh-vuh.
PHARISEES. *Fair*-ih-seez.
SADDUCEES. *Sad*-you-seez.
SYRIANS. *Sear*-ee-unz.

---

agement that a final deliverance—freedom from sin's captivity—would come with the Messiah.

The *one crying in the wilderness* is John the Baptist, who preaches boldly as he moves through the wilderness of Judea, northwest of the Dead Sea. God's people must mend their ways and turn back to God. What prepares *the way of the Lord* is John's message of the need to repent. See the next verse.

II. Need for Repentance (Mark 1:4-6)

John is a startling person, and he preaches a startling message. People flock into the desolate wilderness to be scolded by him. Though his words are sharp, they ring true: people need to repent!

A. Message (v. 4)

4. John did baptize in the wilderness, and preach the baptism of repentance for the remission of sins.

Part of John's ministry of preparation is to *baptize* people *for the remission of sins*. Note the connection between these ideas in Acts 2:38. There is no record that John has priestly authority to intercede for sins, and the water has no magical power to cleanse spiritually. Yet John is authorized by God to issue His invitation and proclaim His promise. God will remit sins—if the people will respond. [See question #1, page 16.]

B. Response (v. 5)

5. And there went out unto him all the land of Judea, and they of Jerusalem, and were all baptized of him in the river of Jordan, confessing their sins.

The people of *Judea* and *Jerusalem* do respond—in large numbers. People come, listen, become convicted, and line up to be *baptized*. Naaman the Syrian commander had dipped seven times in the *Jordan* to be cleansed of his leprosy in response to God's spokesman Elisha (2 Kings 5:1-14; Luke 4:27). Now, hundreds of years later, God's people submit to the demand of a new spokesman. A significant part of their sincere repentance is the *confessing* of *sins*. This is a public admission of guilt.

STARTING OVER

A search of the Internet will reveal numerous online dating services. These services promise that life can be enriched with a new relationship. There are online services for people with widely varying interests. For example, Christians looking for marriage partners have Web sites designed to appeal just to them. (Someone in your class may have met his or her spouse this way.)

As important as finding the right marriage partner may be, John was offering something even more significant to his audience: the opportunity to start life over in one's relationship with God. John promised to those who accepted his baptism that God would forgive their sins.

That promise was something his audience needed, regardless of marital status, age, or any other demographic. Having sins forgiven is of far greater long-term importance to our well-being than finding the right person to marry.   —C. R. B.

C. Messenger (v. 6)

6. And John was clothed with camel's hair, and with a girdle of a skin about his loins; and he did eat locusts and wild honey.

John does not look like any typical rabbi! His appearance makes him seem out of place in any gathering of learned Pharisees or wealthy Sadducees. His clothing shows that he cares nothing for the conventions of society. His sharply worded message is not designed to win him any friends.

John's garments are woven of coarse *camel's hair*, commonly worn only by poor people. The clothing and wide leather belt link him with Elijah (2 Kings 1:8). [See question #2, page 16.] In fulfillment of the prophecy of Malachi 4:5, John the Baptist comes as Elijah to issue the call to repentance (Mark 9:9-13). *Locusts* are permissible under Jewish dietary laws (Leviticus 11:21, 22). This diet plus his austere clothing serve as a rebuke to the physical and spiritual softness of God's people.

III. Object of Repentance (Mark 1:7, 8)

What matters most to John is not a comfortable life, but his message regarding the Messiah.

A. Messiah's Worthiness (v. 7)

7. And preached, saying, There cometh one mightier than I after me, the latchet of whose shoes I am not worthy to stoop down and unloose.

John is keenly aware of his own unworthiness in relation to the coming Messiah. See Malachi 3:1.

B. Messiah's Action (v. 8)

8. I indeed have baptized you with water: but he shall baptize you with the Holy Ghost.

John immediately follows the analysis of his own worthiness in relation to that of the coming Messiah (v. 7) with an assessment of their respective roles. As we see John preaching in this wilderness setting about Jesus' baptism *with the Holy Ghost*, we recall Old Testament connections between the Spirit and Israel's experiences in the wilderness during the exodus (Isaiah 63:11-14). The coming action by the Messiah can be seen as something of a "new exodus"—this exodus being from a spiritual wilderness (Isaiah 32:15; 44:3).

IV. Call for Repentance (Matthew 3:1-3, 7-9)

The Gospel of Matthew also emphasizes John's call for repentance. This is a necessary prelude to the ministry of Jesus.

A. Time for Repentance (vv. 1-3)

1. In those days came John the Baptist, preaching in the wilderness of Judea.

The first two chapters of Matthew set the stage for the appearance of *John the Baptist* and the beginning of the adult ministry of Jesus. Those two chapters thus serve as the backdrop for the phrase *in those days* that opens chapter 3. These are days when a tyrant king kills babies in Bethlehem in a vain attempt to eliminate Jesus. These are days when an innocent family has to flee to Egypt. These are days when the possibility of further persecution causes that family to avoid Judea and make their home in Nazareth.

It is in such days that John the Baptist arrives on the scene. The primary feature of John's ministry is *preaching*. He does not come to do marriage counseling, build small-group ministries, etc.

2. And saying, Repent ye: for the kingdom of heaven is at hand.

In a harsh land, John comes preaching the need to *repent*. He knows the job God has sent him to do, and he zealously carries out his task. Matthew records this part of John's message as that which Jesus himself will soon preach: *Repent ye: for the kingdom of heaven is at hand* (compare Matthew 4:17; 10:7). Before God's rule can come to the hearts of people, some changes have to be made!

The *kingdom of heaven* (called "the kingdom of God" in Mark and Luke) is both God's realm and God's rule over that realm. In other words, it is

---

VISUALS FOR THESE LESSONS

The visual pictured in each lesson (example: page 13) is a small reproduction of a large, full-color poster included in the *Adult Resources* packet for the Fall Quarter. That packet also contains the very useful *Presentation Helps* on a CD for teacher use. The packet is available from your supplier. Order No. 192.

both a kingdom and a kingship. It is a kingdom that is not of this world (see John 18:36). It is a kingship that rules over the hearts of people (see Luke 17:21). The Jews have long awaited a Messiah to establish a political kingdom on earth. Will they be able to accept God's plan instead?

3. For this is he that was spoken of by the prophet Isaiah, saying, The voice of one crying in the wilderness, Prepare ye the way of the Lord, make his paths straight.

Matthew, Mark, and Luke quote exactly the same words from *Isaiah* (see Isaiah 40:3; Mark 1:3; and Luke 3:4; compare John 1:23). That *prophet* had good news for the Jewish nation hundreds of years prior. God has not abandoned them; He will come to their rescue! [See question #3, page 16.]

When Isaiah speaks of the coming of *the Lord*, he refers to more than just God the Father. In this verse there is a clear unity of Father and Son, since it is in the coming of Jesus that the prophecy is fulfilled. Jesus will even say that Isaiah had seen His glory and had spoken of Him (see John 12:41). Scripture contains other examples of this idea of seeing in Jesus the fulfillment of Old Testament statements about *the Lord* (see Psalm 68:18 and Ephesians 4:8; Psalm 102:25-27 and Hebrews 1:10-12).

B. Fruit of Repentance (vv. 7-9)

7. But when he saw many of the Pharisees and Sadducees come to his baptism, he said unto them, O generation of vipers, who hath warned you to flee from the wrath to come?

When the religious leaders arrive, John does not give them a friendly welcome. Although the *Pharisees* are known for their public piety and the *Sadducees* have control of public worship at the temple, John addresses them with contempt. Whether *come to his baptism* means "come in order to be baptized" or "come to where he is baptizing," they have not repented. John sees them as arrogant spectators, not humble participants. In John's eyes they are no better than *vipers* (compare Isaiah 14:29; 30:6; Matthew 12:34).

With bitter sarcasm, John asks how they have found out about *the wrath to come*. His clear insinuation is that they have not been listening to God and are ignorant of His will. They are not sincerely seeking truth, nor even innocently curious about his preaching—they are openly suspicious (see John 1:19-25). [See question #4, page 16.]

8. Bring forth therefore fruits meet for repentance.

Genuine repentance means more than just a mental adjustment. Repentance is a total transformation on the inside that produces a total change of behavior on the outside. Inner change without

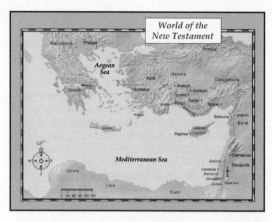

Visual for Lesson 1. *Keep this map posted for the entire quarter for a geographical perspective. It will be particularly helpful for Lesson 5.*

outer change cannot be genuine; outer change without inner change cannot endure.

Thus John the Baptist demands that people *bring forth* the *fruits* that befit *repentance*. As Jesus will later teach, good trees produce good fruit, but bad trees do not (Matthew 7:17). For John the Baptist, the Pharisees and Sadducees are prime examples of bad trees. Any tree (individual or nation) that does not produce the fruit of repentance will be chopped down and burned (see Matthew 3:10; Luke 13:6-9). [See question #5, page 16.]

9. And think not to say within yourselves, We have Abraham to our father: for I say unto you, that God is able of these stones to raise up children unto Abraham.

John knows what the immediate response of the religious leaders will be. When they hear John's call to repentance, they will say to themselves, "Yes, but *we have Abraham* as *our father*." As children of Abraham, they are children of the covenant. They are God's favorites—He surely will not pour out His wrath on them!

In the face of such self-righteous complacency, John has a surprising statement: *God is able* to make covenant children out of *stones*! The Jewish religious leaders should remember that God made the human race out of the dust of the ground in the first place. If He so chooses, He can make people out of rocks. Even more importantly, the Jewish leaders should remember that the covenant with Abraham was God's doing. It was the power and sovereignty of God—not of Abraham—that brought the covenant into existence.

In just a matter of three more years, God will indeed raise up new children to Abraham and His covenant. These children will not come from stones, but from Gentiles. They will not replace the Jews as God's people, but will join repentant Jews in the new covenant of Jesus Christ. In that covenant both Jews and Gentiles will be welcome to join God's community. But repentance comes first.

It is hard for so-called "good" people to repent. People who have complete confidence in their own goodness have a mental block at this point. John the Baptist comes to shake people out of their complacency and make them admit their sinfulness. Those who repent open themselves to the favor of God. Those who do not repent put themselves in a position to receive God's wrath.

"MISTAKES WERE MADE"

We hear halfhearted apologies frequently these days. In some cases the so-called "apology" is phrased something like this: "I regret that someone was offended by what I said or did." What the speaker really means is, "I'm sorry that there is anyone so thin-skinned as actually to have taken offense at my innocuous comments or my perfectly innocent mistake."

A different way to apologize is to say "mistakes were made." Apparently, a mistake is like the weather—it just sort of happens without anyone in particular causing it to be so. This fits our culture's reluctance to accept personal responsibility for any imperfections in thought, word, or behavior. *Sin* is such an old-fashioned concept!

John's message was very different from our modern approach to life. Today, some would request that John apologize for his intemperate language about being snakes that need repentance. After all, that may hurt someone's feelings! But he didn't apologize, because he spoke the truth: we all need to repent to experience God's salvation. —C. R. B.

Home Daily Bible Readings

Monday, Sep. 1—God's Coming Messenger (Malachi 3:1-5)

Tuesday, Sep. 2—A Voice in the Desert (Isaiah 40:1-5)

Wednesday, Sep. 3—A Voice Crying Out (Isaiah 40:6-11)

Thursday, Sep. 4—A Voice of Warning (Matthew 3:4-10)

Friday, Sep. 5—A Voice from Heaven (Matthew 3:11-17)

Saturday, Sep. 6—God's Holy People (1 Peter 2:1-10)

Sunday, Sep. 7—John Prepares the Way (Matthew 3:1-3; Mark 1:1-8)

Conclusion

A. "It's Time to Get Ready!"

Children often need to be told, "Hurry up! It's time to get ready!" Perhaps it's time for church or a special activity; perhaps company is coming. The importance of the event will require fresh clothing and a general cleanup.

The children of God in Judea also needed to get ready. The Messiah was coming, so they needed to wash up and get clean. In their case the cleansing needed to start on the inside with repentance—a change of mind. Only with this spiritual transformation would they be ready for His coming.

John said, "He that cometh after me is mightier than I" (Matthew 3:11), so Jesus was certainly important enough to deserve their preparation. When He came, He invited them into the community that John preached, the community characterized by repentance and forgiveness.

B. Repentance Means Change

Repentance means change: a change of heart and attitude that leads to changed behavior. We must be ready to change, because God himself does not change. As Malachi reminded Israel, "For I am the Lord, I change not" (Malachi 3:6). As James wrote in the New Testament, in the Father there is "no variableness, neither shadow of turning" (James 1:17). God will not compromise His holiness to meet us halfway; therefore, we must repent completely. [See question #6, page 16.]

The opening word of John's message is "Repent!" (Matthew 3:2). The opening word of Jesus' ministry is "Repent!" (Matthew 4:17). The first demand by Peter in his sermon on the Day of Pentecost is "Repent!" (Acts 2:38). Obviously, we must approach God's kingdom through repentance.

Repentance is not a one-time thing, but is continual. When we sin, we are to confess our failure (1 John 1:9). If our hearts grow cold, we repent and return to our first works (Revelation 2:4, 5). The changes inside us must be continuing changes, as God patiently remakes us in His image (Ephesians 4:24; Colossians 3:10). This side of Heaven, we will always need to repent.

C. Prayer

Our Father, we admit our weakness and sinfulness. Help us to change our hearts and mend our ways. May we always be a community of repentance, eager to hear Your voice and to follow Your will. In Christ's name we pray. Amen.

D. Thought to Remember

Make repentance a priority.

Learning by Doing

This page contains an alternative lesson plan emphasizing learning activities. Some of these activities are also found in the helpful student book, Adult Bible Class.

Into the Lesson

Have these four scrambled words in view as learners arrive: *ACEEENNPRT, HIILMTUY, AELSUV, CEEIRSV.* Say to the class, "These four words are the key words of our first four lessons in this study of 'The New Testament Community.' What are they?"

As they unscramble the four—*repentance, humility, values,* and *service*—ask, "Are there other key characteristics you think we should note that describe the essence of the New Testament community, the church?" You may wish to highlight others that are a part of the whole series, such as *evangelistic fervor* (Lesson 8) and *joy* (Lesson 11).

Write as large as possible the word *REPENT* and an exclamation mark on the board. Say, "One of the big words (and ideas) of the Bible is *repent!* And it can hardly be written without the exclamation mark. It must be articulated with urgency."

Distribute four index cards, each having one of these references written on it: Ezekiel 18:30-32; Acts 17:30; 2 Peter 3:9; Revelation 3:3a. Ask the four recipients to find the verses and read them aloud with emphasis. After your four readers finish, say *"Repent!* is the constant, intensive appeal and command of God. Today's lesson reveals that it is repentance that lays a foundation for the New Testament community (the church), our theme for the quarter."

Into the Word

As you introduce today's text, ask, "What is appropriate about using the concept of repentance to begin a series such as this?" The obvious response is that no one becomes a part of the church without repentance. Learners may have additional responses, including Peter's answer to the crowd in Jerusalem on the Day of Pentecost, when the church came into being (Acts 2:38).

Say, "John the Baptist epitomizes the concept of repentance." Draw a simple stick figure on the board and say, "Here is John in simple clothes." Add a sketch of a simple table with two bowls, and say, "Here is John's simple diet." Add a few hills and scrubby bushes and say, "Here is John's simple home." Add a dialogue balloon over the stick figure, and say, "Here is John's simple message," as you write in the word *"Repent!"* Repeat: "John epitomizes the concept of repentance."

Ask the class to explain how each of the following elements of John's life and ministry is established in today's text (or other texts about John, such as Luke 1, 3; Matthew 14) and how each enhanced John's call to repentance (read each in turn):

1. John's life was lived to draw attention to Jesus, not to himself.

2. John did what God called him to do.

3. John lived simply, without extravagance in needs or wants.

4. John confronted sin without hesitation and without fear of those confronted.

5. John's "success" in life was unrelated to money, prestige, comfort, or typical human relationships and pleasures.

Allow freedom of expression, but expect such ideas as the following, numbered to match the five statements above:

1. The Christian's call to repentance includes turning one's focus off of self and onto the person and work of Jesus.

2. God's call for repentance will be followed by a call to fulfill God's will in one's life.

3. A call to repentance is always a call away from materialism and excess.

4. The new covenant call to repentance is a call to speak up for righteousness at every turn, a call to forsake and despise sin.

5. Success in life is not to be judged by worldly accomplishment, but only by the evaluation of the Savior.

Into Life

Call this activity *A Desirable Obituary and Epitaph.* Have one of your good oral readers read aloud Matthew 14:3-12 (on John's death). Then call for your class to write John's obituary and epitaph. You may wish to consider forming several small groups for this activity, but give each the same assignment. After a short time of deliberation and work, call for the results to be read aloud. Ask, "What elements of these would you want others to hear about you following your own death?"

Ask learners to consider whether their own gravestones could be engraved with the words *Repentant One.* Note that it would be an appropriate epitaph for the one whose life was characterized by a lifelong repentance from sin.

Let's Talk It Over

The questions on this page are designed to promote discussion of the lesson by the class and to encourage application of the lesson Scriptures. The answers provided are only discussion starters. Let your class talk it over from there.

1. If John the Baptist were preaching today, in what ways would his message be the same? In what ways would it be different? Why?

In the most important way, the message of John would not be any different: people still need to repent (see Acts 17:30). Also, it is likely that John would have some hard things to say to certain religious leaders of our day.

Yet there would be some notable differences. Today John would loudly proclaim the death and resurrection of Christ, which grants forgiveness. He would repeat Peter's directions on the Day of Pentecost (Acts 2:38). John would proclaim that believers are to draw on the power of the Holy Spirit. Who will be a John the Baptist for today?

2. Why is appearance an unreliable guide for evaluating a person's spiritual state? How do we avoid making a mistake in this area?

John was a true prophet of God who proclaimed the Messiah's coming, yet John wore rough clothing. Elijah, whom John emulated, was also a coarse-looking individual. Jesus is described in Isaiah 53:2 as one who "hath no form nor comeliness; and when we shall see him, there is no beauty that we should desire him."

This is a lesson all of us need to keep relearning. The prophet Samuel learned this lesson when selecting David as the future king of Israel. Samuel had looked on the outward appearance, but the Lord looked at the heart (see 1 Samuel 16:7). King Saul had good looks (1 Samuel 9:2), but turned out to be a spiritual dud.

3. In what ways are the circumstances of John's day similar to our own? How are the circumstances different? Why is this analysis important?

No matter what era of history we are in, sin is a problem. The human need for repentance never changes. Our day is much more technologically advanced than was John's, but with every technological advance come ways to use that technology in sinful ways.

John prepared the people of his day for Jesus' first appearance; we are here to prepare people for His second appearance. Thus the content of our message will be different in that regard. Also, John's particular method of preaching may not work today, given cultural differences between then and now. But preaching in and of itself will always be important.

4. How do we reconcile John's harsh language ("generation of vipers") with the call to have our speech "be always with grace, seasoned with salt" (Colossians 4:6)?

Certainly there is a time when "a soft answer turneth away wrath" (Proverbs 15:1). Yet we must recognize that at times a hard, confrontational answer is what is needed. Knowing *what* to say is important, of course. But knowing *how* to say it often requires much discernment and spiritual maturity.

A safe guide may be to try the soft answer first. If it is not heeded, then the hard answer may be what is needed. Do not be surprised if you need to "shake off the dust under your feet" (Mark 6:11) in protest to a lack of godly response.

5. How can we tell if a person's repentance is genuine? Or should we even be evaluating or judging such matters? Why, or why not?

Repentance is more than just a mental or emotional response; it is a change in mind-set that results in certain actions and behaviors. John told the people coming for repentance that they needed to bear fruit in keeping with repentance. Jesus said that we would know people by their fruits (Matthew 7:16).

It is such fruits that are the best indicators of the heart of a person. Good trees (in our case, truly repentant trees) will produce good fruit. Bad trees will show themselves to be bad when their fruits are examined. But before we go around examining the fruits others, we surely should examine our own!

6. What changes have you made in your life as a result of your own repentance?

Responses will be highly individualized, of course. But responses can be divided into two categories: things that the repentant person has *started* doing and things that he or she has *stopped* doing. If the responses tend to be one-sided in either direction, gently challenge your learners to think about the other area as well.

Community of Humility

DEVOTIONAL READING: Hosea 11:1-4.

BACKGROUND SCRIPTURE: Matthew 1:18–2:23.

PRINTED TEXT: Matthew 1:18-25; 2:13-15.

Matthew 1:18-25

18 Now the birth of Jesus Christ was on this wise: When as his mother Mary was espoused to Joseph, before they came together, she was found with child of the Holy Ghost.

19 Then Joseph her husband, being a just man, and not willing to make her a public example, was minded to put her away privily.

20 But while he thought on these things, behold, the angel of the Lord appeared unto him in a dream, saying, Joseph, thou son of David, fear not to take unto thee Mary thy wife: for that which is conceived in her is of the Holy Ghost.

21 And she shall bring forth a son, and thou shalt call his name JESUS: for he shall save his people from their sins.

22 Now all this was done, that it might be fulfilled which was spoken of the Lord by the prophet, saying,

23 Behold, a virgin shall be with child, and shall bring forth a son, and they shall call his name Immanuel, which being interpreted is, God with us.

24 Then Joseph being raised from sleep did as the angel of the Lord had bidden him, and took unto him his wife:

25 And knew her not till she had brought forth her firstborn son: and he called his name JESUS.

Matthew 2:13-15

13 And when they were departed, behold, the angel of the Lord appeareth to Joseph in a dream, saying, Arise, and take the young child and his mother, and flee into Egypt, and be thou there until I bring thee word: for Herod will seek the young child to destroy him.

14 When he arose, he took the young child and his mother by night, and departed into Egypt:

15 And was there until the death of Herod: that it might be fulfilled which was spoken of the Lord by the prophet, saying, Out of Egypt have I called my son.

GOLDEN TEXT: And thou Bethlehem, in the land of Judah, art not the least among the princes of Judah: for out of thee shall come a Governor, that shall rule my people Israel.—Matthew 2:6.

Lesson Aims

After participating in this lesson, each student will be able to:

1. Describe the difficulties facing Mary and Joseph in the times immediately before and after the birth of Jesus.

2. Contrast the humble circumstances of the family into which Jesus was born with the wealth and power of others included in the narratives.

3. Describe one way to model the faithful humility of Joseph.

Lesson Outline

INTRODUCTION
    A. Proud As a Peacock
    B. Lesson Background
  I. HUMILIATING PROBLEM (Matthew 1:18, 19)
    A. Mary's Problem (v. 18)
      A Problem or a Privilege?
    B. Joseph's Problem (v. 19)
 II. DIVINE SOLUTION (Matthew 1:20-25)
    A. Announcement (vv. 20, 21)
    B. Fulfillment (vv. 22, 23)
    C. Agreement (vv. 24, 25)
III. DIVINE PROTECTION (Matthew 2:13-15)
    A. Vengeful King (v. 13)
    B. Faithful God (vv. 14, 15)
      Seeking Refuge
CONCLUSION
    A. Humility as a Fruit
    B. Humility as a Command
    C. Prayer
    D. Thought to Remember

Introduction

A. Proud As a Peacock

For three days in October of 1971, dignitaries feasted in Persepolis at one of the biggest parties in the history of the world. More than 60 crowned royalty and heads of state from 5 continents came to celebrate the 2,500-year history of the Persian (Achaemenian) Empire and to honor its head, the Shah of Iran. They feasted on sumptuous food and drank the world's finest wine. The cost (in 1971 dollars) was about $100 million.

Decorating the great room were images of the peacock, the symbol of the empire. The Shah of Iran, proud as a peacock, was decked out in his finest jewels and medals. It was a grand moment for the ruler who sat on the Peacock Throne.

But "pride goeth before destruction, and a haughty spirit before a fall" (Proverbs 16:18). In less than eight years the Shah would be driven into exile. About one and one-half years after that he would be dead. Looking at the banquet in retrospect, perhaps it was fitting that the main course for the final night was stuffed peacock. Earthly glory is fleeting, and God has ways of reversing people's situations (Matthew 20:16).

B. Lesson Background

Jesus didn't rule His people from an earthly Peacock Throne. He came as a baby to be placed in an animal's feed trough; that was God's way of preparing for the church.

God was preparing a community of faith from the very beginning. Old Testament Israel would usher in the Messiah, who would bruise the serpent's head (Genesis 3:15) and bless "all families of the earth" (12:3). To be prepared for Messiah's arrival, the Jewish nation was made distinct—a separate people. They were given the temple, the law, and animal sacrifices. All of this was to prepare for Christ's coming and to encourage understanding of the need for His sacrifice on the cross.

Throughout the pages of the Old Testament, the Jews are often powerless. They endured centuries of slavery in Egypt, generations of warfare with their neighbors, and a lifetime of exile in Babylon. They were God's chosen people, but they lived in difficult circumstances.

It was appropriate, then, that when Messiah finally came He should be of lowly birth. His nation was being trodden under the boot of Rome; his family was struggling with poverty and an out-of-wedlock pregnancy. Jesus would know rejection. He fully embraced God's community of humility; truly He was "meek and lowly in heart" (Matthew 11:29). He did not love the people of this community because of their great worth; rather, they had great worth because He loved them.

I. Humiliating Problem (Matthew 1:18, 19)

From the beginning of creation, the plan of God has been for one man and one woman to unite as husband and wife (Genesis 2:24). Although today's secular world does not consider chastity to be a supreme virtue, the people of God's Old Testament covenant did. For a woman to have a child outside of marriage is a sinful disgrace in that era. Therefore, when God sends His Son to be conceived within an unwed mother, it creates a problem!

A. Mary's Problem (v. 18)

18. Now the birth of Jesus Christ was on this wise: When as his mother Mary was espoused to Joseph, before they came together, she was found with child of the Holy Ghost.

Matthew begins his Gospel with a lengthy genealogy, tracing the ancestry of the *Christ* back to Abraham (Matthew 1:1-17). Following this genealogy, Matthew explains the unusual circumstances of *the birth of Jesus.*

It is customary for Jewish girls of the time to be *espoused*, or legally promised to be married, in their early teens. The man to whom such a girl is espoused is usually some years older, having established himself in a career. During the year-long engagement, the girl lives with her parents and has no sexual contact with the man. The betrothal or espousement is a solemn commitment. It can be broken only by death or legal divorce.

During their period of engagement, Mary and Joseph do not come *together* in sexual union. Nevertheless, Mary is *found* to be *with child.* At first the pregnancy is known only to Mary, of course. But the scandal of her condition cannot be hidden for very long from Joseph, her parents, and the whole community of Nazareth. Mary knows that her child has been conceived through the Holy Spirit (see Luke 1:26-38), but Joseph and everyone else apparently do not. [See question #1, page 24.]

A PROBLEM OR A PRIVILEGE?

It is no secret that modern culture is schizophrenic about how we should regard whatever it is that resides in a woman's womb during pregnancy. Typically, a woman who wants to have a baby knows without doubt that she is carrying a *baby.* A woman who experiences what is sometimes called a crisis pregnancy is encouraged by those who advocate unrestricted access to abortion to use euphemisms such as *fetus.*

One unusual battle in these fetal wars is fought by parents who want their baby, but whose child is stillborn. They can obtain a death certificate, but they want a birth certificate so they can have some tangible evidence of the life they had hoped to bring into the world. How amazingly different are these attitudes about the value of a baby's life!

Mary had a humiliating problem: she had to endure reproach for being pregnant while unmarried. Today, Mary would receive abundant advice on how to get rid of her "problem" pregnancy quickly and without guilt. Instead, Mary accepted her problem as a privilege because she knew her child was a gift from God.   —C. R. B.

B. Joseph's Problem (v. 19)

19. Then Joseph her husband, being a just man, and not willing to make her a public example, was minded to put her away privily.

When the pregnancy becomes known, Mary's problem becomes Joseph's problem. As *her husband* (in terms of espousal), he cannot ignore the fact that she carries a child who is not his. He is a *just man*, dedicated to upholding the righteousness demanded in the law of God. And yet he cares so much for her that he simply is *not willing* to expose her to *public* contempt and ridicule.

The Law of Moses has a provision for dealing publicly with wives suspected of adultery (see Numbers 5:11-31). The law permits divorce (Deuteronomy 24:1), and Joseph feels that he has no option but *to put her away* with such a divorce. Even so, out of kindness he can at least do it as privately as possible. This will allow Joseph to be righteous before the law while exercising mercy at the same time. [See question #2, page 24.]

II. Divine Solution (Matthew 1:20-25)

God himself has the task of reconciling justice and mercy. Justice demands that the law be fulfilled, but mercy calls for forgiveness. The primary example of justice and mercy meeting is at the cross. In the case before us, the divine solution is simply a fuller explanation of the facts, leading to Joseph's acceptance of God's plan.

A. Announcement (vv. 20, 21)

20. But while he thought on these things, behold, the angel of the Lord appeared unto him in a dream, saying, Joseph, thou son of David,

---

How to Say It

ACHAEMENIAN. Ah-kuh-*mee*-nee-un.
AHAZ. *Ay*-haz.
BETHLEHEM. *Beth*-lih-hem.
HEROD. *Hair*-ud.
IMMANUEL. Ih-*man*-you-el.
ISAIAH. Eye-*zay*-uh.
JOSHUA. *Josh*-yew-uh.
JUDAH. *Joo*-duh.
MICAH. *My*-kuh.
NAZARETH. *Naz*-uh-reth.
PERSEPOLIS. Pur-*sep*-puh-lis.
SEPTUAGINT. Sep-*too*-ih-jent.

fear not to take unto thee Mary thy wife: for that which is conceived in her is of the Holy Ghost.

For a time after the disheartening discovery, Joseph ponders *these things*, trying to decide what he should do. Then one night while he is sleeping, *the angel of the Lord* appears to him *in a dream*. Because of its source, it is no ordinary dream! Joseph remembers it in exact detail, and he has no question that the messenger is from Heaven. God uses dreams in Bible times to communicate in special circumstances. This circumstance qualifies!

The angel addresses Joseph as *thou son of David*, a reminder that he is part of the royal lineage. (This may make Joseph even more reluctant to accept an illegitimate child as his own.) The fact that an angel is doing the explaining and not Mary herself is intriguing. There is no hint that Mary has tried to explain her situation to Joseph. Who would believe her anyway? Thus the need for divine communication. [See question #3, page 24.]

21. And she shall bring forth a son, and thou shalt call his name JESUS: for he shall save his people from their sins.

The baby is to be a boy, and *his name* is already selected. The name *Jesus* is the equivalent of the Hebrew name *Joshua* in the Old Testament. It is a derivative of the verb meaning "to save."

This baby, conceived of God's own Spirit, will be the Savior of God's people. Unlike the hero-kings of old who saved Israel from various foreign enemies, this Son of David will *save his people from their sins*. He will save them from the penalty of sin by taking their place in death; He will save them from the power of sin by living in their hearts. But fuller explanation of all that will have to wait.

B. Fulfillment (vv. 22, 23)

22. Now all this was done, that it might be fulfilled which was spoken of the Lord by the prophet, saying.

God does not play "catch up" with history. He does not wait to see what happens and then react. God has a master plan that has been determined from the beginning; He shapes the events of world history to bring about His will. Thus God announced through Isaiah, over 700 years in advance, that the Messiah was to be born. *All this*—the conception, the angelic announcement, the birth—is done so that His will is accomplished and His word *fulfilled*.

23. Behold, a virgin shall be with child, and shall bring forth a son, and they shall call his name Immanuel, which being interpreted is, God with us.

Centuries after the prophecy of Isaiah 7:14, a miracle will happen: *a virgin* will conceive. In addition to the name *Jesus*, this boy will bear the designation *Immanuel*. That's a Hebrew word that means *God with us*. Although no one has ever seen God (John 1:18), Jesus comes to show us God in the flesh. [See question #4, page 24.]

While belief in the virginal conception is a stumbling block for some people, it is foundational to understanding who Jesus is. If He were bound by all natural laws, such a conception would be impossible. But if He is also God, the one who ordains and controls natural laws, such a conception is both possible and appropriate. Just as His resurrection from the dead sets Jesus apart from all others at the end, so His conception within a virgin sets Him apart at the beginning.

Isaiah 7:14 is one of the most famous prophecies in the Old Testament. While its meaning in Matthew is clear, its interpretation in the context of Isaiah's day is controversial. In that setting, King Ahaz is told to ask for a sign that God will defeat Judah's enemies, but Ahaz refuses. Therefore, God says that He will give a sign anyway, despite Ahaz's refusal.

Some scholars hold that the Hebrew word for *virgin* in Isaiah 7 should be translated "a young woman" instead, since the Hebrew can be taken both ways. The idea is that the child of some such woman is to be a sign to Ahaz. We know now, however, that something grander is in view. The pronoun *you* is plural in Isaiah's words, "the Lord himself shall give you a sign." It is not just to Ahaz, but also to all the house of David (even in coming centuries) that the sign will be significant.

With this understanding, it is proper to translate the Hebrew word as *virgin*. This rendering is supported by the Greek translation of the Old Testament, known as the Septuagint. That ancient translation, which comes into being long before Christ is born, uses the distinct Greek word for *virgin*. Like many other prophecies of the Old Testament, Isaiah 7:14 is not fully understood until God brings it to pass.

C. Agreement (vv. 24, 25)

24. Then Joseph being raised from sleep did as the angel of the Lord had bidden him, and took unto him his wife.

When *Joseph* awakens from his *sleep*, he has complete confidence that what he has experienced is a divine communication, not just an ordinary dream. He also knows that *the angel of the Lord* must be obeyed. Without further hesitation he accepts Mary as *his wife*. In the custom of the day this means that he takes her from her parents' home to live in his own home. In the eyes of the people of Nazareth, they are husband and wife.

25. And knew her not till she had brought forth her firstborn son: and he called his name JESUS.

Even now, however, Joseph still does not have marital relations with Mary. This underscores her virginal state. It is not until after she has *brought forth* her baby that Joseph and Mary consummate their marriage. God later blesses Joseph and Mary with other children (see Matthew 13:55, 56).

Jesus is not born in Nazareth, but in another little village: Bethlehem (see Micah 5:2 and Matthew 2:1-6). There Joseph and Mary lay the child in a lowly manger (see Luke 2:1-7). In obedience to the angel's decree, they name their boy *Jesus*. Now God has taken up residence among people!

III. Divine Protection (Matthew 2:13-15)

God protects Joseph from making the mistake of putting away an innocent woman. In an additional act of providence, God then protects this holy family from the sinister plot of King Herod. In the first 12 verses of chapter 2, Matthew relates how wise men come from the East to see the newborn king. They follow a star westward to Jerusalem and ask, "Where is he that is born King of the Jews?" (Matthew 2:2).

They are told that Scripture says the child is to be born in Bethlehem. Before they leave for the village, King Herod tells them to be sure to come back and inform him where to find the child. After seeing Jesus and presenting gifts to Him, however, the wise men are warned by God's angel not to return and tell Herod.

A. Vengeful King (v. 13)

13. And when they were departed, behold, the angel of the Lord appeareth to Joseph in a dream, saying, Arise, and take the young child and his mother, and flee into Egypt, and be thou there until I bring thee word: for Herod will seek the young child to destroy him.

After the wise men leave, it is time for *the angel of the Lord* to warn Joseph as well. This is the third *dream* in the first two chapters of Matthew.

Egypt is a good place to go to escape. Egypt is fairly close, it has a large Jewish population, and Herod's jurisdiction does not extend there. This is not the first time that Egypt has been a place of refuge (Genesis 46; 1 Kings 11:40).

This king, known in history as Herod the Great, is indeed capable of murderous rage. He even has his own sons put to death out of fear that they will try to wrest the throne from him. The danger to Mary's little child is very real. Without divine intervention the baby Jesus will be slain

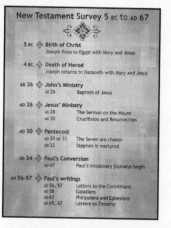

Visual for Lesson 2

Post this timeline alongside the map from Lesson 1 for the entire quarter.

along with other babies in Bethlehem (see Matthew 2:16). [See question #5, page 24.]

B. Faithful God (vv. 14, 15)

14. When he arose, he took the young child and his mother by night, and departed into Egypt.

In immediate obedience to the command from God, Joseph escapes *by night* with Mary and Jesus. Their hasty departure shows how urgent the situation is. The trip to *Egypt* undoubtedly is quite a financial hardship. However, they have just received expensive gifts. So in God's providence they not only have the warning to flee, they also have the means.

Matthew's reference to Jesus in these verses as *the young child* is an indication that Jesus is no longer a newborn infant, as he was at the time of the shepherds' visit (see Luke 2:8-18). We should note that when the wise men find Jesus, He and his family are in a "house" (Matthew 2:11), no longer in a temporary residence with the livestock.

15. And was there until the death of Herod: that it might be fulfilled which was spoken of the Lord by the prophet, saying, Out of Egypt have I called my son.

Herod the Great dies in 4 BC after reigning more than 30 years. (This date is a reminder that our modern calendar is based on an incorrect estimate of how many years it has been since the birth of Christ.) At the time of Herod's death, Jesus is a little boy no more than one year old, living in Egypt. When the angel finally gives the all-clear signal (Matthew 2:19), the family returns to Nazareth.

The return from refuge in Egypt is also a remarkable fulfillment of prophecy. Over 700 years earlier, Hosea had written, "When Israel was a child, then I loved him, and called my son out of Egypt" (Hosea 11:1). In saying this, Hosea showed that the return of God's people from Egypt to the promised land under Moses and Joshua was both a historical fact and a prophetic picture. Once more God brings His child up from Egypt—and this time the child is Jesus.

A repeated theme in these verses about the birth of Jesus is the humble and helpless circumstances of those involved. This teaches us important things about the parents, about Jesus, and about God. The parents are part of a community of humility— people who know they cannot rely on their own resources and power. Coming to join and shape that community, Jesus shows that He intends to embrace His humanity completely. God shows that His providential care is sufficient to keep His community safe as He watches over all these events.

SEEKING REFUGE

Seeking refuge for political or other reasons has a long history. Old Testament law created cities of refuge, and ancient Egyptian and Greek law also recognized the principle of granting asylum. In Christian times, the concept developed even further, with England's King Ethelbert making laws governing sanctuary in about AD 600. As the concept of asylum developed, church buildings became havens of refuge, sometimes even for felons!

Our text today pictures the plight of three political refugees. They had done nothing wrong, but their very existence was deemed a threat by the paranoid King Herod. What an irony that Joseph and his family were unsafe in their homeland and had to seek refuge in Egypt, where their ancestors had once been slaves! Another irony is that Herod, who cared little for God's plan for the people of

Israel, became an unwitting agent for the fulfillment of a messianic prophecy.

God still grants refuge to His people in the twenty-first century. See Hebrews 6:18.—C. R. B.

Conclusion

A. Humility as a Fruit

Apple trees produce apples; pear trees make pears. It is only natural that fruit trees should bear fruit. That is their design and the purpose of their creation (Genesis 1:11). If a fruit tree does not bear fruit, something is very wrong (Luke 13:9).

God's community naturally should bear the fruit of humility. Just as Jesus described himself as meek and lowly of heart (Matthew 11:29), we who follow in His footsteps should also be meek and humble. When God's Spirit lives in our hearts, it is only natural that we will produce a harvest of God-like qualities. Included in this fruit of the Spirit are "gentleness" and "meekness" (Galatians 5:22, 23). These traits should grow in the Christian heart as naturally as the flowers on the hillsides, as naturally as the fruit on healthy trees.

B. Humility as a Command

But humility is also a command. This means we cannot take it for granted that humility will become part of our nature automatically. Paul exhorted Christians to walk "with all lowliness and meekness" (Ephesians 4:2) and "in lowliness of mind" to "esteem other[s] better than themselves" (Philippians 2:3). James admonished his readers to "humble yourselves in the sight of the Lord" (4:10). Peter commanded "be clothed with humility: for God resisteth the proud, and giveth grace to the humble" (1 Peter 5:5). While humility should grow in us naturally as the fruit of the Spirit, it must also be cultivated actively in obedience to God's command.

When Jesus became a man, He humbled himself (Philippians 2:5-8), setting an example for us to follow. If we are to have the mind of Christ, we must follow Him in this attitude of humility. Only then will we properly be known as God's community of humility.

C. Prayer

Our Father, forgive our foolish pride. Teach us to walk humbly in Your sight. Remind us of Your providential care, so that we will not trust in ourselves. In the name of Jesus our Savior and our example, amen.

D. Thought to Remember

Model humility.

Home Daily Bible Readings

Monday, Sep. 8—God's Care for His People (Hosea 11:1-9)

Tuesday, Sep. 9—The Right to Be Children of God (John 1:10-14)

Wednesday, Sep. 10—Foolish and Wise; Weak and Strong (1 Corinthians 1:26-31)

Thursday, Sep. 11—Gifts from God's Spirit (1 Corinthians 12:4-13)

Friday, Sep. 12—Members of the Body (1 Corinthians 12:14-27)

Saturday, Sep. 13—The Kingdom of God's Son (Colossians 1:9-14)

Sunday, Sep. 14—God with Us (Matthew 1:18-25; 2:13-15)

Learning by Doing

This page contains an alternative lesson plan emphasizing learning activities. Some of these activities are also found in the helpful student book, Adult Bible Class.

Into the Lesson

Display the incomplete phrase on the board as class members arrive: "Proud As a _____." Also have displayed a simple cutout of a peacock, with "feathers" as separate pieces stuck to the body. (Recruit an artistic class member to prepare this for you; a simple Internet search for "peacock pattern" will provide what you need.)

Ask the class to complete your phrase and then ask, "What is it about a peacock that could and should tend to humble it?" For each suggestion offered, "pluck" a tail feather from your cutout. Some of your students may mention such truths as "a peacock has very limited flight ability," "a peacock has a shrill, unmelodious cry," "a peacock has a very small natural habitat," and "a peacock is largely for show." When the bird's tail is somewhat bare, remark, "Our peacock has about as much to be proud of as we flawed and weak humans—no matter how smart, how handsome, or how prosperous we are."

Summarize "Proud As a Peacock" from the lesson Introduction (p. 18). Mention the pride that was obvious in the Shah of Iran's great party of 1971, which was a conspicuous display of pride if there ever was one. (*Option:* There are photographs of this party on the Internet; print some off and pass them around.) Contrast that example with the simple birth and lifestyle of Jesus, King of kings.

Into the Word

Write *Humility Factors* on the board. Ask the class, "What is it that keeps us humble?" Write responses on the board. Add the following if no one mentions them: 1. Dilemmas that challenge our perspective; 2. Submitting to God's will when it seems to contradict our common sense; 3. Unexpected immorality among family or friends; 4. Disruptions to our well-thought-out plans; 5. Having to accept the consequences of the foolishness of others; 6. Needing to depend on others for simple survival—that is, financial inadequacy.

Once you have a list, ask your class to identify similar humbling connections in today's text and context. Related to the first entry above, certainly Joseph's limited human perspective could not determine the proper way to deal with what he considered to be "Mary's sin"; his decision

had to be corrected by divine intervention. Further, Joseph's needing to deal with Mary's seeming infidelity, as related to the third entry above, is another connection. Someone may note the need of Joseph and his family to escape because of Herod's evil plan, changing their own good intention to return to Nazareth immediately, as related to the fourth and fifth entries. Also, the holy family's need of the magi gifts to support a trip to Egypt (Matthew 2) is related to the sixth entry.

The connections you point out may encourage your learners to add other "humility factors" to the list as they relate to the situation of Joseph and his family. Wrap up by noting that Joseph had every reason to be humble. He was poor. He was put into a hard dilemma, beyond his limited perspective to comprehend. He was forced to change his plans by an evil ruler.

Say, "We may find ourselves in similar straits. Without sufficient resources to do everything we need to do, with our plans being challenged constantly by the ever-present work of that evil ruler Satan, we must depend upon God's revelation and His protection."

Continue: "Do you feel humble? Are you ready to depend on Him?" Ask your class to repeat these verses from James 4:6, 10 in unison: "God resisteth the proud, but giveth grace unto the humble. . . . Humble yourselves in the sight of the Lord, and he shall lift you up." Encourage your students to memorize these verses this week.

Into Life

Give each learner an adhesive name label onto which you—or someone in your class with calligraphic skill—have written IWTBLJ. Ask the group to speculate as to what the letters represent. After a time, tell them you want it to represent the declaration *I Want To Be Like Joseph.*

Ask your learners to identify godly attributes that today's texts reveal about him. *His kindness in wanting to deal with Mary in private* and *his obedience to God's seemingly unreasonable commands* are possible responses. Your learners will have others. Suggest that on at least one occasion in the coming week your learners wear the label IWTBLJ as a conversation starter and an opportunity to speak of this study in the characteristics of the New Testament community.

Let's Talk It Over

The questions on this page are designed to promote discussion of the lesson by the class and to encourage application of the lesson Scriptures. The answers provided are only discussion starters. Let your class talk it over from there.

1. What was a time when you had to do something that other people ridiculed or otherwise "looked down on"? How did you cope with the situation in a Christian manner?

Mary certainly was placed in a situation by God that everyone in her day would misinterpret; yet she willingly submitted herself to God's plan anyway. There was even a danger (although a slight one, given Roman law) that she would be stoned to death for adultery, as nearly happened with the woman in John 8 (compare Leviticus 20:10).

Yet Mary understood that God had given her this task, and for her it was more important to obey God than to worry about the opinions of others. The apostles also understood this principle (see Acts 5:29).

2. Have you ever been faced with a problem that had more than one possible way of being handled? How did you go about choosing which solution to take?

Joseph certainly had options when presented with the problem of what to do with Mary. He was well within his rights to accuse her publicly of infidelity. Instead he chose the option to spare her by divorcing her quietly. Although Joseph did not know God's plan at that point, he chose the solution that wasn't just "allowed" but showed love and compassion to the one who (apparently) needed it.

In a fallen world, we sometimes may have to choose between "the lesser of two evils." Sometimes that difficult choice has to be made because of our own unholy behavior. The parents of a teenager were consulting a counselor because the daughter had become pregnant out of wedlock. They were wrestling with the difficult choice of keeping the baby or putting the child up for adoption. The wise counselor noted that the choice was difficult because the parents were trying to discover God's second-best plan.

3. Has God ever changed what you were planning? What was the circumstance, and how did things turn out?

Plans get changed all the time, as we all know. Sometimes those plan changes come about for godly reasons, sometimes not.

Joseph's plan to divorce Mary was not according to God's plan, so Joseph's plan got changed. Paul received a vision of a Macedonian asking for help, and so Paul's plan changed (see Acts 16:6-10). We doubt that John ever voluntarily planned to be exiled on Patmos (Revelation 1:9), but whatever else John had in mind was set aside. People whose plans are changed by God do well to accept God's plan over their own. James rightly understood that our plans are subject to the Lord's will. "For that ye ought to say, If the Lord will, we shall live, and do this, or that" (James 4:15).

4. Why is the designation *Immanuel* ("God with us") important to you personally?

Certainly this word should make us realize that we are not alone! God has not left us to our own devices, devices that have failed us time and again. He sent His Son to redeem us.

We can also know that God truly identifies with us, for Jesus took the form of a man. He knew what it was to struggle with temptations. Hebrews 4:15 states that Jesus was tempted in all things like we are. He also knew what it was to suffer pain and to be betrayed, mocked, and experience death. It should bring us great joy to consider that God came to us when we could not go to Him.

5. What was a time when you think that you were divinely protected? How did your level of faith change?

In order for God's plan to continue, He protected the infant child and His parents from wicked Herod. Yet God chose not to extend His divine protection to the babies who were killed in the Bethlehem area. While we at times will still suffer hurt, God has plans for us. He will work His will.

It should not be too difficult to think of times when God has protected you from possible accidents and other disasters or during a time of great need. Sometimes He even protects us from ourselves! He certainly protected David when he was on the run from Saul, for God had a plan for David. But God did not extend physical protection to James in Acts 12:2, perhaps because God's plan was for him to witness through martyrdom. We can take comfort in knowing that God is working His plan in all circumstances.

Community of Values

DEVOTIONAL READING: **Numbers 6:22-27.**

BACKGROUND SCRIPTURE: **Matthew 5:1–7:28.**

PRINTED TEXT: **Matthew 5:1-16.**

Matthew 5:1-16

1 And seeing the multitudes, he went up into a mountain: and when he was set, his disciples came unto him:

2 And he opened his mouth, and taught them, saying,

3 Blessed are the poor in spirit: for theirs is the kingdom of heaven.

4 Blessed are they that mourn: for they shall be comforted.

5 Blessed are the meek: for they shall inherit the earth.

6 Blessed are they which do hunger and thirst after righteousness: for they shall be filled.

7 Blessed are the merciful: for they shall obtain mercy.

8 Blessed are the pure in heart: for they shall see God.

9 Blessed are the peacemakers: for they shall be called the children of God.

10 Blessed are they which are persecuted for righteousness' sake: for theirs is the kingdom of heaven.

11 Blessed are ye, when men shall revile you, and persecute you, and shall say all manner of evil against you falsely, for my sake.

12 Rejoice, and be exceeding glad: for great is your reward in heaven: for so persecuted they the prophets which were before you.

13 Ye are the salt of the earth: but if the salt have lost his savor, wherewith shall it be salted? it is thenceforth good for nothing, but to be cast out, and to be trodden under foot of men.

14 Ye are the light of the world. A city that is set on a hill cannot be hid.

15 Neither do men light a candle, and put it under a bushel, but on a candlestick; and it giveth light unto all that are in the house.

16 Let your light so shine before men, that they may see your good works, and glorify your Father which is in heaven.

GOLDEN TEXT: Seek ye first the kingdom of God, and his righteousness; and all these things shall be added unto you.—Matthew 6:33.

The New Testament Community
Unit 1: Birth of a New Community
(Lessons 1–4)

Lesson Aims

After participating in this lesson, each student will be able to:

1. Tell what kind of person is "blessed," according to Jesus' Sermon on the Mount.

2. Explain the purpose of the Beatitudes in the context of Jesus' ministry.

3. Make a plan to apply one Beatitude to his or her life.

Lesson Outline

INTRODUCTION
  A. Congratulations!
  B. Lesson Background
 I. VALUE OF RIGHT ATTITUDES (Matthew 5:1-6)
  A. Right Teacher (vv. 1, 2)
  B. Right Spirit (vv. 3, 4)
  C. Right Zeal (vv. 5, 6)
 II. VALUE OF RIGHT ACTIONS (Matthew 5:7-12)
  A. Right Responses (vv. 7, 8)
  B. Right Interactions (vv. 9, 10)
    Making Peace
  C. Right Acceptance (vv. 11, 12)
III. VALUE OF RIGHT WITNESS (Matthew 5:13-16)
  A. Our Value As Salt (v. 13)
  B. Our Value As Light (vv. 14-16)
    Shining in the Darkness
CONCLUSION
  A. Are You Happy Now?
  B. Is God Happy Now?
  C. Prayer
  D. Thought to Remember

Introduction

A. Congratulations!

When someone inherits a lot of money, others may say, "How fortunate!" When someone enjoys good health, many think, "What good genetics!" When someone is honored for an achievement, a typical response is, "How happy you must be!" The one word that sums up these responses is *Congratulations!*

When the ancient Greeks expressed such ideas, they used the same word attributed to Jesus in the Beatitudes. We translate it "blessed." They used this word to congratulate parents on their children, to congratulate wise men on their knowledge, and to congratulate rich men on their wealth. For them, these were things of great value.

Whenever we congratulate people, we are making a statement about values. If we congratulate people for being healthy or getting wealthy, we do so because we set high value on such things. By contrast, Jesus congratulated people based on a very different set of values. In His shocking appraisal of the human condition, He called people "blessed" who were poor in spirit and meek and persecuted.

The challenge for followers of Christ is to embrace His values. We must stop admiring people for wealth or achievements that have no value in the sight of God. Instead, we must learn what things have true, eternal value. Then we will be a community of values—God's values.

B. Lesson Background

The Beatitudes form the introduction to the famous Sermon on the Mount. Jesus spoke these words on a mountain in Galilee during the second year of His ministry.

Both Matthew 4:25 and Luke 6:17 state that large crowds followed Jesus at this time in His ministry. Jesus' fame as a miracle worker had spread throughout the region. People came from as far away as Tyre and Sidon to hear Him teach and to be healed of their diseases. Their astonishment increased when they saw Him command unclean spirits to depart from demon-possessed people.

But Jesus had not come primarily to heal the sick and cast out demons. He had come to preach truth in light of the in-breaking kingdom of God. His Sermon on the Mount was both radical and reasonable; it was both spiritually idealistic and sensibly down-to-earth. His words may set ethical standards that are higher than we can personally reach in this life, but no one can claim that His standards are wrong.

I. Value of Right Attitudes (Matthew 5:1-6)

A. Right Teacher (vv. 1, 2)

1. And seeing the multitudes, he went up into a mountain: and when he was set, his disciples came unto him.

Because of Jesus' growing fame, *multitudes* of people come to Him "from Decapolis, and from Jerusalem, and from Judea, and from beyond Jordan" (Matthew 4:25). The people have various motives: some want to be healed, some want to learn about God's kingdom, and some are just curious.

In order to make it possible for such a large number of people to see and hear Him, Jesus goes *up into a mountain.* There, on an elevated spot, Jesus sits down to teach. This is the common posture for a rabbi. It indicates that He is ready to begin teaching and His *disciples* (literally, "students" or "learners") come to hear Him.

2. And he opened his mouth, and taught them, saying.

Without the aid of a public address system, a public speaker in ancient times has to develop a strong speaking voice. In addition, the concise truths that Jesus begins teaching in the Beatitudes can be repeated easily from person to person throughout the crowd. As Jesus begins to teach, it is reasonable to assume that the truths about the kingdom spread like ripples on a pond throughout the multitude.

B. Right Spirit (vv. 3, 4)

3. Blessed are the poor in spirit: for theirs is the kingdom of heaven.

The word *blessed* should not be understood as a word of pity or sympathy. Jesus is not expressing sorrowful compassion for those He is talking about; rather, He is commending them! People who have the character traits and circumstances that Jesus lists are to be congratulated. In God's eyes they are better off, more fortunate, and in the long run happier than anyone else.

The first virtue Jesus commends is to be *poor in spirit.* People who are poor in spirit are aware of their own spiritual bankruptcy. They see their sinfulness; they feel their guilt. People like this are far more likely to turn to God for help than people who are smug in their own goodness. That is why Jesus can look at people like this and announce that they—not the proud and self-righteous—will enter God's community. How much better in the long run to be lowly and saved, than to be proud and lost! [See question #1, page 32.]

Each of the Beatitudes has its own reward. In each instance, the reward has a partial fulfillment

---

How to Say It

CORINTHIANS. Ko-*rin*-thee-unz (*th* as in *thin*).

DECAPOLIS. Dee-*cap*-uh-lis.

ISAIAH. Eye-*zay*-uh.

JERUSALEM. Juh-*roo*-suh-lem.

JUDEA. Joo-*dee*-uh.

MESSIAH. Meh-*sigh*-uh.

SIDON. *Sigh*-dun.

TYRE. Tire.

---

on earth and an ultimate fulfillment in Heaven. The *kingdom* that Jesus promises has both earthly and heavenly aspects. Only those who are poor in spirit are eligible to enter *the kingdom of heaven.*

4. Blessed are they that mourn: for they shall be comforted.

They that mourn does not constitute a second group of people from verse 3. Indeed, all the Beatitudes should be seen as a total description of the kingdom citizen, not a smorgasbord from which we select the ones we like most (or dislike least).

Like the poor in spirit, those who mourn receive God's favor (Isaiah 61:2, 3). Those who mourn for their own sinfulness will be *comforted* by the grace and forgiveness of God. Those who mourn in sorrow or affliction will be comforted by all those who love them in God's community (see 2 Corinthians 1:4). Those who mourn because they have lost houses, family, or lands for the sake of the gospel will be comforted by receiving much more (see Mark 10:29, 30). [See question #2, page 32.]

C. Right Zeal (vv. 5, 6)

5. Blessed are the meek: for they shall inherit the earth.

Meekness is the attitude of people who know their own spiritual poverty. To be *meek* is not to be confused with being servile. The suggestion is one of gentleness. Jesus himself is our best example of this (Matthew 11:29; 21:5). To be meek is to have strength reined in. The meek Jesus certainly is no weakling! Those who are meek are those who are eager to let God take the steering wheel.

Unbelievers may sneer at the promise that the meek *shall inherit the earth.* But as heirs of God and joint-heirs with Christ, the children of God will ultimately inherit all things (see Romans 8:17; compare Psalm 37:9, 11, 29). Even now, a Christian has untold resources at his or her disposal. When all the members of God's community are willing to share their possessions with one another when there is need, every believer has already inherited a vast fortune.

6. Blessed are they which do hunger and thirst after righteousness: for they shall be filled.

Jesus recognizes that at least some in the crowd have come to hear Him because they are hungry and thirsty for *righteousness.* They have a burning zeal, an unsatisfied appetite, to pursue what is right. The world has left them disappointed and unsatisfied; they are tired of living in the midst of wickedness.

For those who really seek righteousness, Jesus has good news: their *hunger and thirst* will be *filled.* By coming to Christ, they can have their sinful slate wiped clean. They can be clothed in

Visual for Lesson 3. *You can use this visual to introduce one or more of the discussion questions on page 32.*

His righteousness. By joining God's community they can have God's own Spirit enable them to rise above their past failures and live a new life. Best of all, in the world to come they will live in complete purity. In Heaven they will finally live in the righteousness that their hearts have so long desired (2 Peter 3:13).

II. Value of Right Actions (Matthew 5:7-12)

A. Right Responses (vv. 7, 8)

7. Blessed are the merciful: for they shall obtain mercy.

Mercy can be expressed in at least two different ways. First, the *merciful* person is forgiving to people who have wronged him or her. Second, the merciful person is compassionate to people who are suffering or needy. In either situation, the merciful person displays a generous spirit.

In return, the merciful person will *obtain mercy* from God. This does not mean that our mercy toward others forces God to be merciful toward us. The idea, rather, is that our merciful attitude toward others becomes an occasion of God's mercy to us. Whether as a sinner in need of forgiveness or as an afflicted person in need of help, God's merciful children will be shown God's mercy.

This Beatitude requires a word of warning. As Jesus elaborates later in the Sermon on the Mount, people who are not merciful and forgiving to others cannot expect God to be merciful and forgiving to them (see Matthew 6:14, 15). We must respond in mercy as we have been shown mercy (see Matthew 18:23-35; James 2:13).

8. Blessed are the pure in heart: for they shall see God.

Those who are *pure in heart* are not polluted with either moral impurity or insincere motives. In both respects they meet the requirements of Psalm 24:3, 4: "Who shall ascend into the hill of the Lord? Or who shall stand in his holy place? He that hath clean hands, and a pure heart; who hath not lifted up his soul unto vanity, nor sworn deceitfully." [See question #3, page 32.]

God wants hearts that respond to Him in total devotion. The person who is pure in heart will seek holiness, "without which no man shall see the Lord" (Hebrews 12:14). The final reward for such a person is to live with God in Heaven, where he or she will look upon God's face (see Revelation 22:4).

B. Right Interactions (vv. 9, 10)

9. Blessed are the peacemakers: for they shall be called the children of God.

Being a peacemaker is often a thankless task. Like policemen trying to settle a domestic dispute, *peacemakers* may find themselves under attack from both sides. Stepping in to help settle disputes for others is not always appreciated.

Furthermore, it is sometimes our own disputes that need the balm of peace. Even though we may have a right to be angry with someone, Jesus calls us to become instruments of peace (Proverbs 15:1; Matthew 5:39). For those in Jesus' audience who expect Messiah to launch a war with Rome, these words must be both shocking and disappointing.

Members of God's community, however, place great value on peace. Like Jesus himself, we try to live at peace with all (see Hebrews 12:14), to break down the walls of hostility (see Ephesians 2:15-17), and to be agents of reconciliation (see 2 Corinthians 5:18-20). People who value making peace will *be called the children of God.* This does not mean that such folks promote "peace at all costs." That is not the model of Jesus (Matthew 10:34; 21:12). Even so, we "seek peace, and pursue it" (Psalm 34:14). [See question #4, page 32.]

MAKING PEACE

Most of us cannot remember a time when there was peace in the Middle East. At various times, American presidents have tried to broker peace in the region. One of the few successful efforts was the Camp David talks of 1978. Those talks ended a 30-year state of war between Israel and Egypt.

However, the situation between Israel and the Palestinians seems to be intractable. The Oslo Accords of 1993 affirmed Palestinian right of self-government. Negotiators won Nobel Peace Prizes.

But that was 15 years ago, and still the strife continues! This situation demonstrates how difficult it is to make peace in a fallen world.

Those who yield to the power of God's Spirit have the greatest chance of being peacemakers. God has made peace with us through the cross. Now it's our turn. Let us "seek peace, and ensue it" (1 Peter 3:11).   —C. R. B.

10. Blessed are they which are persecuted for righteousness' sake: for theirs is the kingdom of heaven.

The last of the eight Beatitudes is the only one with a note of peril. And unlike the others, this Beatitude is expanded into two more verses of explanation (vv. 11, 12, below). Living as a citizen of God's kingdom will draw opposition (compare 2 Timothy 3:12).

Persecution may come in many forms: physical, psychological, social, financial, etc. But the issue here is the reason behind whatever form the persecution takes. Persecution *for righteousness' sake* is the world's response to us for doing the right thing. Those persecuted are still called *blessed*. It is far better to suffer such persecution and enter *the kingdom of heaven* than to avoid persecution by doing the wrong thing and then be punished throughout eternity.

C. Right Acceptance (vv. 11, 12)

11. Blessed are ye, when men shall revile you, and persecute you, and shall say all manner of evil against you falsely, for my sake.

Jesus knows that people of the world will *revile*, *persecute*, and *say all manner of evil against* His followers. If they persecuted the master, they will also persecute His disciples (see John 15:20).

It is important to note that the persecution described by Jesus has two qualifications. First, the accusations in view are those leveled against the disciple *falsely*. It is no virtue to suffer punishment for actual faults (see 1 Peter 2:20). But to "suffer for well doing" is an honor (see 1 Peter 3:17). Second, Jesus speaks of persecution that is suffered for His *sake*. To suffer as a Christian is to bring glory to God (see 1 Peter 4:14-16).

12. Rejoice, and be exceeding glad: for great is your reward in heaven: for so persecuted they the prophets which were before you.

Whatever the form of persecution, those who suffer for Christ are to *rejoice and be exceeding glad*. The apostles learn this lesson well after Jesus ascends. After they are beaten by the Sanhedrin for preaching in the name of Jesus, they go home "rejoicing that they were counted worthy to suffer shame for his name" (Acts 5:41). In their suffering,

the apostles will be like *the prophets* who were also *persecuted* by religious leaders (see Hebrews 11:32-38; James 5:10).

The *reward in heaven* will far outweigh the suffering. If we suffer with Christ, we will also be glorified with Christ (see Romans 8:17). Even though our outward body may perish, we are strengthened inwardly as we look forward to "a far more exceeding and eternal weight of glory" (2 Corinthians 4:17).

III. Value of Right Witness (Matthew 5:13-16)

A. Our Value As Salt (v. 13)

13. Ye are the salt of the earth: but if the salt have lost his savor, wherewith shall it be salted? It is thenceforth good for nothing, but to be cast out, and to be trodden under foot of men.

Salt is an important commodity in the ancient world. Roman soldiers are even paid part of their wages in salt (the origin of the word *salary*). Salt can flavor food, but in a time before refrigeration salt's primary use is to prevent meat and fish from spoiling. Jesus challenges His followers to be *the salt of the earth*, to be a moral disinfectant in society, preserving it from decay.

But the salt of Palestine is often impure, mixed with other minerals. If such a composite gets damp, the actual salt in the mixture can leach out, leaving a residue that is tasteless and useless. If a person's salt has lost its saltiness, how can it be made salty again? Jesus' crowd knows the answer: it can't be done. When they have salt that becomes unsalty, it is *good for nothing*. The saltless residue is worthless dust, so they throw it out.

B. Our Value As Light (vv. 14-16)

14. Ye are the light of the world. A city that is set on a hill cannot be hid.

Throughout Scripture, light versus darkness is symbolic of good versus evil. Jesus calls on His disciples to be *the light of the world*, spiritual beacons showing the way to what is good and exposing the error of what is bad.

On the darkest night even a small light is visible from a great distance. When *a city* is *set on a hill*, that city cannot be hidden if there is light streaming from any of the windows. Jerusalem is certainly a city set on a hill. Is Jesus implying that the holy city has let its light go out?

15. Neither do men light a candle, and put it under a bushel, but on a candlestick; and it giveth light unto all that are in the house.

The whole purpose of *light* is to shine and illuminate. What would be the point of lighting a *candle* (literally, a pottery lamp that burns olive oil) and then hiding it under a basket? The lamp is supposed to be set on a lamp stand so that it will give light to *all that are in the house.* Even a small source of light can penetrate the gloom of the darkest night.

16. Let your light so shine before men, that they may see your good works, and glorify your Father which is in heaven.

Jesus challenges his listeners to let their *light . . . shine before men.* They are not to be ashamed to stand up for moral purity. They are not to be afraid to expose society's indecency. When people see their *good works,* perhaps they will be inspired to leave their own sinful works and follow the better example of right living. Most of all, when the light points the way to God, this will lead people to *glorify* the *Father* who *is in Heaven.* [See question #5, page 32.]

We should note that later in the Sermon on the Mount there is a strong warning against making a show of good works (see Matthew 6:1-20). Thus there is a tension for the sincere Christian in the matter of putting personal piety on display. If one's motive is to be seen and praised by others, then good works become hypocrisy. But if one's motive is to set an example and bring glory to God, then good works are a beautiful part of a redeemed life.

SHINING IN THE DARKNESS

In the beginning when God created light, He called it "good." When the plague of darkness covered Egypt for three days, there was light where the Israelites lived (Exodus 10:21-23). As God led Israel on its march to freedom from Egyptian slavery, He did so with a pillar of fire by night, providing both illumination and protection for His people (Exodus 13:21). When Moses came down from God's presence on Mt. Sinai, his face was so radiant with God's glory that the Israelites were afraid to look at him (Exodus 34:29-35). God likes light. God is light (1 John 1:5).

When Jesus says we are the light of the world, He is saying we must reflect the divine glory and let the world see that we have been with Jesus. Most of us have seen composite photographs taken from space showing what the world looks like at night. The darkness of the oceans and the great landmasses are interrupted by the brilliant lights of the cities of the world. As our world becomes darker morally and spiritually, Christians will become increasingly like those cities shining in the darkness in the photos: they cannot be hidden!

May that light be beautiful, delightful, and excellent.   —C. R. B.

Conclusion

A. Are You Happy Now?

"There! Are you happy now?" We usually hear these words in a sarcastic tone; someone is obviously *not* going to be very happy. But in a more serious vein, the question really does need to be asked. To people whose whole lives have been focused on careers, on social standing, or on stock portfolios, we might ask: Are you really happy now? Have worldly values brought true satisfaction? Or have you been left wondering where you can find a deeper level of satisfaction?

The timeless teachings of Jesus show us eternal values. His Beatitudes may go against the current of modern society, but they are nonetheless true. Real happiness is found in spiritual blessedness.

B. Is God Happy Now?

Each of the Beatitudes represents a shifting of priorities. They teach us to stop putting ourselves first. In the process of learning to live out these values, we will make an important discovery: We find lasting happiness only when we stop trying to please ourselves and start trying to please God. We find the blessed life only when we embrace God's values instead of our own.

C. Prayer

Our Father, teach us what to value most. Lead us to be the kind of people who display kingdom values. Help us to be salt and light in our world, so that others will give glory to Your name. In Jesus' name, amen.

D. Thought to Remember

Be salt! Be light!

Home Daily Bible Readings

Monday, Sep. 15—The Lord's Blessing (Numbers 6:22-27)

Tuesday, Sep. 16—Blessed by the Father (Matthew 25:31-40)

Wednesday, Sep. 17—Wise and Foolish Builders (Matthew 7:24-29)

Thursday, Sep. 18—Sincere Love (Romans 12:9-13)

Friday, Sep. 19—Right Response to Evil (Romans 12:14-21)

Saturday, Sep. 20—Inheriting a Blessing (1 Peter 3:8-15)

Sunday, Sep. 21—Blessing for God's People (Matthew 5:1-16)

Learning by Doing

This page contains an alternative lesson plan emphasizing learning activities. Some of these activities are also found in the helpful student book, Adult Bible Class.

Into the Lesson

As class members arrive, tie a simple "price tag" around the wrist of each. The tags can be home-made with a string attached, bearing a pretend dollar and cents price. Or you can purchase tags at an office supply store. Use any prices you like.

Say, "The world pays close attention to cost. 'How much did (or does) it cost?' may be the most-asked question in the Western world. That can be a legitimate criterion, but every smart consumer knows some things are overpriced, making them bad values. Occasionally, some are underpriced. Today's study is not about price tags, but *values*. What is truly valuable? Jesus answers that question in our text today."

Into the Word

Display an image of Jesus and attach a dialogue balloon with the single word *Congratulations!* written in it. Note, as the lesson writer does, that we congratulate individuals for the things that we value: bringing a new baby into the world, achieving an honor, succeeding in a vocational endeavor, etc. Note that Jesus' *blesseds* are God's way of expressing pleasure at our state of being according to His values.

Distribute copies of the following word-search puzzle with these directions: "God's values are represented in today's text and in other places such as Galatians 5:22, 23, which lists the fruit of the Spirit. Find as many as you can. For each, explain why God would consider the one who has that fruit to be blessed indeed."

```
S G E N O Y M H T I A F B L
S G N I R E F F U S G N O L
E E L S S I N G J O N V H G
N U E F L G B E L E S S T N
S G T I Y O G N V S A S U U
U E E B L O V S S S U E R N
O G M I L D J E Y B H N T A
E T P U E N N T M S U K B E
T Y E S S E I I R Y M E N C
H S R U L S S T C E I E V A
G L A T T S E R R B L M L E
I S N S I H E N C U I E A P
R E C V G M S I N V T O L U
G E E S B P U R I T Y H J L
```

These words can be found in the puzzle: *faith, gentleness, goodness, humility, joy, longsuffering, love, meekness, mercy, peace, purity, righteousness, submissive, temperance, truth.*

You may have your learners work in competitive teams, if you desire. For a real challenge, do not distribute the list of words to be found. Instead, merely inform your learners that they are looking for a total of 15 words.

After all the words are found, spend some time relating them to today's text and to the concept of kingdom values. You can create a question for each of the words found. The questions may be phrased "Where do we find the idea of _____ (if not the exact word) in today's text?"

Into Life

Jesus intended His Sermon on the Mount to give direction to the daily living of those who would follow Him. The Beatitudes are an introduction to godly character and the righteous lifestyle. Give your learners copies of the following list of "personalized paraphrases" of the Beatitudes. Encourage learners to reflect and evaluate themselves this week with these statements in a time of personal meditation and devotion: 1. I am fully aware of my own spiritual bankruptcy; I know both sin and guilt. 2. I sense the deep sadness and loss in my life because of what sin has robbed me of. 3. I am in control of my rebellious spirit; both temper and aggression are reined in. 4. I feel the need for righteousness to fill the emptiness in my daily life; it hurts to fail God. 5. My life is characterized by forgiveness and compassion; my deeds are the natural outcome of generosity that reflects God's loving and giving. 6. Moral degradation and insincerity can find no place in my heart, for holiness is my watchword. 7. In the midst of violence, rancor, and petty disagreement, I want to display the serenity of confidence in God's justice; I want to be a peacemaker. 8. I want my righteousness to be so obvious and pervasive that unrepentant sinners are intimidated and threatened—they will have anxiety in my presence. 9. I am not deterred by sinners lying about me; I will not be detoured by their slights and attacks; I eagerly await the joys of Heaven.

Time allowing, ask for volunteers to relate these paraphrases to the Beatitudes of today's text.

Let's Talk It Over

The questions on this page are designed to promote discussion of the lesson by the class and to encourage application of the lesson Scriptures. The answers provided are only discussion starters. Let your class talk it over from there.

1. What thoughts did you have when you first read about "the poor in spirit"? How has today's lesson changed (or reinforced) that thinking?

In this world it is considered to be a bad thing to be poor in just about anything. Abundance is highly valued in modern culture. To the secular mind, "poor in spirit" sounds like someone who has self-esteem issues and needs counseling.

Yet what Jesus apparently was thinking of was a person who has the right estimation of his or her own spiritual condition. The Bible speaks plainly of how all have sinned (Romans 3:23) and of the consequences of that sin (Romans 6:23). Those who are poor in spirit recognize this and know they need a Savior to help them with their spiritual condition. An awareness of spiritual poverty is a precondition to inheriting Heaven.

2. How can someone be blessed for mourning? How is this the opposite from what the world thinks?

There is undoubtedly more than one answer. It is in the mourning that is connected with godly sorrow that people will find comfort from God. God accepts a broken and contrite heart (see Psalm 51). He can turn the mourning for sin to "the oil of joy" (Isaiah 61:3).

Also, those who mourn over relationships and possessions lost for the cause of Christ can know that they will gain much more in Heaven. Further, "God shall wipe away all tears from their eyes; and there shall be no more death, neither sorrow, nor crying, neither shall there be any more pain: for the former things are passed away" (Revelation 21:4).

3. What are some synonyms for *pure*? How do these words add to your understanding of what purity implies?

Clean is one of the words we might associate with *pure*. Ceremonial cleanness was very important in the Old Testament. There were many rules and regulations to tell the Israelites what made them unclean and how to become clean again. (Many of these regulations are found in Leviticus and Deuteronomy.) One thing was certain: an unclean person could not approach God in worship.

In the New Testament we are also called to be clean and to be "unspotted from the world" (James 1:27). The blood of Jesus is what allows our purity. This is a purity we cannot attain on our own.

4. Why is being a peacemaker so difficult? How can you do better in this area?

Christianity and the world may not see eye to eye on the issues of spiritual poverty, mourning, etc. But on the value of being a peacemaker there is substantial agreement. The world recognizes great achievements in peacemaking by awarding Nobel Peace Prizes, etc. Great peacemakers must break through the me-first agendas of warring parties. Jesus' position on the value of peacemaking is clear.

Peacemakers are what God calls us to be. The reason is that we are His children, and He wants us to be like Him. The Prince of Peace knew the difficulty of peacemaking, for He even gave His life so that peace might once again exist between God and us. This is by far the most important kind of peace there is.

5. Why is it important that your own light not be hidden? How do you make this a priority?

First of all, if we truly wish to be like our Father, we must be light, for He is light (see 1 John 1:5). Light imagery is important in the New Testament. Light shows us the way to go; Jesus used the word *light* to describe himself as one who can show the way (see John 12:35).

Light also exposes the "dirty corners" in ourselves and in others so that we might correct those areas of darkness. Verse 16 of today's text also shows another reason why we need to be a light that is not hidden: so that our good works will be noticed by others and they will look heavenward to recognize and glorify God. Our light should be such that it consistently points to the Father of lights, and not to ourselves.

We make this a priority when we "drill down" to make God's light a priority in even the smallest areas of life. Those small areas (meaning those areas that many of us think aren't that big a deal) can include obeying traffic laws, practicing everyday courtesies, and making sure we leave a proper tip when dining out.

Community of Service

DEVOTIONAL READING: Philippians 2:1-11.

BACKGROUND SCRIPTURE: Matthew 20:1-28; Mark 10:35-45.

PRINTED TEXT: Matthew 20:17-28.

Matthew 20:17-28

17 And Jesus going up to Jerusalem took the twelve disciples apart in the way, and said unto them,

18 Behold, we go up to Jerusalem; and the Son of man shall be betrayed unto the chief priests and unto the scribes, and they shall condemn him to death,

19 And shall deliver him to the Gentiles to mock, and to scourge, and to crucify him: and the third day he shall rise again.

20 Then came to him the mother of Zebedee's children with her sons, worshipping him, and desiring a certain thing of him.

21 And he said unto her, What wilt thou? She saith unto him, Grant that these my two sons may sit, the one on thy right hand, and the other on the left, in thy kingdom.

22 But Jesus answered and said, Ye know not what ye ask. Are ye able to drink of the cup that I shall drink of, and to be baptized with the baptism that I am baptized with? They say unto him, We are able.

23 And he saith unto them, Ye shall drink indeed of my cup, and be baptized with the baptism that I am baptized with: but to sit on my right hand, and on my left, is not mine to give, but it shall be given to them for whom it is prepared of my Father.

24 And when the ten heard it, they were moved with indignation against the two brethren.

25 But Jesus called them unto him, and said, Ye know that the princes of the Gentiles exercise dominion over them, and they that are great exercise authority upon them.

26 But it shall not be so among you: but whosoever will be great among you, let him be your minister;

27 And whosoever will be chief among you, let him be your servant:

28 Even as the Son of man came not to be ministered unto, but to minister, and to give his life a ransom for many.

GOLDEN TEXT: The Son of man came not to be ministered unto, but to minister, and to give his life a ransom for many.—Matthew 20:28.

The New Testament Community
Unit 1: Birth of a New Community
(Lessons 1–4)

Lesson Aims

After participating in this lesson, each student will be able to:

1. Summarize the response of Jesus to the request made by the mother of Zebedee's sons.

2. Compare and contrast the view of greatness held by the mother of Zebedee's sons with that of Jesus.

3. Select an area of Christian service that reflects humility rather than authority.

Lesson Outline

INTRODUCTION
  A. "Service with a Smile!"
  B. Lesson Background
 I. MASTER'S PLAN (Matthew 20:17-19)
  A. Significant Destination (v. 17)
  B. Startling Announcement (vv. 18, 19)
    Betrayal
II. DISCIPLES' PLEA (Matthew 20:20-23)
  A. Outrageous Request (vv. 20, 21)
  B. Courteous Refusal (vv. 22, 23)
III. LESSON OF SERVICE (Matthew 20:24-28)
  A. Usual Abuses (vv. 24, 25)
  B. Unusual Service (vv. 26, 27)
  C. Ultimate Example (v. 28)
    Leading by Serving
CONCLUSION
  A. Service in Its True Beauty
  B. Prayer
  C. Thought to Remember

Introduction

A. "Service with a Smile!"

Service with a Smile! This slogan used to grace the walls of many stores, service stations, and repair centers. Family businesses made this motto a point of pride. But that philosophy now seems antiquated. The world of the twenty-first century seems too busy to care about such things anymore. Both the smile and the personal service have fallen by the wayside.

For Christians, however, a life of service will never go out of style. Much more than just a good business strategy, service is the lifestyle of the master. To walk in the footsteps of Jesus is to walk the path of humble servanthood.

B. Lesson Background

At the point in the Gospel of Matthew that concerns today's lesson, Jesus has nearly reached the end of His three-year ministry. During this time He has healed the sick and fed the hungry. He has given sight to the blind and hearing to the deaf. He has freed the demon-possessed from their demons. He has even raised the dead. While Jesus' miraculous works have given proof that He is the Son of God, they also have given a clear demonstration of the love of God. Jesus has spent His ministry in the service of humanity, showing people the way to God.

Popular excitement was building, even though Jesus was not the kind of Messiah that most people wanted. Official opposition was also building, with the religious authorities trying to find a way to put Jesus to death. The excitement and the animosity reached their peak in Jerusalem, which became the most dangerous place in the world for Jesus to go.

Yet Jesus set a determined course toward the holy city. Jesus knew in advance all the terrible things that were to happen to Him there. He was not caught up helplessly in events beyond His control. He chose to give His life as a ransom for the world, to die in the service of humanity.

As a final lesson on the way, Jesus taught His disciples the value of service. Citizens of the kingdom of Heaven must realize they belong to a community of service, even to the point of giving their lives for the sake of others. (The parallel Gospel account to today's lesson is Mark 10:32-45.)

I. Master's Plan
(Matthew 20:17-19)

A. Significant Destination (v. 17)

17. And Jesus going up to Jerusalem took the twelve disciples apart in the way, and said unto them.

The road *to Jerusalem* is a climb in elevation, hence the phrase *going up*. Jesus has gone there before, but this time is different. Now He is going there to die. The parallel account in the Gospel of Mark shows Jesus boldly leading the way, with the disciples astonished and fearful (see Mark 10:32).

No other city is more appropriate for this trip. The Son of David is going to be put to death in the city that King David had made his capital. The Son of God will die as a sacrifice near the temple of God. At the hands of men, the Son of Man will be put to violent death.

Jesus warned His followers previously that this is going to happen (see Mark 8:31; 9:31). Now He takes *the twelve* apart from the other disciples to give them one last warning. They must understand that the upcoming death on the cross is a necessary part of God's plan.

B. Startling Announcement (vv. 18, 19)

18. Behold, we go up to Jerusalem; and the Son of man shall be betrayed unto the chief priests and unto the scribes, and they shall condemn him to death.

Jesus' favorite self-designation is *the Son of man,* which occurs about 80 times in the Gospels. This somewhat mysterious designation is drawn from Daniel 7:13, 14: "I saw in the night visions, and, behold, one like the Son of man came with the clouds of heaven, and came to the Ancient of days, and they brought him near before him. And there was given him dominion, and glory, and a kingdom."

Jesus probably uses this phrase because it both reveals and conceals. Those with eyes to see and ears to hear will recognize by this phrase that Jesus is the Messiah. Those whose hearts are hardened can only ask, "Who is this Son of man?" (John 12:34).

After the traveling party arrives in the holy city of Jerusalem, Jesus will be *betrayed.* One of His own disciples will turn against Him. We remember that Judas Iscariot, the betrayer, is present among the 12 disciples as these words are spoken. Jesus already knows, even if Judas does not, that this disciple will turn Him over to the Jewish religious authorities in exchange for 30 pieces of silver. [See question #1, page 40.]

The chief priests represent the authority of the temple; *the scribes* (and Pharisees) represent the authority of the synagogues and the law. Thinking they are acting on behalf of God, these authorities will *condemn* Jesus *to death.*

How to Say It

CORINTHIANS. Ko-*rin*-thee-unz (*th* as in *thin*).

HEROD. *Hair*-ud.

JERUSALEM. Juh-*roo*-suh-lem.

JUDAS ISCARIOT. *Joo*-dus Iss-*care*-ee-ut.

MESSIAH. Meh-*sigh*-uh.

PATMOS. *Pat*-muss.

PHARISEES. *Fair*-ih-seez.

PILATE. *Pie*-lut.

SYNAGOGUE. *sin*-uh-gog.

ZEBEDEE. *Zeb*-eh-dee.

BETRAYAL

Betrayal seems to be rampant these days. The TV show *Cheaters* even allows us to watch! A Web site with the slogan "where cheaters are caught red handed" claims that "50–65 percent of husbands and 45–55 percent of wives have had extramarital affairs by the time they are 40."

Of course, this could just be hype to encourage paranoid people to fork over a $20 fee for the organization's investigative services. Then there is the matter of a reward for an informant's information. The Web site advises, "The more money you are willing to pay, the more motivated the informant will be."

We may be disgusted by such a mercenary attitude toward the issue of betrayal. After all, if someone is aware of a betrayal, why does the potential informant have to be paid off to reveal the information (if indeed that is the right thing to do)? Even so, the situation of Judas was even more appalling: he wasn't a mere paid informant, he was a paid perpetrator!

Jesus accepted betrayal by a disciple and chose not to fight His enemies. Knowledge of both the glorious plan of God and the perverseness of human hearts is what kept Jesus true to His mission as our Redeemer. Where do we find ourselves on the scale from complete faithfulness to utter betrayal? How can we determine whether we are Jesus' true or false friends?   —C. R. B.

19. And shall deliver him to the Gentiles to mock, and to scourge, and to crucify him: and the third day he shall rise again.

Under Roman law, the Jewish leaders do not have the authority to put anyone to death. (The stoning of Stephen in Acts 7 is an act of mob violence.) For this reason, those leaders have to *deliver him to the Gentiles* so that a death sentence can be carried out (see John 18:28-32).

The Romans have little respect for the Jews and their laws. With pride in the military power of Rome, they especially have little respect for a so-called "king" who has no power at all. That is why they will *mock* Jesus with the sneering words, "Hail, King of the Jews!" (see Matthew 27:29). They will *scourge* him without mercy. Finally, they will *crucify* Him. Crucifixion is such a slow, horrible death that it is reserved for only the worst of criminals and rebels. Jesus knows exactly what awaits Him at the end of His road.

But Jesus also knows that death will not be the final chapter. On Friday He will die; on Saturday He will lie in the grip of death in a borrowed tomb; but on Sunday—*the third day*—He will *rise again!* On an earlier occasion when Jesus spoke of rising

Home Daily Bible Readings

Monday, Sep. 22—The Humility of Christ (Philippians 2:1-11)

Tuesday, Sep. 23—The Greatest in the Kingdom (Matthew 18:1-5)

Wednesday, Sep. 24—Serving and Following Jesus (John 12:20-26)

Thursday, Sep. 25—Serving Fearlessly (Matthew 10:24-33)

Friday, Sep. 26—Serving in God's Strength (1 Peter 4:7-11)

Saturday, Sep. 27—The Last Will Be First (Matthew 20:1-16)

Sunday, Sep. 28—Service, Not Status (Matthew 20:17-28)

again, His disciples questioned each other to try to discover what Jesus could possibly mean by the words "rising from the dead" (see Mark 9:10). It may be unimaginable and seemingly impossible, but Jesus knows it will happen.

II. Disciples' Plea (Matthew 20:20-23)

A. Outrageous Request (vv. 20, 21)

20. Then came to him the mother of Zebedee's children with her sons, worshipping him, and desiring a certain thing of him.

As if totally oblivious to what Jesus is saying, James, John, and their *mother* come to Him with a selfish request (compare Mark 10:35). The two men, *Zebedee's children*, were among the earliest disciples to follow Jesus (see Matthew 4:21, 22). They are also part of what we call the inner circle of three that had accompanied Jesus when He was transfigured (see Matthew 17:1). In *worshipping him* their underlying motive is to ask Jesus to say that He will grant them a special favor.

A comparison of the lists of women at the cross raises the interesting possibility that the mother of Zebedee's children is Jesus' aunt on His mother's side (see Matthew 27:56; Mark 15:40; John 19:25). If there is such a family connection, it helps explain why the woman is so bold in asking for a special privilege for her sons in the next verse.

21. And he said unto her, What wilt thou? She saith unto him, Grant that these my two sons may sit, the one on thy right hand, and the other on the left, in thy kingdom.

As Mark's Gospel explains in greater detail, the requested favor follows the statement to Jesus, "Master, we would that thou shouldest do for us

whatsoever we shall desire" (Mark 10:35). Rather than blindly agreeing to such an open-ended request, Jesus asks, *What wilt thou?*

Now the mother brings the request out into the open: she wants her boys to *sit* at the *right hand* and at the *left* of Jesus, enjoying seats of special privilege and power in His *kingdom* (compare Psalms 16:11; 45:9; 110:1). She apparently expects that Jesus will soon usher in the long-awaited messianic kingdom (see Acts 1:6). She and her sons probably envision Jesus reigning in majesty and power, and they want in on it! While it may be understandable that a mother would have high hopes for her sons, her request is completely out of line. [See question #2, page 40.]

B. Courteous Refusal (vv. 22, 23)

22. But Jesus answered and said, Ye know not what ye ask. Are ye able to drink of the cup that I shall drink of, and to be baptized with the baptism that I am baptized with? They say unto him, We are able.

Jesus responds with admirable restraint. Instead of rebuking her and the sons with exasperation and anger, He explains that they have no idea what they are asking. Can they *drink of the cup* from which Jesus will drink? Can they *be baptized with the baptism* that Jesus will experience?

Cup is a symbol of the wrath and punishment of God many times in the Old Testament (see Psalm 75:8; Isaiah 51:17; and Jeremiah 25:15-28). Even before the crisis in the Garden of Gethsemane (see Matthew 26:39), they should understand that drinking the cup is a bitter, unpleasant experience. Likewise, to *be baptized* is to be totally engulfed in something (such as the baptism of the Holy Ghost and the baptism of fire in Matthew 3:11). Jesus knows that He will soon be engulfed in a *baptism* of suffering—and it will be such suffering as the disciples cannot begin to imagine!

With the kind of confidence that comes from complete ignorance, the disciples answer, *We are able*. Perhaps they suppose that they are ready for anything, since they have persevered with Jesus through three years of ministry. Perhaps they have an unrealistic idea of their own strength. While it is admirable of them to volunteer to face whatever the future holds, it is also naïve.

23. And he saith unto them, Ye shall drink indeed of my cup, and be baptized with the baptism that I am baptized with: but to sit on my right hand, and on my left, is not mine to give, but it shall be given to them for whom it is prepared of my Father.

Looking into the years that lie ahead, Jesus assures James and John that they will *drink indeed* of His *cup*. They will be engulfed in sufferings far beyond what they can envision. James will be the first apostle to be martyred for his faith, when Herod has him put to death with the sword (see Acts 12:2). John, for his part, will live a long life of service, but will be cast into exile on the Island of Patmos (see Revelation 1:9).

It is not up to Jesus to decide who will *sit on* His *right hand* or on His *left*. Just as the kingdom will be established in the time set by the Father (see Acts 1:7), likewise any positions of authority will be determined by the Father. Just as Jesus cares little for earthly power and the praise of people, so should the disciples stop jockeying for position and learn the lesson of servanthood.

III. Lesson of Service
(Matthew 20:24-28)
A. Usual Abuses (vv. 24, 25)

24. And when the ten heard it, they were moved with indignation against the two brethren.

Are we surprised that the other *ten* are *moved with indignation* against their *two* fellow apostles? Are they indignant because they have not had the opportunity to ask first?

The mind-set of the apostles is clearly revealed not many days later when they gather together in the upper room. Another dispute arises among them as they argue over who will be counted as the greatest (see Luke 22:24). Jesus uses the setting in the upper room to teach a lesson of service. On this later occasion, He will gird himself with a towel and humbly wash their feet (see John 13:3-17). Like most of us today, they are slow to learn the value of servanthood. [See question #3, page 40.]

25. But Jesus called them unto him, and said, Ye know that the princes of the Gentiles exercise dominion over them, and they that are great exercise authority upon them.

As the ten quarrel with the two over who will get seats of power and importance, Jesus calls *them* over. First, He reminds them of the abuses of power that are usual in the political world of which they know. In the world of *the Gentiles*, the rulers always take advantage of their power to *exercise dominion* over their subjects.

Likewise, *they that are great*, meaning the powerful magistrates, *exercise authority* in oppressive ways. Rome is like that; Pilate and Herod are like that; and the people resent them for it. Jesus is thus able to use the question of James, John, and their mother as a teaching moment for all the disciples. Rather than getting distracted about details of a future kingdom, Jesus is more interested in

teaching His disciples how they ought to live right now. The lesson they need is a lesson of service.

The illustration Jesus uses can be found in virtually every society in every era. Whenever a group rises to power and stays in power long enough, power eventually corrupts it. When an oppressed minority becomes the ruling authority, they can become just as oppressive as their predecessors. The abuse of authority seems to be ingrained in human nature. Jesus does not want His church to learn patterns of power from the world. [See question #4, page 40.]

B. Unusual Service (vv. 26, 27)

26. But it shall not be so among you: but whosoever will be great among you, let him be your minister.

The standard abuse of authority by those who climb the ladder to power is not to be the model of the followers of Christ. Instead, whoever has the ambition to *be great* should become a mere servant. To minister to the needs of others is a higher calling than to claim seats of power.

Moreover, we should not interpret this verse to mean that Jesus is teaching a secret route to power. He is not saying that ambitious, power-hungry people can reach their goal more quickly by adopting the guise of servanthood. Becoming a servant is to be a cure—not a clever tool—for those with such ambitions. Just a short time earlier, Jesus had told the rich young ruler how to deal with the money he loved so much (see Matthew 19:16-22). Now Jesus is warning those who love seats of power to abandon their ambition.

27. And whosoever will be chief among you, let him be your servant.

THE KEY TO GREATNESS IS SERVICE

Visual for
Lesson 4

Turn this statement into a question: "Why is service the key to greatness?"

To repeat the lesson, Jesus puts His teaching into even stronger terms. If anyone wants to be *chief among you*, meaning to be number one above all others, then he is to be *your servant* (literally, "your slave"; 1 Corinthians 9:19; 2 Corinthians 4:5). Such a person's unhealthy craving to be recognized as the greatest is to be replaced with a humble willingness to be the least. [See question #5, page 40.]

C. Ultimate Example (v. 28)

28. Even as the Son of man came not to be ministered unto, but to minister, and to give his life a ransom for many.

Appropriately, Jesus offers himself as the ultimate example. As *the Son of man*, He does not come to have people serve Him; rather, He comes to serve them. He does not demand a palace; rather, He chooses a life in which He has nowhere to lay His head (see Matthew 8:20). He seeks neither the praise and approval of men nor a life of power and prestige; rather, He chooses to be meek and lowly (see Matthew 11:29). He chooses a life of service.

Most of all, Jesus chooses to serve by giving His life as *a ransom for many*. All people are sinners and deserve to die (see Romans 3:23; 6:23). Jesus goes to the cross as our substitute, paying our debt as people rightly condemned under law. His *ransom* payment satisfies all the claims that the law holds against us.

Jesus began these verses by warning His disciples that betrayal and death await Him in Jerusalem. Because of an interruption by two disciples and their solicitous mother, Jesus has a great opportunity to teach a lesson about serving others. He concludes this lesson with a return to the beginning fact: He is going to die. In this death He will teach the ultimate lesson of serving others, as the incarnate Son of God takes the place of others and suffers the penalty of death.

LEADING BY SERVING

Robert K. Greenleaf (1904–1990) was Director of Management Research at AT&T for 38 years. His name has become well known in the business world, largely because of his innovative approach to leadership at AT&T. Greenleaf's essay "The Servant as Leader" was published in 1970 and gained for him the reputation as the man who coined the phrase *servant-leadership*. He developed what many saw as a revolutionary idea: leaders lead best by serving those whom they lead.

After retiring from AT&T, Greenleaf founded The Center for Creative Leadership to promote the servant-leader concept (www.greenleaf.org).

He has been called "one of the twentieth century's most innovative thinkers." Yet Christians recognize that Greenleaf simply rediscovered what Jesus talked about in our lesson today.

The world has structured its value system on power almost from the beginning. As a result, ancient and modern cultures esteem people in relation to the amount of power they have. Yet Jesus challenged the status quo and showed us a better way: We who follow Him should find the way of the servant.   —C. R. B.

Conclusion

A. Service in Its True Beauty

Doesn't it seem that the universal goal of people is to serve themselves? Even when they offer service, it usually is to gain a paycheck or some personal advantage.

In complete contradiction to the predominant view of the ancient and modern worlds, Jesus shows us that serving others is God's way. Yet service to be seen and appreciated by other people may result in only that (Matthew 6:5). God's recognition comes from forgetting ourselves as we serve others.

Service in all its true beauty is best seen in the life of Jesus. Even though He had all the power and privileges of Heaven, He emptied himself and came to earth as a man (see Philippians 2:5-8). He had the heart of a servant, gladly humbling himself to serve others. He even lowered himself to the point of dying on a cross between two thieves. His is the life to emulate; His is the mind-set to adopt.

God will reward humble servanthood. He opposes the proud, but He gives grace and approval to the lowly. He honors the faithful disciple who follows in the steps of Jesus and serves Him (see John 12:26). To those who have fed the hungry, clothed the naked, and cared for the sick and imprisoned, the Lord will say, "Inasmuch as ye have done it unto one of the least of these my brethren, ye have done it unto me" (Matthew 25:40).

B. Prayer

Our Father, how quickly we forget the lessons that Jesus taught us about servanthood! Forgive us when we ignore what You are teaching us and think only of our own advancement. Teach us anew to forsake personal ambition and give our lives serving others. We pray in the name of Jesus, who gave His all, amen.

C. Thought to Remember

Embrace servanthood.

Learning by Doing

This page contains an alternative lesson plan emphasizing learning activities. Some of these activities are also found in the helpful student book, Adult Bible Class.

Into the Lesson

Recruit an actress to deliver the following short monologue as class begins. The woman is portraying the mother of James and John.

I once watched my sons follow their father to his fishing boat. What a handsome group of men! I watched them faithfully follow my husband to the synagogue. How I admired them from the women's side! Then one unusual day I saw them follow a stranger . . . away from their father's business, away from their mother's wings of care. What mixed emotions I felt deep within. Oh, I wanted them to share in the Messiah's kingdom, but now I would see them less and less. Now I would lie awake anxiously at night concerned about their safety. The Romans would not understand this Jewish idea, and what they did not understand they viewed with suspicion.

And there was already talk among some Jewish leaders that this Jesus could not be the Messiah, only a pretender. Who knew what they would do? My sons—they could be in perils I knew nothing about. Sometimes I long for the simple Galilean mornings when I saw them off to the Sea of Galilee, full of talk about weather and fish. If I ever have the opportunity, I will speak to Jesus about my boys. He needs to know how special they are, how special they can be.

Thank this "mother of Zebedee's sons," and direct your class's attention to today's text.

Into the Word

Copy and distribute the following list of surprising events and affirmations in today's text. Put the heading *SURPRISE!* at the top. (Though numbered here, the list should be presented without numbers.)

1. Jesus had to tell His disciples of His fate yet again. 2. Jesus knew exactly what would happen to Him in Jerusalem. 3. Jesus had to die, but He would rise to life again. 4. The mother of James and John asked a special position for her sons. 5. James and John affirmed their ability to follow Jesus' steps of suffering and death. 6. Jesus declared that James and John would indeed follow Him in suffering and death. 7. Jesus indicat-

ed that certain places of privilege were not His to give. 8. The other 10 apostles were indignant when they heard of James and John's request, as made by their mother. 9. Jesus declared that the great—the leaders—in His kingdom would be servants. 10. Jesus used himself as the example of a successful life, one of service.

Give this direction: "Much of this text may surprise and startle us. Pick the three truths that are most surprising to you."

Allow time for the task, and then ask several to identify their top three surprises, with an explanation of why they chose them. You are not looking for a particular "correct" sequence. Rather, you are allowing for a discussion of the ideas of the text. If you hear any general agreement on "the most surprising," note that to the class for further reflection.

Into Life

Prepare a large sheet of paper or poster board resembling a want ads page in a newspaper. Put the large heading *Positions Available* at the top. Divide the sheet into two columns.

Give each of your learners an index card with the identification of a typical service task in the local church printed on it. Include those tasks that go wanting in your congregation. Some of the following are nearly always "available": telephoning or visiting senior members who are shut in by health; driving disabled members to appointments (or running errands for them); preparing elements used in Communion services; keeping bulletin boards current and neat; mowing grass in summer and clearing sidewalks in snowy weather; preparing coffee/tea service for various occasions or regular worship hours; handling special mailings of the congregation; preparing food for funeral gatherings; teaching classes; greeting worship attendees; contacting first-time visitors afterward; making "missed you" calls to individuals noted to be absent two or three Sundays.

Give learners time to prepare short, simple "job descriptions and solicitations" and then have some read. Enter all on your *Positions Available* sheet. Give your class first crack at the positions, but also ask permission to post the needs in a conspicuous place in the church building to stir others to service.

Let's Talk It Over

The questions on this page are designed to promote discussion of the lesson by the class and to encourage application of the lesson Scriptures. The answers provided are only discussion starters. Let your class talk it over from there.

1. What are some ways that people betray Christ today? How do we guard ourselves in this regard?

Betrayal and *denial* are related ideas (although outright betrayal is the stronger of the two). Peter exhibited a betrayal of sorts when he denied Jesus (Matthew 26:69-75). A type of betrayal can come when we deny Jesus by our faithlessness. The only one ever completely faithful is God (see 2 Timothy 2:13). All Christians will be guilty of some level of betrayal/denial at some point.

There is no doubt that betrayal hurts, and one can easily imagine the hurt on Jesus' face when He inquired of Judas, "Betrayest thou the Son of man with a kiss?" (Luke 22:48). Yet there can be forgiveness for betrayal and denial (John 21:15-19).

2. If you could characterize the request of James and John's mother with a single word, what would that word be? Why? How do you guard your heart against this attitude?

Some folks may think of the words *inappropriate, selfish,* and *arrogant*. If John and James were related to Jesus by blood, then the word *nepotism* also could come to mind. A link of being blood relatives may have caused the mother to believe that her boys "had first dibs" on the positions of honor.

This is the way of the world, isn't it? Secular thinking is always looking for an angle to promote oneself over another. There is nothing wrong with earning a college degree, gaining some type of certification, etc., to advance in one's career as long as the motives are right. God expects us to do our best in our occupations. A problem with the mother of Zebedee's sons was that her motive was all wrong. Before we embark on a path of self-promotion, we do well to pause and ask ourselves, "Exactly what outcome do I seek, and why do I seek it?"

3. What was a time when you became indignant over the fact of another's advancement? Was your indignation godly or ungodly? Why?

We all seem to have a keen sense of what is *fair* and what is *not fair*. When we examine instances in our own lives when we have become indignant, we may find that it is not really the other person's fairly achieved success that upsets us. Rather, it

may be the fact that the success didn't come to us—thus we think "not fair!" When that happens, the monster called *envy* is not far away.

Romans 12:15 tells us what our attitude should be with another's success: "Rejoice with them that do rejoice." With this attitude, we will praise God for His goodness when we see Him blessing the lives of our friends and family.

4. When was a time you felt that someone was exercising power over you in an oppressive way? How should we respond in such situations?

Whether it be a governmental policy or some ridiculous requirement at the workplace, we all have had to follow instructions that did not make any sense to us and for which our concerns were ignored. Yet we are commanded by God to honor and obey such authorities, since they were put in place by God. Romans 13:1 states: "Let every soul be subject unto the higher powers. For there is no power but of God: the powers that be are ordained of God." Everyone, without exception, is to be subject to those over them. Even though we may not like how some people exercise their authority over us, we are called to obey.

This does not mean blind obedience, however. There are specific times to say *no* to authority, no matter what it costs us (see Acts 5:29).

5. How would you respond if you were asked to become a servant to another?

We would probably start by asking for clarification! *"Servant* like a *butler,* or *servant* like a *slave?"* we might ask. Certainly slavery as practiced by the world deserves its horrendous reputation and our condemnation. Oppression is not what Jesus desired. In the Bible, slavery to sin is something that Jesus came to free us from.

The attitude Jesus calls us to have is one of humility. An attitude of humility leads us to be willing servants. The apostle Paul tells us in Philippians 2 that we are to look out for the interests of others and to consider others more important than ourselves. This God-appointed form of servitude can be very difficult, but it is what is required to be great in the kingdom of God. We are also to be servants (slaves) of righteousness (Romans 6:18).

Empowered Community

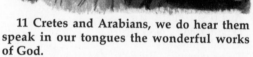

DEVOTIONAL READING: Ephesians 2:11-22.

BACKGROUND SCRIPTURE: Acts 2:1-47.

PRINTED TEXT: Acts 2:1-17a.

Acts 2:1-17a

1 And when the day of Pentecost was fully come, they were all with one accord in one place.

2 And suddenly there came a sound from heaven as of a rushing mighty wind, and it filled all the house where they were sitting.

3 And there appeared unto them cloven tongues like as of fire, and it sat upon each of them.

4 And they were all filled with the Holy Ghost, and began to speak with other tongues, as the Spirit gave them utterance.

5 And there were dwelling at Jerusalem Jews, devout men, out of every nation under heaven.

6 Now when this was noised abroad, the multitude came together, and were confounded, because that every man heard them speak in his own language.

7 And they were all amazed and marveled, saying one to another, Behold, are not all these which speak Galileans?

8 And how hear we every man in our own tongue, wherein we were born?

9 Parthians, and Medes, and Elamites, and the dwellers in Mesopotamia, and in Judea, and Cappadocia, in Pontus, and Asia,

10 Phrygia, and Pamphylia, in Egypt, and in the parts of Libya about Cyrene, and strangers of Rome, Jews and proselytes,

11 Cretes and Arabians, we do hear them speak in our tongues the wonderful works of God.

12 And they were all amazed, and were in doubt, saying one to another, What meaneth this?

13 Others mocking said, These men are full of new wine.

14 But Peter, standing up with the eleven, lifted up his voice, and said unto them, Ye men of Judea, and all ye that dwell at Jerusalem, be this known unto you, and hearken to my words:

15 For these are not drunken, as ye suppose, seeing it is but the third hour of the day.

16 But this is that which was spoken by the prophet Joel;

17a And it shall come to pass in the last days, saith God, I will pour out of my Spirit upon all flesh.

GOLDEN TEXT: They were all filled with the Holy Ghost, and began to speak with other tongues, as the Spirit gave them utterance.—Acts 2:4.

The New Testament Community
Unit 2: Growth of the New Community
(Lessons 5–8)

Lesson Aims

After participating in this lesson, each student will be able to:

1. List the dramatic events that preceded the birth of the church on the Day of Pentecost.

2. Explain the role of the Holy Spirit on the Day of Pentecost.

3. Write a prayer of thankfulness for the presence of the Holy Spirit.

Lesson Outline

INTRODUCTION
 A. Power Outage
 B. Lesson Background
 I. POWER DELIVERED (Acts 2:1-4)
  A. Assembly (v. 1)
  B. Audio Miracle (v. 2)
   Do You Hear What I Hear?
  C. Visual Miracle (v. 3)
  D. Empowerment Miracle (v. 4)
 II. POWER DISPLAYED (Acts 2:5-13)
  A. Confounded (vv. 5, 6)
  B. Cosmopolitan Crowd (vv. 7-12)
  C. Scoffers (v. 13)
 III. POWER PREACHING (Acts 2:14-17a)
  A. Peter Defends (vv. 14, 15)
  B. Prophecy Fulfilled (vv. 16, 17a)
   Too Good to Be True?
CONCLUSION
 A. The Holy Spirit Then and Now
 B. Prayer
 C. Thought to Remember

Introduction

A. Power Outage

The American professor visiting a missions college was excited when he was told that his classroom in a remote location had been fitted with "air-con" (air conditioning). When he had taught there the previous year, the sweltering heat of the tropical nation had caused the sweat to roll off him in a constant flow.

Sure enough, upon arrival in the classroom the teacher spotted the shiny new air-con unit. He was surprised, however, to find that the room was still very hot. Explanation? There was no electricity to that part of the city on that day.

Even the newest, most technologically sophisticated equipment in the world is of no value without a source of energy. A cutting-edge computer with no electricity is good for no more than a doorstop or a plant stand. An expensive car is no more than a lawn ornament if it has no fuel.

The church draws on the energy of its members. It is undergirded by faith, both of past and present Christians. But the church's greatest source of power is God himself. God empowers the church and the individual believer through the work and ministry of His Holy Spirit.

A congregation may construct a lavish palace for worship, but without the presence of the Spirit, it will always be underutilized. A church may recruit many community leaders to its board, but without the Spirit empowering their lives, it will be just another nonprofit organization. A creative church staff may develop an array of programs to appeal to the unchurched community, but without the active work of the Holy Spirit, the effort will resemble the marketing efforts of any business.

B. Lesson Background

Acts is the second volume of work from the author Luke. As in the Gospel of Luke, there is a continuing emphasis on the Holy Spirit in Acts (compare Luke 1:15, 35; 2:25-27; 4:1, 18; 10:21; 12:12 for some examples). Some students have suggested that the theme of the work of the Holy Spirit is so prominent in Acts that the book could be renamed the "Acts of the Holy Spirit" instead of the traditional "Acts of the Apostles."

After Jesus' resurrection, He made various appearances to the believers for a period of 40 days (Acts 1:3). He then left them to go back to Heaven to be with the Father. His final instructions before the ascension included the command for them to wait in Jerusalem until they had received the power of the Holy Spirit (Acts 1:5, 8). This was to be the fulfillment of an earlier prophecy by John the Baptist that Jesus was the one who would baptize with the Holy Spirit and with fire (Luke 3:16).

The first chapter of Acts records what the group of believers did during this waiting period. The group numbered about 120 (Acts 1:15), and they met regularly for prayer (Acts 1:14). They also used this time to select a new apostle, Matthias, to replace Judas Iscariot and return the number of apostles to 12.

Pentecost was a Jewish holiday that occurred in May or early June. It was also called the Feast of Weeks (see 2 Chronicles 8:13). It was to commemorate the giving of the Law to Moses at Sinai 50 days after the Exodus and was thus celebrated 50 days after the last day of Passover week.

Since Passover ended with a Sabbath (Saturday), and 50 days is 7 weeks plus 1 day, that means Pentecost fell on a Sunday, the first day of the week. (For more on Pentecost see Leviticus 23:15-21; Deuteronomy 16:9-11.) In the New Testament era, it was not uncommon for Jewish pilgrims from other parts of the world to visit Jerusalem for Passover and remain in the city the 7 weeks until Pentecost. This is the reason for the many foreign nationalities mentioned in today's lesson.

I. Power Delivered
(Acts 2:1-4)
A. Assembly (v. 1)

1. And when the day of Pentecost was fully come, they were all with one accord in one place.

This particular *Pentecost* is a Sunday about 10 days after Jesus' ascension (compare Acts 1:3). As they have gathered throughout this week and a half, the disciples are together again for fellowship and prayer.

Who is being referred to as *they* in this verse (and therefore the following verses)? Some see it as including only the 12 apostles. Others see it as the larger group of 120 of Acts 1:15, which includes apostles and nonapostles, both men and women. In any case, we may note that the larger group has been meeting every day since Jesus' departure. They are unified. [See question #1, page 48.]

B. Audio Miracle (v. 2)

2. And suddenly there came a sound from heaven as of a rushing mighty wind, and it filled all the house where they were sitting.

How to Say It

ARABIANS. Uh-*ray*-bee-unz.
CAPPADOCIA. Kap-uh-*doe*-shuh.
CRETE. Creet.
CYRENE. Sigh-*ree*-nee.
ELAMITES. *Ee*-luh-mites.
MATTHIAS. Muh-*thigh*-us (*th* as in *thin*).
MEDES. Meeds.
MESOPOTAMIA. *Mes*-uh-puh-*tay*-me-uh (strong accent on *tay*).
PAMPHYLIA. Pam-*fill*-ee-uh.
PARTHIANS. *Par*-the-uns (*the* as in *thief*).
PENTECOST. *Pent*-ih-kost.
PHRYGIA. *Frij*-e-uh.
PONTUS. *Pon*-tuss.

The reader should be careful to notice the details of the story as portrayed by Luke, the author of Acts. The gathered believers are surely startled to hear a loud *sound*, described as a powerful *wind* noise. Those who have been in a dangerously strong windstorm can testify that it is loud, so loud that spoken words are impossible to hear. There is no wind damage here, however, for there is no actual wind. This is a supernatural sound, a supernatural phenomenon. This noise fills the room, meaning everyone present experiences it.

Two symbolic items should be noted here. First, the source of this sound is *heaven*, implying that its origin is God himself. Second, the ancient concept of *wind* is closely related to *spirit*, thus setting the scene for what is about to happen.

DO YOU HEAR WHAT I HEAR?

Many of us suffer a gradual decline in hearing ability as we age. Some tones that are clear to young people may not be heard by older folks. These facts prompted a security firm to develop a device called the Mosquito, which emits a high-pitched tone that older adults cannot hear, but which is said to be "ear-splittingly painful" to young people. The intended use for this device is to play it in places where older folks do not want younger people to gather. Thus the first group will not be bothered by the disconcerting habits, clothing styles, and music of the second group.

However, youth has found a way to get revenge. There is now a high-pitched cell-phone ring tone that most people over a certain age cannot hear. This enables students sitting in a classroom to receive cell phone calls unbeknownst to the teacher. Thus the student can be getting text messages that may range anywhere from idle chatter to answers to the questions on the exam the student is taking at the time.

The sound of a rushing wind on Pentecost was a sound that *everyone* could hear. Its purpose was not to drive people away, nor to deceive anyone. On the contrary, the sound was to draw attention to the fact that God was about to do something spectacular. It drew the crowd to hear the gospel. What the world sees and hears from the church should have a similar effect today.   —C. R. B.

C. Visual Miracle (v. 3)

3. And there appeared unto them cloven tongues like as of fire, and it sat upon each of them.

As with Acts 2:2, this verse is also susceptible to misunderstanding. Just as there is no wind damage to the house, there is no fire damage either. Nothing is burned or even singed. Luke says that those present see *cloven* (divided) *tongues like as of fire*. This is supernatural fire, like the bush Moses experienced—it burned but was not consumed (Exodus 3:2).

The term *tongue* has three potential meanings here. First, it can refer to the small appendage in our mouths that we use to lick ice cream cones (see James 3:5). Second, tongue can also refer to a spoken language, and by extension, to the people group that speaks that language (see Revelation 5:9). Third, the shape of the human tongue can be used to describe the shape of other items. In this case, it is used to describe the tongues (flames) of the supernatural spirit-fire.

The sound of wind provides an audio miracle. The tongues of fire provide a visual miracle. We can only imagine what this actually looks like, but it must be both startling and exciting. As with the wind noise, all present can see that it is being experienced by *each* person present.

D. Empowerment Miracle (v. 4)

4. And they were all filled with the Holy Ghost, and began to speak with other tongues, as the Spirit gave them utterance.

What does it mean to be *filled with the Holy Ghost*? In this particular case, it leads to a supernatural empowerment, the miraculous ability to do something beyond one's normal capability. The effect of the tongues of fire is the ability to speak in *other tongues*, meaning languages unlearned by the believers.

II. Power Displayed
(Acts 2:5-13)

A. Confounded (vv. 5, 6)

5. And there were dwelling at Jerusalem Jews, devout men, out of every nation under heaven.

The location of the previous events is uncertain. The day seems to start in the house where the believers have been meeting (thought to be the house of Mary, the mother of John Mark; see Acts 12:12). The power of the Holy Spirit is surely in this house! Without comment, Luke next allows the action to shift outside to a more public place. This may be a nearby courtyard, marketplace, or even the courts of the temple.

Jews in the New Testament period have emigrated to all the major cities of the Roman world and even beyond. Later in Acts, Paul will encounter Jewish communities in cities he visits (compare Acts 15:21). Many Jews come to Jerusalem to visit, to be educated, or to retire. Both Paul and Barnabas are foreign-born Jews who take up residence in the temple city (see Acts 4:36; 22:3).

6. Now when this was noised abroad, the multitude came together, and were confounded, because that every man heard them speak in his own language.

Sunday, the first day of the week, is a working, business day in the Jewish world. People are out and about, and the city is abuzz with visitors still there for the Pentecost festivities. It is not difficult for the word to spread of extraordinary happenings in or near the believers' meetinghouse. So a crowd gathers quickly.

B. Cosmopolitan Crowd (vv. 7-12)

7. And they were all amazed and marveled, saying one to another, Behold, are not all these which speak Galileans?

If the group that gathers is made up largely of visitors for the Passover-to-Pentecost period, then this is a wealthy, well-educated lot. (To make such a lengthy, time-consuming trip requires lots of money.) They recognize by the believers' appearance that they are from Galilee, considered to be a rural backwater for any sophisticated Jew of this period. For the visitors, it is highly unexpected that *Galileans* could be speaking in all the languages of the known world; see the next verse. [See question #2, page 48.]

8, 9. And how hear we every man in our own tongue, wherein we were born? Parthians, and Medes, and Elamites, and the dwellers in Mesopotamia, and in Judea, and Cappadocia, in Pontus, and Asia.

The widespread geographic origins of this crowd are remarkable. They come from as far east as Parthia (modern Iran) and as far north as *Pontus* (northern shore of modern Turkey).

10, 11. Phrygia, and Pamphylia, in Egypt, and in the parts of Libya about Cyrene, and strangers of Rome, Jews and proselytes, Cretes and Arabians, we do hear them speak in our tongues the wonderful works of God.

The visitors also come from as far south as *Libya* (northern Africa) and as far west as *Rome*, the imperial city. All of the other places mentioned are within these boundaries.

The content of the miraculous message is not given to us directly, but we get a clue in that the foreigners hear of the *wonderful works of God* in their native languages. This may be something like the praise passages from the Psalms (example: Psalm 40:5).

12. And they were all amazed, and were in doubt, saying one to another, What meaneth this?

In the Gospel of Luke, for a crowd to be *amazed* usually means the people have witnessed a miracle of God (see Luke 5:26; 9:43). Here in Acts (also written by Luke), the crowd recognizes that something very out of the ordinary is going on. They assume that God does not perform miracles capriciously, however, and are left wondering, "Why? What's going on here?"

C. Scoffers (v. 13)

13. Others mocking said, These men are full of new wine.

Although all are amazed, not everyone sees the hand of God in this. Some deride the believers. They are not only country bumpkins, they are drunk! What do you expect from mere Galilean peasants?

New wine does not mean unfermented grape juice; such would not be wine. It is wine that is not fully cured and is still very sweet. Such beverage is cheap and crude. [See question #3, page 48.]

III. Power Preaching
(Acts 2:14-17a)

A. Peter Defends (vv. 14, 15)

14. But Peter, standing up with the eleven, lifted up his voice, and said unto them, Ye men of Judea, and all ye that dwell at Jerusalem, be this known unto you, and hearken to my words.

As in the selection of the twelfth apostle in Acts 1:15-26, Peter assumes the role of leader and spokesman for the apostles and therefore the entire group of believers. We can imagine a very dramatic moment here. God has just displayed His miraculous power. A crowd has gathered, made up of citizens from across the Roman world and beyond. The crowd has reacted with either scoffing or a desire to know more. All eyes are on Peter, and all ears are tuned in to hear him. [See question #4, page 48.]

15. For these are not drunken, as ye suppose, seeing it is but the third hour of the day.

Peter first addresses the scoffers and uses logic to point out that this is the least likely time of day for drunkenness. The *third hour* is about nine o'clock in the morning. The all-night party drunks will be either sobered up by this time or still asleep in their drunken stupor. It is too early to have started drinking again; certainly for such a large group to be drunk in public at this hour is unthinkable.

Peter's command of the situation also dispels the notion of any drunkenness on his own part. He is lucid and in total command of the situation. The scoffers probably count him as one of the intoxicated, since it is highly likely that he is participating in the miracle of tongues.

B. Prophecy Fulfilled (vv. 16, 17a)

16, 17a. But this is that which was spoken by the prophet Joel; And it shall come to pass in the last days, saith God, I will pour out of my Spirit upon all flesh.

Peter, a Jew, answers his all-Jewish audience in a very Jewish manner: he quotes Scripture. This particular quotation is a prophecy from *the prophet Joel.* There are two important fulfillments from this passage that Peter intends his audience to hear.

First, the spiritual outpouring is a sign of *the last days,* meaning a new era of salvation. The key to this comes at the end of Joel 2:28-32 as quoted by Peter: "And it shall come to pass, that whosoever shall call on the name of the Lord shall be saved" (Acts 2:21). God's favor and promise of salvation is not to be confined to the Jews, but will be extended to *all flesh* (all people). Peter himself may not fully understand the scope of all this just yet, given his experiences and statements as recorded in Acts 10.

Second, the sign of this new era is the gift of the Holy *Spirit* to God's people. The Spirit was not unknown in Old Testament times. King David said "Cast me not away from thy presence; and take not thy Holy Spirit from me" (Psalm 51:11). Even so, there was no sense that God's Spirit was shared by all of Israel. Now, because of the atoning work of Jesus, the Spirit is freely available. Just a bit later, in Acts 2:38, Peter will explain that the gift of the Holy Spirit is available to all who come to Christ on Christ's terms. The result, then, of Christ's work on the cross and His ascension to glory is forgiveness of sin and spiritual renewal (compare Acts 3:19). [See question #5, page 48.]

Visual for Lesson 5. *Post this visual alongside the map from Lesson 1 as you discuss how the gospel has spread across the globe through the centuries.*

TOO GOOD TO BE TRUE?

Randall W. Harding gave generously to his church and sang in the choir. He owned an investment firm, which he called *JTL*—"Just the Lord"—in which his ministers and fellow church members invested large sums of money. It was all too good to be true: Harding and his accomplices stole more than $50 million from their clients. One man in the church personally lost $500,000 to Harding's fraudulent dealings.

North American Securities Administrators Association (an organization devoted to investor protection) says religious-based investment scams are becoming a massive problem. Between 1998 and 2001, the toll was $2 billion. Trinity Foundation (www.trinityfi.org), an organization that searches for fraud in televangelism, says that part of the problem is the "prosperity gospel." The belief that faithful Christians are rewarded with earthly wealth is becoming more common in mainstream churches.

What Peter promised on Pentecost was not physical wealth, but something more valuable by far: salvation through the gift of God's Spirit. Earthly poverty left behind is not nearly as important as sin forgiven. The first is temporal, based sometimes on faith in untrustworthy humans; the latter is eternal, guaranteed by God's faithfulness. It's a promise *not* "too good to be true"!   —C. R. B.

Conclusion

A. The Holy Spirit Then and Now

A soccer association once purchased a large, commercial lawn mower to cut the grass on its playing field. Despite the mower's cost and the claims of its manufacturer, those using it felt it was severely underpowered. They complained unrelentingly.

It wasn't until many months after the purchase that a mechanic changing the cutting blades discovered that one of the spark plug wires was not connected. The mower's two-cylinder engine should have provided plenty of muscle, but it had been operating only at half power. After the wire was connected, the operators were amazed at how it roared through the densest grass almost effortlessly.

Many churches have ignored the ministry of the Holy Spirit to the point where they are operating on half power (or less). We may hope that a careful study of the Holy Spirit's dynamic role on the Day of Pentecost may remedy this power deficit. One of the great promises shared by all Christians is the ministry of the Holy Spirit in our lives. The New Testament teaches that the presence of the Holy Spirit in the life of a believer is both a seal of God's salvation and a taste of our future glory with Him (see Ephesians 1:13, 14).

Acts has much to teach us concerning the Holy Spirit's role in the church. In Acts, the Holy Spirit was a source for power and boldness among the early Christians (see Acts 4:8, 31; 13:9). The gift of the Holy Spirit is closely associated with baptism into the name of Jesus (Acts 2:38, 39; 19:1-7). The Holy Spirit is with the disciples at their times of greatest need (Acts 7:55; compare Romans 8:26). The Holy Spirit directed the evangelistic activities of Paul (Acts 13:2; 16:7). It was a gift shared by the brothers and sisters of the new churches that Paul planted: "And the disciples were filled with joy, and with the Holy Ghost" (Acts 13:52).

Today we can be bolder and more effective as people who share the gospel, if we will lean on the power of the Holy Spirit. This will not take the place of personal initiative and knowledge of God's Word. But as in the book of Acts, the Holy Spirit is the avenue God employs to have unremarkable persons do mighty things in His name and for His glory.

B. Prayer

Father in Heaven, You are the source of spiritual power, renewal, and comfort in our lives through the ministry of Your Holy Spirit. We err greatly when we try to "go it alone," without the Spirit's help. Remind us again not to neglect this precious gift. May we draw upon Your Spirit to be bold in sharing the good news about Jesus Your Son. It is in His name we pray, amen.

C. Thought to Remember

The Holy Spirit still empowers.

Home Daily Bible Readings

Monday, Sep. 29—Fellowship with God and Man (1 John 1:1-4)

Tuesday, Sep. 30—Prophecy Fulfilled (Acts 2:22-36)

Wednesday, Oct. 1—Community Established (Acts 2:37-47)

Thursday, Oct. 2—"Receive the Holy Spirit" (John 20:19-23)

Friday, Oct. 3—One Body in Christ (Romans 12:3-8)

Saturday, Oct. 4—The Coming of the Holy Spirit (Acts 2:1-13)

Sunday, Oct. 5—Signs of the Last Days (Acts 2:14-21)

Learning by Doing

This page contains an alternative lesson plan emphasizing learning activities. Some of these activities are also found in the helpful student book, Adult Bible Class.

Into the Lesson

Write the phrase *Power Outage* on the board. Display pictures of power lines downed due to ice storms, hurricanes, or tornados (easy to find on the Internet, in magazines, etc.).

Ask learners to recall an instance when they had to go without power for a significant period of time. Help them recall the occasions and causes. But more importantly, have them note the problems a power outage caused and the inconvenience (and danger) it posed to them and their family.

Some may mention how they were "saved" by generators. Remind them that portable generators are temporary fixes, since they are not expected to supply power indefinitely. Make a transition by saying, "Trying to live the Christian life without the power of the Holy Spirit is an even bigger problem. Let's take a trip back to the Day of Pentecost to remind ourselves again of the Spirit's power."

Into the Word

Say, "The Christians in the book of Acts recognized and relied on the power of the Holy Spirit." Ask your class to turn to Acts 2:1-17. Have students work either individually or in study groups of two or three for the following exercise.

Distribute paper and pencils. Say, "To understand the passage, we need to know what the Feast of Pentecost was." Write the following passages on the board and ask students (individually or in their groups) to summarize them: Exodus 23:16; 34:22; Leviticus 23:9-16; Numbers 28:26; Deuteronomy 16:9-11. Ask students what significance they see in the fact that the church began during this "firstfruits" observance (one of the names for Pentecost; also known as Feast of Harvest and Feast of Weeks).

Students also need to realize that Peter's sermon was delivered to a diverse audience. Ask, "How is Peter's audience described in Acts 2:5-13?" Follow up with, "How does this temporary gathering compare with your community? Why is this comparison important?" (Those living in diverse communities may react to this text rather differently from those whose communities are less diverse.)

Next, ask the class to form study groups of three or four. Instruct them to write a summary of the work of the Holy Spirit on the Day of Pentecost as described in Acts 2:1-17a. Once they have done so in their study groups, ask each group to share one item on their lists with the class. Write each observation on the board as it is given.

Next, ask the study groups to look up the following passages to see what else the Holy Spirit does in the life of the believer. (You may wish to write these on the board or on a handout, but don't list the italicized answers.)

Acts 2:38, 39 *(indwells us)*
Acts 13:52 *(associated with joy)*
Romans 8:26, 27 *(involved in our prayers)*
Galatians 5:18, 25 *(leads us)*
Ephesians 1:13, 14 *(seal of our salvation)*

Ask students to share responses. Write the responses (which should be similar to the italicized answers above) on the board.

Continue the discussion by saying, "The people of the first-century church recognized and acknowledged the work of the Holy Spirit. They depended on His power to direct their lives and empower their congregations. How do we compare?"

Into Life

Prior to class, write the following five phrases on strips of paper: *Acknowledgment of the Spirit's Indwelling, Experience of the Joy of the Spirit, Accepting the Spirit's Involvement in Prayer, Allowing the Spirit to Lead,* and *Finding Comfort in the Spirit's Assurance of My Salvation.*

Make as many five-statement sets of these phrases as you have students. Give each student a set of strips. Ask them to place them in order of the most recognized personal spiritual experience (at the top) to the least experienced one (at the bottom).

Once they have done this, ask them to form groups of three or four and discuss their rankings. Ask, "Why are your lists ranked as they are? How can you encourage one another to grow in the ranking that is bottom-most?"

Close with a prayer of thankfulness for the presence of the Holy Spirit. As students depart, you can pass out three-prong adapters as a reminder of the need to be "plugged into" the Holy Spirit. (These adapters are available at low cost from hardware stores.)

Let's Talk It Over

The questions on this page are designed to promote discussion of the lesson by the class and to encourage application of the lesson Scriptures. The answers provided are only discussion starters. Let your class talk it over from there.

1. Why is it important that the members of your church be of one accord? How can your church's members demonstrate this unity, and what will happen when they do?

God is a God of unity in the essence of His own being, for He exists as three persons in one. We reflect the nature of God as we demonstrate unity in the church. Jesus expressed the desire that His followers demonstrate this unity in His prayer to the Father in John 17:20, 21: "Neither pray I for these alone, but for them also which shall believe on me through their word; that they all may be one; as thou, Father, art in me, and I in thee, that they also may be one in us: that the world may believe that thou hast sent me."

Unity in the church opens the door for people to believe the gospel. Unity in Christ is seen when all we do points to Christ and not to ourselves, our personal preferences, or to human leaders.

2. What are some works of the Holy Spirit that cause amazement today?

The most amazing thing is changed lives as the Holy Spirit works in those lives. To go from being self-centered and worldly to exhibiting a lifestyle that reflects the fruit of the Spirit of "love, joy, peace, long-suffering, gentleness, goodness, faith, meekness, temperance" (Galatians 5:22, 23) is a marvelous thing.

The fruit of the Spirit can reveal itself in various ways. The Holy Spirit working in a husband and wife who have been fighting and threatening divorce, but who are now living in sacrificial love for one another, points to an amazing work in that marriage. Racial reconciliation in the name of Christ is another demonstration of the Spirit's power. Sudden release from the bondage of an addiction is yet another. The list can go on.

3. How is the work of the Holy Spirit misunderstood or misinterpreted by the secular world?

The secular world does not understand many of the things that Christians understand. A selfless love, prompted by the Holy Spirit, is misinterpreted as one person trying to curry favor with another so he can get his way. Spirit-filled Christians who take an activist stand against things such as homosexuality or abortion are seen as hard-hearted or mean-spirited. In reality, these Christians are looking out for the good of others.

It's vital that Christians not allow the misunderstanding of others to discourage them in their faith. Just as the work of Jesus was misunderstood and therefore mocked by the onlookers (see Matthew 27:39), so Christians can expect the same reaction and treatment.

4. What are some ways that Christians can respond to attacks or questions from those who oppose the gospel?

Standing in a united front on the Day of Pentecost, Peter and the eleven showed how to respond to being misunderstood or attacked: Peter was ready to give an answer, being set for the defense of the gospel (see Philippians 1:17; 1 Peter 3:15). He was also able to use logic very well.

One of the important things followers of Christ need to do is to live in such a way that there is no evidence to support the attack when someone wants to attack or confront them (see 1 Peter 3:16). When we are persecuted and suffer for the sake of Christ, we remember that, like Paul, we may be "troubled on every side, yet not distressed; we are perplexed, but not in despair; persecuted, but not forsaken; cast down, but not destroyed" (2 Corinthians 4:8, 9).

5. How is Peter's response in Acts 2:16, 17 similar to Jesus' response in Luke 4:4, 8, 12? Why is this important to us?

Christians often are ill-prepared to respond to questions non-Christians ask. Because of this we try to make up answers on the fly or state personal opinion. Peter did not express his personal opinion in this text. He did not seek to explain what was happening by saying what he thought about the situation. Instead he went to the Word of God and allowed that to be his source of authority.

This response was the same approach in Luke 4:4, 8, 12, where Jesus was confronted by Satan in the wilderness. Too often Christians depend upon their own opinions or powers of persuasion in confronting issues in life. What is most important is that we know the Word of God and that we have the Word in our hearts and minds (compare Hebrews 4:12).

Growing Community

DEVOTIONAL READING: Acts 1:3-11.

BACKGROUND SCRIPTURE: Acts 6:1-15; 8:1-8.

PRINTED TEXT: Acts 6:1-15.

Acts 6:1-15

1 And in those days, when the number of the disciples was multiplied, there arose a murmuring of the Grecians against the Hebrews, because their widows were neglected in the daily ministration.

2 Then the twelve called the multitude of the disciples unto them, and said, It is not reason that we should leave the word of God, and serve tables.

3 Wherefore, brethren, look ye out among you seven men of honest report, full of the Holy Ghost and wisdom, whom we may appoint over this business.

4 But we will give ourselves continually to prayer, and to the ministry of the word.

5 And the saying pleased the whole multitude: and they chose Stephen, a man full of faith and of the Holy Ghost, and Philip, and Prochorus, and Nicanor, and Timon, and Parmenas, and Nicolas a proselyte of Antioch;

6 Whom they set before the apostles: and when they had prayed, they laid their hands on them.

7 And the word of God increased; and the number of the disciples multiplied in Jeru-

Oct 12

salem greatly; and a great company of the priests were obedient to the faith.

8 And Stephen, full of faith and power, did great wonders and miracles among the people.

9 Then there arose certain of the synagogue, which is called the synagogue of the Libertines, and Cyrenians, and Alexandrians, and of them of Cilicia and of Asia, disputing with Stephen.

10 And they were not able to resist the wisdom and the spirit by which he spake.

11 Then they suborned men, which said, We have heard him speak blasphemous words against Moses, and against God.

12 And they stirred up the people, and the elders, and the scribes, and came upon him, and caught him, and brought him to the council,

13 And set up false witnesses, which said, This man ceaseth not to speak blasphemous words against this holy place, and the law:

14 For we have heard him say, that this Jesus of Nazareth shall destroy this place, and shall change the customs which Moses delivered us.

15 And all that sat in the council, looking steadfastly on him, saw his face as it had been the face of an angel.

GOLDEN TEXT: The word of God increased; and the number of the disciples multiplied in Jerusalem greatly; and a great company of the priests were obedient to the faith.—Acts 6:7.

The New Testament Community
Unit 2: Growth of the New Community
(Lessons 5–8)

Lesson Aims

After participating in this lesson, each student will be able to:

1. Describe the controversy between the Grecian and Hebraic Jews in the first-century church.

2. Give a modern example of a church controversy that parallels the one in today's text.

3. Make a plan to solve the problem in aim #2.

Lesson Outline

INTRODUCTION
  A. "How to Do Church"
  B. Lesson Background
I. PROBLEM ARISES (Acts 6:1)
  A. Rapid Growth (v. 1a)
  B. Perceived Inequity (v. 1b)
    Differences in Perception
II. PROCESS DEVELOPS (Acts 6:2-7)
  A. Situation Analyzed (v. 2)
  B. Process Proposed (vv. 3, 4)
  C. People Appointed (vv. 5, 6)
  D. Ministry Multiplied (v. 7)
    New Ways of Doing Things
III. PREACHER PRODUCED (Acts 6:8-15)
  A. Stephen Causes Controversy (vv. 8-10)
  B. Stephen Charged (vv. 11, 12)
  C. Stephen Prosecuted (vv. 13-15)
CONCLUSION
  A. Leaders in Today's Church
  B. Prayer
  C. Thought to Remember

Introduction

A. "How to Do Church"

What sort of organizational structure should a church have? Who should its leaders be? How should the structure and the leaders be put in place? These are ongoing questions for any church. It is natural that a church will reflect some of the leadership and organizational traditions of her culture. There are, however, biblical principles that *must* serve the church in any situation or age.

The book of Acts is rightly seen as something of a template for "how to do church." This is because the first-century church was largely formed by the efforts of the apostles. They were authorized by Jesus and empowered by the Holy Spirit to establish the church. We must presume that the apostles understood Jesus' intentions and that their decisions to meet the challenges that confronted the first-century church are still valid ways of understanding "how to do church" today.

Today's lesson involves the trials that arose in a growing church. Church growth brings both blessing and difficulty. What do you do when you outgrow your assembly space? How do you assimilate new believers from diverse backgrounds into the body of Christ? What happens when your church outgrows her leadership structure? Perhaps a church of 20 can make consensus decisions after a potluck dinner on Sunday afternoon, allowing all members to present their opinions and ideas, but does this work for a church of 500 or 5,000?

Acts does not give definitive answers to these specific questions. But the principles we find in Acts 6 still are required reading for guiding the church in its selection of leaders.

B. Lesson Background

In the fourth century BC, Alexander the Great led his Greek armies to conquer much of the ancient world. This was more than a military conquest. Alexander and his people saw themselves as missionaries for the Greek way of life. They considered Greek culture superior to other cultures. This included the Greek language, Greek philosophy, and Greek lifestyle (including athletic training). This Greek culture is referred to as *Hellenism*.

At the time of Acts, Hellenism had gained adherents throughout the Roman Empire. Consider that Paul wrote his letter to the Romans in Greek, even though he was writing to the center of the Latin, Roman world. Paul knew that everyone in that church would understand Greek because Hellenism had a deep influence on the imperial city.

Hellenism had made inroads into Judaism, even in Palestine and Jerusalem. We see this among the 12 disciples of Jesus, 2 of whom have Greek names (Andrew and Philip; see John 12:20-22). Adoption of Hellenism was probably more prevalent among Jews of the Diaspora, meaning those living outside Palestine (see James 1:1). Greek ways were fiercely resisted by traditionalist Jews, who saw Hellenism as a threat.

An obvious differentiation between a Hellenistic and a traditional Jew was in the language spoken. Hellenistic Jews spoke Greek and used the Greek translation of Scripture we know as the Septuagint. Traditional Jews in Jerusalem spoke Hebrew or Aramaic, related languages that were the original languages of the Old Testament. Some Jews like Paul were able to bridge the gap, being fluent in both Greek and Hebrew (see Acts 21:37–22:2).

The reality of the existence of Hellenistic and traditionalist Jews forms the backdrop for the story of Acts 6. Since the church had not spread beyond Jerusalem and all its members were Jewish Christians, it is not surprising that this historic rivalry caused friction. Today's church still faces culturally based conflict between members. Thus the steps taken by Peter and the other leaders to resolve this problem are instructive for us.

I. Problem Arises
(Acts 6:1)
A. Rapid Growth (v. 1a)
1a. And in those days, when the number of the disciples was multiplied.

The timing of this story is indefinite, but we assume it is several months after the great events of the Day of Pentecost in Acts 2. The church has continued to grow, despite opposition from the temple leaders in Jerusalem. The total number of believers is apparently in the thousands (see Acts 4:4).

B. Perceived Inequity (v. 1b)
1b. There arose a murmuring of the Grecians against the Hebrews, because their widows were neglected in the daily ministration.

The first-century church feels a deep sense of responsibility to care for her *widows*. Because of the social dynamics of the day, widows are especially vulnerable persons, with no government social services available (see James 1:27; compare 1 Timothy 5:3-16).

As explained in the Lesson Background, the conflict here is deeper than an administration problem. It has roots in the dispute between Hellenistic and traditionalist Jews, a conflict that has simmered in Jerusalem for two centuries. Many churches since then have experienced conflict between traditionalists and those who are new or different.

Those who expect to find a conflict-free history in the apostolic church of the book of Acts will be disappointed. As long as there is sin in the world, human egos and agendas will lead to conflict. We are naïve to think we can avoid all conflict. We are wise to study godly ways to resolve disputes, however, and not to let them wreck a congregation.

Whether there is an intentional slight of the Hellenistic widows by the food stewards is unknown. What is most significant is that there is a *perception* that this is being done on purpose. Such a perception will not long exist in any church without resulting in division or open conflict. [See question #1, page 56.]

DIFFERENCES IN PERCEPTIONS

A San Diego woman's husband died in an airplane crash, and she received a settlement of millions of dollars. Some years later, she decided she wanted to remarry. So she hired a dating service that claimed to have a "select worldwide clientele," whose financial status would be anywhere from "comfortable" to "extremely wealthy."

The fees charged by the service were certainly in keeping with the kind of matches it promised. The widow paid $30,000 up front and promised to pay an equal amount if she found a mate. The right man was never provided, so she sued the dating service for breach of promise. She later met her "true love" on an Internet dating site. It cost $30!

What a person in one situation views as desperate a person in another situation may look at with indifference. We don't know if the widows in the Jerusalem church were looking for new husbands per se. Their desperation was much more basic than that of the woman noted above: they needed food! The frustration of "the Grecians" had to do with perception that the church was not meeting needs in an evenhanded way. This became the church's first recorded intercultural crisis.

Try this. First, make a list of the three most important needs of people in your church that you believe are going unmet and why. Then ask two other people to do the same thing. Finally, compare the three lists. You may be surprised at the differences in perceptions!   —C. R. B.

II. Process Develops
(Acts 6:2-7)
A. Situation Analyzed (v. 2)
2. Then the twelve called the multitude of the disciples unto them, and said, It is not reason that we should leave the word of God, and serve tables.

The apostles do not let the conflict simmer. They take active steps to resolve it.

First, they do some prioritizing: they decide that the ministry of *the word of God* is their own primary task. Nothing else should distract them from this. Having done this analysis, they bring the findings to the larger congregation. In effect, they say, "We can't do everything and we shouldn't neglect preaching and teaching, so we need to find some other people to *serve* the food."

B. Process Proposed (vv. 3, 4)
3. Wherefore, brethren, look ye out among you seven men of honest report, full of the Holy Ghost and wisdom, whom we may appoint over this business.

The apostles recognize an important leadership principle here: delegation. When a church grows, the original cadre of leaders will not be adequate to meet the demands of the larger organization. They will need help. The apostles are not shirking their responsibilities. They still retain ultimate authority. They want qualified persons whom they may *appoint* to the task. [See question #2, page 56.]

The five criteria for the new workers are laid out: *seven* total (should not overstaff or understaff), *of honest report* (these men have a good reputation), *full of the Holy Ghost* (spiritually minded and mature), wise (demonstrating the ability to make good decisions), and available to be appointed (having a willingness to serve).

4. But we will give ourselves continually to prayer, and to the ministry of the word.

There is an important play on words in this verse. The apostles will not "serve tables" (Acts 6:2). Rather, they will focus their work on the *ministry of the word*. The word *serve* comes from the same word group as *ministry* in these two verses. The cumulative impact of this is to say "some will serve food to stomachs, but we will serve the Word of God to souls." [See question #3, page 56.]

The noun from the word group at issue is sometimes rendered as *deacon* in other passages. For this reason, some Bible students see this passage as the origin of the office of deacon in the church, although that is not specifically stated as such. We recognize that the New Testament concept of deacon includes the idea of "servant."

C. People Appointed (vv. 5, 6)

5. And the saying pleased the whole multitude: and they chose Stephen, a man full of faith and of

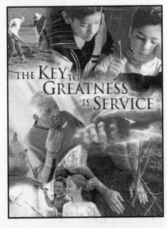

Visual for
Lesson 6

Point to this visual as you ask your learners to list examples of Christ-centered service.

the Holy Ghost, and Philip, and Prochorus, and Nicanor, and Timon, and Parmenas, and Nicolas a proselyte of Antioch.

How the congregation chooses these men is not specified. In democratic societies, we assume this is done through some type of election. More likely, however, is that it is done through acclamation and consensus during the group meeting.

The list is significant for three reasons. First, all of the men have Greek names, indicating a special concern to accommodate the Hellenistic widows. Second, the first two are destined for larger roles in Acts. Stephen's story as a fiery preacher follows almost immediately. Philip's story as an evangelist comes in chapter 8. Philip reappears briefly much later as the father of four remarkable daughters (Acts 21:8, 9). Third, the man *Nicolas* is identified as being from Antioch. This is a foreshadowing of the great city to the north of that name, which plays a pivotal role in the later events of Acts (see Acts 11:19-30).

6. Whom they set before the apostles: and when they had prayed, they laid their hands on them.

The commencement of this new ministry is signaled by a public ceremony of installation. The seven are prayed over by the leaders *(the apostles)*. This is accompanied by the physical act of laying *hands on them*, an act of blessing and a symbolic authorization. This is an act of "ordination," meaning a setting apart of individuals for specific service for the church.

D. Ministry Multiplied (v. 7)

7. And the word of God increased; and the number of the disciples multiplied in Jerusalem greatly; and a great company of the priests were obedient to the faith.

Unresolved church fights inevitably stop church growth. A church with feuding members is an unattractive place for potential participants. The Jerusalem church is able to overcome this bump in the road, however, and the result is significant growth.

The widespread nature of this growth is indicated by the fact that *priests* are now becoming believers. The priests of Jerusalem are of the Sadducee party and do not believe in the resurrection of the dead (see Acts 23:8). For them to believe the gospel means they now accept the resurrection of Jesus, a dramatic denial of their traditions.

NEW WAYS OF DOING THINGS

Would you believe that God now takes credit cards? To be more precise, some churches do. Debit cards too! Stevens Creek Community Church in Martinez, Georgia, was among the first to take advantage of online technology to help its members give more regularly (and more generously). The 1,100-member church installed ATMs ("automatic tithe machines") in 2005.

The minister says giving went up 18 percent. Giving to the church is as easy as paying for groceries: punch in your phone number and PIN, then indicate the amount of your offering. One church member says, "This church gets how I live." Other churches apparently do too (although some accept only debit cards in order to help members stay away from the debt that comes with credit car usage). Love the idea or hate it, it definitely is a new way of doing things.

The Jerusalem church didn't have the technology we have, but they were not afraid to try new ways. When their benevolent program was revealed to be flawed, they changed procedures. The result was that the widows received the attention they needed, the apostles were free to perform the ministry God had called them to, and the church continued to grow.   —C. R. B.

How to Say It

ALEXANDRIANS. Al-ex-*an*-dree-unz.
ANTIOCH. *An*-tee-ock.
ARAMAIC. *Air*-uh-*may*-ik (strong accent on *may*).
CILICIA. Sih-*lish*-i-uh.
CYRENIANS. Sigh-*ree*-nee-unz.
DIASPORA. Dee-*as*-puh-ruh.
GRECIANS. *Gree*-shunz.
HELLENISM. *Heh*-leh-nih-zim.
LIBERTINES. *Lib*-er-teens.
NICANOR. Nye-*cay*-nor.
PARMENAS. *Par*-meh-nas.
PROCHORUS. *Prock*-uh-rus.
SADDUCEE. *Sad*-you-see.
SANHEDRIN. *San*-huh-drun or San-*heed*-run.

III. Preacher Produced
(Acts 6:8-15)

A. Stephen Causes Controversy (vv. 8-10)

8. And Stephen, full of faith and power, did great wonders and miracles among the people.

The story now takes an unexpected turn: one of the table servers, *Stephen*, quickly gains a reputation as a wonder worker. He is a man of great *faith* and spiritual *power*. The presence of the Holy Spirit in his life is so pronounced that special things happen (see Acts 6:5, above). He is the first Christian who is not one of the 12 apostles to be used by God to perform miraculous signs *among the people*. [See question #4, page 56.]

9, 10. Then there arose certain of the synagogue, which is called the synagogue of the Libertines, and Cyrenians, and Alexandrians, and of them of Cilicia and of Asia, disputing with Stephen. And they were not able to resist the wisdom and the spirit by which he spake.

Libertines are slaves who have been given their liberty (freedom). They are commonly called *freedmen* and are an important component of Roman society. History tells us that Felix, the governor mentioned in Acts 23 and 24, is a freedman.

There are many synagogues in Jerusalem at this time—more than 400 by one estimate. Two of them seem to be involved in disputing with Stephen: the Libertine/Cyrenian/Alexandrian *synagogue* and the Cilician/Asian synagogue. It is likely that a young Jew from Tarsus in Cilicia is a member of this latter group: Saul of Tarsus. Saul (later

the apostle Paul) may have the opportunity to confront Stephen directly. No one prevails over the mighty Stephen, however, not even Saul. This perhaps explains Saul's consent to Stephen's death (Acts 7:58; 8:1).

Some students think that these synagogues are made up of non-Hellenistic Jews. If so, the accommodation of the Hellenistic Jews within the church is not seen as a positive development by the members of such synagogues. Combined with the powerful acts of Stephen, this group now sees the church as a significant threat.

B. Stephen Charged (vv. 11, 12)

11. Then they suborned men, which said, We have heard him speak blasphemous words against Moses, and against God.

Suborned testimony is testimony that has been illegitimately influenced. The primary charge against Stephen is that he is a blasphemer on two counts (compare Jesus' trial, Matthew 26:65). To speak *against Moses* is to speak against the Jewish law; to speak *against God* is to deny the essence of the Jewish religion.

12. And they stirred up the people, and the elders, and the scribes, and came upon him, and caught him, and brought him to the council.

In many respects, Stephen's trial is a replay of Jesus' trials. A mob is stirred up, and the accused is thrown before the high *council* of the Jews, the Sanhedrin. As with Jesus, we have the sense of a rushed process.

C. Stephen Prosecuted (vv. 13-15)

13. And set up false witnesses, which said, This man ceaseth not to speak blasphemous words against this holy place, and the law.

When the charges are presented, a new item is added. Stephen is now presented as having made threats against the *holy place,* meaning the Jerusalem temple (compare Jeremiah 26:11). Many of the members of the Sanhedrin are of the Sadducee party, the party of the Jerusalem priests. For them, a threat against the temple is more than a religious matter; it challenges their livelihoods (compare John 11:48).

14. For we have heard him say, that this Jesus of Nazareth shall destroy this place, and shall change the customs which Moses delivered us.

Jesus said that the temple is not the only place for worship (see John 4:21-24). Paul will later say that God does not dwell in temples made by humans (Acts 17:24). Stephen will make similar points in his speech to follow (see Acts 7:47-49). The accusers pile on the charge that Jesus and Stephen advocate departure from the *customs* of *Moses,* meaning the law and its traditional interpretation. These charges are more than religious; they question the national loyalty of Stephen. This is the equivalent of charging a U.S. citizen with wanting to tear up the Constitution and raze the White House. It is treason.

15. And all that sat in the council, looking steadfastly on him, saw his face as it had been the face of an angel.

What does an angel's *face* look like? We wish we knew! Some think that this may be a type of glow or brightness. Others interpret it to mean Stephen has a look of supreme inner peace.

Whatever it is physically, we are to understand it as a supernatural presence that accompanies Stephen during his trial. At his time of greatest testing and challenge, God has not forsaken him. [See question #5, page 56.]

Home Daily Bible Readings

Monday, Oct. 6—No Other Name (Acts 4:1-12)

Tuesday, Oct. 7—What We Have Seen and Heard (Acts 4:13-22)

Wednesday, Oct. 8—Boldness to Speak the Word (Acts 4:23-31)

Thursday, Oct. 9—Falsehood Exposed (Acts 5:1-11)

Friday, Oct. 10—Obedience to God (Acts 5:27-39)

Saturday, Oct. 11—Scattered but Not Silenced (Acts 8:1-8)

Sunday, Oct. 12—Full of the Spirit and Wisdom (Acts 6)

Conclusion

A. Leaders in Today's Church

Acts 6 does not serve as a precise blueprint as to how churches should put leadership into place, for it does not include many details that we would find useful. By observing the process, however, we can see at least three principles that churches today can follow in leadership decisions.

First, the leaders of the first-century church were servants. The seven were chosen to serve as food stewards. The apostles chose to relinquish this task and focus on their calling of serving the Word of God. This concept of leading by serving is part of the Christian worldview. Most societies experience a leader as someone who expects to be served. In the church, leaders are to put self-interests aside and seek to minister to the needs of the members and the community.

Second, moral qualities (some prefer the stronger word *qualifications*) of leaders are important. The personal list used in Acts 6 includes having a good reputation, spiritual maturity, demonstrated ability to make wise decisions, and availability for service (that is, commitment). Other places in the New Testament give additional qualities (1 Timothy 3:1-13; Titus 1:5-8). The newspaper in my city recently ran a story about an elder at a prominent church who was arrested for sexual abuse of foster children and possession of child pornography. What a horrible witness for the church! Moral qualities are important.

Third, the selection of the seven in Acts 6 involved input from the congregation and approval by the existing leaders. A healthy church will have a balance of these two. New leaders should not be chosen merely by a powerful minister or elder. This leads to favoritism and power bases. On the other hand, simply letting the general congregation choose leaders can lead to popularity contests. Acts 6 does not explain fully the way the Jerusalem church accomplished this balance, and each congregation should decide its own process. But input from both "above" and "below" will result in leaders who have the full confidence of all.

B. Prayer

God, Your Son is our great leader and Your Holy Spirit is our guide. We seek to follow You and learn from You daily. We trust You to furnish leaders for Your church who are qualified and approved by You. We pray in the name of Jesus, our Savior, amen.

C. Thought to Remember

Use biblical principles to choose church leaders.

Learning by Doing

This page contains an alternative lesson plan emphasizing learning activities. Some of these activities are also found in the helpful student book, Adult Bible Class.

Into the Lesson

Write the word *Conflict* on the board for students to see as they arrive. This will allow them to think about this word until class starts. Ask, "What is your initial reaction when you see this word? Is it always harmful and negative, or can it be beneficial and positive? Why?" Jot responses on the board. Direct students' focus to conflict within Christianity, perhaps by asking, "How and when is conflict evident in Christianity?" You may get responses focusing on doctrinal differences, denominational boundaries, and preferences in worship style.

Next, focus attention on your particular congregation by asking, "What conflicts has this congregation experienced through the years?" Have your students share the possible causes and the outcome of those conflicts without mentioning names. (Caution! You may wish to not use this question if it will aggravate old or current wounds. If you think that will be the case, stick with discussing conflict within Christianity as a whole.)

Make a transition by saying, "Conflict is nothing new to Christianity. Even in the book of Acts, the earliest Christians were in conflict with one another. One of the first conflicts involved a matter of how a benevolence ministry was (or was not) being done."

Into the Word

Make a handout of the following questions. You can also make an overhead transparency or PowerPoint® slide of them if you prefer. Ask your class to form study groups of four to six. Distribute the handouts and pencils. Say, "Congregational growth brings challenges. This was the case in Acts 6:1-7." Instruct your groups to read Acts 6:1-7 and respond to these questions:

1. What were the causes of the conflict? *(v. 1)*

2. Why didn't the apostles want to serve tables? *(vv. 2, 4)*

3. Who selected the persons to be the food stewards? *(v. 3)*

4. What were the criteria for the selection of people to serve? *(v. 3)*

5. By what procedure did those selected receive their responsibility? *(v. 5a)*

6. How is Stephen described? *(v. 5);* how does this description compare with the one in Acts 6:8?

7. How do we know the decision was acceptable to the apostles? *(v. 6)*

8. What is the result when ministry is shared by more people? *(v. 7);* how does this compare with the situation in verse 1?

Write responses on the board as space allows. Your learners may provide more than one valid response to a question.

Make a transition by saying, "Not only was there conflict within the church, but within the wider community as well." Turn students' attention to Acts 6:8-15. Help them see Stephen as a linchpin to the narrative: he was one of the seven selected in the first half of chapter 6 and arrested in the latter half of the chapter.

While students are still in their study groups, ask them to read Acts 6:8-15 and respond to the following questions:

1. Why would Stephen be drawing the attention of the Jews? *(v. 8)*

2. What "kind" or nationality of Jews most likely were the strongest in opposition of Stephen? *(v. 9)*

3. Why do you think the Jews of that particular background or nationality were disturbed by Stephen's ministry?

4. What do we learn about human nature as we consider how Stephen was treated? *(vv. 10-14)*

5. Should we expect God to cause our faces to appear as Stephen's? Why, or why not? *(v. 15)*

Into Life

Return to the word *conflict.* Ask your class to reflect again on cases where conflict is harmful or beneficial, negative or positive. After some ideas are offered, stress that the answer really lies in the approach to resolving conflict. Emphasize that conflict can be helpful when it is met with *resolution* rather than *regret.* A conflict resolved can yield a congregation strengthened.

Ask, "How can we help our congregation avoid unnecessary conflicts from starting in the first place? What will be your part in helping our congregation's leaders address conflict constructively?" Allow open discussion; jot ideas on the board. However, be cautious about allowing the discussion to focus on an ongoing conflict, especially if emotions are running high. Close with prayer for each student to play a part in resolving conflict.

Let's Talk It Over

*The questions on this page are designed to promote discussion of the lesson
by the class and to encourage application of the lesson Scriptures. The answers
provided are only discussion starters. Let your class talk it over from there.*

1. What are some sources of disputes within the church? Why are disputes so prevalent? How should we respond?

Just as the feeling of bias caused the dispute in the Jerusalem church in our text, so this same feeling can plague the church today. Sometimes these feelings are based on reality—people actually are being discriminated against. But sometimes those feelings are not based on reality—people feel they are being discriminated against when that is not the case. But the feeling is there nonetheless.

Either way, the problem has to be addressed. It must not be allowed to fester. Proper response means more than addressing the surface problem, which in today's text is the issue of food for certain widows. Proper response addresses the underlying problem, which in today's text is the perception of bias. If the dispute is because of selfishness or envy, a good dose of teaching from Ephesians 2:1-5 may be in order.

2. What can you do to help your church's leadership set up the church's divisions of labor properly so that the purpose of the church is accomplished?

It all starts with having a servant's mind-set. This will help us be aware of the various needs that exist within the church. After this, we can look within the fellowship (and within ourselves) to discern who is best suited to perform different kinds of service. A spiritual gifts survey or talent and interest survey may be helpful at this point.

After the need is assessed and the workers are selected, there should be some training for the service in question. Also, the church needs to be sure to supply the resources and encouragement needed by those who serve so they can fulfill their service successfully.

3. How can we implement today the apostles' model of an appropriate way to deal with criticism and conflict?

The apostles first took time to listen to the problem instead of ignoring it; we can do the same. Then they recognized the validity of the need of food for widows and the elimination of a perception of bias; we should evaluate situations properly as well. Then they took the time to explain the need for role distinctions; clear communication is a must yet today. Then they solicited the cooperation of the congregation in solving the problem; this is still our model.

The apostles were cautious to be sure that the "tyranny of the urgent" did not get in the way of doing the main thing of the church: ministering spiritually through the Word and prayer. In doing this, the 12 were able to maintain leadership in the church while releasing ministry to others.

4. What are some principles we can learn from the life of Stephen about how God uses people who are involved in the ministry of the church?

When a servant of God proves himself or herself faithful in one area, God may very well use that person in another area of even greater importance. In the Parable of the Talents, we see that the one who was faithful proved himself worthy of more opportunities to serve. "His lord said unto him, Well done, thou good and faithful servant: thou hast been faithful over a few things, I will make thee ruler over many things: enter thou into the joy of thy lord" (Matthew 25:21).

Those who humble themselves in faithful service are also exalted by God (see Matthew 23:12). We may say that Stephen's martyrdom (not in today's text) was his greatest service to God.

5. What are practical ways for twenty-first-century Christians to respond when suffering reproach for the name of Christ? Why should we respond in those ways?

This world teaches that when you are insulted, you are justified in defending yourself or even retaliating. But the teaching of Scripture is that we are to turn the other cheek (Luke 6:29). This may take the form of how we use (or *don't* use) electronic tools such as blogs and e-mail.

Jesus said, "Blessed are ye, when men shall revile you, and persecute you, and shall say all manner of evil against you falsely, for my sake. Rejoice, and be exceeding glad: for great is your reward in heaven: for so persecuted they the prophets which were before you" (Matthew 5:11, 12). Scripture teaches that we are blessed and God is glorified when we respond in a proper way (see 1 Peter 4:14).

Transformed Community

October 19
Lesson 7

DEVOTIONAL READING: Galatians 1:11-24.

BACKGROUND SCRIPTURE: Acts 9:1-31.

PRINTED TEXT: Acts 9:1-11, 16-19a.

Acts 9:1-11, 16-19a

1 And Saul, yet breathing out threatenings and slaughter against the disciples of the Lord, went unto the high priest,

2 And desired of him letters to Damascus to the synagogues, that if he found any of this way, whether they were men or women, he might bring them bound unto Jerusalem.

3 And as he journeyed, he came near Damascus: and suddenly there shined round about him a light from heaven:

4 And he fell to the earth, and heard a voice saying unto him, Saul, Saul, why persecutest thou me?

5 And he said, Who art thou, Lord? And the Lord said, I am Jesus whom thou persecutest: it is hard for thee to kick against the pricks.

6 And he trembling and astonished said, Lord, what wilt thou have me to do? And the Lord said unto him, Arise, and go into the city, and it shall be told thee what thou must do.

7 And the men which journeyed with him stood speechless, hearing a voice, but seeing no man.

8 And Saul arose from the earth; and when his eyes were opened, he saw no man: but they led him by the hand, and brought him into Damascus.

9 And he was three days without sight, and neither did eat nor drink.

10 And there was a certain disciple at Damascus, named Ananias; and to him said the Lord in a vision, Ananias. And he said, Behold, I am here, Lord.

11 And the Lord said unto him, Arise, and go into the street which is called Straight, and inquire in the house of Judas for one called Saul, of Tarsus: for, behold, he prayeth.

. . . .

16 For I will show him how great things he must suffer for my name's sake.

17 And Ananias went his way, and entered into the house; and putting his hands on him said, Brother Saul, the Lord, even Jesus, that appeared unto thee in the way as thou camest, hath sent me, that thou mightest receive thy sight, and be filled with the Holy Ghost.

18 And immediately there fell from his eyes as it had been scales: and he received sight forthwith, and arose, and was baptized.

19a And when he had received meat, he was strengthened.

**Oct
19**

GOLDEN TEXT: Ananias . . . said, Brother Saul, the Lord, even Jesus, that appeared unto thee in the way as thou camest, hath sent me, that thou mightest receive thy sight, and be filled with the Holy Ghost.—Acts 9:17.

The New Testament Community
Unit 2: Growth of the New Community
(Lessons 5–8)

Lesson Aims

After participating in this lesson, each student will be able to:

1. Describe Saul's conversion experience.

2. Compare and contrast Saul's conversion experience with his or her own.

3. Identify one individual who needs Christ and suggest a way to facilitate his or her conversion.

Lesson Outline

INTRODUCTION
  A. Conversion Experiences
  B. Lesson Background
  I. DEATH-DEALER NAMED SAUL (Acts 9:1, 2)
    A. Murderous Heart (v. 1)
    B. Ambitious Spirit (v. 2)
      Murders, Ancient and Modern
 II. DESTINATION CALLED DAMASCUS (Acts 9:3-9)
    A. Confronted and Humbled (vv. 3, 4)
    B. Surprised and Judged (vv. 5, 6)
    C. Blinded and Confused (vv. 7-9)
III. DISCIPLE NAMED ANANIAS (Acts 9:10, 11, 16-19a)
    A. Fear, Then Obedience (vv. 10, 11, 16)
    B. Blessing, Then Fellowship (vv. 17-19a)
      Saving an Endangered Species
CONCLUSION
  A. Transformations
  B. Prayer
  C. Thought to Remember

Introduction

A. Conversion Experiences

Personal testimony is a popular and useful way to share the gospel with others. The general pattern is simple. First, you relate the "where I was" part; that is, what your life was like before you became a believer. Second, you tell about the "what happened" element, or what the circumstances were that brought you to faith. Third, you share the "where I am now" part: what life is like as a Christian and how you have been transformed.

There is incredible power in such a personal testimony, and every believer should be ready to "give an answer . . . [for] the hope that is in you"

(1 Peter 3:15). On Christian radio and television, one may hear many stories of dramatic spiritual encounters that brought unbelievers to faith in a decisive and rapid fashion. The pages of church history are full of testimonials about the conversion experiences of famous figures. These stories serve as both an inspiration to us and as helps in appreciating that God is living and active in the world today.

But for every celebrity testimony of faith's rescue from a wasted life, there are many believers who have never lived lives of debauchery. For every story of a homeless street person instantly freed from destructive addictions and hopelessness, there are droves of Christians who have never experienced such rapid transformations. There are those studying this lesson who surely have no real sense of ever *not* having been a Christian.

The recognition of the existence of "lifelong" believers is but one reason to treat the Damascus road experience of Saul with great care. While all believers will have moments of new, direction-changing insight, very few will have an experience comparable to the experience of Saul. Even so, Saul's experience has much to teach us.

B. Lesson Background

The man who comes to be known as *the apostle Paul* is introduced in Acts as *Saul,* a primary instigator of the mob action that led to the stoning of Stephen (Acts 7:54–8:1; 22:20). He is described as a young man in Acts 7:58, probably in his late teens or early twenties. We usually date this incident about AD 34, so we can surmise that Saul was born around AD 15. He was sent to Jerusalem to study under the famous rabbi Gamaliel (Acts 22:3). It is unlikely that Saul ever had any direct contact with Jesus before the crucifixion, for he never mentions anything like this in his many letters.

Saul was his given name, in honor of the first king of Israel. Like King Saul, he was from the tribe of Benjamin (Philippians 3:5). He was a "Diaspora" Jew, having been born outside Palestine, in Tarsus of Cilicia (Acts 21:39). This was a large Greek city some 400 miles north of Jerusalem. It is not surprising, then, to learn that he also had a Roman name, Paul (Acts 13:9), and that his father had obtained Roman citizenship for the family (Acts 22:27, 28).

Despite being born far from the center of Judaism, Saul had become a rabid partisan for the faith. Since he was not a Levite, he could not be a priest. So he became, in his mind, the next best thing: a Pharisee (Acts 23:6). The Pharisees were a lay movement among first-century Jews. Pharisees taught the Jewish law in an uncompromising way.

We can understand, therefore, how Saul's love for Judaism and its traditions drew him to Jerusalem, the center for all things Jewish. Once there, however, this ambitious young man found it necessary to prove himself. He found a way to do this by pleasing the Jewish elite in the holy city through vicious persecution of their greatest threat: Christ's church (see Galatians 1:13, 14). Such violent behavior was not characteristic of first-century Judaism. It was brought forth by fervent devotion and unrestrained ambition coupled with the devious conduct of Saul's Jewish masters.

By the time of Saul's conversion, the Jerusalem church had progressed through several stages. It was begun in a spectacular fashion (Acts 2), but met with immediate opposition from the Jewish leaders (Acts 3, 4). The church had experienced a very difficult internal matter resulting in the deaths of two members (Acts 5:1-11). It had reorganized to minister more effectively to its growing membership (Acts 6). A dynamic young preacher, Stephen, was killed after he infuriated the Jewish leaders (Acts 7). Further threats of death had caused some church leaders to exit Jerusalem. Then the church had spread to nearby Samaria (Acts 8). At this point, Saul comes on the scene.

I. Death-Dealer Named Saul (Acts 9:1, 2)

What is it about some people's faith that makes them believe that killing religious opponents is a righteous act? For Christians serving under the lordship of the Prince of Peace, religious murder is almost beyond comprehension. Yet we see it with alarming frequency in our world today. We should not be surprised to learn that religious murder occurred in the ancient world too, even within Judaism.

A. Murderous Heart (v. 1)

1. And Saul, yet breathing out threatenings and slaughter against the disciples of the Lord, went unto the high priest.

Saul has been personally involved in persecuting Christians (Acts 8:3; 9:13). To describe Saul as *breathing out* murderous threats shows how completely obsessed he has become with eliminating Christians. This despicable condition is the reason Saul can later describe himself as the chief of sinners (1 Timothy 1:15).

No less astounding is the complicity of *the high priest* Caiaphas, the number one Jew in the entire world. Annas, the high priest deposed by the Romans, is still considered to have high priestly authority as well (see Acts 4:6). This evil old man, father-in-law of Caiaphas, instigated the trials that led to the death of Jesus (John 18:13, 24). Caiaphas and Annas seem to lack any moral restraint in regard to crushing the Christian movement.

B. Ambitious Spirit (v. 2)

2. And desired of him letters to Damascus to the synagogues, that if he found any of this way, whether they were men or women, he might bring them bound unto Jerusalem.

The Roman government is amazingly tolerant of actions the Jewish leaders are taking. At this time there is a significant Jewish population in *Damascus*, thus there is a plurality of *synagogues* there. Saul's business is to find members of the Jewish-Christian community and bring them to *Jerusalem* for trial. Such aggressive actions surely strike a note of terror in the infant church.

The Christian movement is referred to here as the *way*, a common designation in Acts. This is *way* in the sense of "road" or "path." For believers, it is "the way of salvation" (Acts 16:17) or "the way of the Lord" (Acts 18:25). It is the prophesied "way of life" (Jeremiah 21:8). [See question #1, page 64.]

The desperation of Saul's mission is shown by the fact that he intends to bring back both *men* and *women*. In the ancient world, women would not usually be considered important enough for such measures. This shows that Saul knows of women who are an important part of the church.

MURDERERS, ANCIENT AND MODERN

The infamous Arellano Félix Organization, a drug cartel in Mexico, once controlled a multi-million-dollar drug business through torture, murder, political assassinations, and the corruption of

---

How to Say It

ANANIAS. An-uh-*nye*-us.

ARAMAIC. *Air*-uh-*may*-ik (strong accent on *may*).

ARELLANO FÉLIX. Aw-ray-*yawn*-oh *Fay*-leaks.

CAIAPHAS. *Kay*-uh-fus or *Kye*-uh-fus.

CILICIA. Sih-*lish*-i-uh.

DAMASCUS. Duh-*mass*-kus.

DIASPORA. Dee-*as*-puh-ruh.

GAMALIEL. Guh-*may*-lih-ul or Guh-*may*-lee-al.

LEVITE. *Lee*-vite.

PHARISEE. *Fair*-ih-see.

SAMARIA. Suh-*mare*-ee-uh.

SYNAGOGUES. *sin*-uh-gogs.

TARSUS. *Tar*-sus.

Mexican law enforcement. The cartel murdered more than 2,000 people in 2006, the final year it was able to act with impunity.

With help from American authorities, the cartel leaders were arrested. Then, only a few weeks into his presidential term in 2007, the newly elected president of Mexico extradited 11 accused narcotics traffickers to the United States. Their money and connections would buy no favors from authorities in American courts and prisons.

Like the leaders of this cartel, the Jewish leaders had little moral compunction against violently neutralizing anyone who threatened their positions. They controlled the lives of the Jewish people and would do almost anything to stay in power. In league with the high priest, Saul of Tarsus became the rising star in the evil plot against the Christians. Sometimes those who claim to be on God's side commit horrendous acts! We must always be on guard against them lest *they* turn out to be *us*.   —C. R. B.

II. Destination Called Damascus (Acts 9:3-9)

Saul is sent to Damascus, about 150 miles northeast of Jerusalem. By this time these two ancient cities have experienced various periods of friendship and hostility for over 1,000 years (and still do today). Since both cities are under Roman rule in the first century, a period of peaceful relations exists. This expedition undoubtedly is well funded. The trip will take a week or more.

A. Confronted and Humbled (vv. 3, 4)

3. And as he journeyed, he came near Damascus: and suddenly there shined round about him a light from heaven.

Since the traveling party is *near Damascus*, it has been on the road for several days by this point. The party is stopped by a powerful, supernatural *light* as it approaches the destination. This is at midday, about noon (see Acts 22:6). The brilliant, heavenly light is seen by Saul and all of his companions (Acts 22:9).

4. And he fell to the earth, and heard a voice saying unto him, Saul, Saul, why persecutest thou me?

Some think that Saul's "falling" is from a horse. Whether walking or riding, the proud young firebreather now finds himself flat on the ground.

The *voice* speaks to Saul in the Hebrew (or Aramaic) tongue (Acts 26:14). The risen Christ is not limited to any particular language, but He uses Saul's mother tongue for a purpose. The obviously supernatural encounter is not with a pagan

god or demon. It is with the Jewish God, and He is making an accusation against the self-assured Saul: you are working against me! The Son of God already knows Saul's motive, so that is not the purpose of the question. He asks the confrontational question to force Saul into a reckoning for his murderous actions.

B. Surprised and Judged (vv. 5, 6)

5. And he said, Who art thou, Lord? And the Lord said, I am Jesus whom thou persecutest: it is hard for thee to kick against the pricks.

Saul's worst fears must be realized here. In a flash he understands, "I'm on the wrong side!"

Jesus uses a striking expression to describe Saul's behavior. He is like the stubborn ox that kicks whenever its driver attempts to guide it by using a poker in its rear haunch. The obstinate animal resists being guided and wants to proceed on its own path, no matter how wrong or dangerous.

This indicates that Saul has had previous opportunities to accept the truth of the church's message about Jesus. Saul had listened to Stephen's speech that revealed the guilt of Jerusalem's Jewish elite. Saul surely had been one of those in the angry mob who put his hands over his ears as a sign of disrespect and defiance to Stephen's message (Acts 7:57). This time, however, rejecting Jesus will not be so easy. [See question #2, page 64.]

6. And he trembling and astonished said, Lord, what wilt thou have me to do? And the Lord said unto him, Arise, and go into the city, and it shall be told thee what thou must do.

In an instant Saul changes from a sworn enemy of Jesus to a believer. His response shows this in two ways. First, he addresses Christ as *Lord*, an indication of respect and submission. Second, he displays an obedient heart, asking, *what wilt thou have me to do?* The Lord puts this new faith to the test by issuing certain instructions.

C. Blinded and Confused (vv. 7-9)

7, 8. And the men which journeyed with him stood speechless, hearing a voice, but seeing no man. And Saul arose from the earth; and when his eyes were opened, he saw no man: but they led him by the hand, and brought him into Damascus.

All the travelers have seen a light, but only Saul is blinded. This is a miraculous blindness, indicating that while there are several witnesses to this event, Saul is its target. Any horses present may have run off in fear, thus the proud, self-reliant young man is required literally to "walk by faith," for he is *led* by *the hand* to nearby *Damascus*.

9. And he was three days without sight, and neither did eat nor drink.

The blindness does not go away with the mere passage of time. Saul responds with the godly practice of fasting. This is accompanied by fervent, focused prayer (see v. 11, below). We may say that God has put Saul in "time out"!

III. Disciple Named Ananias (Acts 9:10, 11, 16-19a)

We have no record of how the Christian faith has spread to Damascus. That it indeed has is evidenced by Saul's awareness of the presence of disciples in the city—thus his mission to bring them to Jerusalem for trial and punishment. God often has people in places we don't expect. This is a lesson that Saul (as Paul) learns later in Corinth (Acts 18:10).

A. Fear, Then Obedience (vv. 10, 11, 16)

10. And there was a certain disciple at Damascus, named Ananias; and to him said the Lord in a vision, Ananias. And he said, Behold, I am here, Lord.

This is the second *Ananias* we meet in Acts. The first one, "Bad Ananias," was put to death earlier by God for lying to the church about a financial matter (Acts 5). This one, "Good Ananias," is a devout man with a positive reputation in the Jewish community (Acts 22:12). His name's Old Testament meaning is "the Lord is gracious." The Lord is gracious to Ananias by entrusting him with the task of working with Saul. The level of trust is shown in that Ananias receives *a vision,* a relatively rare event in the Bible.

11. And the Lord said unto him, Arise, and go into the street which is called Straight, and inquire in the house of Judas for one called Saul, of Tarsus: for, behold, he prayeth.

Saul is staying at a home on the *street* called *Straight,* which is a long, colonnaded thoroughfare during this period. There is a certain irony for Saul to be on this street, for the term *straight* can have the sense of "straightforward" or "full disclosure." It is like the patient telling his doctor, "I want you to be straight with me." Saul's eyes are to be opened to the light again, but his mind and heart are to be opened to the full reality of the risen Christ and the mission for which he has been chosen.

16. For I will show him how great things he must suffer for my name's sake.

Not all of the news is pleasant. Saul is being called to *suffer* some great things (see 2 Corinthians 11:23-28). [See questions #3 and #4, page 64.] He will no longer lead against Christians those well-funded police actions that have the blessing of the high priest.

Visual for Lesson 7

Point to this visual as you ask, "How is a spiritual transformation like the emergence of a butterfly?"

B. Blessing, Then Fellowship (vv. 17-19a)

17. And Ananias went his way, and entered into the house; and putting his hands on him said, Brother Saul, the Lord, even Jesus, that appeared unto thee in the way as thou camest, hath sent me, that thou mightest receive thy sight, and be filled with the Holy Ghost.

Ananias understands his visit with Saul to have three purposes. First, he announces that he has come to represent *the Lord, even Jesus.* This is a fulfillment of Saul's earlier directions, that if he goes to Damascus and waits, Jesus will tell him what to do. Saul is not abandoned.

Second, Ananias is to be the instrument by which Saul's *sight* is restored. Third, Saul will begin to taste of the precious gift of Christianity: the presence of *the Holy Ghost.* Despite all of his piety and devotion as a Pharisee, Saul has never experienced this spiritual blessing. His exhaustive study of Scripture and his loyal obedience to the great Jewish leaders of his day have not given him this gift.

SAVING AN ENDANGERED SPECIES

Only 200 American peregrine falcons were left in North America in 1970. This predatory species was still on the endangered list 10 years ago. Today there are more than 3,000 of the birds, thanks to captive breeding programs and the banning of DDT.

Many of these falcons now nest on high-rise towers and bridges in cities across the continent. Their survival rate in urban settings is only 40 percent, due in part to dangers the fledglings face in learning to fly among tall buildings and from falling to the ground in heavily trafficked streets. Some bird-watchers in Salt Lake City risk their lives to save the young birds. Wearing bright orange vests, the volunteers rush into traffic to keep cars from killing the fledglings.

We wonder if Ananias initially felt as those volunteers do today. To his point of view, he probably saw himself being required to rush out and place himself between helpless Christians and an oncoming truck (Saul of Tarsus). Ananias was aware of Saul's reputation as a persecutor of Christians. Ananias even raised an objection to God's call (Acts 9:13, 14). But when God said *Go!* Ananias acted in faith. God still expects His people to act that way. —C. R. B.

18. And immediately there fell from his eyes as it had been scales: and he received sight forthwith, and arose, and was baptized.

Saul's healing is described as being like *scales* falling *from his eyes*. These must be something like biggish pieces of dry skin flaking off. [See question #5, page 64.]

We should not assume that Saul knows instinctively that he should be *baptized*. Doubtlessly, Ananias shares with him the significance of the act of water baptism for a believer (Acts 2:38), and again Saul obediently submits.

19. And when he had received meat, he was strengthened.

Meat is here used in the older sense of food in general. After three days, Saul is weak with hunger. Ananias wisely recognizes that he needs to care for his new brother physically as well as spiritually.

Conclusion

A. Transformations

Earlier this month I heard a woman speak of coming to faith as a "lightning bolt" conversion. By this she meant that she had had an experience that changed her from a sin-loving unbeliever to a godly believer overnight. I have no reason or need to question her testimony. Her life of service to the Lord is by itself a testimony to her faith.

Yet I knew another woman, recently passed away, who was as close to a lifelong Christian as any person I have ever known. She was brought up in a Christian home by godly parents, and she easily and naturally accepted Jesus as her Lord and Savior when she was old enough to understand faith. She married a fine Christian man, and the marriage produced a son who is a strong believer.

She told me once that she never really experienced a period of doubt or despair, although she

had many heartaches and tragedies in her life. She had never felt a need to "find herself" by exploring options outside the will of God. She died peacefully, having quietly demonstrated a life well lived in the Lord.

Many believers fall somewhere between these two extremes. But however we come to Christ, the life of faith is a long road. Sometimes it is full of doubts—doubts about God and about our true devotion to Him. When things get hard, we can be overcome by selfishness and our tendencies to want to save ourselves. The Christian life is not a quick dash, however. It is a marathon.

While Paul's conversion was full of drama, we should also remember that the Lord chided him for kicking against the pricks (Acts 9:5). Saul had resisted the overtures of the Lord more than once. He had hardened his heart to reject the message of Stephen and had taken satisfaction in his death. We also know that Saul/Paul had periods of doubt and depression in his ministry (see 2 Corinthians 1:8). Yet the Lord did not give up on him, patiently bringing him to a faith that could say, "For to me to live is Christ, and to die is gain" (Philippians 1:21). May we say the same.

B. Prayer

O Lord, please continue to be patient with us. May we use our experiences to strengthen our trust in You. May our faith grow each day as we learn to trust You more. And may our unbelieving friends and relatives see a faith in us that would draw them to You. We pray this in the name of Jesus, amen.

C. Thought to Remember

God still transforms people.

Learning by Doing

This page contains an alternative lesson plan emphasizing learning activities. Some of these activities are also found in the helpful student book, Adult Bible Class.

Into the Lesson

Ask students to form study groups of three or four. Say, "Please share your conversion experience with others in the group. If someone is not yet a Christian, they can either listen or share why they are now attending a Sunday school class." Suggest they focus their discussions on who led them to Christ, why they felt compelled to accept Christ as Savior, and any other details (possibly even humorous) of their conversions that may be of interest.

After 10 minutes or so, ask your learners if they detect common elements among the conversion experience stories. Write these on the board. After this time of sharing, note that while conversion experiences are personal, they also have common elements. These elements concern the recognition of a need and a sense of being unable to help oneself. Make a transition by saying, "One of the most startling conversions in the New Testament is that of Saul. Let's examine his experience."

Into the Word

Request that your students once again get into study groups; distribute paper and pencils. Ask students to read Acts 9:1-5 within their groups. Then let them start with these easy questions about "preconversion Saul." (You can put these on the board or reproduce them on a handout. The Scripture references may be either included or not.)

1. How would you describe Saul's attitude toward Christianity at the outset? *(9:1, 2)*

2. What event caused Saul to reconsider his attitude? *(9:3-5)*

These won't take long to answer—just a few minutes. Move through the responses rapidly, adding your own observations as appropriate.

Then ask students to write down some ways to describe "preconversion Saul" and discuss their descriptions. After 10 minutes or so, ask students to share with the entire class the observations on their lists. Add any descriptions that they may have missed. Possible answers include the following: *threatening (v. 1), murderous (v. 1), against God (v. 1), zealous (v. 2), persecutor (v. 4)*.

Now ask your students to answer the following questions about "postconversion Saul" of Acts 9:6-11, 16-19a. (Again, you can put these on the board

or reproduce them on a handout. The Scripture references may be either included or not.)

1. How did Saul receive the good news of Jesus Christ? *(9:6-9)*

2. What was Saul's physical problem and how did it get resolved? *(9:8, 9, 18)*

3. What did Saul do immediately after his blindness was healed? *(9:18, 19a)*

Then ask students to write down some ways to describe "postconversion Saul" and discuss their descriptions. After 10 minutes or so, ask students to share with the entire class the observations on their lists. Add any descriptions that they may have missed. Possible answers include the following: *humbled (v. 6), submissive (v. 8), fasted (v. 9)*.

Compare how Saul was perceived according to Acts 9:13, 14 with how God perceived him in 9:15 and with how Ananias saw him in 9:17. Point out that conversion changes our relationship with God and others.

Make a transition by saying, "In some ways Saul's conversion is different from ours, but in other ways it is similar." Let's explore these differences and similarities.

Into Life

Keep students in their study groups. Ask the following questions. (Again, you can put these on the board or reproduce them on a handout.)

1. Which elements of your own conversion experience were like those of Saul's, if any? Did you have something remotely like a Damascus Road experience that heightened your spiritual awareness? Who was your Ananias, if anyone?

2. Which elements of your conversion experience were unlike those of Saul's?

Expect that most answers will focus on conversions being less dramatic than was Saul's.

Next, turn your students' attention outward. Ask them to think of someone who needs to hear the gospel and be converted to Christ. What commitment will the respondent make to reach out to him or her?

Invite students to pair off for a time of prayer. The prayer is to have two emphases. First, it is to be for the individuals of whom they are thinking. Second, it is to be for the one praying that God will grant him or her the right opportunity and boldness to share the good news.

Let's Talk It Over

*The questions on this page are designed to promote discussion of the lesson
by the class and to encourage application of the lesson Scriptures. The answers
provided are only discussion starters. Let your class talk it over from there.*

**1. What does it mean to you to be a part of
the way?**

In Acts 19:9, 23; 22:4, the early followers of
Christ were spoken as being of *that way* or *this way.*
Being considered as following *the way* is a direct
connection with how Christ spoke of himself in
John 14:6: "I am the way, the truth, and the life."

When we think of being part of *the way,* we may
think of it being the way to Heaven. That is certainly true. Yet while we want it to be a way of
comfort and peace, it is important to see that *the
way* takes us through persecution and conflict as
well. To follow Jesus, "the way," is to share in His
sufferings along the way (Romans 8:17).

**2. In what ways have you "kicked against
the pricks" in your relationship to Jesus? What
caused you to repent?**

Through His written Word, God seeks to provide direction for our lives. He gives principles
for us to live by and proper examples to follow.
When we refuse to live in God's way, we are kicking against the pricks.

Titus 1:16 provides a look at those who claim
to be followers of Christ but are actually kicking
against Him: "They profess that they know God;
but in works they deny him, being abominable, and
disobedient, and unto every good work reprobate."
The writer of Hebrews states that it is impossible
for those who have tasted the gift of salvation and
then willfully and deliberately rebel (kick against
the pricks) to be restored, because "they crucify to
themselves the Son of God afresh, and put him to
an open shame" (Hebrews 6:6).

**3. In what ways has God's call differed at times
from the ways we have called people to become
followers of Christ? What do we do to correct the
mismatch?**

In issuing invitations for people to become followers of Christ, it's tempting to paint a picture
of "now all your troubles are over." Some Christians encourage this kind of thinking by holding
to the philosophy "If it doesn't make me happy, it
must not be from God, because God wants me to
be happy."

While we may want to focus on calling people
to a safe environment, Jesus calls people to be willing to suffer for Him. While we may wish to call
people to a peaceful life, Jesus leads His followers in a way that often results in strife and persecution (Luke 14:26; 21:17). We dare not create
fantasies to appeal to people when Jesus presents
reality. We share in both comfort and sufferings
(2 Corinthians 1:7).

**4. How do you respond when God asks you to
do something uncomfortable? How have such situations caused you to grow spiritually?**

We do not like to be bound by anything; we like
to be free. As a result, Christians may find themselves avoiding the path to which Christ calls us.
We can be guilty of having the same attitude as
that of the rich young ruler (Mark 10:17-23).

Sometimes we may try to negotiate with God.
Or instead of committing ourselves to get involved
in the lives of other people, we want to pay someone else to do the work of ministry. When God
calls us to go to others with His message or to
offer kindness, we may think that we have more
important things to do, implying that those people
are not worthy (Luke 10:25-37). Our attitude can
become much like that of the Pharisees!

**5. What are some of the figurative "scales" that
have fallen from your eyes so that you were able
to see Jesus more clearly?**

The world is a strong influence on Christians.
There are false teachings that creep into the lives
of Christians and the church that cloud our understanding of Christ and His way. Pluralism and
postmodernism are strong influences in our culture. The teaching that one religion is as good as
another and that all lead to the same place in the
end becomes adopted by some in the church. Such
teachings deny Jesus as the only way through
whom people come to the Father.

There are those who claim Christ, yet teach
"another gospel" (2 Corinthians 11:4; Galatians
1:6). Such "gospels" in the twenty-first century
may include the notion that God wants all His
followers to be materially blessed and that prosperity is a sign of spirituality. Under this kind of
philosophy, Jesus himself would not be considered spiritual, since He had no place to lay His
head (Luke 9:58)!

Evangelistic Community

DEVOTIONAL READING: Matthew 28:16-20.

BACKGROUND SCRIPTURE: Acts 13.

PRINTED TEXT: Acts 13:1-12.

Acts 13:1-12

1 Now there were in the church that was at Antioch certain prophets and teachers; as Barnabas, and Simeon that was called Niger, and Lucius of Cyrene, and Manaen, which had been brought up with Herod the tetrarch, and Saul.

2 As they ministered to the Lord, and fasted, the Holy Ghost said, Separate me Barnabas and Saul for the work whereunto I have called them.

3 And when they had fasted and prayed, and laid their hands on them, they sent them away.

4 So they, being sent forth by the Holy Ghost, departed unto Seleucia; and from thence they sailed to Cyprus.

5 And when they were at Salamis, they preached the word of God in the synagogues of the Jews: and they had also John to their minister.

6 And when they had gone through the isle unto Paphos, they found a certain sor-cerer, a false prophet, a Jew, whose name was Bar-jesus:

7 Which was with the deputy of the country, Sergius Paulus, a prudent man; who called for Barnabas and Saul, and desired to hear the word of God.

8 But Elymas the sorcerer (for so is his name by interpretation) withstood them, seeking to turn away the deputy from the faith.

9 Then Saul, (who also is called Paul,) filled with the Holy Ghost, set his eyes on him,

10 And said, O full of all subtilty and all mischief, thou child of the devil, thou enemy of all righteousness, wilt thou not cease to pervert the right ways of the Lord?

11 And now, behold, the hand of the Lord is upon thee, and thou shalt be blind, not seeing the sun for a season. And immediately there fell on him a mist and a darkness; and he went about seeking some to lead him by the hand.

12 Then the deputy, when he saw what was done, believed, being astonished at the doctrine of the Lord.

Oct
26

GOLDEN TEXT: When they had fasted and prayed, and laid their hands on them, they sent them away.—Acts 13:3.

The New Testament Community
Unit 2: Growth of the New Community
(Lessons 5–8)

Lesson Aims

After participating in this lesson, each student will be able to:

1. Summarize the events that led up to Barnabas and Saul's mission trip and what happened while they were on Cyprus.

2. Compare and contrast the experiences of the church at Antioch and of Barnabas and Saul with modern churches and individuals involved in short-term missions.

3. Describe one way he or she will support the local church's mission program.

Lesson Outline

INTRODUCTION

   A. Has the Church Outgrown Missions?
   B. Lesson Background

I. PLANNED EXPANSION (Acts 13:1-3)

   A. Leadership Listens (vv. 1, 2)
   B. Leadership Acts (v. 3)

II. PREACHING EXPEDITION (Acts 13:4, 5)

   A. Strategic Destination: Cyprus (v. 4)
      Going Home
   B. Strategic Target: Synagogues (v. 5)

III. POWER ENCOUNTER (Acts 13:6-12)

   A. Sorcerer Is Met (vv. 6, 7)
   B. Sorcerer Challenges (v. 8)
   C. Sorcerer Is Overcome (vv. 9-12)
      Confronting Evil

CONCLUSION

   A. Missions Today
   B. Prayer
   C. Thought to Remember

Introduction

A. Has the Church Outgrown Missions?

A generation ago, the North American church was very enthusiastic about "missions." A substantial portion of the budget was devoted to the support of missionaries. Missionary speakers were frequent guests in the Sunday morning pulpit. Missions conferences were guaranteed to draw large crowds. The regular members in the pew were encouraged by reports of conversions and church planting in exotic, distant lands.

Things have changed. While churches still contribute large amounts of money to causes outside their walls, many such causes would not have been defined as "missions" in previous years. Missionaries find it hard to schedule speaking engagements in churches while home on furlough, for schedules are packed and preachers guard their pulpits. Some would say that the church has moved beyond the missionary efforts of the post–World War II period, and that she has outgrown (or at least rethought) missions as previously understood.

As we ponder this change, it will be helpful to see missions within a biblical framework. The church is called to the task of evangelism (see Matthew 28:19, 20; Acts 5:42). As understood historically, *missions* suggests something more than general evangelism. Missions is intentional and strategic cross-cultural evangelism. This requires specialized training, enormous commitment, and generous funding.

The need for churches to support missionary efforts has not changed. Today's lesson tells the story of a little church far, far away and long, long ago that pioneered the idea of strategic cross-cultural evangelism. The resultant missionary activity had an impact that is still felt today.

B. Lesson Background

Antioch of Syria was one of the great cities of the ancient world. This city was founded in 300 BC by Seleucus, one of the generals of Alexander the Great. The city was named in honor of Antiochus, the father of Seleucus. It became the capital city for the Seleucid dynasty. The city sat on the banks of the Orontes River, about 15 miles from the Mediterranean coast.

The city seems to have had a Jewish community from the beginning, and this grew to such a large number that the Jews of Antioch were allowed to have a large measure of self-government. In Paul's day, Antioch had become the administrative capital of the eastern Roman Empire. It was a very cosmopolitan city, having a mixture of Greek, Roman, Arabian, and Jewish cultural influences. Estimates put the population of Antioch in this period at half a million people, making it the third city of the empire, behind Rome and Alexandria.

It is not surprising that the new faith in Jesus as the Jewish Messiah had spread to the large Jewish community in Antioch (see Acts 11:19), which numbered between 25,000 and 65,000 at the time. Unlike the Jerusalem church, the Antioch congregation seems to have been an early adopter of the right of non-Jews to be full members of the church (Acts 11:20). These believers were also the first to be called *Christians* (Acts 11:26), meaning "of the

Christ party." This name quickly gained popularity and has been a primary designation for the followers of Christ ever since.

When the leaders of the Jerusalem church heard about the church in Antioch, they sent Barnabas to investigate (Acts 11:22). However, rather than impose the authority of the Jerusalem church upon the church in Antioch, Barnabas joined their leadership team. Realizing Antioch's need for a first-rate teacher, Barnabas remembered his old friend Saul (Paul), who was in his hometown of Tarsus. So Barnabas went to Tarsus, some 100 miles away, and brought Saul back to Antioch (Acts 11:25, 26). Saul was encouraged by Barnabas and the challenges of the Antioch ministry.

The scope of this ministry was shown when the Antioch church sent support to Jerusalem for famine relief (Acts 11:28-30). This successful trip by the team of Barnabas and Saul sets the scene for today's lesson about a far more significant journey.

I. Planned Expansion
(Acts 13:1-3)

Progress in evangelistic work does not happen by accident. God uses various circumstances to advance His kingdom. For example, the death of Stephen caused some members of the Jerusalem church to scatter. This provided new opportunities to preach the gospel (see Acts 11:19). This was unplanned from their perspective, but used by God anyway.

At other times, evangelistic efforts are enhanced by careful, strategic planning. In today's lesson, we see the leaders of the Antioch church make a momentous missions decision based on a prompting by the Holy Spirit.

A. Leadership Listens (vv. 1, 2)

1. Now there were in the church that was at Antioch certain prophets and teachers; as Barnabas, and Simeon that was called Niger, and Lucius of Cyrene, and Manaen, which had been brought up with Herod the tetrarch, and Saul.

The leaders in this *church* are described as *prophets and teachers* (compare Acts 11:27; 15:32). A prophet speaks for God as a result of the influence of the Holy Spirit. A teacher expounds scriptural doctrine. We do not need to understand these roles as mutually exclusive, for doubtlessly there were "teaching prophets" in the early church.

The order of the names in this list is revealing. *Barnabas,* listed first, is assumed to be the most important. We know nothing of the middle three, but the details are interesting for each. *Simeon*

is *called Niger*, which means "black"—probably indicating that Simeon is a black man. *Lucius* is from Cyrene on the North African coast. *Manaen* had been a childhood companion of one of the Herod family. This is probably Herod Antipas, ruler of Galilee (Luke 3:1), who presided over one of the trials of Jesus (Luke 23:7).

The last to be mentioned is *Saul*, with whom we are well acquainted by this point in Acts. His position in the list, however, indicates that he is the least recognized (and perhaps the youngest, about 30 years old) of these five leaders. How quickly Saul's reputation will change!

2. As they ministered to the Lord, and fasted, the Holy Ghost said, Separate me Barnabas and Saul for the work whereunto I have called them.

In Acts, Luke (the author) presents the Holy Spirit almost like other individuals in the story line. We almost get the impression that people are at a morning leadership prayer meeting and *the Holy Ghost* is at the table with them, occupying one of the chairs! This is not Luke's intent, however. He wants to show the intimacy that this leadership group has with God's Spirit. Although it is not explained, we can assume that one of the leaders serves as prophet to give voice to the intentions of the Holy Spirit.

Notice who is chosen to go from the church to do evangelism in other places: two of the absolutely top people in the congregation. This is not a church trying to get an unappreciated preacher to consider mission work. These two are not misfits who find it difficult to get along with other people. Nor are they young idealists in search of adventure. Barnabas is perhaps the wealthiest member of the Antioch church (Acts 4:36, 37) and Saul the best educated. Those who are commissioned by churches to do cross-cultural evangelism should be the church's very best. [See question #1, page 72.]

How to Say It

ANTIOCH. *An*-tee-ock.
CYRENE. Sigh-*ree*-nee.
DIETRICH BONHOEFFER. *Dee*-trick *Bon*-hoe-fur.
ELYMAS. *El*-ih-mass.
LUCIUS. *Lew*-shus.
MANAEN. *Man*-uh-en.
NIGER. *Nye*-jer.
ORONTES. Awe-*rahnt*-eez.
PAPHOS. *Pay*-fus.
SELEUCIA. Sih-*lew*-shuh.
SELEUCUS. Suh-*loo*-kuss.
SERGIUS PAULUS. *Ser*-jih-us *Paul*-us.

B. Leadership Acts (v. 3)

3. And when they had fasted and prayed, and laid their hands on them, they sent them away.

The ceremony of commissioning Barnabas and Saul is presented with little detail, but we assume that it takes place in the presence of the full congregation. This is logical because those sent out as missionaries are still accountable to their mother church, and everyone there should know what is going on.

Missionaries need accountability, for theirs can be a lonely road. Saul's willingness to be held accountable is shown by his return to Antioch at the end of the first two missionary journeys (see Acts 14:26; 18:22).

II. Preaching Expedition
(Acts 13:4, 5)

Talking about missions is nice, but *doing* missions is the bottom line. The leaders in Antioch act upon the plan without significant delay.

A. Strategic Destination: Cyprus (v. 4)

4. So they, being sent forth by the Holy Ghost, departed unto Seleucia; and from thence they sailed to Cyprus.

Divine approval for this endeavor is shown by Luke's comment that they are *sent forth by the Holy Ghost*. Barnabas, Saul, and the others have a high sense of discernment regarding the will of God, so they act on it. *Seleucia* is Antioch's port city, about a dozen miles away. [See question #2, page 72.]

Why do they go to *Cyprus*? This island is the original home of Barnabas (Acts 4:36), so at least two factors come into play. First, Barnabas surely has a

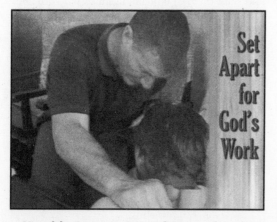

Visual for Lesson 8. *Start a discussion by asking, "How well are we doing in following biblical principles in setting people apart for service?"*

burden for his own people to hear the message of salvation. Second, this is known territory for Barnabas, making the target location seem less intimidating. He will be able to use his network of friends and relatives to provide accommodations in a day when there are no hotels as we think of today.

GOING HOME

"Over the river and through the woods, to Grandmother's house we go; the horse knows the way to carry the sleigh through the white and drifted snow." Many of us remember that tune from childhood, even if we didn't take that exact path to our grandparents' home for Thanksgiving Day.

This song has a winsome attraction to many of us. The idea takes us back to the pleasant days of childhood, when our lives were simpler. We may think of loving figures who were there to make us feel welcome and important. That's what grandparents are for, isn't it?

We don't know whether Barnabas visited his grandparents' house when he and Saul went to Cyprus for their mission. Barnabas may have been pulled by some of the same feelings many of us have regarding where we grew up. But the purpose for the trip was not to take a trip down memory lane. The mission was to bring the message of Jesus to others. That's the task for all of us, however near to or far from home we are.   —C. R. B.

B. Strategic Target: Synagogues (v. 5)

5. And when they were at Salamis, they preached the word of God in the synagogues of the Jews: and they had also John to their minister.

Salamis is the major port on the eastern end of Cyprus, about 160 sea miles from Seleucia. It has a substantial Jewish population, with archaeological evidence of more than one synagogue. There is regular shipping activity between these two cities, with the voyage taking two or three days if there are favorable winds. Here we learn that young *John* Mark, a relative of Barnabas, goes along (compare Acts 12:25). Later in Acts we learn that Mark abandons Barnabas and Saul in the middle of this trip (Acts 15:38).

The specific strategy of Barnabas and Saul is revealed here. These two have decided to use their own "Jewishness" as a way to get into unfamiliar synagogues; this will give them ready audiences for their preaching. The apostle Paul will practice this strategy throughout his missionary travels: he arrives in a new city, finds a synagogue, shows up on the Sabbath, and attempts to show his fellow Jews that Jesus is the Messiah on the basis of Scripture (example: Acts 17:1, 2). [See question #3, page 72.]

III. Power Encounter
(Acts 13:6-12)

Modern missionaries have stories about "power encounters" they have experienced. This is where there is a direct assault by the forces of Satan. In such cases, the missionaries are powerless on their own and must rely on the Holy Spirit to protect them. These power encounters are crucial events for the people in deciding whether the God of the gospel is more powerful than the "gods" of this world.

A. Sorcerer Is Met (vv. 6, 7)

6. And when they had gone through the isle unto Paphos, they found a certain sorcerer, a false prophet, a Jew, whose name was Bar-jesus.

Barnabas and Saul work their way westward to the Roman administrative capital of *Paphos*. It is about 100 miles from Salamis. But the trip likely takes several weeks, for the team probably waits for Sabbath opportunities along the way as the primary means to share the good news about Jesus in the synagogues.

It is probable, then, that the team encounters this *sorcerer* in a synagogue. Here he has established himself as a prophet, having great sway over the people. Nevertheless, the missionaries recognized him for what he really is: *a false prophet,* in league with Satan. His name is ironic, for *Bar-jesus* means "son of Jesus" or "son of Joshua." Yet he is in utter rebellion against everything taught by Jesus or by Joshua (compare Joshua 24:15).

A sorcerer is one who practices witchcraft. The law teaches that such persons are to be put to death (see Exodus 22:18; compare Deuteronomy 18:10). Yet this man is not only tolerated by the Jewish community, he seems to be a leader!

7. Which was with the deputy of the country, Sergius Paulus, a prudent man; who called for Barnabas and Saul, and desired to hear the word of God.

Bar-jesus has become a confidant of *Sergius Paulus,* the leading authority (proconsul) of the entire island province. This encounter is a partial fulfillment of Jesus' promise to Saul that he will appear before "kings" (Acts 9:15), for Sergius Paulus is as close to a king as Cyprus can offer. Sergius Paulus is known to us from nonbiblical sources as a member of a leading family of the city of Rome. His name appears on an ancient inscription found in Turkey that confirms his title of proconsul. We can assume that he has ties with the Jewish synagogue (thus his relationship with Bar-jesus) and is therefore interested to learn more about the message of the missionaries.

B. Sorcerer Challenges (v. 8)

8. But Elymas the sorcerer (for so is his name by interpretation) withstood them, seeking to turn away the deputy from the faith.

Elymas may be the Aramaic version of "magician," thus showing that Bar-jesus has assumed an exotic, one-name moniker like some celebrities do today. This is similar to Simon the magician in Acts 8:10, who goes by the title "the great power." Here, the sorcerer quickly realizes the threat posed by the missionaries. So he seeks to protect Sergius Paulus from them in order to maintain his own position of influence. [See question #4, page 72.]

C. Sorcerer Is Overcome (vv. 9-12)

9. Then Saul, (who also is called Paul,) filled with the Holy Ghost, set his eyes on him.

Luke (the author of Acts) presents a scene of high drama. *Paul* does not back down or cower from the threatening sorcerer. Paul engages him with direct eye contact, demanding his full attention.

Paul is ready to do his first mighty deed of power, and Luke chooses the moment to make a change. Without comment, the Jewish name *Saul* becomes the Greco-Roman *Paul.* This is also a point of change in the leadership of the team. From this point forward, it is no longer "Barnabas and Saul" (Acts 13:7), but rather "Paul and his company" (Acts 13:13). While Barnabas is still important, the mantle of leadership is passed!

10. And said, O full of all subtilty and all mischief, thou child of the devil, thou enemy of all righteousness, wilt thou not cease to pervert the right ways of the Lord?

Paul passes judgment on Bar-jesus quickly with three condemnations. First, Bar-jesus is the source of *subtilty* and *mischief,* meaning he continually distorts the truth. While he seems powerful and authoritative, he is lying and leading his followers astray. Second, Bar-jesus is a *child of the devil,* indicating that his source of supernatural power is not God, but Satan. Third, Bar-jesus is an *enemy* and perverter of God's righteous standards. [See question #5, page 72.]

CONFRONTING EVIL

Adolf Hitler's rise to power in Germany in the 1930s placed the church in a dilemma. One element in German Protestantism welcomed Hitler with open arms and pushed a proposal that would have forbidden "non-Aryans" in ministry positions.

Dietrich Bonhoeffer (1906–1945) became a heroic figure opposing such perversion of the gospel. He led in the establishment of a minority movement, called *the Confessing Church,* to attempt to remain free from Nazi control. Bonhoeffer was executed for his strong stand in the face of the evil that was consuming his nation.

When Paul confronted Elymas in the power of the Spirit, it was with that same kind of straightforward determination. Paul "called evil by its first name" (as the saying goes). From time to time we need to ask ourselves, "What issues does the church need to speak against today, and what is the best way to do so?"　　　　　—C. R. B.

11a. And now, behold, the hand of the Lord is upon thee, and thou shalt be blind, not seeing the sun for a season.

Bar-jesus is cursed with blindness. Paul does not claim any power for himself in this situation, but attributes this punishment to *the hand of the Lord*. This is the second time we encounter God's striking someone blind in the book of Acts. The first one was Paul himself (chapter 9)! But this case is presented in very different terms.

11b. And immediately there fell on him a mist and a darkness; and he went about seeking some to lead him by the hand.

Paul had been blinded by a brilliant light (Acts 9:3), symbolically overcome by the glory of the risen Christ. By contrast, the sorcerer is blinded by a cloud of *darkness*. A further contrast is seen in the sorcerer's groping for someone to help him and the apparent lack of response. On the Damascus road, Paul's friends had quickly helped him and led him into the city (Acts 9:8).

12. Then the deputy, when he saw what was done, believed, being astonished at the doctrine of the Lord.

The power encounter is over, and the Holy Spirit has prevailed. *The deputy* (Sergius), an intelligent person, understands the implications of the

defeat and humiliation of his former friend. The Roman proconsul respects this teaching, which is confirmed with spiritual power. That causes him to be amazed by *the doctrine of the Lord*, meaning the message of Paul. He is now a receptive audience for what Paul wants to preach.

Conclusion

A. Missions Today

In Paul's day, a missions trip involved getting a group together, rounding up a little money, receiving the blessing of the church, and then booking passage on a wooden boat. How much more complex are these things today! Now we must worry about passports and visas, about forwarding agents and tax ID numbers, about proper equipment and shipping, about health care and education for children, about language learning and e-mail access—the list goes on and on. All of this is expensive, very expensive. While the cost of living in some foreign countries may be low, the cost of having a missionary on-site is not.

While such details of mission work may have changed dramatically in the last 2,000 years, basic strategy has not. Missionaries are those who are called to find people who do not have the gospel, make effective contact with them, and preach the good news so that they too may become disciples of our Lord Jesus Christ.

But aren't there many legitimate needs close to home that cry out for funding? When such an objection arises, remember that we do missions for two basic and interconnected reasons. First, we do them because being Christlike means that we have compassion upon the multitudes of unsaved (compare Matthew 14:14). Second, we do them because the Lord Jesus has commanded that the gospel be taken to all peoples (Matthew 28:19).

When we gain this perspective, we will begin to experience what used to be called a "passion for the lost." From this perspective, support of Christian missions moves to a high place on our priority list. We must support cross-cultural evangelism with our attention, our prayers, and our finances.

B. Prayer

Mighty God, who reigns over all the earth, may we never be guilty of hoarding the gospel, of keeping it for our community and ourselves. May we share it freely by our support of ministries dedicated to taking the good news to the ends of the earth. We pray this in Jesus' name, amen.

C. Thought to Remember

Either be a missionary or support one.

Home Daily Bible Readings

Monday, Oct. 20—Vacancy Filled (Acts 1:15-26)

Tuesday, Oct. 21—Go, Proclaim the Good News (Matthew 10:1-15)

Wednesday, Oct. 22—Persevere in Persecution (Matthew 10:16-25)

Thursday, Oct. 23—Life Found in Giving It (Matthew 10:32-39)

Friday, Oct. 24—Hope in the Living God (1 Timothy 4:6-16)

Saturday, Oct. 25—Salvation Sent to the Gentiles (Acts 28:25-31)

Sunday, Oct. 26—Set Apart for God's Work (Acts 13:1-12)

Learning by Doing

This page contains an alternative lesson plan emphasizing learning activities. Some of these activities are also found in the helpful student book, Adult Bible Class.

Into the Lesson

Write the word *GLOCAL* on the board, in capital letters. Ask students what they think this word means. If no one knows, say that it is a combination of *global* and *local;* this is a term that is gaining in popularity. It refers to something that we do both near (locally) and far (globally).

Remind the class that missions are something we conduct both near and far. Then form the class into study groups of three; provide each group paper and pencils. Ask groups to explore through dialogue how your congregation is *glocal* in its approach to missions.

After a few minutes, write on the board the words *Global* and *Local*. Then summarize the results of the group discussions under those two categories. Ask your learners to explain the relationship between the two. For example, efforts at local evangelism and benevolence (outreach) are parallel to our efforts at global evangelism and benevolence (missions). Make a transition by saying, "The church in Acts was also a *glocal* community, with the local congregation sponsoring missions."

Into the Word

Divide the class into study groups of between four and six. Provide paper and pencils for each study group. Ask groups to read Acts 13:1-3 and answer this question: "What do we know about the church at Antioch and how was it engaged in missions?"

After a few minutes, call for conclusions. You may hear responses such as *the church had teachers and prophets (v. 1); they worshiped (v. 2); they fasted (v. 2); they ordained missionaries by setting them apart and laying hands on them (vv. 2, 3); they fasted and prayed for missionaries (v. 3); they sent them off with financial support implied for a later date (v. 3).*

Ask the class this general question: "If you had to describe the church at Antioch in one word or one short phrase, what would it be?" Write their responses on the board as a means of summarizing the treatment of the first half of the passage.

Once this is complete, turn your students' attention back to the text. Ask them to read Acts 13:4-12 in their study groups. Pose the following questions. (You can have these on prepared handouts, or just write the questions on the board; do not include the italicized verse designations.)

1. In what manner did the Holy Spirit send the missionaries? *(v. 4)*

2. Where was the first actual mission stop on that first missionary journey? *(v. 5)*

3. Did the team work alone, or were others assisting them? *(v. 5)*

4. What resistance did Saul and Barnabas encounter? *(vv. 6-8, 10)*

5. What kind of person resisted the message of the gospel? *(vv. 6, 8)*

6. How did Saul/Paul respond to that resistance? *(vv. 9-11)*

7. What was the result of the "power encounter"? *(v. 12)*

8. Why was the deputy amazed? *(v. 12b)*

After giving the study groups a few minutes, move rapidly through the questions and answers. Once again, write the words *Global* and *Local* on the board. Ask the study groups (or the class as a whole) to reflect on the church at Antioch and the mission work of Saul and Barnabas under each of these two categories (Acts 13:1-12).

After a few minutes, call for reflections; write them on the board. Make a transition to the next portion of the lesson by saying, "Let's use your thoughts to reflect on how our church sends or supports missionaries."

Into Life

Prior to class, collect information on your congregation's support for missions. If possible, bring photos of missionaries, copies of their newsletters, etc. Some of this may be available on the Internet or from your church's mission committee (if your church has one). Also bring a globe or map of the world. Pass around the newsletters, etc., to the study groups; ask them to skim the material.

After a few minutes, ask for descriptions of the mission work they are now acquainted with, perhaps noting on the globe or world map where that missionary serves. For each one ask, "In what way does our congregation support that mission?" Write responses on the board. *(Alternative: Ask someone who is closely connected with your church's missionary support to give a presentation on that effort.)* Close with prayer that focuses on "glocal" action.

Let's Talk It Over

The questions on this page are designed to promote discussion of the lesson by the class and to encourage application of the lesson Scriptures. The answers provided are only discussion starters. Let your class talk it over from there.

1. Why does the church often fail to send her "best" into full-time Christian service? What can we do to correct the problem?

There are many fine young people (and some in midlife) who could be excellent preachers, youth ministers, and missionaries. Others could be effective teachers for Christian colleges and schools. But often they are not encouraged to pursue these opportunities because a career of Christian service is not looked upon as prestigious.

Others are discouraged by Christian parents because those parents know some of the difficulties and pitfalls of Christian ministry and do not want their children to have to endure these problems. In addition, churches that fail to respect, honor, and pay a living wage to their ministers are providing a disincentive for people from their church to enter Christian service. A study of 1 Timothy 5:17 can begin the solution.

2. In what ways have you been guilty of resisting the promptings of the Holy Spirit? How have you overcome this tendency?

Some think that following the lead of the Holy Spirit is risky business. To follow the Spirit's lead will take us out of our comfort zones. We may fear the questions and criticism of others as we act on the promptings of the Spirit.

At times we fail to respond to the Holy Spirit's leading because we are overly cautious about the origin of the prompting. "Is this really from the Holy Spirit, or is it simply my own desires at work?" we ask—and rightly so! Sometimes those who are in leadership positions want to move forward, since they believe the Holy Spirit is leading them. But there may be someone in the church who has a strong influence in opposition to what the leaders want to do. Fear of offending this person causes some churches to fail to move out by faith.

Yet fear of offending the Holy Spirit should be the greater fear. The problem of resisting the Holy Spirit is noted in Acts 7:51.

3. Which elements of Saul's evangelism strategy can you personally use today, if any? Why?

All Christians can be involved in practicing lifestyle evangelism. We can each respond to the needs of friends and neighbors who are not Chris-

tians and by this demonstrate the love of Christ. This is foundational.

Beyond that, one's personal evangelism strategy is an issue of giftedness. A Christian may hear the name of a well-known evangelist and think, "I cannot be a success in evangelism because I am not like that person." There may be some who are more gifted in the area of evangelism than we are, but God simply asks us to be faithful to what we have been given, to be faithful to who we are in Christ.

4. In what ways have others tried to distract you from the faith? How do you resist?

Sometimes Christians are intimidated by non-Christians. This intimidation may take the form of verbal or physical persecution. Sometimes a Christian may be threatened with the loss of a job for failing to go along with some unethical business practices. Because of the pressure to advance in one's career or the pressure simply to keep food on the table, a Christian may cave in.

Other times Christians become discouraged and leave the faith because of spiritually immature Christians who are abusive toward others in the church. Being part of a small group whose members encourage one another in the faith can help.

5. What parts of Paul's response to Bar-jesus can we still use today in reply to the enemies of the cross? Which elements should we not use? Why?

In a day where political correctness and tolerance are such strong issues, it seems out of place to take a strong stand against sin and (especially) against the sinner. Though there is truth in the statement often made by Christians that we are to "hate the sin, yet love the sinner," we need to be careful not to allow this idea to keep us from confronting the sinner.

Just as David was confronted and rebuked by Nathan (2 Samuel 12), those who sin need to be rebuked and corrected. Even so, we realize that Paul may have been granted an ability that the Holy Spirit has not granted us: the ability to see into the heart of an individual. If that's the case, we would exercise caution in using language as strong as Paul's.

Unity in the Community

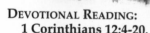

DEVOTIONAL READING:
1 Corinthians 12:4-20.

BACKGROUND SCRIPTURE: 1 Corinthians
12:3-21; Ephesians 4:1-16.

PRINTED TEXT: Ephesians 4:1-16.

Ephesians 4:1-16

1 I therefore, the prisoner of the Lord, beseech you that ye walk worthy of the vocation wherewith ye are called,

2 With all lowliness and meekness, with long-suffering, forbearing one another in love;

3 Endeavoring to keep the unity of the Spirit in the bond of peace.

4 There is one body, and one Spirit, even as ye are called in one hope of your calling;

5 One Lord, one faith, one baptism,

6 One God and Father of all, who is above all, and through all, and in you all.

7 But unto every one of us is given grace according to the measure of the gift of Christ.

8 Wherefore he saith, When he ascended up on high, he led captivity captive, and gave gifts unto men.

9 (Now that he ascended, what is it but that he also descended first into the lower parts of the earth?

10 He that descended is the same also that ascended up far above all heavens, that he might fill all things.)

11 And he gave some, apostles; and some, prophets; and some, evangelists; and some, pastors and teachers;

12 For the perfecting of the saints, for the work of the ministry, for the edifying of the body of Christ:

13 Till we all come in the unity of the faith, and of the knowledge of the Son of God, unto a perfect man, unto the measure of the stature of the fulness of Christ:

14 That we henceforth be no more children, tossed to and fro, and carried about with every wind of doctrine, by the sleight of men, and cunning craftiness, whereby they lie in wait to deceive;

15 But speaking the truth in love, may grow up into him in all things, which is the head, even Christ:

16 From whom the whole body fitly joined together and compacted by that which every joint supplieth, according to the effectual working in the measure of every part, maketh increase of the body unto the edifying of itself in love.

GOLDEN TEXT: Unto every one of us is given grace according to the measure
of the gift of Christ.—Ephesians 4:7.

The New Testament Community
Unit 3: Challenges in the New Community
(Lessons 9–13)

Lesson Aims

After participating in this lesson, each student will be able to:

1. State the source, expression, and goal of church unity as identified in today's text.

2. Contrast the way gifts can be used to unify the body with what happens when they are used to show differences.

3. Suggest a way to unify his or her congregation in one area of church life.

Lesson Outline

Introduction

A. The Divided Church

If you consult the telephone directory for any larger city, you will find a bewildering array of churches. Why are there so many? On the one hand, the answer to this is very complicated and involves understanding the historical origins for every different church. On the other hand, these historical answers usually have a simple, common thread: established churches divide when they cannot agree over issues such as control, organization, or doctrine. Over the centuries, these divisions are multiplied and perpetuated until it becomes difficult even to estimate how many different varieties of churches there are.

Today, we seem to accept the divided church as a given. While there are signs that this attitude is being challenged, we still are far from presenting the church of our Lord Jesus Christ as a united body to an unbelieving world.

It does not have to be this way. On the night He was betrayed, Christ prayed for the unity of the church so that the world would believe the church's message about salvation in Him (John 17:21). Similarly, the lesson this week is a strong testimony to the apostle Paul's belief in a united church.

The biggest challenge of Paul's day was from those who wanted to make or continue to promote certain distinctions between Jew and Gentile within the church. While our reasons may be different, the principles given by Paul are still of great value in freeing ourselves from the divided church mentality that is so pervasive today.

B. Lesson Background

Ephesians, Philippians, Colossians, and Philemon form a group of Paul's letters known as *the Prison Epistles*. These letters are so called because each mentions Paul's being held prisoner or in chains (example: Ephesians 3:1; 4:1). We believe that Paul wrote these letters while awaiting his trial in Rome during the period AD 61–63.

All are quite useful for the church today, since Paul takes up issues of a timeless nature. Times have changed, but people haven't, so we are able to find much in these letters that feels like they have been written precisely for the benefit of the twenty-first-century church.

As with many of Paul's letters, Ephesians follows the format of opening with a presentation of doctrinal teaching, followed by application of that teaching in the life of the individual and the church. In Ephesians, this shift takes place at the beginning of chapter 4.

In the first three chapters of this letter, Paul discusses the church's foundation in the plan of God (Ephesians 1:11, 12); Paul explains Christ's role in breaking down the dividing wall between Jews and Gentiles (Ephesians 2:14); and he calls his readers to recognize that Christ is the head of His church, and the church is His body (Ephesians 1:22, 23). These points are all at odds with a divided church. Therefore, chapter 4 begins Paul's expression of the vital, unitary nature of the church.

I. Worthy Walk
(Ephesians 4:1-6)

A. Walking Our Vocation (v. 1)

1. I therefore, the prisoner of the Lord, beseech you that ye walk worthy of the vocation wherewith ye are called.

Vocation is not a misspelling of our annual vacation week at the beach. Vocation is related to the word *vocal* and literally means "calling." Today, we often associate vocation with an employment category, the job a person holds at any one time. The Bible teaches a much deeper sense of vocation, however, as a lifelong calling.

Paul's language emphasizes this by describing it as the vocation to which we have been *called*. To be called is to be invited to an event or task. As Christians we have been invited to live our lives according to the standards of God, and we have accepted this invitation with all our hearts.

We may have many jobs and various careers over a lifetime, but Christians have a single vocation: to live with and for Christ (see Galatians 2:20; Colossians 2:6). This life *walk* extends to work, play, family, school, and entertainment— to whatever we do. We do not walk in a *worthy* manner when we dishonor the name of Christ and betray the trust He has put in us. When we walk/live for ourselves alone, we do so as enemies of Christ (see Philippians 3:18). [See question #1, page 80.]

B. Walking Our Unity (vv. 2, 3)

2. With all lowliness and meekness, with long-suffering, forbearing one another in love.

Paul characterizes the Christian walk with four related concepts. All of these are based on the idea of not seeking to put ourselves first, but instead placing priority on the needs of others. We live lives of *lowliness* (humility) and *meekness* (gentleness, non-aggressiveness). We are *long-suffering* (patient). We act with loving forbearance (refusing to become irritated over the minor faults and failings of others). See also Colossians 3:12, 13.

How to Say It

AGABUS. *Ag*-uh-bus.

COLOSSIANS. Kuh-*losh*-unz.

CORINTHIANS. Ko-*rin*-thee-unz (*th* as in *thin*).

EPHESIANS. Ee-*fee*-zhunz.

PHILEMON. Fih-*lee*-mun or Fye-*lee*-mun.

PHILIPPIANS. Fih-*lip*-ee-unz.

THESSALONIANS. *Thess*-uh-*lo*-nee-unz (strong accent on *lo*; *th* as in *thin*).

---

3. Endeavoring to keep the unity of the Spirit in the bond of peace.

If we practice a lifestyle of self-denial and love for others, our efforts at *unity* within the church are more likely to be successful. It is when individuals jockey for control and self-interest that the church becomes a fractured fellowship. If we expend all of our energy on fighting with our brothers and sisters, we have lost sight of our calling. Part of this calling is to "have *peace* one with another" (Mark 9:50; compare Colossians 3:15; 1 Thessalonians 5:13).

The church filled with strife is not a church practicing *unity of the Spirit*. Paul's language indicates that this is a spiritual problem. It requires the offenders to get right with God if peace and unity are to be achieved. [See question #2, page 80.]

C. Walking Our Oneness (vv. 4-6)

4. There is one body, and one Spirit, even as ye are called in one hope of your calling.

Paul often uses the metaphor of a human *body* to represent the church (see 1 Corinthians 12:27). Elsewhere Paul asks, "Is Christ divided?" (1 Corinthians 1:13). The logical answer to this question is "no, certainly not." There was and is only one Jesus Christ. Therefore, Paul begins his famous list of "seven ones" by reminding his readers that there is but *one body*, the body of Christ, the church. In Ephesians, this is especially the united church of Jewish and Gentile believers (see 2:14-16).

One body is thus appropriate to be first in a list that Paul chooses to illustrate church unity. In all of this, Paul is showing the folly of a divided church. From God's perspective, the church is one whether we like it or not!

A further example of this is that the church is given *one Spirit*, the Holy Spirit of God. There are not various Holy Spirits for the different denominations of the church. There is only one. Also, the church is motivated by *one hope*, its call to eternal salvation through Jesus Christ. [See question #3, page 80.]

THE BASIS FOR UNITY

An Internet search of the topic "Christian unity" results in thousands of hits. One such unity site says, "Our mission is to reach out to those who many churches often overlook. We want to see barriers torn down. It's not about how you look. It's not about the style of music you like. It's more than a denominational label. It's about Jesus. Period." Sounds a lot like the New Testament, doesn't it?

Problems arise if the unity is sought on the basis of human preconceptions. For example, one Christian unity Web site appeals to homosexuals of a specific racial/ethnic group because of the "sacredness of all life." Many Christians will wonder if the message on sexuality matches what the Bible says. We may also question whether unity in the church can be achieved by targeting only one racial group.

The unity Paul talks about is not to be found in focusing on the "hot button" issues that society squabbles over. Rather, that unity is grounded firmly in the nature of God. That fact should determine how we model our behavior, for it is our Christian behavior that reveals we are God's children. —C. R. B.

5, 6. One Lord, one faith, one baptism, one God and Father of all, who is above all, and through all, and in you all.

One Lord in this context is Jesus, the one we serve as the head of the church (Ephesians 1:22). Logically, then, there is only *one faith*, because Paul is speaking of faith in the Son of God (Galatians 2:20; Ephesians 4:13). There is only one faith because there is only one Son of God, the Lord Jesus.

Further, there is only *one baptism*: baptism into Christ. According to Paul, "as many of you as have been baptized into Christ have put on Christ" (Galatians 3:27). There can be only one baptism because there is only one Christ. With this understanding, Paul ties baptism to full identification with Christ.

That there is only *one God* is the cornerstone of Jewish faith (Deuteronomy 6:4). This has not changed with the advent of Jesus as the Son of God. Christians believe there is only one God. The Christian doctrine of the Trinity is not a denial of the oneness of God.

Visual for Lesson 9. *Start a discussion by asking, "Which area of unity gives us the most problem? How do we improve in this regard?"*

Paul uses marvelous imagery to describe the complete oneness of God. God is the *Father of all*, the source and creator of all things. There exists nothing made by a rival god, because there is no rival creator. Paul then uses three prepositional phrases to describe God's presence everywhere: *above all, through all,* and *in you all.* This is not a statement that "everything is God." Rather, it summarizes Paul's belief that God is universally present and influential in everything we do.

II. Gracious Gifts
(Ephesians 4:7-13)
A. Gifts of Measured Grace (v. 7)

7. But unto every one of us is given grace according to the measure of the gift of Christ.

Having urged his readers to understand God's intention that they walk in unity of purpose, Paul now proceeds to show how unity is a key to the functioning of the church. The first point of unity that Paul mentions is that each member of the church has been *given grace.* The underlying idea is "gift," something not earned. This gracious gift is bestowed upon each believer in accordance with Christ's *measure,* meaning the Lord determines the specifics of this gift.

What is the gracious gift being talked about? Certainly we understand salvation is a gift that cannot be earned (see Ephesians 2:8), but that does not seem to be what Paul is talking about here. He is referring to gifts that will lead to the success and unity of the church. This is explained more clearly in 1 Corinthians 12:4-7. The point is that Christ provides His church with gifted people to do the necessary ministries; this should lead to the unity of the body. [See question #4, page 80.]

B. Gifts from Christ's Victory (vv. 8-10)

8. Wherefore he saith, When he ascended up on high, he led captivity captive, and gave gifts unto men.

Paul illustrates his point by using powerful imagery drawn from Psalm 68. In this psalm we get the picture of the conquering king returning to his city. Yet Jesus is not returning from the killing fields, but has risen from the grave. Jesus has not vanquished a foreign army, but death itself. Moreover, Jesus does not receive tribute *gifts* from others; rather, He gives gifts to them.

9, 10. (Now that he ascended, what is it but that he also descended first into the lower parts of the earth? He that descended is the same also that ascended up far above all heavens, that he might fill all things.)

Finally, Jesus does not sit on an earthly throne, but reigns from Heaven so that *He might fill all things*. Nothing is beyond the reach of His power.

C. Gifts of Special Leaders (v. 11)

11. And he gave some, apostles; and some, prophets; and some, evangelists; and some, pastors and teachers.

We should remember that the theme of this section is the God-ordained unity of the church. If we keep this in mind, we can see that the emphasis here is not upon giving special endowments to individuals, but more upon providing certain categories of leaders for the work of the church as a whole. Christ providentially supplies *apostles, prophets, evangelists, pastors and teachers* for the ongoing ministry of His body, the church.

Apostle is a word implying "one sent out with authority to do a certain task." The New Testament seems to limit this term to those commissioned by Jesus personally. This includes the original 12 disciples (see Luke 6:13) and a very few others (Acts 14:14). It is unlikely that every first-century church has an apostle, indicating that Paul has the larger church in mind at this point.

Prophets are those who are given a special word from God to communicate to the church. An example in Acts is Agabus (Acts 11:27, 28; 21:10). Whether or not Christ still provides prophets to His church is a matter of some controversy today. We can see, however, that the ministry of prophets became less important as the Word of God became available as the written New Testament.

Evangelists are those who proclaim the gospel message through preaching. Timothy is known as an evangelist (2 Timothy 4:5) as is Philip (Acts 21:8). This may take several forms in today's church. One example of an evangelist is the modern "church planter," who seeks to evangelize a community by establishing a new church.

Some students see the last two designations on Paul's list as separate functions; other students think that Paul is referring to a single function of "pastor-teacher." A pastor is a shepherd who tends to the needs of the flock. In the first-century church, the word *elder* is used interchangeably with the words *shepherd* and *overseer* (see Acts 20:17-28; similarly 1 Peter 5:1, 2). This office of the church provides the stability of oversight, bolstered by strong teaching. It is important for Paul that each church has elders (see Acts 14:23).

D. Gifts for Ministry Fulfillment (vv. 12, 13)

12. For the perfecting of the saints, for the work of the ministry, for the edifying of the body of Christ.

Paul's point is that God provides leaders as the church needs them. The result is that ministry is accomplished and the church is edified. Edification is the act of building an edifice. In this context, *for the edifying* means "for building up" the body of believers. This is done by comprehensive teaching, by mutual love, and by encouragement and support for all believers. This is the *work of the ministry*. This purpose remains the same today.

13. Till we all come in the unity of the faith, and of the knowledge of the Son of God, unto a perfect man, unto the measure of the stature of the fulness of Christ.

Is there a goal in all of this? Yes. The goal is to have a church so unified that there is perfect agreement on all matters *of the faith*. This is not agreement imposed on them, but agreement arrived at after careful and intensive study and prayer. This is the church that will waste no time on doctrinal squabbles because all will be in agreement. This church will be the *perfect man*, the ideal body of Christ.

Unfortunately, this church has never come about. It did not exist in Paul's day, and it cannot be found today. It is still an ideal and a goal for which we must strive, now and in the future.

III. Talking Truth (Ephesians 4:14-16)

A. Deception Protection (v. 14)

14. That we henceforth be no more children, tossed to and fro, and carried about with every wind of doctrine, by the sleight of men, and cunning craftiness, whereby they lie in wait to deceive.

The goal of unity within the body of Christ will not be achieved accidentally. Paul now gives some concrete application of ways to break out of the cycle of church disunity.

Paul's plea is, "Grow up! Stop being spiritual babies!" (See 1 Corinthians 14:20.) In the fable of Jack and the Beanstalk, the gullible Jack traded away the family cow for "magic" beans. That story turned out well, but most stories of gullibility don't. As in Paul's day, there are still those who foist false *doctrine* upon the church. A mature, unified body is much more likely to resist such foolishness. Doctrine is not like the *wind*, sometimes strong, often gusty, ever shifting. Doctrine and faith need to be stable and reliable.

MORE OF THE SAME?

The International Chivalric Order Solar Tradition is one of many doomsday cults that have arisen throughout Christian history. One of Solar

Tradition's leaders claims to be Christ. This cult is a mixture of Christianity, New Age, and alternative medicine.

Death is said to be an illusion, and reincarnation takes place on other planets. According to authorities in Canada, France, and Switzerland, mass murder and suicide involving cult members have taken place. Some of these events include a reenactment of the Last Supper.

All this fits what Paul was talking about: crafty teachers who deceive others, often by mixing truth with error. Paul calls on the body of Christ to resist these. We do so first of all by taking Paul's word to Timothy as our own: "Take heed unto thyself, and unto the doctrine; continue in them: for in doing this thou shalt both save thyself, and them that hear thee" (1 Timothy 4:16). Then we lovingly proclaim the truth. See the next verse below.   —C. R. B.

B. Verbal Enrichment (v. 15)

15. But speaking the truth in love, may grow up into him in all things, which is the head, even Christ.

What do we do if someone is spreading false teaching? Does our desire for unity mean that we just put up with it and keep quiet? Paul points out that this attitude is what keeps the church in the infantile stage. If the body of Christ is to *grow up,* false teaching must be confronted and refuted (see Titus 1:9). This must not be done as a personal attack, but at the level of *truth.*

Truth is from God and will withstand any human attack. The person with truth on his or her side need not fear being exposed as devious. Christians are to love truth (compare 2 Thessalonians 2:10) and to take joy in truth (1 Corinthians 13:6). Yet we make sure we speak the truth in love.

Home Daily Bible Readings

Monday, Oct. 27—Drawn by God's Power (Acts 8:12-25)

Tuesday, Oct. 28—Drawn from a Distant Land (Acts 8:26-38)

Wednesday, Oct. 29—Drawn from Rebellion (Acts 22:3-16)

Thursday, Oct. 30—Drawn to be Christians (Acts 11:19-26)

Friday, Oct. 31—Drawn from Among All People (Acts 17:22-28)

Saturday, Nov. 1—Worthy of the Calling (Ephesians 4:1-6)

Sunday, Nov. 2—Joined Together in Christ (Ephesians 4:7-16)

C. Body Bonding (v. 16)

16. From whom the whole body fitly joined together and compacted by that which every joint supplieth, according to the effectual working in the measure of every part, maketh increase of the body unto the edifying of itself in love.

For Paul, the church that lives in unity is like a properly functioning human body. It has arms, legs, etc., that work as a coordinated whole.

Paul notes three characteristics of the united church as he closes this part. First, it will *increase* or grow. It will be adding new members and those members will be maturing spiritually. Second, it will be self-edifying. This is not the same as self-congratulatory. It means, rather, that in well functioning churches teachers will teach, elders will shepherd, and evangelists will preach. And all will be blessed.

Third, all of this will be permeated with an atmosphere of *love* for one another. The church should be known as a place were every member is loved (see John 13:35). [See question #5, page 80.]

Conclusion

A. The Unity of the Church

This may be a discouraging lesson for some who serve a church that is wracked with strife or for those who have been victims of church warfare in the past. The key to overcoming this problem is "speaking the truth in love." Many cantankerous church people are ready and willing to speak their understanding of the truth, not allowing for differences of opinion on relatively unimportant matters. They have the "truth" part, but not the "love" part.

On the other hand, there are those who want to avoid conflict at all cost and just love everyone 24/7. For them, "love" means never correcting a misguided or misinformed brother or sister.

Would you rather be in a church that has truth but no love or a church having love but no regard for truth? We shouldn't have to make this choice. Unity comes through good teaching of correct doctrine, done without arrogance or disrespect. Unity comes when the love of Christ is shared and practiced by every member.

B. Prayer

O God, the one who is over all, through all, and in all things, we pray today that You would make our hearts long for unity and peace between all who believe in our Lord Jesus. It is in His name we pray, amen.

C. Thought to Remember

Work and pray for church unity.

Learning by Doing

This page contains an alternative lesson plan emphasizing learning activities. Some of these activities are also found in the helpful student book, Adult Bible Class.

Into the Lesson

Begin class with a brainstorming session. Tell your students that they have two minutes to name as many different denominations and fellowships of Christians (or those who claim the name of Christ) as they can.

Ask someone whose watch can count down the seconds to say *start* and *stop*. Have a volunteer write down all the names that are mentioned. Accept all answers, without rejecting names of groups that might be considered cults. After two minutes, count the number of groups named.

Then say, "Even in such a short time, you were able to name quite a few groups. The number would be even larger if we began to name all the subgroups within each denomination. In spite of all the things that divide us, we know it is our Lord's desire for His body, the church, to be one. Let's look at today's text to see what we can do to help promote unity."

Into the Word

Before class write the following Scripture references on five separate pieces of paper:

> Ephesians 4:1, 2
> Ephesians 4:7, 8
> Ephesians 4:9, 10
> Ephesians 4:11, 12
> Ephesians 4:14, 15

Distribute one sheet each to five of your students. Ask them to be prepared to read the verses aloud. Write these references on the board: *Ephesians 4:3-6, 13, 16.*

To introduce the reading of the Scripture text say, "Because our lesson is about unity, we are all going to work together to read today's text. Please turn to Ephesians 4. So that we will all read in unison, please read from the *King James Version;* if you don't have that version, please share with someone who does. The verses we will all be reading together are listed on the board. Five people will be reading the other verses from Ephesians 4:1-16."

Ask the student who has Ephesians 4:1, 2 to begin. After verse 16 is read in unison, use the Lesson Background to introduce the book of Ephesians. Then divide your class into small groups and distribute the following assignments on handouts.

Assignment #1: Live a Worthy Life. Read Ephesians 4:1-6. 1. List ways that we can "walk worthy of the vocation" or calling we have as Christians; discuss how these qualities contribute to church unity (vv. 1-3). 2. List the "seven ones" Paul names as reasons for Christians to be united; discuss how a proper understanding of each will increase Christian unity (vv. 4-6).

Assignment #2: Receive Gifts of Grace. Read Ephesians 4:7-13. 1. Name some of the "gifts" Christ has given His church (vv. 7-11); how do these gifts help the church function with unity? 2. Discuss how well our church is practicing "the unity of the faith" (vv. 12, 13); what will be accomplished by Christians using their gifts and working together?

Assignment #3: Speak the Truth in Love. Read Ephesians 4:14-16. 1. Name ways that church unity can be harmed by false doctrine (vv. 14, 15); how can "speaking the truth in love" help prevent church quarrels and disunity? 2. Discuss how a healthy body illustrates a church that works well together (v. 16); in what ways can a lack of unity keep a church from growing?

Discuss conclusions. Allow time for each group to share one quality that a Christian should have that will help him or her work well with others.

Into Life

Tell the following story: "A Christian man who did not like fences had a backyard that was totally fenced in. It happened because the neighbor behind him and on each side of him had fenced in their yards. Even so, he made up his mind to continue to be the best neighbor he could by shoveling their driveways, watching their houses while they were gone on vacation, and inviting them to swim in his pool."

Then ask, "If we compare the people in that story with our church, are we more likely to be the ones building fences or the one trying to be a good neighbor in spite of the fences? Give reasons why you think so." Then ask, "What are some things we are doing or could be doing to reach across those fences?"

Close your class time with a prayer for church unity. Challenge each learner to ask for God's help in finding and promoting ways to help fulfill Christ's prayer for the unity of His church.

Let's Talk It Over

The questions on this page are designed to promote discussion of the lesson by the class and to encourage application of the lesson Scriptures. The answers provided are only discussion starters. Let your class talk it over from there.

1. How do you attempt to "walk worthy" in Christ?

As we consider walking worthy in Christ, we must remember that we are not worthy of what Christ has done for us. Our salvation is by grace, not something we deserve. But being in Christ demands that we live lives that honor Him—lives worthy of bearing the name of Christ.

We effectively walk this Christian life in the Spirit as we flee from sin. Paul tells the Galatians (5:16) that in walking in the Spirit they will not fulfill the lusts of the flesh. We also walk worthy of Christ when we walk in love as Christ did (see Ephesians 5:2). Christlikeness is the goal of walking in Christ (see 1 John 2:6).

2. Why does maintaining unity in the church seem so difficult at times? How do we stay on the alert for this problem?

The first sin ever committed destroyed the relational unity between God and humans. This temptation came to Adam and Eve because of rebellion against God by one of His angels. The sin in both of these circumstances was pride.

The pride of self-promotion continues to be the culprit in the disunity among people. Failing to consider others as more important than self (Philippians 2:3) causes us to look with a condescending attitude toward those with whom we should be establishing godly relationships. The desire to exalt self often results in demeaning others. When selfishness replaces selflessness in the church, disunity is not far behind.

3. Thinking of church-to-church cooperation, how can you promote the unity that Paul envisioned?

We may start by answering this question with a question: Do we spend more of our time focusing on areas of disagreement or focusing on areas of agreement? This question applies both within a congregation ("intrachurch") and between congregations ("interchurch").

It is imperative that we find areas of agreement with others of the Christian faith, then work with them for the advancement of the kingdom. This can be done as local churches band together to work on projects that promote the glory of God.

Such programs can involve, for example, sharing the volunteer staffing load at a crisis pregnancy center. In this way churches can work together against the forces of Satan. Churches of different doctrinal convictions can become a united force to stand against issues that Christians agree are in contradiction to the Word of God.

4. What spiritual gifts do you have, and how can they be used to develop unity within your particular church?

God gives gifts to each person in His body, the church, for the benefit of all (1 Peter 4:10). When each person uses his or her spiritual gift or gifts, the load of ministry is shared. This relieves any one person or a few people from being burdened with the heavy load of the work of the church. For unity to happen, the church must function as a body (1 Corinthians 12).

This practice of mutual ministry within the church not only benefits the church as a whole, but each person as well. As you use your particular gift, you are becoming more of what God desires you to be. Teachers help students as they teach, and students help the teacher to experience the grace of God as they follow the teaching received. Each grows as he or she encourages another in the Christian walk.

5. In what ways does the effectual working of each person in the church lead to an increase in love? Or is it the other way around: an increase in loving attitudes leads to effectual working? Explain.

Most people take care of their physical bodies in various ways. Similarly, we are to care for the body of believers of which we are a part: our local church. As the members of the body demonstrate proper love and concern for one another, they begin to understand and express more of the love of Christ (Ephesians 3:17-19). It is as we demonstrate loving behavior toward those who differ from us that the love Christ wants becomes most evident.

As those in the church express love to one another by mutual ministry, love blossoms. The world will be drawn to the church and to Christ as a result when it sees the church functioning this way.

Conflict in the Community

DEVOTIONAL READING: Romans 10:5-17.

BACKGROUND SCRIPTURE: Galatians 2:1–3:29.

PRINTED TEXT: Galatians 2:9-21.

Galatians 2:9-21

9 And when James, Cephas, and John, who seemed to be pillars, perceived the grace that was given unto me, they gave to me and Barnabas the right hands of fellowship; that we should go unto the heathen, and they unto the circumcision.

10 Only they would that we should remember the poor; the same which I also was forward to do.

11 But when Peter was come to Antioch, I withstood him to the face, because he was to be blamed.

12 For before that certain came from James, he did eat with the Gentiles: but when they were come, he withdrew and separated himself, fearing them which were of the circumcision.

13 And the other Jews dissembled likewise with him; insomuch that Barnabas also was carried away with their dissimulation.

14 But when I saw that they walked not uprightly according to the truth of the gospel, I said unto Peter before them all, If thou, being a Jew, livest after the manner of Gentiles, and not as do the Jews, why compellest thou the Gentiles to live as do the Jews?

15 We who are Jews by nature, and not sinners of the Gentiles,

16 Knowing that a man is not justified by the works of the law, but by the faith of Jesus Christ, even we have believed in Jesus Christ, that we might be justified by the faith of Christ, and not by the works of the law: for by the works of the law shall no flesh be justified.

17 But if, while we seek to be justified by Christ, we ourselves also are found sinners, is therefore Christ the minister of sin? God forbid.

18 For if I build again the things which I destroyed, I make myself a transgressor.

19 For I through the law am dead to the law, that I might live unto God.

20 I am crucified with Christ: nevertheless I live; yet not I, but Christ liveth in me: and the life which I now live in the flesh I live by the faith of the Son of God, who loved me, and gave himself for me.

21 I do not frustrate the grace of God: for if righteousness come by the law, then Christ is dead in vain.

**Nov
9**

GOLDEN TEXT: There is neither Jew nor Greek, there is neither bond nor free, there is neither male nor female: for ye are all one in Christ Jesus.—Galatians 3:28.

Lesson Aims

After participating in this lesson, each student will be able to:

1. Describe Peter's error and Paul's remedy for that error.

2. Explain how modern Christians can make an error similar to Peter's.

3. Repent of any hint of hypocrisy and/or legalism that he or she may be harboring.

Lesson Outline

Introduction

A. Legalism and Exclusion

"My dress looks old-fashioned." "I'll appear silly in this outfit." "I'll look foolish if I have to pray in front of people." "I don't want anyone to see my bald spot." "I look fat in a bathing suit."

Isn't it amazing how much our awareness of the perception of others influences what we do? This is not all bad. I, for one, am glad that we are still taught that certain things "are not done in public." The bad side is that fear of embarrassment may keep us from doing the brave thing, the right thing. *Peer pressure* is a slippery concept, but we have all experienced it. As adults, we realize that peer pres-

sure is not just something we felt in junior high school. Adults can be utterly captive to the expectations of others, whether helpful or harmful.

In the Christian community (the church), behavioral expectations can have many beneficial effects in teaching us to maintain a lifestyle pleasing to God. But sometimes expectations within the church can get off track and lead to damaging legalism and exclusionary practices. Today's lesson concerns the most famous example of this in the history of the church. It was an apostle vs. apostle conflict: Paul's public confrontation of Peter in Antioch.

B. Lesson Background

Unlike many of his letters, Paul did not address the book of Galatians to the church in a particular city. Galatia was a Roman province in the central highlands area of modern Turkey. Paul and Barnabas had evangelized this area on the first missionary journey, including the cities of Pisidian Antioch, Iconium, Lystra, and Derbe (Acts 13, 14). These cities were the likely recipients of the book, which was intended to be circulated among them and read to all the churches.

Galatians very likely was written after the Jerusalem Council of Acts 15, which occurred around AD 51. Many scholars believe that Galatians 2:1-10 is Paul's account of what happened when he attended that council. In this passage, Paul is careful to say that he did not need permission from anyone in Jerusalem to preach to the Gentiles, but he still wanted their sanction and tacit agreement not to oppose his message. He noted that they had nothing to add to his message (2:6) and that God had ordained Paul to preach to Gentiles as Peter was chosen to preach to Jews (2:7).

Not everyone was on board with this arrangement, however. Earlier, some Judaizers had infiltrated the churches founded by Paul. They taught the members that they were required to follow the Jewish law (Galatians 2:4). Despite the decision of the Jerusalem Council not to require circumcision, this Judaizing had continued. It wreaked havoc in the churches. The churches were confused. Should their men be circumcised? Was the Jewish law still in effect? Paul's exposition of this matter is the heart of the book of Galatians.

I. Concord in Jerusalem (Galatians 2:9, 10)

Galatians 2 is Paul's account of his trip from Antioch to Jerusalem (with Barnabas and Titus) to seek vindication for his preaching to the Gentiles. The key issue on the table both here and in Acts

15 is circumcision. Galatians shows us that Paul brings along a Gentile, Titus, who is not required to be circumcised (Galatians 2:3). Instead, Paul believes he has support from the leaders in Jerusalem to continue his ministry.

A. Mutual Recognition (v. 9a)

9a. And when James, Cephas, and John, who seemed to be pillars, perceived the grace that was given unto me, they gave to me and Barnabas the right hands of fellowship.

James is the brother of Jesus (Mark 6:3). This particular James also is the author of the book that bears his name. By this time, he has emerged as a leader of the Jerusalem church (Acts 12:17; 15:13). *Cephas* is the Aramaic version of Peter's name (John 1:42). Why Paul calls him Cephas here and Peter elsewhere (Galatians 2:7, 8) is unknown.

John is the brother of James the apostle; that particular James was killed by King Herod Agrippa in about AD 44 (Acts 12:1, 2). John may have been the youngest of the original 12 disciples. By now, though, he is a mature leader of the Jerusalem church.

Paul identifies these three as the *pillars* of the Jerusalem church, meaning the recognized leaders. These men are famous, even legendary, because of their close relationship with Jesus before His death and resurrection. Paul has not had this relationship. It must bring relief and comfort, then, for the trio to extend their *right hands* to Paul and *Barnabas*. This is a sign of *fellowship,* recognition, and acceptance.

B. Mutual Mission (vv. 9b, 10)

9b. That we should go unto the heathen, and they unto the circumcision.

The agreement is summarized in two parts. First, there is a type of comity arrangement: Paul and the Antioch church will direct their evangelistic efforts to *the heathen* (meaning Gentiles),

---

How to Say It

ANTIOCH. *An*-tee-ock.
ARAMAIC. *Air*-uh-*may*-ik (strong accent on *may*).
CEPHAS. *See*-fus.
CORNELIUS. Cor-*neel*-yus.
DERBE. *Der*-be.
GALATIANS. Guh-*lay*-shunz.
HEROD AGRIPPA. *Hair*-ud Uh-*grip*-puh.
ICONIUM. Eye-*ko*-nee-um.
LYSTRA. *Liss*-truh.
PISIDIAN. Pih-*sid*-ee-un.

---

while Peter and the Jerusalem church will focus on *the circumcision* (meaning Jews). This shows a very Jewish way of thinking, for Jews traditionally divide the entirety of humanity into two parts: Jews and non-Jews. [See question #1, page 88.]

10. Only they would that we should remember the poor; the same which I also was forward to do.

The second part of the agreement is the ongoing concern of both the Antioch church and the Jerusalem church to take care of *the poor.* There is to be a balance between evangelism and benevolence. The Antioch church has already demonstrated this by bringing an offering to Jerusalem to help with famine relief (Acts 11:28-30). Paul will continue collecting money for the Judean relief effort with churches he will plant elsewhere (see 1 Corinthians 16:1).

II. Conflict in Antioch (Galatians 2:11-14)

The meetings in Jerusalem seem to end on a high note of agreement and cooperation (Acts 15:1-35). Not long afterward, though, it seems as if the agreements there were never made!

A. Peter Yields to Pressure (vv. 11-13)

11. But when Peter was come to Antioch, I withstood him to the face, because he was to be blamed.

We do not know why *Peter* comes *to Antioch.* This is no small journey, being something of a 400-mile trip. It is often assumed that he comes to investigate the church in Antioch on behalf of the leaders in Jerusalem.

From Paul's perspective, Peter is *to be blamed,* meaning that Peter is in the wrong about something. He goes on to explain Peter's misdeed.

12. For before that certain came from James, he did eat with the Gentiles: but when they were come, he withdrew and separated himself, fearing them which were of the circumcision.

Even if the issue of *circumcision* was resolved at the Jerusalem Council (Acts 15), the Judaizing party is still alive and active. The key issue at stake here is fellowship as demonstrated by eating together.

From the Jewish perspective, there is a strong tradition to share meals with other Jews only. This tradition is based on the fear of becoming ritually unclean by associating with Gentiles (see Acts 10:28). From the Gentile perspective, this is unacceptable elitism. If they are truly equal brothers and sisters with the Jewish Christians, then eating together should not be a problem.

Paul's words evoke feelings of disappointment and betrayal. He has just mentioned that while he was in Jerusalem he was given the right hand of fellowship, a seeming endorsement of his ministry to the Gentiles. Yet now, two of the principals in that agreement apparently have reneged. James has sponsored a delegation from Jerusalem that separates itself from the Gentiles, at least at mealtime. Peter is caught in blatant hypocrisy, enjoying Gentile fellowship for a time, but then rejecting it when he feels pressure from the James delegation.

Exactly why Peter is afraid is not stated. But his failure to live up to his earlier commitments shows a certain shallowness of character. We can compare this with Peter's report of his ministry concerning the household of Cornelius, a Gentile. There too the criticism was over eating with Gentiles (Acts 11:2, 3). At that time, Peter rightly defended his fellowship with Gentiles as being the will of God (Acts 11:17). [See question #2, page 88.]

13. And the other Jews dissembled likewise with him; insomuch that Barnabas also was carried away with their dissimulation.

Paul's language is particularly harsh! The term behind *dissembled* carries the sense "to be together as hypocrites." The extremity of the situation is shown when Paul mentions that even *Barnabas* has become involved in this hypocrisy.

What is unexplained is the power of the pressure that has been brought to bear on the Jewish Christians of Antioch by the Jerusalem group. With the defection of Barnabas, we are left to think that Paul stands alone as the sole Jew who is willing to have complete fellowship with the Gentile Christians of the Antioch church!

B. Paul Confronts Hypocrisy (v. 14)

14. But when I saw that they walked not uprightly according to the truth of the gospel, I said unto Peter before them all, If thou, being a Jew, livest after the manner of Gentiles, and not as do the Jews, why compellest thou the Gentiles to live as do the Jews?

The *truth of the gospel* is that God makes no distinction between Jews and Gentiles when it comes to the offer of salvation (see Acts 10:34, 35; 15:9; Romans 2:11). If God makes no distinction, neither should we. This is why Paul can write a little later, "There is neither Jew nor Greek, . . . ye are all one in Christ Jesus" (Galatians 3:28).

It is easy to imagine that this is an intense, public confrontation *(before them all)*. Paul understands that the churches he has started, which have many Gentile members, are on the verge of being disavowed. The Judaizers have twisted the situation to give this message to Gentiles: "OK, you don't have to be circumcised, but we won't eat with you unless you are. Thus you will always be excluded from true, full acceptance."

We should understand that at this particular point in history there is no comparison between Peter and Paul when it comes to influence and reputation. Peter had walked and talked with the Lord. Peter is seen as the leading apostle. It is Peter who had faced down the Jewish authorities in the earliest days of the church. Two decades after the resurrection, Peter is a legendary leader.

Paul, on the other hand, is still "a bit of an unknown" in AD 51. His famous letters are yet to be written. He has the stain of having been a zealous persecutor of the church. He is from Tarsus, hardly the mainstream of Judaism. And he is associated with the Antioch church, seen by some in Jerusalem as out of control. It takes a lot of courage for Paul to confront Peter! While the exact nature of the controversy (Judaizing) is long gone today, the church still experiences a similar need for confrontation when important truth is at stake.

PRETENSE

Hypocrite! How the world loves to throw this word at Christians who stumble. Faultfinders enjoy it all the more when the one who stumbles is a Christian leader found guilty of sexual sin. The most recent (as of the time of this writing) high visibility sin of this nature came in late 2006 when Ted Haggard, a minister of a megachurch in Colorado, was "outed" by a homosexual escort with whom he had been involved.

Haggard had been known for his strong advocacy of legislation that would outlaw gay marriage, thus the hypocrisy. His problems were compounded by his admission that he had bought drugs from the escort (although denying ever using them). Haggard lost his reputation because his unbiblical actions did not match his biblical words.

The apostle Peter had preached the gospel to Cornelius, a Gentile (Acts 10). Peter strongly defended his actions when questioned. However, Peter also demonstrated how easy it is to become something less than what we proclaim. None of us is immune to this temptation. —C. R. B.

III. Crucified with Christ (Galatians 2:15-21)

Paul is now at his most passionate, for he knows what is at stake.

A. Dead End of Legalism (vv. 15, 16)

15. We who are Jews by nature, and not sinners of the Gentiles.

Paul admits that *Jews* have not engaged in the depths of sin that is common among *the Gentiles* of his day. Many things that are considered immoral by Jews are perfectly acceptable for non-Jews in the Greco-Roman environment. This is particularly true of sexual behavior, where pagans do not condemn homosexual behavior or prostitution. For this reason, Paul characterizes the Gentiles as *sinners*. But read on, for Paul does not stop there.

16a. Knowing that a man is not justified by the works of the law, but by the faith of Jesus Christ.

The hallmark of being a Jew is having the Law of Moses and keeping it faithfully (compare John 7:19). But no one is able to keep *the law* perfectly (see Acts 15:10; compare James 2:10). Justification cannot be earned. It must be received as a gift through our *faith* in the Lord *Jesus Christ* (Romans 1:17; Galatians 3:11; Ephesians 2:8, 9).

16b. Even we have believed in Jesus Christ, that we might be justified by the faith of Christ, and not by the works of the law: for by the works of the law shall no flesh be justified.

Paul knows that up until the time of Christ the Jews had the best system for maintaining a correct relationship with God. Yet the Jewish Christians know (or should know) that that system ultimately is inadequate to gain them justification. When they realize that *works of the law* cannot earn salvation, the value of such works takes on a different perspective. While keeping these practices still may be essential to being a Jew, they have no specific claim on Gentiles. [See question #3, page 88.]

THE WAY OF WORKS, OR THE WAY OF CHRIST?

Modern orthodox Jews want to know *exactly* how to keep each of Judaism's 613 commandments (or *mitzvot*). Of those 613 (the actual count varies somewhat), 248 are positive "do's" and 365 are negative "do not's." Web sites such as www.askmoses.com offer plenty of advice in this regard. Attention to minute detail of the law allows some to think that they are in charge of their salvation.

The spirit of *works salvation* that typified much of Judaism in New Testament times still lives on. Christians both now and in New Testament times have fallen into this trap.

However, Paul—that most Jewish of all Jews—says explicitly that our salvation is not based on "the works of the law," but "by the faith of Christ." Work-it-out-rules-keeping will never erase our sins in the eyes of God.   —C. R. B.

B. Living Way of Justification (vv. 17-19)

17. But if, while we seek to be justified by Christ, we ourselves also are found sinners, is therefore Christ the minister of sin? God forbid.

Visual for Lesson 10. *Point to this visual as you ask, "How do we foster oneness in Christ? What behaviors and attitudes work against oneness?"*

Paul now returns to the situation of Peter. If a Jewish Christian eats with a Gentile, he or she is "sinning" according to the Jewish law. If *Christ* and Paul promote this fellowship, are they promoting sin? Is then Christ a *minister of sin*, one who serves sin?

As he frequently does, Paul uses a technique of reducing the argument to the absurd. Is Christ, who gave His life as a sin offering (Hebrews 9:28), now an advocate for sin? *God forbid*. Of course not! Neither Peter nor Paul is sinning by eating with the Gentile believers.

18, 19. For if I build again the things which I destroyed, I make myself a transgressor. For I through the law am dead to the law, that I might live unto God.

The law has taught Paul many things, including the nature of sin itself (Romans 7:7). The law is not sin, but it defines sin. Furthermore, Paul's experience with the law has taught him that the law is a *dead* end. No one can be saved by the law, because no one can keep it fully and perfectly.

For Paul, then, the great sin is not in following the law, but in believing and teaching that it is a necessary part of being a Christian believer. If Paul were to fall into this trap, he would be making himself to be a *transgressor*. This word has the sense of a "nonkeeper" of the law. Ironically, then, Paul concludes that he will be violating the spirit of the law if he requires Gentiles to keep it.

C. Death and Life in Christ (vv. 20, 21)

20a. I am crucified with Christ: nevertheless I live; yet not I, but Christ liveth in me.

We are *crucified with Christ* so that we will be freed from the enslavement of sin (Romans 6:6).

This understanding applies to Jews and Gentiles alike. The old self is controlled by lust, by sinful passions (Ephesians 4:22). The new life is controlled by *Christ,* for He lives in us. By uniting with Christ through faith, we have a renewal that leads to becoming the man or woman God created us to be, a person in God's image (see Colossians 3:10). [See question #4, page 88.]

A beautiful example of this is found in the practice of baptism: a believer is immersed in water, thus reenacting the death of Christ. Being lifted out of the water is seen as a type of resurrection, being raised to a new life (Romans 6:4; Colossians 2:12).

20b. And the life which I now live in the flesh I live by the faith of the Son of God, who loved me, and gave himself for me.

Christ, then, is Paul's master and Lord. Paul lives for Christ, but Christ does not control him by threats or legalistic rules. Paul is controlled and motivated by the love of Christ as demonstrated on the cross.

There is nothing more important to Paul than God's demonstration of love through Christ's death. This is why Paul can characterize his preaching as "Christ crucified" (1 Corinthians 1:23), which Paul acknowledges to be a "stumblingblock" (offense) to the Jews. It couldn't be that simple, could it? What about all these rules you need to keep? Is it really possible that we can have decent behavior and true, rich fellowship on the basis of our mutual love and faith in Christ? For Paul, the answer is *yes.*

21. I do not frustrate the grace of God: for if righteousness come by the law, then Christ is dead in vain.

Paul concludes with a final zinger: If we go the path of legalism, believing rules-keeping makes one righteous, then we have destroyed the gospel by nullifying the death of Christ. We are saying, "Jesus, You didn't really need to die for me. I'll just clean up my act and justify myself. Self-righteousness is the better way." If self-justification were possible in God's eyes, the entire mission of Jesus to be the sacrificial Lamb of God (John 1:29) was unnecessary. May we never come to the point of despising the death of Christ in this way! [See question #5, page 88.]

Conclusion

A. Extremes

Ironically, libertines (rule scoffers) and legalists share a common trait: both desire to be in control. Libertines want to be in control of their own lives without any restrictions or rules. Legalists want to extend their control over others and have everyone behave according to their expectations. Both would be advised to let God be in control, because of course He is. Our puny attempts to retain control are really acts of defiance against God.

As we let God be in control, we realize that there are three primary factors at work to bring us into conformity with God's standards. First is the Word of God. The Bible is full of advice, examples, and demands for how we should live. We should live lives of holiness (2 Corinthians 7:1; 1 Peter 1:15, 16).

Second, we should follow the examples of mature, proven Christian leaders (1 Corinthians 11:1). There is no quicker way to disillusion a new believer than for him or her to discover hypocrisy among the church's leaders. (This is a topic of next week's lesson.)

Third, we should allow the Holy Spirit to work in our lives to transform and renew us (Titus 3:5). Our constant plea should not be "behave to get right and stay right with God" but "love and obey God because you already are right with Him." If we are truly sold out to Him, our lives will be filled with spiritual fruit.

B. Prayer

Holy Father, guard us from a spirit of pride when our behavior meets Your desires, from a spirit of discouragement when we fail You, and from a spirit of judgment when we disagree with the actions of others. Help us to love You more dearly, every day. We pray this in the name of the Lord Jesus, amen.

C. Thought to Remember

Focus on Christ,
not on the expectations of others.

Home Daily Bible Readings

Monday, Nov. 3—Dissension and Debate (Acts 15:1-5)

Tuesday, Nov. 4—Evidence of God's Work (Acts 15:6-11)

Wednesday, Nov. 5—Basis for Unity (Acts 15:12-21)

Thursday, Nov. 6—Confession That Saves (Romans 10:5-9)

Friday, Nov. 7—Same Lord Is Lord of All (Romans 10:10-17)

Saturday, Nov. 8—Not Running in Vain (Galatians 2:1-10)

Sunday, Nov. 9—Living by Law or Faith (Galatians 2:11-21)

Learning by Doing

This page contains an alternative lesson plan emphasizing learning activities. Some of these activities are also found in the helpful student book, Adult Bible Class.

Into the Lesson

Ask your class to break into small groups. Distribute a copy of the following scenario to each group and ask students to discuss it.

"Your best friend, Scott, works for a major tobacco company in the public relations department. His job is to ease people's fears about the dangers of smoking. Yet you know Scott quit smoking years ago because of all he learned about the health hazards of smoking. Although he's a Christian, he seems to have no conflicts about what he does. Would you confront him about his hypocrisy? If so, what would you say? What factors would determine how successful you would be?"

After a few minutes, ask groups to share their conclusions. Then say, "In today's lesson, Paul faced a similar dilemma when Peter, his fellow apostle, acted hypocritically toward the Gentile Christians. Let's see how Paul handled it."

Into the Word

In the week before class, ask a student to prepare a five-minute report on who the Judaizers were and what they believed. Provide this person with a copy of "Legalism and Exclusion" from the lesson's Introduction and the Lesson Background (p. 82). Ask the student to give this report to begin the Bible study.

Then say, "As we just heard, the Judaizers were legalists who were insisting that the Gentile Christians comply with the Jewish law. At one point Peter caved in to their demands, and Paul confronted him. Today we're going to imagine that Paul is being interviewed by a reporter for the Christian newspaper *The Antioch Anchor.* Provide answers to the interview questions as if you were Paul."

Divide the class into small groups. Give each group one of the three sets of questions below. (Note: The third set of questions is the most difficult and deals with doctrinal issues, so distribute that set accordingly.) Circulate among the groups and offer help as needed.

Interview Questions, Part 1: Concord. Paul, help me understand how this conflict between you and Peter developed. In the beginning didn't you reach agreement on several issues? What was the reason you met with Peter and the others for the council in Jerusalem? *(Acts 15:1, 2)* What did you decide about compelling the Gentiles to be circumcised?

(Acts 15:22-29; Galatians 2:1-5) How did you agree to divide the preaching of the gospel? *(Galatians 2:7-9)* In what way did you seal your agreement? *(v. 9)* What are your feelings about the Jerusalem leaders' instructions to remember the poor? *(v. 10)*

Interview Questions, Part 2: Conflict. So, Paul, help me understand how this problem between you and Peter developed. What were Peter's relations with the Gentile Christians like when he first came to Antioch? *(Galatians 2:12)* How and why did that change? *(v. 11)* What were some of the negative effects of Peter's actions? *(vv. 13, 14a)* Why did you think it was necessary to confront Peter publicly? *(vv. 11, 14)*

Interview Questions, Part 3: Conclusion. Paul, I understand that you used some very compelling arguments to confront Peter. Help me understand them. First, if a Christian isn't justified by keeping the law, then on what basis is he or she justified? *(Galatians 2:15, 16)* Second, isn't the law a good thing? What's the big deal about asking Gentiles to live by it? *(vv. 17-19)* Third, what do you mean that you are "crucified with Christ"? What does that have to do with not keeping the law? *(v. 20)* Fourth, what's the worst aspect of the false teaching you opposed? *(v. 21)*

Ask for one volunteer for each set of questions to come to the front and give "Paul's" response as you read the above statements and questions.

Into Life

Before class use modeling dough to make two three-inch circles with unhappy faces. Leave one out to harden; the other should be kept soft. Show the two faces and say, "Although both the Judaizers and Peter were hypocrites in the way they treated the Gentile Christians, there was a difference between them. The Judaizers had hardened their position, and no one could convince them they were wrong. *[For dramatic effect, tap the hardened dough so that its hard quality is audible.]* But Peter realized his mistake, and his heart was still soft enough to accept Paul's correction."

Reshape the unhappy face on the soft dough into a happy face. Then say, "Let's have a moment of silent prayer as we ask the Lord to keep our hearts soft and open to His correction in the week ahead."

Let's Talk It Over

The questions on this page are designed to promote discussion of the lesson by the class and to encourage application of the lesson Scriptures. The answers provided are only discussion starters. Let your class talk it over from there.

1. Does the principle of outreach we see here still apply in the twenty-first century? Why, or why not?

Dividing the world into "Jew and non-Jew" is not the best way to channel our evangelistic efforts today. For starters, that "non-Jew" category is too broad. There are clearly identifiable groups under that umbrella that will require different methods of presenting the gospel.

However, the principle of division of labor still stands. We realize that no one person is able to reach everyone. Also, cultural responses to presentations of the gospel vary. One people group may be reached more readily by an evangelist who is more confrontational, while that approach may turn away others from both the messenger and the message.

2. In what ways have you seen the church of the twenty-first century mimic this sin of bias of the first-century church? How do we guard against this?

When we read a passage like this, we may shake our heads in disbelief that such a thing could happen, especially among these early church leaders for whom we have such respect. But while we express our dismay, we may be doing something similar.

There are churches that support foreign missions strongly but do not lift a finger to support the needs of certain segments of their own community. On a person-to-person basis, don't most of us draw conclusions about whom we would or would not like to sit with at church potluck dinners? The solution: next time make a conscious effort to sit with someone you have never sat with before!

3. What was a time when you caught yourself living as if your salvation were based on works instead of on faith in Christ? How did you put this kind of thinking behind you?

We often find it easier to live by a set of rules than to live a life of faith. Rules are tangible. If we have rules, we can just check off those things on our list that we have fulfilled; then we feel good (even prideful) about ourselves.

Sometimes the way people come to Christ fosters a rules-keeping view of the Christian life. If we

teach a set of steps to complete for one to receive salvation (as if one were keeping a list of commandments), then the new convert may expect to continue to progress in the faith by following even more prescribed steps. The bottom line: When we put more emphasis on *what we must do* than on *what God has done*, we risk promoting the concept of works-salvation.

4. How do you demonstrate in your life that you have been crucified with Christ and that it is now Christ living in you?

We live in a world that calls on us to look out for ourselves. The world teaches us to promote self and to do what we feel like when we feel like it. The life we are called upon to live in Christ goes against the teaching of this world.

We live for Christ as we forsake sin. Romans 6:11 tells us: "Likewise reckon ye also yourselves to be dead indeed unto sin, but alive unto God through Jesus Christ our Lord." All that we do should be done as if being done for the Lord (Romans 14:8). Our love for our brothers and sisters in Christ is another demonstration of this. In 1 John 3:14 we read: "We know that we have passed from death unto life, because we love the brethren."

5. Why is it important not to "frustrate the grace of God"? What preventive steps can we take in this regard?

The obvious reason stated in the text is that we risk making Christ's death in vain. Yet there are "collateral" reasons why we need to be careful not to frustrate the message of grace. One problem involves confusing the gospel message in the minds of those who are outside of Christ. There is no other religion in the world that has Christianity's concept of grace. Nullifying grace in favor of works puts Christianity down at the level of other religions.

When that happens, we end up establishing a standard of salvation or a standard for living that is contrary to the will of God. Jesus condemned the Pharisees for a similar attitude when He said, "For they bind heavy burdens and grievous to be borne, and lay them on men's shoulders; but they themselves will not move them with one of their fingers" (Matthew 23:4).

Joy in the Community

DEVOTIONAL READING: **Psalm 46.**

BACKGROUND SCRIPTURE: **Philippians 3:3–4:9.**

PRINTED TEXT: **Philippians 3:17–4:9.**

Philippians 3:17-21

17 Brethren, be followers together of me, and mark them which walk so as ye have us for an ensample.

18 (For many walk, of whom I have told you often, and now tell you even weeping, that they are the enemies of the cross of Christ:

19 Whose end is destruction, whose God is their belly, and whose glory is in their shame, who mind earthly things.)

20 For our conversation is in heaven; from whence also we look for the Saviour, the Lord Jesus Christ:

21 Who shall change our vile body, that it may be fashioned like unto his glorious body, according to the working whereby he is able even to subdue all things unto himself.

Philippians 4:1-9

1 Therefore, my brethren dearly beloved and longed for, my joy and crown, so stand fast in the Lord, my dearly beloved.

2 I beseech Euodias, and beseech Syntyche, that they be of the same mind in the Lord.

3 And I entreat thee also, true yokefellow, help those women which labored with me in the gospel, with Clement also, and with other my fellow laborers, whose names are in the book of life.

4 Rejoice in the Lord always: and again I say, Rejoice.

5 Let your moderation be known unto all men. The Lord is at hand.

6 Be careful for nothing; but in every thing by prayer and supplication with thanksgiving let your requests be made known unto God.

7 And the peace of God, which passeth all understanding, shall keep your hearts and minds through Christ Jesus.

8 Finally, brethren, whatsoever things are true, whatsoever things are honest, whatsoever things are just, whatsoever things are pure, whatsoever things are lovely, whatsoever things are of good report; if there be any virtue, and if there be any praise, think on these things.

9 Those things, which ye have both learned, and received, and heard, and seen in me, do: and the God of peace shall be with you.

GOLDEN TEXT: The peace of God, which passeth all understanding, shall keep your hearts and minds through Christ Jesus.—Philippians 4:7.

The New Testament Community
Unit 3: Challenges in the New Community
(Lessons 9–13)

Lesson Aims

After participating in this lesson, each student will be able to:

1. Describe the life that Paul says results from following the godly example that he and others set.

2. Compare and contrast earthly joy with the joy of the Christian.

3. Make a plan to correct one area in his or her life that is deficient in Christian joy.

Lesson Outline

INTRODUCTION
 A. No Joy in Mudville
 B. Lesson Background
 I. WALKING TOGETHER (Philippians 3:17-21)
 A. Walking Like Paul (v. 17)
 B. Walking Toward Destruction (vv. 18, 19)
 C. Walking Toward Glory (vv. 20, 21)
 II. STANDING TOGETHER (Philippians 4:1-3)
 A. Stand in Security (v. 1)
 B. Stand in Harmony (vv. 2, 3)
  In the Race Together
 III. REJOICING TOGETHER (Philippians 4:4-9)
 A. Consistent Joy (v. 4)
 B. Consistent Readiness (vv. 5, 6)
 C. Consistent Peace (v. 7)
 D. Consistent Virtue (vv. 8, 9)
  Consistency: A Paste Jewel?
CONCLUSION
 A. Twenty-First-Century Joy
 B. Prayer
 C. Thought to Remember

Introduction

A. No Joy in Mudville

In the classic poem "Casey at the Bat," Ernest Lawrence Thayer weaves a tale about two small-town teams engaged in a heated battle of baseball. The story focuses on the final chance for the heroes from Mudville to win the game.

Down two runs in the final inning of play, they have managed to put a couple of men on base. Now their most powerful hitter, the mighty Casey, has come to bat with the opportunity to win the game. But, alas, there is no victory for the team

that afternoon, for as Thayer put it, "There is no joy in Mudville. Mighty Casey has struck out."

Fans of every sport can testify to the empty feeling that follows the loss of a big game or match by a favorite team. The partisan passions of competition can give us great highs and lows. Beyond sports, however, many people live this way in general. Life is an emotional elevator, up one day and down the next. This is a very difficult way to live, and it exacts a heavy emotional and spiritual toll.

Churches can be like this too; however, it works a little differently. In many churches, the "good times" are in the past. We look back at old joy, but we never seem to realize current joy. Both the past victories and the current losses are greatly amplified.

A joyless church is not what Christ intended. Paul taught, "The kingdom of God is not meat and drink; but righteousness, and peace, and joy in the Holy Ghost" (Romans 14:17). Is your life or your church a place of which it could be said, "There is no joy in Mudville"? If so, this lesson will offer some biblical principles to bring joy back into your world.

B. Lesson Background

Paul's letter to the Philippian church was written while he was imprisoned in Rome, awaiting his trial before Caesar. This is where we leave Paul at the end of the book of Acts. Therefore, we date the letter sometime around AD 63.

Philippi was located in the Roman province of Macedonia, in the northeast section of modern Greece. By the time Paul visited Philippi on his second missionary journey (Acts 16:12; early AD 50s), the city had become an important Roman/Latin center in that Greek area. It was designated as a Roman colony, giving its residents special privileges. Many of the citizens of Philippi were descendants of Roman legionnaires who settled there after their terms of service in the army were finished.

Paul's first visit to Philippi included a time in jail. The miraculous deliverance of Paul and Silas resulted in the conversion of the jailer and his family (Acts 16:23-34). Another prominent convert in this church was a wealthy woman named Lydia (Acts 16:14).

Paul seemed to have maintained a close relationship with the Philippians over the years that followed. He remembered that they had supported him financially after he left them (Philippians 4:15, 16). The church even sent assistance to Paul while he was under house arrest in Rome. This came in the form of money and a helper named Epaphroditus (Philippians 2:25; 4:18).

This visit by Epaphroditus was the occasion for Paul's letter to the Philippians. The apostle had learned of several problems that were plaguing the church. One of these was infighting among some prominent members of the congregation. This public feuding had drained the congregation of its joy. Our lesson this week explores Paul's remedy for joy-restoration and shows how his words are still applicable today.

I. Walking Together (Philippians 3:17-21)
A. Walking Like Paul (v. 17)

17. Brethren, be followers together of me, and mark them which walk so as ye have us for an ensample.

Often we ask children, "What do you want to do when you grow up?" More telling though is the question, "Whom do you want to be like when you grow up?" Children often have a person whom they seek to emulate. Sometimes it is a healthy role model—a virtuous parent or family friend. Sometimes it is a church leader who "walks the talk" of being a Christian. Unfortunately, sometimes a sleazy celebrity is appealing because of wealth and notoriety.

The Philippians' memories of Paul are still fresh enough for him to exhort them to *be followers* of him. This is because Paul strives to follow Jesus Christ (see 1 Corinthians 11:1; 1 Thessalonians 1:6). For those who do not know Paul, he advises that they watch leaders who are known to be following Paul's *ensample* (example). Most people will never achieve Christlikeness by reading books. They need solid role models.

B. Walking Toward Destruction (vv. 18, 19)

18. (For many walk, of whom I have told you often, and now tell you even weeping, that they are the enemies of the cross of Christ.

Paul offers a quick aside to speak about negative role models. This is very personal for Paul, literally causing tears to well up in his eyes as he writes. These people are *enemies of the cross of Christ* and thus are Paul's enemies as well. He is not speaking abstractly, but has specific, unnamed individuals in mind who are probably known to some of the Philippians. Elsewhere, Paul does name some people like this (see 1 Timothy 1:20, 2 Timothy 4:10). [See question #1, page 96.]

19. Whose end is destruction, whose God is their belly, and whose glory is in their shame, who mind earthly things.)

Paul describes these enemies in four ways. First, they are headed to *destruction*. This serves as a

warning to the Philippians not to follow them, for theirs is not the way of life. Second, Paul says their *God is their belly*. This means they are not controlled by the Holy Spirit, but by the appetites of the flesh. If our life goal is gratification of carnal desires, we sink deeper and deeper into depravity (see Romans 7:18).

Third, the enemies find *glory* in *shame*. They celebrate that which should embarrass them. How true this rings today in our celebrity culture, where people become famous for strident immorality! Fourth, these false leaders *mind earthly things*, meaning that they have lost any sense of spirituality and live selfishly and materialistically. They walk oblivious to the danger of the destructive life they choose and celebrate.

C. Walking Toward Glory (vv. 20, 21)

20. For our conversation is in heaven; from whence also we look for the Saviour, the Lord Jesus Christ.

The Greek word translated *conversation* is quite rare in the New Testament, appearing only here. It comes from the political sphere and has the sense of "citizenship." As Philippi is a colony of Rome in Paul's day (Acts 16:12), so also the church is an outpost of the homeland of Heaven, the residence of our *Lord Jesus Christ*. We await His return to end this separation finally.

This is one of the most important truths of the Christian worldview. That is, with all of its heartaches, trials, disappointments, broken relationships, and struggles, this world is not our final home. Christ will take us home, and we will be with Him forever (1 Thessalonians 4:17). We take joy in believing that our home in glory will remove us from the tears of this life (see Revelation 21:4). [See question #2, page 96.]

How to Say It

CAESAR. *See*-zer.
CORINTHIANS. Ko-*rin*-thee-unz (*th* as in *thin*).
EPAPHRODITUS. Ee-*paf*-ro-*dye*-tus (strong accent on *dye*).
EUODIAS. You-*o*-dee-us.
LYDIA. *Lid*-ee-uh.
MACEDONIA. Mass-eh-*doe*-nee-uh.
PHILIPPI. Fih-*lip*-pie or *Fil*-ih-pie.
PHILIPPIANS. Fih-*lip*-ee-unz.
SHALOM *(Hebrew)*. shah-*lome*.
SILAS. *Sigh*-luss.
SYNTYCHE. *Sin*-tih-key.
THESSALONIANS. *Thess*-uh-*lo*-nee-unz (strong accent on *lo; th* as in *thin*).

21. Who shall change our vile body, that it may be fashioned like unto his glorious body, according to the working whereby he is able even to subdue all things unto himself.

One aspect of this glorious future that is particularly precious to Paul is the promise of a resurrection *body*. We do not understand this completely, but Paul teaches us that our new bodies will be like the body of Christ after His resurrection (1 Corinthians 15:49). They will be imperishable and immortal (15:53). They will be suitable for an eternity in Heaven with God. They will be without disease, injury, or defect. The final terror of humanity—death—will be vanquished (15:26), for Christ will be the complete master of all things (Philippians 2:10, 11).

II. Standing Together (Philippians 4:1-3)

A. Stand in Security (v. 1)

1. Therefore, my brethren dearly beloved and longed for, my joy and crown, so stand fast in the Lord, my dearly beloved.

Paul describes his *beloved* Philippians as his *joy and crown*. He takes great satisfaction in their continued faithfulness and good works. He is able to pray about them with joy (see Philippians 1:3-6), believing in their endurance to the end. They are his crown in the sense that we say righteous children are jewels on the crown of a faithful mother. This is not the crown of power or dominion, but of reward for a job well done. It is the award crown given to the victor in athletic contests, the laurel of honor.

Paul switches metaphors from walking (living) to standing (persevering). To *stand fast in the Lord* is an act of faith in Christ. It is a unifying act, for the Philippians all have the same Lord. The result of this is to give them security in their fellowship, the "safety in numbers" effect. Paul is not telling them to "go along with the crowd," but to stand together with others who are following Christ. [See question #3, page 96.]

B. Stand in Harmony (vv. 2, 3)

2. I beseech Euodias, and beseech Syntyche, that they be of the same mind in the Lord.

A specific conflict in the Philippian church involves two prominent women. (*Euodias* means "pleasant fragrance"; *Syntyche* means "shared fate.") Their spat has become public, and the result is some kind of partisan mess. Paul wisely points to the only real solution: remember your commonality *in the Lord*. This does not necessarily include ironing out all their points of disagreement.

3. And I entreat thee also, true yokefellow, help those women which labored with me in the gospel, with Clement also, and with other my fellow laborers, whose names are in the book of life.

We can only guess at the historical references here. Some suggest that the *true yokefellow* is Lydia of Acts 16:11-15, but not mentioned by name in this letter. That is just a guess, however. It is more important to note that Paul lifts up the value of ministry done by *those women*. Today, one need not look far in most churches to find the invaluable contributions made by women.

The *Clement* mentioned here is unknown to us. It is unlikely that he is the Clement who later becomes a recognized leader of the church in Rome. Clement is a common name in the Roman world. It means "merciful one" (think of the word *clemency*).

Paul refers to his beloved Philippian believers as having their names written in *the book of life*. The only other place where this expression is used in the New Testament is in the book of Revelation. Having one's name recorded in the book of life makes one exempt from eternal punishment (Revelation 20:15). It is comforting to think that our salvation is recorded in Heaven and not subject to our day-by-day inconsistencies. This is also another factor in the church's unity in Christ: our common destiny. This begs a question: If I am going to spend eternity with this person, shouldn't I be working on getting along with him or her now?

IN THE RACE TOGETHER

There seems to be no limit to what can be accomplished when people work together. Look at father and son Dick and Rick Hoyt. Rick was brain-damaged at birth, having been strangled by the umbilical cord. Doctors urged the parents to put the boy in an institution. They refused.

When Rick was 11, a computer was adapted so Rick could "talk." When a high school classmate was paralyzed in an accident and a charity run was organized for him, Rick said (aided by his computer), "Dad, I want to do that." Thus began their mutual career of marathon running, with Dick pushing Rick in a wheelchair. They've now completed over 200 triathlons. In the process, Rick saved his dad's life. After Dick had a mild heart attack, the doctors said, "If you were not in such great shape, you'd have died 15 years ago."

Paul tells us of those who "ran the gospel race" with him, yet two found it hard to do so (or at least hard to do so with each other). Paul strongly urged those two to find a way to show that Christ was first in their lives. When we run together, we find mutual blessing.
                                                    —C. R. B.

III. Rejoicing Together (Philippians 4:4-9)

A. Consistent Joy (v. 4)

4. Rejoice in the Lord always: and again I say, Rejoice.

Paul gives the entire church a simple command to be joyful. This is not a contingent command based on a particular circumstance. Paul calls for unconditional rejoicing. There is no need to wait for something beneficial. Paul knows that the Christian life should always be joyful, even under the most difficult circumstances. Similar admonitions are found frequently in the Psalms, such as "Be glad in the Lord, and *rejoice*, ye righteous: and shout for joy, all ye that are upright in heart" (Psalm 32:11).

There is great unity to be found in laying down our weapons and joining together in joyful praise to God. We can release our fears and doubts as we fulfill our created purpose of glorifying God. In a world full of doleful and self-absorbed people, it is wonderful to encounter a person with the deep-seated joy that Paul speaks of here. This joy is contagious, and soon we find that we "rejoice with them that do rejoice" (Romans 12:15). [See question #4, page 96.]

B. Consistent Readiness (vv. 5, 6)

5. Let your moderation be known unto all men. The Lord is at hand.

Moderation in this sense is the opposite of harshness. Here it has the sense of being gentle. Paul does not command the Philippians to be gentle, however. He assumes they are. Their gentle moderateness should be self-evident to all.

This idea is at odds with the infighting for which Paul chastises them. The sharp disagreements between members must be resolved so that nonbelievers will take note. Paul gives a further motivation for getting the conflicts resolved: *The Lord is at hand.* Do they want to be found bickering when Jesus comes to take them home?

6. Be careful for nothing; but in every thing by prayer and supplication with thanksgiving let your requests be made known unto God.

Careful in this context doe not mean "cautious," but "full of cares" or "anxious." Paul reminds his readers that they are foolish if they worry about everything (compare Matthew 6:25).

Worry and anxiety may be symptomatic of the lack of *prayer*. One of the functions of prayer is to give us a release for our worries by communicating our concerns to God. Peter taught that we should cast all our cares on God, because He cares for us deeply (1 Peter 5:7). This may be done cor-

Visual for Lesson 11

Point to this visual as you ask, "How is church harmony like the performance of a symphony?"

porately for the whole church (what Paul has in view here) or by the individual believer.

C. Consistent Peace (v. 7)

7. And the peace of God, which passeth all understanding, shall keep your hearts and minds through Christ Jesus.

For Paul, *peace* has a larger significance than "lack of hostility." It is the Jewish idea of *shalom*, meaning our general well-being. There can be no greater sense of personal well-being than in knowing God loves us, cares about us, and will provide for us. [See question #5, page 96.]

D. Consistent Virtue (vv. 8, 9)

8. Finally, brethren, whatsoever things are true, whatsoever things are honest, whatsoever things are just, whatsoever things are pure, whatsoever things are lovely, whatsoever things are of good report; if there be any virtue, and if there be any praise, think on these things.

There is a popular song that tells us to remember our favorite things if we want to be happy. Paul's advice here is similar, but much deeper. He exhorts the Philippians to find joy in the simple virtues of life: truth, honesty, justice, purity, beauty, commendability. If these are characteristics that we want in our lives, we should celebrate when we see them demonstrated by others.

The sad fact is that modern society often fears truth, lacks honesty, perverts justice, ridicules purity, exploits beauty, and disregards the need for a good reputation. We, as believers, can do better. We can take joy when we see these virtues displayed, even among nonbelievers, for we know that all virtue has its ultimate source in God.

9. Those things, which ye have both learned, and received, and heard, and seen in me, do: and the God of peace shall be with you.

Paul ends this section as he began (Philippians 3:17): by urging the Philippian community of believers to follow his example. Paul does not say this because he believes his own conduct is perfect, but because he is fully devoted to serving Christ. Life dedicated to Christ will yield rest in the storm, the comforting presence of God.

CONSISTENCY: A PASTE JEWEL?

"A foolish consistency is the hobgoblin of little minds, adored by little statesmen and philosophers and divines." So said Ralph Waldo Emerson (1803–1882). William Allen White (1868–1944) said, "Consistency is a paste jewel that only cheap men cherish." On the other hand, another sage was more on target: "Without consistency, there is no moral strength." And Francis Bacon (1561–1626) said, "Consistency is the foundation of virtue."

Many Christian thinkers throughout the ages have been of the latter opinion, trying to tie all biblical doctrines together into a consistent whole. We seek for a view of what the Bible teaches that is marked by harmony and free of contradictions. We intuitively realize that teaching that is lacking in harmony can lead us into behavior that is inconsistent with God's faithfulness and our Christian profession.

Paul urges us to be—here's that word again—consistent in our joy, our readiness for the Lord's return, the well-being that comes from experiencing God's love and care, and in the virtuous life that springs from devotion to Christ. Consistency in Christian commitment is a jewel. But it is not cheap, nor should it be rare!   —C. R. B.

Home Daily Bible Readings

Monday, Nov. 10—God Is Our Refuge (Psalm 46)

Tuesday, Nov. 11—Partnership in God's Grace (Philippians 1:3-11)

Wednesday, Nov. 12—Rejoice! Christ Is Proclaimed (Philippians 1:12-18)

Thursday, Nov. 13—To Live Is Christ, and to Die Is Gain (Philippians 1:19-26)

Friday, Nov. 14—Working Side by Side (Philippians 1:27-30)

Saturday, Nov. 15—Citizens of Heaven (Philippians 3:17–4:1)

Sunday, Nov. 16—The Peace That Guards (Philippians 4:2-9)

Conclusion

A. Twenty-First-Century Joy

As we near the time for Christmas merchandising, we begin to see the word *Joy* sprinkled on holiday items everywhere. Business-wise, this is safe. Who can object to such a happy little word? In the Christian faith, however, joy has a much deeper significance than being a commercial tagline. In the context of the Christmas story, joy is the response to the wonderful news that Jesus the Messiah has been born, that God has put on human flesh to take away the sins of the world.

The Bible teaches that joy is much more than a happy feeling experienced by Christians once a year. Joy is to be an ongoing characteristic of the Christian believer, a deep-seated attitude that does not depend on the fortunes of this life. Joy is part of who we are as God's children. Yet many Christians live lives where joy is rare. Many churches are joyless places. The apostle Paul saw this situation in the church at Philippi, one of his most beloved congregations.

For Paul, joy is our proper and natural response to the love and grace of God. Since God's love does not waver or change, our inner joy and peace can be strong and stable. We can be joyous even when our lives are going through sorrow or unhappiness. This is why James can make the seemingly contradictory statement "count it all joy when ye fall into divers temptations" (James 1:2). If our eyes and hearts are turned to Jesus, we should experience His joy. But if we are diverted into squabbling with brothers and sisters, that joy can evaporate easily.

Think, then, of your own life and your relationship to others in your church. Are you a positive influence in bringing joy into the lives of others? Have you lost your own sense of peace in joyful service to the Lord and to His church? Are you a person of whom it could be said, "She is always rejoicing"? Don't leave this lesson without resolving to be a rejoicer in all your tasks, roles, and responsibilities.

B. Prayer

God of peace and joy, we praise You in the unity of our spirits. We thank You for Your love and grace, so undeserved but so appreciated. May we find unity and peace among our fellow believers, and may that translate into joy in our lives. We pray this in the name of the Prince of Peace, our Lord Jesus Christ, amen.

C. Thought to Remember

Joy is possible with or without happiness.

Learning by Doing

This page contains an alternative lesson plan emphasizing learning activities. Some of these activities are also found in the helpful student book, Adult Bible Class.

Into the Lesson

Write the following contradictory quotations on the board:

People drain me, even the closest of friends, and I find loneliness to be the best state in the union to live in. (Margaret Cho, comedienne, from her weblog)

Doing things together is more important than doing things alone. (Henri Nouwen, from his book *Spiritual Direction*)

Read both quotes aloud. Then ask your class to break into small groups and talk about these two statements. Ask them to give reasons why they agree or disagree with each one. After a few minutes, ask for a few people to share their thoughts.

Then say, "Most of us will find ourselves shifting from one to the other at various points in life. But overall, our lives as Christians are meant to be shared with others. Today we're going to look at the joy we can experience through fellowship with other Christians."

Into the Word

Use the Lesson Background to introduce briefly the situation that prompted Paul to write the letter to the Philippians. Note some of his experiences in Philippi. Then say, "A person who is sitting in prison might be excused for being discouraged and for writing a letter to match that mood. But that's not at all what we will hear in Paul's letter." Ask for two volunteers to read Philippians 3:17-21 and Philippians 4:1-9. Then ask the class what mood they sense in Paul's letter. Expect such answers as "hopeful" and "joyful."

Before class, create a chart on letter-sized paper with these three column headings: *Scripture, Joy Killers, Joy Givers*. Down the left column, make rows numbered 1 through 10. List on those lines the following 10 passages from Philippians, 1 each per line: 3:17; 3:18, 19; 3:20, 21; 4:1-3; 4:4; 4:5; 4:6; 4:7; 4:8; 4:9. Include on the first row two sample answers: *Joy Killer*—"Being led astray by someone's bad example"; *Joy Giver*—"Having a godly mentor or role model to whom you can go for counsel."

Divide the class into small groups (or have them stay in the groups previously formed) and distribute copies of the chart. Say, "Read the verses and come up with things people might do that would either kill their joy or give them joy. The first one is done as a sample. Try to come up with at least one Joy Killer and one Joy Giver for each line." (*Alternative approach:* If pressed for time, assign half of the groups to write Joy Killers and the other half to write Joy Givers.)

Possible answers are as follows. For *Joy Killers:* 2. Developing unhealthy, self-indulgent habits; 3. Focusing all one's attention on life on earth; 4. Fighting among ourselves; 5. Being overcome by doubts and fears; 6. Trying to "win" through intimidation; 7. Trying to handle all your problems yourself; 8. Allowing emotions to control our hearts; 9. Dwelling on the negative aspects of life; 10. Living life your own way. For *Joy Givers:* 2. Walking by the Spirit and not by the flesh; 3. Looking forward to the joy of Heaven; 4. Working as a peacemaker to help resolve conflict; 5. Rejoicing in spite of circumstances; 6. Overcoming a bad habit of self-indulgence; 7. Turning every worry into a prayer; 8. Focusing on God and the peace He gives; 9. Seeing the good in people; 10. Studying Scripture and living by it.

At the end of 10 minutes, go down through the chart and ask groups to give their answers. Make the point that the way to joyful living is to share our lives with God and other Christians.

Into Life

Early in the week, think about a difficult time in your own life (or the life of someone you know well) when Christians were there to give you their loving support. Tell that story at this time, emphasizing how much better the situation was because Christians helped support you (or the other person). Either ask for volunteers from the class to share stories, or ask students to break into pairs and share stories with each other.

Distribute the following commitment statements and ask students to sign them, if they wish:

This week I will look for opportunities to share my life with one other Christian, especially one who is currently going through a difficult time.
Signed _____.

Encourage your students to take these commitments with them and follow through on them before next Sunday.

Let's Talk It Over

The questions on this page are designed to promote discussion of the lesson
by the class and to encourage application of the lesson Scriptures. The answers
provided are only discussion starters. Let your class talk it over from there.

1. How do you recognize improper spiritual role models, who walk as enemies of the cross of Christ? How do you guard yourself against following them?

There are many celebrities in the entertainment and sports world who are poor role models for Christians or anyone else. Christians often are able to discern this, and they refuse to follow such role models, even though the performance ability of the person is respected.

But there also are those who claim the name of Christ and are poor role models. Some celebrity Christian speakers and bands put on a good show on the stage, yet their main focus may be their own personal advancement. Demands for special treatment and exorbitant fees for their speeches or concerts contradict the message they present from the stage. The forthright question "Who really is being exalted here?" is our first line of defense against choosing such folks as role models.

2. How can the truth that *this world is not our home* be misrepresented? What dangers are to be avoided when we consider this?

Truly, this world is not our permanent home. We realize that our permanent home is in Heaven. But we must be careful not to neglect the needs of this world while awaiting Heaven. Christians and churches can be guilty of adopting a fortress mentality and refusing to interact with this world.

The key is to learn how to live out the prayer of Jesus in John 17:15, 16: "I pray not that thou shouldest take them out of the world, but that thou shouldest keep them from the evil." The church is to find ways to be an influence for Christ in the world through ministry to those who are in physical, emotional, and spiritual need. The words of C. T. Studd (1860–1931) should guide our efforts: "Some wish to live within the sound of church or chapel bell; I want to run a rescue shop within a yard of hell."

3. In what ways does the church need to do better in standing fast in the world today? What is your part in this corrective?

Standing fast, being firm in one's beliefs and convictions, is needed in a world that embraces the "truth is relative" idea of postmodernism. From political correctness run amok to lascivious behavior so readily accepted, the world needs a moral compass that is based on ethical absolutes. The only place this can be found is in the church.

Opportunities exist for the church to make a difference in all communities. Churches may need to confront abortion clinics. Public school boards, which are often hotbeds of political correctness and "tolerance," may need to have Christians come to meetings and make bold yet loving pleas for biblical morality. Taking a firm stand must begin, though, within the walls of the church.

4. Is it really possible to rejoice always? Why, or why not?

How easy it is to focus on what is going wrong in life! Our joy can evaporate when we get life out of focus. When things aren't going as we want them to, life seems unpleasant.

But Scripture reminds us that when we have our priorities right, we can have joy. This is seen in Romans 14:17: "For the kingdom of God is not meat and drink; but righteousness, and peace, and joy in the Holy Ghost." We caution ourselves against thinking that joy is to be equated with happiness. Though there may be things that make us unhappy, we can still find joy. We remember that when we go through trying circumstances, we are sharing in the sufferings of Christ (see 1 Peter 4:12, 13).

5. How has the peace of God kept you strong and faithful to the Lord?

Stories here will be highly individual. Yet all of us have times in life when we feel as if everything is falling apart. It is hard to find answers to the trials we are going through. The solutions the world proposes and the pat answers that some well-meaning Christians provide may hurt more than they help.

It is in times of weakness and seeming hopelessness that God does His best work. God's peace is made evident to us in the gracious help of a friend, even if it comes in the form of someone just sitting with us without saying a word. God's peace comes over us as we gather with other Christians to worship God. We also feel the peace of God as we learn to rest in Christ.

Leadership in the Community

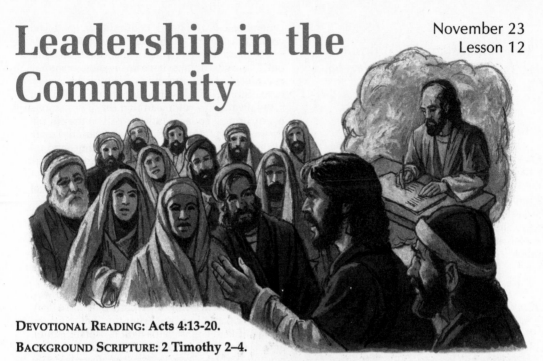

DEVOTIONAL READING: Acts 4:13-20.

BACKGROUND SCRIPTURE: 2 Timothy 2–4.

PRINTED TEXT: 2 Timothy 2:1-3; 3:14–4:5.

2 Timothy 2:1-3

1 Thou therefore, my son, be strong in the grace that is in Christ Jesus.

2 And the things that thou hast heard of me among many witnesses, the same commit thou to faithful men, who shall be able to teach others also.

3 Thou therefore endure hardness, as a good soldier of Jesus Christ.

2 Timothy 3:14-17

14 But continue thou in the things which thou hast learned and hast been assured of, knowing of whom thou hast learned them;

15 And that from a child thou hast known the holy Scriptures, which are able to make thee wise unto salvation through faith which is in Christ Jesus.

16 All Scripture is given by inspiration of God, and is profitable for doctrine, for reproof, for correction, for instruction in righteousness:

17 That the man of God may be perfect, thoroughly furnished unto all good works.

2 Timothy 4:1-5

1 I charge thee therefore before God, and the Lord Jesus Christ, who shall judge the quick and the dead at his appearing and his kingdom;

2 Preach the word; be instant in season, out of season; reprove, rebuke, exhort with all long-suffering and doctrine.

3 For the time will come when they will not endure sound doctrine; but after their own lusts shall they heap to themselves teachers, having itching ears;

4 And they shall turn away their ears from the truth, and shall be turned unto fables.

5 But watch thou in all things, endure afflictions, do the work of an evangelist, make full proof of thy ministry.

GOLDEN TEXT: The things that thou hast heard of me among many witnesses, the same commit thou to faithful men, who shall be able to teach others also.—2 Timothy 2:2.

Nov
23

The New Testament Community
Unit 3: Challenges in the New Community
(Lessons 9–13)

Lesson Aims

After participating in this lesson, each student will be able to:

1. Summarize Paul's charge to Timothy.

2. Tell how Paul's concern with raising up a new generation of leaders is relevant to the twenty-first century church.

3. Construct a biblical process of leadership training.

Lesson Outline

INTRODUCTION
  A. Two-Tim-Two-Two
  B. Lesson Background
I. LEADERS WHO LAST (2 Timothy 2:1-3)
  A. Lasting by Grace (v. 1)
  B. Lasting by Replication (v. 2)
  C. Lasting by Toughness (v. 3)
    Strong Leadership
II. LEADERS WHO ARE GROUNDED (2 Timothy 3: 14-17)
  A. Grounded in Tradition (v. 14)
  B. Grounded in Scripture (vv. 15, 16)
  C. Grounded in Good Works (v. 17)
III. LEADERS WHO ARE FAITHFUL (2 Timothy 4:1-5)
  A. Faithful to the Lord (v. 1)
  B. Faithful to the Task (v. 2)
  C. Faithful to the Ministry (vv. 3-5)
    Scratching Itching Ears
CONCLUSION
  A. Passing the Baton
  B. Prayer
  C. Thought to Remember

Introduction

A. Two-Tim-Two-Two

Several years ago, there was a leadership training program popular in some churches that used 2 Timothy 2:2 as its touchstone: "the things that thou hast heard of me among many witnesses, the same commit thou to faithful men, who shall be able to teach others also." In one church, this was made into a catchy slogan: *2-Tim-2-2*. This helped people remember that text and the core teaching on which the program was based: training across

generations. Provision for continuity in good leadership must take a multigenerational view.

The church is always one generation from dying out. To survive, it must have an ongoing, unending program of identifying and nourishing the leaders of the future. This is very difficult to visualize for some people. Do you mean that those impetuous, overly critical college students will be the church leaders of the future? Yes. Do you mean that some of those flaky teenagers whose piercings and tattoos we disapprove of will be the church leaders of the future? Yes. Do you mean that those spoiled, pampered children will be the church leaders of the future? Yes. Remember: *2-Tim-2-2*.

B. Lesson Background

Timothy first appears in Acts during Paul's second missionary journey, in about AD 51 (Acts 16:1-3). Timothy was probably a teenager at the time. Amazingly, Timothy's mother, Eunice, and his grandmother, Lois (see 2 Timothy 1:5), allowed Timothy to leave his home and become a traveling companion of Paul. Timothy then emerged as one of Paul's most important coworkers, often entrusted with important visits to churches, representing Paul (see Acts 19:22). Paul described Timothy as his "beloved son, and faithful in the Lord" (1 Corinthians 4:17).

Paul wrote 2 Timothy in about AD 67, shortly before his death in Rome. It was thus something like 16 years after their first meeting, and Timothy was far beyond being the raw teenager whom Paul initially took under his wing. Timothy became the primary leader of the important church in Ephesus, founded by Paul on the third missionary journey (Acts 19:8-10). Although 2 Timothy does not say specifically that Timothy was still in Ephesus as we see in 1 Timothy 1:3, we assume this to be the case for this letter too. We can imagine, then, that Paul was writing to his beloved protégé who was at the time the ancient world's version of a megachurch minister in his 30s.

Timothy is described as an "evangelist" (2 Timothy 4:5), literally a "preacher of good news." Whether because of this title or due to his association with Paul, Timothy seems to have been accorded extraordinary authority to oversee leadership issues in the Ephesian church. This is seen more in 1 Timothy, where Paul encouraged Timothy to be engaged in corrective actions with poor or deviant leaders (see 1 Timothy 1:3). In 2 Timothy, Paul's emphasis is more upon the leadership example to which Timothy should aspire (see 2 Timothy 3:14).

The book of 2 Timothy is a treasure for those who strive to have effective and godly leaders within the church. It is the mature reflection of the apostle "Paul the aged" (Philemon 9) as he faces death and the prospects for the church's survival without his guidance. He was not discouraged. He was ready to entrust leadership to Timothy's generation. Paul knew that Timothy would be called on to do the same thing later (should the Lord delay returning).

I. Leaders Who Last
(2 Timothy 2:1-3)
A. Lasting by Grace (v. 1)

1. Thou therefore, my son, be strong in the grace that is in Christ Jesus.

Where do *strong* leaders find their strength? Even for tough people, the inner reservoir of strength can dry up. Paul testifies in his letters that his strength comes from the Lord, not himself (see 1 Timothy 1:12). This is a matter of faith, of trusting in *the grace* and mercy of God as seen in Jesus Christ. There is great, reassuring strength in being faithful, in knowing one is within the will of God. When we trust God in this way, we claim the Lord's promise that He will never leave or forsake us (Joshua 1:5; Hebrews 13:5). [See question #1, page 104.]

Most of us have seen leaders apparently lose strength and burn out. What some people see as *burnout* is seen by others as God's way of driving someone back to Him. Burnout occurs when we lose hope, when our abilities and capacities seem unequal to the task, and no solutions are evident. When we turn back to God and quit depending on our own strength, we can understand Paul's paradoxical statement, "When I am weak, then am I strong" (2 Corinthians 12:10).

B. Lasting by Replication (v. 2)

2. And the things that thou hast heard of me among many witnesses, the same commit thou to faithful men, who shall be able to teach others also.

Recently, my household endured the experience of replacing a water heater. I can't really complain about the old unit since it had gone several years past its warranty. It had served its useful lifespan and needed replacing.

Leadership is like that too. Even the most enduring leaders do not escape the process of aging and the eventuality of death. The church needs to replenish its leaders constantly. The wise church is the one that understands this need and acts on it. When it does, it will not find itself with a leadership vacuum.

Paul identifies two parts to the process of leadership replication. First, the current leader must be

sure of what he is doing and teaching. For Timothy, this refers to what he has heard from Paul. For us, it is solid knowledge of God's Word and God's will for the church.

Second, the current leader must identify future leaders who have three important characteristics. Uppermost, they must be *faithful*. They must have a track record demonstrating their commitment to the cause of Christ. They should exhibit a lifestyle of Christlikeness. Next, they must be teachable. Good leaders never outgrow this quality. They remain learners for a lifetime. The stubborn person who is resistant to correction or instruction is a poor choice to be a leader. Finally, they must be capable of teaching the next generation of leaders. Young leaders must have an eye to even younger potential leaders. [See question #2, page 104.]

C. Lasting by Toughness (v. 3)

3. Thou therefore endure hardness, as a good soldier of Jesus Christ.

The phrase *endure hardness* translates a word found only here and at 2 Timothy 1:8 in the New Testament. There it is translated "be thou partaker of the afflictions." Paul is never remiss about warning his younger disciples that the cause of Christ can be a tough life. It will be met with opposition and persecution. People are generally resistant to the truth that they are sinners and need a Savior.

A *good soldier* is one who focuses on duty. A Roman soldier of Paul's day is expected to endure extreme deprivation. He sleeps on the ground, eats what is available, and marches long hours carrying heavy equipment. The Roman legions do not tolerate grumblers. Thus, Paul balances his advice

Visual for Lesson 12. *As you discuss verse 2, point to this visual and ask, "In what ways are you able to teach others?"*

to find strength in the grace of Christ (v. 1) with a call for leaders who are tough. Strong leaders must not be thin-skinned, easily cowed by criticism and uncooperative church members.

STRONG LEADERSHIP

Some regard Winston Churchill (1874–1965) as the most important world leader of the World War II era. He demonstrated the capacity of strong leadership very early in life. In the Boer War in South Africa, he escaped after being taken captive. He won elections in the early 1900s and received a succession of prestigious appointments. He fought in World War I. Churchill was never one to take timid stances, and his political fortunes reversed several times in the decades that followed.

As Hitler came to power in 1933, Churchill advocated British rearmament and opposed appeasement policies. When Nazi Germany began marching across Europe, King George VI appointed Churchill to be Britain's prime minister. Churchill led the British people courageously through the darkest hours of the war. He was also one of the first leaders to recognize the growing threat of the Soviet Union.

One of Paul's admonitions to Christians who would be leaders was that they must be able to endure great difficulty. Faithful leadership sometimes demands that we take unpopular stances on vital issues, steadfastly maintaining our principles when it may not seem expedient to do so. Combining that stance with grace in leadership can require both wisdom and great effort.

—C. R. B.

II. Leaders Who Are Grounded (2 Timothy 3:14-17)

A. Grounded in Tradition (v. 14)

14. But continue thou in the things which thou hast learned and hast been assured of, knowing of whom thou hast learned them.

How to Say It

ECCLESIASTES. Ik-*leez*-ee-*as*-teez (strong accent on *as*).
EPHESIAN. Ee-*fee*-zhun.
EPHESUS. *Ef*-uh-sus.
EUNICE. U-*nye*-see or *U*-nis.
GALATIANS. Guh-*lay*-shunz.
HABAKKUK. Huh-*back*-kuk.
LOIS. *Lo*-is.
PHILEMON. Fih-*lee*-mun or Fye-*lee*-mun.
SOCRATES. *Sock*-ruh-teez.

We may turn Paul's statements into questions: What have you *learned*? From *whom* have you learned it? Often, the measure of a person is found in knowing who his or her teachers were. Who were the influential educators in this person's training?

The student likely will follow in the footsteps of the teacher. For this reason, Paul reminds Timothy to remember that he has had good teachers. They have taught him solid doctrine. This is more than a self-reference by Paul. Paul is well aware that the earliest teachers in Timothy's life were his faithful mother and grandmother (2 Timothy 1:5). A family tradition of faithfulness is a powerful gift. [See question #3, page 104.]

B. Grounded in Scripture (vv. 15, 16)

15. And that from a child thou hast known the holy Scriptures, which are able to make thee wise unto salvation through faith which is in Christ Jesus.

A traditional responsibility of Jewish fathers is to see to the education of their sons. Since Timothy did not have a father to provide a Jewish education (see Acts 16:1), he had been a likely candidate to fall through the cracks and not receive grounding in the essentials of Scripture.

Fortunately, this was not the case, for his mother and grandmother had not neglected his religious training. In the fractured families of our day, these duties may fall similarly upon the female household heads. There is great virtue in teaching children Scripture as early as they are able to learn. The sage advice to "remember now thy Creator in the days of thy youth" (Ecclesiastes 12:1) still applies. This will happen only if parents shoulder this responsibility.

The *holy Scriptures* Paul has in mind are what we Christians call the Old Testament. Paul uses the Old Testament frequently, both in his letters and in his public presentations (see Acts 17:2). His key doctrine of justification by faith, which is in mind here *(salvation through faith)*, is grounded in two key Old Testament passages: Genesis 15:6 and Habakkuk 2:4 (see Romans 1:17; 4:3; Galatians 3:6, 11).

16. All Scripture is given by inspiration of God, and is profitable for doctrine, for reproof, for correction, for instruction in righteousness.

Paul reminds Timothy of the nature of *Scripture*. In so doing, Paul gives us the clearest statement of the doctrine of scriptural inspiration in the entire Bible. First, he states the essence of Scripture: it is *given by inspiration of God,* literally it is "God-breathed." When God breathed into the human body He had formed, Adam became a living soul (Genesis 2:7), and Paul surely has this idea in mind. The Bible is like no other book or literature in that it is enlivened by God. It is "quick" and "powerful" (Hebrews 4:12). Therefore it rightly deserves the designation "word of life" (Philippians 2:16).

Next, Paul goes on to list four important functions of Scripture. First, it is *profitable for doctrine*, meaning that it is a reliable source of information for Christian teaching. Second, Scripture is profitable *for reproof*, meaning it is a consistent guide to identify erroneous teaching. All teaching and preaching in the church should be measured by the standard of what Scripture says.

Third, it is profitable *for correction*. It is not sufficient to single out false teaching. A correct alternative should be presented, and this should come from Scripture. On a personal level, there is a self-correcting aspect to Scripture as we read it and apply it to our own lives. This is the basis of the fourth scriptural function, *instruction in righteousness*. While the pursuit of self-righteousness is folly, God still expects His people to live and love His standards of purity and morality. Our only reliable source for understanding God's expectations of righteousness is the Bible itself. We seek lives and churches in which "righteousness [runs down] as a mighty stream" (Amos 5:24).

C. Grounded in Good Works (v. 17)

17. That the man of God may be perfect, thoroughly furnished unto all good works.

The ancient Greek philosopher Socrates said, "The unexamined life is not worth living." Paul is saying that life is worth living only if it is examined, corrected, and enriched by the standard of Scripture. We are not *perfect* in the sense of sinless behavior, but in the sense of being *thoroughly furnished* or equipped to perform godly actions in any circumstance. It is through our commitment to knowing and following the standards of Scripture that we may be recognized as people *of God*. It is such people who are to be church leaders. [See question #4, page 104.]

III. Leaders Who Are Faithful (2 Timothy 4:1-5)

A. Faithful to the Lord (v. 1)

1. I charge thee therefore before God, and the Lord Jesus Christ, who shall judge the quick and the dead at his appearing and his kingdom.

Accountability in leadership can be difficult. Church leaders spend many hours engaged in unobserved activities (surfing the Internet, etc.). The leader who takes undue advantage of this may

live as a hypocrite for years before being detected. Timothy himself is many miles from his mentor, and Paul has no direct control over Timothy's day-to-day doings.

Paul's solution, then, is for Timothy never to forget his ultimate accountability to God. There will be a time of judgment, and it will cut through all deceptions (see Acts 17:31).

B. Faithful to the Task (v. 2)

2. Preach the word; be instant in season, out of season; reprove, rebuke, exhort with all long-suffering and doctrine.

When should we *preach* the gospel? Any chance we get! Preaching *the word* does not go out of fashion and will never become obsolete. There were some in the twentieth century who believed that the age of preaching was past, but they have been proven wrong. There will always be a need for public proclamation of the good news about Jesus Christ. Leaders, whether preachers or not, must see this as the primary task of the church. Those who are called to preach must feel a fire in their hearts that cannot be quenched, whose only outlet is faithful preaching.

Leadership can require confrontation, which is implied in the terms *reprove, rebuke,* and *exhort.* Leaders in the church cannot allow serious error to grow and become strong. Leaders must be watchful and patient in guarding correct doctrine. The church may have diversity in membership, but should have unity in the faith.

C. Faithful to the Ministry (vv. 3-5)

3, 4. For the time will come when they will not endure sound doctrine; but after their own lusts shall they heap to themselves teachers, having itching ears; and they shall turn away their ears from the truth, and shall be turned unto fables.

Does this sound familiar? Paul uses the striking metaphor of *itching ears* for future audiences. By this he means they will tolerate only those *teachers* who please them, who scratch them where they want to be scratched. [See question #5, page 104.] They want to leave a teaching session feeling satisfied rather than being challenged to change. They won't want to hear *the truth*, because it will demand that they change their behaviors and attitudes.

The antidote for this is *sound doctrine*, literally "healthy doctrine." This is doctrine that leads to spiritual vigor. The opposite of this is to teach *fables*, things from a fantasy world that will threaten no one. There always have been teachers who pander to their audiences and teach only things that will not cause friction within the body. But sin must be confronted (v. 2). If not confronted, its malaise will infect the whole congregation and destroy it from within.

SCRATCHING ITCHING EARS

Kirby Hensley (1911–1999) incorporated the Universal Life Church (ULC) in 1962. Millions of people followed him. He once wrote, "The biggest enemy that man has today, in the free world, is the church. All life wants the same things. It wants to be free, it wants food, and it wants sex . . . in that order! That is heaven when you have it and it is hell when you don't have it." The ULC's only belief is "To do that which is right."

Do you recognize all this as standard American "do your own thing" doctrine? Would you be surprised to learn that the founder of this "church" had started several evangelical churches in his earlier days?

The problem, of course, is that once Scripture is jettisoned as the authority, anything goes. And among ULC members, that is exactly what happens. In church services, anyone can preach anything, as in one recent service in which a "minister" (everyone there is a "minister") denounced the Bible as "a guide that is totally out of date."

This is exactly what Paul feared would happen if the church strayed from true doctrine. Itching ears want to be scratched. The world has plenty of leaders who recognize this and have created fables to attract their followers.   —C. R. B.

5. But watch thou in all things, endure afflictions, do the work of an evangelist, make full proof of thy ministry.

Paul's final words in this section are for Timothy's ears, but ring true for anyone committed to ministry. Timothy is called to be watchful, careful, and clearheaded. There will always be those who seek to bring him down. He is expected to *endure afflictions,* not to be surprised or deterred by the hardships of ministry. This may include emotional, physical, or financial suffering for the cause of Christ.

Timothy must never stray from doing *the work of an evangelist,* which is bringing people to Christ. Ministry has many tasks, and it is easy to be sidetracked from the most important thing: saving lost souls through the power of the gospel.

Finally, Paul tells his protégé to *make full proof of thy ministry* (compare Colossians 4:17). He means that Timothy should work his ministry to the fullest. He should fulfill the great potential that Paul saw in him some 16 years before.

Conclusion

A. Passing the Baton

A relay race is a team effort that requires the tricky maneuver of handing a baton from one runner to another. Sometimes the baton is fumbled, and the runners must slow down. Sometimes the baton is dropped, and the runners stop. But if the runners trust each other and practice together, the baton may be passed with runners sprinting at nearly full speed. Thus the winning team is one that is successful in passing the baton, even if its runners are not as fast as some of its competitors.

The leadership needs of the church are best served when there are smooth transitions. Veteran leaders must realize when their time is ending; then they can ready themselves and the congregation for change. If they stay too long and refuse to pass the baton, they hinder the work of the church.

Younger leaders must understand the need for training and the value of experience. They must not alienate older leaders, but instead draw upon their wisdom and knowledge. When these transitions are made according to the biblical model, the church will not miss a step. She will proceed with the ministry to which Christ has called her.

B. Prayer

O Lord, give us strong leaders. Give us leaders who are grounded in Your Word. Give us leaders who will guard their lives from sin. Give us leaders who will love the lost and seek them out for salvation. Give us leaders who are willing to pass the baton when the time is right. We pray this in the name of Jesus Christ. Amen.

C. Thought to Remember

Is your church getting ready to pass the baton?

Home Daily Bible Readings

Monday, Nov. 17—Power, Self-discipline, Love (2 Timothy 1:3-7)

Tuesday, Nov. 18—Not Ashamed! (2 Timothy 1:8-14)

Wednesday, Nov. 19—The Power of the Gospel (Romans 1:8-17)

Thursday, Nov. 20—The Unchained Word of God (2 Timothy 2:8-13)

Friday, Nov. 21—An Approved Worker (2 Timothy 2:14-19)

Saturday, Nov. 22—Equipped for Every Good Work (2 Timothy 3:14-17)

Sunday, Nov. 23—Preach the Word! (2 Timothy 2:1-3; 4:1-5)

Learning by Doing

This page contains an alternative lesson plan emphasizing learning activities. Some of these activities are also found in the helpful student book, Adult Bible Class.

Into the Lesson

Start the class by saying, "For the past three weeks we've talked about qualities we need to develop in order to have a strong community of believers. In addition to unity, the courage to confront, and joy, today's quality is important for a healthy church now and in the future. See if you can unscramble this 10-letter word."

Write *ADEEHILPRS* on the board. If students need help unscrambling the word *leadership,* give them clues, such as the first or last letters. (*Alternative:* Have the scrambled word already written on the board as students begin to arrive. This will serve to start discussion in and of itself.)

Say, "Let's look at several passages from Paul's second letter to Timothy to see what advice he has on how to develop leadership in the church."

Into the Word

Write today's Scripture reference for the lesson on the board: *2 Timothy 2:1-3; 3:14-17; 4:1-5.* Distribute copies of the following *Agree-Disagree* activity (but do not distribute the suggested answers, which are in parentheses). Ask students to work together in small groups or study pairs to complete it. Say, "Read through today's text. Then go through each of these statements about what makes a good leader and write A or D to indicate if you think the apostle Paul would *agree* or *disagree* with it. Indicate the verse that best supports your answer; there should be one verse for each statement."

1. A good leader can teach others about salvation even without any real background in the Scriptures. *(Disagree, 3:15)* 2. To survive as a church leader, a person needs to be tough, able to handle criticism, and competent to deal with church crises. *(Agree, 2:3)* 3. To serve a congregation effectively, a minister needs to stress good planning over good preaching. *(Disagree, 4:2)* 4. A leader must depend primarily on personal inner resources to help solve problems. *(Disagree, 2:1)* 5. All leaders need to remember that one day they will be held accountable by God. *(Agree, 4:1)* 6. A leader should never forget that the primary part of ministry is bringing lost souls to Jesus. *(Agree, 4:5)* 7. The thing that's important is *what* you learn, not *whom* you learn it from. *(Disagree, 3:14)* 8. The ability to train others to be leaders is an impor-

tant quality for a good leader to have. *(Agree, 2:2)* 9. The Bible can teach leaders about righteousness. *(Agree, 3:16)* 10. A preacher can best serve the congregation by having sermons that are crowd-pleasers. *(Disagree, 4:3)* 11. Leaders should be thoroughly prepared to handle potential problems and help the church grow. *(Agree, 3:17)*

As you ask the various groups to share their answers, some of them may have different answers from what is indicated. Allow for this possibility, since some questions may be understood in various ways. But use the lesson commentary to help your class understand the foundational principle(s) taught in each verse.

Follow up on this activity with a discussion on the importance of preparing future leaders for the church. Ask, "Did you notice a sense of urgency in Paul's instructions to Timothy? Paul knew his time was about up, so his last letter to his protégé was full of practical advice to help Timothy continue to develop as a strong leader of the church. This advice also can be very useful to us as we consider how to develop leadership for our church."

Then ask, "How important is it for the leaders of our church to train young people for future leadership? What are some of the qualities we should be developing?" (Make a list on the board.) "What kinds of activities or programs could help us develop these qualities in our young people? How much of a sense of urgency do we have in this regard?"

Into Life

Choose one of the following activities to conclude today's lesson. Select the one that best suits the interests and abilities of your students.

Option #1: Distribute stationery or small thank-you notes. Ask students to think of someone in the church who demonstrates the kind of leadership qualities Paul encouraged Timothy to have. Suggest that they thank these individuals for their leadership and praise them specifically for one or more of their leadership strengths.

Option #2: In small groups, ask students to talk about those who have been mentors in helping them develop their strengths. Ask them to talk about the methods used by the mentor. Then have them identify a young person in the congregation with whom they would be willing to develop a relationship and act as a mentor.

Let's Talk It Over

The questions on this page are designed to promote discussion of the lesson by the class and to encourage application of the lesson Scriptures. The answers provided are only discussion starters. Let your class talk it over from there.

1. What are some ways that God's grace has kept you strong in your faith?

Remembering the promises of God is one way to remain strong in the faith. God has promised that He will never leave nor forsake His people (Hebrews 13:5).

We can feel defeated when we realize how far short of the mark we fall in serving and pleasing God as we should. In those times we receive strength in knowing that God forgives (1 John 1:9). God gives us strength as we remember the resurrection of Jesus and realize that we share in that resurrection power (Philippians 3:10).

2. What are some ways you can help pass the mantle of church leadership on to the next generation?

Start by examining your attitude and perspective. Every generation, it seems, looks upon the following generation as being far worse than theirs is. We can have very short memories when it comes to our own lives as adolescents and young adults. It is important to remember how we bristled at the blanket condemnation by our parents and grandparents on all young people. Then we can avoid the same attitude. We must take time to commend our young people instead of condemning them.

The most foundational thing in developing the next generation of church leaders is to model them the Christian life at all times. When young people see Christians acting in unchristian ways, leadership and faith development are hindered.

3. What are some things or attitudes that you have discovered impedes your progress of continuing on in the things you have learned? How do you overcome these impediments?

We remember that we are locked into spiritual warfare with the forces of evil, with Satan himself. Alongside all the good seed of knowledge that Christians receive, Satan is there with his army of deceivers trying to snatch it away (Matthew 13:19). Titus 3:3 reminds us that "we ourselves also were sometime foolish, disobedient, deceived."

Some claim to be speaking God's Word, but they twist and distort the Scriptures. Failing to examine the Word daily will make us easier targets for false teaching. Our growth in Christ will be inhibited.

Coupling our knowledge with our faith is a vital safeguard (see 2 Peter 1:5).

4. How do you live your life in such a way that you demonstrate belief in the inspired and inerrant Word of God?

Many claim to believe the Bible to be the Word of God. They say they believe it from cover to cover and are upset when someone questions its authority and authenticity. Yet some of these same people will forsake the teaching of God's Word as they follow their own desires; in that case, their actions don't match their stated beliefs. Such folks run the risk of "having a form of godliness, but denying the power thereof" (2 Timothy 3:5).

For one who believes in the Word of God, the best way to express this belief is in action, not simply talk. Christian belief is not seen in going to endless Bible studies just to soak in all of the Word we can. It is seen in *practicing* the principles taught in that Word (James 1:22). True acceptance of the truth of God's Word means allowing it to influence the way we live, the decisions we make, and the priorities we have in our day-to-day lives.

5. How do we guard ourselves against the tendency to listen to teachers who do little more than scratch us where we itch?

At times people have wrong perceptions of what a preacher of the gospel should be. Sometimes we say someone doesn't "look like" a preacher, and thus we ignore what he says. Another preacher can have a powerful stage presence, so we accept him. This is the "scratch" to the "itch" of an image-driven culture.

We avoid this problem by being like the noble Bereans of Scripture. These are the ones who "received the word with all readiness of mind, and searched the Scriptures daily, whether those things were so" (Acts 17:11).

We do the same when we look past image and take into account what is actually being said. A strong stage presence is helpful when it is used to enhance communication of the truth of God's Word. But we must guard ourselves against allowing a preoccupation with image to override a concern for sound doctrine.

Grace in the Community

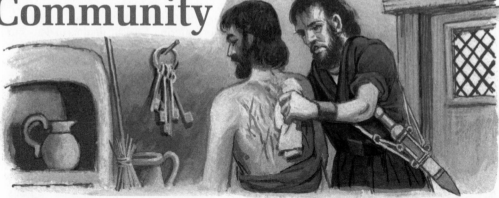

DEVOTIONAL READING: 1 Corinthians 1: 18-25.

BACKGROUND SCRIPTURE: 2 Corinthians 11:16–12:10.

PRINTED TEXT: 2 Corinthians 11:17, 21b-30; 12:9, 10.

2 Corinthians 11:17, 21b-30

17 That which I speak, I speak it not after the Lord, but as it were foolishly, in this confidence of boasting.

. . . .

21b Howbeit, whereinsoever any is bold, (I speak foolishly,) I am bold also.

22 Are they Hebrews? so am I. Are they Israelites? so am I. Are they the seed of Abraham? so am I.

23 Are they ministers of Christ? (I speak as a fool,) I am more; in labors more abundant, in stripes above measure, in prisons more frequent, in deaths oft.

24 Of the Jews five times received I forty stripes save one.

25 Thrice was I beaten with rods, once was I stoned, thrice I suffered shipwreck, a night and a day I have been in the deep;

26 In journeyings often, in perils of waters, in perils of robbers, in perils by mine own countrymen, in perils by the heathen, in perils in the city, in perils in the wilderness, in perils in the sea, in perils among false brethren;

27 In weariness and painfulness, in watchings often, in hunger and thirst, in fastings often, in cold and nakedness.

28 Beside those things that are without, that which cometh upon me daily, the care of all the churches.

29 Who is weak, and I am not weak? who is offended, and I burn not?

30 If I must needs glory, I will glory of the things which concern mine infirmities.

2 Corinthians 12:9, 10

9 And he said unto me, My grace is sufficient for thee: for my strength is made perfect in weakness. Most gladly therefore will I rather glory in my infirmities, that the power of Christ may rest upon me.

10 Therefore I take pleasure in infirmities, in reproaches, in necessities, in persecutions, in distresses for Christ's sake: for when I am weak, then am I strong.

GOLDEN TEXT: I take pleasure in infirmities, in reproaches, in necessities, in persecutions, in distresses for Christ's sake: for when I am weak, then am I strong.—2 Corinthians 12:10.

The New Testament Community
Unit 3: Challenges in the New Community
(Lessons 9–13)

Lesson Aims

After participating in this lesson, each student will be able to:

1. List some of Paul's sufferings.

2. Explain how God's grace and power can protect us in times of human weakness.

3. Apply 2 Corinthians 12:9, 10 to one area of his or her life in the week ahead.

Lesson Outline

INTRODUCTION
  A. No Pain, No Gain
  B. Lesson Background
I. PAUL'S BOASTS IN STRENGTH (2 Corinthians 11:17, 21b-30)
  A. Boasting in Foolishness (v. 17)
    Telling Stories
  B. Boasts of Background (vv. 21b, 22)
  C. Boasts in Trials (vv. 23-27)
  D. Boasts in Concern (vv. 28-30)
    Curriculum Vitae
II. PAUL'S STRENGTH IN WEAKNESSES (2 Corinthians 12:9, 10)
  A. Sufficiency in Grace (v. 9)
  B. Pleasure in Pain (v. 10)
CONCLUSION
  A. It Can't Get Any Worse?
  B. Prayer
  C. Thought to Remember

Introduction

A. No Pain, No Gain

The world of athletic competition has contributed a modern proverb to us: *no pain, no gain.* Originally, this spoke to the need for intense, painful training as preparation for competition and victory. The saying is now applied to everything from financial matters, to academic pursuits, and even to weight-loss programs. The principle is that sacrifice and delayed gratification can lead to better results in the long run.

Yet most people do not willingly endure hardship. If I have the choice of sitting in a hard, metal chair or a soft, comfortable recliner, I'm likely to choose the recliner. If I can swap my rattletrap, old car for a newer, more reliable model, I'm inclined to make the switch. I would rather do yard work on a pleasant, sunny day than a cold, wet one. Choosing hardship for hardship's sake is seen as aberrant, unhealthy behavior.

To choose the Christian life, however, is to make a choice for suffering. Christ called us to deny our own desires and follow Him while shouldering our own cross (Matthew 16:24). A central belief of the church is that persecution and suffering in the present life will be replaced by great reward in Heaven (see Matthew 5:12).

Unlike the training athlete, though, we cannot always pick our pain. Hardships may come at us from unexpected places, hitting us where we are weak and vulnerable. This week's lesson looks at some very personal words from Paul on this subject. Paul suffered greatly over a lifetime of ministry, yet he always counted it as joy to serve Jesus (see Acts 20:24). Our stories will be different, but we too may find joy in serving the Lord in the midst of difficulties.

B. Lesson Background

Paul first visited the city of Corinth on his second missionary journey in about AD 52. He founded the Corinthian church and stayed with it for about 18 months (Acts 18:11). He befriended a Jewish Christian couple, Priscilla and Aquila, with whom he stayed and shared in their occupational task of making tents (Acts 18:1-3). The Corinthian church was a rich mix of Jews and Gentiles. Being in a large, cosmopolitan city, it had members with widely varying backgrounds and social status.

During Paul's third missionary journey, he settled in Ephesus for about three years (Acts 19; 20:31). Located across the Aegean Sea from each other, Ephesus and Corinth shared regular communications and commerce. While Paul was in Ephesus, he learned of several issues that were troubling the Corinthian church. So he wrote to help correct the problems.

The book of 2 Corinthians is especially concerned with outside teachers who have come to Corinth. These men have established themselves by minimizing Paul and his teachings and claiming to be more authoritative than Paul. Paul sarcastically referred to these men as "the very chiefest apostles," a description they may have used for themselves (2 Corinthians 11:5; 12:11). Paul was not frightened by their tactics, and he was never willing to claim anything less than full apostolic authority.

In this week's lesson, we find Paul responding to these opponents by giving his credentials. His résumé is not full of degrees and honors, however, but of multiple instances of suffering for the gospel. His point is that his ability to survive hardship was not due to his own personal strength, but to the grace of God that had sustained him throughout his ministry.

I. Paul's Boasts in Strength (2 Corinthians 11:17, 21b-30)

Boasting is normally seen as an unpleasant mannerism. Paul views boasting as dangerous. He is particularly negative about any boasting that implies that we earn God's favor by our good deeds (see Romans 4:2). Boasting is also to be avoided when it is based on outward appearances (2 Corinthians 5:12).

It is a little surprising, then, that Paul goes on a boasting spree in this part of 2 Corinthians! However, when we examine the text closely we will learn why Paul seems to boast. We will understand where his heart really is.

A. Boasting in Foolishness (v. 17)

17. That which I speak, I speak it not after the Lord, but as it were foolishly, in this confidence of boasting.

One way to expose foolish behavior is to exaggerate it. Paul's rivals (see the description of them in the Lesson Background) seem to have a propensity for *boasting*. Paul responds with some big-time bragging of his own. In so doing, he intentionally plays the part of a fool. What follows are numerous boasts in what is sometimes called the Fool's Speech.

We should not miss what lies behind this for Paul. He knows full well that a boasting match is foolish and that any confidence gained by tooting one's own horn is false. His response, then, is not so much true boasting, but a self-defense against the arrogant and unjust attacks of his opponents. At the same time, he fights fire with fire to show the shallowness and weakness of their claims and character.

How to Say It

AEGEAN. A-*jee*-un.
AQUILA. *Ack*-wih-luh.
CORINTH. *Kor*-inth.
CORINTHIANS. Ko-*rin*-thee-unz (*th* as in *thin*).
DEUTERONOMY. Due-ter-*ahn*-uh-me.
EPHESUS. *Ef*-uh-sus.
GENTILES. *Jen*-tiles.
LYSTRA. *Liss*-truh.
PRISCILLA. Prih-*sil*-uh.

TELLING STORIES

Aesop, who lived in the sixth century BC, was famed for his fables. Who among us doesn't remember hearing "The Tortoise and the Hare" and "The Boy Who Cried Wolf" as a child? One of his lesser-known fables is "The Boasting Traveler."

It seems that a man who had traveled widely was given to much boasting about his journeys and exploits (just like some modern travelers). He told of heroic things he had done in foreign lands. For example, he said that in Rhodes he had demonstrated athletic prowess so great that no one else could leap anywhere nearly as far as he had. He claimed that many had seen him do so, and he could call them as witnesses, if need be.

A man in the audience replied, "Sir, if this is all true, there is no need for witnesses. Simply pretend this is Rhodes and leap for us." There was no reason the bragging traveler could not repeat his fabled jump for his current audience—unless, of course, the story was not true!

Most people are tempted to boast occasionally. However, someone has wisely observed, "When we sing our own praises, we invariably pitch the tune too high." Paul was not doing this. He was speaking truthfully in order to put to shame his critics, who were magnifying their own credits to the harm of the church. —C. R. B.

B. Boasts of Background (vv. 21b, 22)

21b, 22. Howbeit, whereinsoever any is bold, (I speak foolishly,) I am bold also. Are they Hebrews? so am I. Are they Israelites? so am I. Are they the seed of Abraham? so am I.

As will be shown abundantly, Paul is as *bold* as anyone is. With the terse statement *I am bold also* Paul casts down the gauntlet to those who challenge his commitment and credentials. He is inferior to no one in his service to Christ.

First, Paul's authority cannot be trumped just because his opponents are Jewish Christians. Paul is as Jewish as one can be. He uses three synonyms to describe this: Hebrew, Israelite, and *seed of Abraham*, all pointing to the same thing. Paul's Jewish heritage is undeniable.

C. Boasts in Trials (vv. 23-27)

23. Are they ministers of Christ? (I speak as a fool,) I am more; in labors more abundant, in stripes above measure, in prisons more frequent, in deaths oft.

Paul now focuses his "boasting" upon his ministry credentials. He measures himself in several ways. First, he claims to have worked harder than his opponents have *(labors more abundant)*. Second, Paul has received far more *stripes*, so many he can't remember them all (example: Acts 16:23). The word behind *stripes* is similar to the word *plague,* and it indicates a blow to the body. If administered by a whip, this will leave a stripe on the flesh.

Third, Paul has been jailed more often (example: Acts 16:24). There are hints in Paul's letters that he is arrested many times for community disruptions in various places where he preaches the gospel (see Romans 16:7). Fourth, Paul declares that he has often been around death. This is his way of saying that he has been in deadly danger many times (2 Corinthians 1:9, 10). [See question #1, page 112.]

We should not miss Paul's tone here. He reminds us that he is speaking *as a fool,* meaning as one who has lost his mind. Paul's bragging is not normally acceptable behavior. It is necessitated by the tactics of his opponents. If they think they can win a war of credentials, they have awakened a slumbering giant who will overwhelm their claims of superiority.

24. Of the Jews five times received I forty stripes save one.

We lack the historical specifics to identify all of these instances, but we are not in the "countless" stage here. First, Paul carefully remembers abuse he has suffered from *the Jews.* These had been instigated by various synagogues that he angered because of his claims about Jesus. *Five times* he received the synagogues' most severe punishment: forty lashes with a whip (see Deuteronomy 25:1-3). It is customary for the Jews to withhold one of these blows, perhaps to avoid a miscount—thus *forty stripes save one.*

25a. Thrice was I beaten with rods.

Paul also remembers three times when he was *beaten with rods,* or what we might call "caned." This is less severe, but still tortuous. These may have been punishments inflicted by Gentiles. [See question #2, page 112.]

25b. Once was I stoned.

One time Paul suffered mob violence in the form of a stoning. This was instigated by out-of-town Jews in Lystra during Paul's first missionary journey (Acts 14:19). Stoning is intended to cause death. Paul's escape from this intended execution can be seen only as miraculous (Acts 14:20).

25c. Thrice I suffered shipwreck, a night and a day I have been in the deep.

Paul has been the victim of *shipwreck* on three occasions thus far. We know of one shipwreck in Acts, the shipwreck at Melita (or Malta; Acts 27:14–28:1). This will occur about AD 61, several years after 2 Corinthians is written. So it is not one of the three in view here. We can only imagine the over-

whelming sense of hopelessness caused by drifting in the ocean for many hours, far from land.

26. In journeyings often, in perils of waters, in perils of robbers, in perils by mine own countrymen, in perils by the heathen, in perils in the city, in perils in the wilderness, in perils in the sea, in perils among false brethren.

Travel in the ancient world is neither easy nor safe. Paul lists eight types of danger he has braved in traveling for the sake of the gospel. First, he has experienced dangerous water hazards. Paul is talking about rivers in mentioning *perils of waters,* not sea voyages. Many rivers are unbridged in his day, and ferrying in small boats is always risky.

Second, Paul recognizes the continual threat of bandits who haunt the remote roadways. Third, the apostle is consistently hounded and threatened by Jewish opponents, who follow him to stir up trouble (example: Acts 17:13). Fourth, Paul is also at risk from *the heathen* (Gentiles), some of whom see his message as a threat to their way of life (see Acts 16:20, 21).

Paul goes on to list three geographic scenarios he frequently encounters: in a *city,* out in the *wilderness* on his travels between cities, and on the ocean in a boat. He has already illustrated some of the dangers in each place: Jewish opponents in the cities, bandits in the wilderness, and shipwrecks on the sea. Paul is saying that no matter where he goes, he faces danger. He cannot escape it, nor does he try.

Finally, Paul mentions the danger that must hurt him the most: *false brethren.* It is one thing to be on guard against known enemies. It is another thing to find out that your enemies are people whom you thought were friends. This is a subtle warning to the Corinthians: they dare not allow "the very chiefest apostles" to turn their hearts against Paul!

27. In weariness and painfulness, in watchings often, in hunger and thirst, in fastings often, in cold and nakedness.

Paul now illustrates his sufferings by listing things that affect his physical body. He lives with *weariness and painfulness,* meaning he is always tired and he always hurts. He experiences frequent *watchings,* meaning nights with little or no sleep. He does not travel luxury class.

On the most basic level, Paul has days with nothing to eat or drink. He has to depend on the kindness of those he meets. Sometimes he receives no welcome hospitality. He has no warm bed and has to sleep "rough."

Nakedness here means having inadequate clothing, not being bare naked. Sleeping outdoors with light clothing leaves Paul with *cold,* restless nights.

This contributes to his feelings of being tired to the bone. If anyone has reason to complain about aching joints, it's Paul.

D. Boasts in Concern (vv. 28-30)

28. Beside those things that are without, that which cometh upon me daily, the care of all the churches.

The previous things are external assaults on the physical body. Paul is a tough old bird, and he won't let physical dangers and hardship slow him down. What burdens Paul more is his constant concern for the churches he has founded.

This pressure never eases for Paul. Will his churches remain faithful? Will they endure? Will they abandon Paul? This shows the apostle's great love and concern for the Corinthian church in particular. This is a church that has a special place in Paul's heart (2 Corinthians 7:3), a church for which he has a godly pride (2 Corinthians 7:4). He loves them with a shepherd's heart.

29. Who is weak, and I am not weak? who is offended, and I burn not?

Paul's deep love for the Corinthians is illustrated in two ways. First, he empathizes with their weaknesses. When they feel pain, he shares their pain.

Second, he is sensitive to what offends them. This is offense in the sense of a "stumblingblock," something that causes one to fall. Paul is passionate on this point. He will *burn* with indignation if someone tries to lead his beloved Corinthians astray. He will do whatever he can to protect his brothers and sisters in Christ. [See question #3, page 112.]

30. If I must needs glory, I will glory of the things which concern mine infirmities.

Paul winds up this Fool's Speech with an ironic summary of what he will *glory* in (boast about). He does not boast about his brilliance, eloquence, great knowledge, extensive accomplishments, or celebrity status. He makes the seemingly foolish statement that he will boast only about his *infirmities*. He refuses to use the tactics of bragging and instead turns the reader's attention to his weaknesses and trials. Paul's desire is that the Corinthians will see through him to the source of his strength: the empowering grace of Christ.

CURRICULUM VITAE

When a person applies for a job, the prospective employer looks for a statement of his or her job experience. For a "blue collar" job, this may be a list of previous employers and dates of employment. A "white collar" position requires a résumé. In the academic job market, the term used is *curriculum vitae,* literally, "the course of (one's) life."

The purpose of such a document is to show the applicant to be a strong candidate for the job. The person seeking a position as a college professor, for example, would include his or her academic pedigree, which is all those cryptic letters such as MA, PhD, EdD, etc. These give clues as to how much money one has spent, energy one has burned, and educational hoops one has jumped through to satisfy the academic world that one actually knows something about the subject one hopes to teach. Naturally, previous teaching and research experience are also listed.

Paul literally gives us a record of "the course of his life." In this case, it is not merely academic. And it is not to *get* a job; he already *has* one—he is an apostle! Rather, his record is the story of his heritage in Judaism, the sufferings he had endured for the cause of Christ, and his ongoing concern for his fellow Christians. The facts of Paul's life demonstrated his faithfulness. What do the facts of our lives demonstrate?   —C. R. B.

II. Paul's Strength in Weaknesses (2 Corinthians 12:9, 10)

Paul's youth was characterized by zeal and ambition (see Galatians 1:14). He must have felt cocky and self-sufficient when the high priest appointed him to lead a group of enforcers to Damascus (Acts 9:1, 2). Yet the Lord humbled him with blindness on that journey and has kept him humble ever since. Paul has learned that human strength is always inadequate to do the ministry to which one is called. Paul now moves beyond foolish talking to speak of one of the great paradoxes of the Christian life: when we are weakest, then we are strongest.

Home Daily Bible Readings

Monday, Nov. 24—Persecution in the World (John 16:25-33)

Tuesday, Nov. 25—Similar Suffering (1 Thessalonians 2:13-16)

Wednesday, Nov. 26—Present Suffering, Future Glory (Romans 8:18-25)

Thursday, Nov. 27—Through Many Hardships (Acts 14:21-23)

Friday, Nov. 28—Sharing Christ's Sufferings (1 Peter 4:12-19)

Saturday, Nov. 29—Come to Our Help! (Psalm 44:17-26)

Sunday, Nov. 30—Made Perfect in Weakness (2 Corinthians 11:16-18, 21-30; 12:9, 10)

A. Sufficiency in Grace (v. 9)

9. And he said unto me, My grace is sufficient for thee: for my strength is made perfect in weakness. Most gladly therefore will I rather glory in my infirmities, that the power of Christ may rest upon me.

Paul has been confessing a personal matter. He has a "thorn in the flesh" (2 Corinthians 12:7). We are not told what this is, but it may be a debilitating physical condition such as poor eyesight or difficulty walking. For Paul it is more than an irritant, because he sees it as a barrier to being as effective in ministry as he wants to be. He has prayed to be healed from this condition, but his request has been denied.

Why would this man, who heals others, be denied personal healing? The answer is that God has been using the infirmity to humble Paul and to teach him the power of *grace*. The person who recognizes his or her many weaknesses becomes a ready tool whom God can use. We believe that "all things work together for good to them that love God" (Romans 8:28), even our weaknesses. God can use any person with a willing and obedient spirit. In the end, Paul takes no credit for his remarkable ministry career. As he says, "By the grace of God I am what I am" (1 Corinthians 15:10). [See question #4, page 112.]

B. Pleasure in Pain (v. 10)

10. Therefore I take pleasure in infirmities, in reproaches, in necessities, in persecutions, in distresses for Christ's sake: for when I am weak, then am I strong.

Paul's identity and self-worth cannot be separated from his dedication to the service of Christ. For

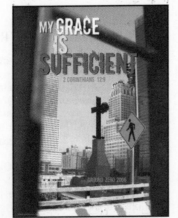

Visual for
Lesson 13

Use this visual to connect verse 9 to a modern event: the 9/11 terrorist attacks.

Paul, suffering for Christ is a privilege (Philippians 1:29). He puts this very simply later when he states, "For to me to live is Christ, and to die is gain" (Philippians 1:21). [See question #5, page 112.]

The body of Christ is full of *weak* people. We are disabled, disturbed, diseased, distressed, and dying. Paul calls the Corinthians to recognize God's strength coming out of human weakness. We too should hear his plea. We can support and help one another through the grace and mercy of God. We can bear one another's burdens with the spiritual strength that only Christ will grant to each believer.

Conclusion

A. It Can't Get Any Worse?

More than once I have heard people in the middle of terrible circumstances say, "Well, it can't get any worse than this." Let us not fool ourselves. It can always get worse. We can be driven to our knees and then knocked flat by life's circumstances. On any given Sunday, churches are populated by men and women who have been beaten up terribly all week. Although we rarely share the true depths of our troubles, many of us live day to day with fears. Joy can be elusive and fleeting.

"Why does God allow suffering?" is a popular question. A better question may be, "How does God use suffering?" The Bible teaches that all people suffer at one time or another. God may use our suffering to "break" us. Just as a horse has no value for human use until it is "broken," we are not useful to God until we have been broken, for God is able to use "a broken and a contrite heart" (Psalm 51:17).

The psalmist teaches us not to be afraid to walk through the "valley of the shadow of death" because God is always with us (Psalm 23:4). Paul teaches that the church should be a community of shared suffering and joy (1 Corinthians 12:26). May we always walk with God, and may we walk with our brothers and sisters through those dark nights of the soul.

B. Prayer

Father, our boasting is ridiculous when we consider Your power and magnificence. Our suffering is minor in light of Your grace. When we feel strong, help us to understand that we are still weak. Your grace is sufficient for us. May our confidence be in You and You alone. In Jesus' name we pray, amen.

C. Thought to Remember

We are weak without the grace of Jesus Christ.

Learning by Doing

This page contains an alternative lesson plan emphasizing learning activities. Some of these activities are also found in the helpful student book, Adult Bible Class.

Into the Lesson

Before class, write the following list on the board: *accidentally on purpose, baggy tights, cold sweat, definite maybe, escaped inmate, forgotten memories, gentleman bandit, icy hot, jumbo shrimp, kosher ham, ladies' man.*

When you're ready to begin, say, "Do you know what such phrases are called?" Someone should recognize these as *oxymorons.* Ask the class if they can think of any other oxymorons to add to the list; write them on the board.

Then say, "We have two oxymorons in our lesson text today, as Paul talks about *pleasurable suffering* and *strong weakness.* Let's take a look at today's text and see how he was able to harmonize these seemingly self-contradictory ideas."

Into the Word

The following activity compares the kinds of suffering a modern Christian might complain about with the kinds of suffering Paul experienced. Create a two-column chart on letter-size paper. Title it *You Think That's Bad!* The column headings are *Christian Complainer* and *Paul's Experiences.*

Put the following quotes on separate rows down the left column: 1. "I had to go down to the city jail at midnight to bail out a kid from my youth group." 2. "I tried to intervene when I saw a man abusing his wife, and I got punched in the nose." 3. "The tent I slept in for Family Camp weekend leaked, and I ended up sick." 4. "While driving to visit shut-ins, my windshield was cracked by a rock thrown up by an 18-wheeler." 5. "The kayak I was in on a young adult outing overturned; I got soaked and lost my water bottle." 6. "I'm so tired of the half-hour drive to church each Sunday." 7. "Every time I go to the downtown mission to work in the soup kitchen, I'm afraid I'll be robbed." 8. "No more all-night sleepovers at the church building for me! I need my eight hours." 9. "If they don't start increasing the heat in the auditorium, I won't be back!" 10. "Being the chairperson for the Missions Committee is really a heavy burden!"

Distribute copies of the chart to your students and ask them to form small groups to work on completing it. Say, "Often we think we have good reason to complain when our Christian service results in suffering. However, if we compare our suffering with what Paul experienced, his will top ours every time. Use the list of Paul's hard times from 2 Corinthians 11:23-30 to find corresponding (but much worse) experiences for which Paul could say, 'You think that's bad; listen to what happened to me!'"

Allow time for groups to share their examples from the text. Expected answers are 1. "in prisons more frequent" (v. 23); 2. "five times received I forty stripes save one" and "thrice was I beaten with rods" (vv. 24, 25); 3. "in deaths oft" (v. 23); 4. "once was I stoned" (v. 25); 5. "thrice I suffered shipwreck, a night and a day I have been in the deep" (v. 25); 6. "in journeyings often" (v. 26); 7. "in perils of robbers" (v. 26); 8. "in weariness and painfulness, in watchings often" (v. 27); 9. "in cold and nakedness" (v. 27); 10. "the [daily] care of all the churches" (v. 28).

Into Life

Distribute all three of the following case studies to all the small groups. Ask each group to select one of the case studies and suggest an ending in which the grace of Christ is demonstrated and those who are weak become strong.

Case Study #1. A father who has been out of work for several months has just run out of unemployment benefits. Although he has looked for work, he has been unsuccessful and now is very discouraged. The family has exhausted its savings and has no money for next month's rent. Family members share their worry with their small group.

Case Study #2. After her husband dies, a woman tries hard to maintain the home in which she has lived for many years. However, she has no family close by to help her. As her arthritis becomes worse, she is no longer able to do the yard work. She tells a Christian friend how sad she is because she thinks she will have to sell her home and move into a condo.

Case Study #3. Parents of a teenage daughter with serious emotional problems struggle to find a therapy or program that will help her. They finally locate an excellent facility, but it is outside their price range and far from their home. They ask their church family for prayer support as they try to find a solution to their dilemma.

Close by asking for volunteers to suggest how they will apply 2 Corinthians 12:9, 10 to one area of life in the week ahead.

Let's Talk It Over

The questions on this page are designed to promote discussion of the lesson by the class and to encourage application of the lesson Scriptures. The answers provided are only discussion starters. Let your class talk it over from there.

1. In what ways do we sometimes find ourselves in harm's way as followers of Christ? How are these the same as or different from the dangers that Paul faced?

The difficulties we face in our walk with Christ usually do not compare exactly with those Paul speaks of. Yet there are still difficulties. One is the potential for economic harm. When a Christian stands for biblical principles, this may put him or her at odds with an unscrupulous boss. Failing to go along with the company plan can mean the loss of a job. At other times the harm may be the loss of friendships when we refuse to go along with the crowd in participating in some unchristian entertainment or lifestyle. But there is nothing we can go through that other Christians before us haven't faced as well. God still reigns.

2. Do you think that it is possible to prepare for suffering physically for one's faith? Why, or why not?

Bum Phillips, who was head coach of the Houston Oilers from 1975 to 1980, was once asked why he didn't have his team practice in freezing weather in preparation for games that would take place in such a climate. His response? "You can't practice being miserable."

When applied to Christianity, that may be true regarding bodily preparation, but what about mental preparation? In many cultural settings, there is not a lot of concern about the possibility of facing physical persecution for living a life of faith. But this could lead to a false sense of security and make one mentally unprepared should persecution come. Therefore, the first step in mental preparation for persecution is to acknowledge that persecution can happen.

Beyond this, one can do no more (and should do no less) than live a life of faithfulness daily. When we are faithful in the day-to-day Christian life, this strengthens us for the more difficult times (see James 1:3-5). Consistency in the spiritual disciplines of Bible reading, prayer, study, worship, etc., is a must.

3. What are some practical ways to demonstrate solidarity with those saints who are enduring persecution in the world today?

From Afghanistan to China, from Indonesia to the Sudan, physical persecution against Christians is real. Much of the persecution stems from religious groups that have no tolerance for any view besides the one they profess. The reporting of these persecutions is sadly lacking in much of today's news.

As a first order of business, Christians can make themselves aware of what is happening among other Christians in the world. Then we will be able to pray in an informed way for them. Information is available, for example, at the Web site www.persecution.org. Christians can also make government officials in their own nation aware of what is happening elsewhere. This can result in intervention of a political or economic nature against those nations where persecution exists.

4. What are some ways that God's strength is made perfect in your own weakness?

When Christians face difficulties or become aware of weaknesses, naturally we want an immediate fix for the problem. But God may not want to "fix" the problem! He may have a bigger plan in mind.

As we seek God to work in and through our weaknesses, we can practice patience. Scripture reminds us that "they that wait upon the Lord shall renew their strength; they shall mount up with wings as eagles; they shall run, and not be weary; and they shall walk, and not faint" (Isaiah 40:31). Trusting God's knowledge of what is best for us allows us to find strength in our weakness. Just as we realize that we are not able to save ourselves, but rather rely on God's grace, so we learn to trust Him in all things.

5. What is the significance of the phrase "for Christ's sake" in your own life?

Certain cultures place much emphasis on the individual and promote the idea that the individual should look out for self first. In the church, we may slip into adopting this outlook. When that happens, Christians are guilty of allowing culture to force them into its mold. Better is it to approach life from the view of Christ. This means humbling self and preferring others above self (see Romans 12:9-21). That's what Christ did on the cross.

Winter Quarter 2008–2009

Human Commitment
(Character Studies)

Special Features

Lessons

Unit 1: Commitment to the Messiah

Unit 2: Old Testament People of Commitment

Christ and Creation

Unit 1: The Promise of New Life

About These Lessons

People have varying levels of commitment to all kinds of things. This fact is very useful, because it reveals where a person's heart truly lies. Are we committed to the right things? The winter lessons provide the confrontation we need in this regard.

Dec 7

Dec 14

Dec 21

Dec 28

Jan 4

Jan 11

Jan 18

Jan 25

Feb 1

Feb 8

Feb 15

Feb 22

Mar 1

Quarterly Quiz

The questions on this page may be used in several ways: as a pretest at the beginning of the quarter; as a review at the end of the quarter; or as a review after each lesson. The questions are based on the Scripture text of each lesson (King James Version). **The answers are on page 116.**

Lesson 1

1. Mary's song of praise in Luke 1 is similar to a prayer of what Old Testament woman? (Ruth, Hannah, Deborah?) *1 Samuel 2:1-10*

2. Mary said that all future generations would call her _____. *Luke 1:48*

Lesson 2

1. Of whom was Elisabeth the mother? (Zechariah, John the Baptist, Joseph?) *Luke 1:60*

2. Mary and Elisabeth were pregnant at the same time. T/F. *Luke 1:36*

Lesson 3

1. The sign to the shepherds that the Messiah had been born was that they would find a baby lying in a _____. *Luke 2:12, 16*

2. What was the initial reaction of the shepherds to the appearance of the angel? (fear, great joy, indifference?) *Luke 2:9*

Lesson 4

1. John the Baptist promised his audience that the Messiah would baptize with the Holy Ghost and with _____. *Luke 3:16*

2. Which group did John the Baptist tell to stop doing violence to others? (publicans, Pharisees, soldiers?) *Luke 3:14*

Lesson 5

1. The midwives told Pharaoh that they could not kill the male babies because the mothers gave birth before they arrived. T/F. *Exodus 1:19*

2. The problems of the children of Israel began when there was a new king over Egypt who did not know about _____. *Exodus 1:8*

Lesson 6

1. What was Rahab's occupation? (spy, cook, harlot?) *Joshua 2:1*

2. Rahab was the only resident of Jericho who was not killed when the city was destroyed by the Israelites. T/F. *Joshua 6:23*

Lesson 7

1. What was the first thing that crossed into the Jordan River before the nation of Israel? (ark of the covenant, pillar of fire, soldiers?) *Joshua 3:6*

2. On the day before crossing the Jordan River, Joshua told the people that they must _____ themselves. *Joshua 3:5*

Lesson 8

1. What was the king of Bashan a remnant of? (family of the Pharaohs, giants, tribe of Melchizedek?) *Joshua 13:12*

2. Some of the tribes of Israel received an inheritance of land on the east side of the Jordan River. T/F. *Joshua 13:7, 8*

Lesson 9

1. The Shunammite woman perceived that Elisha was a _____ man. *2 Kings 4:9*

2. Who was Gehazi? (Elisha's mother, Elisha's servant, Elisha's wife?) *2 Kings 4:12*

Lesson 10

1. Nathan told David a story about a poor man who kept a _____ as a pet. *2 Samuel 12:3*

2. As a result of his sin of adultery with Uriah's wife (Bathsheba), David's child died. T/F. *2 Samuel 12:14, 18*

Lesson 11

1. What would allow Esther to avoid death if she entered the king's court without being summoned? (king holds out his golden sceptre, king says "all is forgiven," king stands up from the throne?) *Esther 4:11*

2. Esther asked the Jews of Shushan to ____ for three days in preparation for her visit to the king. *Esther 4:16*

Lesson 12

1. Who died in the year that Isaiah received his vision of God's throne in Heaven? (Isaiah's wife Gehazi, the prophet Habakkuk, King Uzziah?) *Isaiah 6:1*

2. Isaiah had a live coal touched to his mouth by one of the _____. *Isaiah 6:6, 7*

3. Isaiah felt unworthy in the presence of God because he said he was a man with an unclean heart. T/F *Isaiah 6:5*

Note: Questions for the 13th lesson are printed with the spring quarter. See note on page 216.

Extras, Bits, and Stars

by Lloyd M. Pelfrey

IT WAS A PREMIER SHOWING of a Hollywood movie. Much of it had been filmed in a small town in Missouri, which had been transformed to appear as it may have been 150 years before. The theater chosen for the presentation was in a nearby town, and the management was willing to cancel its regular programming for the special event.

The persons present included some of the stars in the movie, bit players (at least one line of spoken dialogue), and the extras. The extras were volunteers from that part of the state. It was evident that most in attendance did not come to see the celebrities, but to see themselves in their minor roles in a major movie.

High-visibility events are often arranged so that politicians, generals, sports stars, etc., receive special recognition. Often overlooked are those ordinary people whose workaday efforts make it possible for others to receive that special recognition and honor. Every Christian has a role or function to fulfill before God. The daily outcome depends on whether the person is faithful in completing the tasks as assigned by God. Failure to fulfill the tasks compromises the functioning of the whole body, as the apostle Paul makes clear in 1 Corinthians 12:14-26.

The lessons for this quarter emphasize the theme of commitment. Some of the lessons are about individuals whose names are well-known to students of the Bible. Other lessons present people who have only "bit" roles. Nevertheless, those roles are important in accomplishing God's redemptive plan.

The quarter is unusual in that there are only 12 Sundays from the beginning of December through the end of February. The conscientious teacher or student who regularly uses these lessons is aware that there are normally three units of study for a quarter (one for each month) that total 13 lessons. That is not the case this time. There are only two units of study, and the second unit extends for two months.

Unit 1: December
Commitment to the Messiah

This month's lessons are from the book of Luke. There are three lessons about certain people associated with Jesus' birth: Mary, Elisabeth, and the shepherds. The fourth lesson is about John the Baptist. In **Lesson 1** Mary is at the home of Elisa-beth, and she responds to Elisabeth's greeting with an extended expression of praise. This reminds us of the song of thanksgiving by Hannah when she gave her son (Samuel) for service at the tabernacle. Mary's statement begins with herself, continues with praises of the Lord, and concludes by reviewing ways that the Lord has blessed Israel and the seed of Abraham.

Lesson 2 is based on the verses immediately prior to those used for Lesson 1. Elisabeth is one of the "bit players" in the New Testament's storyline. Even so, she is God's instrument to be the mother of John the Baptist, who was the forerunner of Jesus. In the midst of anticipating motherhood and the personal changes in her life, she receives an unexpected visitor—Mary, who is also pregnant. This prompts her to burst into an inspired statement of praise.

Their names are unknown to us, but the shepherds who were keeping watch over their flock by night also had roles to fulfill. In **Lesson 3** the study focuses on their receiving an announcement by an angel, the praise by a heavenly host, and the responses of the shepherds. Only one statement of the shepherds is recorded, but the events of that night cause them to return to their regular duties with joy and praise.

John the Baptist came in the spirit and power of Elijah (Luke 1:17). **Lesson 4** depicts the dynamic challenges of John as he spoke for God to prepare the way for the Messiah. John's purpose was to shake a spiritually lethargic people into repentance in preparation for the ministry of the Son of God on the planet that God loves. John's effectiveness was demonstrated in the responses of the people who came to hear him.

Unit 2: January and February
Old Testament People of Commitment

Lesson 5 offers us the names of two women of commitment: Shiphrah and Puah (Exodus 1:15). They were the midwives who feared God more than they feared the pharaoh of Egypt, and they would not put male infants to death. They demonstrated that loyalty to God can bring conflicts in the commitments of life.

Yes, even a prostitute can examine the evidence and come to faith in the one true God. That is Rahab in **Lesson 6**. This lesson will show us how she befriended and sheltered two Israelite spies.

That was a dangerous thing to do! But she committed herself to keeping her part of an agreement that ended up saving herself and her family. She later married an Israelite and became the mother of Boaz (Matthew 1:5), who was the husband of Ruth in the book of Ruth. In the New Testament, Rahab is praised for her faith (Hebrews 11:31) and her works (James 2:25).

"Instant gratification" was not a part of the life of Joshua! In **Lesson 7** we see him ready to lead Israel into Canaan after 40 years of faithful service and commitment in the desert. The promises made by God to Israel were about to be fulfilled. In faith Joshua gave the command to begin crossing the Jordan, even though it was in flood stage. The task before him seemed impossible, but he had learned that God rewards those who seek Him (Hebrews 11:6).

Lesson 8 involves another mother, the mother of Samson. It is reasonable to think that her spiritual walk did not begin with this encounter with the angel of God. But her experience that we see in this lesson intensified her awareness that her life had implications for God's plan. She was promised that she would bear a son, who was to be reared as a Nazarite. He would deliver his people from the Philistines. She may have wondered how her son would gather and lead the army that would do this. Little did she know how he would become a one-man army!

Sometimes Christians are accused of serving God for the benefits they expect to receive. **Lesson 9** is about an Israelite woman who gave of herself without expecting to receive anything in return. Her name is not known. She is simply designated as *the Shunammite woman*. She befriended Elisha and prepared the ideal guest room: a prophet's chamber for the man of God to use whenever he came that way. For her faithfulness, however, she received the promise of a son. The promise was fulfilled.

It is sometimes dangerous to be a preacher or prophet for God. In **Lesson 10,** we see the prophet Nathan being given the task of confronting King David with his sins. As Nathan pronounces those famous words "Thou art the man," he probably wonders about the response. Will it be retaliation or repentance? Psalm 51 demonstrates that David responded correctly with repentance. But not everyone has that reaction when confronted with personal sin.

Lesson 11 features Esther's dramatic and dangerous response when she was challenged by Mordecai to enter the presence of the king. Her goal was to request that the king spare the lives of her people—the Jews who lived throughout the Per-

sian Empire. Her commitment led her to ask that others join with her in fasting for three days prior to her bold move.

The final lesson of the quarter is about Isaiah, one of the great prophets in the Old Testament. **Lesson 12** recounts the call of Isaiah in which he saw God and His holiness. This contrasts vividly with the sinfulness Isaiah saw in himself. To "see" God forces us to see ourselves for what we are. We may look good when we compare ourselves with others, but to compare ourselves with God should cause repentance. A desire to serve Him completely will follow. We will say, with Isaiah, "Here am I; send me."

Only a Nail?

For want of a nail the shoe was lost,
For want of a shoe the horse was lost,
For want of a horse the rider was lost,
For want of a rider the battle was lost,
For want of a battle the kingdom was lost,
And all for the want of a horseshoe nail.

This famous rhyme may go back to the fourteenth century. It speaks of a domino effect that leads to a great loss. The rhyme is designed to teach faithful, lasting commitment to a task, for the negative consequences of shirking duties may multiply many times over.

The nails in the hands of Jesus are also important. They not only bound Him to the cross, but they also served to confirm faith for Thomas and others (Luke 24:39, 40; John 20:25-28). As these lessons lead into the season when Christ's death and resurrection are especially remembered, may we find in ourselves a resurgence of commitment that has positive effects into eternity.

Answers to Quarterly Quiz
on page 114

Lesson 1—1. Hannah. 2. blessed. **Lesson 2**—1. John the Baptist. 2. true. **Lesson 3**—1. manger. 2. fear. **Lesson 4**—1. fire. 2. soldiers. **Lesson 5**—1. true. 2. Joseph. **Lesson 6**—1. harlot. 2. false, Rahab's relatives were also saved. **Lesson 7**—1. ark of the covenant. 2. sanctify. **Lesson 8**—1. giants. 2. true: Reuben, Gad, and half of Manasseh. **Lesson 9**—1. holy. 2. Elisha's servant. **Lesson 10**—1. lamb. 2. true. **Lesson 11**—1. king holds out his golden sceptre. 2. fast. **Lesson 12**—1. King Uzziah. 2. seraphim. 3. false, he said he was a man of "unclean lips."

The Focus of Commitment

by Ronald L. Nickelson

BACK IN MY HIGH SCHOOL DAYS, I was quite fascinated with the game of chess. The combination of mental challenge and competition was irresistible to me. I would spend hours studying the intricacies of the game. I dreamed of becoming a grand master.

Well, it's now some 35 years later, and I have never come close to earning the designation *grand master*! But that fact does not cause me to view my hours of playing chess as wasted. To the contrary, the game of chess has taught me at least one invaluable life lesson: there's a big difference between *playing to win* and *playing to not lose*.

Unlike most athletic competitions, a tie game (called *a draw*) is very possible in chess. Everyone who sits down to play a game of chess knows this. It is a fact that can influence one's style of play greatly. Thus chess players—particularly those who compete at the higher levels—must face this question squarely: "Which is more important to me: *winning* or *not losing*?" Those who focus on not losing tend to have timid, passive styles of play. And this fact is not limited to the game of chess.

In War

Ed Rasimus flew an F-105 Thunderchief fighter-bomber during the Vietnam War. In 2003, he wrote a book entitled *When Thunder Rolled* to describe his experiences. F-105 pilots were expected to fly 100 combat missions against the enemy; after that, they could go home, transferring to much safer flying assignments. We may not be surprised to learn that the first 10 of those 100 missions "were deadly because of fear, lack of experience, and unfamiliarity with the whole pattern of war" (p. 256).

What we may find quite surprising, however, is the fact that the last 10 missions of those 100 were almost as dangerous as the first 10 in terms of the likelihood of being shot down. As Ed Rasimus describes it, at least part of the problem was an increase in timidity. No one wanted to take an unnecessary chance on being shot down on, say, his 99th mission. But such increased caution led to "indecision and apprehension."

The problem was a shift in mind-set from a commitment to winning to a commitment to not losing. Yet the cruel irony is that such a shift made those pilots even more likely to lose! I have discovered that the same is true in chess; others have found it to be true in the business world.

In Business

In years past, we have offered illustrations in the pages of this commentary involving the business strategies of Henry Ford and of the Montgomery Ward company. Henry Ford, for his part, was a hard-charging innovator in his early days. The design, cost, and production methodology of his Model T automobile were breakthroughs in the early part of the twentieth century.

But as time moved on, Henry Ford became cautious. He held on to the Model T as his company's flagship product for too long—18 years! The competition began to pass him by. The Model A that he eventually introduced to replace the Model T was almost "too little, too late." Long before his death in 1947, Henry Ford had shifted from being concerned with winning to being concerned with not losing. But it was that very shift that caused his company to lose ground.

The story of the Montgomery Ward company reads much the same. Following World War II, Americans began moving to the suburbs. Sears, Roebuck, and Co. followed them there, while archrival Montgomery Ward decided on a much more conservative strategy. That strategy seemed to be something like, "Get all you can, can all you get, and sit on the can." Montgomery Ward went bankrupt in 1997 and closed down in 2001.

In Christianity

So, what does the distinction between *being committed to winning* and *being committed to not losing* have to do with the Christian walk? Luke 19:11-27 offers us the answer.

That passage relates Jesus' famous Parable of the Ten Pounds. Before departing for "a far country," a certain nobleman entrusted his servants with money. Some servants multiplied their money many times over and were richly rewarded. But one particular servant merely put the money aside for safekeeping. When the master returned, that servant produced the money safe and sound. As a result, he was called "wicked" and ended up losing everything.

This quarter's lessons challenge our commitment in Christ. Are we committed to *winning* as we step out on faith? Or are we more concerned with *not losing* as we walk by sight? "The just shall live by faith: but if any man draw back, my soul shall have no pleasure in him" (Hebrews 10:38).

COMMITMENT Counts!

Mary
Luke 1:26-56

Elisabeth
Luke 1:39-45

Shepherds
Luke 2:8-20

John the Baptist
Luke 1:57-80

Midwives
Exodus 1:15-22

Rahab
Joshua 2:1-21; 6:17-25

Joshua

Samson's Mother
Judges 13:1-24

A Shunammite Woman
2 Kings 4:8-37

Nathan
2 Samuel 12:1-23

Esther
Esther 4:9-17

Isaiah
Isaiah 6:1-13

Expanding Your Preparation

Using Internet Resources

by Eleanor Daniel

MANY TEACHERS long for added resources to guide them in their study and preparation for teaching adults. Their personal resources have limitations, some more than others. Some do not live near a library that offers much in the way of biblical study resources.

But these limitations need not be a hindrance to effective preparation to teach—not in this day and age—if you have access to the Internet. Imagine expanding your resources exponentially! You can do it with the resources at your fingertips via the Internet.

[Special note: the listing of Internet sites in this article is not necessarily an endorsement of everything to be found on those sites. Some sites undoubtedly have been created by those who hold very different doctrinal convictions from your own. The watchword is "use discretion"!]

Resources for Nearly Any Lesson

Don't have a concordance? Not to worry, just go to www.biblegateway.com. This resource will allow you to search for key words and topics. Another helpful resource is www.answers.com. This site provides information for a variety of areas, not just religious studies. When you arrive at the page, click on the link for the two-minute tour. Once there, click on Content Library, where one of the choices is Religion. This section features, among other things, a Bible dictionary as well as comparative readings of Bible texts.

A third resource is www.bible-history.com. A long list of categories appears to the left of the screen. Some of these may aid your preparation. This site also includes a number of church history resources. A fourth general resource is the Resource Pages for Biblical Studies that is found at www.torreys.org/bible. Here you can find pages that examine texts and translations, electronic publications, and material relating to the social aspects of the Mediterranean world.

Standard Publishing has two Web sites that you will find helpful. To gain access to articles and essays in *The Lookout* magazine, go to www.lookoutmag.com. There you will find three weekly columns: Day by Day with the Bible, This Week with the Word, and The Lesson and Life. As the titles imply, these provide daily readings, brief notes on the text, and application of the weekly text to life.

Another resource from Standard Publishing is a treatment of the lesson each week at www.christianstandard.com, which is the home page of *Christian Standard* magazine. One of the topics on the menu is Sunday School Lesson, which features an essay that develops the lesson for the week.

Resources for This Quarter's Lessons

An avid Bible student will find many helpful resources from the list above to aid in teaching the lessons for the quarter. However, some resources may be of even greater help.

Lesson 1: Mary Praises God. Much has been written about Mary, the mother of Jesus. Some of this is quite factual, some is quite fanciful, with much in between. For interesting artwork, go to campus.udayton.edu/mary//gallery.html. Some material you find that deals with Mary in various places will overlap with information on Elisabeth, useful for **Lesson 2: Elisabeth Honors the Messiah.**

Lesson 3: Shepherds Glorify God. Who were the shepherds? An overview of shepherds and their lives in Bible times can be found at www.bibletexts.com/topical.htm; once you get there, click on the Shepherd link.

Lesson 4: John the Baptist Preaches God's Message. Questions and answers about John the Baptist are provided at www.pbs.org; once you get there, just type in "John the Baptist" (with quotation marks) in the little search box and hit *go*. References to John the Baptist in the Bible and in the writings of Josephus may be found at members.aol.com/fljosephus/JohnTBaptist.htm.

Lesson 5: Midwives Serve God. Your students may desire to know something about the skills and responsibilities of midwives in the ancient world. Go to a search engine such as Google and type in "ancient midwives" (with quotation marks). There will be dozens of hits.

Lesson 6: Rahab Helps God's People. The site www.jewishencyclopedia.com offers background material on Rahab and Jericho (type those two names into the search box). For more information on Jericho, try www.christiananswers.net and www.jewishvirtuallibrary.org. They can provide information about archaeological discoveries pertaining to the site.

Lesson 7: Joshua Leads Israel. Find a helpful overview on the book of Joshua and related material at www.biblehistory.net/Joshua.pdf. The site www.bible-history.com makes available maps showing the land of Palestine at the time of Joshua.

Lesson 8: Samson's Mother Prepares and **Lesson 9: A Shunammite Woman Hosts Elisha.** The site www.jewishencyclopedia.com offers information for both these lessons. In particular, you may want you to dig deeper into the meaning and significance of the Nazarite vow.

Lesson 10: Nathan Confronts David. The site www.newadvent.org is an online Catholic encyclopedia. When you get there, click on the *N* at the top, then click on Nathan to see a profile of that prophet.

Lesson 11: Esther Risks Her Life. Introductory material for the Book of Esther may be found at www.gotquestions.org; just search for the name of that book when you get there. Further information may be found at www.otgateway.com.

Lesson 12: Isaiah Answers God's Call. Coming back again to www.answers.com, you can get the biography of this prophet by typing his name on the search line. A very useful feature of this site is the many links that will take you elsewhere should you wish to do more research on Isaiah and his times.

Sites Providing Helps for Presentation

The lesson commentary you are now using provides many helpful illustrations, teaching outlines, teaching notes, and presentation methods. Power-Point® slides are available on the *Presentation Helps* CD in the *Adult Resources* packet. Even so, you may want to explore additional ideas to help you shape and present your lesson. Some helpful sites are:

www.bibleteachingnotes.com
www.bible.org/index.php
www.mintools.com/teaching-ministry.htm

These resources are not tied to any specific lesson. They will provide continuing help to enhance your teaching.

Criteria for Selecting Internet Resources

Just as every book on a topic in a library is not necessarily useful for every purpose, the same is true of Internet resources. Also remember that Internet resources can be posted far more easily than books can be published, making it possible for anyone to distribute any notion or falsehood via the Internet easily. For example, problems with www.wikipedia.org have been noted in this regard. So be selective in what you use. Here are a few guidelines:

• Make sure to explore general resources (such as those listed in the first section above). Tried and true Bible dictionaries, maps, and treatments of history such as those at Bible Gateway will generally serve you well.

• Treatments of texts such as those found on *The Lookout* and *Christian Standard* sites are also good places to begin. These are not exhaustive treatments of the text, to be sure, but they provide a tone and direction that can serve as a helpful comparison with other material you find.

• When you find unfamiliar ideas and theories, see how those square with accepted resources. If they disagree, search a bit more to see if you find the unfamiliar view critiqued by other sites.

• Information from Web sites by biblical studies professors at reputable colleges and seminaries often are good to use for comparison with ideas acquired from other, lesser known sites.

• Discuss your findings—especially those of which you are uncertain—with your minister or another knowledgeable Bible teacher in your congregation.

Even after you've had opportunity to determine the worth of the material, it's still vital to "be selective." In fact, it is only after you have done your evaluation of a site's material are you equipped to be selective.

Conclusion

Internet resources expand your opportunities for study and presentation of Bible lessons. The Internet provides a library at your fingertips. But one additional caution is in order: *There are no shortcuts to good preparation.*

Internet sites, as much information as they may give you, cannot prepare for you. You have to search-and-read, assess the validity of the information, assemble (and sometimes discard) that information, and weave what is useful and relevant into your presentation. A Web site cannot determine the key idea you will emphasize in the lesson. Nor can it shape the outline or choose the teaching methods and illustrations. A big pile of information left unorganized is just that.

In other words, you still have to do the hard work of preparation if you want to teach effectively. But if you use your expanded study possibilities wisely and prepare well, you will enjoy the fruits of your labor as you present effective Bible lessons.

Mary Praises God

DEVOTIONAL READING: 1 Samuel 2:1-10.

BACKGROUND SCRIPTURE: Luke 1:26-38, 46-55.

PRINTED TEXT: Luke 1:46-55.

Luke 1:46-55

46 And Mary said, My soul doth magnify the Lord,

47 And my spirit hath rejoiced in God my Saviour.

48 For he hath regarded the low estate of his handmaiden: for, behold, from henceforth all generations shall call me blessed.

49 For he that is mighty hath done to me great things; and holy is his name.

50 And his mercy is on them that fear him from generation to generation.

51 He hath showed strength with his arm; he hath scattered the proud in the imagination of their hearts.

52 He hath put down the mighty from their seats, and exalted them of low degree.

53 He hath filled the hungry with good things; and the rich he hath sent empty away.

54 He hath holpen his servant Israel, in remembrance of his mercy;

55 As he spake to our fathers, to Abraham, and to his seed for ever.

GOLDEN TEXT: My soul doth magnify the Lord, and my spirit hath rejoiced in God my Saviour.—Luke 1:46, 47.

Human Commitment
Unit 1: Commitment to the Messiah
(Lessons 1–4)

Lesson Aims

After participating in this lesson, each student will be able to:

1. List three elements of praise in Mary's song.
2. Explain one connection between Mary's song and the Old Testament.
3. Write a four-line praise stanza.

Lesson Outline

INTRODUCTION
   A. Short- and Long-term Commitments
   B. Lesson Background
 I. LORD'S BLESSINGS MAGNIFIED (Luke 1:46-48)
   A. Expression of Worship (vv. 46, 47)
   B. Expression of Amazement (v. 48)
 II. LORD'S ATTRIBUTES APPRECIATED (Luke 1: 49, 50)
   A. Acknowledgment of Power (v. 49a)
   B. Acknowledgment of Holiness (v. 49b)
   C. Acknowledgment of Mercy (v. 50)
      Our Merciful God
III. LORD'S FAITHFULNESS EXTOLLED (Luke 1:51-55)
   A. Recognition of Power (v. 51)
      Which Strength Is Most Important?
   B. Recognition of Justice (vv. 52, 53)
   C. Recognition of Aid (v. 54)
   D. Recognition of Trustworthiness (v. 55)
CONCLUSION
   A. Mary as an Example for Christians
   B. Prayer
   C. Thought to Remember

Introduction

A. Short- and Long-term Commitments

Recently, I signed up for a new cell phone. I was told that if I made a two-year commitment, I would get a deep discount on the phone I wanted. This meant that I had to sign up for one of the phone company's service plans. If I canceled this plan and switched to another carrier before the end of the two years, I would have to repay the discount on my new phone. Therefore, I made a commitment that was not based on the wonderful service of the cell phone company, but primarily on my desire to save a few hundred dollars.

Since this was my fourth cell phone obtained under these kinds of circumstances, I had no problem in making the commitment. In my mind, 24 months was relatively short-term, not an odious condition for a substantial savings. The clock began ticking toward the end of this commitment the day I signed the agreement. Every month when I pay the bill, I will reduce the length of this commitment by one twenty-fourth. At the end of the two years, I expect that my phone will be a technological fossil, and I will shop for a new phone and a new plan; I will be willing to make a new commitment.

Many years ago, God led me to a woman who became my wife. When we were married, the minister asked us if we were committed "for richer, for poorer" and "in sickness and in health." The commitment was for "so long as you both shall live." We have kept that commitment to each other. We understood it as a long-term commitment with no exact end date. We still intend to be married until we are parted by death.

When I was a teenager, I made a commitment to Jesus Christ. This was not an altogether easy commitment for me to make, because I knew this would determine the direction of my life. But on one particular day, I made a vow to serve Jesus and to trust Him as my Savior. I publicly promised this and was baptized into Christ on that same day. I really had no idea what all this commitment would require of me and where it would lead me. But it is a commitment with no end point. I intend to serve Jesus every day of my life and to live with Him for all eternity.

B. Lesson Background

Today's lesson comes from Luke's account of the events leading up to the birth of Jesus the Messiah. The calendar system devised to begin with this birth is off by a few years, so we date today's text as having taken place about 5 or 6 BC. The two main characters in this part of Luke's story are Mary, a young woman from Nazareth, and Elisabeth, her older relative.

Nazareth was a Jewish village in the Galilee region, about 70 miles north of Jerusalem and 15 miles west of the Sea of Galilee. We are not told the name of Elisabeth's city, just that it was in the Judean hill country (Luke 1:39, next week's lesson). Some think that Elisabeth and her husband, Zechariah, lived in the village of En Karem, located a few miles west of Jerusalem. Today, En Karem is the location of several churches and shrines associated with John the Baptist (the son of Elisabeth and Zechariah).

This week's lesson is about what happened when Mary visited Elisabeth. Mary's ability to make such a trip is a bit of a puzzle to us. Mary was yet to be married, so she was very young, perhaps 15 or 16 years old. For a young village girl to go from Nazareth to En Karem alone would have been unthinkable. Some students propose that Mary's family was relatively wealthy, and therefore she was safely accompanied by servants. Others suggest that Mary spent her early years in Jerusalem, with the journey from Jerusalem to En Karem being no more than a day's excursion. Mary thus could have made this trip many times. But these are just guesses.

Although the age gap between Mary and Elisabeth was 30 years or more, the two seem to have had a special bond that transcended generations. Both had become pregnant in miraculous ways, and Mary was eager to share with Elisabeth. Pregnant women, especially first-timers, often have a tie of fellowship that is difficult for others (especially men) to appreciate. This special bond is an important factor in both this and next week's lessons.

I. Lord's Blessings Magnified (Luke 1:46-48)

When Mary arrives at the home of Elisabeth, the older woman blesses the younger. That is the subject of next week's lesson. Mary's "Song of Praise" in response is famous in the world of music and literature. Writers have used it as the basis for devotional contemplation and reflection. Music composers have made it into glorious choral masterpieces such as Johann Sebastian Bach's "Magnificat" (that being the first word of the Song of Praise in the Latin translation).

The Song of Praise shows affinities to Hannah's prayer in the Old Testament (1 Samuel 2:1-10). Both are beautiful expressions of devotion to God and praise for His power.

A. Expression of Worship (vv. 46, 47)

46, 47. And Mary said, My soul doth magnify the Lord, and my spirit hath rejoiced in God my Saviour.

Mary begins her Song of Praise with recognition of how blessed she is to have been chosen by God to give birth to the Messiah. We see the strong character of this young woman, who, rather than being terrified by an unplanned pregnancy, is ecstatic in her praise to the Lord.

Right away we should notice that the Song of Praise is filled with parallel lines (that is, two lines that express the same concept in different words). This is the primary characteristic of Hebrew poetry, often found in the Psalms and other places. Mary's use of this ancient technique shows both the excellence of her mind and the beauty of her *soul*.

To *magnify the Lord* does not imply that Mary thinks she is able to increase the size of God, for the concept of "size" does not apply to our creator. We magnify God by lifting up our praise for Him, by proclaiming His greatness more and more. This concept is found frequently in the Old Testament (see 2 Samuel 7:26; Psalm 34:3; 69:30).

The concept of spiritual joy is another well-known theme in the Bible. Often joy is associated with the presence of God's Holy Spirit (see Luke 10:21; Acts 13:52; 1 Thessalonians 1:6). Paul taught that joy was part of "the fruit of the Spirit" (Galatians 5:22). Here, Mary finds cause for rejoicing *in God* her *Saviour.* She finds joy and comfort in the role she has been assigned in God's plan. [See question #1, page 128.]

B. Expression of Amazement (v. 48)

48. For he hath regarded the low estate of his handmaiden: for, behold, from henceforth all generations shall call me blessed.

A *handmaiden* is literally a female slave. This is the term that Mary applied to herself when she first understood God's call and submitted to it back in Luke 1:38. She makes no demands and sets no conditions for her submission. She has a heart of pure commitment that is marvelous for us to contemplate.

Mary is undeterred by her *low estate,* meaning her humble circumstances. Many factors contribute to making her an unlikely choice to be a primary tool for God's mighty purposes. She is very young, thus she has had little chance to earn the trust and respect of her community to this point. She probably has minimal education. She is from a village far from Jerusalem, the center of Israelite power and tradition.

None of this matters for the soul who is truly willing to serve God with all her heart, strength,

---

How to Say It

BABYLON. *Bab*-uh-lun.
BABYLONIANS. Bab-ih-*low*-nee-unz.
EN KAREM. In Kuh-*rim*.
GALILEE. *Gal*-uh-lee.
HAMAN. *Hay*-mun.
HANNAH. *Han*-uh.
JEREMIAH. Jair-uh-*my*-uh.
MAGNIFICAT. Mag-*nif*-ih-cot.
MESSIAH. Meh-*sigh*-uh.
NAZARETH. *Naz*-uh-reth.
ZECHARIAH. Zek-uh-*rye*-uh (strong accent on *rye*).

and mind. Mary has a measure of prophetic insight, for she is able to rejoice in the fact that future generations will see her as specially *blessed*.

II. Lord's Attributes Appreciated (Luke 1:49, 50)

Effective praise needs specifics. The great praise passages of the Bible are full of reasons to praise God. This can include both the divine attributes and the mighty deeds of the Lord. Mary now personalizes her praise for the ways God has worked in her life.

A. Acknowledgment of Power (v. 49a)

49a. For he that is mighty hath done to me great things.

Confessing that God *is mighty* is the acknowledgment of God's all-powerful nature (compare Genesis 17:1; Revelation 1:8). Prophetically, this characteristic is to be attributed to the Messiah, who himself is to be called "mighty God" (Isaiah 9:6).

B. Acknowledgment of Holiness (v. 49b)

49b. And holy is his name.

Perhaps we associate holiness with quietness, meekness, and passivity. We make such an association when we think of the personality traits of people whom we consider to be especially *holy*. Yet the Bible often connects the power of God with His holiness (example: Revelation 4:8). The unfathomable power of God is unique and incomparable. He is the all-powerful creator, separate from His creation. *Holy is his name!*

C. Acknowledgment of Mercy (v. 50)

50. And his mercy is on them that fear him from generation to generation.

The Old Testament speaks of God punishing iniquity across generations (see Exodus 34:7; Numbers 14:18). But Mary chooses to speak of the Lord's continuing *mercy* that *is on them that fear him* as she thinks across the generations. [See question #2, page 128.]

Modern people usually associate *fear* with evil things. We are terrified by deep depravity and criminality. The fear of the Lord has nothing to do with evil, however. To fear God is a matter of pure respect and reverence. It is to understand our position of weakness and neediness in relation to God.

This is the starting point for a life of wisdom (Psalm 111:10). To fear God is more than just a wise course, however. It is our duty (Ecclesiastes 12:13).

OUR MERCIFUL GOD

Matthew McGee, age 14, nearly drowned one Saturday a few years ago. He and Preston Harp were surfing at Torrey Pines State Beach near San Diego when something went wrong. No one knows what happened, but Preston looked around and couldn't find Matthew. Finally, he saw Matthew floating facedown in the water. Preston dragged Matthew toward shore and two cardiologists who were walking along the beach ran to help save the boy's life.

The next day, Matthew was back at the beach, this time to be baptized (as he had previously planned). Matthew's minister referred to the doctors and friend who saved him and said, "You're here today because God has a plan." Whether or not we agree with the minister's doctrine, we can agree that God's mercy acted upon Matthew that unforgettable day.

When God offered Mary His plan for her life, she could have said, "No thanks. That sounds like too much trouble for me." Instead, she praised God for having done "great things" for her. She may have seen in her pregnancy a predicament with insuperable social difficulties. However, she rejoiced at the mercy God had shown her in giving her this opportunity. Her life would count for more than it ever would have otherwise. What mercies of God have made a difference in your life?   —C. R. B.

III. Lord's Faithfulness Extolled (Luke 1:51-55)

The way of the world is that the rich and powerful often take advantage of the poor. This oppression is decried by the Old Testament prophets, who teach that God is Lord of both rich and poor. "Hear this word, ye . . . which crush the needy. . . . The Lord God hath sworn by his holiness, that, lo, the days shall come upon you, that he will take you away with hooks" (see Amos 4:1, 2).

In the eyes of God, a ruler must be just (2 Samuel 23:3) and must be a champion for the poor and

---

VISUALS FOR THESE LESSONS

The visual pictured in each lesson (example: page 125) is a small reproduction of a large, full-color poster included in the *Adult Resources* packet for the Winter Quarter. That packet also contains the very useful *Presentation Helps* on a CD for teacher use. The packet is available from your supplier. Order No. 292.

needy (Psalm 72:4). The Lord's unwavering commitment to the weak and helpless is an expression of His faithfulness to men and women. In the final section of the Song of Praise, Mary worships God for His faithfulness.

A. Recognition of Power (v. 51)

51. He hath showed strength with his arm; he hath scattered the proud in the imagination of their hearts.

The strong *arm* is an Old Testament figure for the active justice of God. Jeremiah foretold that God would be on the side of the Babylonians against the rebellious Jews in the battle for Jerusalem in 586 BC. God would "fight against [the Jews] with an outstretched hand and with a strong arm, even in anger, and in fury, and in great wrath" (Jeremiah 21:5). In battle, the *scattered* army is the defeated army (Jeremiah 52:8).

Mary understands that God is working actively to knock *the proud* off their high horses. This is not a physical, blood-and-guts battle as in 586 BC. It is waged at the seat of pride, *the imagination* of the heart. In this, Mary perhaps sees the spiritual nature of the future ministry of the child she carries. Jesus will wage a battle for souls. Just as God always prevailed in the past, His mighty faithfulness will win this battle too. [See question #3, page 128.]

WHICH STRENGTH IS MOST IMPORTANT?

Statistics show that babies whose birth weight is less than 5.5 pounds have a much higher mortality rate than normal-weight infants. Underweight infants are often premature, lacking the normal developmental time in the womb. If such children survive, they are at risk for numerous physical and mental abnormalities, as well as a shortened life expectancy. The risk is even worse for severely underweight newborns of less than 3.3 pounds.

By this standard, a 13 pound, 6 ounce baby born in 2004 to a 35-year-old mother in Monterrey, Mexico, should be a "poster child" for health and longevity! (Amazing as this is, it is not the record.) Generally speaking, a relatively large baby carried to full term has developmental advantages over premature, smaller babies.

As Mary anticipated the nature of her yet-to-be-born son's future, she envisioned Him acting in the mighty power of the Lord in some way. Whatever her baby's birth weight, it was His future spiritual strength that occupied Mary's attention. Good prenatal care is important for a child to have the strength to survive outside the womb. But how many parents-to-be think also of the spiritual strength their children should have?   —C. R. B.

Visual for Lesson 1. *This visual depicts the personalities of this quarter's lessons. Keep it posted all quarter to provide commitment reminders.*

B. Recognition of Justice (vv. 52, 53)

52. He hath put down the mighty from their seats, and exalted them of low degree.

Modern people enjoy tales of triumph by underdogs. Ancient people likely are no different. We may think of Esther, the clever and faithful Jewish girl who resisted the intrigues of the powerful Haman with the result that Haman was destroyed. Also compelling are the stories of Daniel and his companions, who resisted the decrees of the mighty kings of Babylon.

Equally loved are the stories of ancestors who rose from humble beginnings to positions of great power. Joseph went from being a slave in prison to being the master of Egypt. David left the solitary life of a shepherd to become a great king. The irony of Jesus' life is that in His greatness He becomes the servant of all (see Mark 9:35). Paul tells us that Jesus left His secure place in Heaven and humbled himself to become a man. God has now exalted Jesus above all others (Philippians 2:6-9).

53. He hath filled the hungry with good things; and the rich he hath sent empty away.

This role reversal of the *rich* and the poor is continued (compare 1 Samuel 2:5; Psalm 107:9). Later in Luke, Jesus teaches that the poor will be blessed and their hunger will be satisfied (Luke 6:20, 21). In contrast, Jesus says the rich will be turned away hungry (Luke 6:24, 25).

The coming of God's Messiah is to be a working out of His justice, bringing good news to the poor. When Jesus reads Scripture in the synagogue of His hometown Nazareth, He picks this passage: "The Spirit of the Lord is upon me, because he hath anointed me to preach the gospel to the poor" (Luke 4:18).

C. Recognition of Aid (v. 54)

54. He hath holpen his servant Israel, in remembrance of his mercy.

Holpen is an older English form meaning "helped." We should remember that helping the nation of *Israel* is first and foremost in the ministry of Jesus. Jesus will later teach that He is primarily sent "unto the lost sheep of the house of *Israel*" (Matthew 15:24).

The coming of the promised Messiah is to be understood as an act of great *mercy* to the nation in accordance with God's promises; God will indeed "perform the mercy promised to our fathers" (Luke 1:72). Israel has learned the lesson that it cannot survive without God's mercy, as shown in His consistent aid for the nation.

A strong theme in the Old Testament is the necessity of "waiting" for the Lord to show His mercy to the people. "And therefore will the Lord wait, that he may be gracious unto you, and therefore will he be exalted, that he may have mercy upon you: for the Lord is a God of judgment: blessed are all they that wait for him" (Isaiah 30:18; compare Luke 2:25). Now this mercy has been shown in the womb of Mary. This part of the waiting is over! [See question #4, page 128.]

D. Recognition of Trustworthiness (v. 55)

55. As he spake to our fathers, to Abraham, and to his seed for ever.

Mary ends her Song of Praise by recalling the most basic and central of Israel's heritage of promises from God. This is the promise *to Abraham* that his descendants *(his seed)* are to become a great nation. "And I will make of thee a great nation, and I will bless thee, and make thy name great; and thou shalt be a blessing" (Genesis 12:2; compare 17:7; 22:17).

Mary recognizes that God keeps His promises. This is the essence of trustworthiness. For this poor, pregnant teenager of "low estate," the trustworthiness of the Lord is the lifeline she needs to sustain her. [See question #5, page 128.]

Conclusion

A. Mary as an Example for Christians

Are you committed to too many things? Do you find yourself running between church, school, family, job, hobbies, sports, social events, band concerts, shopping, fitness clubs, and many other commitments? Has anyone ever told you that you must learn to say *no* when asked to do more things? If this describes you, you may have a problem with overinvolvement, but this is not necessarily a commitment problem.

True commitment is not a scheduling problem. It is not measured by the level of one's busyness. Commitment, rather, is a deep matter of the heart. It involves both a selfless willingness to serve and a clear sense of priorities. Ironically, commitment to God does not always mean "Let's get busy right now." Commitment to the Lord starts with slowing down and carefully discerning His will and His work.

Think about that: commitment begins with slowing down! If we take the opposite path, the path of "diving right in," we run the risk of missing what God may be trying to tell us through the subtle clues that He likes to give. We may become more and more inefficient as we become more and more frantic in our busyness.

This quarter's lessons will teach us much about commitment. They will do so by examining the lives of important Bible characters. Mary was one who slowed down and took time to praise God. She was faithful to Jesus throughout His life and did not abandon Him even at His execution. She is pictured after the resurrection as a person of deep faith and prayer (Acts 1:14). These are the reasons we still should call Mary "blessed."

B. Prayer

Heavenly Father, when we see the praise that poured from Mary's heart, we cannot help but be moved. This young woman loved You very dearly. May our hearts become like hers, full of joy in serving You. May we never lose the wonder of being allowed to serve You. We pray this in the name of Mary's son Jesus, Your Messiah. Amen.

C. Thought to Remember

Make Mary's praise your own.

Home Daily Bible Readings

Monday, Dec. 1—The Prayer of Hannah (1 Samuel 2:1-10)

Tuesday, Dec. 2—Gabriel's Announcement (Luke 1:26-33)

Wednesday, Dec. 3—Mary's "Let It Be" (Luke 1:34-38)

Thursday, Dec. 4—Simeon and Mary (Luke 2:25-35)

Friday, Dec. 5—Do What He Tells You (John 2:1-11)

Saturday, Dec. 6—Praying with the Disciples (Acts 1:6-14)

Sunday, Dec. 7—Praise for God's Mercy (Luke 1:46-55)

Learning by Doing

This page contains an alternative lesson plan emphasizing learning activities. Some of these activities are also found in the helpful student book, Adult Bible Class.

Into the Lesson

Do one or both of the following activities.

Activity #1. Brainstorm a list of commitments that people make. Give a few examples, such as a two-year commitment to a cell phone plan or a commitment in marriage that includes "in sickness and in health." Write responses on the board.

Make the transition to the next activity (or to the Into the Word segment) by saying, "Some commitments are for a brief time period. Others involve serious and difficult responsibilities. But our greatest commitment is one that we make to the Lord. This lesson begins a series of examples of people who have demonstrated 'carry through' with their commitments—even when the commitment brought great stress. One of these examples is Mary, the mother of Jesus."

Activity #2. Give the students hymn books or song books with Christmas songs. Ask them to identify lines or phrases that speak of Mary, the mother of Jesus. Write these lines on the board. Make the transition to the Into the Word segment by saying, "Mary is a main character in the Christmas story. Mary's faith, as she faced social ridicule and gossip, is also an excellent model for accepting and completing a commitment to the Lord."

Into the Word

Begin the Bible study with a brief lecture on the background of today's lesson. Then group your students into three teams and distribute the supplies noted at the end of each assignment below. Also give teams photocopies of their assignments. Each team will report its findings to the rest of the class.

Team #1. Your task is to prepare a poster listing three major elements of Mary's praise. Then search Mary's "Magnificat" and find words or phrases she uses to describe God's character or actions that are expressions of praise. List these words or phrases under each of the three major elements of praise. (Supplies needed: poster board, marker, a photocopy of the lesson outline from the lesson commentary.)

Team #2. Your task is to explain some of the key words or significant concepts that Mary uses in her "Magnificat." Use the lesson commentary to help prepare your explanations. List the following words or phrases on the poster board and be ready to explain their significance to the class: "magnify" (v. 46); "rejoiced" (v. 47); "low estate" (v. 48); "holy is his name" (v. 49); "fear him" (v. 50). (Supplies needed: poster board, marker, a photocopy of the lesson commentary on verses 46-50.)

Team #3. Your task is to discover and explain the significance and depth of Mary's commitment that she indicates in verses 48-50. Jot the clues to this commitment, along with your notes, on the poster board. Be ready to explain your discoveries to the class. (Supplies needed: poster board, marker, lesson commentary on verses 48-50.)

Into Life

Ask the following three discussion questions and jot responses on the board. If your class is large and open discussion will take too much time, assign one question to each of three small groups. After a few minutes of small-group discussion, have a representative of each group summarize its conclusions. (You may find it saves time and increases understanding to put these questions on a handout ahead of time.)

1. What does Mary's "Magnificat" teach us about the type of person God chooses to use in accomplishing His will? What traits does God need in His servants?

2. Mary faced huge hurdles in fulfilling God's will for her. What does her song teach us about commitment to God, even in the face of hurdles?

3. What are some hurdles people face in today's world that may challenge their commitment to the Lord?

Next, challenge the class with a creative writing activity. Say, "Think of the commitment each of you has made to God. Many times we face deep hurdles in keeping our commitment to Him. But there is also great joy in keeping it. Along these lines, write one new verse to the tune of a familiar Christmas song."

Tell the class that they may find ideas from the notes on the posters or the lists on the marker board. Here is an example of a song by one suffering from arthritis, to the tune of "Away in a Manger":

My Savior, I love you; in my heart you reign!
I need you to help me be faithful in pain.
Discouragement tempts me; I wonder "why me?"
Then, Jesus, I remember, a new body I'll see.

Let's Talk It Over

The questions on this page are designed to promote discussion of the lesson by the class and to encourage application of the lesson Scriptures. The answers provided are only discussion starters. Let your class talk it over from there.

1. What was a time when you were so happy that you felt like bursting forth in song? Why were you happy, and what song did you want to sing?

Mary's heart was filled with the joy of being chosen by the Lord for special service. Her spontaneous expression of joy and faith must have pleased her Lord. We are encouraged to express ourselves "in psalms and hymns and spiritual songs, singing and making melody" in our hearts to the Lord (Ephesians 5:19). There are times when our expressions of joy must be in song; no other form of communication will do.

There is no limit to the number of songs that could be mentioned. Some songs that express joy are secular. The melodies of movie sound tracks are etched in our brains. But how much better it is to meditate on Christian songs! Secular songs of joy focus on self; Christian songs of joy focus on God. This distinction has something to say about how we answer the question *What song did you want to sing?*

2. How could Mary, young as she was, speak with such confidence about God's great mercy and other attributes? What does this tell us about the capabilities of teenagers today?

Mary must have had a good understanding of the Old Testament. Her song of praise is much like Hannah's prayer in 1 Samuel 2:1-10. The parallels are striking. Good hymnody will flow from good doctrine. When we are saturated in the Word of God, our praise will be fueled by the Word of God. It is evident that Mary knew the Word of God.

Mary's understanding also suggests that she had received good religious training, probably from her parents. Like Timothy, she may have been taught the truths of Scripture from an early age (2 Timothy 1:5). Never underestimate the influence that parents have on their children!

3. What one word would you choose to describe Mary's attitude as revealed in her song? Why did you choose that word?

Your students may answer with a word that describes a fruit of the Spirit as listed in Galatians 5:22, 23. Mary was loving, joyful, peaceful, long-suffering, and gentle. She was faithful, full of goodness, and meek. These characteristics are evidence that the Holy Spirit was prominent in her life.

There are many other words that could come to mind. Committed, worshipful, and obedient are just three. Students will respond to this question based on how the Scripture communicates to their own situations. At one level, the Word of God speaks the same truth to everyone. At another level, it speaks a personalized message to those who seek to understand its practical applications.

4. How is God showing His mercy in your own life right this moment?

Answers will be highly personal, of course. You may round out the discussion by stressing how blessed we are to see the love of God manifested in Mary's life. This glimpse should help us understand the great love He has for us.

In a broad sense, God's most merciful act is to extend to us that He extended to Mary: the invitation to participate in His work as He enters our lives. He desires to use each of us as vessels for His holiness. Saying *yes* to God's invitation ought to fill us with genuine praise. God has been merciful to us through the incarnation of Christ within us.

5. As you consider the qualities of God described in Mary's song, what was an occasion where you saw one of those specific qualities displayed? What was your reaction?

The Lord has done "great things" for many of your students. God has proved himself mighty in hundreds of ways! Some individuals have seen complete medical recovery when doctors offered little hope. Others have seen broken relationships restored. Some of your students may have had a financial burden lifted through an unexpected source. The blessing can seem the greatest when the times seem the darkest.

In our lifetimes, we have seen some of what Mary sang about come to pass. We have seen ungodly rulers providentially removed from their positions. Our God has fed the hungry and ministered to the widow and the orphan. Indeed, God has been merciful to us. This might be a good opportunity to count our blessings.

Elisabeth Honors the Messiah

December 14
Lesson 2

DEVOTIONAL READING: Isaiah 7:10-14.

BACKGROUND SCRIPTURE: Luke 1:5-24, 39-45.

PRINTED TEXT: Luke 1:39-45.

Luke 1:39-45

39 And Mary arose in those days, and went into the hill country with haste, into a city of Judah;

40 And entered into the house of Zechariah, and saluted Elisabeth.

41 And it came to pass, that, when Elisabeth heard the salutation of Mary, the babe leaped in her womb; and Elisabeth was filled with the Holy Ghost:

42 And she spake out with a loud voice, and said, Blessed art thou among women, and blessed is the fruit of thy womb.

43 And whence is this to me, that the mother of my Lord should come to me?

44 For, lo, as soon as the voice of thy salutation sounded in mine ears, the babe leaped in my womb for joy.

45 And blessed is she that believed: for there shall be a performance of those things which were told her from the Lord.

GOLDEN TEXT: Elisabeth was filled with the Holy Ghost: and she spake out with a loud voice, and said, Blessed art thou among women, and blessed is the fruit of thy womb.—Luke 1:41, 42.

Human Commitment
Unit 1: Commitment to the Messiah
(Lessons 1–4)

Lesson Aims

After participating in this lesson, each student will be able to:

1. Retell the story of the meeting between Mary and Elisabeth.

2. Explain the role of faith in the life of one who is used by God in significant ways.

3. Express appreciation to one other person for how God is working in his or her life.

Lesson Outline

INTRODUCTION
    A. Commitment
    B. Lesson Background
I. HASTY VISIT (Luke 1:39, 40)
    A. Mary Departs (v. 39)
       Making Haste
    B. Mary Greets (v. 40)
II. SUPERNATURAL SIGNS (Luke 1:41)
    A. The Unborn Leaps (v. 41a)
       Heightened Awareness
    B. The Spirit Stirs (v. 41b)
III. GREAT BLESSINGS (Luke 1:42-45)
    A. Selection of Mary (v. 42)
       Blessing Mary
    B. Son of Mary (vv. 43, 44)
    C. Steadfastness of Mary (v. 45)
CONCLUSION
    A. Qualifications for Service
    B. Prayer
    C. Thought to Remember

Introduction

A. Commitment

Many years ago, a college-aged war protester was photographed holding a sign that said, "Nothing is worth dying for." This picture was on the front page of many newspapers, and his claim generated lively discussion on campuses. It is one thing to protest a war; it is quite another thing to claim that nothing is worthy of absolute allegiance. To die for something is the ultimate commitment. The question at the time was this: Was this sign an expression of a world whose only absolute commitment was to noncommitment?

This quarter's lessons seek to help us understand commitment from a biblical perspective. *Commitment* is difficult to define adequately and tricky to evaluate initially. Sometimes, we have no idea of the breadth or the depth of a commitment until it is put to the test, for in the end commitment must be demonstrated rather than simply verbalized. The groom who is truly committed to his bride will honor his vows of fidelity to her. The woman who is committed to her children will sacrifice her time, her comfort, and even her personal happiness to see them thrive. The believer committed to his church will give his time and money to it in significant ways.

Last week's lesson looked at the commitment of Mary, the mother of Jesus. This week, we consider another player in the drama surrounding Jesus' birth: Mary's relative Elisabeth. These two women have much to teach us about commitment, both to God and to each other.

B. Lesson Background

In the Jewish households of the ancient world, the birth of a baby was no less a special event than it is today. The "barren woman" of Old Testament times was a married woman who failed to get pregnant. Her lack of children was a huge disappointment to her husband. Furthermore, it was the cause of pain in her own life; it was an unfilled void. Therefore, there was great joy when a woman who had been childless for many years was blessed with children (see Psalm 113:9). This barren-woman-become-mother was the situation of Elisabeth in today's lesson. She understood her pregnancy in old age not as an inconvenience, but as a blessing (Luke 1:25).

Today's text takes this joyous commitment of two mothers to their unborn sons and factors in their deep commitment to God and His plan for the nation of Israel. The women experienced miraculous pregnancies—pregnancies that could be only God's work. They were both affected by angelic visitations. They both had husbands who struggled to come to terms with these events. And in the end they both submitted fully to God's will and allowed their bodies to become vessels for the working out of His will.

The opening narrative of Luke tells the story of Zechariah and Elisabeth. They were a married couple who believed that parenthood had passed them by. They were no younger than age 40, for they were described as being "well stricken in years" (Luke 1:7). It would be unusual in Elisabeth's day for a woman to experience a first pregnancy even in her late twenties or her thirties. Women married very young, and if there were no pregnancy within a year or two of the consummation of a marriage, the woman was considered to be *barren*, unable to have children.

Both Zechariah and Elisabeth were from Judaism's priestly tribe, the Levites (Luke 1:5). Zechariah was a member of the priestly course of Abijah, 1 of 24 such divisions. Members of each of these divisions served as temple workers for a week at a time in Jerusalem on a twice-yearly rotation. These priests lived elsewhere the rest of the year.

Elisabeth is described as being of "the daughters of Aaron," meaning the daughter of a priest. Zechariah was dutiful to serve at the Jerusalem temple when his division's time came up (Luke 1:8). We may surmise that since they had not been granted children, they had directed their devotion toward this type of service.

I. Hasty Visit
(Luke 1:39, 40)

Most people have had to make a "quick trip" at some point in their lives, a hasty excursion that didn't allow for much advanced planning. Such trips are occasioned by unforeseen emergencies or special opportunities. Today's text begins with such a journey.

A. Mary Departs (v. 39)

39. And Mary arose in those days, and went into the hill country with haste, into a city of Judah.

Previously, *Mary* was visited by the angel Gabriel. Mary learned during that visitation that she was to be the mother of the Messiah. Her initial response was to submit to God's will and offer herself as a servant (Luke 1:38). Although she demonstrated great faith in this surrender of her life, she was troubled (Luke 1:29). The angel also told Mary that her relative Elisabeth was experiencing God's grace in a miraculous pregnancy of her own (Luke 1:36).

How to Say It

FORTUNA. For-*too*-nuh.
GABRIEL. *Gay*-bree-ul.
HANNAH. *Han*-uh.
ISAAC. *Eye*-zuk.
JUDAH. *Joo*-duh.
MANOAH. Muh-*no*-uh.
PRUDHOE. *Prew*-doe.
REBEKAH. Reh-*bek*-uh.
ZECHARIAH. *Zek*-uh-*rye*-uh (strong accent on *rye*).

There are few options available to Mary when it comes to finding someone in whom to confide. Elisabeth has not experienced a virginal conception (she has been married for many years), yet her pregnancy in old age is also miraculous. Such a pregnancy is understood in the Old Testament as a sign of a son who will be appointed by God for a special function. This was the case of the sons of Sarah (Genesis 17:19), Rebekah (Genesis 25:21), the wife of Manoah (Judges 13:3-5), and Hannah (1 Samuel 1:5, 20).

On the other hand, Mary's pregnancy is unique. There is no reason to tag her as *barren* since she has not yet consummated her marriage. A virginal conception is without precedent and is understood as a key fulfillment of the prophecy of Isaiah 7:14 (compare Genesis 3:15).

As Mary reaches Elisabeth's house, which is located in a certain *city of Judah,* we see these two women stand together at this point in history as beautiful, devoted souls. Their lives are dramatically changed by God's touch. [See question #1, page 136.]

MAKING HASTE

How long do you think it would take you to drive from the northernmost point in Alaska to the southernmost tip of Florida? Here's a hint: the distance from Prudhoe Bay, Alaska, to Key West, Florida, exceeds 5,400 miles. In 2004, it took Gary Eagan of Salt Lake City only 100 hours to make the trip on a motorcycle.

Also imagine riding a motorcycle some 2,900 miles from New York City to San Francisco in 47 hours and 41 minutes. Michael Kneebone did just that, in the process setting a 24-hour endurance record of 1,704 miles. One might imagine that the speed limit was broken along the way!

Mary and Elisabeth lived in slower-moving times, making their world a much smaller place than ours, figuratively speaking. They would have been surprised at the distance we can travel in a single hour. Haste is a relative idea. Mary's journey "in haste" would be agonizingly slow to us today. Yet its purpose was certainly nobler than either of the two time-and-distance achievements noted above! Do we have the perspective to acknowledge this fact?   —C. R. B.

B. Mary Greets (v. 40)

40. And entered into the house of Zechariah, and saluted Elisabeth.

The house of Zechariah may be quite small, with just one primary room. Upon entering, Mary finds the goal of her journey: *Elisabeth.* Although the text indicates the salutation is verbal (Luke 1:41,

44), the word translated *saluted* carries the idea of an embrace. Thus we can imagine the scene of the teenager spilling out many words and hugging her elderly relative, whose body is well along with her own pregnancy.

Elisabeth hid her pregnancy for the first five months (Luke 1:24), and its news may not have traveled to Elisabeth's kin in Nazareth until after the angelic announcement (Luke 1:36). Yet for Elisabeth's part, there seems to be no surprise that Mary has come to visit her. [See question #2, page 136.]

II. Supernatural Signs
(Luke 1:41)

God's involvement does not stop with the two miraculous pregnancies. The special presence of God enlivens the reunion of Elisabeth and Mary.

A. The Unborn Leaps (v. 41a)

41a. And it came to pass, that, when Elisabeth heard the salutation of Mary, the babe leaped in her womb.

The detail revealed in this verse is remarkable. Pregnant women normally experience movement of their unborn babies (compare Genesis 25:22), but this is different. When Elisabeth realizes who her visitor is, Elisabeth's baby (who will come to be known as John the Baptist) leaps *in her womb.*

John's assigned function is to be the forerunner of the Christ and to identify Him to others. Incredibly, he seems to begin this ministry even before his birth! This places John in the prophetic tradition of the great Jeremiah, who acknowledged that God knew him and set him apart for ministry before his birth (Jeremiah 1:5). John is indeed "filled with the Holy Ghost, even from his mother's womb" (Luke 1:15).

The ancient Jews understand the baby in the womb as a true person, capable of having a relationship with God (Psalm 139:13; compare Hosea 12:3). While the relationship between God and an unborn baby is very simple, it is understood to be pure and holy. Therefore, Elisabeth simply cannot ignore the powerful sign she receives from her womb. She takes great joy in the message of her son.

The son of Zechariah and Elisabeth becomes the prophetic figure who plays a vital part in God's messianic plans. The Old Testament had prophesied the coming of an Elijah-like figure to prepare Israel for the coming of the Christ (Malachi 4:5). Luke, in particular, emphasizes the importance of John's ministry, even in his second book (Acts 13:24, 25; 19:3, 4).

John serves several functions in the Gospels. He preaches a strong ethical message that causes the people to examine their lives and repent of their sin. He performs baptisms. He publicly identifies Jesus as the Messiah and points people to Him (see John 1:29-34).

HEIGHTENED AWARENESS

The heightened security awareness since September 11, 2001, created trouble for a man in Escondido, California. A fire engineer was standing outside a business establishment when two men walked by carrying a gas can. They asked where they could buy diesel fuel for their car. As the men passed by, the fire engineer's small radiation detector went off.

A few minutes later, the men returned and the monitor sounded again. The alarm sounded a third time when the fire crew drove by the man's car. Since diesel fuel can be used for making bombs and the detector was indicating a radiation source, the engineer called the sheriff, who stopped the driver. The car was free of radiation, but the driver himself set off the detector. The (confirmed) explanation was unexpected, but simple: he had received a radiation treatment for a medical condition earlier in the day.

Elisabeth had no high-tech device to alert her of Mary's condition. Nevertheless, the Spirit provided a heightened awareness to the baby developing in Elisabeth's womb. Thus the baby could detect (although at a very elemental level) the coming of the Messiah! Why do you think so many full-grown adults are unable to detect the presence of the Messiah today?   —C. R. B.

B. The Spirit Stirs (v. 41b)

41b. And Elisabeth was filled with the Holy Ghost.

The Gospel of Luke reveals a great interest in the Holy Spirit (see Luke 3:16; 4:1; 11:13; 12:12). Elsewhere as here, Luke presents a person as being *filled with the Holy Ghost* in order to utter a prophecy (see Luke 1:67; compare 2:25, 26). Therefore, Elisabeth's words that follow constitute a divinely inspired word from God. She is acting in a prophetic manner on this occasion.

III. Great Blessings
(Luke 1:42-45)

In the Bible, to be *blessed* is a sign of God's favor. It is more than the fortunate results of our hard work or the unexpected favorable outcome of a stressful situation. By contrast, to the pagans of the ancient world a *blessing* is a gift of good fortune from a god or goddess (such as the goddess *Fortuna*) that can be bestowed or withheld capriciously according to the whims of the fictitious deity.

We refer to the blessings of the Bible as *beatitudes,* and there are many examples (Numbers 24:9; Psalm 118:26; etc.). Jesus himself gives blessings numerous times in the Gospel of Luke (examples: Luke 6:20-22; 7:23; 14:15). Elisabeth's blessings are not gifts from her, but constitute a prophetic recognition of God's favor upon Mary and the baby in her womb.

A. Selection of Mary (v. 42)

42. And she spake out with a loud voice, and said, Blessed art thou among women, and blessed is the fruit of thy womb.

Elisabeth's words are not privately whispered to Mary, but proclaimed loudly enough to be heard by anyone nearby. Elisabeth does not waste words, but pronounces a simple blessing on Mary and a second blessing on Mary's child.

Why, though, should Mary be considered to be *blessed*? [See question #3, page 136.] An evaluation of her circumstances according to twenty-first century sensibilities could say that she has been cursed. She is very young, pregnant, and unmarried. We know from another account that her future husband's first reaction to her pregnancy is to ponder canceling the betrothal, which is the same as divorce (Matthew 1:19).

If Joseph carries out this action, Mary's chances of marriage and a "normal" life will be almost nil. Her son will be born illegitimately. She will be stuck with a taint in the small town of Nazareth for the rest of her difficult life. The answer to our question about why Mary should be considered blessed is given in the next part of Elisabeth's prophetic utterance.

BLESSING MARY

Protestant Christians (as well as those who prefer to be known as simply *Christian*) have tended to keep verse 42 at arm's length. The reason for this avoidance is due to the fact that the Roman Catholic Church has made the passage into a ritual of praise for the Virgin Mary and has attached certain questionable doctrines to it. But is this reason enough for us to shy from acknowledging Mary's special blessedness for bearing the child who would become the Messiah?

Think about it: Would we refuse to drive an automobile because cars are used by certain people in ways we disapprove of? Would we demand that police officers be disarmed because some people use firearms carelessly? If members of a group

Visual for Lesson 2. *Point to this visual as you ask, "In what ways does this image speak to the blessings of belief?"*

we disapprove of brush their teeth, does that mean we refuse to brush ours?

Elisabeth set an example for us when she pronounced a blessing on Mary. Mary was indeed blessed by the Lord. She had been honored with the sacred task of bringing the chosen one of Israel into the world so that He might become the Savior of the world. For certain, we should not *worship* Mary (or any other human being). But there is a measure of respect that is due her from all who love and serve the child she bore. After all, if God approved of this young woman's life and character, shouldn't we?
　　　　　　　　　　　　　　　　—C. R. B.

B. Son of Mary (vv. 43, 44)

43, 44. And whence is this to me, that the mother of my Lord should come to me? For, lo, as soon as the voice of thy salutation sounded in mine ears, the babe leaped in my womb for joy.

Elisabeth clearly understands the root cause of blessing in this situation. Mary, her young relative, has been chosen to be *the mother of* the Lord! [See question #4, page 136.]

The New Testament speaks often of God's divine plan of providing for human redemption by sending His Son (see John 3:16, 17; Galatians 4:4). Yet we can think of many other ways in which the Son of God could have come into the world. He could have appeared as a full-grown man, ready to begin His work on day one. He could have been born into one of the wealthy households of Jerusalem, where He would have had easy access to the venues of power and influence. He could have come to earth on a cloud of glory, giving instant credibility to His mission by the nature of His appearance.

But God chooses none of these avenues for the advent of the Lord Jesus. The Messiah begins His human existence in the womb of a peasant girl from an insignificant village of poor reputation (John 1:46). From Mary and Elisabeth we learn that no person who is willing to serve God should underestimate his or her value. God does not look upon our outward appearance or circumstances. The Lord looks instead at our hearts (see 1 Samuel 16:7).

C. Steadfastness of Mary (v. 45)

45. And blessed is she that believed: for there shall be a performance of those things which were told her from the Lord.

Mary has the one requirement that God needs to make His plan work: faith. She is *blessed* because she believes. [See question #5, page 136.] Her submission to God's will leads to the fulfillment of the angel's fabulous predictions for her son. Her boy will grow to be the true heir of David's throne, to preside over an eternal kingdom, and to be understood as the Son of God himself (see Luke 1:33-35).

It is difficult for us to appreciate fully how key Mary's role is in all of this. At this stage, the creator of the universe entrusts His plan to save sinful humankind to a teenaged girl of simple yet powerful faith. We marvel at this plan, even twenty centuries later.

Conclusion

A. Qualifications for Service

An elderly friend of mine once confided to me that his early goal in life had been to become a fighter pilot in the Air Force. As a young boy he had done all he could to prepare himself. He had read voraciously and knew extensive details about every plane in active service. He had worked to keep himself fit so he would be able to pass a physical.

Eventually, he applied and was accepted into a pilot training program. In the end, though, he washed out because his eyesight was slightly below the necessary standard. He went on to have a productive career in another field and to raise a family of wonderful children, but the desire of his heart was denied because he did not meet the standards of qualification.

What sorts of qualifications do we need to enlist in the service of the Lord? Today's lesson is about two key players in the divine drama of human salvation, and we can learn much by examining their lives. We don't know about their eyesight, but we do know that both lived in tiny villages and probably had minimal educations.

Neither Elisabeth nor Mary could bring great influence or wealth to the task of ministry, but both possessed loving, submissive hearts. They were women of faith, and they were committed to each other. They did not permit rivalry to enter their relationship. Because of these and other factors, God trusted them to be the mothers of John the Baptist and Jesus the Christ.

The basic qualifications for God's service are commitment to the Lord and commitment to His people. Such commitment finds its source in faith. But this is not "blind faith" as the world might think of when it hears the word *faith*. This is faith based on evidence. Both Elisabeth and Mary had evidence from Israel's history. They also had the evidence of their miraculous pregnancies.

God can always use one who has submitted to His authority and strives to do His will. As another marvelous woman of faith, Christina Rossetti (1830–1894), wrote, "What can I give him, poor as I am? . . . [I] give my heart."

B. Prayer

Everlasting Father, may we find encouragement in the examples of two of Your great servants, Mary and Elisabeth. Their circumstances were humble, yet their hearts were rich. As Mary was pronounced blessed for her faith, may we continue to receive Your bounteous blessings as we too walk in faith. And should You need us for a task as great as You entrusted these women with, may we be found worthy. We pray these things in the name of Mary's son, our Savior, Jesus Christ. Amen.

C. Thought to Remember

God still blesses faithful, committed people.

Home Daily Bible Readings

Monday, Dec. 8—Do Not Pass By Your Servant (Genesis 18:1-8)

Tuesday, Dec. 9—Hope for the Barren (Genesis 18:9-14)

Wednesday, Dec. 10—Righteous and Blameless (Luke 1:5-11)

Thursday, Dec. 11—The Promise of a Son (Luke 1:12-20)

Friday, Dec. 12—The Lord's Favor (Luke 1:21-25)

Saturday, Dec. 13—Faith in God's Promises (Luke 1:39-45)

Sunday, Dec. 14—He Is to Be Called John (Luke 1:57-63)

Learning by Doing

This page contains an alternative lesson plan emphasizing learning activities. Some of these activities are also found in the helpful student book, Adult Bible Class.

Into the Lesson

Prepare the classroom by hanging a banner over the door saying *Welcome to Lessons on Commitment Through the Fine Arts!* Hang four signs from the ceiling (or post on various walls) that read *Storytelling, Crafts, Sculpture,* and *Portraits.* Put a group of three to five chairs in circles near each sign. (Larger classes may have two groups for each activity; smaller classes will take fewer chairs.)

Warmly greet students as they enter the room, pointing out the variety of signs displayed. Ask students to be seated near one of these signs. Begin the class by showing a poster with the heading *And Baby Makes Three.* Point out that choosing to have a child means parents will be making many commitments. Ask the class to call out commitments that will be made in the course of rearing that child.

Write on the board "Commitments to . . ." followed by class responses. Make the transition to Bible study activities by telling the class, "Choosing to have a child is a serious commitment. Today's text records the joyful commitment of two mothers to their unborn sons and to God's will. Today we'll focus on the model in Elisabeth's commitment to God."

Into the Word

Give each team one of the following assignments and the supplies noted below their instructions.

Storytelling. Your task is to tell the story of Zechariah and Elisabeth to the class as though you were telling the story to an 8-year-old child. You may have one storyteller or use several people's voices in the story. Quickly read Luke 1:5-24, 36-49. Outline the important points and note the emphasis you wish to make in the story. (Supplies needed: notepaper.)

Crafts. Your task is to use the supplies in the bag supplied to quickly create items to serve as reminders or clues to the background of Zechariah, Elisabeth, and John. You will find these clues in the photocopy of the Lesson Background. Create at least one item for each person. Be ready to show your crafts to the class and explain their significance. Remember that your goal is to help the class understand the background of these people so that they can appreciate this family's commitment to God. (Supplies needed: a bag filled with small pieces of cloth, 20–30 craft sticks, glue, craft paper, a few paper clips, two markers, cotton balls, and a photocopy of the Lesson Background from the lesson commentary.)

Sculpture. Your task is to create a small sculpture that represents Mary's mission in visiting Elisabeth. Read Luke 1:39-45 to determine your conclusions as to why the visit occurred. Be ready to explain your sculpture and its representation to the class. (Supplies needed: modeling dough.)

Portraits. Read Luke 1:36-45. Your task is to create a portrait of faith. Draw or sketch Elisabeth (a "stick woman" portrait is OK), incorporating items that demonstrate her faith and commitment to God. Feel free to add speech bubbles, labels, or captions to the portrait. Your goal is to discover and portray clues to Elisabeth's faith and commitment. (Supplies needed: poster board, pencil, and markers in various colors.)

Encourage each team to work very quickly. After the teams make their presentations to the class, make the transition to the application by telling the class, "Honoring our commitment to God often requires strength and determination. Let's talk about people who have modeled that determination."

Into Life

Brainstorming Activity #1. Remind the class that life is filled with many commitments, some of which may interfere with our commitment to God. An example: a commitment to a large house payment may interfere with monetary gifts to God. Ask the class to brainstorm a list of commitments that may hinder commitment to the Lord.

Brainstorming Activity #2. Point out that heaping guilt on the class for failing to keep commitments to the Lord is not the goal. Rather, we wish to encourage continuing growth in our walk with God. The example of Elisabeth is meant to be an encouragement. We also often find wonderful models of commitment to the Lord in people we know. Allow class members to share examples of people they know who have demonstrated godly commitment. List observations on the board.

Conclude with two prayers by volunteers. One is to be a prayer of thanksgiving for models of godly commitment. The other is to be a prayer petitioning God's help and patience as your students strive to become more Christlike.

Let's Talk It Over

The questions on this page are designed to promote discussion of the lesson by the class and to encourage application of the lesson Scriptures. The answers provided are only discussion starters. Let your class talk it over from there.

1. Why was it important for Mary to visit Elisabeth soon after the angel's message? In what ways should Mary's haste serve as a model?

The issue may be just as much one of "where Mary was leaving" as it was "where Mary was going." Although she had not yet begun to "show," she knew she eventually would. An unmarried woman who was expecting a baby was a disgrace to her family as well as to her faith. Thus Mary may have felt the need to get away from her home community for a time in order to find some emotional and spiritual confirmation.

The visit to Elisabeth provided Mary with that emotional and spiritual confirmation. There undoubtedly were wagging tongues in Nazareth as Mary's pregnancy began to "show" later on. When that happened, Mary was able to draw on Elisabeth's emotional and spiritual confirmations after having returned to Nazareth to live among disapproving friends and family members.

We also recall that Mary had received word from the angel that Elisabeth was expecting a baby. That news itself—not to mention the manner in which it was delivered—would have drawn Mary to Elisabeth. Elisabeth had been waiting a long time to experience motherhood, and this could be a shared joy. Godly joy should be shared quickly!

2. What spiritual benefits have you received from a relationship with an older relative?

Probably all of us have a favorite older relative. We have been blessed by his or her wisdom and guidance. We have learned valuable lessons that will not soon be forgotten.

This fact should cause us to aspire to be a blessing to all relatives, but especially to younger ones. Those of us who are aunts and uncles have opportunities to make a significant impact on nieces and nephews. Often they will listen to us when they will not heed their own parents. Be sensitive to the fact that some of your class members may be rearing their own grandchildren. That's a great challenge, and those grandparents need Christian affirmation.

3. What causes you to want to celebrate? How does what we celebrate reveal our values and priorities?

God has been good to your students—they need to be reminded of this. This question will give them an opportunity to recall their blessings. We often share our prayer requests, but unfortunately we don't program much of our Sunday school time to share our praises. During that Sunday school prayer-request time, we may throw in as an afterthought, "Oh, we'll take praises too." The prayer requests can outnumber the praises by 10 to 1 or more!

Yet praise reports build our faith. God has healed us. Our spiritual lives are enriched. God has calmed minds and lifted people from despair and depression. He has restored broken relationships. We have seen people delivered from sin, addictions, and death. The list is endless! God has provided for your students and cared for them up until this very day. He will continue to bless them. Remind them of these facts.

4. How are we blessed in ways Mary and Elisabeth were not?

Mary and Elisabeth had the Old Testament plus direct revelation from an angel. We, on the other hand, have the revealed, written, and completed New Testament! What greater blessing could there be? Elisabeth probably didn't live long enough to know "the end of the story" in terms of the fullness of New Testament revelation. Mary may have lived long enough for that (through the end of the first century), but she certainly never had the New Testament in the handy book format that we are privileged to enjoy today.

We also can reflect on the Spirit's movement through 2,000 years of church history, something unavailable to Mary and Elisabeth. If your students neglect to mention these two blessings in favor of mentioning modern technological marvels, etc., they will need a gentle reminder!

5. What Christian will you express appreciation to for how he or she is blessed? Will you choose an older or a younger person? Why?

Busyness works against being able to take time to express appreciation for being blessed. Christmas cards may be a convenient way of affirming blessings during the upcoming holiday season, but it's all too easy to "hide behind" those cards as a substitute for personal visits.

Shepherds Glorify God

December 21
Lesson 3

DEVOTIONAL READING: Psalm 107:1-15.

BACKGROUND SCRIPTURE: Luke 2:1-20.

PRINTED TEXT: Luke 2:8-20.

Luke 2:8-20

8 And there were in the same country shepherds abiding in the field, keeping watch over their flock by night.

9 And, lo, the angel of the Lord came upon them, and the glory of the Lord shone round about them; and they were sore afraid.

10 And the angel said unto them, Fear not: for, behold, I bring you good tidings of great joy, which shall be to all people.

11 For unto you is born this day in the city of David a Saviour, which is Christ the Lord.

12 And this shall be a sign unto you; Ye shall find the babe wrapped in swaddling clothes, lying in a manger.

13 And suddenly there was with the angel a multitude of the heavenly host praising God, and saying,

14 Glory to God in the highest, and on earth peace, good will toward men.

15 And it came to pass, as the angels were gone away from them into heaven, the shepherds said one to another, Let us now go even unto Bethlehem, and see this thing which is come to pass, which the Lord hath made known unto us.

16 And they came with haste, and found Mary and Joseph, and the babe lying in a manger.

17 And when they had seen it, they made known abroad the saying which was told them concerning this child.

18 And all they that heard it wondered at those things which were told them by the shepherds.

19 But Mary kept all these things, and pondered them in her heart.

20 And the shepherds returned, glorifying and praising God for all the things that they had heard and seen, as it was told unto them.

GOLDEN TEXT: The shepherds returned, glorifying and praising God for all the things that they had heard and seen, as it was told unto them.—Luke 2:20.

Human Commitment
Unit 1: Commitment to the Messiah
(Lessons 1–4)

Lesson Aims

After participating in this lesson, each student will be able to:

1. Recite from memory the message of the angels to the shepherds.

2. Explain the significance of God's choice of the shepherds to receive the angel's announcement of the Messiah's birth.

3. Suggest a way to "spread the word" about Jesus in a fresh and compelling manner.

Lesson Outline

INTRODUCTION
  A. New Baby News
  B. Lesson Background
 I. EXCITEMENT (Luke 2:8-12)
  A. Shepherds (v. 8)
  B. Angel (v. 9)
  C. Gospel (vv. 10-12)
 II. INFORMATION (Luke 2:13-15)
  A. Angel Army (vv. 13, 14)
    Glories in (or from) the Heavens
  B. Shepherds' Quest (v. 15)
III. ENCOUNTERS (Luke 2:16-20)
  A. Messiah Is Found (v. 16)
  B. Messiah Is Proclaimed (vv. 17, 18)
  C. Messiah Is Pondered (vv. 19, 20)
    Memory
CONCLUSION
  A. The Word Became Flesh
  B. Prayer
  C. Thought to Remember

Introduction

A. New Baby News

A new baby is born! How do you let people know of this joyous event? There are many different ways, both old and new. Years ago, it was traditional for men to hand out cigars to let their friends know there was a new child in the household. (For non-smokers this might be a bubble gum or candy cigar, in either blue or pink.) Within a few days, the record of the birth would be published in the town newspaper, efficiently informing those who kept track of such things.

When mother and baby were home from the hospital, she might hand-address birth announcements and mail them to all the appropriate friends and relatives. It was not uncommon for a business owner to post a message on the reader board, letting all those who drove past know "It's a girl!" or "It's a boy!" Informally, the community grapevine could quickly convey the news: "Did you hear that Linda and Ryan just had another boy?" A tradition in many churches was to have a rose in a vase on the pulpit, accompanied by an announcement from the preacher and a note in the bulletin.

Times have changed, but the desire to let people know about a birth has not. Now the news of a birth may be instantly communicated to grandparents via cell phone cameras. Digital pictures of the newborn may be e-mailed on the day of the birth. Details may be posted on a family Web site within hours. Birth announcements may be done through some type of e-card system that is paperless, cheap, and quick.

None of that existed in the first century AD. But we may safely assume that all of the normal channels of communication of the ancient world were working to announce the birth of Mary's son. Grandparents in Nazareth would have learned, although it would have taken several days for the news to travel there.

In addition, God chose two extraordinary methods to announce the birth of Jesus. First, He revealed a new star, which was noticed by ancient stargazers. This figures into the story of the wise men and is told in the second chapter of the Gospel of Matthew. Second, God sent angels to give the news to some local shepherds that very night. This is the story that is told in the second chapter of the Gospel of Luke, and that is the focus of today's lesson.

B. Lesson Background

Understanding today's lesson hinges on appreciating the role of shepherds in the ancient world. In this period, flocks of sheep or goats were common sights throughout Palestine. Much of the land was unsuitable for cultivation because of rocky conditions or the steepness of the slopes. As a result, many families, even those who lived in the cities and villages, owned flocks. The animals were both a source of income and a tangible asset of wealth.

The flocks were tended by shepherds, who came to the task from several different sources. Some shepherds of the time were simply the children of the owner, doing menial work for the greater benefit of the family. Others could be relatives in need of employment. In these cases, there was a strong family motivation to guard and care for the flock.

Shepherd duty was generally unpleasant. Hours were long. There was little protection from the rain, sun, and cold. The meals were sparse. Daily routine could include leading the flock for several miles to be watered and to find adequate forage. The opportunity for social niceties such as meeting with friends was rare. Small flocks were tended by a single shepherd, who may have had only a dog for companionship.

If appropriate family resources were inadequate for shepherd duty, the owner could be forced to hire men for the task. This was considered to be one of the lowest levels of employment possible, and the men who took such jobs were seen as untrustworthy (see John 10:12, 13). We do not know if the shepherds of today's lesson were from the category of young family members or from the loathed journeyman shepherd class.

Bethlehem had a reputation for shepherds and flocks that extended back to the time of David (1 Samuel 16:11). During the time of Jesus, the flocks of Bethlehem were a main source for lambs that were sold to Passover pilgrims in nearby Jerusalem. A Jewish historian of this period by the name of Josephus estimated that 100,000 lambs were sacrificed in Jerusalem on Passover (compare 1 Kings 8:63; 2 Chronicles 35:7). This made sheep a big business! Therefore, we may assume that such large flocks were tended by a mix of family children and hirelings.

A most unexpected thing happened to the shepherds of today's story: they were visited by an angel! While we sometimes think that the Bible is full of angels, such visitations are relatively rare. Luke has a special interest in this area. He records three angelic appearances during the events leading up to the birth of Jesus (to Zechariah, to Mary, and to the shepherds). An angel ministered to Jesus in the garden (Luke 22:43). Angels witnessed to the women at the empty tomb (Luke 24:23). Likewise, in Acts (Luke's second book) angels were encountered as a means of direction

and protection for the people of the first-century church (examples: Acts 5:19; 8:26).

I. Excitement
(Luke 2:8-12)

A. Shepherds (v. 8)

8. And there were in the same country shepherds abiding in the field, keeping watch over their flock by night.

There is nothing glamorous about being a shepherd. It is a 24/7 job that is filled with inactivity and tedium. But then, one *night*, it is the most exciting job in the world!

The sheep are settled down for the night, perhaps in some type of enclosure. The shepherds may be consuming a sparse evening meal around a fire. We should not think in terms of a blazing bonfire, such as we might see at family camp or a pep rally. Wood is scarce and valuable. This fire (if there is one) is likely small, smelly, and smoky, using dried sheep dung for fuel. Such a tiny fire provides little illumination for the shepherds, so the blazing stars above are visible in all their glory, just as on most other nights (assuming a cloudless sky).

B. Angel (v. 9)

9. And, lo, the angel of the Lord came upon them, and the glory of the Lord shone round about them; and they were sore afraid.

While we usually assume that *the angel of the Lord* simply "appears out of nothing," the language *came upon them* implies that the angel walks up to the shepherds. At the proper instant, though, the angel is revealed to them with supernatural glory. This includes bright light, for Luke says *the glory of the Lord* shines.

The deep darkness of the shepherds' night, broken only by the glow of a (perhaps) small fire, starlight, and moonlight is suddenly penetrated by a heavenly blaze. It is not surprising that they are *sore afraid*! Remember: at this point there is only one angel, which is probably all the shepherds' hearts can stand. [See question #1, page 144.]

C. Gospel (vv. 10-12)

10. And the angel said unto them, Fear not: for, behold, I bring you good tidings of great joy, which shall be to all people.

The first two words of *the angel* echo Gabriel's words to Zechariah (Luke 1:13) and to Mary (Luke 1:30). This greeting does not negate the awe-inspiring appearance of the angel, but it informs the shepherds that the angel means them no harm.

How to Say It

BETHLEHEM. *Beth*-lih-hem.
GABRIEL. *Gay*-bree-ul.
JERUSALEM. Juh-*roo*-suh-lem.
JOSEPHUS. Jo-*see*-fus.
MESSIAH. Meh-*sigh*-uh.
NAZARETH. *Naz*-uh-reth.
ZECHARIAH. *Zek*-uh-*rye*-uh (strong accent on *rye*).

What the angel says next is difficult to render into English. We should note that in the original text the phrase *bring you good tidings* is a verb and *great joy* is the object of that verb. The idea is something like this: "I have a good announcement for you: a great joy for *all* the *people* has come."

11. For unto you is born this day in the city of David a Saviour, which is Christ the Lord.

What is this "great joy"? It is the announcement of a birth. The angel includes four reasons why this birth is joyous.

First, it has taken place in David's *city*, Bethlehem (1 Samuel 16:4-13). Even the uneducated shepherds understand this as a fulfillment of the many promises to King David regarding an eternal throne (example: Psalm 89:3, 4). Thus, this is the announcement of a royal birth.

Second, this baby is to be *a Saviour,* one to deliver oppressed Israel. This may lead the shepherds to think the baby will be a warrior-king, not realizing that the Savior's mission is spiritual rather than political (compare Matthew 1:21).

Third, the baby is the *Christ,* the Messiah. These two words, one Greek and one Hebrew, both mean "the anointed one." This signifies that He is chosen and sent by God with special authority and empowerment.

Finally, the baby is *the Lord.* This is surely puzzling to the shepherds, for this is a title the Jews reserve for God himself. How can a baby in Bethlehem be God? Such is the mystery of the incarnation of Christ, the foundational Christian belief that Jesus is both fully human and fully God. As an author, Luke does not lead his readers to this conclusion after many chapters, but states the divinity of Jesus with Him yet a tiny baby.

12. And this shall be a sign unto you; Ye shall find the babe wrapped in swaddling clothes, lying in a manger.

The term *swaddling clothes* does not indicate anything special. On the contrary, this way of caring for the baby is the usual method. Mary has no fine silken baby clothes available. There is no fuzzy sleeper suit for Jesus. There are no disposable diapers. What Mary has are strips of cloth, perhaps six or eight inches wide, to wrap Him in. The fact that Mary lays the baby down rather than holding Him indicates that He is a content child. This perhaps confirms the words of the carol: "No crying He makes" (at least not yet!).

The unusual detail for the shepherds is that a *manger,* an animal feed trough, has been appropriated for the baby to sleep in. There is no wooden cradle or even a large basket. This fact directs the shepherds to search for the new king in places where livestock feed. They probably are aware of every possible stable, so in the small village of Bethlehem this will take relatively little time to locate.

II. Information
(Luke 2:13-15)
A. Angel Army (vv. 13, 14)

13. And suddenly there was with the angel a multitude of the heavenly host praising God, and saying.

If the shepherds are terrified by the appearance of a single angel, the turn of events we see here must tax their emotions to the limit! They are now chosen to glimpse even greater glory to help them understand the magnitude of the birth in Bethlehem.

We usually picture verse 13 as describing the night sky instantly filled with an angel choir. Yet such a display would surely be noticed by others, and it seems that only these shepherds are involved. The description *heavenly host* indicates beings from Heaven, but not necessarily that they are in Heaven or in the sky. Perhaps this *multitude* covers the immediate hillside.

The word *multitude* indicates a group larger than can be counted easily. The biblical term *host* is often a military term, for when God wreaks vengeance on the earth, He is the "Lord of hosts" (see Isaiah 1:24). Thus what the shepherds witness is more of an angel army—an army of heavenly worshipers—than it is an angel choir.

14. Glory to God in the highest, and on earth peace, good will toward men.

This army does not talk of war, though, but of *peace.* God is not coming with vengeance, but to initiate peace *on earth.* This will come about through God's offer of His Son, a sacrifice for human salvation, a peace offering (see Ephesians 2:14). The angels are not announcing the end of war between nations, for we still see that today. They are celebrating the end of war between God and sinful humanity. In this all glory goes to God, for this is a work solely of Him. It is an act of pure grace.

GLORIES IN (OR FROM) THE HEAVENS

We've all seen those amazing pictures of far-off galaxies captured by the Hubble space telescope. Launched in 1990 and updated with new technology several times, it circles the Earth about every hour and a half at an altitude of 360 miles. The size of Hubble's main mirror would make it only a medium-size telescope if it were on the ground. But since the Hubble's view is not distorted by the atmosphere, it is more powerful than any earthbound telescope.

The official Hubble Web site (http://hubble.nasa.gov) has scores of pictures captured by the telescope. These remind us of the scriptural truth that "The heavens declare the glory of God; and the firmament showeth his handiwork" (Psalm 19:1). The images that Hubble has allowed us to see were not available to humanity before 1990. Yet the image the shepherds saw on that holy night long ago negates any technological arrogance that we may find ourselves wallowing in!

What the shepherds saw was unique in history. The biblical description that we have of this event is never updated by better technology, nor need it be. The picture of God's glory seen by the shepherds is timeless. Even as we read of it 2,000 years later, its message still speaks with clarity of God's marvelous grace.   —C. R. B.

B. Shepherds' Quest (v. 15)

15. And it came to pass, as the angels were gone away from them into heaven, the shepherds said one to another, Let us now go even unto Bethlehem, and see this thing which is come to pass, which the Lord hath made known unto us.

The *shepherds* are alone again, and the inky darkness has returned. They do not wait for more signs or instructions, though. They decide that they should find the baby *now*. No waiting until morning. No long discussion. No worrying about the sheep. *Let us now go!* There is an urgency befitting this marvelous occasion. [See question #2, page 144.]

III. Encounters
(Luke 2:16-20)

A. Messiah Is Found (v. 16)

16. And they came with haste, and found Mary and Joseph, and the babe lying in a manger.

The shepherds arrive in the stable within hours of the birth, for the stopgap measure of using the *manger* as a baby bed has not been updated. All of this happens on one glorious night. In this case, the many pictures that have been painted of the holy family in the stable may be accurate, for this scene likely includes domestic animals and the soft glow of light from an oil lamp.

B. Messiah Is Proclaimed (vv. 17, 18)

17. And when they had seen it, they made known abroad the saying which was told them concerning this child.

After the dramatic appearance of the angels, the shepherds do not need to see the baby in order to believe the message that the Christ has been born. But now the shepherds are eyewitnesses,

Visual for Lesson 3. *This visual depicts one setting in which to share the good news. Can your learners name others?*

and they waste no time in letting everyone in the village know the news. They are locals; as such, they know all the residents. So the entire town probably has the news by daybreak. In a sense, these shepherds become the first evangelists, the first to proclaim the Christ to others. [See question #3, page 144.]

18. And all they that heard it wondered at those things which were told them by the shepherds.

"To wonder" means to not understand fully and yet to marvel. For the author Luke, this is a reaction from those who witness the miraculous (see Luke 8:25; Acts 2:7).

The villagers indeed have many things to wonder at and many questions to ask. Have these *shepherds* lost their minds? Why would God choose their little town? Is it possible that God's Messiah, the new king, really has been born in a stable? Do angels make visits to sheep fields? Undoubtedly, some villagers believe and some don't. Many probably just shake their heads and don't know what to think. [See question #4, page 144.]

C. Messiah Is Pondered (vv. 19, 20)

19. But Mary kept all these things, and pondered them in her heart.

Luke has a special interest in *Mary,* and some scholars believe he may have talked with her while gathering information to write his Gospel (compare Luke 2:51). Luke does not speak of Joseph this way.

The fact that Mary ponders the implications of God's activity indicates that she is trying to sort things out. What does all this mean? Such pondering is still done today by all who are confronted with the claims of Jesus. Each must reach a conclusion about what His advent means. Will they submit in faith, or will they resist in unbelief?

MEMORY

Those of us who are passing (or have passed) through middle age know all about the issue of memory loss. We walk from one room of the house into another and ask ourselves, "Now why did I come into this room?" A comedian suggested that there's just the same amount of memory in the world that there always has been, but modern life has shifted the memory banks from humans to computers!

Computers have at least a couple of types of memory. One is RAM, or "random access memory." RAM allows our computers to access information as long as the power is on. ROM, or "read-only memory," stores information that is not lost when the power is off. This kind of memory allows our computers to work when we turn them back on. RAM can be compared with how our minds work when we are awake. ROM might be compared to what happens when we arise in the morning and find that our brains still work!

When Mary "pondered . . . in her heart" the things that happened the night Jesus was born, she was preparing herself for a lifetime of considering the meaning of that momentous event. We wonder how much and how often such issues occupied her thoughts. Certainly her "ROM" never let her forget anything about Jesus as Christ, especially His crucifixion and resurrection. And we may be sure that at times her "RAM" was in overdrive trying to make sense of everything!

When Christ comes into our own lives, we enter on a lifelong journey of reflection regarding what the person and work of Jesus means. If we don't engage in that reflection on a regular basis, something is wrong!   —C. R. B.

20. And the shepherds returned, glorifying and praising God for all the things that they had heard and seen, as it was told unto them.

The faith of the *shepherds* is quickly translated into worship. After taking the news to all their friends and family, they return to their sheep. They return as changed people, though, having the joy of God in their hearts. It has not been a dream or a hallucination. Everything the angels said is true. [See question #5, page 144.]

Conclusion

A. The Word Became Flesh

This is the last lesson before Christmas, and it continues our look at aspects of the birth of Jesus as recorded in the Gospel of Luke. Luke is a master at narrative characterization. That is, Luke writes in such a way that the readers get to know the people of his story and gain insights into these characters very quickly. This lesson focuses on some unnamed men and boys who would have seemed unusual candidates for attention in the ancient world: field shepherds. For a brief moment, Luke brings us into their world to witness a marvelous work of God.

God's plan for human salvation required that His divine Son become a human being. Without being human, Jesus would not have been able to die for the sins of the world. God decided that this necessitated Jesus' birth by a woman, and His years as a baby, toddler, and child. Jesus was not to be like the mythical Greek gods, who emerged fully grown from the sea or a cave.

While we bow the knee to the newborn king at Christmastime, we recall that we are worshiping God among humankind. He is the Word become flesh (John 1:14). "Oh come, let us adore Him!"

B. Prayer

Our Father in Heaven, things haven't changed that much since Jesus was born. We, like the shepherds, are awed by the magnitude of Your gift. We ponder and try to understand the depth of Your love, but it is beyond our ability to comprehend. So we continue to offer You our praise and give You all the glory. May You always reign over us. We pray these words through the name of Your Son, Jesus the Messiah. Amen.

C. Thought to Remember

The good news of Jesus' birth
is still precisely that!

Home Daily Bible Readings

Monday, Dec. 15—God's Plan Fulfilled (Isaiah 46:8-13)

Tuesday, Dec. 16—The King of Glory (Psalm 24)

Wednesday, Dec. 17—Who Is Like the Lord? (Psalm 113)

Thursday, Dec. 18—Praise the Lord (Psalm 148)

Friday, Dec. 19—Glory Forever (Romans 16:25-27)

Saturday, Dec. 20—Mary's First Baby (Luke 2:1-7)

Sunday, Dec. 21—Glory to God! (Luke 2: 8-20)

Learning by Doing

This page contains an alternative lesson plan emphasizing learning activities. Some of these activities are also found in the helpful student book, Adult Bible Class.

Into the Lesson

Decorate the room with balloons, ribbons, baby paraphernalia, and a large poster with the heading *It's a boy!* Begin the lesson by reminding the class of the excitement parents feel when they bring a new baby into the world.

Parents have used varied and creative ways to announce births down through the years. Ask the class to list some of these. Write the answers below the poster heading *It's a boy!* If you have parents in the class, ask them how they announced the birth of their children. Answers may include balloons and a sign in the front yard, mailed announcements, e-mails and personal Web sites, a rosebud presented at church, etc.

Make the transition to Bible study by telling the class that the birth of Jesus was also good news. God's birth announcement, however, tops any announcement we've ever seen since.

Into the Word

You will need to recruit students early in the week for the following activities. Give each of four students or teams you recruit one of the following assignments. Provide photocopied material to the individual students or teams as indicated.

1. Lesson Background (one person). First, study the attached photocopy of the Lesson Background for Luke 2:8-20. Then prepare a brief presentation for the class (no more than five minutes) that describes the role and significance of shepherds in the ancient world.

2. Conversations (team). You are part of a team of at least three people. Your task is to dramatize today's passage. One or more team members will narrate the text itself. At appropriate points before, during, and after the narration, other team members will "fill in the blanks" with the imagined conversations among the shepherds (1) before the angel appears, (2) as the shepherds walk to Bethlehem's manger, and (3) as the shepherds leave the nativity scene. You may include prophecy, their emotions, their speculations, etc.

3. Angels (one person). Your task is to prepare a very brief (three to four minute) presentation about angels in the Bible. You may build your remarks from the photocopy of the Lesson Background for this Sunday's lesson. A concordance of the Bible will also be very useful.

4. Sheep as the people of God (one person). Your task is to prepare a very brief presentation (no more than five minutes) that compares the people of God with sheep. What are the implications of this analogy? You might begin your study with John 10. [Note to the teacher: if you wish to shorten this segment of the lesson, the fourth assignment is the one to leave out.]

Ask each team to report or make presentations in the order listed above.

Into Life

Ask the following discussion questions:

1. "The angels announced they had good news of great joy. Why was this announcement such good news?" As the class responds, make sure to glean the important reasons listed in the lesson commentary and write them on the board: it was the announcement of a royal birth, the birth of a Savior, and the birth of the Christ or Messiah.

2. "What are ways that Christians may capitalize on the Christmas season to share this good news with those who have not accepted Jesus?" Write the answers on the board. Two possible ideas: always send greeting cards that have a Christian message, and extend invitations to Christ-focused concerts or programs.

Create certificates that feature the following resolution, which is printed at the top center:

Since Christmas is the celebration of Christ's birth; and

Since the Savior's birth is good news to all humanity; then

I do hereby resolve that for the next few days and for next year's Christmas season I will do the following . . .

Use a computer to put the wording into an interesting font. If your budget allows, use "certificate looking" paper. You can purchase this at office supply stores. Give each learner a certificate.

Ask each to reconsider the ideas you've shared in today's lesson and decide which ones they will apply personally for this and/or next year's Christmas seasons. They can write these ideas on the certificate, take it home, and place it where they will see it often. When this Christmas is over, they should pack it away with the ornaments, to be rediscovered next Christmas.

Let's Talk It Over

The questions on this page are designed to promote discussion of the lesson by the class and to encourage application of the lesson Scriptures. The answers provided are only discussion starters. Let your class talk it over from there.

1. Throughout church history, people have claimed to have received angelic visitations. How should we evaluate these claims?

Some people believe with a certainty that they have seen an angel. Magazines are now available that relate the stories of those who believe they have interacted with angels. We don't have a precise biblical description of angels, so it might be difficult to know whether we have ever met an angel based on appearance.

The starting point for evaluating claims of angelic visitation is to ask ourselves *why* God would initiate such visitations today. If the claimed angelic visitation merely results in a reaffirmation of something that's already in the Bible, we may logically wonder "What's the point?" If the claimed angelic visitation results in additional revelation, over and above what's already in the Bible, then we're on dangerous ground indeed! (See Revelation 22:18.)

Hebrews 13:2 encourages us to "be not forgetful to entertain strangers: for thereby some have entertained angels unaware." If the word *angels* is being used literally, then the passage implies that angelic visitations are still possible, even likely. But that word *unaware* means that the angels are not recognized as such during the course of the events. This passage does not encourage us to seek out angels (which would imply being able to recognize them) for the purpose of being hospitable to them.

2. If you were a shepherd who heard the angelic announcement of Christ's birth, in what ways do you think your reactions would both mirror and differ from the shepherds' reactions?

We would certainly share their astonishment. I might have said, "Did you see what I saw, or was I dreaming?" Some might wonder, "Why me? With so many people in the world, why was I chosen to receive this announcement?" Students might express that they would have been afraid to tell anyone about the experience for fear of ridicule.

The question should lead students to discuss how we should respond to the movement of God's Spirit in our lives. It is normal to have some fear mingled with joy at God's unknown. We trust God, but at times it is difficult to wait in order to see exactly what He intends to do.

3. How will you share the supernatural message of Christ's birth this Christmas season?

The shepherds reported the truth of Christ's birth to everyone they met. This is the natural reaction of true belief. Because our lives have been changed by Christ, it is natural to tell others of our joy.

It seems to be increasingly difficult to communicate the truth of the gospel at Christmas or any other time. We hesitate because we are fearful of offending nonbelievers. Nevertheless, the message still needs to be communicated. Your students may choose to share the good news through a heartfelt e-mail or card, although such methods are easy to "hide behind" when a face-to-face communication is what is needed. Encourage your students to evaluate what their Christmas decorations communicate. Some may need to replace Santa with a nativity scene.

4. We have heard the message of Christ's birth many times. How can we renew our enthusiasm for this message?

Those of us who are longtime Christians have been exposed to the story of Christ's birth many times. As such, we may take it for granted. Perhaps this supernatural event may not be as exciting to us as it once was. If we are not thrilled at hearing again of the birth of Christ, it will be evident in the way we live.

The cure is to enter into the narrative again, like little children hearing it for the first time. If your church has a drama team or choir for the Christmas story, join it! (Undoubtedly it's too late for this year, so plan for the next.) This experience can refresh your enthusiasm.

5. Why is it significant that the shepherds returned to their flocks? How does this action speak to us today?

Life goes on. Christ does make a change in us, but not necessarily in our immediate circumstances. The shepherd's workaday responsibilities did not disappear because of the angel's message. In the same way, our lives can seem rather mundane even though we have this tremendous good news inside of us. Be encouraged! Know that Christ has changed you for eternity, from the inside out.

John the Baptist Preaches God's Message

DEVOTIONAL READING: Psalm 51:10-19.

BACKGROUND SCRIPTURE: Luke 3:1-20.

PRINTED TEXT: Luke 3:7-18.

Luke 3:7-18

7 Then said he to the multitude that came forth to be baptized of him, O generation of vipers, who hath warned you to flee from the wrath to come?

8 Bring forth therefore fruits worthy of repentance, and begin not to say within yourselves, We have Abraham to our father: for I say unto you, That God is able of these stones to raise up children unto Abraham.

9 And now also the axe is laid unto the root of the trees: every tree therefore which bringeth not forth good fruit is hewn down, and cast into the fire.

10 And the people asked him, saying, What shall we do then?

11 He answereth and saith unto them, He that hath two coats, let him impart to him that hath none; and he that hath meat, let him do likewise.

12 Then came also publicans to be baptized, and said unto him, Master, what shall we do?

13 And he said unto them, Exact no more than that which is appointed you.

14 And the soldiers likewise demanded of him, saying, And what shall we do? And he said unto them, Do violence to no man, neither accuse any falsely; and be content with your wages.

15 And as the people were in expectation, and all men mused in their hearts of John, whether he were the Christ, or not;

16 John answered, saying unto them all, I indeed baptize you with water; but one mightier than I cometh, the latchet of whose shoes I am not worthy to unloose: he shall baptize you with the Holy Ghost and with fire:

17 Whose fan is in his hand, and he will thoroughly purge his floor, and will gather the wheat into his garner; but the chaff he will burn with fire unquenchable.

18 And many other things in his exhortation preached he unto the people.

GOLDEN TEXT: Bring forth therefore fruits worthy of repentance.—Luke 3:8.

Human Commitment
Unit 1: Commitment to the Messiah
(Lessons 1–4)

Lesson Aims

After participating in this lesson, each student will be able to:

1. Recall several points of emphasis in the preaching of John the Baptist.

2. Tell why the points in lesson aim 1 were relevant to John's culture and continue to be relevant today.

3. Express a specific plan to implement at least one of John's points in his or her own life.

Lesson Outline

INTRODUCTION
  A. Wilderness Wise People
  B. Lesson Background
 I. COMING WRATH (Luke 3:7-9)
  A. Snakes (v. 7)
  B. Stones (v. 8)
  C. Judgment (v. 9)
    Judging Evil
II. COMING COMMUNITY (Luke 3:10-14)
  A. Sharing Community (vv. 10, 11)
  B. Honest Community (vv. 12, 13)
  C. Civil Community (v. 14)
    Soldiers, Then and Now
III. COMING MESSIAH (Luke 3:15-18)
  A. People Expect (v. 15)
  B. John Prepares (v. 16a)
  C. Messiah Judges (vv. 16b-18)
CONCLUSION
  A. Actions That Count
  B. Prayer
  C. Thought to Remember

Introduction

A. Wilderness Wise People

Throughout Christian history, some believers have chosen to withdraw from society. Isolation has allowed them to ponder deep questions, meditate, and pray without interruption; often this has involved voluntary poverty in order not to be distracted by worldly desires. Some have retreated in this way for a few weeks or months, then have returned to "civilization." Others have done this as a long-term lifestyle, preferring never to return.

One of the earliest of these religious hermits was an Egyptian Christian named Anthony (or Antony), who lived about AD 251–356. Anthony is recognized as the first to organize the many hermits of Egypt into communities, the beginning of the monastic movement that flourished in the Middle Ages.

An inspiration for Anthony and others like him was John the Baptist. John did not go to the cities to preach. Rather, the people sought him out in the wilderness. There he roared at them about the need for serious life change. This phenomenon of seeking answers from a wilderness wise man is at the center of today's lesson.

B. Lesson Background

As we study the Bible, we learn that God's plan for a Messiah required much preparation. God chose a nation (Israel) to be His holy people (Deuteronomy 7:6); this nation was to embody God's holy laws and worship Him alone (10:20). God's plan for a Savior was gradually revealed to Israel through prophets. The Messiah would be an heir of King David (Jeremiah 23:5). By the time of Jesus, the people of Israel had been anticipating the advent of God's Messiah for hundreds of years.

Luke is alone among the Gospel authors in giving information about the origin of John the Baptist. Luke mentions that John was "in the deserts" before his public ministry began (Luke 1:80). We should not understand this as a reference to a place with large sand dunes, tumbleweeds, and pounding heat. Instead, John's ministry took place "about Jordan" (Luke 3:3).

A deserted place is sometimes called *wilderness* in the Bible (compare Luke 3:2). Both Galilee and Judah had a lot of open territory that was inhabited by wild animals and few people (see Mark 1:13). John is presented as one who preferred to be out there by himself. He foraged for his own food and wore rough clothing (Matthew 3:4).

John was not the only Jew of his day to live a wilderness life. Others abandoned "normal" life to set up communities in the desert. The most famous of these was at Qumran. That community gave us the Dead Sea Scrolls. There are important differences between John and those who lived at Qumran. Whereas those at Qumran speculated about the Messiah, God used John to introduce Him. Inhabitants of Qumran withdrew to prepare themselves for the Messiah, but John's task was to prepare the nation of Israel for Him (Luke 1:16).

Although the Dead Sea Scrolls shed some light on the circumstances of John's day, they do little to help us understand this enigmatic figure, who dressed and acted so out of the ordinary. [See question #1, page 152.] For this, we turn to Luke.

I. Coming Wrath
(Luke 3:7-9)

A. Snakes (v. 7)

7. Then said he to the multitude that came forth to be baptized of him, O generation of vipers, who hath warned you to flee from the wrath to come?

The *wrath* of God is not a popular or comfortable topic today. We want to focus on a loving God, not an angry God. Yet the Bible, both Old and New Testaments, is loaded with references to the wrath of God (examples: Jeremiah 10:10; Romans 1:18). Two connections are often present in such texts.

First, the wrath of God is connected with God's righteous judgment (Romans 2:5). God's anger is His response to evil and sin (see Romans 13:4). Second, the wrath of God is often associated with the wilderness experience of the nation of Israel. Because of disobedience and lack of faith, the wrath of God came upon Israel, and they wandered in the wilderness 40 years before entering the promised land (Deuteronomy 9:7). Surely, some of John's audience who go out to the wilderness to hear him remember this detail from their history.

Multitude is an inexact term, but it indicates a large crowd—probably several hundred. John is not an itinerant preacher going from town to town (contrast Luke 10:1). Rather, the people are leaving their cities and villages to come to him in the wilderness *to be baptized of him.* [See question #2, page 152.] Even people from Jerusalem come to see him (John 1:19).

There is nothing warm or accommodating about John's personality. He questions the motives of the crowd. He insults them by calling them a *generation of vipers*—poisonous snake-people. He challenges them to be sure their motives are not false. Are they coming because they want a new experience? Do they really understand how important it is to be prepared for the coming Messiah?

B. Stones (v. 8)

8. Bring forth therefore fruits worthy of repentance, and begin not to say within yourselves, We have Abraham to our father: for I say unto you, That God is able of these stones to raise up children unto Abraham.

John wants the people to know that the old ways of thinking are no longer valid (if they ever were). Being a descendant of *Abraham* does not give a Jew immunity from the judgmental wrath of God. The creator God can always form for himself a new people who are not Israelites.

We can imagine John illustrating this by lifting a smooth stone from the Jordan River and reminding the audience that God can take rocks and make them into people for His glory. God formed Adam from dirt (Genesis 2:7) and showed Ezekiel that He could form people from dry, old bones (Ezekiel 37). *Fruits worthy of repentance* are more important than biological descent.

C. Judgment (v. 9)

9. And now also the axe is laid unto the root of the trees: every tree therefore which bringeth not forth good fruit is hewn down, and cast into the fire.

In warning the people, John shifts to another analogy: the periodic elimination of unproductive *trees* from an orchard. The ancient orchard tender is not sentimental when it comes to such trees. Unfruitful trees take up valuable space and water. When it is clear that a tree is barren, it is taken out. Even the stump is removed. Only then can a new tree be planted in its place. The barren tree, whose primary purpose should be *fruit* production, is then suitable only for a one-time use as firewood.

The purpose of being one of God's people is to serve Him. If a person produces no good works, then he or she is not serving. John is not teaching that good works will save one from God's wrath. Rather, John is saying that works are a measure of the heart. God demands a repentant heart, and this should lead to works of service.

JUDGING EVIL

A reluctance to judge any person as *bad* is prominent today. A generation has been raised on a moral diet of "there are no bad people, only bad actions."

A Christian college professor was comparing the Marquis de Sade's view that humans are "cruel

Visual for
Lesson 4

While discussing verse 8, point to this visual and ask, "What fruits does God expect from us?"

beasts" with Jean-Jacques Rousseau's perception that people are "noble savages." The class much preferred Rousseau's view. The professor asked if class members could name anyone they would judge to be *evil*. In response to the ensuing silence, he suggested Hitler, Stalin, and Hussein. No one was willing to call any of these men *evil*, although it was acknowledged that "they did bad things."

John had no difficulty making such judgments, and—this is important—he did it on the basis of a person's failure to bear the fruit of godliness. Jesus tells us in Matthew 7:1-5, 15-20 about the right and wrong ways of judging.   —C. R. B.

II. Coming Community
(Luke 3:10-14)

A. Sharing Community (vv. 10, 11)

10. And the people asked him, saying, What shall we do then?

Doubtless, some reject John's message and go their way with unrepentant hearts. But many are convinced that he is telling the truth. They want to know more. Luke presents three groups who question John further, each asking *What shall we do?*

For Luke, *the people* is one specific group of these three. These are common folk, the peasant population. They have taken John's message to heart and desire further, specific instructions. Sometimes today we are guilty of repeating vague generalities (such as, "Just love Jesus more") without helping immature believers with the specifics. We too need to have good answers for the person who asks, "What shall I do?"

11. He answereth and saith unto them, He that hath two coats, let him impart to him that hath none; and he that hath meat, let him do likewise.

John's foundational answer is "quit being selfish!" There are enough *coats* to go around if we share. There is plenty of *meat* (food) if we refuse to hoard.

The sharing heart is found in the person who does not even covet his or her own possessions. Sharing is an act based in a repentant heart. This is probably a difficult message for some of John's hearers. The messianic community that John anticipates will be a fellowship where physical needs are met through the generosity of its members (Acts 4:32). [See question #3, page 152.]

B. Honest Community (vv. 12, 13)

12. Then came also publicans to be baptized, and said unto him, Master, what shall we do?

The second of John's three groups are *publicans*. These are Jews employed by the Romans to assist in gathering taxes from the people. Publicans are particularly despised in Jewish society because they are viewed as collaborators with the hated overlords. Publicans are often guilty of outrageous corruption. They are found frequently in Luke's Gospel (see Luke 5:27-30; 7:29).

Publicans seem to be rather obvious in their unrighteous lifestyle, for Luke contrasts them with the Pharisees, the self-righteous paragons of the community (see Luke 18:10). Jesus is criticized for His willingness to fellowship with publicans (Luke 7:34). One of the later disciples, Levi (Matthew), is a publican (Luke 5:27). Luke also relates the beloved story of a short publican named Zaccheus, who is a convert of Jesus (Luke 19:1-10). These social outcasts also come to John for more instructions about their repentance.

13. And he said unto them, Exact no more than that which is appointed you.

The Roman system of taxation is rife with graft and kickbacks. While the people hate the Romans, they also fear them. This makes it easy for the publicans to charge more than is due in taxes and pocket the extra for themselves. While not legal, such practices are generally accepted.

As with many countries today, this means that not all taxes paid make it to the public treasury. The publicans are justifiably vilified by the community. John's instruction: quit being greedy! Don't use your authority to extort money for yourselves! This will show everyone that they have had a change of heart.

C. Civil Community (v. 14)

14a. And the soldiers likewise demanded of him, saying, And what shall we do?

The third group that comes to John is made up of *soldiers*, professional military men. It is possible that these are Jews serving in the Roman military or in the private army of King Herod Antipas. More likely, though, is that these are Romans (Gentiles). At any rate, it must shock the common people to see these proud men seeking help with their spiritual lives. Roman soldiers play important parts in the gospel storyline (Luke 7:1-10; 23:47; Acts 10; etc.).

14b. And he said unto them, Do violence to no man, neither accuse any falsely; and be content with your wages.

Roman soldiers are battle-hardened, often brutal men. The Roman army is an army of occupation in Palestine. Such soldiers are often required to do police-type enforcement rather than wage war (sound familiar?). Occupiers can easily see the citizens of the defeated country as helpless targets for extortion. John's instruction to the soldiers is that they not give in to the common practice of bullying citizens in various ways in order to extort money from them. They are to be *content* with the pay they receive, not misusing their authority to enrich themselves.

SOLDIERS, THEN AND NOW

The United States entered the Iraq War to accomplish various objectives, including removing the barbaric Saddam Hussein from power. However, America's moral high ground was called into question by the Abu Ghraib prison scandal of 2004.

Under Hussein's rule, that prison was the site of torture and execution of Iraqi dissidents. Later, we came to realize that reprehensible behavior does not know national boundaries. Photos came to light showing some smiling American soldiers— male and female—posing over Iraqi prisoners who were shackled in dehumanizing postures. The scandal called into question the character of some American military personnel. By inference on the part of America's enemies, it also brought into disrepute the claimed virtue of Western, "Christian" civilization.

The scandal reminds us that atrocities and abuse are common during times of war and military occupation. This problem goes way back. The Roman soldiers of Jesus' time certainly had no reputation for saintly behavior. This is why John called on them to repent of abusing the citizens of the country they occupied. All Christians are "soldiers of the cross" (compare Philippians 2:25; Philemon 2). Our warfare is spiritual in nature (Ephesians 6:12). Do we discredit Christianity by the way we conduct ourselves during this struggle?   —C. R. B.

III. Coming Messiah
(Luke 3:15-18)

A. People Expect (v. 15)

15. And as the people were in expectation, and all men mused in their hearts of John, whether he were the Christ, or not.

The powerful wilderness preacher stirs up the passions of the people. [See question #4, page 152.] Because of this, they begin to wonder whether *John* might be the Messiah they await. The dynamism of John raises hopes. As they have allowed John to be authoritative for them in spiritual matters, now they are considering following him in a tangible, perhaps political, way.

B. John Prepares (v. 16a)

16a. John answered, saying unto them all, I indeed baptize you with water.

John's answer to the crowd's messianic musings is to define his role within the larger picture of

God's plan. John's job is to *baptize*. This certainly means the physical act of baptism, but that act must be seen as part of the broader issue of repentance. His task is to get the people to recognize their sin problem.

C. Messiah Judges (vv. 16b-18)

16b. But one mightier than I cometh, the latchet of whose shoes I am not worthy to unloose.

John also explains his relationship with the coming Messiah. Despite the admiration of the crowd, John knows that he is not the main act in God's drama. His ministry points to the Messiah. John knows that his own fame will fade, for later he says, "He must increase, but I must decrease" (John 3:30).

Shoes for John are sandals, and he is asserting that he is unworthy even to untie the straps of the Messiah's footwear. This makes sense to a Jewish crowd, who sees much of their world in terms of clean and unclean. John recognizes the sin in his life and understands the great gulf between himself, a sinner, and the pure and sinless "Lamb of God" (compare John 1:29).

16c, 17. He shall baptize you with the Holy Ghost and with fire: whose fan is in his hand, and he will thoroughly purge his floor, and will gather the wheat into his garner; but the chaff he will burn with fire unquenchable.

The term *baptize* in John's day means to be fully immersed. John's water baptism is connected with cleansing of the heart (repentance). He foretells that the coming Messiah will be able to do much more than water baptisms. The Messiah will provide an immersion in *the Holy Ghost* and in *fire*.

Luke does not understand this baptism (immersion) with the Holy Spirit to happen during the earthly ministry of the Messiah. After the resurrection, Jesus reminds the disciples of this promise, and He tells them to wait just a few more days (Acts 1:4, 5). The great Day of Pentecost brings about the

---

How to Say It

ABRAHAM. *Ay*-bruh-ham.
ABU GHRAIB. Uh-boo Grayb.
HEROD ANTIPAS. *Hair*-ud *An*-tih-pus.
JEAN-JACQUES ROUSSEAU. Zhon-Zhok Ru-*so*.
JEREMIAH. Jair-uh-*my*-uh.
LEVI. *Lee*-vye.
MARQUIS DE SADE. Mar-kee deh *Sod*.
MESSIAH. Meh-*sigh*-uh.
MESSIANIC. mess-ee-*an*-ick.
QUMRAN. Koom-*rahn*.
ZACCHEUS. Zack-*key*-us.

fulfillment of the promise, for the Holy Spirit comes upon the disciples in a process that appears like fire descending from Heaven (Acts 2:3, 4).

Peter associates the outpouring of the Holy Spirit on the Day of Pentecost with "the last days" (Acts 2:17). The supernatural manifestation of the Spirit directly precedes the promise of the gift of the Spirit to those who come to Jesus on His terms (Acts 2:38, 39).

18. And many other things in his exhortation preached he unto the people.

Luke ends this section by reminding us that his presentation of John is brief and selective. There are *many other things* said by this powerful preacher to the crowds who come to hear him. Luke indicates that these are exhortations, meaning moral encouragements to the people to give up their many sinful ways and work out their repentance.

We wish we had more of the preaching of this mighty man of God. It is easy to accept Jesus' evaluation of John as "much more than a prophet" (Luke 7:26). He is a unique player in God's divine drama of human salvation. [See question #5, page 152.]

Conclusion

A. Actions That Count

"I promise! I'll never drink again!" These might be the words of a destructive alcoholic attempting to negotiate his way through yet another crisis caused by his drinking. The problem is that for many families this has a hollow ring, for they have heard it before. They might love the alcohol addict dearly, but his poor choices affect others too. They want more than words, no matter how sincere.

Home Daily Bible Readings

Monday, Dec. 22—More Than a Prophet (Luke 7:24-29)

Tuesday, Dec. 23—A Witness to the Light (John 1:6-9)

Wednesday, Dec. 24—A Voice in the Wilderness (John 1:19-28)

Thursday, Dec. 25—John's Testimony (John 1:29-34)

Friday, Dec. 26—A Shining Lamp (John 5:30-35)

Saturday, Dec. 27—I Must Decrease (John 3:22-30)

Sunday, Dec. 28—Call to Repentance (Luke 3:7-18)

They want change. They want the person who promises to quit drinking . . . *to quit drinking!*

Repentance is a nonexistent topic in some churches. Part of this stems from a reaction to the preaching of the past, which was often overly moralistic. Preachers of a previous generation were expected to condemn everything from card playing to mixed swimming. However well-intentioned this might have been, the emphasis was upon behavior rather than repentance. Social pressure was applied to church members that required strict standards of *do's* and *don'ts*—and woe to the errant sinner who violated this code!

This system is based on fear, and fear is not a good motivator for the long term. Eventually we become numb to threats, and they lose their effectiveness. Behavioral change that is long lasting must come from a different source. True godly living comes from the heart. I do the right thing because I want to do the right thing, not because I am afraid of the consequences of violation.

John the Baptist understood this very well. He was called to prepare Israel for God's Messiah. He did not see this as getting them to clean up their lives for the sake of appearances. He saw this as effecting a change in heart. When he called Israel to repentance, he wasn't just saying, "Cut down on sinning." He demanded "fruits worthy of repentance" (Luke 3:8), the outward signs of a positive inward change.

Today, the Messiah still comes into the hearts of men and women. Jesus understands us in our weaknesses. His heart is broken by our self-destructive sinning. But he wants much more than "less sin." He wants a changed heart, a repentant heart. He desires more than a person saying, "I won't sin anymore." He wants the heart that repents and affirms, "I don't want to sin anymore." Until we get to that point, we have not fully repented, for repentance involves the whole person, not just specific behaviors.

B. Prayer

God of all creation, judge of the living and the dead, we do not fear judgment because we have been redeemed by the blood of Jesus. May we never take our salvation for granted by disregarding how You expect us to live. Instead, may Your Holy Spirit continue to mold and shape us toward being ones who bear much fruit that is pleasing and acceptable to You. We pray this in the name of the One whom John the Baptist pointed to, Your Son, Jesus. Amen.

C. Thought to Remember

John's challenge to repent endures.

Learning by Doing

This page contains an alternative lesson plan emphasizing learning activities. Some of these activities are also found in the helpful student book, Adult Bible Class.

Into the Lesson

Neighbor Nudge. Begin this lesson by observing that most Christians have had spiritual mentors: those who have served as models, encouragers, or counselors in their spiritual lives. Ask the class members to identify such people from their lives and share that information with someone sitting close to them. They should tell the name of the person and how that person has been a positive influence.

Make the transition to Bible study by telling the class, "Very few people of either the first century or today thought (or think) of John the Baptist as someone to emulate. Nor did John the Baptist counsel people to copy his lifestyle. Even so, we will find three groups of people who valued this wilderness preacher and sought his advice."

Into the Word

Before class begins, ask a class member to serve as an interviewer of John the Baptist. You or someone else will play the part of John while the interviewer asks questions. "John" may choose to put on a costume beard and a burlap bag in preparation for being interviewed.

Ask the interviewer to read and ask the following questions. You will find answers to the questions in the Lesson Background and lesson commentary. Before you begin this activity, have a class member read today's printed text.

1. "John, we all know you as a preacher from the wilderness. Are there other people who have chosen the lifestyle of a religious person? If so, tell us about them."

2. "John, you often seem to be angry with God's chosen people. You even called one of your crowds a 'generation of vipers'! What makes you so upset with the Jewish people? And what was 'the wrath to come' of which you spoke?"

3. "When you told the crowd to bring forth fruits worthy of repentance, what did you mean? And what did you mean by saying God is able to raise up children from stones?"

4. "While not everyone accepted your message, John, there were some who asked for more information. I remember reading that the people or the common folk were asking what they should do. How did you answer them?"

5. "John, when the publicans asked the same question, what did you say to them? And how did you answer the soldiers when they also asked the same question?"

6. "One more question. You preached repentance. That's not a popular word in many churches. Why is repentance still important in 2008?"

7. "Thank you, John, for coming and clarifying the words you preached from Jordan so many years ago. Any last thoughts?"

As "John" removes the beard and robe, remind the class that John's preaching contains some wonderful imagery. Instruct the class members to look at the lesson text for help in answering these questions:

1. What did John intend to communicate by saying he was not worthy of untying Jesus' shoes?

2. What was John's colorful imagery about the wheat meant to teach?

3. Does repentance mean only to *stop* doing things, or is there another dimension to repentance? Explain.

Into Life

Tell the class that they need to let John's call to repentance touch them also. Distribute handouts entitled *Repentance, Change, Grace, and Gratitude* with the questions below. These questions are designed to stimulate personal reflection. Give the class a few minutes to complete the questionnaire, then discuss. If you are running short on time, this can be either a small-group activity or a take-home exercise.

Repentance, Change, Grace, and Gratitude

1. Repentance may include a behavior to stop or start, an ungodly value to change, a priority to correct, etc. If you were to imitate those who heard John speak, what answer would you expect to your question, "What should I do in the year 2009?" In other words, what would John tell you to change or do in your life?

2. We read that John preached a message of the good news as well as a message of God's wrath. In light of this, how would you finish the following statement? "God's grace to me is certainly good news. I make sure to express my gratitude for His grace by _____."

Let's Talk It Over

The questions on this page are designed to promote discussion of the lesson by the class and to encourage application of the lesson Scriptures. The answers provided are only discussion starters. Let your class talk it over from there.

1. What misconceptions do we sometimes draw about a person because of an unusual haircut or manner of dress? How do we avoid this trap?

John the Baptist certainly looked and acted strangely (Matthew 3:4)! Yet despite his outward appearance, he was fully committed to God's program. It is easy to pigeonhole people based on the way they look. Some people won't meet our fashion expectations. We may desire people to look and act a particular way, especially when they come to worship. We avoid this trap by remembering that God looks past external appearance (1 Samuel 16:7).

Yet it can be so difficult to look beyond the outward! We must acknowledge also that appearance can, at times, reveal important things about the inner person. Psychological problems may be evident in those who, for example, dress in "goth" apparel or who engage in extreme kinds of body modification. But lower-key tattoos and body piercings may be no more than harmless fashion statements. Even though the appeal of such things may be hard for some to understand, we must remember that our attitude makes a difference in whether or not the other person will be open to the gospel.

2. Do you think an "outdoor" baptism in a river, lake, or a swimming pool is spiritually more desirable than an "indoor" baptism? Why, or why not?

Some of your students may have been baptized outside. They will want to tell of their experiences. Perhaps some have seen or have heard about folks lining up along the bank, waiting to be immersed in a river or creek. Most baptisms today, however, take place inside church facilities.

Some may think that outdoor baptisms are spiritually superior because they are "more public" than baptisms that happen indoors. Yet an outdoor baptism may be witnessed by few people while an indoor baptism may be witnessed by a hundred or more. What matters is the heart of the one receiving the baptism. The joyously repentant person will want as many people to know about their change as possible!

3. What are some specific ways that repentance can and should be visible in the twenty-first century? Which of these most apply to your own life?

True repentance will be visible. Encourage your students to express what repentance looks like in their own lives. A repentant man might be kinder to his wife. Everyone should become active in church attendance. Language that needs to be cleaned up will be. The list goes on. You might ask for examples of people whose repentance was obvious without necessarily mentioning names.

The apostle Paul had a genuine conversion experience. His repentance is "writ large" in the pages of Scripture. Zaccheus made an immediate turnaround in both thought and deed (Luke 19:8). Watching or listening to Christian broadcasting, one cannot miss the dramatic stories of repentance. The fruits of repentance will differ from person to person, but there will be common elements. Ask students to name some of those elements.

4. In what ways are today's preachers whom we consider "powerful" similar to and different from John the Baptist?

Very few modern-day preachers share John the Baptist's dress and lifestyle! Most of today's preachers dress better, and their diet isn't quite as harsh. The modern sermon should still be God's message, however. Though methods have changed throughout the centuries, the message hasn't. A powerful preacher is one who is true to the Word of God.

Students may suggest other similarities and differences. Stress that when the Word of God is preached in the Spirit of God, people are moved to respond. Preaching God's message can stir people's emotions and cause a change in the way they think (Acts 2:37). The end result should be a change in the person's will; there should be a decision to be obedient to the gospel. That's the sign of having heard a powerful preacher.

5. How can John the Baptist's directions to his original audience help someone today to reach the point of repentance?

Repentance is closely connected with the confessing of sin—after all, sin is what we repent of. Before someone will confess sin, he or she must acknowledge that sin exists. John pointed out both sinful and godly behavior. Placing the two alongside one another allows the hearer to realize the stark contrast between them.

Midwives Serve God

January 4
Lesson 5

DEVOTIONAL READING: Proverbs 16:1-7.

BACKGROUND SCRIPTURE: Exodus 1:8-21.

PRINTED TEXT: Exodus 1:8-21.

Exodus 1:8-21

8 Now there arose up a new king over Egypt, which knew not Joseph.

9 And he said unto his people, Behold, the people of the children of Israel are more and mightier than we:

10 Come on, let us deal wisely with them; lest they multiply, and it come to pass, that, when there falleth out any war, they join also unto our enemies, and fight against us, and so get them up out of the land.

11 Therefore they did set over them taskmasters to afflict them with their burdens. And they built for Pharaoh treasure cities, Pithom and Raamses.

12 But the more they afflicted them, the more they multiplied and grew. And they were grieved because of the children of Israel.

13 And the Egyptians made the children of Israel to serve with rigor:

14 And they made their lives bitter with hard bondage, in mortar, and in brick, and in all manner of service in the field: all their service, wherein they made them serve, was with rigor.

15 And the king of Egypt spake to the Hebrew midwives, of which the name of the one was Shiphrah, and the name of the other Puah;

16 And he said, When ye do the office of a midwife to the Hebrew women, and see them upon the stools, if it be a son, then ye shall kill him; but if it be a daughter, then she shall live.

17 But the midwives feared God, and did not as the king of Egypt commanded them, but saved the men children alive.

18 And the king of Egypt called for the midwives, and said unto them, Why have ye done this thing, and have saved the men children alive?

19 And the midwives said unto Pharaoh, Because the Hebrew women are not as the Egyptian women; for they are lively, and are delivered ere the midwives come in unto them.

20 Therefore God dealt well with the midwives: and the people multiplied, and waxed very mighty.

21 And it came to pass, because the midwives feared God, that he made them houses.

GOLDEN TEXT: The midwives feared God, and did not as the king of Egypt commanded them, but saved the men children alive.—Exodus 1:17.

Human Commitment
Unit 2: Old Testament People of Commitment
(Lessons 5–12)

Lesson Aims

After participating in this lesson, each student will be able to:

1. Summarize the nature of the oppression that the Israelites experienced and its causes.

2. Explain how the example of the Hebrew midwives can strengthen personal resolve.

3. Confess one area where obedience to God has not taken highest priority.

Lesson Outline

INTRODUCTION
A. Lesson in Loyalty
B. Lesson Background
I. KING AND HIS FEAR (Exodus 1:8-14)
A. Issue for Egypt (vv. 8-10)
B. Consequences for Israel (vv. 11-14)
   Blinders
II. MIDWIVES AND THEIR FEAR (Exodus 1:15-21)
A. Declaration by the King (vv. 15, 16)
B. Disobedience by the Midwives (v. 17)
C. Reaction of the King (v. 18)
D. Response of the Midwives (v. 19)
E. Rewards for the Midwives (vv. 20, 21)
   Choosing Between Two Masters
CONCLUSION
A. Consequences
B. Prayer
C. Thought to Remember

Introduction

A. Lesson in Loyalty

It was his first real job, and the wages were much more than the weekly allowance that his parents provided. He was working at a supermarket, and his primary duty was to sack the groceries at the checkout counter. During a slack time, an assistant manager asked the young man to go to one of the aisles to put canned goods on the shelves.

While stocking the shelves, another assistant manager walked by and told the young worker to go and unload a truck that had just arrived with fresh produce. The new employee was enjoying this different project until the first assistant manager saw him and authoritatively asked why he was not stocking the shelves, as he had been instructed. Just at that moment the store manager appeared on the scene and resolved the dilemma by sending the young worker back to sacking duty.

The incident described above illustrates Jesus' affirmation that "no man can serve two masters" (Matthew 6:24). We conclude that Jesus' statement refers to the ultimate authority in each person's life—something much more profound than stocking shelves. The Bible teaches that there are different kinds of loyalties. Examples are relationships to parents (Luke 2:51), wives to husbands (Ephesians 5:22), to the ordinances of government (1 Peter 2:13), to leaders in the church (Hebrews 13:7, 17), and to one another (1 Corinthians 16:16; Ephesians 5:21).

Difficulties develop, however, when authorities have differing expectations. Each person eventually realizes that the authority structures in life must be rank-ordered. The words of a parent have more weight than those of an older sibling. The pronouncements of the principal mean more than the statements of a teacher. Federal regulations may take precedence over the laws of a state or city.

Some kings have claimed to be divine (or at least to have divine rights of authority). The result was a demand for obedience. The issue of loyalty becomes critical, however, when the precepts of God conflict with the orders of a king. That is the issue faced in the lesson for today.

B. Lesson Background

An underlying theme of the book of Exodus is that God keeps the promises that He had made to the patriarchs (Abraham, Isaac, and Jacob) in the book of Genesis. One such promise or prophecy by God was that the descendants of Abraham (or Abram) would endure some 400 years of servitude in a foreign land, where they would suffer oppression (Genesis 15:13; Acts 7:6).

The final chapters of the book of Genesis depict the migration of the family of Jacob from Canaan to Egypt. The date of 1876 BC is often given as the time for this migration that would turn into a stay of 430 years (Exodus 12:40, 41). The Scripture for this lesson tells why the treatment of Jacob's descendants changed from appreciation to persecution during the stay, and it reveals the means by which servitude and oppression became reality.

I. King and His Fear (Exodus 1:8-14)

The first seven verses of the book of Exodus introduce the book as a whole. The seventh verse uses five different verbs to describe the growth of the people of Israel in the region of Egypt called

Goshen. Moses will lead this slave nation, but that is at least 80 years in the future from the events of this lesson.

A. Issue for Egypt (vv. 8-10)

8. Now there arose up a new king over Egypt, which knew not Joseph.

The identity of the *new king over Egypt* is not given. This lesson is written, however, from the perspective that he is one of the early kings of what is designated as Egypt's 18th dynasty. This is the dynasty that regains control of Egypt by driving out the Hyksos, the foreign invaders that ruled Egypt for about 150 years. The fact that *Joseph* had once saved Egypt from the ravages of an extreme drought is but a misty, irrelevant memory for the leaders of the new dynasty. They are concerned only for the present (sound familiar?).

If the new king is not aware of the deliverance that Joseph accomplished, then neither does he know of how God, whom Joseph served, had been behind the chain of events that put Joseph into his place of leadership. It is not in the best interest of a nation when its current leaders do not know of or care about the religious heritage of the nation they are leading.

9. And he said unto his people, Behold, the people of the children of Israel are more and mightier than we.

The new king demonstrates a certain practical wisdom by planting the seed of fear into the minds of *his people.* This ancient tactic is still used as a deviously effective political ploy today. The expression of fear against the nation *of Israel* appears here for the first time. It will be repeated throughout the centuries that follow. [See question #1, page 160.]

It seems that the Israelites and their immediate neighbors are living together peacefully, but the king of Egypt begins his propaganda campaign

How to Say It

ABRAHAM. *Ay*-bruh-ham.
GOSHEN. *Go*-shen.
HYKSOS. *Hik*-sos.
ISAAC. *Eye*-zuk.
MACCABEES. *Mack*-uh-bees.
MOSES. *Mo*-zes or *Mo*-zez.
PHARAOH. *Fair*-o or *Fay*-roe.
PITHOM. *Py*-thum.
PUAH. *Peu*-uh.
RAAMSES. Ray-*am*-seez.
SEMITE. *Seh*-mite.
SEMITIC. Suh-*mih*-tik.
SHIPHRAH. *Shif*-ruh.

to build hostility and distrust. Differences among social groups are easily exploited for the purposes of power and prestige. It is commendable that in America groups such as the Amish live congenially alongside their neighbors, even though there may be very little social interaction.

10. Come on, let us deal wisely with them; lest they multiply, and it come to pass, that, when there falleth out any war, they join also unto our enemies, and fight against us, and so get them up out of the land.

The king gives an invitation to "his people" (v. 9) to *come* and join him in making a decision on how to handle a hypothetical situation. The entire appeal of the king is grounded on fears: that the multiplication of the Israelites will become even greater, that such a large group will be a serious threat if they chose to *fight against* Egypt, and that Israel may decide to go elsewhere. The last-named item leads to speculation that the Israelites are a good source for tax revenues, or perhaps that some of their agricultural products have become staples in the diets of the Egyptians.

Some think that the Hyksos were Semites as are the Hebrews. Under this theory, it is easy to conclude that any similar groups will find natural allies in the Israelites.

B. Consequences for Israel (vv. 11-14)

11. Therefore they did set over them taskmasters to afflict them with their burdens. And they built for Pharaoh treasure cities, Pithom and Raamses.

The oppression of the Israelites begins. First comes a type of enslavement in order to build certain *cities* in Egypt *for Pharaoh.* The duration of such projects may be as long as 20 years. The precise locations of the cities of *Pithom and Raamses* have not been determined today.

12. But the more they afflicted them, the more they multiplied and grew. And they were grieved because of the children of Israel.

The purposes of the oppressive labor are to (1) crush incentive, (2) control the people, and (3) curtail population growth. The resentment of the Egyptians increases when they realize that the results are the opposite of what is planned: the greater the affliction, the greater the multiplication of these feared foreigners. To the Egyptians it becomes a vicious cycle. The first stage of the abuse has failed to achieve its goal. [See question #2, page 160.]

13, 14. And the Egyptians made the children of Israel to serve with rigor: and they made their lives bitter with hard bondage, in mortar, and in brick, and in all manner of service in the field:

all their service, wherein they made them serve, was with rigor.

The second phase of abuse against the Israelite people is to intensify and expand the scope of their labor. Their work *in brick* is to produce building blocks that are slightly over 12 inches square and over 3 inches thick. The bricks of ancient Egypt are usually dried in the sun, about 3 days on each side.

To perform the various tasks of making bricks and to do so in the heat of the sun is intended to be a part of the increased demands. This involves the hauling of water, mixing the clay with water, and shaping the clay to be dried. One ancient document that is a satire about the trades depicts the brick maker with these phrases: dirtier than pigs, clothes stiff with clay, arms are destroyed, washes himself only once a season, and simply wretched. A wall painting from ancient Egypt attributes this statement to a taskmaster who is standing over some brick makers: "The rod is in my hand; do not be idle."

An agricultural component *(service in the field)* is added to the expectations for the Israelites. This could be counted as a third step in the oppression. This type of work is not done in the comfort of an air-conditioned cab on a tractor. Rather, it is arduous, backbreaking labor. It involves all the tasks that accompany the planting, cultivating, and harvesting of grain by primitive methods.

BLINDERS

Slavery began in the New World early in the seventeenth century. By the end of that century, laws had declared enslaved Africans to be "slaves for life." A Virginia law in 1667 declared that even "baptisme doth not alter the condition of the person as to his bondage or freedome."

The life of the slave was a hard one. Labor was difficult and discipline could be severe. We read of benevolent slave-owners, but slavery by definition is brutal in that the slave is denied freedom. The 1667 law noted above demonstrates how slave owners became blinded to Christian morality.

Slavery in the U.S. was outlawed over 140 years ago. But many of the social problems that America struggled with in the twentieth century (and which persist into the twenty-first century) owe their existence to unchristian attitudes developed during the era of slavery—and perpetrated even thereafter.

It was tragic that so many supposedly Christian people could not see the evils of slavery, especially given the Old Testament portrayal of how the Egyptians treated the people of God. How easy it is to read the Bible with blinders on, see-ing only what confirms our preexisting ideas! We must question which unbiblical cultural practices we have turned an unseeing eye toward today.

—C. R. B.

II. Midwives and Their Fear (Exodus 1:15-21)

An important biblical principle is ready to be illustrated in the moral choices made by two women. They must determine whether to obey a pagan ruler or their spiritual convictions. Their moral dilemma will be resolved with the correct decisions, and they will be blessed by God because of their choice.

A. Declaration by the King (vv. 15, 16)

15. And the king of Egypt spake to the Hebrew midwives, of which the name of the one was Shiphrah, and the name of the other Puah.

A fourth stage of oppression is announced by the *king of Egypt.* Two *Hebrew midwives* are named as the ones who are to be the instruments of the next step that is intended to suppress further growth among the Israelites. Their names are Semitic, and this suggests that they also are Israelites (although the language allows the phrase *Hebrew midwives* to mean "midwives over the Hebrews").

It is frequently asked if two midwives are enough to meet the demands of this growing group of people. The answer is probably *no* if they are expected to be in attendance at all the births that take place. It is possible that they are the chief midwives, and that other midwives work under their supervision. It is also possible that the services of a midwife are not always sought, and that the two women are able to provide this service for those who request it.

The modern idea of *midwife* or *midwifery* may suggest different concepts to the reader, depending on one's orientation. It may bring the thought of a nice lady who assists and encourages a mother in the delivery of an infant. Such a person is often termed a "lay" midwife. The word may also refer to an individual who moves beyond a degree in nursing to become a registered or endorsed midwife. At lease one U.S. university offers a program in "midwifery education." *Shiphrah* and *Puah* probably have all the skills available at the time for this profession.

16. And he said, When ye do the office of a midwife to the Hebrew women, and see them upon the stools, if it be a son, then ye shall kill him; but if it be a daughter, then she shall live.

Ancient sources provide several details about the duties of midwives. Their tasks are described as cutting the umbilical cord, washing the infant, rubbing the newborn with salt, and wrapping the baby in cloths. The word given as *stools* may be a reference to two specially shaped stones on which women sit while giving birth.

The king's request is not quite what we call "partial-birth abortion," although there are similarities. The pharaoh is asking the women to use their resources to *kill* male infants. The reason is obvious: males can become part of a fighting force against the Egyptians. [See question #3, page 160.]

B. Disobedience by the Midwives (v. 17)

17. But the midwives feared God, and did not as the king of Egypt commanded them, but saved the men children alive.

We see two kinds of fear in today's lesson. The fear of Egypt's *king* is for his personal position, power, prestige, and pride. The fear of the *midwives* is a godly fear or reverential awe that puts *God* at the center of life. This is "the fear of the Lord [that] is the beginning of wisdom" (Psalm 111:10; Proverbs 9:10). This wisdom enables a person to evaluate situations properly and then make decisions that are pleasing to God.

This verse is the heart of today's lesson. It presents the midwives as making a choice based on what they believe God wants them to do, and not on what the king has ordered. Some things may be legal or politically correct, but they are morally wrong. Ida M. Tarbell reports Abraham Lincoln as saying, "You may burn my body to ashes, and scatter them to the winds of heaven; you may drag my soul down to the regions of darkness and despair to be tormented forever, but you will never get me to support a measure which I believe to be wrong, although by doing so I may accomplish that which I believe to be right."

The opening comments for this lesson developed the thought that every person must learn to prioritize his or her loyalties. The midwives place loyalty to God above loyalty to the king. Shiphrah and Puah, two obscure women living in ancient Egypt, thus provide an example that we see in others through the centuries. They include the companions of Daniel who refuse to bow to an image (Daniel 3:18), those in the intertestamental period who choose death over denying their faith (see the nonbiblical 4 Maccabees), and the apostles who continue to preach Jesus even though commanded not to do so (Acts 4:19; 5:29).

The pressures of many situations are enormous, but God-honoring choices are possible. The results may not be pleasant in the initial consequences that accompany the decision, but they are pleasing to the creator. [See question #4, page 160.]

C. Reaction of the King (v. 18)

18. And the king of Egypt called for the midwives, and said unto them, Why have ye done this thing, and have saved the men children alive?

The king of Egypt is confronted by what seems to be willful disobedience on the part of the *midwives*. His line of inquiry seems to demonstrate that he wants a fair inquiry. His questions are designed to determine if there is a reasonable explanation for what has been happening (compare Daniel 3:14).

D. Response of the Midwives (v. 19)

19. And the midwives said unto Pharaoh, Because the Hebrew women are not as the Egyptian women; for they are lively, and are delivered ere the midwives come in unto them.

It is possible that childbirth may be less difficult for women who endure rigorous lives. If this is the case, then *the midwives* state the truth. Another possibility is that the women speak only part of the truth in that the midwives have determined to be very slow about responding when making their house calls. Under this possibility, the Hebrews are fully aware of the reason for the delay, and it is agreed that each baby will be born and breathing before a midwife arrives.

A third view is that the midwives are telling an outright lie. If so, they are taking what would be called "the lesser of two evils" approach. This means that the midwives realize that telling a lie is a lesser sin (although still a sin) than allowing or causing innocent babies to be murdered. Ultimately, we don't have enough information to know which of the three possibilities reflects what is really going on here. (We will have more to say

Visual for Lesson 5

Use this visual to remind your learners that making right choices can be a lonely experience.

about the "lesser of two evils" concept in next week's lesson.)

E. Rewards for the Midwives (vv. 20, 21)

20. Therefore God dealt well with the midwives: and the people multiplied, and waxed very mighty.

It seems that the king accepts the statements of *the midwives*. The important thing is that the actions of the midwives are pleasing to *God*. The king's plans to stifle population growth are thwarted. God's plans are still on schedule.

The oppression of the people, however, does not end (see the last verse of the chapter and the account of Moses' birth in Exodus 2). But the efforts to practice population control at this time are futile.

21. And it came to pass, because the midwives feared God, that he made them houses.

The *midwives* eventually are blessed with their own children—that's the implication of *he made them houses*. We may say that "they lived happily ever after." Times often will be difficult for the Israelites as the years pass, but for now they have examples of faith and faithfulness of two midwives who fear *God* and are blessed for their decision. [See question #5, page 160.]

CHOOSING BETWEEN TWO MASTERS

Official Roman Catholic teaching has long been opposed to many forms of fertility treatments. In 2007, the senior Catholic prelate in England instructed London's St. John & St. Elizabeth Hospital to cease all such treatments, including abortion referrals. Since 2005, the hospital had been the subject of Vatican concern. At that time it had leased a part of its premises to National Health Services physicians. Since they are British public employees, they are required by law to prescribe contraceptives and the so-called "morning after" pill, and to make referrals for abortions. This put the hospital in the uncomfortable position of having two masters holding conflicting value systems.

Regardless of one's views regarding the Catholic church's doctrine in some of these matters, one can certainly sympathize with the plight of the hospital personnel. A secular government with little concern for biblical teaching is battling a group trying to follow biblical principles as it understands them—and the hospital is caught in the middle.

All this reminds us of the midwives' dilemma: should they obey Pharaoh or their conscience? The situation of the midwives demonstrates that this kind of struggle is not new. The situation of the hospital demonstrates that this kind of struggle is not going away.   —C. R. B.

Conclusion

A. Consequences

The midwives' response to the king's question has more than one possible interpretation, as the commentary notes. But the bottom line is that their fear of the Lord was greater than their fear of the consequences that the king of Egypt could administer.

The results could have been disastrous. We recall that God does not always choose to provide physical protection and blessing for those who take a stand for Him; the martyrdoms of the prophets and the apostles speak to this fact clearly. We thus should not come away from this lesson believing that taking a stand for God will result in an easier or safer earthly life.

But God did choose to bless the two midwives who feared Him. In the final analysis, to hear the words "Well done" is the desired eternal consequence for those who serve Him, no matter the earthly consequence (Matthew 25:21, 23).

B. Prayer

Lord, thank You for this study that has prompted a greater commitment to make godly decisions. We all go through crises in life, and these often offer us choices. The important thing is that we bring glory to You when a crisis comes. This will require courage, but with the power of Your Spirit, we shall prevail. In Jesus' name, amen.

C. Thought to Remember

Pleasing God is the most important thing.

Home Daily Bible Readings

Monday, Dec. 29—Honor Those Who Fear God (Psalm 15)

Tuesday, Dec. 30—Whom Shall I Fear? (Psalm 27:1-6)

Wednesday, Dec. 31—Fear No Evil (Psalm 23)

Thursday, Jan. 1—Delivered from Fear (Psalm 34:4-14)

Friday, Jan. 2—The Friendship of the Lord (Psalm 25:12-21)

Saturday, Jan. 3—Let All Fear the Lord (Psalm 33:8-18)

Sunday, Jan. 4—Courage in the Face of Threat (Exodus 1:8-21)

Learning by Doing

This page contains an alternative lesson plan emphasizing learning activities. Some of these activities are also found in the helpful student book, Adult Bible Class.

Into the Lesson

Present the following as a quiz to your learners. "If you received conflicting orders from the following pairs, whom would you obey? 1. As a child, your schoolteacher or your mother; 2. As a driver, the Department of Transportation highway rules book or a law officer who has stopped your vehicle; 3. Regarding nutrition, a registered nutritionist or a medical doctor; 4. Regarding your car, an independent auto mechanic or the auto mechanic at the new car dealer; 5. Regarding mental health, a secular psychiatrist or a Christian counselor with only a master's degree; 6. Regarding your finances, a tax accountant or an IRS agent; 7. For directions, a map or someone who has lived in that area for six years.

Let the class respond orally. You may expect most answers to begin with, "It depends on . . ." After the discussion runs its course, say, "The midwives in Exodus 1 had no problem deciding what to do in their dilemma regarding whom to obey. Let's examine their story in today's text."

Into the Word

Display a sign with the phrase *Something Old, Something New*. Say, "Some things change; some things stay the same. As I read each verse of today's text, I'm going to ask, 'What's old?' and 'What's new?' Help me make a list." Read the text audibly.

Some responses are fairly obvious. Here are possible answers. Verse 8: *Old*, Joseph's people in the land; *New*, king and government. Verse 9: *Old*, suspicion of alien people in a country; *New*, the insight/observation of the king. Verse 10: *Old*, the concept of choosing sides in a war; *New*, the plan for dealing with the Israelites. Verse 11: *Old*, self-aggrandizement by a monarch; *New*, taskmasters who afflicted the Jews. Verse 12: *Old*, fear and anxiety of the Egyptians; *New*, results of affliction. Verses 13, 14: *Old*, abuse of slaves; *New*, duties and burdens. Verses 15, 16: *Old*, idea of racial extinction; *New*, pharaoh's approach to the midwives. Verse 17: *Old*, disobedience for an ungodly law; *New*, two heroines for God. Verses 20, 21: *Old*, God blesses faithfulness to His will; *New*, midwives establish their own families with children.

Accept all the answers your learners suggest. Some may differ as to whether a phenomenon is old or new, but that will allow discussion of relevant events and decisions. As the group proceeds through the verses, you will be free to add commentary notes as you choose.

Stress that the midwives demonstrate submission to the greater authority. Ask your class, as a group or in smaller groups, to develop an acrostic on the word *midwives*, characterizing their status and faith and deeds. Many possibilities exist, but here is one set of examples (with brief explanation in parentheses).

M — mothers (themselves, v. 21)
I — identified (by name, v. 15)
D — devoted (to God and His people)
W — wise (in response to Pharaoh's inquiry)
I — intransigent (refused to compromise)
V — volitional (free to refuse Pharaoh's order)
E — Egyptian (by birthplace)
S — significant (in God's plan for Israel)

Certainly, other key words can apply, such as *decisive*, *insightful*, and *submissive*.

Into Life

When Peter and John faced a dilemma of authority in the earliest days of the church, they had the answer every Christian needs for such circumstances: "We ought to obey God rather than men" (Acts 5:29; see also 4:19). Teach your class this handy verse for such occasions. Label the fingers one by one with the eight words of that text; then for the last two fingers, use "Acts" and "5:29." Get the class to repeat the exercise in unison at least twice.

Ask the class to consider recent decisions when they should have used the principle of this verse as their deciding factor, but did not. Suggest that this failure and new resolve be a matter of repentant prayer in the coming week's personal devotional times. Give your learners these two commitment statements to consider for those devotional times:

I, _____, *will follow in the footsteps of Shiphrah and Puah, never hesitating to disobey the commandments of people and governments when they clearly conflict with those of God.*

I, _____, *will stand up for God's people when they are threatened by the devil and his agents, and I will actively intervene on their behalf.*

Let's Talk It Over

The questions on this page are designed to promote discussion of the lesson by the class and to encourage application of the lesson Scriptures. The answers provided are only discussion starters. Let your class talk it over from there.

1. In what ways do church leaders fail to exercise proper leadership because of fear? Should we make a distinction between sincere fear and fear that is being used merely to manipulate? How do we guard against this problem?

Use this question with caution if your church has had problems in this area. Point out that in the Old Testament 12 spies were sent to look over the land God had promised. Two of these trusted God to provide victory, but the fearful opinion of the other 10 prevailed—much to God's displeasure.

Some fear is sincerely held. Some fear is expressed falsely, being used only to manipulate. Under either kind of fear, leaders can come up with all kinds of reasons why moving out by faith will not work. Some leaders hold the church back out of fear of what "might" happen. In effect, they are more concerned about *not losing* than they are about *winning.* Jesus had something to say about this; see Luke 19:11-27. (See also p. 117 of this commentary.)

2. How has God worked in your life or in your church to reverse attempts to stop the progress of the gospel?

Daniel was cast into the lions' den. His three friends were tossed into a fiery furnace. Peter was thrown in prison. God did not allow these injustices to stop His plan.

Christians face ridicule. When the Christian does not react in anger and vengeance, the hearts of the persecutors can melt and be drawn to God. A church may become a place of influence in a community that at one time was opposed to having a church there. Church buildings have been set on fire and destroyed, but when Christians respond in forgiveness and faith, people see the real Christ.

3. What was a time when you were asked to do what was wrong in order to meet the desires of someone in authority? How did you respond?

Romans 13 tells us that we are to obey those in authority. However, Peter and John refused to obey an authoritative command to speak no more in the name of Jesus. "Whether it be right in the sight of God to hearken unto you more than unto God, judge ye. For we cannot but speak the things which we have seen and heard" (Acts 4:19, 20).

Together, these two passages tell us that our obligation to obey earthly authority ceases when that authority commands something contrary to God's will. When Peter and John responded as they did, God provided His blessing and the church continued to grow. When we are asked to violate the will of God for the will of people, we must respond not in arrogance or vindictiveness, but rather in simple statements declaring our allegiance to the Word of God.

4. What does it take to make right choices, godly choices, when those choices defy those over us in this world?

Taking a stand against political pressure, economic oppression, or social ostracism is not easy. To do so requires confidence in God that He will remain faithful to His promise never to leave or forsake His people. A wholehearted commitment to that which is right and hatred of that which is wrong or evil is required.

Taking a stand also requires a healthy dose of godly fear. Matthew 10:28 challenges us with these words: "And fear not them which kill the body, but are not able to kill the soul: but rather fear him which is able to destroy both soul and body in hell." It is those who work for righteousness whom God blesses.

5. How has God blessed you because of your faith?

Scripture tells us that "godliness with contentment is great gain" (1 Timothy 6:6). Part of the blessing of God is the contentment we gain when we are godly. The Lord delivers His people from afflictions (Psalm 34:19). He also provides care for His people when they are sick (Psalm 41:3). God has promised to work in all things for good for those who love Him (Romans 8:28).

The greatest blessing in this life for the faithful is that we are God's children (John 1:12). This leads to the ultimate blessing of Heaven itself, the final reward of the faithful (Revelation 2:10). Things that we take for granted, such as safety in travel, protection in our homes, faithful children, and our daily needs being met, should be seen as blessings from a faithful God to His faithful people.

Rahab Helps God's People

DEVOTIONAL READING: Hebrews 11:23-31.

BACKGROUND SCRIPTURE: Joshua 2; 6:22-25.

PRINTED TEXT: Joshua 2:1-4a, 11b-14; 6:22-25.

Joshua 2:1-4a, 11b-14

1 And Joshua the son of Nun sent out of Shittim two men to spy secretly, saying, Go view the land, even Jericho. And they went, and came into a harlot's house, named Rahab, and lodged there.

2 And it was told the king of Jericho, saying, Behold, there came men in hither tonight of the children of Israel to search out the country.

3 And the king of Jericho sent unto Rahab, saying, Bring forth the men that are come to thee, which are entered into thine house: for they be come to search out all the country.

4a And the woman took the two men, and hid them.

. . . .

11b For the LORD your God, he is God in heaven above, and in earth beneath.

12 Now therefore, I pray you, swear unto me by the LORD, since I have showed you kindness, that ye will also show kindness unto my father's house, and give me a true token:

13 And that ye will save alive my father, and my mother, and my brethren, and my sisters, and all that they have, and deliver our lives from death.

14 And the men answered her, Our life for yours, if ye utter not this our business. And it shall be, when the LORD hath given us the land, that we will deal kindly and truly with thee.

Joshua 6:22-25

22 But Joshua had said unto the two men that had spied out the country, Go into the harlot's house, and bring out thence the woman, and all that she hath, as ye sware unto her.

23 And the young men that were spies went in, and brought out Rahab, and her father, and her mother, and her brethren, and all that she had; and they brought out all her kindred, and left them without the camp of Israel.

24 And they burnt the city with fire, and all that was therein: only the silver, and the gold, and the vessels of brass and of iron, they put into the treasury of the house of the LORD.

25 And Joshua saved Rahab the harlot alive, and her father's household, and all that she had; and she dwelleth in Israel even unto this day; because she hid the messengers, which Joshua sent to spy out Jericho.

GOLDEN TEXT: The LORD your God, he is God in heaven above, and in earth beneath. Now therefore, I pray you, swear unto me by the LORD, since I have showed you kindness, that ye will also show kindness unto my father's house.—Joshua 2:11, 12.

Jan 11

<table>
</table>

Human Commitment
Unit 2: Old Testament People
of Commitment
(Lessons 5–12)

Lesson Aims

After participating in this lesson, each student will be able to:

1. State the factors that caused fear for the Canaanites, but faith for Rahab.

2. Give a modern example of someone who has the godly courage of Rahab.

3. Describe how he or she will adopt Rahab's courage in one area of life.

Lesson Outline

INTRODUCTION
   A. Keep Your Word!
   B. Lesson Background
 I. CONCEALING THE SPIES (Joshua 2:1-4a)
   A. Command by Joshua (v. 1)
      Courage at Work
   B. Concern of the King (vv. 2, 3)
   C. Craftiness of Rahab (v. 4a)
 II. COVENANT WITH THE SPIES (Joshua 2:11b-14)
   A. Confession by Rahab (v. 11b)
   B. Concerns of Rahab (vv. 12, 13)
   C. Consolation for Rahab (v. 14)
      Quid Pro Quo
 III. CONTRASTING THE OUTCOMES (Joshua 6:22-25)
   A. Covenant Remembered (vv. 22, 23)
   B. Consequences for Jericho (v. 24)
   C. Compensations for Rahab (v. 25)
      Keeping Promises
CONCLUSION
   A. The Problem with Rahab
   B. Prayer
   C. Thought to Remember

Introduction

A. Keep Your Word!

The three-year-old girl was eager to accompany her father to the supermarket. As the two of them went outside and walked toward the car, the father suddenly stopped. The shopping list was still inside.

The father then made a bargain with his daughter. He told her to stand where she was on the sidewalk and not go onto the grass. If she obeyed, he would buy her a candy bar at the store.

He asked if she understood, and she said *yes.* He asked her what she was going to do, and she said she would not move. In less than a minute her father had returned with the list. At the store the little girl made her selection, and she was thrilled. From previous experiences she had come to expect that her father would keep his word.

Contrast the above account with a scene that was overheard in the same supermarket. A mother promised candy to a son if he would quit reaching for things. When they arrived at the checkout counter, the youngster saw the candy display and asked for his reward. The mother's response was this: "Did you think I would really get anything for you?" The little boy was being shaped to look out for himself and not to take people at their word.

Many do not keep their commitments. In the twenty-first century, as in other centuries, people make promises with no intention of keeping them. In some situations, a person actually intends to do what is promised, but changing circumstances make it inconvenient to follow through. We remember that Jesus said that we will give an account in the judgment for our words (Matthew 12:36, 37).

Today's lesson is a great illustration of pledges being kept. It also involves a great problem—the fact that someone used deception. Attention will be given to that issue in the closing comments.

B. Lesson Background

The book of Joshua begins with the Israelite nation encamped in the plains of Moab, across the Jordan River from Jericho. That city was the first military objective in Canaan. It had been at least 120 years since the Egyptians began the oppression of Israel, as described in the previous lesson. During that time Moses had been born, and he had fled Egypt at the age of 40 (Acts 7:23-29). At the age of 80 (Exodus 3:10; 7:7), Moses was called by God to return to Egypt to lead the Israelites out of Egypt. Moses died at the age of 120 (Deuteronomy 34:7), while the Israelites were camped in Moab (Numbers 21:20).

The stay in the plains of Moab lasted quite some time. During that interval the king of Moab sent for Balaam to come and curse Israel. It was at least a 400-mile trip one way to secure Balaam, and he did not come until the second appeal. These two trips thus required that the king's representatives travel no less than 1,600 miles (Numbers 22).

Israel also fought extensive campaigns against two major groups who lived on the eastern side of the Jordan (Numbers 21:21-35). These were against Sihon and the Amorites (the nearest group to the north and east; Deuteronomy 2:24-37) and against

Og, the king of Bashan, an area east of Galilee. The latter conflict involved capturing 60 cities (Deuteronomy 3:4), and such campaigns take time.

A military census was taken at the end of the wilderness wanderings, with the total number of men available being 601,730 (Numbers 26:51). It seems to have been a custom to keep a large part of the army on the home front, so a much smaller number was available for the conquests in the Transjordan area (that is, the area to the east of the Jordan River). Then came time to cross that river into the promised land (Joshua 3, 4).

I. Concealing the Spies
(Joshua 2:1-4a)

First a bit of reconnaissance is needed. The verses selected for this lesson yield a thrilling account of spying, intrigue, treason, courage, and hope. They primarily involve Rahab (a prostitute in Jericho), two unnamed spies, and Joshua.

A. Command by Joshua (v. 1)

1. And Joshua the son of Nun sent out of Shittim two men to spy secretly, saying, Go view the land, even Jericho. And they went, and came into a harlot's house, named Rahab, and lodged there.

The word *Shittim* represents a place in the plains of Moab. The word is a transliteration from the Hebrew original. If the word is translated, a reasonable rendering is "acacia grove" (see Numbers 25:1; 33:49).

In his careful preparations, *Joshua* sends *two* trustworthy individuals to assess the situation at *Jericho.* Memories of being one of the 12 spies about 39 years prior must be on Joshua's mind (Numbers 13:8, 16), and he does not want the tragedy of that situation repeated. He undoubtedly recalls that the majority report was the wrong one, and that Israel was sentenced to a total of 40 years

---

How to Say It

AMORITES. *Am*-uh-rites.
BALAAM. *Bay*-lum.
BASHAN. *Bay*-shan.
CANAAN. *Kay*-nun.
JERICHO. *Jair*-ih-co.
JORDAN. *Jor*-dun.
MOAB. *Mo*-ab.
MOSES. *Mo*-zes or *Mo*-zez.
QUID PRO QUO. kwid pro kwo.
RAHAB. *Ray*-hab.
SHITTIM. Shih-*teem*.
SIHON. *Sigh*-hun.

---

in the wilderness for their lack of faith and courage. The Hebrew text actually says that he spoke to them *secretly,* and the sending is also in secret.

Joshua 6:23 says that these are young men, and crossing the Jordan when it is in flood stage (Joshua 3:15) requires the vigor of youth. Their choice of a place to lodge is tactically sound: the location on the wall can facilitate an emergency escape (Joshua 2:15; Acts 9:25). It normally will not arouse suspicion for men to be seen going to such a place as Rahab's, which also provides overnight accommodations for travelers.

It is interesting that God uses many people who are often scorned or are weak spiritually to accomplish His ends. The list of such people includes Matthew (a tax collector), Gideon (a fearful person), Moses (a murderer and a refugee in a foreign land for 40 years), Jacob (a deceiver), Samson (someone who has problems with the opposite sex), and Jonah (a reluctant prophet). [See question #1, page 168.]

COURAGE AT WORK

Bond . . . James Bond. With those words the most famous spy in literature has introduced himself numerous times on the silver screen. Bond is the hero of Ian Fleming's 14 novels about him. Bond has been portrayed in numerous films, by 6 actors. He is world famous for his droll humor and his courage and cunning, aided and abetted by amazing, high-tech wizardry.

We note that the Bond character is often interpreted as that of a suave lady's man who has a distinct tendency for committing immorality with beautiful women. Add to that his appetite for alcoholic beverages, and it becomes quite apparent why Christians do not hold James Bond up as a role model for their children!

In one of the Old Testament's stories that could be deemed as rated PG, Joshua's spies found their refuge in the city of Jericho in the home of a prostitute. We may be sure that the spies were neither as photogenic nor as technologically savvy as the actors who have portrayed James Bond. The text is silent as to whether their morals were any better than Bond's. But the spies certainly must have been courageous and cunning, and Israel was blessed by their willingness to risk their lives for the cause of Israel and Israel's God. How many situations today can you name in which God's people are risking their lives for him?   —C. R. B.

B. Concern of the King (vv. 2, 3)

2. And it was told the king of Jericho, saying, Behold, there came men in hither tonight of the children of Israel to search out the country.

We may find it strange to read that cities have kings, but many city-states at this time have leaders who use this title. In this case, a report gets back to *the king of Jericho* about the strangers who have entered his city. Their clothing and their speech perhaps cause them to be identified.

The people of Jericho certainly are aware of the very large encampment that has been on the other side of the Jordan for several months by this time. Merchants surely have brought word that those people are coming to take this land, and that they are convinced that their God promised it to them centuries before (Genesis 13:14, 15). Rahab's statement in verse 10 shows that the inhabitants of the land know how God has led His people through the Red Sea, and how they had defeated the forces of Sihon and Og.

3. And the king of Jericho sent unto Rahab, saying, Bring forth the men that are come to thee, which are entered into thine house: for they be come to search out all the country.

The *king of Jericho* draws an accurate conclusion concerning why *the men* have come, and he also knows that they have *entered* the *house* of *Rahab.* The soldiers do not rush into her house. Instead they demonstrate the courtesy of the time by not entering the dwelling of a woman unless invited to do so. The appeal that they use is based on the elements of fear and patriotism.

C. Craftiness of Rahab (v. 4a)

4a. And the woman took the two men, and hid them.

It is likely that Rahab and *the two men* are aware of the danger of the situation. Thus the precaution of hiding may already be accomplished. The hiding place is on the roof, under stalks of flax that are there to dry (Joshua 2:6, not in today's text).

II. Covenant with the Spies (Joshua 2:11b-14)

The intervening text not included in today's lesson describe how Rahab deceives the king's soldiers who came to her house to seek the spies. She confirms that the spies have been there, but then falsely states that they have already left. She adds that if the soldiers hurry they may be able to overtake the spies. The spies, however, are on top of the house.

A. Confession by Rahab (v. 11b)

11b. For the LORD your God, he is God in heaven above, and in earth beneath.

Women of Rahab's occupation often are very astute. For better or worse, they observe things and people carefully. Rahab knows about the great things that the Israelites have achieved by God's help. Her analysis is that the *God* of Israel is also the God of *heaven above* and *earth beneath.* She wants to be aligned with Him! [See question #2, page 168.]

B. Concerns of Rahab (vv. 12, 13)

12. Now therefore, I pray you, swear unto me by the LORD, since I have showed you kindness, that ye will also show kindness unto my father's house, and give me a true token.

Rahab's faith is strong enough to motivate her to take bold action. So at the risk of her life, she bargains with the spies. Her requests involve what she has done for the spies, on the oath that she wants the spies to *swear,* and on her receiving something that will serve as a reminder and proof of the covenant. The word given as *kindness* is often rendered "love"; it represents a relationship, especially a covenant relationship. [See question #3, page 168.]

Rahab is cited twice in the New Testament for her brave action of receiving the spies and protecting them: once for her faith (Hebrews 11:31) and once for her works (James 2:25). She is also mentioned in Matthew 1:5 as an ancestress of Jesus the Messiah.

13. And that ye will save alive my father, and my mother, and my brethren, and my sisters, and all that they have, and deliver our lives from death.

Rahab's request for safety goes beyond herself. At the appropriate time, she will have to acknowledge to her family what she has done in her unpatriotic deeds, and she surely shares with them the basis of the faith that she has acquired. One definition for faith is that it is "a whole-soul trust in God because of the sufficiency of the evidence." Rahab has examined the evidence, and she has decided for God.

C. Consolation for Rahab (v. 14)

14. And the men answered her, Our life for yours, if ye utter not this our business. And it shall be, when the LORD hath given us the land, that we will deal kindly and truly with thee.

The spies give the first of three conditions with which Rahab must comply. For now, she cannot speak to anyone about what she has done. Joshua 2:17, 18 adds two other components: (1) she must have all of her family in the house with her, and (2) a scarlet cord must be in the window of her house. She is assured that the Israelites will treat her and her family *kindly.* If these conditions are not met, the spies will be free from the oath.

QUID PRO QUO

Quid pro quo is a Latin phrase that means "something for something." It is the essence of contracts, as each side promises to fulfill certain obligations. Promises made in advertising campaigns become *quid pro quo* as the sales pitch becomes something of a contract that says, "Give us your money for this product, and look at all the benefits you'll get in return."

Think, for example, about the VW Beetle—also called "the Bug." The first Bugs to come to America were, by American standards, tiny, exceedingly simple, and terribly underpowered. Perceptions changed in 1959 when a New York advertising firm began promoting this car.

The resulting *Think Small* advertising campaign was voted the No. 1 campaign of all time in 1999 by *Advertising Age*. The campaign poked fun at the elementary nature of the vehicle, but promised that the buyer would end up with important things: high quality, inexpensive operation, and the cachet that came from owning a car that many people could not comprehend. It was a *quid pro quo* that sold millions of cars.

In the *quid pro quo* between Rahab and the spies, each promised something of value that involved physical safety for the parties concerned. Our relationship with Christ is a *quid pro quo* of infinitely greater value: He promises our eternal salvation as we promise to live for Him. Are we as good at articulating this most important of all *quid pro quos* as advertising agencies are at selling cars? —C. R. B.

III. Contrasting the Outcomes (Joshua 6:22-25)

When the spies return to the camp, they share with Joshua the details of their adventure. The most important aspect of their report is that the people of the land are fearful. The narrative between 2:14 and 6:22 includes the accounts of the crossing of the Jordan, the observance of the Passover, the beginning of eating the produce of the land (no more manna!), and of the 13 marching trips around Jericho that lead to its fall and capture.

A. Covenant Remembered (vv. 22, 23)

22. But Joshua had said unto the two men that had spied out the country, Go into the harlot's house, and bring out thence the woman, and all that she hath, as ye sware unto her.

The spies also have told by this time of the commitment that is in effect for Rahab and her family. *Joshua* thus directs *the two men* to rescue the family. He and the spies are men of honor—they keep their word. [See question #4, page 168.]

Visual for Lessons 6 & 11

Use this visual to remind your learners of that most fundamental question: "Who is the Lord?"

23. And the young men that were spies went in, and brought out Rahab, and her father, and her mother, and her brethren, and all that she had; and they brought out all her kindred, and left them without the camp of Israel.

This is the verse that gives the detail that the spies are *young*. These two *men* fulfill the covenant that they have made, and they bring *out Rahab* and her family. (It is interesting to speculate on the emotions of Rahab when she sees the same two men again.) The family cannot be brought into *the camp of Israel* until they are clean ceremonially.

B. Consequences for Jericho (v. 24)

24. And they burnt the city with fire, and all that was therein: only the silver, and the gold, and the vessels of brass and of iron, they put into the treasury of the house of the LORD.

The *city* of Jericho is the first conquest within Canaan. It and its contents are said to be "devoted" to God (Joshua 6:18), and the consequence is that the city is destroyed by burning. All the valuables of the city are to be placed *into the treasury* of *the Lord* (compare Joshua 6:19).

Jericho is one of three cities in the book of Joshua that is destroyed in this way (Joshua 8:2, 28; 11:11, 14). The spoils of the others cities of Canaan belong to the Israelites, but not this one.

C. Compensations for Rahab (v. 25)

25. And Joshua saved Rahab the harlot alive, and her father's household, and all that she had; and she dwelleth in Israel even unto this day; because she hid the messengers, which Joshua sent to spy out Jericho.

Joshua is given the primary credit for sparing *Rahab* and her family. A reason is assigned for her rescue: she had hidden the spies who found refuge with her. She eventually marries one of the men of Judah because she becomes a Gentile in the lineage of Jesus. (There is no evidence to support the romantic conjecture that she marries one of the spies.) The verse before us affirms that Rahab is still alive when this account is written down. [See question #5, page 168.]

KEEPING PROMISES

In March 1990, football coach Bill McCartney (University of Colorado) asked his friend Dave Wardell, "What do you feel is the most important factor in changing a man spiritually, from immaturity to maturity?" Wardell said, "Discipleship." A seed was sown, and in a meeting a few months later at Boulder Valley Christian Church the Promise Keepers (PK) concept came to fruition (www. promisekeepers.org).

PK features a list of seven promises that men should keep. Number three concerns "spiritual, moral, ethical, and sexual purity." This promise—with its emphasis on biblical values—is a great help for men seeking to keep the marriage vows they have made before God to their wives. Since 1990, millions of men have attended PK conferences. The Promise Keepers' call for men to act with integrity can hardly be seen as a negative influence in society!

Keeping promises builds trust. Breaking promises destroys trust. Rahab and the Hebrew spies kept their promises. One result was that this Gentile woman's name would find its place in the lineage of Christ! Where will your kept promises lead you in the service of God?   —C. R. B.

Home Daily Bible Readings

Monday, Jan. 5—The Courage of Faith (Joshua 1:10-18)

Tuesday, Jan. 6—Rahab—Example of Faith (Hebrews 11:23-31)

Wednesday, Jan. 7—Rahab's Declaration (Joshua 2:8-11)

Thursday, Jan. 8—Rahab's Agreement (Joshua 2:15-21)

Friday, Jan. 9—Rahab—Justified by Her Works (James 2:21-26)

Saturday, Jan. 10—Rahab's Legacy—A King! (Matthew 1:1-6)

Sunday, Jan. 11—Rahab's Protection (Joshua 2:1-4, 11-14; 6:22-25)

Conclusion

A. The Problem with Rahab

Were Rahab's deceptions displeasing to God? James 2:25 would lead us to answer that question *no*. Yet scholars have debated this issue through the centuries, and their differing conclusions cause us to think carefully.

First, some affirm that what Rahab did cannot be defended, but her less than perfect background and the pressures of the situation excuse her. John Calvin writes that "Rahab acted wrongly when she told a lie and said that the spies had gone. . . . although God wished the spies to be delivered, He did not sanction their being protected by a lie."

Others have proposed that a lie is to be defined as "a false statement, with wicked or malicious or selfish intent to deceive or mislead." Under this definition, Rahab did not tell an actual lie since her false statements had good motives (compare also the midwives from last week's lesson). This definition, however, does not match the one in Merriam-Webster's dictionary, which says that a lie is "an assertion of something known or believed by the speaker to be untrue with intent to deceive." This is exactly the kind of assertion Rahab made. Notice that the Merriam-Webster definition of a lie does not include the issue of the "goodness" or "badness" of the deceiver's motives.

Others propose that Rahab's deception falls under the "lesser of two evils" idea. Lying is a serious sin (Exodus 20:16; Revelation 21:8). Yet we live in a fallen world, and sometimes we have to make sobering choices. Under this consideration, Rahab made the decision that telling a lie was a lesser evil than allowing the spies to be captured.

The best solution, however, takes into account the God-directed wars in which the Israelites engaged. Since God commanded the taking of human life in those wars, then such killing was not a violation of the command not to murder (Exodus 20:13). If people can kill without sinning in the prosecution of a "just" war, then should they not be able to make false statements without sinning in that same context? May God grant us wisdom and courage to make choices that please Him.

B. Prayer

Almighty God, thank You for the examples of men and women who were prompted by their faith in the choices they made. Give us wisdom today to choose what is pleasing to You and in accord with Your Word. In Jesus' name, amen.

C. Thought to Remember

Our words acquit or condemn us.

Learning by Doing

This page contains an alternative lesson plan emphasizing learning activities. Some of these activities are also found in the helpful student book, Adult Bible Class.

Into the Lesson

Come to class dressed in a dark trench coat (all weather), with the collar turned up around your neck. Wear a man's dark fedora pulled down almost over your eyes. Have dark glasses on. If possible, enter the room after others have arrived, "sneaking" through the door and around objects in the room, with an occasional furtive glance to both sides and behind you.

When you stand/sit in your usual teaching position, say, "Well, I'm dressed for the part. What part is it?" Someone will say "Spy!" and give you the opportunity to comment, "Today's study is about spies who get caught—sort of! Let me introduce you to the one who helped them out." Introduce your "Rahab" of the following activity, and suggest that learners follow along in the texts and the intervening chapters of Joshua.

Into the Word

Recruit an actress to wear a biblical-times robe. She will present the following monologue as if she were Rahab of Jericho. Introduce "Rahab" to your class and suggest that students follow along in today's text to spot relevant facts and suppositions. Also direct them to consider questions they would like to ask your Rahab at the end. It may be helpful to copy and distribute copies of Rahab's monologue at the conclusion to spur further thought and discussion.

Rahab's Monologue

Little did I imagine that a kindness to enemy spies would make me the mother of princes and kings. It was far beyond my imagination to picture my sinful self as an ancestress to a righteous Savior. Oh, I did believe in the God of Israel. The stories those caravan men told us of His power over nature and enemies was enough to convince me. Holding the sea back! Providing food in the wilderness! Fire! Smoke! Oh, my! I should not be surprised at His ability to transform an unworthy, insignificant life.

Think of my surprise when men came from Israel's encampment to my house. Perhaps they came to me because of the fact that my house was along the wall, making an easy escape possible. Perhaps, sadly, it was the fact that traveling men knew my door well, and these two saw themselves blending in in that regard.

I do not know whose loose lips told the king of their presence, no doubt expecting the king's coin to fill his pockets. When I covered the spies with the flax, I assured them that they would not be found in the dark of the night.

My untruth—that they were not in my house—God will forgive. It was a simple bargain: their lives for mine and those of my family. It was a bargain kept in good faith. And so my family and I came to dwell with the people of God. Even more importantly, my family and I became part of the people of God.

· ·

At the conclusion, allow your learners to question Rahab, both for revealed and supposed truths of her story. Be sure your actress is willing to respond to such inquiries.

To get the question and answer time started, you could ask, "Rahab, what particular stories that you heard regarding the work of the Lord God in rescuing His people from Egyptian bondage impressed you the most?"

Into Life

Challenge your class to identify godly people of modern times who have risked all to establish and maintain a relationship with the Lord Jesus. These may be people whose names are unknown to the students, such as Muslims who risk their lives by converting to Christianity.

Call this concluding activity Compared to Rahab. Say, "Most of us think we would come off fairly well if compared with a pagan prostitute. But Rahab sets a high standard for a follower of God! Here's a list of attributes and acts of Rahab. Rate yourself from 0 (not at all) to 5 (completely true) for each of these."

Give each of your learners a copy of the following, with the heading *Compared to Rahab:* 1. I have believed the testimonies about God's mighty works in saving His people. 2. I am escaping the pagan influences of the culture into which I was born and live. 3. I desperately want my family saved from destruction, and I will work boldly to accomplish that. 4. I have made myself a part of the family of God with all the responsibilities of that relationship. 5. I see myself as "giving birth" (spiritually, if not physically) to future "kings" and "queens" of the kingdom of God.

Let's Talk It Over

The questions on this page are designed to promote discussion of the lesson by the class and to encourage application of the lesson Scriptures. The answers provided are only discussion starters. Let your class talk it over from there.

1. In what ways have you seen God use those considered "unworthy" to accomplish His purposes?

When we make a statement of the unworthiness of someone to be used by God, we are in fact sitting as a judge of God. Instead, we should give praise to God for the fact that He chooses to use *any* of us! The fact that He sent Jesus to die for us means that we all fall into the category of being unworthy.

God frequently uses those who appear to be unworthy by the standards of this world. First Corinthians 1:27-29 reminds us that God can use those who seem foolish, weak, base, and despised to demonstrate His wisdom, strength, and majesty. God accomplishes His will by using even those who reject Him; pharaoh is a prime example (Exodus 9:12). We want to make sure we don't fall into this category.

2. What would someone have to see in your church and in your individual life in order to exclaim, "For the Lord your God, he is God in heaven above, and in earth beneath"?

Churches and individual Christians are sometimes guilty of failing to live out their profession of God's power and glory. When churches give in to worldly practices and compromise the basics of biblical teaching, God is not seen as Lord of earth. Instead, slick marketers are seen as the ones to be looked up to as they are viewed as the ones "getting results."

Postmodern philosophy doesn't ask if something is *true,* but rather it asks if something *works.* Thus, those outside of Christ often will not be that interested in the truth that Christians preach. What impresses many unbelievers are *results* and how those results come about. Christians who fail to seek first the kingdom of God (Matthew 6:33), instead pursuing the things of this world, demonstrate that their hope for results is not in the power and provision of God.

3. How can we be more effective in demonstrating kindness?

The fruit of the Spirit in Galatians 5 includes kindness. This fruit can be a rather vague concept for us—hard to get a handle on. There are other Scriptures, though, that help us figure out how to express kindness.

Romans 12:10 states, "Be kindly affectioned one to another with brotherly love; in honor preferring one another." Beyond expressing kindness by preferring others or taking the feelings and needs of others into account, Ephesians 4:32 states that kindness is expressed in forgiveness. Kindness is seen in offering a cup of cold water to the one who is thirsty (Matthew 10:42) or a shoulder to cry on to the one who is distraught (2 Corinthians 1:4). Random acts of kindness performed in anonymity can be a great way to express this fruit of the Spirit in our lives.

4. What is the difference between the ways Christianity and the world view the value of keeping one's word? How do we resist the world's viewpoint?

Most people like to consider themselves to be truthful and honest. Yet many will succumb to the postmodern viewpoint (see question #2 above) that it's important to keep one's word only as long as it "works." Yet our word is at the core of our being. Our faithfulness to our word is the basis of our integrity and reputation. Breaking promises, forsaking marriage vows, and using bankruptcy to get out of debt all are forms of failing to keep our word. To be a person of one's word demands that he or she first take time to consider all promises, vows, or contracts being entered into. Commit yourself only to those things you are fully persuaded are right and that you can honor.

5. How can our faith be effective for saving our own families?

We first have to make a distinction between physical and spiritual "saving." Rahab's act of faith led to the sparing of the physical lives of her family, but did it lead them to accept the God of Israel and thus save them spiritually as well? We don't know for sure, but the right actions of one can have a powerful influence on others.

This is especially so in regard to salvation and Christian living. Remember: God has no grandchildren. Each person must individually make a personal decision for Christ. Yet by example a Christian may influence a family member who is lost to come to Christ. Prayer is a powerful tool in this regard. Also see 1 Corinthians 7:14.

Joshua Leads Israel

DEVOTIONAL READING: Psalm 142.

BACKGROUND SCRIPTURE: Joshua 3.

PRINTED TEXT: Joshua 3:1-13.

Joshua 3:1-13

1 And Joshua rose early in the morning; and they removed from Shittim, and came to Jordan, he and all the children of Israel, and lodged there before they passed over.

2 And it came to pass after three days, that the officers went through the host;

3 And they commanded the people, saying, When ye see the ark of the covenant of the LORD your God, and the priests the Levites bearing it, then ye shall remove from your place, and go after it.

4 Yet there shall be a space between you and it, about two thousand cubits by measure: come not near unto it, that ye may know the way by which ye must go: for ye have not passed this way heretofore.

5 And Joshua said unto the people, Sanctify yourselves: for tomorrow the LORD will do wonders among you.

6 And Joshua spake unto the priests, saying, Take up the ark of the covenant, and pass over before the people. And they took up the ark of the covenant, and went before the people.

7 And the LORD said unto Joshua, This day will I begin to magnify thee in the sight of all Israel, that they may know that, as I was with Moses, so I will be with thee.

8 And thou shalt command the priests that bear the ark of the covenant, saying, When ye are come to the brink of the water of Jordan, ye shall stand still in Jordan.

9 And Joshua said unto the children of Israel, Come hither, and hear the words of the LORD your God.

10 And Joshua said, Hereby ye shall know that the living God is among you, and that he will without fail drive out from before you the Canaanites, and the Hittites, and the Hivites, and the Perizzites, and the Girgashites, and the Amorites, and the Jebusites.

11 Behold, the ark of the covenant of the Lord of all the earth passeth over before you into Jordan.

12 Now therefore take you twelve men out of the tribes of Israel, out of every tribe a man.

13 And it shall come to pass, as soon as the soles of the feet of the priests that bear the ark of the LORD, the Lord of all the earth, shall rest in the waters of Jordan, that the waters of Jordan shall be cut off from the waters that come down from above; and they shall stand upon a heap.

GOLDEN TEXT: The LORD said unto Joshua, This day will I begin to magnify thee in the sight of all Israel, that they may know that, as I was with Moses, so I will be with thee.—Joshua 3:7.

Human Commitment
Unit 2: Old Testament People
of Commitment
(Lessons 5–12)

Lesson Aims

After participating in this lesson, each student will be able to:

1. Describe the different ways that God provided assurances to Joshua and Israel that Joshua was the approved leader.

2. Compare and contrast the manner in which Joshua was approved by God to be the leader of the people with the way leaders are approved in the church today.

3. Determine a specific way the class members, individually or collectively, can honor God's leaders in the local congregation.

Lesson Outline

INTRODUCTION
    A. Leadership Transitions
    B. Lesson Background
 I. PREPARING THE PEOPLE (Joshua 3:1-5)
    A. Changing Locations (v. 1)
    B. Commanded to Follow (vv. 2-4)
      What to Follow
    C. Cleansing Required (v. 5)
 II. PREPARING THE PRIESTS (Joshua 3:6-8)
    A. Carrying the Ark (v. 6)
    B. Commending Joshua (v. 7)
    C. Continuing to Stand (v. 8)
III. PROMISES TO ISRAEL (Joshua 3:9-13)
    A. Military Successes (vv. 9, 10)
      Will We Trust?
    B. Movement of the Ark (v. 11)
    C. Memorials Anticipated (v. 12)
    D. Mountain of Water (v. 13)
CONCLUSION
    A. Choose Your Leaders Wisely!
    B. Prayer
    C. Thought to Remember

Introduction

A. Leadership Transitions

He had been one of those outstanding elders in a local church. He was a businessman, but his real interest in life was God's Word. He loved nothing more than to talk about the Bible at length with preachers and Bible college professors whom he met. With his concordance he had done word studies and researched many topics.

Now, however, he was concerned. His health was declining, and within a short period of time others would have to take his leadership role in the church. He may not have been the chairman, but for years he had been the leader whose wisdom was sought in every situation.

His concerns were expressed in an article that he wrote, "Passing the Mantle." Its title comes from the occasion when Elijah was taken to Heaven in a whirlwind and dropped his mantle (or cloak) to Elisha, who was going to succeed him as the leader of the prophets (2 Kings 2:11-13).

Leadership transitions have two dimensions: the concerns of the one who has been the leader and the concerns of the successor. The former leader may wonder if the successor will bring to ruin what years of work have accomplished; in some cases the one receiving the mantle of leadership does little more than bask in the benefits that are available. The forward momentum slows, and over a period of time there is a reversal of the positive motion that had been in effect. The one giving up leadership also may wonder if the one who follows will do so well that many will question why the previous leader was not able to accomplish as much.

The successor also confronts certain issues. "Can I do as well? Will I fail?" are questions of self-doubt. The new leader may want to change the image or methodology of the organization while wondering how the changes will be received. Some people cannot handle change; others delight in it.

This lesson presents the first leadership challenge that Joshua faced after he succeeded Moses. Moses had been the father of the nation, and he had accomplished much in the 40 years that he was the leader. At times the Israelites rebelled against God and Moses, but Moses always met the challenges.

Would Joshua himself be equal to the obstacles that the nation was to face in Canaan? Assurances had been given (see Joshua 1), but was Joshua up to the job?

B. Lesson Background

The background for this lesson is essentially the same as in the previous lesson about Rahab. Featured here will be a review of references to Joshua during the previous part of his life—the 40 years in the wilderness that were years of preparation for his task as Moses' successor.

The first mention of Joshua occurs just after the initial time that Moses struck a rock for water to flow from that rock (Exodus 17). The Amalekites, a wandering desert group descended from Esau, immediately attacked, perhaps desiring possession of the new water supply. Moses selected Joshua to organize an army out of the inexperienced Israelites to confront the enemy.

Moses needed someone like Joshua, so the next reference to him is as Moses' "minister" or valet (Exodus 24:13). At that time Moses ascended Mt. Sinai to receive the two tablets with the Ten Commandments (see Exodus 20) and the Law in oral form. Joshua was permitted to go beyond the point where Moses instructed the elders to wait for "us" until they returned (Exodus 24:14).

Young Joshua is also mentioned as remaining in what Moses called "the Tabernacle of the congregation," perhaps to care for it as a part of his ministry to Moses (Exodus 33:7-11). In Numbers 13 and 14, Joshua was one of the 12 spies who entered Canaan from the south. That 40-day period turned into 40 years when the Israelites developed the "grasshopper complex" (Numbers 13:33). As the people heard the negative reports of 10 spies, they sided with the majority.

Only Joshua and Caleb of the 12 had the faith needed to forge ahead into Canaan, and they encouraged the people to do so. The people attempted to stone the two "good" spies, but God prevented it (14:10). The penalty was not only 40 years in the wilderness (14:34), but God decreed that 603,548 out the 603,550 men of war would die in the wilderness during the time remaining (see Deuteronomy 2:14). This averaged more than 40 funerals per day, each a reminder of the rebellion against God.

Joshua was designated by the Lord to be Moses' successor. Joshua was "a man in whom is the spirit" (Numbers 27:18), and he was commissioned or ordained by Eleazar (the son of Aaron who became the high priest after Aaron died; 27:19-23). Joshua was filled with the spirit of wisdom because Moses had also "laid his hands upon him" (Deuteronomy 34:9).

In one of Moses' last addresses to the nation, he commended Joshua to the people. He also challenged Joshua to be strong and courageous (Deuteronomy 31:7). At that time the Lord himself commissioned Joshua with the same admonition (31:14, 23) and did so again in Joshua 1. Joshua was God-chosen to lead the people across the Jordan, into the promised land.

I. Preparing the People (Joshua 3:1-5)

The events of the first two chapters of the book of Joshua lead up to the dramatic event about to take place. The people assure Joshua that they will follow him as they had followed Moses. Joshua reminds the two and one-half eastern tribes of their commitment to help in the conquest on the western side of the Jordan River. The incident of the spies and Rahab (last week's lesson) provides the important information that the inhabitants of the land are fearful. All is in readiness.

A. Changing Locations (v. 1)

1. And Joshua rose early in the morning; and they removed from Shittim, and came to Jordan, he and all the children of Israel, and lodged there before they passed over.

The Israelite encampment covers many square miles east of the *Jordan. Early* one *morning* Joshua gives the order, and the people move from where they have been for several months. The special cloud that has given guidance during the wilderness years is not mentioned. The Israelites, however, will have the ark of the covenant to lead the way, even as it did during the wilderness wanderings (Numbers 10:33).

The Jordan is in flood stage at the end of the rainy season and because of the melting snow on the mountains to the far north (Joshua 3:15; 4:18). It is clear that the people must cross this obstacle to enter Canaan. We can surmise that some of the older people who had been teenagers when the Red Sea was crossed 40 years before wonder if God will now repeat that miraculous experience.

B. Commanded to Follow (vv. 2-4)

2. And it came to pass after three days, that the officers went through the host.

The Israelites have *three days* for the leaders of the tribes to receive the critical information from Joshua, make the appropriate arrangements, and

---

How to Say It

AMALEKITES. *Am*-uh-leh-kites or Uh-*mal*-ih-kites.

AMORITES. *Am*-uh-rites.

CANAAN. *Kay*-nun.

ELEAZAR. El-ih-*a*-zar or E-lih-*a*-zar.

GILGAL. *Gil*-gal (G as in *get*).

GIRGASHITES. *Gur*-guh-shites.

HITTITES. *Hit*-ites or *Hit*-tites.

HIVITES. *Hi*-vites.

JEBUSITES. *Jeb*-yuh-sites.

PERIZZITES. *Pair*-ih-zites.

SHITTIM. Shih-*teem*.

SINAI. *Sigh*-nye or *Sigh*-nay-eye.

take their conclusions to the people in anticipation of the upcoming event. Joshua 3:16 indicates that the waters will be rolled back as far as Adam. That is about 16 miles north of the Jericho area. This indicates that the encampment itself covers a very large area for the water to be rolled back so far.

3. And they commanded the people, saying, When ye see the ark of the covenant of the LORD your God, and the priests the Levites bearing it, then ye shall remove from your place, and go after it.

It is quite obvious that not all *the people* can *see* the ark, but they can see each other. There will be a wave effect as the people to the north begin the crossing.

The ark of the covenant represents the presence of *the Lord*, so in one sense it is God himself who is leading the way as *the priests* and *Levites* carry it (compare Deuteronomy 1:32, 33). When the ark is moved, it is covered with the screen (veil) from inside the tabernacle that separates the Holy Place from the Most Holy Place (Numbers 4:5). [See question #1, page 176.]

WHAT TO FOLLOW

The Columbus (Ohio) *Dispatch* recently ran an article about the Civil War flags that various Ohio infantry regiments carried through battle. Every regiment had a national standard (the Stars and Stripes, of course) as well as a flag specifically for that regiment. The flags were emblazoned with various designs—sometimes eagles, sometimes a tree, shields, or other ornamentation. These flags, many of them bullet-ridden, feature the names of various battles the unit experienced. Even 150 years later, these deteriorating flags serve as sad reminders of the hard-won laurels these regiments earned.

Certain men of the regiment were designated as the "color guard." Their responsibility was to carry the flag into battle. Men vied for this role, as it was a position of honor. The regiment was told to "follow the flag." The flag became the symbol of the battle line, the point of assembly, a place to rally in times of confusion. As a result, the men of the color guard often suffered high casualties, as the other side tried to eliminate this badge of regimental identity. Sometimes as many as 15 color-bearers would fall in a single engagement.

To the children of Israel, the ark of the covenant was their "flag" identifying their loyalty to the Lord God. It was the focal point of their identity. Today, we are surrounded by flags, corporate logos, etc., that vie for our loyalty and followership in various ways. The main point of identity for the Christian, however, will always be the cross. We take heart

whenever we look upon it. That's when we realize that Christ has already won the battle. —J. B. N.

4. Yet there shall be a space between you and it, about two thousand cubits by measure: come not near unto it, that ye may know the way by which ye must go: for ye have not passed this way heretofore.

The distance between the ark and the people is to be about 3,000 feet (over half a mile). This does two things: (1) it allows the ark to be seen by a greater number of people, and (2) it teaches that the holiness of God must be respected and revered. It is assumed that this distance applies both to the north and south of the priests as the people cross the riverbed. [See question #2, page 176.]

The ark has another function: to provide direction for the movement of the people in a territory with which they are not familiar. Previously the ark led the march, but the ones carrying it followed the cloud. The word *way* occurs frequently in the Bible. It is often used spiritually to refer to the path in which a follower of God should walk. Jesus applies the word to himself when He says that He is the way (John 14:6). There is one right way and many wrong ways; Joshua is showing the Israelites the right way.

C. Cleansing Required (v. 5)

5. And Joshua said unto the people, Sanctify yourselves: for tomorrow the LORD will do wonders among you.

Joshua instructs *the people* that the special event of the day to come requires other symbolic acts that show respect for *the Lord* and what is about to happen. When the Ten Commandments were given in oral form, a similar cleansing involved a washing of clothes and sexual abstinence (Exodus 19:14, 15). The same requirements are probably applied now.

II. Preparing the Priests (Joshua 3:6-8)

Special instructions are given to the ones who carry the ark. Perhaps they think that for the security of the ark they should hurry to the other side, but God has different plans.

A. Carrying the Ark (v. 6)

6. And Joshua spake unto the priests, saying, Take up the ark of the covenant, and pass over before the people. And they took up the ark of the covenant, and went before the people.

The time has arrived for the nation to enter Canaan—after 40 years. The command is given to *the priests* to *take up the ark* and move so as to be visible to *the people*. [See question #3, page 176.] Children often ask the question when traveling, "Are we there yet?" The Israelites are almost ready to say that they are "there."

B. Commending Joshua (v. 7)

7. And the LORD said unto Joshua, This day will I begin to magnify thee in the sight of all Israel, that they may know that, as I was with Moses, so I will be with thee.

One of the purposes of crossing the Jordan is to assure the people again that Joshua is the rightful leader, and that *the Lord* is *with* Joshua as He *was with Moses*. Joshua 4:14 confirms that the people respond as God intends. The analogy is not made in the Bible, but some see a similarity here to the Red Sea experience in which the people were "baptized unto Moses" (1 Corinthians 10:2). This figure of speech shows a total submission and immersion that recognize the leadership of the appropriate person.

C. Continuing to Stand (v. 8)

8. And thou shalt command the priests that bear the ark of the covenant, saying, When ye are come to the brink of the water of Jordan, ye shall stand still in Jordan.

God's plan is that *the priests* are to enter the *Jordan* River. Then they are just to *stand* there until the people have completed the transition to the other side. The time required to cross the river is not given, but the wide expanse available would allow it to be relatively short. [See question #4, page 176.]

III. Promises to Israel (Joshua 3:9-13)

Many people do not like to go where they have never been. They feel uncertain and at risk. The nation needs assurances that the outcomes will be desirable. Joshua now addresses those concerns.

A. Military Successes (vv. 9, 10)

9. And Joshua said unto the children of Israel, Come hither, and hear the words of the LORD your God.

We assume that *Joshua* delivers the instructions to the representative leaders of each tribe, not to the entire multitude personally. The leaders then pass the message to *the children of Israel*. The fact that the message is first communicated to Joshua by *the Lord* gives it a positive impact.

10. And Joshua said, Hereby ye shall know that the living God is among you, and that he

Visual for Lesson 7

Point to this visual as you ask, "How has God been with you thus far in the new year?"

will without fail drive out from before you the Canaanites, and the Hittites, and the Hivites, and the Perizzites, and the Girgashites, and the Amorites, and the Jebusites.

Another purpose of the passage through the Jordan is that the Israelites will be convinced *that the living God is* with them. Military victories are promised, and the seven nations of Canaan are listed. These are the peoples whom the Israelites will conquer so as to possess the land. There will be other people groups, but these are the stronger groups they will encounter and defeat.

WILL WE TRUST?

Some years ago, I was involved in a 10-day camping experience in the Colorado Rockies. I am not a camper, nor much of a hiker, but the venture sounded like fun, so I committed myself to going. A local company would provide all we needed; all I had to do was to bring clothes for the 10 days. I flew in from several states away, trusting that all would be in readiness.

It was a fun trip. As promised, the camp guide and his company provided all the equipment our group needed. They supplied the tents, sleeping bags, cooking equipment, and all our food. In addition to all the equipment, the guide had thorough knowledge of the terrain. We camped by a river to have easy access to water. We climbed mountains (including one 14,000-foot peak). We followed trails. The guide knew where we were at every point along the way. He was prepared for every step of the trip.

The Lord knew every step of the trip the Israelites would take. He was prepared for every part of that journey. He is also prepared for every step of our journey. But how amazing this is: so many people today will trust a human to lead them through the Rocky Mountains, but they won't trust the God of the universe to lead them through life!   —J. B. N.

B. Movement of the Ark (v. 11)

11. Behold, the ark of the covenant of the Lord of all the earth passeth over before you into Jordan.

Whenever a person is uncertain about going ahead, it is always comforting to have someone else make the first move. In this case it is *the ark of the covenant* that will lead the way.

C. Memorials Anticipated (v. 12)

12. Now therefore take you twelve men out of the tribes of Israel, out of every tribe a man.

There are to be two stone memorials for this event. One will be at the next campsite, which will be named Gilgal (Joshua 4:20), and one will be where the priests stand at the edge of the waters (Joshua 4:9). One man from each tribe is selected to choose the stones in order to build the altars. [See question #5, page 176.]

D. Mountain of Water (v. 13)

13. And it shall come to pass, as soon as the soles of the feet of the priests that bear the ark of the LORD, the Lord of all the earth, shall rest in the waters of Jordan, that the waters of Jordan shall be cut off from the waters that come down from above; and they shall stand upon a heap.

There is not a wall of water on both sides of the people as when the Red Sea was crossed (Exodus 14:22), but only on the upstream side. It is occasioned when *the priests* first place their feet into the water.

Home Daily Bible Readings

Monday, Jan. 12—Military Leader (Exodus 17:8-16)

Tuesday, Jan. 13—Optimistic Spy (Numbers 14:6-10)

Wednesday, Jan. 14—Moses' Successor (Numbers 27:12-23)

Thursday, Jan. 15—Moses' Charge to Joshua (Deuteronomy 31:1-8)

Friday, Jan. 16—The Spirit of Wisdom (Deuteronomy 34:1-9)

Saturday, Jan. 17—The Lord Is with You (Joshua 1:1-9)

Sunday, Jan. 18—Joshua's Leadership Affirmed (Joshua 3:1-13)

Everyone must be amazed and shocked to see the waters retreat for up to 16 miles! Some say that a natural event such as an earthquake is what causes the cessation of the flow, but the text says nothing about an earthquake. There have been occasions when earthquakes have dammed water flow for several hours. But such a naturalistic explanation does not account for the precise timing that we see here.

Joshua—his first act as the sole leader is intended to impress, to glorify God, and to move the nation into the promised land. All these things happen.

Conclusion

A. Choose Your Leaders Wisely!

Ancient Jews did not choose Moses, Joshua, etc., by democratic process. Those men could choose subordinates (example: Exodus 18:24-26), but God is the one who chose the main leaders. Today, God has allowed nations and churches the privilege of choosing their leaders.

Secular books and lectures by motivational speakers often develop the theme of how to be a good leader. But some of the finest thoughts on the qualities and qualifications of being a leader are found in the New Testament. One important passage is Acts 6:3. There the apostles needed others to assume the benevolent task of distributing food to the needy. The required qualifications for the men to be "full of the Holy Ghost and wisdom" may seem to be rather high for such a "menial" chore, but the church must always choose her leaders wisely.

Two other important passages, almost parallel to each other, are 1 Timothy 3 and Titus 1. Listed are attributes that overseers (or elders) in the church should have prior to being given the challenging task of being responsible to give an account for those in their care (see Hebrews 13:17).

Whether it is at the national level or within the church or concerning any group having designated leaders, the admonition is still true: choose your leaders wisely. Another admonition is that leaders should ensure that they are worthy of being followed. Joshua did!

B. Prayer

God, above everything else today, I desire to acknowledge Your leadership and to have the spirit of worship or submission in every part of my life. In Jesus' name, amen.

C. Thought to Remember

Honor your leaders.

Learning by Doing

This page contains an alternative lesson plan emphasizing learning activities. Some of these activities are also found in the helpful student book, Adult Bible Class.

Into the Lesson

Bring in 12 stones of about 2 inches in diameter each; give one to each of the first 12 learners to arrive. (Give more to each if you have fewer than 12 learners.) As class begins, ask those who hold the stones to come to the front and create a pile. Say, "In today's story, a pile of 12 stones is significant. If the 12 stones could talk, each could say a significant truth."

Pick up the stones one by one as you say the following as if you "are there" in the original situation. 1. Israel is one nation, but we are 12 families. 2. This river before us is no barrier to prevent us from obeying God's will. 3. Here we enter the land long promised. 4. Now we end 40 years of wandering. 5. Today we see God's hand as our fathers did at the Red Sea. 6. We need reminders of how God has dealt with us. 7. We succeed only as we show unity in God. 8. These stones represent the ordinary things by which God will do extraordinary things. 9. Here we will have occasion to teach our children about God's power. 10. By these markers our enemies will know we have come to stay. 11. God may ask us to build such memorials for other great occasions in our history. 12. Our touch has made these stones holy, dedicated to God.

If you want to add a bit of dramatic humor, hold each stone to your ear before you "let it speak."

Into the Word

Divide your class into three (or four) smaller groups. Give each group four (or three) of the stones with this direction: "Examine the verses assigned to your group, and identify a foundational truth (for each stone) that allows Israel to succeed in its task. See if you can condense each truth into one or a few words. For example, in verse 1 is found the foundation of *unity*: "all the children of Israel."

Assign the verses in this manner for three groups: vv. 1-4; vv. 5-8; vv. 9-13. If you're using four groups, assign verses this way: vv. 1-3; vv. 4, 5; vv. 6-8; vv. 9-13. Allow the groups six to eight minutes for their decisions, and then ask for reports.

Though a variety of responses can be valid, here are samples: verse 1, foundations of godly leadership (Joshua), unity (as noted), rest before action (camped there); verse 2, foundation of thorough explanations (three days allowed), foundation of

clear communication (leaders passed through the crowd); verse 3, foundation of authoritative leadership (commanded), foundation of careful and clear-cut timing; verse 4, foundation of orderliness (no mad rush forward), foundation of reverence (for the ark as a symbol of God's presence as they maintained distance from it); verse 5, foundation of sanctification, foundation of expectation of God's work; verse 6, foundation of spiritual leadership (the priests go first), foundation of obedience (priests did exactly as told); verse 7, foundation of continuity (Joshua replaces Moses), foundation of God honoring His leaders with respect; verse 8, foundation of conspicuous leadership (priests stand still, in full view); verse 9, foundation of hearing God's Word, foundation of assembly for knowing God's will; verse 10, foundation of sensing God's presence, foundation of acknowledging God and Israel's enemies; verse 11, foundation of history and visual reminders (the ark and its significance to Israel); verse 12, foundation of representation and participation (choosing one from each tribe); verse 13, foundation of faith in God's promises.

Into Life

To provide an opportunity for class members to express their appreciation for congregational leaders, buy or prepare oversized greeting cards with an appropriate *Thank You* theme. Post them around your room and tell the class, "This is a walking-over-Jordan path. Walk by the cards and add a quick sentiment of thankfulness and/or prayerful concern for the leaders to whom they are addressed."

Provide markers with each card. If the cards are posted in a somewhat circular path, learners can start and end at any point.

Lead the way by going to a card yourself and writing a short greeting. Card receivers may include anyone on the church staff—preacher, youth leader, worship leader, musician, administrative assistants, elders and deacons—or volunteers in leadership of specific ministries. Assure your learners that you will see that the cards are delivered to the addressees. (Though your class may include significant ministry leaders, it will be better not to include them as receivers of your cards, for obvious reasons.)

Let's Talk It Over

The questions on this page are designed to promote discussion of the lesson by the class and to encourage application of the lesson Scriptures. The answers provided are only discussion starters. Let your class talk it over from there.

1. What are some times in your life when you've seen God move but you've failed to follow? Why do we fail to act when we should? How do you overcome this problem?

Not a day goes by that God does not put into our lives opportunities to follow His lead. We often ask for God to lead, then fail to follow. Sometimes God's leading is to put us in a position to share our faith with a friend or coworker. But because of fear of saying the wrong thing or just feeling the time is not right, we fail to act.

We may see a neighbor working on a project around the house and sense a compulsion to offer assistance. This compulsion could be God giving us an opportunity to share His love by serving. Instead, we rationalize that we would be intruding, and thus we fail to respond. Our desire to spend what we earn on ourselves keeps us from following the leading of God to help a needy person or a Christian ministry that is having financial difficulties. Any corrective action begins with repentance.

2. Is the idea of maintaining a proper "space" between ourselves and the Lord a valid concept today? Why, or why not?

Being a Christian involves a personal relationship with the creator God. But in that relationship we must never forget that God is the sovereign ruler of the universe and is above us in all things.

At times a Christian's relationship with God may not adequately take this into account. The result may be a flippant attitude toward Him, one that lacks reverence. As we realize that God is "not far from every one of us" (Acts 17:27), we also realize that there is a creator-to-creature "distance" that will never be erased. Failing to pause and consider God's will has its roots in thinking of ourselves as being on His level. That probably happens subconsciously, but it still happens.

3. How is the task of going "before the people" the same today as it was in Joshua's day? How is it different?

Though all Christians stand equally in the eyes of God in regard to salvation, there are still those who have leadership responsibilities in the church that others do not have. All groups need those who have a higher level of maturity to provide direc-

tion. This is so in a family, in a nation, in a business, and in the church.

Leaders with vision help the church stay focused on its purpose. Without this there is chaos and confusion. Everyone ends up doing what he or she feels is the right thing, and feelings are not trustworthy. Teachers are needed to go "before the people" to ensure that the truth of God's Word is being maintained in the church. Without them doctrine becomes no more than the opinion of the most vocal or influential. The Israelites had to wander in the wilderness for 40 years because the wrong opinion of the most vocal people prevailed!

4. What are some areas in which you (or your church) need to get your feet wet? What's holding you back?

Getting one's feet wet is another way of expressing a need to step out of a comfort zone. Churches and Christians are often fearful of taking steps of faith. We see much fear and faithlessness on the part of the Israelites during the exodus, and human nature hasn't changed.

Reaching out to new people, our very mission as a church, often goes lacking. Fear of bringing "those people" into our fellowship inhibits our stepping out. Ministering to Christians who are hurting and caught up in a web of sin can be uncomfortable and time-consuming. But such acts of mercy are necessary if we are to be the people God wants us to be.

5. How can we apply the principle of representative leadership in verses 12 and 13 to the church? Or is the principle we see at work here only a "one-time thing" for the historical situation at hand? Explain.

Since each tribe was to provide one man, we may get the idea of political representation. Yet the leaders from each of the tribes were undoubtedly spiritual models; we may safely assume that the men picked were those of high character.

Too often in the church people think of leaders as those chosen to represent their views and opinions in some sort of business meeting. But church leaders are not representatives of the people to a church board or church council. Instead, they are representatives of God's will to the people.

Samson's Mother Prepares

DEVOTIONAL READING: **Psalm 91.**

BACKGROUND SCRIPTURE: **Judges 13.**

PRINTED TEXT: **Judges 13:1-13, 24.**

Judges 13:1-13, 24

1 And the children of Israel did evil again in the sight of the LORD; and the LORD delivered them into the hand of the Philistines forty years.

2 And there was a certain man of Zorah, of the family of the Danites, whose name was Manoah; and his wife was barren, and bare not.

3 And the angel of the LORD appeared unto the woman, and said unto her, Behold now, thou art barren, and bearest not: but thou shalt conceive, and bear a son.

4 Now therefore beware, I pray thee, and drink not wine nor strong drink, and eat not any unclean thing:

5 For, lo, thou shalt conceive, and bear a son; and no razor shall come on his head: for the child shall be a Nazarite unto God from the womb: and he shall begin to deliver Israel out of the hand of the Philistines.

6 Then the woman came and told her husband, saying, A man of God came unto me, and his countenance was like the countenance of an angel of God, very terrible: but I asked him not whence he was, neither told he me his name:

7 But he said unto me, Behold, thou shalt conceive, and bear a son; and now drink no wine nor strong drink, neither eat any unclean thing: for the child shall be a Nazarite to God from the womb to the day of his death.

8 Then Manoah entreated the LORD, and said, O my Lord, let the man of God which

thou didst send come again unto us, and teach us what we shall do unto the child that shall be born.

9 And God hearkened to the voice of Manoah; and the angel of God came again unto the woman as she sat in the field: but Manoah her husband was not with her.

10 And the woman made haste, and ran, and showed her husband, and said unto him, Behold, the man hath appeared unto me, that came unto me the other day.

11 And Manoah arose, and went after his wife, and came to the man, and said unto him, Art thou the man that spakest unto the woman? And he said, I am.

12 And Manoah said, Now let thy words come to pass. How shall we order the child, and how shall we do unto him?

13 And the angel of the LORD said unto Manoah, Of all that I said unto the woman let her beware.

· · · · · · · · · · · · ·

24 And the woman bare a son, and called his name Samson: and the child grew, and the LORD blessed him.

Jan 25

GOLDEN TEXT: Thou shalt conceive, and bear a son; and no razor shall come on his head: for the child shall be a Nazarite unto God from the womb: and he shall begin to deliver Israel out of the hand of the Philistines.—Judges 13:5.

Human Commitment	

Human Commitment
Unit 2: Old Testament People
of Commitment
(Lessons 5–12)

Lesson Aims

After participating in this lesson, each student will be able to:

1. Summarize the context and events that led to the birth of Samson.

2. Compare and contrast Samson's calling with the requirements of the Christian.

3. Select one requirement from lesson aim #2 and express a specific plan for improving his or her conduct related to that requirement.

Lesson Outline

INTRODUCTION
  A. Experiencing Expectancy
  B. Lesson Background
 I. SETTING DESCRIBED (Judges 13:1, 2)
  A. Suffering of a Nation (v. 1)
  B. Suffering of a Couple (v. 2)
  A Picture of Barrenness
 II. ANGEL APPEARS (Judges 13:3-7)
  A. Making a Promise (v. 3)
  B. Mandating Instructions (vv. 4, 5)
  Drink No Wine
  C. Manoah Informed (vv. 6, 7)
 III. ANGEL REAPPEARS (Judges 13:8-13)
  A. Request by Manoah (v. 8)
  B. Reappearance of the Angel (vv. 9, 10)
  C. Restrictions Reviewed (vv. 11-13)
 IV. SON'S BIRTH (Judges 13:24)
CONCLUSION
  A. The "Bad Boy"
  B. Prayer
  C. Thought to Remember

Introduction

A. Experiencing Expectancy

The conscientious expectant mother in Western culture takes seriously the preparations for the arrival of a baby. The mother-to-be often alters her eating habits, takes more rest, gains weight, thinks about possible names, tells her relatives and close friends, decorates an area, gains weight, prepares a place for the baby to sleep, visits the doctor regularly, gains weight, resolves to avoid alcohol and nicotine, tries to avoid morning sickness,

gains weight, talks to other mothers about what to expect, buys maternity clothes, makes arrangements to continue working or to resign, and begins to secure the necessary clothing and linens.

That's a great list, but the most important element is missing. Nothing is said about a spiritual commitment to rear the child in a godly home, to pray for the faithfulness of the child throughout life, to pray for the child's future spouse, or to make sure there will be Bible story books to read in family devotions. The ultimate goals in the preparation should be to please God and to model Christ in such a way that will enable the mother, the child, and the entire family to spend eternity with Jesus.

In a self-centered society, the unborn and the newborn may not be wanted; they may be cast aside in various ways and for different reasons. At the other end of the spectrum are couples who desperately desire to have children and are unable to do so. In addition, there are those prospective parents who have made all the right preparations, but their newborns are unable to exist outside the womb. Caution is therefore encouraged in the remarks that are made by the teacher and the students who consider this lesson, since it concerns a childless woman who received a message from a heavenly being that she was to have a son.

B. Lesson Background

The previous lesson presented the Israelite nation as it crossed the Jordan River and entered Canaan. The fall of Jericho was followed by two subsequent campaigns, one to the south and one to the north. Data from Caleb's statements in Joshua 14 lead to a conclusion that these campaigns consumed six to seven years of time. The conquered territory was divided among the nine and one-half tribes that settled in Canaan. The tribe of Levi did not receive a territory, but was given 48 cities throughout the land (Joshua 21).

The nation of Israel finally has its land, the laws of God, and the promises of God. God promised that if they would keep His covenant they would be blessed with crops, children, and protection from enemies. There were no taxes to support kings, armies, or national programs—just tithes (which some considered a form of a tax). It was an ideal situation in which to "live happily ever after."

The Israelites failed to do what they promised. The older generation did not take the lead in teaching the children about God's works (Judges 2:10). Idolatry as practiced in Canaan seemed more exciting and enticing than the righteous demands by God, so the Israelites forsook the Lord and served other gods (Judges 2:11-13).

The book of Judges depicts the cycles of apostasy and renewal. Sin was followed by years of suffering at the hands of foreign nations. Eventually the Israelites appealed to God, and God sent deliverers called *judges.* As each judge died, the cycle repeated (Judges 2:16, 19). The cycle is often described as *sin, sorrow, supplication, and salvation.*

The last of these oppressions involved two different nations: the Ammonites and the Philistines (Judges 10:7). The Philistines' original home was an island in the Mediterranean. Some Philistines had been in the land since the days of Abraham and Isaac (Genesis 21, 26). By the time of today's lesson (about 1125 BC), they were strong in numbers. Their iron weapons were superior to those made of bronze. The Israelites would not enjoy this technology until the days of David, about 1000 BC (compare 1 Samuel 13:19, 20).

God had two answers for this oppression from the west: Samson and Samuel. Both men served late in the period of the judges at about the same time, but in different ways. Samson's home was near Philistine territory, and Samuel lived in the area north of Jerusalem. The births of both involved divine intervention. This lesson features the preparations for the birth of Samson.

I. Setting Described
(Judges 13:1, 2)
A. Suffering of a Nation (v. 1)

1. And the children of Israel did evil again in the sight of the LORD; and the LORD delivered them into the hand of the Philistines forty years.

Each new generation experiments with sin, and God's chosen people do *evil* before *the Lord.* The Hebrew verb has the thought of adding to or increasing the evil. [See question #1, page 184.]

How to Say It

AMMONITES. *Am*-un-ites.
APOSTASY. uh-*pahs*-tuh-see.
CALEB. *Kay*-leb.
CANAAN. *Kay*-nun.
ISAAC. *Eye*-zuk.
JERICHO. *Jair*-ih-co.
JOSHUA. *Josh*-yew-uh.
LEVI. *Lee*-vye.
MANOAH. Muh-*no*-uh.
MEDITERRANEAN. *Med*-uh-tuh-*ray*-nee-un (strong accent on *ray*).
NAZARITE. *Naz*-uh-rite.
PHILISTINES. Fuh-*liss*-teens or *Fill*-us-teens.
ZORAH. *Zo*-ruh.

Sin has its consequences, and the nation is *delivered to the Philistines for a period of forty years.* This type of oppression does not involve an organized payment of tribute from one nation to another. Instead, the invaders first encourage the Israelites in their farming of grain, one of the major items of wealth in that era. Then at harvest time the Philistines arrive and take the results of the Israelite labor.

The Philistines do not take everything; they leave the Israelites enough for seed for the next year. Then the annual raiding parties return. It is up to the Israelites to find something to eat in the interval (compare the earlier situation in Judges 6:1-11).

B. Suffering of a Couple (v. 2)

2. And there was a certain man of Zorah, of the family of the Danites, whose name was Manoah; and his wife was barren, and bare not.

At first it may seem strange to change the topic from national crisis to the concerns of one married couple. The intention, however, is to show that God is preparing to begin a national deliverance through the son of this couple.

Their village is located in the Danite territory of southwestern Judah (Joshua 19:41). The father's name is *Manoah* (which means "rest"); the mother's name is not revealed. Their situation is stated factually, and the accompanying emotional frustrations are not expressed.

A PICTURE OF BARRENNESS

I was born and reared in midwest America. Although I grew up in a semisuburban area, I know some things about farming. My grandfather was a farmer, and when I was just a boy I usually spent a week in the summer on his farm. When I was in Bible college, I had a couple of weekend ministries in rural areas, and the majority of the men in the congregation were farmers. I spent time on their farms and got to know about corn, beans, and livestock.

When I finished graduate school, my first full-time job took me to California. I drove a rented truck, towing our car to get there. Initially I drove through midwestern farmland that was familiar and fruitful. But eventually I came to Utah and ultimately the Bonneville Salt Flats. Here the highway department did not even bother with fences. There was nothing but salt flats—159 square miles of them. There was no vegetation of any kind. It was the most inhospitable place I had ever seen. It was desolate and looked utterly foreboding. Here for the first time I got a first-hand picture of *barrenness.*

I am certain that Manoah's wife never saw the Bonneville Salt Flats. But after seeing that place myself, I have a pretty good idea how she felt. Today, we are surrounded by spiritually barren people. How tragic when they don't even realize their barrenness. Jesus is still the answer. —J. B. N.

II. Angel Appears
(Judges 13:3-7)

A. Making a Promise (v. 3)

3. And the angel of the LORD appeared unto the woman, and said unto her, Behold now, thou art barren, and bearest not: but thou shalt conceive, and bear a son.

The angel of the Lord appears several times in the Old Testament. His very presence makes the ground holy. He accepts worship. The terms used to refer to this being can change from *angel* to *the Lord* and to *God* (Exodus 3:2, 4, 6). When these facts are combined with the admonition of an angel in the book of Revelation that only God is to be worshiped (Revelation 22:8, 9), then most scholars conclude that this special being is deity. Some think that this is an Old Testament appearance of Jesus, but this is speculation. The word *angel* also means "messenger," and this is helpful in understanding the situation.

God is acting in a special way to bring about a deliverance from the oppression by the Philistines. The deliverance begins by the angel's appearance to an unnamed *woman.* This is not the first time for the messenger to appear to a woman. He also appeared to Hagar, Sarah's handmaid, on two occasions many hundreds of years before (Genesis 16:7; 21:17).

The first part of the divine message offers a recognized fact: the woman has no children. The worth of a wife is often evaluated by her ability to have children, and Manoah's wife surely wonders what her husband thinks about her, in spite of any verbal assurances that he gives (compare 1 Samuel 1:1-8). The opening words of the angel bring a reminder of a painful fact.

The conjunction *but* that leads to the second part of the message indicates that God is ready to act, and the element of hope is kindled. The final phrases must create a joyful expectancy.

B. Mandating Instructions (vv. 4, 5)

4. Now therefore beware, I pray thee, and drink not wine nor strong drink, and eat not any unclean thing.

The angel provides special instructions for the expectant mother and for the son that will be born. The words indicate that these things are mandatory. The first restriction prohibits the drinking of fermented beverages. This restriction will remind

the mother-to-be of her special role in God's plan. Perhaps this barren woman is accustomed to "drowning her sorrows," but that is just a guess (compare 1 Samuel 1:12-16).

The law of Moses gives several dietary restrictions to the Israelites about clean and *unclean* foods (Leviticus 11). The message from the angel implies that she knows about these things. The Philistine oppression causes a scarcity of food, and it is possible that unclean food may have been eaten in order to survive. If so, this woman will no longer have that option. [See question #2, page 184.]

DRINK NO WINE

My grandmother was a card-carrying member of the Women's Christian Temperance Union. I grew up in a church that spoke out plainly against the use of alcoholic beverages. I don't want to get involved in a wrestling match over Prohibition, but I do believe the Prohibition effort in American history in the 1920s was never appropriately supported by the government. And statistics indicate that Prohibition worked: the per capita consumption of alcohol before Prohibition was not matched when Prohibition was removed. It was not until the 1970s that alcohol consumption again reached the per capita levels of the 1910s.

Regardless of that, however, it is interesting that even in our libertarian society of today there is strong teaching regarding pregnant women drinking alcohol. Virtually all medical personnel warn against it, pointing out that the pregnant woman's drinking can result in a baby having severe defects. Heavy drinkers can bear children with *fetal alcohol syndrome,* a permanent condition.

Modern knowledge in this regard may cause us to speculate why Samson's mother was told to avoid wine and other strong drink. Was God's concern that Samson be born from an alcohol-free pregnancy an issue of avoiding fetal alcohol syndrome? We don't know. Perhaps the main issue was to see if Manoah's wife would pass a holiness test. Our obedience to God is not conditioned on full understanding.   —J. B. N.

5. For, lo, thou shalt conceive, and bear a son; and no razor shall come on his head: for the child shall be a Nazarite unto God from the womb: and he shall begin to deliver Israel out of the hand of the Philistines.

The promise of *a son* is repeated, and two factors are added. First, the son is to be a *Nazarite.* The guidelines for a Nazarite (man or woman) are given in Numbers 6:2-6. During the time of the vow, a Nazarite may not get a haircut. A Nazarite may not consume anything that is from a grapevine—beverage, raisins, skin, or seeds. Going near a dead person is forbidden. Samson is to be a Nazarite *unto God from the womb;* Samson's mother shares the same restrictions (Judges 13:14; compare 1 Samuel 1:11; Luke 1:15). [See question #3, page 184.]

The other new item gives the purpose for Samson's life: he will *begin* the process of ending the oppression of *the Philistines.* The responsibility of rearing the child with such a purpose in view must be a part of every parental decision about him.

C. Manoah Informed (vv. 6, 7)

6. Then the woman came and told her husband, saying, A man of God came unto me, and his countenance was like the countenance of an angel of God, very terrible: but I asked him not whence he was, neither told he me his name.

Manoah's wife has a different response from that of Sarah, Abraham's wife (Genesis 18). This *woman* does not laugh, and there is no indication of disbelief. She quickly goes to share the good news with *her husband,* and her first words to him show that what she heard is genuine and must be accepted.

She describes the messenger vividly, and the effect is to credential both the messenger and the message. Both are *of God.* She is so overwhelmed that there is no record that she questions this heavenly message in any way.

7. But he said unto me, Behold, thou shalt conceive, and bear a son; and now drink no wine nor strong drink, neither eat any unclean thing: for the child shall be a Nazarite to God from the womb to the day of his death.

As the woman relays the message, two things are missing from what she heard originally: the reference to the razor and the purpose of the *son* that is to be born. But she adds a fact not found in verse 5: she refers to *the day of his death.* It may be assumed that this was a part of the original communication. This may produce the thought that Israel's deliverance will involve her son's death.

III. Angel Reappears
(Judges 13:8-13)
A. Request by Manoah (v. 8)

8. Then Manoah intreated the LORD, and said, O my Lord, let the man of God which thou didst send come again unto us, and teach us what we shall do unto the child that shall be born.

The request by *Manoah* shows that the couple earnestly desires to rear this special son in a way pleasing to God. Some have accused Manoah of not fully believing his wife's report, but the text does not even hint that his prayer is offered in doubt.

Visual for Lesson 8. *Point to this visual as you ask, "How have you prepared yourself in January to serve God for the rest of 2009?"*

B. Reappearance of the Angel (vv. 9, 10)

9. And God hearkened to the voice of Manoah; and the angel of God came again unto the woman as she sat in the field: but Manoah her husband was not with her.

There is a certain irony in that after *Manoah* prays for a return visit the angel comes to *the woman* instead of to Manoah. Manoah's wife is not in her dwelling. She is out *in the field.* It seems reasonable that she has returned to the spot of the previous manifestation, and her vigil is rewarded by the reappearance of the messenger. That field surely becomes a very special place for the remainder of her life.

10. And the woman made haste, and ran, and showed her husband, and said unto him, Behold, the man hath appeared unto me, that came unto me the other day.

The woman must be concerned that the messenger will depart before she returns, for after the earlier revelation (vv. 3-5) he did not remain to give the revelation to Manoah personally. It is reasonable to assume that she is given assurances that this time he will stay in order to be able to communicate directly with *her husband.*

C. Restrictions Reviewed (vv. 11-13)

11. And Manoah arose, and went after his wife, and came to the man, and said unto him, Art thou the man that spakest unto the woman? And he said, I am.

Manoah immediately drops whatever he is doing and quickly accompanies *his wife* to the field. We assume she has run to him, and they go in haste to receive the confirmation and expansion of the earlier message.

Manoah has questions, and *the man* has answers. The first question is designed to establish that this is the same being that provided a message of shocking joy. The answer affirms that he is one and the same.

12. And Manoah said, Now let thy words come to pass. How shall we order the child, and how shall we do unto him?

Manoah is persuaded that the *words* of the previous revelation will be accomplished. At this point he demonstrates that he and his wife want to be the best parents they can possibly be. They are willing to accept the responsibility, but they want to be certain that what they do will work toward fulfilling the purposes of God. Manoah's request should be a part of the thoughts of every godly couple who have the awe-inspiring task of rearing a child. [See question #4, page 184.]

13. And the angel of the LORD said unto Manoah, Of all that I said unto the woman let her beware.

The response of *the angel of the Lord* does not provide any additional details. A warning is sounded that the mother must do *all* that was expressed to her initially. She is the one who must safeguard her pregnancy by avoiding certain food and drink.

We may assume that this mother-to-be has the primary task of teaching *her* son during his early years. This may include telling him, at the right time, about his special purpose for God's people. Both husband and wife may wonder about the timing and the methods.

IV. Son's Birth
(Judges 13:24)

24. And the woman bare a son, and called his name Samson: and the child grew, and the LORD blessed him.

The verses in the interval between sections of the printed text are also fascinating. The conversation among the three continues, and at the conclusion there is a miraculous disappearance of the divine being.

The days of expectant waiting come to an end. The child of promise is born, and the couple's mission in caring for *Samson* begins. Some parts of his rearing will be difficult—to explain why he cannot have grape juice while others can, why his hair must not be cut, etc. During this time, Samson himself also experiences a time of expectant waiting, probably wondering how and when he will deliver Israel.

The divine assessment of Samson's youth is that he *grew, and the Lord blessed him.* The wording is similar to what is said about others whose births

are prominent in the Bible. These include Samuel (1 Samuel 3:19), John (Luke 1:80), and Jesus (Luke 2:40, 52). [See question #5, page 184.]

Conclusion

A. The "Bad Boy"

One woman said that as a child she was captivated by the bad-boy image of Samson, and that she felt guilty for this. As an adult she came to realize that Samson is listed as a hero of the faith (Hebrews 11:32). This caused her to understand that the important thing is the faith of the individual, and that sinless perfection is not a requirement in order to be used of God to serve Him.

In December 1917, a home for boys was established in Omaha, Nebraska. The oft-repeated philosophy of the founder was "There is no such thing as a bad boy." The founder resolved that encouragement, care, and love would be applied to prepare disadvantaged boys to serve God and humanity. Every parent can easily do an assessment to see that those qualities are being provided for his or her children. Preparing a child for eternity involves much more than providing food, a roof, and a bed. God still prepares to use people from their birth. And the work of parents is a key part of that preparation—His preparation.

B. Prayer

Almighty God, I resolve today to help prepare someone else for eternity with you. May I allow your Word to teach me how I am to do that. In Jesus' name, amen.

C. Thought to Remember

God may prepare someone through you.

Home Daily Bible Readings

Monday, Jan. 19—Special Vows to the Lord (Numbers 6:1-8)

Tuesday, Jan. 20—Disobeying God (Judges 2:1-5)

Wednesday, Jan. 21—A New Generation (Judges 2:6-10)

Thursday, Jan. 22—Results of Unfaithfulness (Judges 2:11-17)

Friday, Jan. 23—Judges Raised Up by God (Judges 2:18-23)

Saturday, Jan. 24—An Offering to the Lord (Judges 13:15-23)

Sunday, Jan. 25—The Promise of a Deliverer (Judges 13:1-13, 24)

Learning by Doing

This page contains an alternative lesson plan emphasizing learning activities. Some of these activities are also found in the helpful student book, Adult Bible Class.

Into the Lesson

Buy or make a baby shower announcement and invitation. Create enough so that each learner in your class will have one. A class member who enjoys computer design projects might be willing to create these for you.

Fill the invitations with information from the text regarding Samson and his family. The following may be included: "It's going to be a boy!" "Proud Parents: Mr. & Mrs. Manoah"; "Date: Sunday, January 25, 2009"; "Time: [fill in your class time]"; "Please: No gifts; God will provide them." If your budget allows, mail them to class members to arrive before today's class; otherwise, hand them out in class a week in advance.

Into the Word

Collect the following objects before class: an "over the hill" gag birthday notion featuring *Age 40* prominently; bride and groom figure for wedding cake; angel figurine; wine glass or canned ham; razor (make sure it has a safety cap) or hair clippers; a *Hello, my name is . . .* badge that is not filled in; small replica tombstone; small "praying hands" charm or pin; picture of a wheat field; a running shoe; a question mark from a child's magnetic set (or simply hand drawn); a book on parenting; a picture of a *Do Not Enter* sign; a baby doll in a blue blanket. Soliciting select items from class members is a good option.

To establish the context for today's study, summarize the Lesson Background. Then send all 14 objects in random order around the class, one quickly following another. As the items return to you, place them where they can be seen by the group. You will be asking learners to relate each object to a particular verse at the end.

Give each student a sheet of paper. Ask them to write the numbers 1 though 13 as well as the number 24 down the side (to represent the verse numbers of today's text). Then they are to write object descriptions beside the appropriate verse number. If needed, give them one object as an example: the "over the hill age 40" gag notion relates to verse 1 and the 40 years of Philistine dominance.

Allow time for the class to associate all 14 objects. Then, verse-by-verse, have them identify their choices. Give opportunity for comments and questions you may want to introduce.

The following object matches are the intended ones: verse 2—the wedding cake figures for Manoah and his "bride"; verse 3—the angel figurine for the angel of the Lord; verse 4—the wine glass (or canned ham) for the Nazarite abstentions; verse 5—the razor or hair clippers for the child's need to leave his hair uncut; verse 6—the blank "hello, my name is . . ." badge for the anonymous angel; verse 7—the tombstone replica for the fact the child's vow will be "until death"; verse 8—the praying hands for Manoah's plea to the Lord; verse 9—the picture of a wheat field for Manoah's wife out in the field; verse 10—the running shoe for the wife running back to get Manoah; verse 11—the question mark for Manoah's urgent question to the angel; verse 12—the parenting book for Manoah requesting child-rearing advice; verse 13—the picture of a *Do Not Enter* warning sign for the angel's repetition of the instructions; verse 24—the baby doll for the birth of Samson.

Into Life

Put the following list of requirements on the board. These were requirements for Samson to fulfill his call by the Lord:

- *avoid intoxicating drink*
- *maintain ceremonial cleanliness in diet*
- *make calling obvious by the length of uncut hair*
- *rescue God's people*
- *maintain his relationship with God to the end of his life*

Ask your class, "How do you see each of these requirements as relating to the requirements God has for us?" Let the answers be spontaneous. Expect some disagreements. One learner may say, "Well, I don't see some of those applying at all; we are not under the old law, so ceremonial foods are irrelevant." To this another learner may respond, "Yes, but we are to keep ourselves free from drunkenness, and we are expected to keep our bodies holy unto Him."

Allow this back-and-forth agreement and disagreement. Some learner will surely see the evangelistic, lifelong nature of the Christian's calling. After the discussion has run its course, ask class members to ask themselves the vital question *How am I doing?* in relationship to God's requirements for the New Testament era.

Let's Talk It Over

The questions on this page are designed to promote discussion of the lesson by the class and to encourage application of the lesson Scriptures. The answers provided are only discussion starters. Let your class talk it over from there.

1. Why do God's people have such a difficult time remaining faithful? How do we guard our faithfulness?

It's a story repeated throughout the history of the people of God. We see it in biblical accounts, we read about it in history, and we all know personally of people who at one time were faithful to the will of God, but for some reason turned away. Backsliding, apostasy, reversion to the world, or whatever name it goes by, hurts each time you see it (or commit it).

Some people forsake God because of pride. They get caught up in wanting things their way and even thinking they have a better idea than God. Others forsake God because they get swept up in a certain moment and forget God's blessings in the past and His promises for the future. A church that provides a good teaching and fellowship network can minimize this danger.

2. What do you think God expects of parents today as they prepare for the birth of a child?

A lot of attention is put into planning for the birth of children; this involves baby showers, setting up rooms, and attending birthing classes. But more attention can be given to pondering the spiritual life of the child before the birth takes place. Will the parents-to-be consider spiritual nutrition as important as physical nutrition?

Parents can make a conscious decision to dedicate themselves to bringing up children in the fear of the Lord. This involves, among other things, taking advantage of Christian education opportunities from the child's earliest days. Praying regularly for them is part of the process—probably the most important part.

3. What does God ask of His people today to demonstrate they are set apart to Him? How are these like and unlike the "set apartness" requirements for Samson?

Living a Christian lifestyle has its challenges. There is so much pressure to conform to the world. Sometimes Christians buy into the idea that "to get along you have to go along."

God's people are called to live in this world, but not to follow the patterns or ways of this world. Christians are to be different from the world (John 17:13-19). Christians are called on to "have no fellowship with the unfruitful works of darkness" (Ephesians 5:11). A transformed life is the aim of followers of Christ. This involves refusing to conform to the way of the world (Romans 12:2). *Personal holiness* is the thumbnail summary of this idea (1 Peter 1:15, 16).

4. What are some areas where we need to say to the Lord, "Now let thy words come to pass"?

We know from Scripture that the Word of the Lord is true and trustworthy. Jesus taught in the model prayer to pray for God's will to be done and for the kingdom of God to come on earth as it is in Heaven (Matthew 6:10). Knowing that God will be faithful to His Word and His will should cause us to pray the words of Scripture.

We can pray that we will be His witnesses in the world (Acts 1:8). Our prayer can be for our leaving worry behind and trusting God to provide our needs (Matthew 6:33). The words of God concerning how His people are to care for others and meet the needs of one another can be an area where we seek God's Word and God's will to come to pass. Joining John the apostle, we can also pray for the return of Jesus to come to pass (Revelation 22:20). That certainly will happen whether we pray for it or not, but praying for it allows us continually to submit ourselves to God's plan.

5. What are some of the ways that God has blessed the children in your church? How often do you praise Him for those blessings?

It is easy sometimes to see the bad in children. The bad stands out, and we end up focusing on fixing the bad instead of nurturing and praising the good.

Also, we may not praise God as we should in this area because of a tendency to take for granted the ways that God blesses children. The good health that so many of our children have is taken for granted until a serious illness arises. We then pray for their health. How about a daily praise to God for the health blessing He already gives? Churches continue to exist from generation to generation because God has blessed children with a heritage of faith that they are willing to pass on as they become adults.

A Shunammite Woman Hosts Elisha

February 1
Lesson 9

DEVOTIONAL READING: Luke 6:32-36.

BACKGROUND SCRIPTURE: 2 Kings 4:8-17.

PRINTED TEXT: 2 Kings 4:8-17.

2 Kings 4:8-17

8 And it fell on a day, that Elisha passed to Shunem, where was a great woman; and she constrained him to eat bread. And so it was, that, as oft as he passed by, he turned in thither to eat bread.

9 And she said unto her husband, Behold now, I perceive that this is a holy man of God, which passeth by us continually.

10 Let us make a little chamber, I pray thee, on the wall; and let us set for him there a bed, and a table, and a stool, and a candlestick: and it shall be, when he cometh to us, that he shall turn in thither.

11 And it fell on a day, that he came thither, and he turned into the chamber, and lay there.

12 And he said to Gehazi his servant, Call this Shunammite. And when he had called her, she stood before him.

13 And he said unto him, Say now unto her, Behold, thou hast been careful for us with all this care; what is to be done for thee? wouldest thou be spoken for to the king, or to the captain of the host? And she answered, I dwell among mine own people.

14 And he said, What then is to be done for her? And Gehazi answered, Verily she hath no child, and her husband is old.

15 And he said, Call her. And when he had called her, she stood in the door.

16 And he said, About this season, according to the time of life, thou shalt embrace a son. And she said, Nay, my lord, thou man of God, do not lie unto thine handmaid.

17 And the woman conceived, and bare a son at that season that Elisha had said unto her, according to the time of life.

Feb
1

GOLDEN TEXT: She said unto her husband, Behold now, I perceive that this is a holy man of God, which passeth by us continually. Let us make a little chamber, . . . and it shall be, when he cometh to us, that he shall turn in thither.—2 Kings 4:9, 10.

Human Commitment
Unit 2: Old Testament People
of Commitment
(Lessons 5–12)

Lesson Aims

After participating in this lesson, each student will be able to:

1. Describe the relationship between Elisha and the Shunammite woman.

2. Tell how the Shunammite's example of service without expectation of reward is an example for Christians today.

3. Identify one need that another person has and commit to meeting that need.

Lesson Outline

INTRODUCTION
  A. Christian Hospitality
  B. Lesson Background
I. NEED MET (2 Kings 4:8-10)
  A. Stopovers (v. 8)
  B. Observation (v. 9)
  C. Plan (v. 10)
II. APPRECIATION EXPRESSED (2 Kings 4:11-13)
  A. Acceptance (v. 11)
  B. Conversation (vv. 12, 13)
    Among My People
III. DESIRE GRANTED (2 Kings 4:14-17)
  A. Suggestion (v. 14)
  B. Prediction (vv. 15, 16)
  C. Realization (v. 17)
    Too Good to Be True?
CONCLUSION
  A. The Immediate Picture
  B. The Larger Picture
  C. Prayer
  D. Thought to Remember

Introduction

A. Christian Hospitality

The exhortation to hospitality is part of the fabric of New Testament Christianity. We are to be "given to hospitality" (Romans 12:13) and offer "hospitality one to another without grudging" (1 Peter 4:9). Hospitality is one of the marks of a righteous person (see Job 31:32).

In the first century AD, hospitality was to characterize a church leader's home (1 Timothy 3:2). It was also to be the mark of a godly widow's home

(1 Timothy 5:10). In one of the most intriguing statements ever made about hospitality, Hebrews 13:2 says, "Be not forgetful to entertain strangers: for thereby some have entertained angels unawares." Have you ever entertained an angel? Would you know it if you did?

Unfortunately, the concept of hospitality has eroded among Christian homes. When missionaries come to visit on furlough, don't we convince ourselves that it would be better for everyone concerned to put them up in a motel? Yet there are still those who have the means, ability, and desire to practice hospitality on a regular basis. My wife is one of those. We decided several years ago to purchase a larger house in order to be better able to practice hospitality.

Because of my position as a Bible college professor, we have many occasions to host students, missionaries, visiting professors, and friends who are simply passing by. Getting acquainted with complete strangers, renewing old friendships, etc., is a blessing to our lives. Yes, there are some costs in terms of time and money, plus a little inconvenience. But nothing compares with the blessing of knowing fellow Christians for the first time, renewing a friendship that goes back to college days, or giving a student a place to stay for a week while he or she takes an intensive class at college.

B. Lesson Background

Today's story from 2 Kings is part of a larger series of stories about Elisha in chapter 4. Here we have the accounts of the widow's oil (vv. 1-7), the poisoned stew (vv. 38-41), and the multiplication of bread for a hundred men (vv. 42-44). These stories are themselves part of a larger complex of accounts about Elisha and the consequences of his prophetic ministry among the kings of Israel (2 Kings 2–13).

Elisha was a prophet of Israel in the time of the divided kingdom (the kingdom of Israel to the north and the kingdom of Judah to the south). Today's lesson concerns perhaps the time around 840 BC. Elisha's ministry started when his mentor, Elijah, was taken up into Heaven in a whirlwind (2 Kings 2:11). The combined ministries of Elijah and Elisha fought against the influences of Baalism, its priests, and the kings who worshiped Baal.

The place of today's story is well known. Shunem is located near the plain of Jezreel in the tribal territory of Issachar, about five miles north of the town of Jezreel itself (Joshua 19:18). It was at Shunem that the Philistines had gathered to do battle with the Israelites as led by Saul and his sons, who had gathered at Gilboa (1 Samuel 28:4);

that had taken place something like 170 years in the past by the time of today's lesson. It is from this place that the beautiful Abishag came; she cared for King David at the end of his life (see 1 Kings 1:1-4).

Apparently the land around Shunem was productive and fertile. It allowed the Shunammite woman and her husband of today's lesson to experience a measure of wealth, for they had servants to work their fields (see 2 Kings 4:18-20).

I. Need Met
(2 Kings 4:8-10)

A. Stopovers (v. 8)

8. And it fell on a day, that Elisha passed to Shunem, where was a great woman; and she constrained him to eat bread. And so it was, that, as oft as he passed by, he turned in thither to eat bread.

Elisha probably lives where Elijah had lived before him. If so, the location is on the highest part of Mount Carmel. This site is part of a mountain range that parallels the Jezreel valley at a northwest angle until it juts out into the Mediterranean Sea. From there one can see a good portion of the Jezreel valley.

Elisha makes regular trips from the mountain through that valley and on to the Jordan valley, perhaps visiting various prophetic groups located at Bethel, Jericho, and Gilgal (see 2 Kings 2:1-18). On such visits, Elisha passes through *Shunem*. The Hebrew is interesting in that the woman is called *a great woman*, but this does not refer to size! All Hebrew scholars agree that this refers to

---

How to Say It

ABISHAG. *Ab*-ih-shag.
BAAL. *Bay*-ul.
BETHEL. *Beth*-ul.
ELIJAH. Ee-*lye*-juh.
ELISHA. Ee-*lye*-shuh.
GEHAZI. Geh-*hay*-zye (G as in *get*).
GILBOA. Gil-*bo*-uh (G as in *get*).
GILGAL. *Gil*-gal (G as in *get*).
ISSACHAR. *Izz*-uh-kar.
JERICHO. *Jair*-ih-co.
JEZREEL. *Jez*-ree-el or *Jez*-reel.
MEDITERRANEAN. *Med*-uh-tuh-*ray*-nee-un (strong accent on *ray*).
PHILISTINES. Fuh-*liss*-teens or *Fill*-us-teens.
SACAGAWEA. Sah-kuh-jeh-*wee*-uh.
SHUNAMMITE. *Shoo*-nam-ite.
SHUNEM. *Shoo*-nem.

---

a well-to-do woman, a woman of wealth. Perhaps she married into this wealth in an arranged marriage, for her husband is much older than she (see v. 14, below).

The Shunammite woman encourages Elisha to stop for a meal. This is her regular practice, and it is a great gesture of hospitality. Elisha's only other option is to camp out, as there are no reasonably nice motels and restaurants as we are used to today. Her house is the ideal place to be at the end of a day's journey (perhaps 25 miles from Elisha's starting point).

For hospitality to be accepted, it must not only be genuinely offered, it must also be "pushed." From experience, I know that for hospitality to be received requires a subtle form of aggressiveness if polite refusals are to be overcome. Many people have difficulty accepting hospitality. But when it is genuinely offered and we feel *constrained,* well . . . there is no way to refuse! Such is Elisha's case. [See question #1, page 192.]

B. Observation (v. 9)

9. And she said unto her husband, Behold now, I perceive that this is a holy man of God, which passeth by us continually.

After (apparently) several visits by Elisha, the woman shares with *her husband* her thoughts about the special traveler. We take for granted that Elisha's servant, Gehazi, is with him, but it is Elisha himself who is scrutinized here.

This woman is an astute judge of character in that she correctly evaluates Elisha to be *a holy man of God.* Somehow she perceives an aura of the divine about him. The text does not tell us exactly how she comes to this conclusion, but she is able to discern Elisha's character and persona probably from his manner of speech and behavior over the course of several visits.

My own wife seems to have an uncanny ability to discern the true character of people, even complete strangers. When she has "a feeling" about someone, I listen! Whatever this ability is, the Shunammite woman seems to have it. I wish we knew her name, but in this life she can be known to us only as "the Shunammite woman."

C. Plan (v. 10)

10. Let us make a little chamber, I pray thee, on the wall; and let us set for him there a bed, and a table, and a stool, and a candlestick: and it shall be, when he cometh to us, that he shall turn in thither.

In consultation with her husband, the Shunammite woman suggests making a more comfortable place for Elisha to stay when he visits. *On the wall* means that the room is built up on the roof. Roofs have various practical uses in ancient times (compare Joshua 2:6; 1 Samuel 9:25; Acts 10:9). So to build a room up there is not a surprising thing to do.

In that room, the prophet Elisha will be able to enjoy the comforts of a *bed,* some kind of a *table* at which he can read and write, and a *stool* or chair for sitting. *Candlestick* refers to the oil lamps of various sizes and shapes used in ancient times. Such a lamp is a shaped item of pottery, having a pinched neck for holding a wick to burn the olive or sesame oil that is stored in the base. Elisha's rooftop room will be completely walled on all sides with a roof of its own.

Some Christians today speak of making an "Elisha room" for visiting missionaries and others who need hospitality. While we don't call it an "Elisha room," my wife and I have placed a comfortable single bed in my basement office; it can function as a bedroom since it is located conveniently next to the basement bathroom. Such an arrangement encourages a mind-set of hospitality, for it is always available when needed. [See question #2, page 192.]

II. Appreciation Expressed
(2 Kings 4:11-13)

A. Acceptance (v. 11)

11. And it fell on a day, that he came thither, and he turned into the chamber, and lay there.

The extraordinary hospitality arranged by the Shunammite woman and her husband provides Elisha a bit of comfort, convenience, and privacy as he journeys to and fro in the land. Elisha does the right thing: he accepts the hospitality! Those who are gifted to offer hospitality do so without thought of reward. The best way to honor such a person is to accept the gift graciously, without raising a fuss. [See question #3, page 192.]

B. Conversation (vv. 12, 13)

12, 13a. And he said to Gehazi his servant, Call this Shunammite. And when he had called her, she stood before him. And he said unto him, Say now unto her, Behold, thou hast been careful for us with all this care; what is to be done for thee? wouldest thou be spoken for to the king, or to the captain of the host?

For the first time, Elisha's servant, Gehazi, enters this particular storyline. He is a "go between" for the prophet and the hospitable woman. Perhaps Elisha thinks his direct conversation with the woman will skew her response, and thus she will not answer as freely as she might otherwise. Eli-

sha is very much appreciative of what she has done and wants to return the kindness, so he asks, *What is to be done for thee?* He even suggests some kind of intervention with *the king* or *captain* of the army on her behalf.

What we don't know is how these ideas can help the woman or her husband. Some suggest that talking to the king will relieve the woman's husband from some kind of onerous civic duty or from paying excessive taxes. Others suggest that Elisha is thinking ahead to some kind of "welfare" from the civic authorities for the time when the woman's husband will die, since he is already advanced in age (v. 14, below). Whatever Elisha has in mind, his ideas suggest that he has influence with the highest authorities in the land, just as his mentor Elijah had.

13b. And she answered, I dwell among mine own people.

The woman's response reveals to us a part of her character. She has an independent streak since her reply *I dwell among mine own people* signifies something like "we can take care of ourselves." She sees no need for a reward. She has not gone out of her way to offer hospitality to Elisha because of anticipation of reward. [See question #4, page 192.]

AMONG MY PEOPLE

Most Americans have heard of Sacagawea. She was the Indian woman who accompanied Lewis and Clark on their trip to the American West in 1804. She served as a valuable guide in various instances on the cross-continental trek. At one point she was extremely helpful in enabling the expedition to get horses from her native tribe.

Once the trip was over, Captain William Clark invited her and her trapper-husband to live near St. Louis in order to provide educational opportunities for their son. They lived near the city for five years, then decided to move back to the West. Conflicting evidence emerges at this point, but one documented theory contends that she returned to her native tribe in Wyoming. There she was a respected and influential member, living until 1884, almost to age 95. She lies buried on the Wind River Indian Reservation, and a monument marks her grave.

She had helped explorers cross the continent, while she carried an infant along the way. She saw the Pacific Ocean, recrossed the mountains, and lived in the world of a different culture for five years in Missouri. But then she returned to her native land, and for the next 70 years earned a special place in her tribe. She easily could have identified with the comment of the Shunammite woman, "I dwell among mine own people." Christians can use that statement to examine their own allegiance. For example, if we prefer to be somewhere other than church on Sunday morning, that may be revealing about who we view as our "own people."   —J. B. N.

III. Desire Granted
(2 Kings 4:14-17)
A. Suggestion (v. 14)

14. And he said, What then is to be done for her? And Gehazi answered, Verily she hath no child, and her husband is old.

The scenario of this verse suggests that the woman has left the rooftop room with "Thanks, but no thanks!" on her lips. Whatever intervention Elisha could have used with those in authority to help this household is now off the table. The woman has declined all possibility of material reward for her extensive hospitality.

But Elisha will not take *no* for an answer! He wishes to reward this extraordinary woman somehow, and so he brainstorms with *Gehazi*, his servant. Aha! The woman does have a need: she is barren. There is no one to carry on the family name and inheritance, that is, to maintain the family title to their property.

The fact that *her husband is old* strongly suggests that the possibility of her having a child is steadily diminishing as the years pass. Cases of barrenness are well known from Israel's history (see the cases of Sarah, Genesis 18:10-12; Manoah's wife, Judges 13:2; and Hannah, 1 Samuel 1:2). [See question #5, page 192.]

B. Prediction (vv. 15, 16)

15. And he said, Call her. And when he had called her, she stood in the door.

We presume that the Shunammite woman goes back to her daily routine after the conversation of verse 13. To her mind, her service to Elisha can stand for what it is.

Yet Elisha requires his servant to *call her* a second time. So she meets the prophet up on the roof, in the doorway to the special hospitality room. Elisha has made up his mind.

16a. And he said, About this season, according to the time of life, thou shalt embrace a son.

Elisha earlier had offered to "pull strings" with earthly authorities to reward the woman. Now Elisha goes beyond that, since the statement *thou shalt embrace a son* must include making an appeal to God himself. To this we may compare similar prophetic promises in Genesis 18:10; Judges 13:3; and Luke 1:13.

Visual for Lesson 9. *Start a discussion by turning this statement into a question: "How does (or should) our generosity imitate that of God?"*

16b. And she said, Nay, my lord, thou man of God, do not lie unto thine handmaid.

This kind of reward is the furthest thing from the woman's mind! Thus her response *Nay, my lord, thou man of God, do not lie unto thine handmaid.* She cannot believe it. To be rewarded with a child is beyond comprehension or even imagination, given her situation.

C. Realization (v. 17)

17. And the woman conceived, and bare a son at that season that Elisha had said unto her, according to the time of life.

For a barren *woman* with an elderly husband, Elisha's promise becomes the greatest reward possible! No one should offer hospitality with the thought, "OK, now what am I going to get out of this?" We don't get the slightest hint that the woman ever thinks, "If I build Elisha a room, my husband and I will end up with a child." Godly people offer hospitality to please God. Yet God may surprise us with unexpected blessings.

TOO GOOD TO BE TRUE?

There is an old saying, "If something sounds too good to be true, it probably is." But every now and then life pulls a surprise. The 1999 movie *Music of the Heart* tells the story of Roberta Guaspari, who was teaching music in three inner-city schools in East Harlem, New York City, when the funding for her program was cut in 1991.

Parents, community leaders, and others banded together to raise the money to provide funding so the program could continue. They decided to hold a charity concert highlighting the accomplishments of her students. Arrangements were made to rent an auditorium for the planned concert, but then everything seemed to fall apart when those in charge of the auditorium backed out of the agreement.

A fellow worker on the project then suggested that the concert be held at Carnegie Hall. It took a while for the coworker to convince Roberta that this was not a joke, that she did indeed have contacts at Carnegie Hall who were willing to grant the use of the hall for this nonprofit venture. In addition, some famous musicians joined forces with the students. It was too good to be true—but it was true. Holding the concert in that famed location brought even more attention and financial support.

The concert was a sensation, and Roberta's music program continues to this day as Opus 118 (www.opus118.org). The opportunity held out by Roberta's coworker seemed too good to be true; it had to be a joke. Similarly, the Shunammite woman told Elisha, "Do not lie unto thine handmaid." But sometimes God delights in blessing us in unexpected ways. Will we be ready to praise Him when He does?   —J. B. N.

Conclusion

A. The Immediate Picture

The Shunammite woman of today's lesson was wealthy, but not miserly. She used her wealth to accommodate a prophet in his difficult journeys by giving him a special room. This provided Elisha respite from the heat, a bed for the evening, food and drink, and a light by which to read and/or write.

This woman knew when to speak and when to keep silent before a "holy man of God." She

Home Daily Bible Readings

Monday, Jan. 26—The Call of Elisha (1 Kings 19:15-21)

Tuesday, Jan. 27—The Prophet's Mantle (2 Kings 2:9-15)

Wednesday, Jan. 28—Elisha's Prayer for a Child (2 Kings 4:27-37)

Thursday, Jan. 29—The Death of Elisha (2 Kings 13:14-20)

Friday, Jan. 30—Jesus Speaks of Elisha (Luke 4:23-30)

Saturday, Jan. 31—Welcoming a Prophet (Matthew 10:40-43)

Sunday, Feb. 1—Blessed by Blessing (2 Kings 4:8-17)

asked for no favors, even from a powerful prophet. When offered certain rewards, she declined without suggesting any alternative ideas. She stressed that she relied solely on her own resources to sustain herself.

This woman was also a practical realist. When given the promise of a son, she offered a response of disbelief. She knew all to well, both from observation and personal experience, what the laws of nature meant in terms of her childless status. But the God who created the laws of nature can surprise us.

B. The Larger Picture

Today's text of 2 Kings 4:8-17 is an introduction to the larger story of 2 Kings 4:8-37. The miraculous arrival of a son brought great joy to his mother. Then one day the boy died in his mother's arms, possibly of a brain aneurysm or sunstroke—no one really knows why (vv. 19, 20).

Even then, the woman did not ask Elisha to bring the boy back from the dead. She simply wailed "Did I desire a son of my lord? did I not say, Do not deceive me?" (v. 28). The Shunammite woman had not sought a reward for her hospitality. And when her son—the greatest treasure a barren woman could have—died, she was inconsolable. Yet she did not sit alone keeping her grief to herself. Instead, she sought out the one person on earth who was the right one to seek: Elisha, the man of God.

Elisha performed extraordinary actions to bring the child back from the dead (vv. 29-37). Perhaps the story tells us as much about Elisha (his godly power and authority) as it does about the Shunammite woman (hospitality without thought of reward). People who have no thought of reward talk and act like the Shunammite woman. They do not feel anyone who has been a recipient of their hospitality owes them anything. Yet God sees and knows (Matthew 25:35, 36).

C. Prayer

Father, teach us to practice hospitality to one another without complaining. May we offer hospitality even to (or especially to) strangers in need. May we offer our best and our most with no thought of personal gain, so that others may be encouraged along the way of life. Remind us continually that the hospitality we offer is as unto Jesus himself. May this be all to Your honor and glory. In Jesus' name. Amen.

D. Thought to Remember

The practice of hospitality
never goes out of style.

Learning by Doing

This page contains an alternative lesson plan emphasizing learning activities. Some of these activities are also found in the helpful student book, Adult Bible Class.

Into the Lesson

Have the following coded message displayed as learners arrive. Call it *A Good Motto for Godly People.* (Emphasize the word *good* as you say it.) Message: BMGLE EMMB DMP EMB'Q QYIC. This is a letter-substitution code for "Doing good for God's sake."

If the group struggles a bit, suggest that they identify the word *good,* figure out the code from that word, and go from there. (The code is that each letter is replaced by the one that comes two letters after it in the alphabet; for example, B=D.) Once the motto *doing good for God's sake* is deciphered, say, "That's the theme for today's study: a person doing good because it pleases God."

Into the Word

Copy the following questions onto strips of paper, one question per strip. Distribute them randomly to your learners. Inform students that they are to figure out which verse of today's text the questions relate to.

- *Where is Shunem?*
- *What made the woman "great"?*
- *What was the woman's attitude regarding feeding Elisha?*
- *How often did Elisha stop by?*
- *How did the woman characterize Elisha?*
- *How would the woman conclude that there was something special about Elisha?*
- *With whom did the woman share her insight about Elisha's character?*
- *Where was Elisha's room to be built?*
- *What furnishings did the woman want to provide for Elisha?*
- *Did Elisha ever use the room?*
- *When was it that Elisha decided he should do something for the woman?*
- *Who was with Elisha?*
- *What possible rewards did Elisha first offer his hostess?*
- *How did the woman first reject Elisha's offer?*
- *When Elisha turned to Gehazi for a suggestion, what did the servant note?*
- *What does the age of the woman's husband have to do with anything?*
- *What custom did the woman follow when she went to Elisha's room?*

- *Who asked the woman to come to see Elisha?*
- *When was the woman to bear the prophesied son?*
- *In what special way would this woman greet her newborn son?*
- *What did the surprised woman accuse Elisha of when he made his prediction?*
- *In what "season" was the woman's son born?*

After you have distributed the strips, read the text aloud, stopping at the end of each verse. When you pause, ask, "Who has a question?" When a student reads the question that relates to the verse you have just read, answer it. This will enable a thorough overview of the text.

If a student reads a question that you or others do not think applies to the verse at hand, additional opportunity for discussion is offered. Be sure to prepare in advance to answer all the questions, using the lesson commentary and your own study. Though the questions are given here in verse order, make sure you shuffle the slips of paper before you distribute them.

At the end of this exercise, summarize the rest of the story as told in verses 18-37. Note that the woman was rewarded more than once.

Into Life

Say, "The United States, as other countries, has a 'hospitality industry' that provides places for travelers to lodge and dine. But this use of the word *hospitality* changes its meaning from "freely offered service" to "service in anticipation of a profit." How can we as a class retain the meaning of *hospitality* to be the same as that of the Shunammite woman and her husband?"

As your class offers ideas, be alert for vague generalities such as "we should be more willing to open our homes." Challenge your students to suggest specifics that include advance preparation in anticipation of offering hospitality.

Give each learner a small magnetic strip that you have lettered *DG4GS.* (Such rolls of magnetic strip are available at office or education supply stores.) Suggest that each student adhere his or her strip in a prominent place this week, as a reminder that we must *Do good for God's sake.* Remind them that the one doing good neither seeks nor needs a reward.

Let's Talk It Over

The questions on this page are designed to promote discussion of the lesson by the class and to encourage application of the lesson Scriptures. The answers provided are only discussion starters. Let your class talk it over from there.

1. What are some specific ways we can and should practice hospitality?

When we recognize that all we have are gifts from God, then we can follow Peter's instructions to "use hospitality one to another without grudging" (1 Peter 4:9). The second element necessary to be able to practice this grace is to have eyes that are aware of needs. This means staying alert to what is going on around us. Providing overnight accommodations to those who need it is but one way of "distributing to the necessity of saints" (Romans 12:13).

We can practice hospitality more effectively when our concern is to invite people into our homes instead of trying to impress them with our houses. But rather than thinking only narrowly in terms of opening our homes, the bigger picture is that of opening up our lives.

2. What are benefits we receive when we practice hospitality? Or is such a question even appropriate? Explain.

Jesus tells us to give without expecting anything in return (Luke 6:35). But in almost the next breath He says to "give, and it shall be given unto you; good measure, pressed down, and shaken together, and running over, shall men give into your bosom" (Luke 6:38).

We may begin to sort out this tension by acknowledging that many of the benefits we receive when we minister to others are of an intangible nature. It may be a hug or handshake, a smile, a tear of joy, or a heartfelt thank you. The joy of knowing that we have pleased God is the major benefit. Many who go into a situation to offer assistance for those who are in need often end up saying they were ministered to and blessed in a stronger way than what they felt they provided for others.

3. Why do some people refuse to accept hospitality when it is offered? How do we overcome this problem in ourselves and in others?

People may refuse to accept hospitality out of pride. The U.S. is often known for its culture of *rugged individualism*. Such a cultural outlook frowns at "accepting charity," which an acceptance of hospitality may be seen as. Another refusal may be along the lines of, "No, don't do that

for me. I should be helping you" (rarely expressed so bluntly, but often implied). That response may reveal a condescending attitude. Others refuse to accept hospitality when it is offered because they "don't want to put anybody out."

But accepting hospitality provides a great way to understand a little more of God's offer of grace to us all, because we are all unworthy of His gift. And sometimes the greatest help we can be to someone is to accept his or her offer of help! That allows him or her to exercise the gift. To refuse may hurt the one trying to be helpful.

4. In what areas do you need to practice more contentment?

Paul models for us what it means to practice contentment in Philippians 4:11, 12. Yet many of us live in cultures that do not even know the meaning of the word *contentment*! So many of us desire the newest, the best, the biggest, or the most prestigious of things. We envy someone who has more. Much advertising is based on appealing to this desire.

Figuring out how to learn "godliness with contentment" (1 Timothy 6:6) is the starting point for a cure. Instead of buying into the schemes of marketers, we need to buy into the plan of the Master. Perhaps each of us should print out the following Scripture and put it someplace where we will see it often: "Better is little with the fear of the Lord, than great treasure and trouble therewith" (Proverbs 15:16).

5. What are some specific ways that we can help others who feel they do not want or need our help? How do we avoid the danger of having a "rescuer mentality" as we make our list?

Sometimes people may feel they do not need help when they really do. Pride, a problem already noted in question #3, may cause them to fail to acknowledge this. Practicing acts of secret service by anonymously dropping off a bag of groceries or sending a gift card for a restaurant, gas station, or grocery store may help without causing embarrassment. Yet there may be times when we want to do something for others who really do not need assistance. Knowing the difference in the situations requires discernment.

Nathan Confronts David

DEVOTIONAL READING: Psalm 51:1-9.

BACKGROUND SCRIPTURE: 2 Samuel 11:1–12:15.

PRINTED TEXT: 2 Samuel 11:26–12:7a, 13-15.

2 Samuel 11:26, 27

26 And when the wife of Uriah heard that Uriah her husband was dead, she mourned for her husband.

27 And when the mourning was past, David sent and fetched her to his house, and she became his wife, and bare him a son. But the thing that David had done displeased the LORD.

2 Samuel 12:1-7a, 13-15

1 And the LORD sent Nathan unto David. And he came unto him, and said unto him, There were two men in one city; the one rich, and the other poor.

2 The rich man had exceeding many flocks and herds:

3 But the poor man had nothing, save one little ewe lamb, which he had bought and nourished up: and it grew up together with him, and with his children; it did eat of his own meat, and drank of his own cup, and lay in his bosom, and was unto him as a daughter.

4 And there came a traveler unto the rich man, and he spared to take of his own flock and of his own herd, to dress for the wayfaring man that was come unto him; but took the poor man's lamb, and dressed it for the man that was come to him.

5 And David's anger was greatly kindled against the man; and he said to Nathan, As the LORD liveth, the man that hath done this thing shall surely die:

6 And he shall restore the lamb fourfold, because he did this thing, and because he had no pity.

7a And Nathan said to David, Thou art the man.

. . . .

13 And David said unto Nathan, I have sinned against the LORD. And Nathan said unto David, The LORD also hath put away thy sin; thou shalt not die.

14 Howbeit, because by this deed thou hast given great occasion to the enemies of the LORD to blaspheme, the child also that is born unto thee shall surely die.

15 And Nathan departed unto his house. And the LORD struck the child that Uriah's wife bare unto David, and it was very sick.

Feb
8

GOLDEN TEXT: The thing that David had done displeased the LORD.
And the LORD sent Nathan unto David.—2 Samuel 11:27; 12:1.

Lesson Aims

After participating in this lesson, each student will be able to:

1. Retell the story of Nathan's rebuke of David.

2. Explain why the method of Nathan's rebuke is or is not a model of Christian rebuke today.

3. Write a prayer that acknowledges God's awareness of all he or she does.

Lesson Outline

Introduction

A. Confronting Leadership

Many years ago I was involved in an interim ministry that brought me into a circle of leaders of a small but influential church. I was enjoying my preaching ministry with this church until the day came that I received a phone call from one of the church's leaders. A fellow leader, an elder in the church, stood accused by the police of "bad behavior" in a public restroom. Others were involved, and it was all caught on videotape. There had to be a confrontation.

Two other leaders and I went to the home of the accused elder. Though we could not see the videotape ourselves, the facts were confirmed by a detective. We expected a confession from this person, and we were prepared to help this individual through the difficulty with prayer, counseling, and forgiveness. He would be given a chance to overcome whatever triggered the "bad behavior."

But there was no confession. In fact, just the opposite occurred. The person denied the accusation by the police. He then began to accuse us of overstepping our boundaries with regard to his personal life. After a couple of hours of heated discussion with no confession or hope of receiving one, we had to ask for the person's resignation. We requested that he cease all leadership activities in the church.

We still offered hope for that person should he change his mind about confessing. He did not. The sad part of this story is that within a few years this individual died of a disease. To my knowledge he never confessed to anyone. Hopefully he made peace with God, but certainly there was no reconciliation with the church family.

The above scenario has been repeated many times in the churches where I have served. I have discovered that confronting a leader is difficult and not always successful. Yet it must be done, since leaders are to be "blameless" (Titus 1:7), "of good behavior" (1 Timothy 3:2), and "have a good report of them which are without" (1 Timothy 3:7).

Nathan was called by God to be a prophet to the dynasty of David. In fact, Nathan had given David good news about his dynasty that it would last "for ever" (2 Samuel 7:16). But later Nathan had to confront David with an accusation. This confrontation is the subject of today's lesson.

B. Lesson Background

At the time of today's lesson, the Israelite army was fighting against the Ammonites. The date was about 990 BC. The particular part of the war that is a backdrop for us is a siege of the Ammonite capital, Rabbah. This was located at the site of the modern city of Amman, Jordan. Situated at the sources of the Jabbok River, the city was about 40 miles east of Jerusalem. The Ammonites were distantly related to Israel by means of Lot's younger daughter (Genesis 19:38).

With a good general directing his army, a king could stay home to take care of administrative concerns or personal matters. David had such a man in Joab. He was a fierce and unrelenting warrior, at that time very loyal to David. Thus David could stay home during the war.

One day while home, David seemed to have enjoyed a nap on the roof (compare 1 Samuel 9:25). After waking, he began to walk around the roof, perhaps enjoying the cool breeze as he looked over his city (2 Samuel 11:2).

The highest point of the city was, of course, Mount Zion, upon which the tent of the ark of the covenant was placed. (Solomon would later build the temple on that spot.) Next to the mount on the south side was David's palace. Thus, David's palace rooftop would have been the second highest position overlooking the small city of David (probable size: about 2,000 people within 12 acres). This is how David could have observed activity on a nearby rooftop (2 Samuel 11:2b).

What David saw was a woman (Bathsheba) performing a ritual bath for purification (see 2 Samuel 11:4; compare Leviticus 15:19-24). David may have known Bathsheba's family, for her father was Eliam (2 Samuel 11:3), one of David's "mighty men" (23:34) and the son of one of David's counselors (see 15:12; 16:23).

King David's notice of Bathsheba quickly turned to lust. He ended up committing adultery. The adultery resulted in a pregnancy (11:5). So David ordered that Bathsheba's husband, Uriah, be placed in a position that would result in his death. Then David took Bathsheba as his own wife.

Before that, David had tried to influence Uriah a couple of times to go to his own house before returning to battle. That way everyone (except David and Bathsheba) would think that the baby was Uriah's. But Uriah's sense of honor kept him from spending time with his wife (11:6-13). Little did Uriah know that it was his sense of honor that sealed his fate (11:14-17), as he carried his own death warrant back to Joab.

How to Say It

AMMONITE. *Am*-un-ite.

BATHSHEBA. Bath-*she*-buh.

ELIAM. Ih-*lye*-am.

JABBOK. *Jab*-uck.

MESOPOTAMIAN. *Mes*-uh-puh-*tay*-me-un (strong accent on *tay*).

OMNIPOTENT. ahm-*nih*-poh-tent.

OMNIPRESENT. *ahm*-nih-*prez*-ent (strong accent on *prez*).

OMNISCIENT. ahm-*nish*-unt.

PHARAOHS. *fair*-ohs or *fay*-roes.

RABBAH. *Rab*-buh.

SOLOMON. *Sol*-o-mun.

URIAH. Yu-*rye*-uh.

YAHWEH *(Hebrew)*. *Yah*-weh.

The hypocrisy of the report of Uriah's death and David's equally hypocritical response (11:18-25) only made the affair more disgusting to Yahweh God: "But the thing that David had done displeased the Lord" (11:27b). Thus, God used His prophet Nathan to confront David.

I. Stage Is Set
(2 Samuel 11:26, 27)

A. Mourning (v. 26)

26. And when the wife of Uriah heard that Uriah her husband was dead, she mourned for her husband.

The deaths of great personalities such as Moses (Deuteronomy 34:8) and Aaron (Numbers 20:29) resulted in periods of mourning of 30 days. But the usual length of mourning for the dead is a week (Genesis 50:10). We may presume that this mourning is no exception.

It is clear that Bathsheba mourns for *her husband,* but does she mourn for her situation as well? She is pregnant. She is at the mercy of the king. He is to blame for her situation, and it is not clear what will become of her. [See question #1, page 200.] We easily wonder how willing an accomplice Bathsheba has been in this sordid affair. Did she reveal herself deliberately on the roof? Could she have refused the king's advances? Such questions will not be answered in this lifetime. But one thing is certain: David is guilty!

B. Marriage (v. 27)

27. And when the mourning was past, David sent and fetched her to his house, and she became his wife, and bare him a son. But the thing that David had done displeased the LORD.

After a brief seven days (the time of *the mourning*), *David* hurriedly has Bathsheba brought to his palace. There, in perhaps a private ceremony, a wife is added to his harem. No one will be the wiser, so he thinks.

Indeed, *a son* is born to David. Someone's careful calculation may reveal the birth to be (seemingly) a bit premature. Yet the public probably thinks this son to be special, since he is potentially a future king. But the inexplicable has happened. How can a man "after [God's] own heart" (1 Samuel 13:14) commit such violations of God's law? Here we see adultery, murder, and even coveting another man's wife—three of the Ten Commandments broken by Israel's ruler!

Does David forget that the God he serves is all-knowing? All of us have to ask ourselves the same question when we contemplate deliberately sinning against God. What are we thinking? Indeed, the abstract adjectives to describe our God as *omniscient* (all-knowing), *omnipresent* (present everywhere), and *omnipotent* (all-powerful) have very practical implications. There is nothing we say, do, or think about that God does not know. Yes, God knows! The stage is set for the prophet's entrance.

A DISPLEASING ACT

Several years ago at the university where I teach, we had a certain outstanding student. He was bright, ambitious, and a persuasive speaker. When he was 16 and still in high school, he was the host of a radio talk show. For a while he was billed as the nation's youngest host of a regular radio program. He was articulate, creative, imaginative, and interesting.

In school he was academically gifted and did well in his classes. But he had a constant desire to be in the spotlight. Now that he was surrounded by other equally gifted intellectuals, he didn't have the monopoly he once enjoyed. So he created new opportunities to acclaim himself. At one time he claimed that while he was ill the Vice President of the United States came to his dorm room to wish him good health. It soon became obvious that the whole thing was a bold-faced lie. Other actions added to this, and he was soon asked to leave school.

It's a well-known proverb that one fly in the ointment ruins the whole jar. A person can have numerous redeeming qualities, but one bad quality left unchecked can compromise all the others. This young man had many obvious talents, yet one disturbing personality characteristic reversed public opinion of him. His displeasing actions changed how he wanted others to receive him to the exact opposite. The same was true, to an extent, of David (see 1 Kings 15:5). May it not be true of us.
—J. B. N.

II. Drama Is Acted Out (2 Samuel 12:1-7a)

A. Prophet Sent (v. 1a)

1a. And the LORD sent Nathan unto David.

The fact that the baby is already born by this point means that God waits several months before sending *Nathan* to confront *David*. Nathan is a prophet of the court (2 Samuel 7). Such prophets have ready access to the king, but their commitment can involve unpleasant and dangerous tasks. Prophets can be dismissed, imprisoned, or even put to death for telling the king what he does not want to hear (1 Kings 22:1-18; Jeremiah 26:7-9, 20-23). But when the Lord sends you, you go!

B. Prophet Narrates (vv. 1b-4)

1b. And he came unto him, and said unto him, There were two men in one city; the one rich, and the other poor.

The godly prophet is always an advocate for justice and truth. Thus it is not out of character for Nathan to present a tale of injustice to the king for his consideration. The story definitely catches David's attention, as we shall see. Whether David views it as a parable or a real story, he is engaged in thinking it through. [See question #2, page 200.]

2. The rich man had exceeding many flocks and herds.

The description of *the rich man* is completed with very few words. Quite simply, this is a guy who has much more than he needs. Yet one should be careful here. It is not a sin to be rich. What happens to the rich is that in their abundance they may become arrogant and exhibit a sense of superiority over those with lesser means. Money or riches become power. And power corrupts. How well the poor understand this because they are the victims of the abuse of power by the rich.

The rich, on the other hand, hardly see themselves in this light. They are innocent of any crime, for they have "worked hard" for their wealth. That outlook can be true, but rationalizing certain methods for obtaining wealth is very easy!

3. But the poor man had nothing, save one little ewe lamb, which he had bought and nourished up: and it grew up together with him, and with his children; it did eat of his own meat, and drank of his own cup, and lay in his bosom, and was unto him as a daughter.

The focus of the story is on the situation of *the poor man*. He has no significant material possessions except *one little ewe lamb*. That's all he has, and he cherishes the little animal. It has grown up with *his children* and has become part of the family, as any pet lover understands.

By contrast, the animals that are in the "flocks and herds" of the rich man are not pets. They are no more than business assets to him. Were he to lose 25 or 50 percent of them, he may get angry. But his reaction would not be that of sadness over a lost relationship.

4. And there came a traveler unto the rich man, and he spared to take of his own flock and of his own herd, to dress for the wayfaring man that was come unto him; but took the poor man's lamb, and dressed it for the man that was come to him.

Near Eastern custom requires elaborate hospitality for travelers (examples: Genesis 18:1-8 and Judges 13:15). Yet rather than sacrifice one *of his own flock,* the rich man inexplicably takes *the poor man's* pet *lamb!* (We remember that David "took" the wife of Uriah; 2 Samuel 11:4.)

Apparently the rich man has such power that his servants have no problem taking with impunity what truly belongs to the poor man. Then a complete stranger eats the meat of the beloved pet. Nathan's words are carefully chosen. [See question #3, page 200.]

C. King Reacts (vv. 5, 6)

5, 6. And David's anger was greatly kindled against the man; and he said to Nathan, As the LORD liveth, the man that hath done this thing shall surely die: and he shall restore the lamb fourfold, because he did this thing, and because he had no pity.

David takes the bait! The hook sinks deeply into *David's* own mouth as he utters words of moral outrage, even with an oath—*as the Lord liveth.* The rich *man* deserves to *die,* but at a minimum he must restore *fourfold.* [See question #4, page 200.] This reveals that David knows the law of God (see Exodus 22:1; compare Luke 19:8). But knowledge of the law does not always translate into obedience to that law, as David's reprehensible behavior demonstrates thus far.

As a bit of speculation, perhaps David sees in this rich man what he bitterly hates in himself: abuse of power, greed, lust, scorn for the rights (and even the lives) of others. That has been his life for several months. It is in this light that David indicts and sentences at the same time.

What David most hates is the fact that the rich man has *no pity.* David, who is declared to be a man after God's own heart, rages against a rich man he considers to be heartless. Little does David realize that he has just indicted and sentenced himself!

D. Prophet Accuses (v. 7a)

7a. And Nathan said to David, Thou art the man.

The four words *thou art the man* are really just two words in the Hebrew: "You the-man" (with *the* and *man* as a single word). How powerful this succinct statement is! Everything comes to a head right here. Nathan's commitment to God is confirmed in this statement. Nathan's life is on the line, for he is confronting a king who is a recent murderer. If David is willing to have one of his most loyal soldiers (Uriah) killed to cover adultery, why not also kill a prophet who offers personal insult?

In verses 7b-12 (not in today's text), Nathan demonstrates the Lord's full knowledge of the situation. The criticism of David is relentless. Nathan

Visual for Lesson 10. *Start a discussion by pointing to this visual as you ask, "What stands have you taken for God?"*

has made his choice. Now it is time for David to make his.

III. Punishment Is Announced (2 Samuel 12:13-15)

A. Confession (v. 13a)

13a. And David said unto Nathan, I have sinned against the LORD.

We may compare David's response to Nathan with King Saul's response to Samuel in 1 Samuel 15:20, 21. When confronted with wrongdoing, Saul made excuses. David, on the other hand, admits his wrongdoing when confronted. A longer version of David's confession is found in Psalm 51. [See question #5, page 200.]

B. Relief (v. 13b)

13b. And Nathan said unto David, The LORD also hath put away thy sin; thou shalt not die.

Back in verse 5, David had condemned the rich man's behavior as worthy of death. Yet the Lord in His mercy has decided that David will *not die.*

C. Judgment (vv. 14, 15)

14. Howbeit, because by this deed thou hast given great occasion to the enemies of the LORD to blaspheme, the child also that is born unto thee shall surely die.

While David's confession brings him personal forgiveness, the course of events his choices set in motion remains unchanged. The most immediate consequence will be the death of David and Bathsheba's first *child.* Further, the Lord proclaims to David (through Nathan) that "the sword shall never depart from thine house. . . . Behold, I will raise up evil against thee out of thine house" (2 Samuel 12:10, 11).

The effect of David's behavior reaches far beyond himself and those close to him. His actions bring shame to the Lord by giving *the enemies* of God *occasion* to *blaspheme*. We do well to remember that there is a difference between *forgiveness* and *freedom from consequences*. To be forgiven (either by the Lord or by a person) does not necessarily mean that all consequences are wiped out.

OCCASION TO BLASPHEME

All of us are representatives of something. Whether we like it or not, people who identify us with a particular cause, social niche, etc., draw conclusions about that cause or niche from our actions. While traveling in Europe, I have sometimes been embarrassed by the insensitive comments of fellow American travelers. It is no wonder that many people of the world think in terms of "ugly Americans." The actions and comments of a few reflect negatively on the entire country.

This is seen particularly in the alleged activities of some American military personnel. Please don't misunderstand me. I believe that the overwhelming majority of those who serve in the armed forces are decent folks who represent the U.S. in a good light. But it doesn't take many negative occurrences to cast a bad light on all military personnel and the entire country. Think of the atrocities in Iraq against civilians and prisoners. Accusations of rape by U.S. military personnel have disturbed residents of Okinawa for years. In all such instances, the reputation of America is smeared.

As Christians, our actions and comments influence how others view God. How often have those actions and words been the occasion of showing

contempt for God? Nathan's judgment was that David's actions had given occasion for the enemies of the Lord to do just that. May we learn this lesson from history so that we will not do likewise.

—J. B. N.

15. And Nathan departed unto his house. And the LORD struck the child that Uriah's wife bare unto David, and it was very sick.

Nathan has done his job. So he goes home, no doubt sick at heart. He knows of the terrible tragedies that await the dynasty of *David* (see 2 Samuel 12:16–24:25). The first of the tragedies will be the death of an innocent child. David bears the blame for this death.

Conclusion

A. Commitments and Consequences

Ancient Egyptian pharaohs considered themselves to be divine and thus answerable to no one. Mesopotamian kings were not much better, thinking that they had at least semidivinity bestowed upon them. Israel's kings were different. Even before the beginning of the institution of kingship, Israel's kings were to be subject to God and God's laws as much as the people were (see Deuteronomy 17:14-20; 1 Samuel 12:14).

Keeping an Israelite king in line with God's will was primarily the work of the prophet. Samuel played that role for Saul. Nathan played that role for David. Nathan's commitment to God's Word and will required him to confront David on the most grievous of sins. David's response of confession and submission was partly due to Nathan's skill in approaching the king. This story should teach us who lead in the church today about the need to confront.

We also must realize that our behavior affects the efforts of the church to win the lost. Sin always affects not only our relationship with God but also our relationships with others (see Galatians 6:1-5).

B. Prayer

Father, have mercy upon us according to Your loving-kindness. We acknowledge our sins and transgressions committed in Your presence. Create in us clean hearts and right spirits. With the restoration of the joy of our salvation, we will help others to acknowledge You in confession and repentance. Accept our broken and contrite hearts. In the name of the Holy One, Jesus. Amen.

C. Thought to Remember

God can use a repentant heart.

Home Daily Bible Readings

Monday, Feb. 2—Lust and Adultery (2 Samuel 11:1-5)

Tuesday, Feb. 3—An Unsuccessful Cover-up (2 Samuel 11:6-13)

Wednesday, Feb. 4—Contrived Murder (2 Samuel 11:14-21)

Thursday, Feb. 5—An Easy Conscience (2 Samuel 11:22-27)

Friday, Feb. 6—A Cry for Forgiveness (Psalm 51:1-9)

Saturday, Feb. 7—A Broken and Contrite Heart (Psalm 51:10-19)

Sunday, Feb. 8—You Are the Man! (2 Samuel 12:1-7, 13-15)

Learning by Doing

This page contains an alternative lesson plan emphasizing learning activities. Some of these activities are also found in the helpful student book, Adult Bible Class.

Into the Lesson

Select one of Aesop's short fables, such as "The Ant and the Grasshopper" or "The Dog in the Manger." (A selection of such fables can be located in a public library or at www.aesopfables.com.) Read your selection to your class. Then ask, "What are the main features of a short story such as this one?" If not mentioned, note such elements as (1) the story has a second, more significant meaning; (2) the story is designed to teach by drawing a reaction; (3) animals or other elements represent human traits and behaviors; (4) such stories are elicited by inappropriate behavior. Once this brief analysis is complete, say, "Today's study includes just such a powerful story, also elicited by bad behavior."

Into the Word

At the core of today's text is the simple but profoundly effective story that Nathan told David. Introduce the New Testament word *parable,* which is a "fictitious story that illustrates a moral attitude or a religious principle" (Merriam-Webster's dictionary).

Give each student a handout with the headings *The Story* and *The Reality* printed over two blank columns. The handouts should also have these subheadings down the left side: 1. The Characters; 2. The Conflict; 3. The Complication; 4. The Resolution.

Move down the column labeled *The Story* and have students identify storyline elements for each of the four subheads as those elements are given in the text (example: one of the story characters is the rich man). Then move down the column labeled *The Reality* and ask your class to identify the "real life" references of the subheadings. Most will have very obvious responses (example: the rich man in Nathan's story represents King David).

Ask at each point, "How does this particular story element reflect reality?" For example, one could say that both "the rich man" story character and the king had more than they needed; each had a place of prominence in society; both would likely have visitors seek them out because of their positions; both had neighbors of lesser means and authority.

Also ask at each point, "How does this particular story element differ from reality?" A potential response is that a king has much greater authority than a generic "rich man" and thus greater respon-

sibility. Another potential observation is that David's declaration of capital punishment was not carried out in real life against David (although the child himself died).

Your learners may enjoy creating their own parable. This will help them see how brilliant Nathan's parable is, since these kinds stories can be difficult to write in such a way that they are both (1) succinct and (2) achieve the intended effect. Make copies of the incomplete story below and give one to each learner. Say, "Try your hand at composing a similar story for the circumstances of 2 Samuel 11 and 12."

> *There were two ____ in one ____. One was __ and the other was ____. The ____ had many, many ____. The other had only one ____. Yet that one ____ was like a ____ to its ____. Once a visiting ____ came to see the ____. Though the ____ had much/many ____, that person took the other's ____ and ____ it for the visitor. Then the ____ became angry and said, "_____!"*

Into Life

Ask a weaving-arts craftsperson in your church to prepare a few of the yarn decorations called "the eye of God." Display these as you approach the end of class. If you cannot obtain the decorations themselves, find pictures of them on the Internet and print them off to pass around.

Ask, "Who can identify this craft by its common name?" If no one does, go ahead and identify it. Then say, "Some may object to calling these decorations 'the eye of God' on the ground of superstitious or pagan belief. But those who hang these on their walls find them to be good reminders that God is all-seeing. This is a piercing truth that confronted King David (compare Genesis 16:13, 14)."

Ask your class to repeat the following prayer with you, a line at a time, either aloud or silently. "O God who sees, I know You see me. / Forgive me when I embarrass You. / Forgive me when I disappoint You. / Thank You for Your eye that sees me in love and grace. / Thank You for being present in my days. / Thank You for being present in my nights. / Your omniscience is a restraint for me. / Your eye of knowledge is my comfort. / O God who sees, thank You for seeing my need and sending Your Son. / In the name of Jesus who knows me, amen."

Let's Talk It Over

The questions on this page are designed to promote discussion of the lesson by the class and to encourage application of the lesson Scriptures. The answers provided are only discussion starters. Let your class talk it over from there.

1. What conflicting emotions and challenges do you think Bathsheba faced in mourning her dead husband? How are these the same or different from grief you have felt?

Guilt is typically part of the grieving process, though usually that guilt is more a sense of regret ("I wish I had called her more," "I should have been there," etc.) than culpability. Was Bathsheba aware that David had engineered Uriah's death? If so, she undoubtedly had much to regret because of her own complicity. Her adultery and pregnancy certainly shaped her mourning period.

Whenever guilt is part of grief, we can use it to reshape our future. If we did not spend enough time with a sick parent, then that guilt can prompt us to spend more time with a sick friend. If there is some actual sin against a loved one now deceased, then confession and repentance are necessary steps to spiritual healing (see 1 John 1:9).

2. When you have to tell a friend, family member, or boss something that he or she will not want to hear, how do you approach the conversation? Is Nathan's approach valid for us today? Why, or why not?

Without doubt, Nathan's approach was right for him because he was inspired by God to use it. Some say that Nathan's approach is not valid today because it is manipulative. Whether that proposal is right or wrong, the fact is that there are times when we have to confront someone with an uncomfortable truth.

The first thing to do is examine the purity of our own motives (see Proverbs 27:6: "Faithful are the wounds of a friend; but the kisses of an enemy are deceitful"). We then present the truth in a way that can lead the other person to see the truth on his or her own. (Remember this old saying: "A man convinced against his will is of the same opinion still.") The technique you use should allow for the possibility of the relationship to continue or even grow. The technique should also allow for the possibility to see that you are the one who is wrong because you have overlooked something important.

3. What are some ways that people exploit the poor in our world today? What should our response be?

Wealth does not always result from the exploitation of others, but it may. Sometimes wealth makes people believe they deserve things—even if they get those things at the expense of others. We also need to define *wealth* and *poverty* carefully. In Western democracies, most middle-class and even many of the poor are wealthy compared with people in underdeveloped nations.

This fact should cause us to consider whether we ourselves are the exploiters. For example, do we expect to be able to purchase inexpensive shoes without concern that they may be made by child labor in foreign countries? If we do not consider the effects that our actions have beyond our own borders, then perhaps we too are guilty of exploiting others.

4. What purposes have you seen punishment and restitution serve when dealing with sin?

Ideally, restitution repays the victim while punishment corrects the sinner (or at least keeps the sinner from committing more crime). Yet we all know that many crimes and sins involve complex situations. For instance, how could the rich man "repay" the emotional loss of a beloved pet even onefold, let alone fourfold? The crime in the story was more than taking an animal; any number of new lambs would not replace the lamb that the poor man loved.

Restitution cannot restore lost innocence or dead children. Punishment may reduce the likelihood of a person's repeating a crime, but it cannot change the past. Considering how we struggle with these matters in our world should make us appreciate again the power of God's grace!

5. How does our treatment of people affect our relationship with God?

David committed adultery with Uriah's wife and then arranged for Uriah's death, but said, "I have sinned against the Lord." John wrote, "If a man say, I love God, and hateth his brother, he is a liar: for he that loveth not his brother whom he hath seen, how can he love God whom he hath not seen?" (1 John 4:20). God takes our relationships with each other very seriously! All evil done to others dishonors Him because each is created in His image.

Esther Risks Her Life

DEVOTIONAL READING: **Philippians 1:20-30.**

BACKGROUND SCRIPTURE: **Esther 4, 5.**

PRINTED TEXT: **Esther 4:1-3, 9-17.**

Esther 4:1-3, 9-17

1 When Mordecai perceived all that was done, Mordecai rent his clothes, and put on sackcloth with ashes, and went out into the midst of the city, and cried with a loud and a bitter cry;

2 And came even before the king's gate: for none might enter into the king's gate clothed with sackcloth.

3 And in every province, whithersoever the king's commandment and his decree came, there was great mourning among the Jews, and fasting, and weeping, and wailing; and many lay in sackcloth and ashes.

· · · · · · · · · · · · · · · ·

9 And Hatach came and told Esther the words of Mordecai.

10 Again Esther spake unto Hatach, and gave him commandment unto Mordecai;

11 All the king's servants, and the people of the king's provinces, do know, that whosoever, whether man or woman, shall come unto the king into the inner court, who is not called, there is one law of his to put him to death, except such to whom the king shall hold out the golden sceptre, that he may live: but I have not been called to come in unto the king these thirty days.

12 And they told to Mordecai Esther's words.

13 Then Mordecai commanded to answer Esther, Think not with thyself that thou shalt escape in the king's house, more than all the Jews.

14 For if thou altogether holdest thy peace at this time, then shall there enlargement and deliverance arise to the Jews from another place; but thou and thy father's house shall be destroyed: and who knoweth whether thou art come to the kingdom for such a time as this?

15 Then Esther bade them return Mordecai this answer,

16 Go, gather together all the Jews that are present in Shushan, and fast ye for me, and neither eat nor drink three days, night or day: I also and my maidens will fast likewise; and so will I go in unto the king, which is not according to the law: and if I perish, I perish.

17 So Mordecai went his way, and did according to all that Esther had commanded him.

**Feb
15**

GOLDEN TEXT: Go, gather together all the Jews that are present in Shushan, and fast ye for me, and neither eat nor drink three days, night or day: I also and my maidens will fast likewise; and so will I go in unto the king, which is not according to the law: and if I perish, I perish.—Esther 4:16.

Human Commitment
Unit 2: Old Testament People of Commitment
(Lessons 5–12)

Lesson Aims

After participating in this lesson, each student will be able to:

1. Summarize the life situations of Esther and Moredecai.

2. Give an example of how Esther's situation is paralleled in the twenty-first century.

3. Describe how he or she will adopt Esther's courage in one area of life.

Lesson Outline

INTRODUCTION
    A. Risky Commitments
    B. Lesson Background
I. PENDING DOOM (Esther 4:1-3)
    A. Reaction of One (vv. 1, 2)
        Dressing for Whom?
    B. Reaction of Many (v. 3)
II. IMMINENT DANGER (Esther 4:9-11)
    A. Hatach's Report (v. 9)
    B. Esther's Response (vv. 10, 11)
III. SHARP RETORT (Esther 4:12-14)
    A. Warning (vv. 12, 13)
    B. Logic (v. 14)
        Such a Time
IV. FIRM RESOLVE (Esther 4:15-17)
    A. Instructions Sent (vv. 15, 16)
        If I Perish
    B. Instructions Implemented (v. 17)
CONCLUSION
    A. Commitments and Risks
    B. Prayer
    C. Thought to Remember

Introduction

A. Risky Commitments

The fabric of American society came under severe strain in the 1960s and early 1970s. Unrest presented itself on several fronts. The Civil Rights movement swept the land. Protests against the Vietnam War grew ever stronger. The assassinations of President John F. Kennedy, his brother Robert Kennedy, and Dr. Martin Luther King, Jr., rocked the sensibilities of the nation. President Richard Nixon's paranoia concerning his political

"enemies" led him into the debacle of Watergate. This led in turn to Nixon's resignation as president lest he be impeached. Gerald Ford found himself in the highest office of the land without having solicited a single vote.

Former President Ford died on December 26, 2006. During his funeral he was eulogized by both Democrats and Republicans for his humility and skill in bringing healing to the nation. Part of that process was accomplished when President Ford pardoned Richard Nixon so that the country would not have to endure years of judicial procedures.

That move turned out to be political suicide. Yet President Ford was determined to do the right thing for the country at a time when the country so badly needed it. Many who eulogized him mentioned that he was the right man at the right time in the right place. Could it have been by divine intervention?

There are people who make commitments that place their careers or even their lives at great risk. But if the cause is noble and right, the risks are worth it. Our study of Queen Esther examines her reaction to a crisis. Her predecessor, Queen Vashti, had committed career suicide by taking a stand on a certain issue (Esther 1). For Esther, the stakes were much higher.

B. Lesson Background

The book of Esther tells the story of the origin of a Jewish festival called *Purim* (see Esther 9). With this beautifully written story in hand (from about 460 BC), the Jews came to celebrate a festival each year that commemorated the victory of the Jews over the evil plot of Haman, who wanted to exterminate all Jews in the Persian empire.

The setting is during Ahasuerus's reign over Persia. Also known as Xerxes, this man ruled that empire from 486 to 465 BC. This vast empire stretched from the borders of India to Ethiopia (upper Nile region; Esther 1:1). The king's palace was located at Shushan (or Susa), the winter residence for the Persian monarchs. Both Daniel and Nehemiah had connections with this city (see Nehemiah 1:1; Daniel 8:2).

The story begins with an elaborate banquet held by the king to show off his vast riches and power. Through a series of events, Queen Vashti was deposed. The search for a new queen resulted in Esther's being chosen. She was the adopted daughter of her relative Mordecai (see Esther 2:7), a Jew. Mordecai forbade Esther from revealing her cultural identity (Esther 2:10).

A few years later, Haman, one of the king's nobles, was promoted. Haman then devised a plan to exterminate the Jews (Esther 3). With half-truths and a bribe, Haman convinced the king to go along with the plan. The date was set (3:13), and the king's edict went out to all the provinces. Then King Ahasuerus and Haman sat down and drank together, perhaps to celebrate (3:15).

I. Pending Doom
(Esther 4:1-3)

A. Reaction of One (vv. 1, 2)

1. When Mordecai perceived all that was done, Mordecai rent his clothes, and put on sackcloth with ashes, and went out into the midst of the city, and cried with a loud and a bitter cry.

Having heard and/or read of the dreadful decree of the king and the political background to it, *Mordecai* does the expected thing: he tears his outer garment and puts on *sackcloth* (goat or camel hair). *Ashes* on the head identify one with the dead.

Such actions are well established in Scripture (examples: 1 Samuel 4:12; 2 Samuel 1:2; 3:31). Weeping and wailing are common gestures of mourning (contrast the "stiff upper lip" of modern Westerners during funerals). Mordecai's grief may include a sense of responsibility at refusing to bow to Haman (Esther 3:1-5), since that is what has set off Haman's rage against the Jews in general (3:6).

2. And came even before the king's gate: for none might enter into the king's gate clothed with sackcloth.

It is obvious that in Mordecai's desperate crying he is not just wandering aimlessly through the city streets. He goes to the only place where he can hope to find relief or some kind of justice: *the king's gate.*

Archaeological excavations at Shushan have identified a gatehouse about 100 yards east of the main palace. The passageway through the gate is about 50 feet long. Four towers grace the outside of the structure, and 4 pillars of about 40 feet high decorate the 12,000-square-foot chamber through which the passageway enters the palace complex. An inscription ordered by Ahasuerus identifies it as having been built by his father, Darius. So the word *gate* signifies much more than a mere "doorway"!

Supplicants of all kinds go to the king's gate in order to seek justice from the only person who can make it happen. So it is with Mordecai. But before anyone can *enter into* the gate and approach the king, the person has to be properly cleaned and attired. Dress codes are nothing new!

DRESSING FOR WHOM?

George Bryan Brummel, better known as Beau Brummel, was born in 1778 to a middle-class family in London. Through various connections, he was soon rubbing shoulders with sons of the highest aristocratic families in England. His wit brought him the friendship of the eldest son of King George III, later to be commonly known as the Prince Regent when he was the caretaker of the government during his father's bouts with insanity.

An astute observer of clothing fashions, Beau Brummel soon gained the reputation of being *the* social arbiter of good taste in men's dress. This was at the height of the Napoleonic Wars, and anything French was regarded with suspicion in England. Brummel emphasized the cut of the garment and the quality of the fabric rather than fancy trim, a French affectation. He also played a major role in making trousers popular, compared with the earlier knee breeches. Further, Brummel gave special attention to neckwear.

The bright colors of the previous decades were out of date, replaced by the plain, dark colors in well-cut coats and jackets that Brummel preferred. To appear in outmoded garments was a social disgrace and could lead to being snubbed. Many of us are familiar with the dress codes that are printed in employee handbooks. But dress codes also can come in the form of "social peer pressure," and this is nothing new!

Was Mordecai aware of the fact that he could not gain admission through the king's gate wearing sackcloth? Probably. Ultimately, however, Mordecai was not dressing for an audience with an earthly king, but the heavenly one.   —J. B. N.

B. Reaction of Many (v. 3)

3. And in every province, whithersoever the king's commandment and his decree came, there was great mourning among the Jews, and fasting, and weeping, and wailing; and many lay in sackcloth and ashes.

How to Say It

AHASUERUS. Uh-haz-you-*ee*-rus.

DARIUS. Duh-*rye*-us.

HAMAN. *Hay*-mun.

HATACH. *Hay*-tak.

MORDECAI. *Mor*-dih-kye.

NAPOLEONIC. Nuh-*poe*-lee-*ahn*-ick (strong accent on *poe*).

NEHEMIAH. *Nee*-huh-*my*-uh (strong accent on *my*).

PERSIA. *Per*-zhuh.

PURIM. *Pew*-rim.

SHUSHAN. *Shoo*-shan.

SUSA. *Soo*-suh.

VASHTI. *Vash*-tie.

XERXES. *Zerk*-seez.

The Jews throughout the 127 provinces of Persia (Esther 1:1) react to the king's edict in the same manner as Mordecai, with an additional element: they fast. Perhaps Mordecai fasts as well, but the text doesn't tell us. [See question #1, page 208.]

Usually when Jews fast, it is accompanied by prayer, and prayer always has God as its focus. Yet one of the peculiar characteristics of the book of Esther is that it does not mention God's name at all. For that matter there is no mention of worship or sacrifice either.

Some decry this phenomenon and declare the book of Esther to be of little religious value. Others, however, see a unique literary device to show how God's sovereignty is exercised in every detail of life so that His will is worked out through human endeavor and decisions. I prefer the latter opinion. Indeed, it will take divine intervention in order to save the Jews from an edict that, according to the text, cannot be reversed (see Esther 8:8).

II. Imminent Danger
(Esther 4:9-11)
A. Hatach's Report (v. 9)

9. And Hatach came and told Esther the words of Mordecai.

Hatach is a eunuch (chamberlain) assigned to care for *Esther* (Esther 4:5). He looks after her every need. Since *Mordecai* refuses to be comforted with new clothes instead of the sackcloth he is wearing (4:4), Esther sends Hatach to find out the what and why of his despair (4:5).

Every detail is given to Hatach by Mordecai, including an explanation of the written decree declaring the date for the annihilation of the Jews in Persia (4:7, 8). On top of the explanations, Mordecai encourages Esther (through Hatach) to intercede on behalf of her people, the Jews, before the king (4:8b). After Hatach tells Esther *the words of Mordecai,* she has a decision to make.

B. Esther's Response (vv. 10, 11)

10, 11. Again Esther spake unto Hatach, and gave him commandment unto Mordecai; All the king's servants, and the people of the king's provinces, do know, that whosoever, whether man or woman, shall come unto the king into the inner court, who is not called, there is one law of his to put him to death, except such to whom the king shall hold out the golden sceptre, that he may live: but I have not been called to come in unto the king these thirty days.

Esther's response to *Mordecai* through *Hatach* informs Mordecai about her dilemma. She can initiate an audience with the king only at the risk of her life. If she goes ahead, she will be spared only if the king holds out his *golden sceptre*.

It has been a month since she has been summoned into the king's presence. Why not wait a little longer? After all, the plan for genocide is 11 months away (Esther 3:7). Why not go through proper channels?

The "proper channels" may be the problem! Leaders of countries have certain assistants who act as figurative "gatekeepers" to determine who is allowed an audience with the leader and who is not. If Haman is himself this gatekeeper (what we may call a *chief of staff* today), then he undoubtedly will deny her an audience if he figures out what she is trying to do. No, Esther has to approach the king without being summoned, possibly incurring a *death* sentence in the process. [See question #2, page 208.]

III. Sharp Retort
(Esther 4:12-14)
A. Warning (vv. 12, 13)

12, 13. And they told to Mordecai Esther's words. Then Mordecai commanded to answer Esther, Think not with thyself that thou shalt escape in the king's house, more than all the Jews.

The faithful Hatach reports *Esther's words* back to *Mordecai.* But Esther's hesitation draws a warning from Mordecai. If Esther thinks she will be exempt from the planned extermination of the Jews because she lives in the king's palace as a queen, she can *think* again!

The passage of four or five years has perhaps cooled the king's ardor for Queen Esther, evidenced by the passing of a month without her being summoned. [See question #3, page 208.] The king's extermination order applies to all *Jews,* without exception. She may have been successful at concealing her cultural heritage so far, but can that go on permanently?

B. Logic (v. 14)

14. For if thou altogether holdest thy peace at this time, then shall there enlargement and deliverance arise to the Jews from another place; but thou and thy father's house shall be destroyed: and who knoweth whether thou art come to the kingdom for such a time as this?

The edict is for the extermination of "all the Jews" (Esther 3:6), and that includes Esther in the king's palace. There will be no exemption once her heritage is discovered. If Esther does not act, God will act through someone else or in another way yet unseen, but Esther will die in her neglect of this opportunity. Esther must not overlook the possibility that God has placed her in the king's palace *for such a time as this.*

In other words, Esther has the opportunity to save her people. Jewish history is rich with examples of God raising up deliverers. Think of Joseph, Moses, and the various judges. Esther must act. It is her destiny to do so. [See question #4, page 208.]

SUCH A TIME

There was a joke that made the rounds in the early 1970s about what the presidents of the United States have taught us. Kennedy taught us it's dangerous to be president. Johnson taught us it's dangerous to have a president. Truman taught us anybody could be president. Eisenhower taught us we don't need a president.

There is some truth to each of these four statements, but the comment about Eisenhower is a bit unkind. Granted, he represented a very laid-back presidency. Yet he was also aggressive in defending pro-American regimes in Taiwan and Lebanon. He was also aggressive in promoting civil rights by sending troops to integrate the schools of Little Rock, Arkansas.

Modern critics have complained that the Eisenhower presidency was too pro-business. But the country had just come through a devastating world war, with governmental price controls over everything. The country was ready for a more relaxed governmental posture. Indeed, Eisenhower may have been the exact kind of president the country needed in the 1950s.

Who knows but that Eisenhower had come to the presidency for just such a time as that? God is still the God of all history. And He may place any of us in situations in order to accomplish His divine purposes!   —J. B. N.

IV. Firm Resolve
(Esther 4:15-17)

A. Instructions Sent (vv. 15, 16)

15, 16a. Then Esther bade them return Mordecai this answer, Go, gather together all the Jews that are present in Shushan, and fast ye for me, and neither eat nor drink three days, night or day.

Esther's mind is made up! She will act out of a sense of duty and destiny. She devises a plan that starts with a complete *fast*: no food or drink for *three days.* Although God's name is not mentioned in the book of Esther, fasting in the Old Testament is preparation for vigorous prayer to God (compare Ezra 8:21, 23; Nehemiah 1:4; Psalm 35:13; Daniel 9:3). Esther asks that *all the Jews* in *Shushan* gather together for concentrated fasting.

Visual for
Lessons 6 & 11

Use this visual to return to this question from Lesson 6: "Who is the Lord?"

16b. I also and my maidens will fast likewise; and so will I go in unto the king, which is not according to the law: and if I perish, I perish.

Esther is a true leader. She does not ask her fellow Jews to do something that she will not do. So she and her *maidens* (though they probably are not Jews) *will fast* as well.

Her determination to approach *the king* in violation of Persian custom is complete, and her risky commitment is the famous *If I perish, I perish* (compare Genesis 43:14; Daniel 3:16-18). Esther commands those around her. Mordecai and others will submit to her requests. [See question #5, page 208.]

IF I PERISH

On the Gettysburg battlefield of July 2, 1863, Union General Daniel Sickles extended his line, without orders, in a salient that he thought would protect the Union left. Instead, he was battered by Confederate forces; his lines were broken and a whole brigade of Confederate soldiers began charging toward a gap in the Union lines.

Union General Winfield S. Hancock saw the danger and looked for troops to fill the gap. He knew more soldiers were soon to arrive, but the needed reinforcements would not come onto the scene for another 10 minutes. Those 10 minutes could spell disaster for the whole Union army.

Hancock saw the First Minnesota Infantry and ordered it into the line. That unit ran into position. The First Minnesota was 262 men facing a Confederate brigade that started the day with 1,800. They were heavily outnumbered.

The Minnesotans charged, stopped the Confederates, and continued to fire until being overrun.

But they had bought precious time. Union reinforcements arrived, the line was stabilized, and the Confederates proceeded no further. In this furious onslaught, the First Minnesota Infantry suffered 215 men killed, wounded, or missing—casualties exceeding 80 percent.

Those who ordered the charge knew it was a suicidal mission. Those being ordered to charge may have known it too. But it was the only way to save the Union line. As the colonel of the regiment observed, "It was a sacrifice that must be made." Sometimes it is very obvious what has to be done, and we can only state, with belief in the ultimate cause, "If I perish, I perish." May God give us the strength to say just that when that time comes.

—J. B. N.

B. Instructions Implemented (v. 17)

17. So Mordecai went his way, and did according to all that Esther had commanded him.

This verse refers to the gathering of the Jews in Shushan to fast (and, undoubtedly, to pray). But Esther's plan sets in motion the following: She approaches the king and is accepted (Esther 5:1, 2). She offers a banquet with Haman present, effectively neutralizing him (5:3-5). Haman continues to be enraged because Mordecai refuses to bow down to him (5:9, 10). Haman's wife suggests a gallows be made 75 feet high upon which all will be able to see Mordecai's dead body. The gallows is built (5:11-14).

The king has insomnia, thus he requests the history books of his reign be read to him. (Do history books put you to sleep?) He ends up hearing about the conspiracy that Mordecai uncovered to save the king's life and that Mordecai was never rewarded (6:1-3). Mordecai is ironically honored in the very manner that Haman anticipated being honored himself (6:4-13).

Esther requests a second banquet with the king and Haman present (6:14–7:2). She exposes Haman as the man who seeks to slaughter the Jews, being careful not to implicate the king himself, although he is privy to the plan (7:3-6). Haman pleads with Esther for his life (7:7b, 8a). From a distance, the king interprets Haman's actions as molesting the queen (7:8b). Haman is quickly hanged on the very gallows that he had erected for Mordecai (7:9, 10).

The rest of the story comes to a fitting conclusion in Esther 8–10. Mordecai replaces Haman in position, power, and property (8:1, 2). The Jews are allowed to defend themselves, and they do it successfully, even for an extra day (8:13–9:17). Thus begins the celebration of Purim (9:18-32). A final tribute is given to Mordecai (chapter 10).

Conclusion

A. Commitments and Risks

Even though God's name is not mentioned in the book of Esther, one comes away from reading the book with the thought of how great God is. "Is any thing too hard for the Lord?" (Genesis 18:14). He reverses the irreversible!

Mankind may propose, but God disposes. Esther was willing to risk her life for the worthy cause of saving her fellow Jews. By God's providence, Esther became queen at just the right time to intercede. God today may arrange circumstances for faithful people to be in special positions at just the right time to effect important change.

Commitment to personal integrity for great causes often carries with it great risk—perhaps to one's career or even to one's life. Maybe God has placed you in a unique position "for such a time as this." Are you willing to make a commitment that risks all?

B. Prayer

O Lord our God, we pray that You will raise up leaders in our homes, our churches, and our country who will make commitments to accomplish Your will on this earth, although it will require great risks. Give us the courage of Esther to carry through with our own commitment to Your plans. May we, like Mordecai, encourage those who need to make such commitments. In the name of Jesus, the one who gave all for us. Amen.

C. Thought to Remember

The greatest risk
is in not following God's plan.

Home Daily Bible Readings

Monday, Feb. 9—The Search for a Queen (Esther 2:1-11)

Tuesday, Feb. 10—A New Queen (Esther 2:15-18)

Wednesday, Feb. 11—A Plot Thwarted (Esther 2:19-23)

Thursday, Feb. 12—An Evil Edict (Esther 3:7-13)

Friday, Feb. 13—The Evil Intent Revealed (Esther 7:1-10)

Saturday, Feb. 14—The People Rescued (Esther 8:3-8)

Sunday, Feb. 15—If I Perish, I Perish (Esther 4:1-3, 9-17)

Learning by Doing

This page contains an alternative lesson plan emphasizing learning activities. Some of these activities are also found in the helpful student book, Adult Bible Class.

Into the Lesson

Have on display a collection of small boxes wrapped as if they contained gifts. If available, use paper with Jewish symbols such as the star of David and the tablets of the Ten Commandments. On the table where you place the boxes, include items related to games of chance: dice, a spinner with numbered sections, a bingo wheel (the type that mixes and distributes numbers), a dreidel (a toy top with Hebrew letters, used in certain games), and a discarded lottery ticket are possibilities. (Do not include items your class would find offensive.)

As class begins, ask if anyone can explain why you have such items on display. If no one knows, introduce the class to the Jewish celebration of Purim, instituted after Esther and Mordecai rescued the people of God. The holiday involves giving gifts. And its name, *purim,* is the Hebrew word in the book of Esther to indicate the lots cast to determine the infamous day for the planned execution of the Jews.

Into the Word

Establish four groups of not more than four people; if your class is larger, repeat the group assignments below. Label your groups *Bad News, Hesitations, Options,* and *Decision.* Prepare and distribute the following discussion sheets.

Bad News Group: Read Esther 4:1-3. These verses picture the reaction to the king's decree to schedule the killing of all Jews in Persia. We no longer tear our clothes, cry loudly in the streets, and wear sackcloth and ashes on the reception of such potentially bad news. What do we do instead? Was Mordecai's action outside the king's gate a political act? What political acts are appropriate for the godly when bad laws are enacted, especially those regarding life and death and the freedom of worship and faith?

Hesitation Group: Read Esther 4:9-11. The tendency to self-protection may cause one to hesitate when action is obviously needed, as in Esther's case. What was reasonable about Esther's hesitancy? What was unreasonable? What are some of the factors that typically keep "good people" from acting in bad circumstances? What are some of the "everybody knows" issues (see v. 11a) that keep you from aggressively pursuing God's truth and justice?

Options Group: Read Esther 4:12-14. How common is the "I am the exception" thinking that Mordecai accuses Esther of? What are some examples? In what kinds of circumstances will Mordecai's "If you don't do it, God will do it in some other way" warning be appropriate and inappropriate? In what ways is Mordecai's challenge regarding a personal "right time" a valid and useful challenge to every believer? Have you ever sensed that God has put you in the right place at the right time to do something significant for Him? Explain.

Decision Group: Read Esther 4:15-17. Does Esther's plan for days of prayer and fasting demonstrate faith or doubt? How so? Is Esther's recounting of the potential death penalty (v. 16b) an appeal for sympathy, a cry for a change of plans, or an appeal for strength in cooperation? Is Esther's "If I perish, I perish" an expression of fatalism or faith? Christian martyrs through the centuries have found their faith worth dying for; do you sense that in contemporary Christians? If not, how do you explain that?

Let each group report both their questions and their conclusions in the sequence of the verses.

Into Life

Give each learner a name tag featuring the large letters *E C* in red and the much smaller letters *H P* in black. The letters *H P* should be confined, respectively, within the spaces of the larger *E* and *C.* Tell your class that the *E C* stands for "Esther's courage" and *H P* stands for "Haman's plan." Point out that Esther's holy courage was bigger than Haman's unholy plot.

Ask the class to suggest other words for the two sets of letters, words that reflect the Christian's need to stand against the deadly plans of the devil himself. Give them an example: *E C* equals "every Christian"; *H P* equals "Hell's poison." Challenge students to wear the tags at some point this week to provide an opportunity to recall the Bible study to someone who asks.

Option: Purchase a small dreidel for each class member as a reminder of today's story and of God's concern for His people in every circumstance. Some craft and hobby stores sell small dreidels very inexpensively. As an alternative, download from the Internet a picture of a dreidel; give a copy of the picture to each student.

Let's Talk It Over

The questions on this page are designed to promote discussion of the lesson by the class and to encourage application of the lesson Scriptures. The answers provided are only discussion starters. Let your class talk it over from there.

1. What is the worst news you have ever heard? What did your reaction to that news say about your Christian character?

Many will focus on something personal: the death of a family member, the illness of a child, the infidelity of a spouse, the loss of a career, the diagnosis of cancer, etc. Some will answer this in a more national or global sense: the worst news was 9/11, the Darfur genocide, Hurricane Katrina, the election of the "wrong" person, etc.

Just as individual as our judgments of the "worst" news are, our reactions to the news will differ greatly. One person hears of a death and sinks quietly into a chair, while another hears the same news and runs from the room screaming in distress. One reacts to a national disaster with despair, while another finds determination.

There may be some "wrong" ways to react to news, but it is always "right" to allow the situation to draw us closer to God. Mordecai and the Jews reacted to news of the planned genocide with grief, but their grief served to bring them together before God.

2. What is the most difficult thing you have ever asked someone to do? What was the outcome?

Many of us never need to ask others to take great risks. Some, however, must do that regularly. A fire captain asks his crew to enter a burning building. A police sergeant tells his team to enter a home where gunfire was heard. A colonel sends his men into battle. An aid agency sends a doctor into a plagued village.

But secular examples aside, we recall that churches send missionaries to countries that are hostile to Christianity. Sometimes their lives are the price paid. But ultimately it is God who is asking them to go. God probably surprised Esther with her situation and with Mordecai's request. God may surprise us as well.

3. What was a time when you knew you were not welcome, but you asserted yourself anyway and began a conversation?

Most of us can read the subtle (or not so subtle) hints that we are not welcome. Eyes avert, conversations change or end, awkward silences ensue. Sometimes, of course, we are overly sensitive and misread cues that don't really exist. And there are times when we barge right in regardless of the welcome we are or are not receiving.

Sometimes, though, the level of welcome does not matter. It does not matter how I feel about a person if she has come to tell me that the building is on fire! Although we need to be sensitive to the feelings and sensibilities of others, important matters may demand that we move past those feelings and speak directly. When we confront a sinning Christian in redemptive love, our message may be unwelcome but needed. When we challenge someone's commitment, we may receive an initial cold shoulder, but the experience will be worth it if it helps soften a hard heart.

4. When was a time you realized a purpose or destiny for yourself? What led to that recognition?

When we think of the word *destiny*, we should not necessarily think of tasks as grandiose as Esther had. For example, a mother may find that her destiny or purpose is teaching her children about Jesus. A salesman may find his purpose is raising the ethical values of his department. A teacher may find her mission is giving children hope and purpose.

God has general tasks and expectations that are the same for everyone (example: 1 Peter 1:15, 16). He also gifts people for specific purposes. Whether that purpose or destiny is very public or one that influences only a select few, God knows the outcome. The child you teach may become a Billy Graham! God may not reveal to us the ultimate results of our service. We can be sure, though, that our work for Him is never in vain.

5. What was a time when you fasted in addition to praying for something? What was the outcome?

Fasting adds intensity to our prayer life. On a physical level, the longing for food becomes a prompter to prayer. As we weaken physically, we recognize more perfectly our need to rely solely on God. Spiritually, fasting connects us more closely with God the provider and sustainer. Prayer may move God to act; the Bible clearly shows us God choosing to respond to the prayers of His people. Prayer may also move us toward God. Fasting added to prayer demonstrates sincerity.

Isaiah Answers God's Call

DEVOTIONAL READING: Revelation 4.

BACKGROUND SCRIPTURE: Isaiah 6.

PRINTED TEXT: Isaiah 6:1-8.

Isaiah 6:1-8

1 In the year that king Uzziah died I saw also the Lord sitting upon a throne, high and lifted up, and his train filled the temple.

2 Above it stood the seraphim: each one had six wings; with twain he covered his face, and with twain he covered his feet, and with twain he did fly.

3 And one cried unto another, and said, Holy, holy, holy, is the LORD of hosts: the whole earth is full of his glory.

4 And the posts of the door moved at the voice of him that cried, and the house was filled with smoke.

5 Then said I, Woe is me! for I am undone; because I am a man of unclean lips, and I dwell in the midst of a people of unclean lips: for mine eyes have seen the King, the LORD of hosts.

6 Then flew one of the seraphim unto me, having a live coal in his hand, which he had taken with the tongs from off the altar:

7 And he laid it upon my mouth, and said, Lo, this hath touched thy lips; and thine iniquity is taken away, and thy sin purged.

8 Also I heard the voice of the Lord, saying, Whom shall I send, and who will go for us? Then said I, Here am I; send me.

Feb 22

GOLDEN TEXT: Also I heard the voice of the Lord, saying, Whom shall I send, and who will go for us? Then said I, Here am I; send me.—Isaiah 6:8.

Human Commitment
Unit 2: Old Testament People of Commitment
(Lessons 5–12)

Lesson Aims

After participating in this lesson, each student will be able to:

1. Retell the story of Isaiah's vision of the Lord.

2. Compare and contrast Isaiah's commissioning with modern calls to ministry.

3. Ask God for guidance in one area where he or she needs to "go" for Jesus.

Lesson Outline

INTRODUCTION
  A. Commitment to a Call
  B. Lesson Background
 I. LORD'S HOLINESS (Isaiah 6:1-4)
  A. Exalted One (v. 1)
    Visions or Imagination?
  B. Flying Seraphim (v. 2)
  C. Crying Seraphim (v. 3)
  D. Shaken Posts (v. 4)
    A Powerful Voice
II. ISAIAH'S SINFULNESS (Isaiah 6:5-8)
  A. "Woe" (v. 5)
    Realization—Or Lack Thereof
  B. "Lo" (vv. 6, 7)
  C. "Go" (v. 8)
CONCLUSION
  A. A Call to Commitment
  B. Prayer
  C. Thought to Remember

Introduction

A. Commitment to a Call

I grew up in a home devoid of spiritual instruction or Bible teaching. I was led to Christ by concerned Christians who saw to it that I attended Bible school, morning worship, and youth group meetings. Wanting a better life than what I had experienced in my own home, I made a decision at the age of 14 not only to become a Christian but also to commit myself to (what was called in that day) "full time" Christian service.

The two calls blended together for me. I prayed this prayer: "Lord, if You are there, I want to become a Christian; but not only a Christian, I want to be a preacher, if that is Your will." It was a simple prayer, honest, but ignorant of what it all meant in the long run. I did want a Christian life, a Christian home, and a Christian vocation. I did not know *how* God would do all this, but I did know the *why*! I was being called by God not only to become a Christian but also to become a minister, somehow to give my life in service to God through the church.

I was baptized in a lake on Easter Sunday of 1957. That was my first step in a commitment to a call that would take me far beyond my abilities or dreams as they existed at the time. While in high school I had to give up several opportunities in other areas of life in order to fulfill my commitment to go to a Bible college for ministry education. The rest is history.

Even though my ministry career moved toward the academic life, my commitment to the call to preach continues. I preach interim ministries and usually try to help struggling churches through difficult times. God has placed me in a position to influence many toward His mission in the world. The need has never been greater. God may not call people today in the way He called Isaiah, but God still calls.

B. Lesson Background

Isaiah began his prophetic ministry to the southern kingdom of Judah in about 740 BC. By that time, Judah had been separated from the northern kingdom of Israel for nearly 200 years.

Isaiah lived in an era of rampant sin. The sin of God's people was so great that even the message of the prophet would only increase their lack of perception and understanding (Isaiah 6:9, 10). Great devastation of the land would result from the people's exile by a powerful enemy (6:11, 12). Only a remnant ("holy seed") would survive (6:13).

Isaiah's ministry began right at the time King Uzziah passed off the scene. Uzziah (also called Azariah in 2 Kings 14:21; 15:1; compare 2 Chronicles 26:1) had a long reign of 52 years (792–740 BC; see 2 Kings 15:2; 2 Chronicles 26:3). He was considered to be a "good" king by the biblical writers. However, he did not eradicate the high places where the people offered sacrifices and burned incense (see 2 Kings 15:4).

Uzziah also had a problem of pride (2 Chronicles 26:16-20). Uzziah's pride can be traced to his military might and military success. He had developed a sophisticated system that enabled Judah to field a powerful army. Uzziah successfully resisted all foreign threats of the time (see 2 Chronicles 26:6-15). Perhaps this pride "leaked over" into the people and contributed to their disdain of the one true God.

Although the king's son had been the acting king for some time (2 Chronicles 26:21-23), Uzziah's death was a time of transition in at least a psychological sense. Such a transition can create unrest as people try to take advantage of various opportunities, real or imagined. It was in this context that Isaiah saw the vision of God on His throne.

I. Lord's Holiness
(Isaiah 6:1-4)
A. Exalted Throne (v. 1)

1. In the year that king Uzziah died I saw also the Lord sitting upon a throne, high and lifted up, and his train filled the temple.

Uzziah dies in about 740 BC. Thus we are able to date Isaiah's vision rather exactly. The death of the *king* and the changes that this brings to the nation are critically important. Jotham, Uzziah's son, succeeds his father as king. He turns out to be a "good" king as noted in 2 Chronicles 27. But spiritual corruption pervades Judah, as the larger context of Isaiah makes clear.

Most Bible students think this vision occurs when Isaiah goes to the temple to worship on some occasion, perhaps to pray concerning the crisis of Uzziah's death or near death. The wording of the verse before us allows us to see how the earthly *temple* and the position of an earthly king can blend with the heavenly *throne* scene. The Israelites envision God reigning in Heaven, seated on a throne, but His footstool is located in the Holy of Holies between the cherubim on top of the ark of the covenant (see Psalm 97:1, 2; 99:1; 132:7; 1 Chronicles 28:2). This necessarily places the vision somewhere close to the temple.

Isaiah recognizes Yahweh God as his master and *Lord.* He is "the King, the Lord of hosts" (Isaiah 6:5, below). The Hebrew text suggests that the Lord is the one who is *high and lifted up,* not the throne. But both are high and lifted up! Isaiah

will later describe the suffering Servant with the same Hebrew words, translated as "exalted and extolled" (Isaiah 52:13) and again with reference to God himself as "high and lofty" (Isaiah 57:15). [See question #1, page 216.]

The throne is a heavenly throne. This kind of scene is connected, in various ways, with Yahweh God from the beginning of His revelation of himself to His people (see Exodus 24:10, 16, 17). Throne visions and descriptions occur in other places in the Bible as well (see 1 Kings 22:17-23; Psalm 11:4; 47:8; 103:19; Ezekiel 10; Matthew 5:34, 35; Revelation 4, 5).

His train relates to the skirts of God's royal robes. This is the loose-flowing part from the waist down, which fills the temple. This points to the heavenly temple, which somehow has properties of the earthly temple. Since the train fills the temple, the implication is that there is no place for Isaiah to move! All he can do is stand still in reverence and awe.

VISIONS OR IMAGINATION?

Over the centuries, Roman Catholicism has recorded numerous instances of people who have claimed a vision of the Virgin Mary. John J. Delaney in his book *A Woman Clothed with the Sun* records eight of these, beginning with Guadalupe, Mexico, in 1531, and including Lourdes in 1858 and Fatima in Portugal in 1917. In all these cases, people's lives were changed by their alleged encounters.

Or think of Martin of Tours, who lived in the fourth century. While a soldier in the Roman army, he once saw a half-clothed beggar shivering in the winter's cold. Martin cut off half of his cloak and wrapped it around the beggar. The following evening, Martin thought that Jesus, wearing the halved cloak, appeared to him. Martin's life was changed. When he finished his military service, he became a priest, then a monk, and ultimately a bishop.

It is easy for us to question whether these alleged encounters with Mary and Jesus actually happened. But one thing cannot be argued: the people who had these experiences went through dramatic life changes. It seems to be impossible to meet heavenly beings (real or imaginary) and remain the same. How much more must this have been true for Isaiah, whose vision definitely was real! Meeting Jesus in the pages of Scripture today should have the same effect. —J. B. N.

B. Flying Seraphim (v. 2)

2. Above it stood the seraphim: each one had six wings; with twain he covered his face, and with twain he covered his feet, and with twain he did fly.

How to Say It

AZARIAH. Az-uh-*rye*-uh.
CHERUBIM. *chair*-uh-bim.
GUADALUPE. *Gwa*-duh-loop.
ISAIAH. Eye-*zay*-uh.
JOTHAM. *Jo*-thum.
LOURDES. Lurdz.
MANASSEH. Muh-*nass*-uh.
SERAPH. *sair*-uhf.
SERAPHIM. *sair*-uh-fim.
UZZIAH. Uh-*zye*-uh.
YAHWEH *(Hebrew).* Yah-weh.

Above the throne, perhaps on both sides, are *seraphim*. Here and in verse 6 are the only places in the Bible where this term is used. Created beings connected to God's throne or presence are called by various names. These include *cherubim* (see Ezekiel 10; Psalm 80:1; 99:1), *sons of God* (see Job 1:6; 2:1; 38:7), *angels* (Psalm 148:2; Hebrews 1:6, 7), and *hosts* (Psalm 89:8; 103:21).

We have no idea what seraphim look like, but that doesn't stop artists from offering ideas! Ancient cultures depict creatures having human bodies, two wings at the shoulders, and four below the waist. Carvings of winged creatures have been found incorporated onto both sides of kings' thrones, called "cherub thrones." They represent guardians to the throne.

The word *seraph* comes from a verb that means "to burn." This word is connected with the snakes of Numbers 21:6, where it is translated "fiery." The idea is that the serpents' bites burned; thus some think that seraphim are serpent-like in appearance. But note here that the seraphim are able to stand and that they have wings.

Certainly the seraphim are designed to revere God and glorify Him. Seraphim seem to be like the angels as described by the book of Hebrews: "And of the angels he saith, Who maketh his angels spirits, and his ministers a flame of fire" (Hebrews 1:7) and "Are they not all ministering spirits, sent forth to minister for them who shall be heirs of salvation?" (Hebrews 1:14). As to the number of seraphim present, we do not know. (The Hebrew language makes words plural by adding -*im* to the end.) There have to be at least two for antiphonal praising (v. 3, next).

They cover their faces with two wings, for the Lord's glory cannot be looked upon directly. They also cover their *feet,* for reasons unknown. They *fly* with one pair of wings, signifying readiness to do the bidding of the majestic king at a moment's notice.

C. Crying Seraphim (v. 3)

3. And one cried unto another, and said, Holy, holy, holy, is the LORD of hosts: the whole earth is full of his glory.

The text does not say the seraphim are singing. Rather the idea is that one is calling out to another in an antiphonal manner (see Deuteronomy 27:26). Whether they are crying out or singing the words, they are certainly praising *the Lord of hosts.* The threefold expression *holy, holy, holy* is the Hebrew way of expressing a strong superlative: Yahweh of hosts is the holiest of all! (Contrast an improper use of a threefold expression in Jeremiah 7:4.) The Lord of hosts is designated as "the Holy One of Israel" more than two dozen times in the book of Isaiah. [See question #2, page 216.]

The phrase *the whole earth is full of his glory* reminds us that the particulars of creation show us something about God (see Psalm 19:1; Romans 1:20). The ultimate manifestation of God's glory is Jesus Christ (see John 1:14). God reveals His glory to His people through Jesus (Colossians 1:27).

D. Shaken Posts (v. 4)

4. And the posts of the door moved at the voice of him that cried, and the house was filled with smoke.

The awe-inspiring scene of this vision reaches a climax as the *posts* that hold the doors in place begin to shake. It is because of the thunderous sound of praise coming from the seraphim as they cry out one to another! The *smoke* is presumably the smoke from the altar of incense, which in the earthly temple stands just before the Holy of Holies (Exodus 30:6; 40:5). Not only are Isaiah's eyes filled with an incredible vision and his ears reverberating with the sound of praising seraphim, but also his nose detects the familiar aroma of fragrant incense. Isaiah's whole being is shaken by this encounter.

A POWERFUL VOICE

When I was little, I had a toy electric train set. One year for Christmas somebody gave me a voice-activated control that would enable me to "talk" to the train, making it go, stop, and even back up. I was pretty impressed until I learned that a person could just say "phfft" into the microphone to put the train through the normal rotation of commands. My voice wasn't as powerful as I had initially thought!

But technology has improved. Now we can control TVs and other electronic gadgets through genuine voice recognition. That same technology allows me to order prescription drugs over the telephone. I do this by speaking my name, certain identifying numbers, and the name of the medication. The order then arrives at my door within a few days—all without my having talked to a human being.

We can stand in awe of our technology of voice recognition and activation! But are we as awestruck when we read of doorposts shaking as the voice of a seraph proclaims the glory and holiness of God? Does reading those words cause you to shake just a bit? What we find most awe-inspiring says a lot about what we most value.   —J. B. N.

II. Isaiah's Sinfulness (Isaiah 6:5-8)

A. "Woe" (v. 5)

5. Then said I, Woe is me! for I am undone; because I am a man of unclean lips, and I dwell in the midst of a people of unclean lips: for mine eyes have seen the King, the LORD of hosts.

Nothing will make a person more aware of his or her own sinfulness than being in the presence of the sinless, holy God. Having experienced the presence of the Holy One of Israel and knowing the sinfulness of Israel (perhaps the reason Isaiah 1–5 was placed before the call in Isaiah 6), Isaiah becomes acutely aware of his own sinfulness.

The word *woe* here is spelled differently in the Hebrew than the *woe* pronounced by Isaiah upon the people for their sins in Isaiah 5:8, 11, 18, 20, 21, 22. Here Isaiah expresses a helpless feeling— "Alas!" He says *I am undone.* The word *undone* has the sense of "to be destroyed." In other words, Isaiah is saying he is doomed to die!

Isaiah gives three reasons for this conclusion. First, he is *a man of unclean lips.* The lips represent the life of a person. The words that come across one's lips reveal a person's true character (Job 6:30; 27:4; Psalm 12:2; 59:12; etc.). Isaiah cannot stand up to God's holiness.

Second, Isaiah dwells *in the midst of a people of unclean lips.* He knows that his own country and culture are corrupt to the core, and he feels he is part of its sinfulness. Third, his *eyes have seen the King, the Lord of hosts.* People do not expect to see God and live (compare Genesis 32:30; Exodus 33:20; and Judges 13:22).

A true evaluation of one's sinful condition is the beginning of a commitment to God. Without this confession, God cannot work His grace in the life of a servant. "Be merciful to me, Lord, a sinner!"

REALIZATION—OR LACK THEREOF

Many today are obsessive about cleanliness. Just think about how much hand sanitizer we use. How different from the days of my childhood! Back then, I often wondered why it was necessary to take a bath once a week. Even when I had been playing outdoors all week in the summer, with its heat, humidity, and dirt, I didn't think I needed a bath.

I've reformed since then, but I still think that there are people who sometimes go too far. I read recently that Germany has a "cleaning week," where tenants are required to sweep the pavement in front of their apartment buildings. In the United Kingdom, 58 percent of those who hire domestic cleaning help admit that they tidy up before the cleaners arrive. One society matron in America instructed her staff to change the bed sheets daily, even if the beds had not been used by guests. A woman on a talk show recently confessed that she can't hold her daughter's hand because she is afraid she will get germs.

Marketers push products that claim to be much better than soap. One product is a "cleansing bar" made with olive leaf extract, which supposedly "deep cleans" to remove oil, dirt, and dead skin. Another product is made with marine oils that are "bio-compatible," allegedly cleansing the pores without disrupting the skin's natural balance. Still another has mink oil and Vitamin E.

All this in an effort to get clean or, somehow, "more than" clean? Physical cleanliness is important, but spiritual cleanliness is infinitely more vital! Yet spiritual cleanliness won't happen until we first acknowledge the need. Isaiah realized his need. Do we realize ours?   —J. B. N.

B. "Lo" (vv. 6, 7)

6, 7. Then flew one of the seraphim unto me, having a live coal in his hand, which he had taken with the tongs from off the altar: and he laid it upon my mouth, and said, Lo, this hath touched thy lips; and thine iniquity is taken away, and thy sin purged.

The *seraphim* are there to do God's will immediately and quickly. The symbolic act that we see accomplished by one of these creatures is interpreted by the seraph's own words. The word *Lo* is usually translated "behold" in other contexts. It is an important word, sometimes left out of modern translations. It should not be. It is saying: "Pay attention, look, note this! Something very important has happened to you, Isaiah!"

Then, in perfect Hebrew parallelism, the seraph declares that Isaiah's *iniquity/sin* is *taken away/ purged.* It is fitting that Isaiah's *lips* are purified with fire, for only when his lips are clean can he speak for God. This becomes Isaiah's motivation for ministry throughout his life. He knows the dark shadows of sin from which he has emerged by God's grace.

This purging, or what we may call forgiveness, motivates Isaiah to respond to his call (next verse). Forgiveness should still provide the motivation to commit to a call. And commitment leads us to sacrifice. [See question #3, page 216.]

C. "Go" (v. 8)

8a. Also I heard the voice of the Lord, saying, Whom shall I send, and who will go for us?

Not only does Isaiah see the Lord on His throne, now he hears the voice of the Lord: *Whom shall I send, and who will go for us?* Much has been made of the *us* to argue for the doctrine of the Trinity (God in three persons). While I would never deny this doctrine as revealed clearly in the New Testament, it seems best to see the *us* at this point to be referring to God (the King) speaking in the divine council with seraphim and even Isaiah present. Thus the use of the word *us* serves to bring everyone into the deliberations (compare 1 Kings 22:19-21; Jeremiah 23:18, 22).

8b. Then said I, Here am I; send me.

Up until this time Isaiah has not been able to respond to God appropriately. But now with the vision having shaken his soul and his sins having been forgiven, Isaiah is compelled to respond to God's challenge to be His servant, His prophet.

When we respond appropriately to God's grace and His call, we too will say *Here am I, send me.* We will not react as Moses did initially when he responded to the Lord's call by requesting that the

Visual for Lesson 12. *Use this visual as the backdrop for this pointed question: "Do you pray for opportunities to say 'Here am I; send me'?"*

Lord send someone else (Exodus 4:13). [See question #4, page 216.]

Conclusion

A. A Call to Commitment

Isaiah responded decisively to God's call without knowing exactly where the call would lead him. Isaiah immediately found himself thrust into a ministry of futility, preaching to a spiritually deaf and blind people who remained that way after his preaching (see Isaiah 6:9-13; compare Matthew 13:14, 15; Acts 28:26, 27). Isaiah was met with unbelief (Isaiah 7:9-13). Even when there was a certain amount of faith exhibited, human shortsightedness and sinfulness prevailed (see Isaiah 39:8).

Isaiah understood that the true servant of God must be prepared to give his or her life for the larger purpose of God's plan. When the servant (Jesus) comes and gives His life on behalf of the world (Isaiah 53:12), then those who have been forgiven much can respond to God's call, "Here am I, send me!" Indeed, Isaiah never turned back from his commitment. Tradition says that Isaiah was murdered by the evil king Manasseh, who allegedly put him inside a hollow log and had it sawn in two (see Hebrews 11:37).

This should lead us to ask what sacrifices we are willing to make in order to fulfill our Christian vocational commitments. Are we willing to go beyond the limits of human endurance, trusting in the strength of God? When we commit to God's call, there is comfort in knowing that God will provide the resources, strength, and courage to go beyond our natural thoughts and abilities.

Could Isaiah have refused God's call? We don't know. Such a question is dangerous in any case, because it may tempt us to toy with the possibility of refusing God's call when it comes to us. Moses tried at first to refuse God's call. What if Moses had been "successful" in doing so? God would have found someone else. Would you really want to be the one who said *no* to the God who has said *yes* to you through Jesus?

B. Prayer

O Lord, please forgive our foolish ways and purge us of our sin. Purify us so that we may respond positively to Your call whenever and wherever it may come. Give us the courage and strength of the Holy Spirit to say, "Here am I, send me!" In the name of our Savior, Jesus. Amen.

C. Thought to Remember

Heed God's call.

Learning by Doing

This page contains an alternative lesson plan emphasizing learning activities. Some of these activities are also found in the helpful student book, Adult Bible Class.

Into the Lesson

Arrange with someone who is out of sight of the class to call you on a cell phone just as class begins, interrupting the procedure. Carry on a conversation with a person whom you repeatedly call "Hi." Include such comments as, "This is not a good time," and "What's that buzzing sound in the background . . . sounds like a flock of hummingbirds," and "Well, I'm awfully busy right now," and "It sounds like my doing that would be pointless."

Say good-bye to your caller and say to the class, "Sorry about that. Calls come at the most inopportune times, you know. And some seem so pointless when your caller asks you to do something even he admits is pretty much futile." Make the transition to your study by affirming, "Isaiah got just such a call. It's recorded in our text today in Isaiah 6:1-8."

Into the Word

Divide your class into groups of four to six. Give each a sheet labeled *Steps from Sinfulness to Holiness* that shows a stair-step line of at least five "steps." Give this direction to all the groups: "When Isaiah realized God's holiness and his own sinfulness, he was on his way to being a committed servant of the Lord. Use today's text to determine 'steps' that lead from sinfulness to holiness and service. While you don't need to put your steps in order, consider developing a first-to-last sequence."

Allow a few minutes for each group to develop its own "stairway." Though you can expect a variety of responses, some of the following ideas may be offered:

- *We need to see God for who He is, the reigning king of the universe (v. 1).*
- *We need an understanding of the existence of a spiritual world beyond this one (v. 2).*
- *We must see the glory of the Lord in what He has created (v. 3).*
- *We must be shaken by the presence of God, as the temple was shaken (vv. 3, 4).*
- *We must be aware of our own mortality (v. 5).*
- *We need to be struck by the corrupt nature of our culture (v. 5).*
- *We need to have our sins forgiven (vv. 6, 7).*
- *We must hear the Word of God (v. 8).*
- *We must put ourselves in line with God's will as did Isaiah when he said "Send me!" (v. 8).*
- *We need to realize that God has a concern for all His children.*

After six to eight minutes, let each group report its list. Both similarities and differences will open the way for further questions and discussions. If any have their "steps" in a sequence, ask for an explanation as to how one step must come before/ after another.

Alternative: put the possible observations listed above on strips of paper, one observation per strip. Do not put the verse numbers on the strips. Give each group a full set of strips. Have each group put their strips into the stairstep sequence. When everyone is finished, compare and contrast the results.

Into Life

Tell your class that you want them to "recall the call" that you had on your cell phone at the beginning of class. Ask them to remember what they overheard. As they relate elements, comment and challenge them to make a commitment to God's call in and on their own lives.

Note these elements, as the class responds:

1. Your call was from "Hi," an allusion to the God on high who has the authority to command, but the love to invite.

2. The call came at "not a good time," with a note that God's call does not need to be convenient from our perspective; it needs only to be opportune from His perspective.

3. The sound of hummingbirds was an allusion to the seraphim; their task—as ours—was to declare God's holiness and glory.

4. The seeming futility of the task called for was a reference to God's knowledge of the predicted limited response to Isaiah's work; such a factor may be irrelevant to God's call to us—the call to obey and serve, not necessarily to "succeed."

With these observations in mind, call for class members to offer sentence prayers reflecting the truths learned and noted. You may choose to begin with such a prayer as, "God, standing in Your presence humbles me."

As your students depart, stand at the doorway of your classroom and say "Go for God" to each student as he or she leaves.

Let's Talk It Over

*The questions on this page are designed to promote discussion of the lesson
by the class and to encourage application of the lesson Scriptures. The answers
provided are only discussion starters. Let your class talk it over from there.*

**1. What is the greatest thing you have ever seen?
What in your value system causes you to characterize that particular thing as "the greatest"?**

Greatest can be taken in various senses. Some
may think immediately of an object of large size,
such as the Grand Canyon, Niagara Falls, or Mount
Everest. Others may think of things with significant
historical meaning or political consequence, such
as the pyramids in Egypt or the Great Wall of China.
Those who have lived through the stress and fear of
a hurricane or tornado may mention that.

In Isaiah's eyes, though, the greatness of the
Lord sitting on a throne made every created thing
pale in comparison. Those in your class having the
most spiritual maturity may say that the greatest
thing they have ever seen is a profession of faith,
a baptism, etc.

**2. What effect has God's holiness had upon
you? What are some ways you can share that
impact with others?**

God's holiness should affect us profoundly, compelling us to live holy lives of our own, convicting
us of our own sinfulness, inspiring us to delight
in His presence. Seraphim could not remain silent
after experiencing that holiness, nor should we.

God's holiness draws our awe. If our awe does
not result in speaking words of edification to other
Christians or speaking to the world in evangelism,
then perhaps we have not experienced His holiness as we ought. We may not experience God's
holiness in the same way that the seraphim did,
but we can acknowledge that "the whole earth is
full of his glory."

**3. Other than God's forgiveness of our sins,
what is the greatest act of forgiveness you have
seen or heard of? What impact did that forgiveness have on the one who was forgiven?**

Occasionally we hear of a victim's family forgiving a murderer, a large debt being forgiven, or
two warring factions ending a conflict. In our grace-deprived world, though, such resolutions are much
rarer than we would like. "Victim impact statements" in courtrooms are often filled with expressions of anger, hostility, and vindictiveness.

Acts and expressions of forgiveness (which
rarely make newspapers' front pages) transform

relationships. Marriages are saved when spouses
forgive. Families are saved when children and parents forgive. Churches are saved when leaders and
members forgive. These acts of forgiveness may
not change the history of the world, but they regularly change the lives of both the forgiver and
the forgiven.

**4. What is the most significant thing you have
ever committed to do for God? What inspired you
to make that commitment?**

The prophet Isaiah may show us almost every
reason people commit to a cause. He comes into
the presence of greatness. He realizes that he is less
than he needs to be. Someone helps him, and he
experiences renewal. He sees the challenge, recognizes his purification, and seizes the opportunity.

Our world has many causes that demand
wholehearted commitment. Some of those causes
are evil (example: terrorist suicide attacks). Other
causes are not inherently evil, but are unworthy of
the commitment level they require (think of some
of the silly things people do to get themselves into
the *Guinness Book of World Records*). In a world
with so many lost causes and so many causes that
should be lost, God's question resounds: "Whom
shall I send, and who will go for us?" God awaits
the answer.

TEACHER: PLEASE NOTE

Each quarter of study normally has 13
Sundays as well as 13 lessons in this commentary. The current, winter quarter, however, has only 12 Sundays, while the spring
quarter to follow has 14. Production constraints require that we deal with this quirk
of the calendar by taking the first lesson of
the spring quarter (the lesson for March 1)
and including it as the 13th lesson of the
winter quarter.

For that reason, you will see that the lesson that begins immediately following this
one is designated "Lesson 1." The lesson for
March 8, which appears as the opening lesson for the spring quarter, is correctly designated "Lesson 2," and so forth.

A New Spirit

DEVOTIONAL READING: **2 Corinthians 3:1-11.**

BACKGROUND SCRIPTURE: **Ezekiel 11:14-21.**

PRINTED TEXT: **Ezekiel 11:14-21.**

Ezekiel 11:14-21

14 Again the word of the LORD came unto me, saying,

15 Son of man, thy brethren, even thy brethren, the men of thy kindred, and all the house of Israel wholly, are they unto whom the inhabitants of Jerusalem have said, Get you far from the LORD: unto us is this land given in possession.

16 Therefore say, Thus saith the Lord GOD; Although I have cast them far off among the heathen, and although I have scattered them among the countries, yet will I be to them as a little sanctuary in the countries where they shall come.

17 Therefore say, Thus saith the Lord GOD; I will even gather you from the people, and assemble you out of the countries where ye have been scattered, and I will give you the land of Israel.

18 And they shall come thither, and they shall take away all the detestable things thereof and all the abominations thereof from thence.

19 And I will give them one heart, and I will put a new spirit within you; and I will take the stony heart out of their flesh, and will give them a heart of flesh:

20 That they may walk in my statutes, and keep mine ordinances, and do them: and they shall be my people, and I will be their God.

21 But as for them whose heart walketh after the heart of their detestable things and their abominations, I will recompense their way upon their own heads, saith the Lord GOD.

GOLDEN TEXT: I will give them one heart, and I will put a new spirit within you; and I will take the stony heart out of their flesh, and will give them a heart of flesh.—Ezekiel 11:19.

Christ and Creation
Unit 1: The Promise of New Life
(Lessons 1–5)

Lesson Aims

After participating in this lesson, each student will be able to:

1. Summarize Ezekiel's message to the exiles in Babylon and the remnant left in Jerusalem.

2. Explain the concept of the "hard heart" as Ezekiel uses it.

3. Describe one area of spiritual hardness in his or her life and suggest one way to correct it.

Lesson Outline

INTRODUCTION
  A. Hard Hearts, Hard People
  B. Lesson Background
I. GREEDY HEART (Ezekiel 11:14, 15)
  A. Ezekiel Receives the Word (v. 14)
  B. Ezekiel Informed of Attitude (v. 15)
II. PROTECTIVE HEART (Ezekiel 11:16)
  A. The Lord Scatters (v. 16a)
  B. The Lord Protects (v. 16b)
    Sanctuaries
III. DIVIDED HEARTS (Ezekiel 11:17-21)
  A. Gathering (v. 17)
  B. Cleansing (v. 18)
  C. Softening (vv. 19, 20)
    A Heart of Flesh
  D. Chastening (v. 21)
CONCLUSION
  A. Hard or Soft?
  B. Prayer
  C. Thought to Remember

Introduction

A. Hard Hearts, Hard People

We hear a lot about *heart health* these days. Medical people have long known that the human heart is a tireless workhorse, pumping the blood that nourishes and cleanses every cell in our bodies. A heart may beat 100,000 times a day or more, and it does this without any conscious effort on our part. If the beating becomes irregular or weak, it is a sign of grave problems. Damage to the heart can lead to disability or death. Thus, heart disease is serious business, and taking care of one's heart is (or should be) a major concern.

Heart specialists have identified a rare medical condition that they call *restrictive cardiomyopathy*. This condition occurs when the walls of the heart stiffen, resulting in a heart that is unable to do its pumping job effectively. A person with this condition will have poor circulation and an overworked heart. This person often will be tired all the time and not be able to tolerate even minor physical activity. In the modern medical world, such a person may become a candidate for a heart transplant.

Restrictive cardiomyopathy is a rare condition. But a hardened spiritual heart is not rare. It is an ancient problem, documented thoroughly in the Bible. The spiritually hard heart is a tragic part of the Bible's storyline. The hard heart has aligned itself against God.

The Bible uses other figures of speech to describe this condition. The ancient Jewish people were accused of being "uncircumcised in the heart" (see Jeremiah 9:26; compare Acts 7:51). The people had ears that were "uncircumcised" (Jeremiah 6:10). They were often chastised for being "stiffnecked" (see 2 Chronicles 30:8).

We can observe that times have not changed that much. All too many people stumble through life with hard hearts, as hard people. They are seemingly impenetrable, neither giving nor receiving overtures of God's love and grace.

As the condition of restrictive cardiomyopathy may call for a physical heart transplant, so the condition of the spiritually hard heart calls for a big change. This change implants a will that is softened to God's purposes. This understanding of the spiritual heart transplant stands at the core of today's lesson from the book of Ezekiel.

B. Lesson Background

When we discuss the history of the people of Israel, we perhaps think of the Babylonian exile as a period beginning with the destruction of Jerusalem and its temple in 586 BC. A careful reading of the Old Testament, however, shows that various stages of the exile occurred earlier than this.

In 605 BC, Nebuchadnezzar, the premier general of the Babylonian armies, defeated the Egyptian armies (see 2 Chronicles 35:20; Jeremiah 46:2). The eventual result was the elimination of Egyptian influence on Jerusalem and the land of Judah, to be replaced by Babylonian domination.

Soon after that battle, Nebuchadnezzar succeeded his father as the king of Babylon. King Nebuchadnezzar made a personal visit to Jerusalem a few years later (about 597 BC) to subdue the rebellious city. The result was that the Babylonians looted the temple and carried the Jewish king, Jehoiachin, into captivity (see 2 Kings 24:10-16). The Babylonians also took "the mighty of the land" (2 Kings 24:15). We are fairly certain that Ezekiel was one of these, taken to Babylon before the destruction of Jerusalem in 586 BC.

In 593 BC, Ezekiel received a vision from God that called him to be a prophet (Ezekiel 2:1-8). He prophesied to other Jews in Babylon (the exiles) before, during, and after the destruction of Jerusalem in 586 BC. This destruction was catastrophic for the Jews because the marvelous temple of Solomon was demolished and its holiness was profaned (although the Jews themselves had done a rather thorough job of profaning the temple). All the sacred worship items were either destroyed or carried away to Babylon as booty.

The background of Ezekiel's ministry is the failure of the Jews to listen to the Lord. The sin of Jerusalem was numbingly deep, the depravity of the people was shockingly pervasive. All that was left was a catastrophe so colossal that it could not be ignored by the rebellious nation. Ezekiel's job was to interpret this disaster for the people. The central theme of his messages was that through God's great calamity, the people would come to "know that I am the Lord," a phrase repeated numerous times in the book (example: Ezekiel 11:12).

I. Greedy Heart
(Ezekiel 11:14, 15)

When a certain billionaire was asked, "How much money is enough?" his answer was "just a little more." Our tendency to greed, if left unchecked, becomes insatiable and consuming. Greed moves beyond a simple unwillingness to share as it becomes a passion to acquire the possessions of others, even by dishonest or immoral means.

A. Ezekiel Receives the Word (v. 14)

14. Again the word of the LORD came unto me, saying.

The phrase *the word of the Lord came unto me* appears dozens of times in this book, indicating Ezekiel's unmistakable vocation as a prophet. The Lord's Word is usually presented as a personal message to Ezekiel, although it naturally contains broader significance for the exiles to whom Ezekiel preaches.

B. Ezekiel Informed of Attitude (v. 15)

15. Son of man, thy brethren, even thy brethren, the men of thy kindred, and all the house of Israel wholly, are they unto whom the inhabitants of Jerusalem have said, Get you far from the LORD: unto us is this land given in possession.

This message to Ezekiel gives a picture of what is being *said* back in *Jerusalem*, hundreds of miles to the west. The *brethren* who have been left behind (the ones who have not been carried into exile) are not mourning the fate of their exiled fellow Israelites. Rather, they are celebrating their apparent good fortune. The phrase *far from the Lord* means far from the temple city, the site of the Lord's worship. This prophecy comes before the destruction of the temple in 586 BC (see Ezekiel 33:21).

The *kindred* who have been left in Jerusalem see a great opportunity. Rather than pray or work for the return of the exiles, their arrogance causes them to wish their countrymen "good riddance." Now they can seize the exiles' lands and possessions. Such ghoulish behavior is shocking to Ezekiel and his fellow exiles. [See question #1, page 224.]

II. Protective Heart
(Ezekiel 11:16)

God certainly knows that His corrective actions will be painful. Although He may jolt us out of our comfortable, sinful life pattern, He does not forsake us. The Lord is presented throughout Scripture as a God who protects the faithful (examples Psalm 41:2; Nahum 1:7). Ezekiel and his fellow exiles have been through a time of trauma, with more yet to come. Yet God has not forgotten them.

A. The Lord Scatters (v. 16a)

16a. Therefore say, Thus saith the Lord GOD; Although I have cast them far off among the heathen, and although I have scattered them among the countries.

This presents the longer view of the Israelite people and their captivity experience. Beginning about 740 BC, the ruthless kings of Assyria had begun to pick apart the northern kingdom of Israel, first deporting the tribes of Reuben, Gad, and Manasseh (1 Chronicles 5:26).

This continued until the fall of the northern kingdom in its entirety in 722 BC. The tribes remaining were resettled in various cities (2 Kings 17:6). Although the Assyrian kings never conquered Jerusalem, they doubtlessly seized some of the citizens of outlying Judah in their military campaigns.

There is no record of the 10 northern tribes ever returning to the promised land in any great numbers, in contrast with the people of the southern kingdom of Judah. At the point now when Ezekiel prophesies, many of Judah and Jerusalem are in exile, with many more to share that fate in a few short years.

How to Say It

ASSYRIA. Uh-*sear*-ee-uh.
BABYLON. *Bab*-uh-lun.
BABYLONIAN. Bab-ih-*low*-nee-un.
CARDIOMYOPATHY. *Kar*-dee-oh-my-*ah*-puh-thee.
CHALDEANS. Kal-*dee*-unz.
EZEKIEL. Ee-*zeek*-ee-ul or Ee-*zeek*-yul.
HABAKKUK. Huh-*back*-kuk.
JEHOIACHIN. Jeh-*hoy*-uh-kin.
JOSIAH. Jo-*sigh*-uh.
JUDAH. *Joo*-duh.
MANASSEH. Muh-*nass*-uh.
NAHUM. *Nay*-hum.
NEBUCHADNEZZAR. *Neb*-yuh-kud-*nez*-er (strong accent on *nez*).
REUBEN. *Roo*-ben.
ZECHARIAH. *Zek*-uh-*rye*-uh (strong accent on *rye*).

Some of those specialize in particular species, such as turkeys, foxes, horses, reptiles, rabbits, monkeys, turtles, chimpanzees, or donkeys. Some are more generic, providing safe places for migrating waterfowl, fish, or various forms of marine life. In 2006 there were 547 wildlife refuges in America's 50 states. Sanctuaries in India offer protection for jungle cats and elephants. Sanctuaries in Africa provide a protected natural habitat for a variety of wild animals—elephants, lions, antelope, and even the hyena.

What all wildlife sanctuaries have in common is the idea of *protection*. And given the stress-laden world in which we live, the idea of protection is something that immediately grabs our attention. Notice that that is exactly what God promises through the words of Ezekiel. Those dispossessed from Judah, wherever they were, would be in a sanctuary under God's protection. We serve a God who does not change. He still offers sanctuary to those who will accept it.   —J. B. N.

B. The Lord Protects (v. 16b)

16b. Yet will I be to them as a little sanctuary in the countries where they shall come.

God will not abandon His people, despite their dire situation. Even in exile, God provides *sanctuary* for them. The Hebrew word translated *sanctuary* here also is used for the holy parts of the tabernacle (Exodus 25:8, 9) and the temple (1 Chronicles 22:19). This is seen as the place where God dwells among His people, with the understanding that God's ultimate sanctuary is in Heaven.

Thus, this promise of sanctuary has a dual significance for the exiles. First, it symbolizes the fact that God is still present among them, even though they are hundreds of miles from Jerusalem. God will still meet them, even though they no longer have access to the temple. Second, we should remember that a sanctuary is a holy place. This means that the exiles can still be holy—a holy people to God. God's holiness is not confined to Jerusalem, but can be found wherever they may go. [See question #2, page 224.]

Before we move on, we should pause to note that *little* should not be taken to mean "small" or "miniature." Rather, the idea is that of being sanctuary for "a little while."

SANCTUARIES

When Christians use the word *sanctuary*, we often think of a part of a church building where we gather for worship. The secular world, on the other hand, probably most often connects the word *sanctuary* with wildlife. Wildlife sanctuaries abound, nationally and internationally.

III. Divided Hearts
(Ezekiel 11:17-21)

Ezekiel next pictures God's great promise of restoration. But God is not interested in just getting the residents of Jerusalem home. He wants change. They must return with new hearts.

A. Gathering (v. 17)

17. Therefore say, Thus saith the Lord GOD; I will even gather you from the people, and assemble you out of the countries where ye have been scattered, and I will give you the land of Israel.

The promise of God to give the land of Canaan to Israel originated with Abraham, over 1,400 years earlier (Genesis 12:7). The exile to Babylon in effect takes the land away.

The promise before us has two parts. First, God promises to *gather* His people. He will not lose track of them. At the appropriate time, the Lord will *assemble* those who have been *scattered*. Second, God will *give* back to them *the land of Israel*. The land certainly is not being given permanently to the Babylonians. God had given it to Abraham and his descendants, and that promise is still at work in the midst of exile.

B. Cleansing (v. 18)

18. And they shall come thither, and they shall take away all the detestable things thereof and all the abominations thereof from thence.

The *abominations* are the *detestable* idols. Many of these had been shamefully introduced into the temple courts by King Manasseh (see 2 Kings 21:1-

9). Although King Josiah later had attempted to eradicate these abominations (2 Kings 23:12), the course of the nation had been infected with pagan idolatry too deeply. Jeremiah, who preaches in Jerusalem while Ezekiel is in Babylon, understands that the exile and temple destruction are a direct result of the grievous religious depravities of Manasseh (see Jeremiah 15:4).

From a historical perspective, the exile seems indeed to cleanse Israel of the temptation to idol worship. Jesus does not condemn idolatry among the Jews, because the Jews of His day do not practice idolatry (although they have other issues that displease God). The shock therapy of the Babylonian exile turns out to be brutal but effective.

C. Softening (vv. 19, 20)

19. And I will give them one heart, and I will put a new spirit within you; and I will take the stony heart out of their flesh, and will give them a heart of flesh.

The purposes of God are seen clearly in several descriptions. The people are to receive *one heart*. This is a unifying act to eliminate the confusion and cross-purposes that have plagued them. Another way to say this is that they will receive a *new spirit*. This evokes memories of God's act in creating humankind, at which time He breathed into the inanimate body the breath (spirit) of life. By receiving a new spirit, they are to be reconnected with their creator. In so doing, God promises to remove their *stony heart*. This is the heart that has been hardened against Him.

A later prophet gives the causes of the exile as the people's refusal to listen to God's messenger prophets. Zechariah most colorfully describes this as the people making "their hearts as an adamant stone" (Zechariah 7:12). Their hearts are set against God's will for the nation. Yet God, the master heart surgeon, intends to remove this stony, ill-functioning heart from them. [See question #3, page 224.] God will replace the stony heart with a *heart of flesh*. The heart of flesh is the living, vibrant heart.

These descriptions boil down to the same thing: God wants people "after his own heart" (compare 1 Samuel 13:14; Acts 13:22). He can mold and shape such people for His purposes. God wants hearts that love His people as much as He loves them. He wants hearts that seek holiness and justice and that delight in glorifying God with worship and actions.

A HEART OF FLESH

In the 1962 movie *The Music Man*, the women of River City tell con man Harold Hill that he

Visual for
Lesson 1

Point to this visual as you ask, "Why is a new spiritual heart more important than a physical one?"

should not pay much attention to Marian Paroo, the town librarian. She advocates reading dirty books (such as Chaucer) and has connived with the town's friendless philanthropist to have all the books for the library given to her. According to one woman, if the librarian's heart were melted down, one would find a lump of lead, cold as steel.

Marian indeed is a bit of a martinet initially. She gives Harold the brush-off when he first flirts with her, and she runs the library with a no-nonsense respect for the rules. But then Harold transforms the personality of Marian's little brother from a self-conscious, shy, lisping wallflower to that of an outgoing, energetic little boy. Marian's "cold as steel" heart melts, and she falls in love with the fast-talking imposter.

Armed with a reference book that proves Harold's degree is a fake, she tears out the incriminating page before handing the book to the mayor. Harold is finally apprehended in his scam after he has had his selfish heart softened by Marian. For her part, she defends him and challenges the town to appreciate what he has accomplished. She too finally has a soft heart, a heart of flesh.

Those kind of fictional tales make for great entertainment, don't they? The problem, though, is that the people listening to Ezekiel thought him to be no more than an entertainer (see Ezekiel 33:32). Yet Ezekiel was serious, and Ezekiel was right: the hard heart exists, and it can be replaced with a soft one. But repentance comes first. That requirement never changes.   —J. B. N.

20. That they may walk in my statutes, and keep mine ordinances, and do them: and they shall be my people, and I will be their God.

God is not introducing any new expectations. He simply wants His people to follow the *statutes* and *ordinances* that they have had all along. He wants the people not to act hypocritically as they *do them*. Zechariah summarizes these expectations as the need for true judgments, the practice of mercy and compassion to one another, an end to oppressing the weak, and abandoning schemes to do evil (Zechariah 7:9, 10). Ezekiel's expectations are no different, for all of these things are covered in the Law of Moses. [See question #4, page 224.]

To *be* God's *people* was the primary purpose for the creation of the nation of Israel in the first place. That's why God had called Israel out of Egyptian bondage (Exodus 6:7). This fact is at the center of what makes (or should make) Israel to be holy, a people called out from the nations to serve the Lord. God's intent is that Israel be His chosen, beloved people, and that He will be *God* to them in a unique way (see Leviticus 26:12). This plan is still intact in the prophetic words of Ezekiel. This is preparation to usher in the Messiah.

D. Chastening (v. 21)

21. But as for them whose heart walketh after the heart of their detestable things and their abominations, I will recompense their way upon their own heads, saith the Lord GOD.

How will the people know if they have the new *heart*? Ezekiel warns them that if they persist in their idol worship, they can be sure that their heart is not renewed. It is still the stony heart obsessed with going after its own desires while disregarding God. This is the heart that God cannot work with, because the person stubbornly persists in rebellion. [See question #5, page 224.]

Home Daily Bible Readings

Monday, Feb. 23—Evil Hearts (Genesis 6:1-8)

Tuesday, Feb. 24—Willing Hearts (Exodus 25:1-9)

Wednesday, Feb. 25—Defiant Hearts (Deuteronomy 2:26-30)

Thursday, Feb. 26—Obedient Hearts (Deuteronomy 5:28-33)

Friday, Feb. 27—Proud Hearts (Deuteronomy 8:11-20)

Saturday, Feb. 28—Loving Hearts (Deuteronomy 10:12-21)

Sunday, Mar. 1—One Heart, a New Spirit (Ezekiel 11:14-21)

Ezekiel later expresses God's actions against such rebellious people this way: "According to thy ways, and according to thy doings, shall they judge thee, saith the Lord God" (Ezekiel 24:14). These are chilling words. No one can stand up against the absolute judgment of a holy God. Our only hope lies in accepting God's offer of a new heart. When we do, we end up yielding our will to Him.

Conclusion

A. Hard or Soft?

It is considered a negative thing to be called *soft* in many situations. If we "play soft" in athletics, it means we are pushovers or we aren't trying hard enough. If a person is called "soft in the head," he or she is thought to be mentally unstable.

By contrast, we often value things that are *hard*, don't we? Perhaps we admire someone who courageously "takes a hard line" on some matter. We equate hardness with strength. Yet in matters of the spirit, God desires that we have soft hearts. He seeks those who have submissive spirits that will yield to His will. He cannot use the person who defies Him. To resist God's will is an act of rebellion that adds "sin to sin" (Isaiah 30:1).

In the case of Judah, God was unwilling to let the nation's rebellion continue. Instead, God chose to "break" His people by allowing the Babylonians to humiliate and enslave them. He did not do this because of His respect for the Babylonians (also called *Chaldeans*), for they are described as a "bitter and hasty nation" (Habakkuk 1:6). Rather, He used the Babylonian nation as a tool in His larger plan.

Many Christians are able to recount a long battle against the will of God before their conversion. God had to "break" them for His service. They had to come to the point that they could pray, "Not my will, but thine, be done" (Luke 22:42). Only broken people can be God's holy servants. Are you still fighting God? Is your heart soft or hard toward His will?

B. Prayer

Merciful Father, may You forgive our constant resistance to Your will. We pray that You give us new hearts again, hearts that are in harmony with Your desires and directions. May You continue to change us, transforming us into the likeness of Your Son, in whose name we pray. Amen.

C. Thought to Remember

Hard heart or soft heart—
it's your choice.

Learning by Doing

This page contains an alternative lesson plan emphasizing learning activities. Some of these activities are also found in the helpful student book, Adult Bible Class.

Into the Lesson

Buy some small candy hearts and distribute one to each learner who arrives. Say, "Don't eat this . . . yet!"

As class begins, say, "Each person who can identify a common phrase or cultural expression with the word *heart* in it can keep his or her candy heart. Who wants to be first?" Such expressions as *stouthearted, coldhearted, warmhearted, broken heart, bleeding heart, heart attack, heart of gold, softhearted, hard-hearted, cut to the heart, heartless, hearts on fire, the cockles of your heart, heartbeat, heart transplant, heartthrob, heart's desire,* and others will "rescue" their candy hearts.

If you like, make a running list as words and phrases are offered. If a few students fail to say a heart phrase and are in danger of losing their candy, ask the class, "Well, should I be hard-hearted and take their candy . . . or should I 'have a heart'?"

Into the Word

Say, "Ezekiel 11:14-21 is a covenant statement. It follows Ezekiel's heartfelt expression of concern for God's people, 'Ah Lord God! wilt thou make a full end of the remnant of Israel?' As typical of covenants, two parties are agreeing to fulfill certain conditions and responsibilities."

Provide paper and pencils to all students. Ask each to make two columns on the paper, putting these two headings at the top: *What God Does* and *What God's Children Do.* Direct students to look at today's text in order to fill out both sides. Your learners will quickly see that it is a one-sided covenant, for mostly it is a picture of a loving God actively seeking the redemption of His wayward children.

Beginning with verse 16, your learners should note that God does the following. (Some of the ideas overlap, since there is repetition in the terminology and phrasing.)

- *has cast the people far away*
- *has scattered His people among other peoples*
- *continues to be a sanctuary for them*
- *will gather them*
- *will bring them back home*
- *will give them back a homeland, their "old" homeland*
- *will give them a pure undivided heart*
- *will restore a new, fresh spirit*

- *will replace their hard hearts with soft hearts of love*
- *will simply and profoundly be their God*
- *will repay those who do not reject idolatry and evil*

Your learners should see that God's children must destroy all the vile images and practices of other gods (repent!). In so doing, the people will give themselves to obeying the righteous expectations of God. The people must simply and fully be God's people, in word and deed.

Ask your class how this covenant compares with other covenants God has made with His people, including (especially!) the new covenant in Christ. Learners will easily see the foundational similarities: the covenant is at God's initiative; it has both blessings and curses; it is relationship-based; it expects a turning from evil and a commitment to righteousness; it is to be a matter of the heart and a matter of the head, featuring both laws and willful choices.

Into Life

Introduce your class to Moh's Hardness Scale, a standard scientific rating of the density/hardness of minerals. This scale goes from the softest, 1 (talc) to the hardest, 10 (diamond). Prepare copies for all your learners of the following rating scale. Distribute them and ask students to rate themselves from 1 to 10 as soft (Christlike) to hard (purely self-centered and resistant to the Spirit).

generous	*stingy*
kind	*harsh*
serene	*angry*
polite	*rude*
thankful	*discontent*
patient	*impatient*
gracious	*demanding*
pure thinking	*impure thinking*
bold	*timid*
meek	*aggressive*
forgiving	*vindictive*

Make this suggestion: "Consider the area of life and relationship where you need a little (or a lot) of the Spirit's softening." Then ask, "What spiritual disciplines will you commit yourself to that will help you in the area of becoming softer in a spiritual sense?"

Let's Talk It Over

The questions on this page are designed to promote discussion of the lesson by the class and to encourage application of the lesson Scriptures. The answers provided are only discussion starters. Let your class talk it over from there.

1. What was your response the last time a friend or family member disappointed you? Was that a godly or an ungodly response? How can you do better?

Try to imagine the feelings of a soldier returning home to discover that his job is gone, his fiancée has married another, and his car has been stolen. Would those feelings be magnified if his job were taken by his brother, his fiancée had married his best friend, and his car had been taken by an old buddy he went to high school with? The most painful wounds sometimes come from those who are closest to us. The word *betrayal* may come to mind.

For the Israelites in exile, it must have been even worse. They had seen their land invaded, their homes destroyed, their countrymen enslaved, and their nation subjugated. Then their old neighbors and friends turned against them, wishing them "good riddance." When tragedy strikes someone close and barely misses us, a strict cause-and-effect logic—along the lines of "They didn't escape but I did, so God favors me more than He favors them"—must be resisted. Instead, it's time to pray.

2. What are some ways that God has been a sanctuary for you in your own life?

Answers will be highly personal, of course. Point out that God's promise to Ezekiel was a promise of presence. No matter where the exiles were, no matter what they faced, God would be in their midst. Although those remaining in Jerusalem thought the exiles to be rejected by God, the actual situation among the exiles was that they were not far from the Lord. The Lord remained with them as a sanctuary.

Christians are not exempt from hardship. In our times of challenge and change, in our experiences of loss and longing, God is always there. He never leaves, He never forsakes. He never abandons, He never turns away. For those times when it seems as if God is far away, remember this: He is not the one who has moved.

3. What are some identifying characteristics of a stony heart? How can we tell whether we have a heart of stone in our own souls? How do we go about correcting this problem?

Jesus' teaching on the mote and the beam (Matthew 7:1-5) cautions us that we may see the signs of stony hearts in other lives before we acknowledge them in ourselves. Knowing God's Word without obeying it, being aware of people's needs without feeling compassion, and putting selfish desires ahead of God's priorities are among the indicators that a spiritual heart transplant is needed.

4. How would a nation obedient to God's statutes and ordinances be different from nations that are not? What would it look like if a people truly lived as "God's people"?

Godly people live differently from the ungodly. People who are truly godly care about the poor. They do all they can to work for their own living and for the improvement of others. They give generously. They pray. They strive to live in peace, but not at the cost of justice.

Although we may barely be able to imagine what a nation fully committed to these principles might be like, we nevertheless can commit ourselves to God's ideals. Instead of worrying about changing others, we focus on changing ourselves. That's the best way to function as facilitators of change in our homes and communities.

5. How can God's warning that He will "recompense their way upon their own heads" be both a source of encouragement and concern for believers today?

For the Jews in exile, having heard about their countrymen taking advantage of the situation, the thought of God bringing the consequences of sin on the heads of sinners might have given some comfort. But that cold comfort would have come as they slept on foreign soil, brought far from home by a hostile army. They knew firsthand how effectively God could "recompense their way upon their own heads."

Christians look forward to the Day of Judgment, when God will correct all injustice finally and fully. That fact is comforting. Even so, we dare not hope for that day in a malicious, "payback" sense. We ourselves once walked the dark path of sin, and we deserve God's "payback" as much as anyone. By Jesus' blood we have life instead. Remember: God is not willing that any should perish.

Spring Quarter 2009

Christ and Creation

Special Features

Lessons

Unit 1: The Promise of New Life

Unit 2: The Dawn of New Life

Unit 3: The Fruits of New Life

About These Lessons

The phrase *new life* (which occurs in the title of each unit of study in this quarter's lessons) strikes people in different ways. Those who are "at rock bottom" are desperate for some kind of new life. Those who are "flying high" see no need for a new life. But we all need a new life! This quarter's lessons will show us the why, the how, and the results of the only kind of new life that counts.

Mar 8

Mar 15

Mar 22

Mar 29

Apr 5

Apr 12

Apr 19

Apr 26

May 3

May 10

May 17

May 24

May 31

Quarterly Quiz

The questions on this page may be used in several ways: as a pretest at the beginning of the quarter; as a review at the end of the quarter; or as a review after each lesson. The questions are based on the Scripture text of each lesson (King James Version). ***The answers are on page 228.***

Lesson 1*

1. What were the "abominations" of Jerusalem that Ezekiel condemned? (foreign wives? violations of the law? idols?) *Ezekiel 11:18*

2. For Ezekiel, the "stony heart" is found in the person who stubbornly resists God. T/F. *Ezekiel 11:19*

Lesson 2

1. Ezekiel prophesied that the Messiah would bring a covenant of _____. *Ezekiel 34:25*

2. What miraculous precipitation did Ezekiel prophesy? (showers of blessing? rain in a dry and thirsty land? snow in summer?) *Ezekiel 34:26*

Lesson 3

1. Ezekiel taught that God was concerned because His _____ had been profaned among the heathen nations. *Ezekiel 36:22, 23*

2. What would the Spirit of God enable the people of Israel to do? (worship in holiness? gain victory over enemies? keep God's laws?) *Ezekiel 36:27*

Lesson 4

1. Ezekiel presents the "valley of dry bones" like an ancient battlefield where no one buried the dead. T/F. *Ezekiel 37:1, 2*

2. Ezekiel was told to _____ upon the dry bones. *Ezekiel 37:4*

Lesson 5

1. In chapter 47, Ezekiel has a vision of a ____ coming out of the temple. *Ezekiel 47:1*

2. What is the sign that the Dead Sea has been "healed"? (deep blue color? cool winds come from it? abundant fish in it?) *Ezekiel 47:10*

Lesson 6

1. The Roman soldiers offered Jesus _____ to drink while he was on the cross. *Luke 23:36*

2. The superscription over Jesus on the cross was written in Greek, Hebrew, and what other language? (Egyptian? Persian? Latin?) *Luke 23:38*

Lesson 7

1. The first person to enter the empty tomb of Jesus was Peter. T/F. *Luke 24:3, 12*

2. At least five women went to the tomb to attend to the body of Jesus. T/F. *Luke 24:10*

Lesson 8

1. Jesus told the disciples to "tarry" in Jerusalem because Galilee was unsafe. T/F. *Luke 24:49*

2. Jesus explained how the law and the apocrypha applied to Him. T/F. *Luke 24:44, 45*

Lesson 9

1. What was Aeneas to do after being healed? (visit a priest? make his bed? pray?) *Acts 9:34*

2. The name *Dorcas* is an alternate name for *Tabitha*. T/F. *Acts 9:36*

Lesson 10

1. What are believers sealed with? (works? prayer? Holy Spirit?) *Ephesians 1:13*

2. Paul teaches that in Christ, God has made known to us the _____ of his will. *Ephesians 1:9*

Lesson 11

1. Paul says that believers have been created in Christ for what purpose? (good works? the praise of His glory? a place in Heaven?) *Ephesians 2:10*

2. Paul says that salvation is not the result of good works. T/F. *Ephesians 2:9*

Lesson 12

1. In Ephesians, Paul claims to be less than the least of all _____. *Ephesians 3:8*

2. Paul teaches the Gentiles that all his tribulations are to their shame. T/F. *Ephesians 3:13*

Lesson 13

1. Paul calls husbands to love their wives as Christ loved the _____. *Ephesians 5:25*

2. Paul says that the husband who loves his wife also loves what? (Christ? the body of believers? himself?) *Ephesians 5:28*

Lesson 14

1. Paul wants us to be strong in the Lord. T/F. *Ephesians 6:10*

2. Paul presents our struggle against evil spiritual forces as a cosmic battle. T/F. *Ephesians 6:12*

*Note: Lesson 1 is printed with the winter quarter.

The Full Story

by John C. Nugent

ISTORY TEACHES that all that is worthwhile can be terribly distorted. Love is deformed into lust. Lifelong marriage is reduced to a temporary legal arrangement. Medical treatment is hijacked by insurance companies.

Christian faith is no exception. Kings have used it to advance human empires, philosophers to showcase human wisdom, and politicians to get elected. Indeed, Christianity has suffered so many distortions that evangelists in our day feel compelled to spend as much time defending the faith against misunderstandings as they do proclaiming the gospel itself. Startled by this negative momentum, many Christians wonder what to do about it.

This quarter's lessons provide the solution to this dilemma: teach and preach the entirety of the Bible's message. This quarter we will look at three crucial junctures in biblical narrative. First is the Old Testament's anticipation of Christ. Next will be Christ's fulfillment of that expectation. Finally will come the church's response to Christ.

Distortions of Christianity result from ignoring one or more of these junctures. Many misrepresent Jesus by tearing Him away from the Old Testament and relocating Him in their preferred context. Others corrupt the faith by embracing the Jesus of Old Testament prophecy, but severing discipleship from membership in churches committed to living out the New Testament's instructions. Still others embrace the church as a social club, failing to take seriously the significance of Christ's life and death for the course of history.

This quarter of study certainly does not discuss every important event in Scripture. Even so, this quarter represents a biblical response to the distorted versions of Christianity that plague the church's witness today.

Unit 1: March
The Promise of New Life

We begin with the book of Ezekiel. This sixth-century prophetic book captures a key moment in the Old Testament story. Through the remarkable prophet Ezekiel, God challenged Israel to live faithfully during a painful period of exile. He also encouraged them to wait expectantly for God's intervention to restore them fully.

Like many of the Old Testament prophets, Ezekiel's vision roots Israel's hope in the fuller biblical time line. The Israelites did not arrive on the scene out of thin air in the sixth century BC. God had been working with them since the calling of Abraham some 14 centuries prior. Apart from this broader context, Ezekiel as a book makes little sense, nor does the work of Jesus.

Lesson 1 (printed with the winter quarter) begins this series on a note of hope. Exile was not to be God's last word for Israel. He promised both to restore Israel to her land and to equip her with a new heart and new spirit.

Israel's hope and help continue in **Lesson 2.** Ezekiel assured the people that God would not only bring them back to a rich and plentiful land, He also would send them a royal shepherd. This Messiah would guide Israel and protect her from whatever wolves would attack.

In **Lesson 3,** we will see God remind Israel that her restoration was to be not only for her own sake. God's work with Israel was to have global ramifications as well. Through Israel, God planned to make a name for himself among the nations. God had an important mission for Israel in the world.

In **Lesson 4,** we will see God use a startling visual image to illustrate Israel's hope. Like a jumbled pile of dry bones being realigned and re-enfleshed, God planned to gather His scattered people and renew them with His spirit. Though Daniel 12:2 makes clear that God plans resurrection for individuals, Ezekiel was more concerned with the reconstitution of God's people as a whole.

The future that God planned for His people is quite marvelous, as **Lesson 5** demonstrates. In this study we will examine Ezekiel's grand vision of a miraculous river flowing from the temple. This river furnishes life wherever it flows.

Unit 2: April
The Dawn of New Life

Israel's Old Testament hope, as expressed in Ezekiel, would have been empty were it not for its fulfillment in Christ. Unit 2 focuses on Luke's account of Christ's saving work from His death to His ascension. All of Scripture up to this juncture has been pointing toward these pivotal events. All Scripture that follows points back to them as the key events that changed world history.

The cross of Christ is rightly a focal point of Christian meditation. We learn in **Lesson 6** that even while He was dying Christ was concerned both to save those around Him and to extend God's grace to those who were trying to destroy Him.

Christ's death on the cross would have been merely the sad conclusion to an extraordinary life had God not raised Him from the dead. **Lesson 7** is about the wonderful events surrounding the empty tomb and how the disciples first received the astounding news that the Lord had risen.

Lesson 8 focuses on the two key events marking the transition from Christ's earthly work to that of the church: Jesus' commission to His disciples to be His witnesses and Jesus' ascension into Heaven. Without the ascension, the church's mission would not be possible.

In **Lesson 9,** we see the ascended Christ continue His work through the church. Both by word and by deed, apostles such as Peter and saints such as Tabitha showed Christ's love to people in need. Their witnesses inspire our own lives of faith and service.

Unit 3: May
The Fruits of New Life

The Old Testament pointed toward Christ's saving work, and Christ completed this work with the utmost faithfulness. Now it is the church's turn to reflect on that work and make it the center of her life. No person can live out Christ's work alone. When Christ came, He gathered 12 disciples in order to form the core of a new Israel. Like old Israel, God requires that we conform our lives to His will. The apostle Paul teaches us in Ephesians what new life in Christ is to look like.

Lesson 10 appropriately begins this series with praise to God. We could never be God's children were it not for His adopting us and commissioning us to bear His name. Since Christ made this adoption possible, He remains the center of our hope and the source of our inheritance. We are helplessly unworthy and can only respond, like Paul, with praise.

Lest we fail to appreciate what Christ has done for us, **Lesson 11** will remind us that, before Christ, we were "dead people walking." We were enslaved to the fallen powers at work in this world, unfit for the inheritance prepared for us. Though nothing we can do will make us worthy, God has given us worthwhile work to do. We were not adopted for the sake of privilege, but chosen for the sake of witness.

Lesson 12 will teach us that our adoption as believers is far from ordinary! The mystery of Christ that Paul proclaimed meant Jews and Gentiles becoming coheirs in Christ—brothers and sisters in the faith. Christ not only broke down the wall between humans and God, He also made it possible for people groups who were formerly at odds with one another to be unified.

The new life made possible by Christ reaches into our everyday relationships, as **Lesson 13** will demonstrate. There we will learn that peace between people groups also means peace among family members. All of our relationships are (or should be) transformed by the love of Christ.

Though Christ won the decisive victory against sin and death on the cross, the battle is not quite over. Enemies of the cross, who have been mortally wounded, nonetheless continue to wreak havoc in this world. In **Lesson 14,** Paul will show us both the nature of our struggle and the unique equipment God provides to fight the good fight.

Conclusion

When taken in its entirety, the biblical story is powerful and compelling. Minimalist, "sound bite" versions of the Christian faith have plagued us long enough! We need Christians who are conversant with the Old Testament, fluent in the life and work of Christ, and committed to fulfilling the Great Commission in churches that are powered by the same Holy Spirit who enabled the first-century disciples.

Christians who heed what God says to His people in this quarter's lessons will serve as living proof of the gospel's integrity and validity. Conforming our lives to biblical truths is vital. Counterfeit faiths and distortions of Christianity will continue to emerge until Christ returns. This fact requires that we so familiarize ourselves with the genuine article that nothing will separate us from the love of Christ.

Answers to Quarterly Quiz on page 226

Lesson 1—1. idols. 2. true. **Lesson 2**—1. peace. 2. showers of blessing. **Lesson 3**—1. name. 2. keep God's laws. **Lesson 4**—1. true. 2. prophesy. **Lesson 5**—1. river. 2. abundant fish in it. **Lesson 6**—1. vinegar. 2. Latin. **Lesson 7**—1. false (the women entered first, Peter later). 2. true (Luke lists two Marys, Joanna, and "other women," indicating at least two others). **Lesson 8**—1. false. 2. false. **Lesson 9**—1. make his bed. 2. true. **Lesson 10**—1. Holy Spirit. 2. mystery. **Lesson 11**—1. good works. 2. true. **Lesson 12**—1. saints. 2. false (his tribulations are to their glory). **Lesson 13**—1. church. 2. himself. **Lesson 14**—1. true. 2. true.

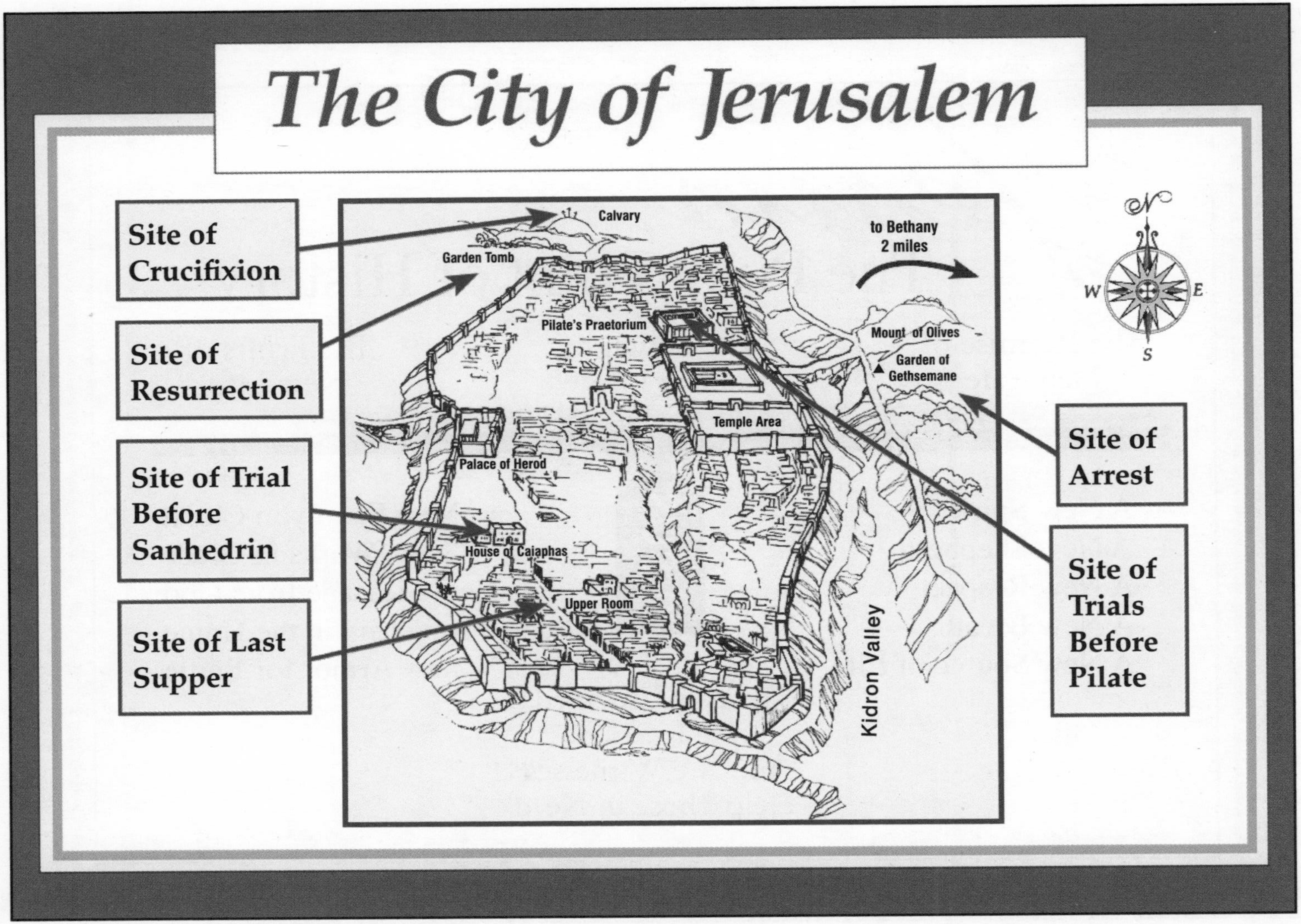

The City of Jerusalem

Site of Arrest

Site of Trials Before Pilate

Site of Crucifixion

Site of Resurrection

Site of Trial Before Sanhedrin

Site of Last Supper

to Bethany 2 miles

Mount of Olives

Garden of Gethsemane

Kidron Valley

Temple Area

Calvary

Pilate's Praetorium

Garden Tomb

Palace of Herod

House of Caiaphas

Upper Room

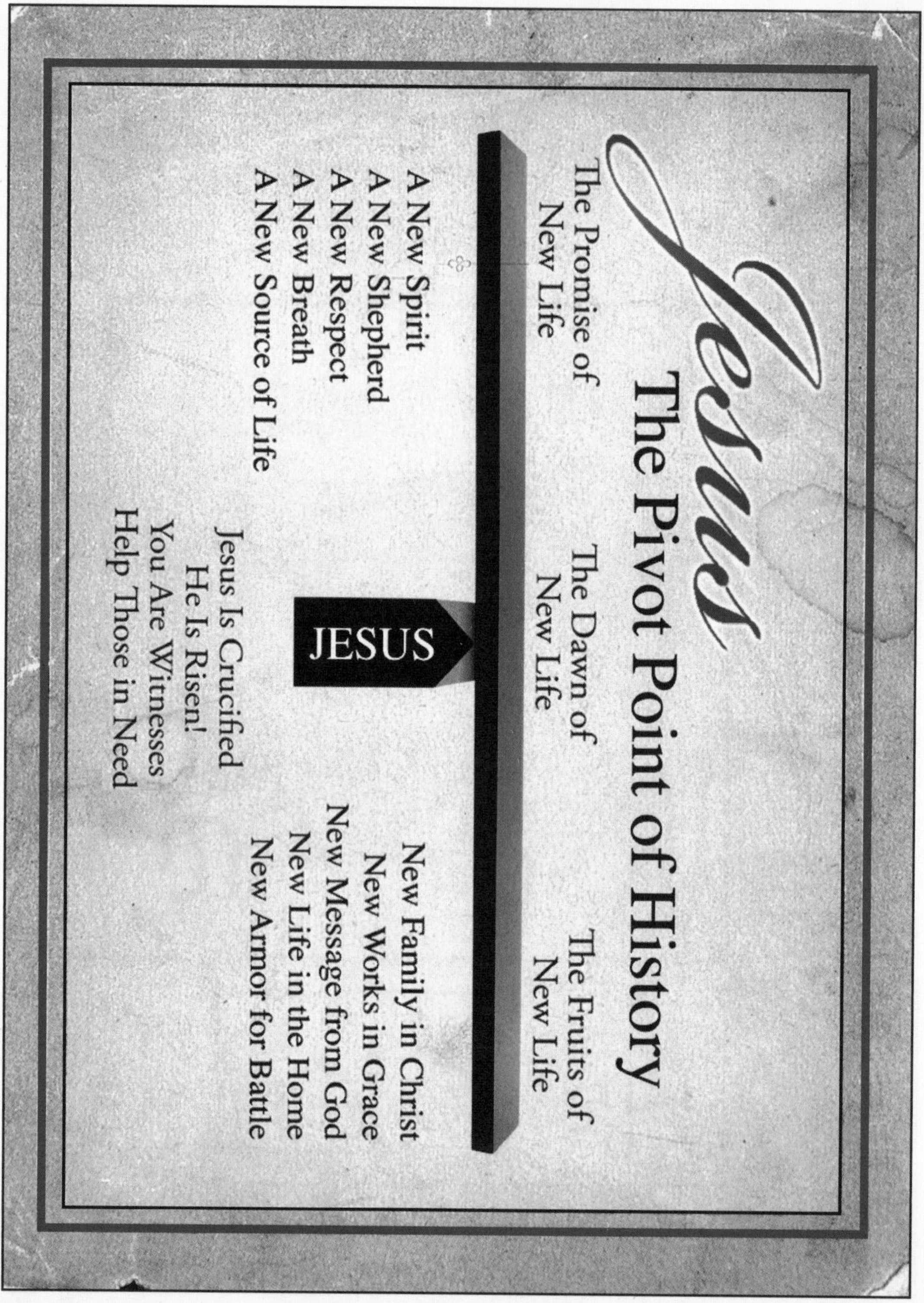

Jesus
The Pivot Point of History

The Promise of
New Life

The Dawn of
New Life

The Fruits of
New Life

A New Spirit
A New Shepherd
A New Respect
A New Breath
A New Source of Life

JESUS

Jesus Is Crucified
He Is Risen!
You Are Witnesses
Help Those in Need

New Family in Christ
New Works in Grace
New Message from God
New Life in the Home
New Armor for Battle

The Medium Is the Message

Tapping the Power of Presentation Tools

by Richard A. Koffarnus

THE EXPRESSION "the medium is the message" was coined by media expert Marshall McLuhan in his greatest work, *Understanding Media: The Extensions of Man* (1964). Although frequently quoted, McLuhan's dictum is commonly misunderstood.

Many assume that McLuhan was (1) speaking strictly of mass-media communication and (2) that "the message" referred to the information presented by these media. Both assumptions are wrong. Worse yet, casual readers may conclude from these two assumptions that McLuhan was arguing that the content presented is less important than the medium that presents it. Nothing could be further from the truth.

According to McLuhan, a *medium* is "any extension of ourselves." For example, a tennis racquet is a medium for extending my arm to the ball, and language is a medium for extending my thoughts to others. A *message*, on the other hand, is more than simply information. Ultimately, it is a change in human attitude or behavior in response to a medium. If I watch a video about evangelism in Haiti and feel compassion for the lost and decide to support a missionary to a third world country, then the message of the video is my change in attitude toward, and decision to support, missions.

Thus, when McLuhan says "the medium is the message," he means that the way to understand the nature of anything we create (a medium) and evaluate its effectiveness is by taking note of the changes it brings about (the message).

Bible School:
Where the Medium Meets the Message

When you think about it, what you teach on Sunday morning is not a lesson, it's a class of students. The lesson is simply the medium by which you extend your thoughts and the truths of Scripture to them. The actual message is the change in your students' attitudes and actions that result from that lesson.

To help you maximize the desired effects of your lesson, Standard Publishing makes available several powerful tools designed to help you reach your students where they are and take them where you want them to go. Among those tools are the PowerPoint® slide presentations for each lesson.

Each presentation contains approximately 20 to 40 slides that include the lesson outline, discussion questions, learning activities, and visuals.

Standard Publishing provides these presentations in four different teachers' resources. If you use the *Standard Lesson eCommentary* (SLeC), the slide presentations are included with the program on CD. The SLeC uses the popular Libronix Digital Library System®, which provides seamless access to dozens of commentaries, Bible translations, and other reference works. As you install the SLeC on your computer, you also install the Standard Publishing Home Page within Libronix so that each lesson and its corresponding handouts, visuals, and PowerPoint® presentation are accessible from a convenient menu.

These same PowerPoint® presentations are also provided on the Presentation Tools CD that is included in Standard Publishing's *Adult Resources* packet. Slide presentations can be copied to a hard drive, CD, or USB flash drive, or they can be shown directly from the Presentation Tools CD. Additionally, Standard Publishing packages the *Adult Resources* packet, including the Presentation Tools CD, in its *Adult Teacher's Convenience Kit*. Finally, you also can get the PowerPoint® presentations via download at www.standardlesson.com.

Putting the Power into PowerPoint®

PowerPoint® is a very flexible presentation program that mimics a slide projector on your computer. There was a time when a "slide show" usually meant a series of still pictures presented to a large crowd in a darkened auditorium. However, the use of PowerPoint® in business and education has shown the versatility of the program in a variety of settings, from small group meetings to large congregations.

Unlike a slide projector, however, PowerPoint® gives you the ability to change fonts and background color for each slide; to add pictures, clip art, animation, video clips, and music to slides; to rearrange slides; and much more at the click of a mouse. PowerPoint® is part of the Microsoft Office Suite® of programs, but it can also be purchased as a stand-alone product. If you simply wish to show pre-made slide presentations (such as those on the Presentation Tools CD) without editing them, you can download Microsoft's free Power-Point® viewer at www.microsoft.com/downloads.

In addition to your computer and the Power-Point® presentation, you will also need a means to display the presentation to your class. For a small group, a large screen monitor may be sufficient. The most flexible display solution, however, is a digital video projector and a projection screen. These are used increasingly in church worship services. Projectors vary widely in display resolution, light output, projection technology, and, accordingly, cost. So do your homework to be sure you get a projector that will meet your needs without breaking your budget.

Tapping the Potential of PowerPoint®

If any medium is an extension of your thoughts, then think of a PowerPoint® presentation as an extension of what you already do as a teacher. That poster you would use in an 8 x 10 classroom is now visible in a room three times as large. When you discuss a person or an event, you can project an applicable picture while you talk. Scripture references and quotations can be displayed while they are read aloud. In other words, whatever you say can be reinforced by what your class sees. And with PowerPoint® you have the additional capability of printing copies of your slide program as handouts so your students can take the lesson home for further study and reflection.

If you prefer to use a discussion approach, as I do in my adult Bible class, you will find questions in the *Adult Resources* slide presentations designed to stimulate discussion. These are taken from the "Let's Talk It Over" sections of the teacher's commentary. Of course, you can add your own questions to these pre-prepared queries. When I ask a question in class, I sometimes get so involved in the discussion that I forget the original question. Having it displayed on screen can help me avoid a "senior moment." It can also be a useful tool to get the discussion back on track when a class member goes off on a tangent.

If you use the learning activities in the teacher's commentary, you will find that many of those activities are also adapted and included as slides in the *Adult Resources* presentations. PowerPoint® slides are a good way to display open-ended questions or agree/disagree statements that invite a student to give a response. Slides are also useful to display the correct answers to puzzles, quizzes, and other exercises that require specific responses. However, some learning activities, such as skits and role playing, may not lend themselves to a slide presentation. Like any tool, PowerPoint® has its strengths and limitations.

Avoiding Pitfalls

For all their power and pizzazz, slide shows often fizzle when it comes to the actual presentation. If you remember a few simple guidelines, however, you can avoid some common mistakes that may spoil your lessons.

First, keep the show brief. A common temptation is to pack too many slides into a single lesson. When that happens, the goal of the presentation can easily become to get through all the slides, rather than to drive home the life-changing message. Allow about one slide per minute of lesson time, and you won't feel rushed to finish.

Second, less is often more. One of the strengths of PowerPoint® is also its greatest weakness. The program has a tempting array of tools that make it far too easy to have words and pictures fade in and out, bounce around the screen like rubber balls, and otherwise thoroughly distract the class. Unless your goal is to entertain, animation should be used to drive home an important point, not simply to amuse. Most of the slides on the *Adult Resources* CD have minimal animation or none at all so that they don't distract from the purpose of the lesson. Use the fireworks sparingly!

Third, keep it simple. Use few words and large letters or pictures on each slide so the class can easily recognize them in a large room. Too many words crammed on a slide make it difficult for the class to remember the content. Likewise, when you use bulleted points, limit the number of bullets to three or four per slide. Generally, sans serif fonts, such as Arial or Tahoma, are easier to read than serif, script, or decorative fonts.

Fourth, don't let the medium supersede the message. Marshall McLuhan argued that we should evaluate the effectiveness of any medium by its message, the change it brings about in its audience. Success is not measured by the "wow" factor of technology, but by its ability to help us achieve our goals. Even the most sophisticated slide show is still just a tool to reach your lesson objectives. As you see the lives of your students brought into conformity with the life of Jesus, then you will know that your teaching is having its desired effect.

Conclusion

Thanks to the influence of Christian writer G. K. Chesterton, Marshall McLuhan converted to the Christian faith in 1937. Thus, it is not surprising that after McLuhan's death in 1980 these words of Jesus were inscribed on his gravestone: "The Truth Shall Make You Free." When you couple the truth of God's Word with the power of presentation tools, the result can set your teaching—and your students—free, indeed.

A New Shepherd

March 8
Lesson 2

DEVOTIONAL READING: John 10:11-18.

BACKGROUND SCRIPTURE: Ezekiel 34.

PRINTED TEXT: Ezekiel 34:23-31.

Ezekiel 34:23-31

23 And I will set up one shepherd over them, and he shall feed them, even my servant David; he shall feed them, and he shall be their shepherd.

24 And I the LORD will be their God, and my servant David a prince among them; I the LORD have spoken it.

25 And I will make with them a covenant of peace, and will cause the evil beasts to cease out of the land: and they shall dwell safely in the wilderness, and sleep in the woods.

26 And I will make them and the places round about my hill a blessing; and I will cause the shower to come down in his season; there shall be showers of blessing.

27 And the tree of the field shall yield her fruit, and the earth shall yield her increase, and they shall be safe in their land, and shall know that I am the LORD, when I have broken the bands of their yoke, and delivered them out of the hand of those that served themselves of them.

28 And they shall no more be a prey to the heathen, neither shall the beast of the land devour them; but they shall dwell safely, and none shall make them afraid.

29 And I will raise up for them a plant of renown, and they shall be no more consumed with hunger in the land, neither bear the shame of the heathen any more.

30 Thus shall they know that I the LORD their God am with them, and that they, even the house of Israel, are my people, saith the Lord GOD.

31 And ye my flock, the flock of my pasture, are men, and I am your God, saith the Lord GOD.

GOLDEN TEXT: Ye my flock, the flock of my pasture, are men,
and I am your God, saith the Lord GOD.—Ezekiel 34:31.

> *Christ and Creation*
> The Promise of New Life
> Lessons 1–5

Lesson Aims

After participating in this lesson, each student will be able to:

1. Describe the future kingdom of peace that Ezekiel prophesied.

2. Tell how this message would have been especially comforting in light of the fall of Jerusalem.

3. Express hope in the future based on his or her relationship with God and, if possible, in contrast with a significant negative event in his or her life.

Lesson Outline

INTRODUCTION
    A. What Does the Future Hold?
    B. Lesson Background
 I. KINGDOM OF THE SHEPHERD (Ezekiel 34:23, 24)
    A. David the Servant (v. 23)
       Shepherds
    B. David the Prince (v. 24)
 II. KINGDOM OF SECURITY (Ezekiel 34:25-29)
    A. Covenant of Peace (v. 25)
    B. Showers of Blessing (vv. 26, 27)
    C. Land of Safety (vv. 28, 29)
III. FLOCK OF GOD (Ezekiel 34:30, 31)
    A. They Are My People (v. 30)
    B. I Am Their God (v. 31)
       Positions
CONCLUSION
    A. The Peaceable Kingdom
    B. Prayer
    C. Thought to Remember

Introduction

A. What Does the Future Hold?

People have always been eager to learn what the future holds. From ancient times there has been a persistent belief that certain individuals were gifted with the ability to see the future, or that certain techniques could be used to learn the answers to questions about the future. This can be seen in the story of Oedipus, a Greek king. At his birth it was prophesied that Oedipus would kill his father and marry his mother. The ancient Greeks believed it was impossible to thwart this prediction.

In our day prediction of the future is a strange mix of superstition and technology. Naïve people still pay for the services of those who will give a reading of their palms or interpret tarot cards for them. Many adults who seem to be otherwise intelligent will not begin the day without consulting the predictions of an astrologer in a horoscope. Others squander money by calling psychic hotlines for answers to questions about the future. On a playful level, most people enjoy reading the inane little comments in fortune cookies, which are often wildly (and hilariously) off base. [See question #1, page 240.]

Our high-tech world has seen the rise of *futurists*. These are intellectuals who boldly predict what the coming decades will be like. Futurists employ sophisticated computer programs and projection models that follow various trends to absurd levels. Yet predictions from the technology world of coming marvels often fail to materialize and are quickly forgotten. This is because human beings, of and by their own capacity, have no way of seeing into the future. Knowing the future is the prerogative of God alone. We can know the future only inasmuch as God chooses to reveal it to us.

In the Old Testament, the prophets of the Lord gave predictions of the future for two primary reasons. First, their predictions might be warnings of the dire consequences for continued disobedience. These were sometimes in the form of conditional prophecies, such as, "this is the future for you if you do not repent and change." Second, the prophets laid out a vision of the future for the purpose of giving hope to the people of God. They showed that the suffering and pain of this world is not the last word. God cares for us, and He will not abandon His people. There is a better time ahead, even a future time without sorrow and regret (see Revelation 21:4).

B. Lesson Background

Several significant things happened in Ezekiel's world since the time of last week's lesson from Ezekiel 11. For one, the prophet had suffered the personal tragedy of the death of his wife (Ezekiel 24:18). Ezekiel's difficult task at that time was not to mourn in public, but to obey the will of God and use the occasion as a prophetic moment in speaking to the people. Although we have no reason to doubt the inner strength of Ezekiel, we can easily understand the deep scars this event left on him. We appreciate that he was a sad and lonely man without his beloved mate. Ezekiel undoubtedly was viewed as odd because of his curious behavior (see Ezekiel 4, 5, and 12). His wife may have been the only one who had understood him.

A second major turning point was the news that the city of Jerusalem had fallen (Ezekiel 33:21). While this news may have been less than surprising given the many prophecies of Jerusalem's demise, the news still would have been shocking and painful to the exiles. Their longing to go back to Jerusalem entered a new phase, for there was no Jerusalem to which they might return. Their beautiful temple, a centuries-old focus of national identity and pride, lay in ruins.

There is a shift in Ezekiel's tone beginning with chapter 33. Up to that point, the prophet had been preaching doom and gloom. Chapter 33 begins to be more hopeful, looking to the future and emphasizing the justice and mercy of God. This is the context for the marvelous vision of the future that is the basis of today's lesson.

I. Kingdom of the Shepherd (Ezekiel 34:23, 24)

A. David the Servant (v. 23)

23. And I will set up one shepherd over them, and he shall feed them, even my servant David; he shall feed them, and he shall be their shepherd.

"The shepherd" is a famous image for the Jewish people. Some of their most celebrated ancestors have been shepherds, including Joseph (Genesis 37:2), Moses (Exodus 3:1), and *David* (1 Samuel 17:34, 35). The metaphor of God as the shepherd of His people is also very ancient and well-known for Ezekiel and the exiles (see Genesis 49:24; Psalm 23:1). The verse before us reveals the shepherd as a prophetic figure, a future player in God's plan for Israel.

We recall David as the young lad who rose from being a lowly shepherd to become the most beloved king of the nation. Ironically, David was almost ignored as a candidate because his father did not think a young boy out tending sheep to be important enough to present to Samuel for anointing (1 Samuel 16:11).

How to Say It

BABYLON. *Bab*-uh-lun.
CORINTHIANS. Ko-*rin*-thee-unz (*th* as in *thin*).
EZEKIEL. Ee-*zeek*-ee-ul or Ee-*zeek*-yul.
JERUSALEM. Juh-*roo*-suh-lem.
MELCHIZEDEK. Mel-*kiz*-eh-dek.
MESSIAH. Meh-*sigh*-uh.
MESSIANIC. Mess-ee-*an*-ick.
OEDIPUS. *Eh*-duh-pus.
OUIJA. *Wee*-juh.
TAROT. *tare*-oh.

In this beautiful prophecy of the Messiah, we see a number of the elements in God's plan. First, there is to be *one shepherd*, not a committee or a dynasty. Ezekiel looks ahead to a single individual to fulfill the prophecy.

Second, the coming one is to be the Lord's *servant*. He will work for God, not for himself. Third, the shepherd of God in some sense will be David. This can refer to lineage. It can also refer to the heart. God cherished David because he had been "a man after mine own heart" (Acts 13:22).

Fourth, the task of the Messiah will be to *feed* God's people. This does not refer to physical food, but spiritual nourishment. The Gospels show us Jesus to be a master teacher who instructs us how to live by His words and His deeds. Fifth, the coming king will shepherd the people, meaning to lead and protect them. [See question #2, page 240.]

A troubling image employed in the Bible is the picture of sheep without a shepherd (see 1 Kings 22:17; Ezekiel 34:8; Matthew 9:36). This invokes the picture of scared animals, wandering aimlessly without protection. Such chaos is not God's intention here.

SHEPHERDS

Montana boasts the seventh largest sheep population in the United States. In 1999 the state raised 370,000 sheep, which is about one sheep for every two people there. Sheep products brought a revenue of over $33 million. Sheep provide wool, meat, and milk (most of which is used to make feta cheese).

Today the industry is highly organized, but in earlier days it was very common for one shepherd to stay with the sheep day and night, all year long. He lived in a covered wagon and saw other people only when the rancher brought supplies to him about once a week. His only companionship beside sheep might have been his working dogs. The shepherds lived on oatmeal porridge, bread, and cheese.

That shepherd was responsible for the total welfare of the sheep. The Old Testament image, the New Testament image, and the agricultural reality are much the same. Today we enjoy the protection of the one great shepherd: Jesus (Hebrews 13:20). But Jesus also uses under-shepherds to do His work. Biblically, these are called *elders* (1 Peter 5:1-4). Pray that God will strengthen you to assist them in their tasks!　　　　　—J. B. N.

B. David the Prince (v. 24)

24. And I the LORD will be their God, and my servant David a prince among them; I the LORD have spoken it.

This verse is subtle, containing an often missed aspect of the purpose of the Messiah. We tend to emphasize the fact that Jesus comes as the Messiah to save us from our sins (Matthew 1:21). But God's messianic project is not just about us; it is about Him too. The planned result is restoration to God so that He may be God to His people. There are to be no more false gods or spiritual infidelity. *I the Lord will be their God.* We are to understand that this is the solemn word of God, for *I the Lord have spoken it.*

Ezekiel's presentation of the coming Messiah adds two elements that are not mentioned in the previous verse. First, the Messiah will be a *prince.* This is a broad term, but does not emphasize the idea of being the son of the king. The prince in this context is more than the king-in-waiting. He is a ruler, one who exercises great authority. Second, Ezekiel promises that the new *David* will be among them. He is not to be some kind of far-off angelic creature. He is to be one of us, a human as David had been (John 1:14).

II. Kingdom of Security (Ezekiel 34:25-29)

A. Covenant of Peace (v. 25)

25. And I will make with them a covenant of peace, and will cause the evil beasts to cease out of the land: and they shall dwell safely in the wilderness, and sleep in the woods.

All godly people long for peace, for rest, and God's plan will culminate in a remarkable *covenant of peace.* We learn later in Ezekiel that this will be an everlasting covenant (Ezekiel 37:26).

The biblical concept of peace is much more than the end of wars between nations. Biblical peace includes personal well-being and prosperity. This comes about only when one is at peace with God. If all people were to be united in their devotion to the Lord, there naturally would be peace.

Peace is a frequent component of the gospel message. The apostles preach the peace of Jesus

---

VISUALS FOR THESE LESSONS

The visual pictured in each lesson (example: page 237) is a small reproduction of a large, full-color poster included in the *Adult Resources* packet for the Spring Quarter. That packet also contains the very useful *Presentation Helps* on a CD for teacher use. The packet is available from your supplier. Order No. 392.

---

for Israel (see Acts 10:36). To go even further, Christ is understood by Paul as embodying this peace (Ephesians 2:14). The author of Hebrews likens Jesus to Melchizedek as the "King of peace" (Hebrews 7:2).

Ezekiel represents this peace to the people by using the image of *evil* (wild) *beasts.* These are deadly animals such as lions, bears, and wolves. It is the shepherd's job to drive these predators away (1 Samuel 17:34, 35), but even this task will be unnecessary if the beasts are content to stay in the woods. By implication, this will also be the end of predatory humans who take advantage of the people (see Proverbs 28:15; Acts 20:29; Jude 12).

B. Showers of Blessing (vv. 26, 27)

26. And I will make them and the places round about my hill a blessing; and I will cause the shower to come down in his season; there shall be showers of blessing.

The picture of God's future kingdom of peace is now presented as a holy hill surrounded by the homes of the faithful. This is the ideal agricultural community, where rain comes at just the right time. There is no drought, no floods. There is no need for irrigation. The crops grow to their greatest potential.

Ezekiel presents this as *showers of blessing,* taking the idea well beyond agricultural paradise. God will make full provision for any needs His people may have. This is a far cry from the exiles' last memories of the Holy Land, with its desolation and despair. [See question #3, page 240.]

27a. And the tree of the field shall yield her fruit, and the earth shall yield her increase, and they shall be safe in their land.

This presentation of agricultural abundance continues with the promise that *fruit* trees will always produce and the fields of *the earth* will yield good crops. Even more important is the promise of safety. In ancient times crop production is long, tedious work. It is not unknown for enemies to sweep down at harvesttime and confiscate a community's food without having done any of the work. This leaves the farmers in a condition of famine (see Judges 6:11). In the prophesied kingdom of peace, there will be no danger from harvesttime marauders. [See question #4, page 240.]

27b. And shall know that I am the LORD, when I have broken the bands of their yoke, and delivered them out of the hand of those that served themselves of them.

The understanding of God's sovereignty will dawn upon the people when they experience their freedom from bondage. The expression *served themselves of them* refers to those who enslave the people. What is envisaged, then, is a new exodus, a freeing of the people of Israel from a new Egypt. In this case, it is release of the exiles from Babylon so they may return to Jerusalem.

C. Land of Safety (vv. 28, 29)

28. And they shall no more be a prey to the heathen, neither shall the beast of the land devour them; but they shall dwell safely, and none shall make them afraid.

This future is now summed up. The people are to live in safety from both human enemies and dangerous animals. They will live in security, an existence without fear. This is not based on their own power or ingenuity, but on the power and protection of their God, the Lord.

29. And I will raise up for them a plant of renown, and they shall be no more consumed with hunger in the land, neither bear the shame of the heathen any more.

The idea of *a plant of renown* is that of amazingly productive harvests. This is presented as more than diligent farming. It is a blessing of God, a supernatural yield of produce.

There will be two results of this abundance. First, hunger will become no more than a memory, for there will always be enough to eat. Second, Israel will gain a new reputation, a new respect from the other nations. She will no longer be a laughingstock (see Psalm 44:13, 14). All of this is a way of describing the "showers of blessing" (v. 26).

III. Flock of God
(Ezekiel 34:30, 31)

A. They Are My People (v. 30)

30. Thus shall they know that I the LORD their God am with them, and that they, even the house of Israel, are my people, saith the Lord GOD.

This future restoration and covenant of peace will be the ultimate sign of God's continuing promise to *Israel,* God's *people.* It is difficult to see all of these promises being fulfilled when some of the exiles are allowed to return to Jerusalem after 538 BC. At that time, the returnees experience harassment from surrounding peoples, crop failure, and a generally tenuous existence. Therefore, we must remember that there is a mixture in this passage of the hoped-for restoration of Jerusalem and the creation of the future messianic kingdom.

While God's covenant with Israel is important, it is not the same thing as God's new covenant with the people of His Christ, the church. For this group, the Jerusalem temple is not essential since God dwells among His people. The people

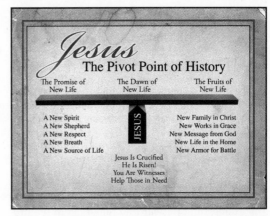

Visual for Lesson 2. *Keep this chart posted the entire quarter so your students can have an overall perspective on these studies.*

of God in the church may truly claim the promise, "I will be their God, and they shall be my people" (2 Corinthians 6:16, from Ezekiel 37:27). [See question #5, page 240.]

B. I Am Their God (v. 31)

31. And ye my flock, the flock of my pasture, are men, and I am your God, saith the Lord GOD.

This prophetic word concludes by coming back to the language of sheep and shepherds. The relationship is clarified bluntly. Just as a shepherd cares for his *flock* of sheep, God cares for His flock of people. No reason is needed to justify this beyond God's declaration.

This is a statement of one of the most beautiful pictures of our relationship with God found in the Bible, a view that appears frequently. The psalmist writes, "We are the people of his pasture, and the sheep of his hand" (Psalm 95:7). Jesus applies the shepherd role to himself, for He teaches that He is "the good shepherd," willing to die for His sheep (John 10:11). Peter writes that Jesus continues this role even after His resurrection, for Christ remains as the shepherd of our souls (1 Peter 2:25).

Furthermore, Peter understands that the role of the Shepherd-Messiah will not be fully realized until Christ comes again. At that time we will see something more than agricultural abundance or safety. At that time, "the chief Shepherd" shall appear to award us a "crown of glory that fadeth not away" (1 Peter 5:4).

POSITIONS

Sometimes people need to be reminded of their position. At the time when my sister lost her husband a number of years ago, her college-age daughter was living with her. After a while my sister began to go on a few dates with a male acquaintance. Her daughter, who was also dating, stated, "Mom, this is great! You have your boyfriend, and I have mine. We can be just like roommates!" My sister then had to sit her daughter down and explain, "I am the mother; you are the daughter. We are not equals in this arrangement." My niece did not like it, but it was necessary to establish who was in charge.

A friend of mine completed his graduate work some time ago. At his oral exams, one of his professors, with whom he had developed a very good relationship, asked some very probing questions that my friend was unable to answer. He passed his exams, but afterward he remarked to the professor about the difficulty of the questions. The professor answered, "Sometimes it's just necessary to establish who is the professor and who is the student."

Adam and Eve were tempted by the possibility that they could become God-like. At the Tower of Babel the people conspired to reach up to Heaven. Sometimes it is necessary for God to remind us that He is God, and we are not. Ezekiel summarizes this passage by stating that we are men, but He is God.   —J. B. N.

Conclusion

A. The Peaceable Kingdom

It must have been easy for the people in exile to conclude either that God was powerless to help Israel or that God had abandoned Israel. We can feel Israel's anguish as expressed in the psalms of the exile. "By the rivers of Babylon, there we sat down, yea, we wept, when we remembered Zion" (Psalm 137:1). "How shall we sing the Lord's song in a strange land?" (Psalm 137:4). Yet God had neither forgotten Israel nor had He forsaken His covenant with them. God was still at work with His plan.

Edward Hicks (1780–1849) depicted God's promise in the painting *The Peaceable Kingdom.* Hicks actually painted several dozen versions of this theme. While Hicks's technique may seem childish to us now, almost cartoonlike, he gives us a beautiful vision of a world at peace. It is a world where babies can play with wild animals and where people of different races can sit down and eat together. Hicks took his inspiration from our lesson's passage and others that present God's future kingdom of peace (see, for example, Isaiah 11:6-9).

Hicks was a Quaker minister, and he had a deep appreciation for the messianic promises of the Bible. He worked in the early days of the new American republic, and he shared the belief that this new nation might be the manifestation of God's millennial kingdom. While this view may have faded over the following decades, Christians should not lose faith in God's promises. We are to live expectantly, with a daily hope that God will act dramatically in the world of humans to advance His kingdom. We are to live confidently, understanding God's love for us and His protective, nurturing grace. And we are to live fearlessly, with the realization that God is far more powerful than our enemies and that our future is secure in His hands.

We can and must live this way despite the fact that God probably will not let us "figure out" the exact details of yet-to-be fulfilled prophecies. This is the essence of a life of faith.

B. Prayer

Loving God, when we read Ezekiel we can feel the anguish that the exiles must have felt in Babylon. We also see how You cared for them and preserved them.

We now better appreciate Your plan for a Messiah, one who comes to save us, feed us, and protect us. We love You for Your grace and Your care for us, given with an abundance that is beyond our ability to comprehend. We thank You for always being faithful, even as we return unfaithfulness for your faithfulness. We pray these things in the name of the shepherd of our souls, Jesus Christ. Amen.

C. Thought to Remember

God's future is one of
abundance, safety, and peace.

Home Daily Bible Readings

Monday, Mar. 2—A Begotten Son (Psalm 2: 4-11)

Tuesday, Mar. 3—The Good Shepherd (John 10:11-18)

Wednesday, Mar. 4—Trusting in the Lord (Psalm 21:1-7)

Thursday, Mar. 5—An Enduring Throne (Psalm 45:1-7)

Friday, Mar. 6—A Righteous King (Psalm 72: 1-7)

Saturday, Mar. 7—An Exalted King (Psalm 110)

Sunday, Mar. 8—You Are My Sheep (Ezekiel 34:23-31)

Learning by Doing

This page contains an alternative lesson plan emphasizing learning activities. Some of these activities are also found in the helpful student book, Adult Bible Class.

Into the Lesson

Ask students to recall times when they received bad news—personal or otherwise—when they were away from home. Some may relate the sudden, unexpected death of a loved one. Others may recall a national tragedy such as the terrorist attacks of September 11, 2001.

After a few are offered, say, "The Jewish captives of Ezekiel's acquaintance received just such bad news: while they languished in a pagan land hundreds of miles from home, their beloved city of Jerusalem had fallen into enemy hands and had been ravaged. It was a hard time, a time of feeling hopeless and powerless, a time of despair. They needed good news . . . and Ezekiel had some, in today's text."

Into the Word

Set up the front of your room with a sign: "Interrogation Room." Recruit three actors to present the following skit. Have labels for the three: *A. Lamb, Good Shepherd,* and *Selfish Shepherd.* A gooseneck floor lamp will add the right ambience to the interrogation scene.

Arrange this setup: "A. Lamb" is seated beneath the lamp and the other two are standing closely over him/her. Give each a copy of the following script that uses ideas from the text in Ezekiel 34:23-31 and from the "bad shepherds of Israel" passage earlier in chapter 34. Have the three present this brief drama for later discussion and comparison to those texts.

Good Shepherd (GS): Tell me, Mr./Ms. Lamb, would you rather have one good shepherd or a whole bunch of mediocre ones?

A. Lamb (AL): Well, I just want someone who cares enough to feed and protect me.

Selfish Shepherd (SS): Whoa! Isn't it true, woolly one, that no matter who the shepherd is, you've gone your own way?

AL: Yes, but . . .

SS: You're not a ram, fleece face; you can't just go butting your way through life!

AL: I was going to say, I sometimes didn't know the way, but some of the shepherds I've had were more interested in their own well-being than in mine.

SS: Oh, like you're the center of the universe. You're just a lamb!

GS: You may be right, Mr./Ms. Lamb. Tell me exactly what you want in a shepherd.

AL: I want cool water and green grass . . . Enough to live . . . I want to feel loved and protected.

SS: *I, I, I*—that's all I'm hearing. Do you ever think about anyone else?

GS: Well, those are reasonable expectations, Selfish. Where, Lamb, do you feel your previous shepherds have failed you in those regards?

AL: Look where I am! A thousand miles from home, in a desert, with no likelihood of ever going back, and with sad news weekly coming from back there. A failure of godly leadership, I'd say.

SS: Whoa again! Hold on there. Blaming others for your predicament? What about your own sins? A little confession—that's all we're after here.

GS: Well, the truth *is* what we want. What is the truth, Mr./Ms. Lamb?

AL: The truth? I'm tired of being afraid—afraid of drought, of wild animals, of approaching armies, of my own evil rulers' shadows. Why do I have to be afraid? What's a shepherd for? All I want is one good shepherd! That's the truth, I confess.

Have someone read all of Ezekiel 34. Then ask the class to compare and contrast the skit with Ezekiel's description of the "shepherds of Israel" and the good shepherd that God describes.

Into Life

Obtain a copy of the lyrics for the song "I Have Confidence" from the musical *The Sound of Music.* (An Internet search will bring a quick copy.) Say, "Ezekiel's message to his people was one of confidence in the future because the future is in God's hands." Remind your class of Maria's sung affirmation (possibly playing a copy of the song aloud) and then ask, "Though Maria's challenge came about because of a hard circumstance—her being asked to leave the abbey—her plan was not without a flaw. What was wrong with Maria's plan?"

Of course, her ultimate comfort was the thought that she had confidence in herself, but such confidence ignores personal inadequacies and God's all-sufficiency. Challenge your class to "sing a different tune" this week, one affirming that they have confidence in God for His future, such as rewording Maria's song to be, "I have confidence in God's plan for my life. Besides which you see, He has confidence in me."

Let's Talk It Over

The questions on this page are designed to promote discussion of the lesson by the class and to encourage application of the lesson Scriptures. The answers provided are only discussion starters. Let your class talk it over from there.

1. How much of a temptation is it for you to try to see into the future by means of fortune-telling tools? What are legitimate ways for Christians to try to discover what the future holds?

Many Christians see no danger in such "harmless fun" as reading their horoscopes, having their palms read, or even playing around with a Ouija board. Yet God commanded the Israelites never to practice abominations such as fortune-telling or sorcery (Deuteronomy 18:10).

Since the Bible is full of information of what the future will be like, Christians can best spend their time by studying God's promises in His Word. We can also pray for the Holy Spirit to give us the wisdom we need to make right decisions that will affect our own futures.

2. How can the image of Jesus as our shepherd give us comfort today?

Although many of Ezekiel's people lived in miserable exile in Babylon (Psalm 137), Ezekiel was able to lift their spirits with the prophecy of a Messiah who would be their loving shepherd. Unlike the wicked shepherds of Ezekiel's day, who took care of only themselves (Ezekiel 34:1-6), we know that our shepherd has our best interests at heart.

When we are weak and helpless, Jesus won't abandon us or take advantage of us; instead, He feels compassion for us (Matthew 9:36). A selfish shepherd makes sure that his own needs are met (Jude 12). But Jesus, our shepherd, lovingly provides everything we need to live life and grow spiritually (2 Peter 1:3). Best of all, we can be confident that He cares for us because He was willing to lay down His life for us (John 10:11).

3. When was a time God showered you with blessings? What circumstances brought this about? What can we do to be more aware of blessings?

It's easy to become oblivious to the many ways that God blesses us each day. Often, the only time we are aware of our blessings is after we lose one of them. A healthy body is never appreciated more than after a prolonged time of illness.

Sometimes it is in the midst of suffering and trials that we are most aware that God is showering us with blessings. When we are grieving the loss of a loved one and our church family rallies round with cards, flowers, food, hugs, tears, and their comforting presence, we feel that God is showering us with blessings through our Christian friends. As we struggle under a financial burden and receive help for daily needs from a variety of sources, we praise God for the love He bestows on us. If we can begin to practice Paul's advice to give thanks in everything (1 Thessalonians 5:18), we can increase our ability to be grateful to God for all the ways He blesses our lives each day.

4. What modern dangers tend to prevent us from feeling safe in our land? How can we use the promises of God to help us feel more secure?

Living far from home and enslaved in a foreign land, the people of God were fearful and insecure. Ezekiel's prophecy that they would be able to dwell safely again in their own homeland must have been a great comfort to these exiles. Today we also need the comfort of God's promises to help us feel safe. Terrorist attacks have shattered our belief that we are safe. The potential of nuclear and germ warfare, plus the reality of moral deterioration of our society, further shake our confidence.

By remembering that we are "strangers and pilgrims on the earth" (Hebrews 11:13), we can gain a new perspective on our situation. While praying for our country and God's blessing on it, we know that our time here is temporary and our true home is in Heaven. The fate of the future of any nation and even the world itself is firmly in God's hands.

5. What are some ways that our church can show that we are God's people and He is our God?

As we take on the characteristics of God and His Son Jesus, we will demonstrate the fact that we are part of God's family. The most obvious way to do this is by obeying Jesus' command to love each other for "by this shall all men know that ye are my disciples" (John 13:35).

As Jesus reached out to social outcasts, so must we (Matthew 25:37-40). Even more importantly, we are to take to the world God's gospel message. He sent His Son to die so that we could be with Him for eternity (John 3:16). What better shepherd could there possibly be?

A New Respect

DEVOTIONAL READING: PSALM 25:11-22.

BACKGROUND SCRIPTURE: Ezekiel 36:22-32.

PRINTED TEXT: Ezekiel 36:22-32.

Ezekiel 36:22-32

22 Therefore say unto the house of Israel, Thus saith the Lord GOD; I do not this for your sakes, O house of Israel, but for mine holy name's sake, which ye have profaned among the heathen, whither ye went.

23 And I will sanctify my great name, which was profaned among the heathen, which ye have profaned in the midst of them; and the heathen shall know that I am the LORD, saith the Lord GOD, when I shall be sanctified in you before their eyes.

24 For I will take you from among the heathen, and gather you out of all countries, and will bring you into your own land.

25 Then will I sprinkle clean water upon you, and ye shall be clean: from all your filthiness, and from all your idols, will I cleanse you.

26 A new heart also will I give you, and a new spirit will I put within you: and I will take away the stony heart out of your flesh, and I will give you a heart of flesh.

27 And I will put my Spirit within you, and cause you to walk in my statutes, and ye shall keep my judgments, and do them.

28 And ye shall dwell in the land that I gave to your fathers; and ye shall be my people, and I will be your God.

29 I will also save you from all your uncleannesses: and I will call for the corn, and will increase it, and lay no famine upon you.

30 And I will multiply the fruit of the tree, and the increase of the field, that ye shall receive no more reproach of famine among the heathen.

31 Then shall ye remember your own evil ways, and your doings that were not good, and shall loathe yourselves in your own sight for your iniquities and for your abominations.

32 Not for your sakes do I this, saith the Lord GOD, be it known unto you: be ashamed and confounded for your own ways, O house of Israel.

GOLDEN TEXT: The heathen shall know that I am the LORD, saith the Lord GOD, when I shall be sanctified in you before their eyes.—Ezekiel 36:23.

Christard and Creation
The Promise of New Life
Lessons 1–5

Lesson Aims

After participating in this lesson, each student will be able to:

1. Tell what God promised to do for Israel, not for their sake, but for the sake of His own holy name.

2. Explain how a Christian's behavior can honor or profane God's name before other people.

3. Determine to honor God's name in one specific way.

Lesson Outline

Introduction

A. Reflective Reputations

Are good reputations important anymore? Our current culture seems to be endlessly infatuated with celebrities who obviously have no concern to maintain a good reputation. Their peccadilloes are paraded in public to a degree that would have been astonishing a generation ago. Rather than put forth even a façade of morality or wholesomeness, some celebrities court a reputation of self-ishness, arrogance, nonaccountability, and general naughtiness.

These obvious facts may lead us to think that "a good reputation" means nothing to a secular culture. But not so fast! The importance of good reputations has made a comeback with the rise of online auctions. There each transaction receives a feedback rating. Those who participate in this world value high positive ratings because this implies trustworthiness. Even a few negative feedbacks can damage a person's standing to the point that buyers will avoid bidding on his or her items.

To combat this, some sellers change their online identities frequently. Yet reputable auction sites have made this tactic difficult. Even in the relative anonymity of the Internet, a reputation for dishonesty may follow a person for a long time.

Growing up, children begin to understand very early that many factors contribute to a person's reputation. Are they mean or kind? Do they tell the truth or tell lies? Can they keep a secret or do they blab it to everyone? These and many other points of natural evaluation are things that form the opinion of their peers about them. In most places the actions of children reflect positively or negatively on their parents. If children are out of control, sullen, and defiant, teachers may assume that their parents are neglectful and inadequate. If children are respectful, cooperative, and happy, teachers will assume that the parents are good people doing a good job.

The Bible teaches that our actions as the people of God reflect upon the Lord God himself. If we are His disobedient or discontented children, then nonbelievers will see our God in a negative light. God's holiness will not allow for this, so He takes remedial action to purge evil from His people. This is what happened to Israel in the time of Ezekiel.

B. Lesson Background

Ezekiel taught that God is very protective of His holy name (Ezekiel 39:25). We may wonder why a name is so important to God. In the biblical world, a person's name was synonymous with that person's reputation. The Bible speaks of glorifying God's name (Psalm 86:9), singing to God's name (Psalm 68:4), praising the name of God (Psalm 99:3), etc. All of these are ways of recognizing the good reputation of God's name and drawing on its power for our lives. We can see the power of the name in the remarkable reference to the Lord's name as "a strong tower," a refuge for the righteous (Proverbs 18:10).

It is for these reasons that the name of the Lord is to be guarded as holy. It is not to be profaned

(Leviticus 22:32) or to be used in vain (Exodus 20:7). These values are (or should be) still important to the people of God. We should treat the name of our God with enormous respect, for this is a sign of our true relationship to Him. Likewise, we should not engage in behaviors that reflect poorly on our God, behaviors that sully His holy name. Hearing people flippantly say "Oh, my God!" should cause us to cringe.

I. The Lord's Holy Name (Ezekiel 36:22, 23)

A. God's Name Profaned (v. 22)

22. Therefore say unto the house of Israel, Thus saith the Lord GOD; I do not this for your sakes, O house of Israel, but for mine holy name's sake, which ye have profaned among the heathen, whither ye went.

A recurring theme in Ezekiel is God's charge that Israel has *profaned* His name (see Ezekiel 20:39; 36:20; 43:8). God has determined that these days are over, and He will no longer allow His name to be defiled (Ezekiel 39:7; 43:7).

Israel is known as the people of its God, the Lord. Yet the behavior of the nation has reflected poorly on her God. The people have created a society that tolerates the random shedding of blood; they also accept the worship of foreign gods and idols (Ezekiel 36:18).

Although God loves the people of Israel, He is unwilling to have His reputation trashed by this society, which shows no respect for Him. The *house of Israel* has forgotten its heritage, its origin, and its covenant (Jeremiah 2:32; Ezekiel 22:12). The Israelites have become just like the

---

How to Say It

ABRAHAM. *Ay*-bruh-ham.
ABRAM. *Ay*-brum.
BABYLONIAN. Bab-ih-*low*-nee-un.
BEATITUDE. Bee-*a*-tuh-tood (*a* as in *mat*).
CORNUCOPIA. kor-nuh-*ko*-pea-uh.
DICHOTOMY. die-*kah*-tuh-me.
EZEKIEL. Ee-*zeek*-ee-ul or Ee-*zeek*-yul.
EZRA. *Ez*-ruh.
ISAIAH. Eye-*zay*-uh.
ISRAELITES. *Iz*-ray-el-ites.
JEREMIAH. Jair-uh-*my*-uh.
LEVITICUS. Leh-*vit*-ih-kus.
NEHEMIAH. *Nee*-huh-*my*-uh (strong accent on *my*).
ZECHARIAH. *Zek*-uh-*rye*-uh (strong accent on *rye*).

---

other nations (Ezekiel 25:8). [See question #1, page 248.]

B. God's Name Sanctified (v. 23)

23. And I will sanctify my great name, which was profaned among the heathen, which ye have profaned in the midst of them; and the heathen shall know that I am the LORD, saith the Lord GOD, when I shall be sanctified in you before their eyes.

The immoral and ungodly conduct of Israel has left God with no alternative but to *sanctify* His *name* by himself. It will be God's actions that will cause the pagan nations to know the power of His name, to know that He is *the Lord*.

To sanctify means "to make holy, to consecrate." We as Christians should understand that we have a responsibility to guard the holiness of God's name. Our actions should not defile the Lord's reputation in the eyes of unbelievers. This is why Jesus taught us to pray to God, "Hallowed be thy name" (Matthew 6:9). The importance of this is shown in that it is the first request of the Lord's Prayer.

In the New Testament, this respect for God's name is extended to Jesus. The name of Jesus is powerful (Acts 3:6; 4:10); His name is associated with holiness (Acts 4:30). It is the power of the name of Jesus that sanctifies and justifies us as believers (1 Corinthians 6:11). [See question #2, page 248.]

CITY ON A HILL

John Winthrop was a Puritan leader in England who became interested in the possibility of establishing a colony in the New World. Chosen as governor of the colony in 1629, he came with the original settlers to the shores of North America in 1630. The voyage across the Atlantic was a tempestuous one, as were virtually all Atlantic crossings in that day. Along the way, Winthrop preached a sermon to the colonists, a sermon that set the course for the future colony.

Winthrop reminded the people that they had to form a community and work together as a unit. "Wee shall be as a Citty upon a Hill," he said, and "the eies of all people are uppon us." If they failed, they would become a story and a byword throughout the world and open the mouths of enemies to speak evilly of the ways of God and all those who professed to follow Him. In order to preserve the colony, they had to follow God's will and thus become a testimony to others. If they failed, God would evict them from the land.

Winthrop's message was that if they were faithful, God would demonstrate to the world His goodness, and pagans would see this as a witness to God's blessing. "Therefore lett us choose life, that wee, and our Seede, may live; by obeying his voice, and cleaveing to him, for hee is our life, and our prosperity." Do these words of more than 300 years ago still have relevance?   —J. B. N.

II. The Lord's Holy People (Ezekiel 36:24-28)

A. Renewed Residence (v. 24)

24. For I will take you from among the heathen, and gather you out of all countries, and will bring you into your own land.

God's primary witness to the pagans is the people He has chosen to be His unique nation— Israel. For the world to understand the nature of a holy God, it is important for His people to be holy themselves. Because of the disgrace and humiliation of the Babylonian exile, this will require total renewal.

The first stage of this renewal process is to be a gathering of the people back to the *land* that was promised to their forefather Abraham (who was previously known as Abram; Genesis 12:7). God intends that this land be occupied by righteous people (Psalm 37:29; Isaiah 60:21). This is reflected in the third Beatitude of Jesus, which promises blessing for the "meek," for they are promised an inheritance of the "earth" or land (Matthew 5:5).

B. Renewed Cleanness (v. 25)

25. Then will I sprinkle clean water upon you, and ye shall be clean: from all your filthiness, and from all your idols, will I cleanse you.

Most of us take *clean water* for granted. We have municipal water supplies that provide abundant, drinkable water from the faucets in our homes. In the ancient world, though, clean water is not as common. Community wells can be brackish, and water from streams may be muddy. Water stored in cisterns becomes disgusting and unhealthy over time. Clean water comes from pristine springs or from rainfall. Good water is seen as a blessing from God (see Numbers 21:16).

This image of renewal is employed by Paul when he speaks of the church being cleansed by water. This water is "the word"; its cleansing power makes the church a perfect bride, "holy and without blemish" (Ephesians 5:26, 27). In the Gospel of John, the figure of "living water" is used for the renewing power of the Holy Spirit (John 7:38, 39).

We are still exceedingly capable of defiling ourselves by worshiping abhorrent *idols*. We may not bow down to carved images of wood as the ancient Israelites did, but allowing anything to displace God on the throne of our hearts is idol worship just the same. True spiritual cleansing must come from God, for even our best efforts at holiness are inadequate (see Isaiah 64:6). [See question #3, page 248.]

C. Renewed Heart (v. 26)

26. A new heart also will I give you, and a new spirit will I put within you: and I will take away the stony heart out of your flesh, and I will give you a heart of flesh.

The renewal project of God includes a "heart transplant." In the Bible, the *heart* is the seat of the will. A hard, *stony heart* is one that has defiantly aligned itself against God and rejects obedience to God's will.

To have a *heart of flesh,* by contrast, means that Israel will have a pliant heart, a will submissive to God. This is also expressed as the presence of the *new spirit,* which is the inner renewal granted by God. Earlier, Ezekiel had prophesied that this new spirit and heart would allow Israel to be considered God's people again (Ezekiel 11:19, 20). [See question #4, page 248.]

D. Renewed Spirit (v. 27)

27. And I will put my Spirit within you, and cause you to walk in my statutes, and ye shall keep my judgments, and do them.

The idea of a renewed human spirit is the subject of Ezekiel's experience in the valley of dry bones (chapter 37, next week's lesson). But the idea of the verse at hand is that of renewal by God's Holy Spirit (Ezekiel 39:29). The ultimate fulfillment of this prediction comes on the Day of Pentecost (see Acts 2:17, 18, which quotes Joel 2:28, 29).

E. Renewed Promise (v. 28)

28. And ye shall dwell in the land that I gave to your fathers; and ye shall be my people, and I will be your God.

God's renewal plan includes restoring Israel to *the land.* This restoration will bring things full circle, making good (again!) on the promise to Abraham (see 1 Chronicles 16:16-18). It is with this return that the land of Canaan will become more than the "promised land"; it is to be seen as the "holy land" (Zechariah 2:12). This designation is still in common use today to refer to Jerusalem and its environs.

The oft-repeated goal of God's plan is given again at the end of this section: *ye shall be my people, and I will be your God.* This was the original intention of God when He freed Israel from the bondage of Egypt, over 900 years prior to this point (Exodus 6:7). This picture appears again near the end of the book of Revelation, where God and His people are united eternally and perfectly.

This promise still resonates with us today, for the church is made up of the people of God. We are His people, and He is our God in every possible way. We, like Israel, are called to guard the holiness of God's name, to protect His reputation from disrepute (Romans 2:24; 2 Thessalonians 1:12).

III. The Lord's Holy Land (Ezekiel 36:29-32)

A. Land of Productivity (vv. 29, 30)

29. I will also save you from all your uncleannesses: and I will call for the corn, and will increase it, and lay no famine upon you.

It is common for people who take a pilgrimage trip to modern Palestine to bring home some soil from the Holy Land. Yet there is nothing magical about this dirt. It does not glow in the dark or cure diseases. The land of Israel in ancient times is not holy because it is enchanted. It is holy because of God's plan for Israel.

Evidence of God's blessing will include abundant *corn,* ensuring that there will be *no famine.* Corn in this sense is not a term for yellow maize, for this field crop came from the western hemisphere and is unknown in Europe or Asia until after the time of Columbus. Rather, the word *corn* refers to field crops in general, such as wheat, millet, lentils, and barley. Crops such as these form the foundation for the food supply of any agricultural society.

30. And I will multiply the fruit of the tree, and the increase of the field, that ye shall receive no more reproach of famine among the heathen.

A rich diet depends on various produce from cultivated orchards of trees. In Ezekiel's time, this includes olives, figs, pomegranates, and dates, as well as nuts such as almonds. In God's renewed and sanctified land, there is to be an abundance of these delightful foods too. None of the surrounding nations, *the heathen,* will be able to criticize or ridicule Israel or Israel's God because of agricultural failure. God's reputation thus will be further enhanced among the nations.

INCREASE OF THE FIELD

California is an amazing place. We associate California with large cities, Hollywood, and beaches. It has all these, to be sure, but it is also the leading agricultural state of the U.S. California has a larger variety of crops and higher yields

Visual for Lessons 3 & 4. *Point to this visual as you ask, "How does the beauty of a sunrise or sunset remind you of the nature of God?"*

per acre than any other state. Its highly automated rice industry produces three times the yield of the labor-intensive paddies in Asia.

The state produces almost the entire national crop of walnuts, almonds, olives, figs, dates, nectarines, pomegranates, and persimmons. It leads the nation in the production of vegetables. California is the nation's leading producer of hay. The state leads the nation in egg and milk production and ranks high in the marketing of cattle and other livestock.

But this has not always been the case. Almost all the above are produced on irrigated land, California having the largest amount of irrigated land in the nation. Until the irrigation systems of the 1930s were developed, much of California was untilled. The soil was fertile, but without water little could be grown. The availability of water has produced a veritable cornucopia of agricultural produce.

Such bounty brings with it the risk of arrogance. Remember: God is the source of all goodness. All human creativity used in bringing about greater abundance exists because of God's permission. And God can withdraw His permission at any time.   —J. B. N.

B. Land of Bad Memories (v. 31)

31. Then shall ye remember your own evil ways, and your doings that were not good, and shall loathe yourselves in your own sight for your iniquities and for your abominations.

Sometimes we do not realize how sick we have been until we get healthy again. In the case of the Israelites, God foresees that His plans for restoration will cause them to be ashamed of their wicked past. They have presumed upon His grace and have caused Him great pain and embarrassment. There will come days when the people of Israel realize what a great disappointment they have been to their Lord (compare Ezra 3:12; Nehemiah 8:9).

When we understand that we have hurt someone deeply, we can have one of two reactions. We can determine that we do not care and harden our hearts against any feelings of remorse. Or we can experience a deep sense of self-loathing that is the beginning of true repentance. This is the godly sorrow that Paul spoke of to the Corinthian church (2 Corinthians 7:10). [See question #5, page 248.]

C. Land of Former Shame (v. 32)

32. Not for your sakes do I this, saith the Lord GOD, be it known unto you: be ashamed and confounded for your own ways, O house of Israel.

There is a bottom line to all of this that may not be completely understandable either to the exiles or to us. This is because we naturally tend to be self-centered and inwardly focused. What God is saying is that the issue is not all about *Israel*. Rather, it is about God and His own purposes. Even without full understanding of this, there will be shame.

When we come to true repentance, we gain an inkling of the pain we have caused God. But we can only imagine how deep this hurt must be. Yet even our imperfect understanding of our shame can help us be determined not to disappoint Him any longer. It is with this renewed heart and spirit that we can begin to serve Him in a worthy manner.

Conclusion

A. The Holy Lifestyle

The holiness of God is so absolute that we are unable to comprehend it fully. Yet it is an essential characteristic in our understanding of our creator and our relationship with Him. God acts from the depths of the utter holiness of His nature.

In the Bible, holiness has two aspects. Holiness includes purity, moral cleanness. In this sense, *holy* is the opposite of *sinful*. But there is another, very important part to biblical holiness. To be holy includes the idea of separation or separateness. God is not the same as His creation. He is separate and holy. He dwells in His holy Heaven (see Deuteronomy 26:15; Psalm 20:6). God is the "Holy One of Israel," a favorite expression of Isaiah (see 12:6).

This idea of holiness as "separateness" is at the core of the Christian life. The followers of Christ

should be known for their different lifestyle in light of the increasing sinfulness of our world. Yet surveys show that there is not much difference between evangelical Christians and the rest of the world when it comes to things like premarital sex, adultery, and divorce. Many things that were considered morally unacceptable a generation ago have found a comfortable home in the lives of church members.

Judson Van DeVenter (1855–1939) wrote the words to a hymn that has been used as an invitation song for thousands of evangelistic services: "I Surrender All." This classic of the faith is a prayer of submission to Jesus as Lord. The phrase "worldly pleasures all forsaken" of the hymn is in tune with this lesson. This is a great expression of the desire to live the holy life.

The lifestyle of a Christian should be visibly different to the nonbeliever. This is to be so even at the risk of coming across as "holier than thou." The reason for such a lifestyle is that the Christian serves a holy master and strives for personal holiness. In this way, we show respect for the holiness of our God's name and seek to bring respect to Him by others.

B. Prayer

Holy Father, we are the ones who violate Your holiness by our sin. We are the ones who cause the need for renewal by our disobedience. We are the ones who must live with the bad memories of our past follies. May You forgive us. May You renew us. May You sanctify us. We pray this in the name of Your Holy Son, Jesus the sinless one, amen.

C. Thought to Remember

God's plans include your holiness.

Home Daily Bible Readings

Monday, Mar. 9—Restored with God's Help (Psalm 60:1-5, 11, 12)

Tuesday, Mar. 10—Restored to Be Saved (Psalm 80:1-7)

Wednesday, Mar. 11—Restored to Our Salvation (Psalm 85:1-9)

Thursday, Mar. 12—Restored to God (Lamentations 5:15-21)

Friday, Mar. 13—Restored Through Repentance (Jeremiah 31:7-9, 16-20)

Saturday, Mar. 14—Restored to Service (Jeremiah 15:15-21)

Sunday, Mar. 15—For the Sake of God's Name (Ezekiel 36:22-32)

Learning by Doing

This page contains an alternative lesson plan emphasizing learning activities. Some of these activities are also found in the helpful student book, Adult Bible Class.

Into the Lesson

Display a simple, cartoon-like figure with a conversation balloon over her/his head. In that balloon write several of the symbols typically used to "disguise" bad language, such as #!&*!$#.

Ask, "Without suggesting specific words, what does such a string of symbols represent?" When someone suggests that they can indicate a person cursing and/or taking the name of the Lord in vain, say, "Yes, and that's part of today's study. But in what other ways do people profane the name of the Lord?" Let learners respond, then move directly to a look at today's text in Ezekiel 36.

Into the Word

To set up the discussion of today's text, assign these references in Ezekiel to different learners, to be read aloud in sequence: 20:39; 36:20; 43:8; 39:7; 43:7. At the end say, "God will defend His honor. He will defend His name. What God does in history is related to His love for His people, but it is first of all to demonstrate who He is." Move to verse 22 of the text.

If you do not use the student books that accompany this series, give your class a markable photocopy of today's text. Say, "In today's text God delineates a covenant He will make with His people. The text is filled with His *I will's*. Go through and underline all the things about which God says, 'I will.'" The preface *I will* (a few times inverted) occurs numerous times in verses 23 through 30.

Let that phenomenon impress your learners, and then say, "When a person understands what God is willing to do, his or her only response will be that of verse 31." Ask a reader to read that aloud. Continue, "Whenever a person sees the goodness and grace of God, the result is a quick awareness of one's own evil ways and wicked deeds. That is the beginning of repentance!"

Say, "Verse 26 speaks of the transformation God will make, if His people truly want to change: He will turn their hearts of stone (being hardhearted) into hearts of flesh (being soft, compassionate, and loving)." Give your learners the following puzzle to solve. They are to start with the word *stone*, then change one letter in the double-underlined position to make a new (real) word for line 2. They are to continue to make similar changes one letter at a time until ending up with the word *flesh*.

```
        S  T  O  N  E
line 2:  __ __ __ == __
line 3:  __ __ == __ __
line 4:  __ __ __ == __
line 5:  __ == __ __ __
line 6:  == __ __ __ __
line 7:  __ __ __ == __
line 8:  __ __ __ __ ==
line 9:  == __ __ __ __
line 10: __ __ __ == __
line 11: __ __ __ __ __
        F  L  E  S  H
```

(The words will be *STORE, STARE, STATE, SLATE, PLATE, PLANE, PLANK, FLANK, FLASK, FLASH*.) Say, "Though some find such a puzzle difficult and exasperating, God finds such changes—from His perspective—easy. And His offer is really to make our difficult changes easy by His Spirit."

Ask your class to identify the either-or dichotomies in each of the verses. For example, in verse 22, God's name will be holy or it will be profaned; in verse 23, the pagans will know God by the behaviors of His people or they will not; in verse 24, either aliens in a strange land or natives at home; in verse 25, either filthy or clean; in verse 26, heart of stone or heart of flesh; verse 27, Spirit-filled or spiritless; verse 28, not a people or the people of God; verse 29, increase (plenty) or famine; verse 30, prosperity or reproach; verse 31, remembering sin or living in it; verse 32, God's glory or Israel's glory. Your class may identify other contrasts.

Into Life

Many traditional hymns and choruses reflect the honor due to the name of the Lord. "Blessed Be the Name" by William Clark and Ralph E. Hudson is one. Recruit a musical class member to lead the class in singing the significant challenges of that song. Then challenge the class: "In what way this week can you honor the name of the Lord? In what way will you do so?"

A common challenge to children in Christian families has been, "Remember who and whose you are!" It is a challenge related to name: the family name and the name of God. Give this challenge to all students as they depart.

Let's Talk It Over

The questions on this page are designed to promote discussion of the lesson by the class and to encourage application of the lesson Scriptures. The answers provided are only discussion starters. Let your class talk it over from there.

1. How can we bring honor to God's name?

Try music! Whether worshiping with fellow believers in church, listening to a Christian radio station on the way to work, or singing as we clean house or do yard work, we can make use of our many opportunities to use music to magnify God's name. Even those without any musical ability can listen to Christian music and agree with the message in their hearts.

More subtle ways to honor God's name would include speaking well of the church and of other Christians, being a good neighbor, practicing financial responsibility, having strong marriages and godly families, and any other actions that reflect well on the God we serve.

2. What can parents do to teach their children to treat God's name with respect?

First of all, parents should be careful to watch their own language. If a slip-up does happen, a quick acknowledgment of what shouldn't have been said and a brief explanation of why it was wrong will also help teach respect for the names of God and Jesus.

Beyond that, parents can be vigilant in monitoring the TV programs, movies, and music that their children are exposed to. When the family is together in public or watching entertainment and profanity is used, there can be a discussion of why their family doesn't use such language. Even discouraging children from developing friendships with other children who are especially prone to bad language can help keep them from developing such habits.

3. What are some blessings of being cleansed by God?

God will not allow any unclean thing in His holy presence. Anyone with the stain of sin will not be able to know God or be close to Him. But the cleansing God provides through the blood of His Son is thorough and complete; it washes away all our sins (1 John 1:7). Through Jesus we have access to God; we even can come into His presence with "boldness" (Ephesians 3:12).

As part of God's family we can bring our requests to the Father with confidence that He will "give [us] good things" because we are His children

(Matthew 7:11). In addition, we have the presence of God's Spirit in our lives and the guidance of God's Word to help keep us "clean" (John 15:3).

4. Which experiences in life cause us to harden our hearts toward God? What can we do to keep them soft and responsive to His Holy Spirit?

Anytime we allow sin to get a foothold in our lives, we begin to harden ourselves against the Holy Spirit and turn a deaf ear to Him (Hebrews 3:8). Our hearts are unreceptive to God's mercy especially when we deny that what we're doing is wrong or make excuses for our actions (1 John 1:8). Allowing the busyness of life to keep us away from church services and personal devotional times makes our hearts a little harder.

Confessing our sins as they occur will help our hearts be more receptive toward the Lord (1 John 1:9). Being willing not only to forgive those who hurt us but also to be kind to them and pray for them will give us tender hearts that are more like the heart of Jesus (Luke 6:27, 28). We can pray David's prayer: "Create in me a clean heart, O God; and renew a right spirit within me" (Psalm 51:10).

5. Once our sins have been forgiven, what benefit is there in continuing to remember them, if any? Is there danger in spending too much time remembering and regretting our sins? Explain.

The Israelites were encouraged to "remember [their] own evil ways" so that they would hate them and repent. Remembering what our lives were like before we experienced God's mercy makes us aware of how much He has done for us. In addition, we are able to use our testimony of the transformation that Christ brought about in our lives to share our stories with both believers and nonbelievers. Paul called to mind his own sins at times (example: 1 Timothy 1:13).

The danger comes when remembering our past sins causes us to condemn ourselves. Once sins are forgiven, our lives should be characterized by joy, not mourning. In Christ "old things are passed away; behold, all things are become new" (2 Corinthians 5:17). Spending too much time dwelling on past sins allows Satan to be our accuser (Revelation 12:10) instead of realizing that there is "no condemnation" of Christ's followers (Romans 8:1).

A New Breath

DEVOTIONAL READING: Romans 6:1-14.

BACKGROUND SCRIPTURE: Ezekiel 37.

PRINTED TEXT: Ezekiel 37:1-14.

Ezekiel 37:1-14

1 The hand of the LORD was upon me, and carried me out in the Spirit of the LORD, and set me down in the midst of the valley which was full of bones,

2 And caused me to pass by them round about: and, behold, there were very many in the open valley; and, lo, they were very dry.

3 And he said unto me, Son of man, can these bones live? And I answered, O Lord GOD, thou knowest.

4 Again he said unto me, Prophesy upon these bones, and say unto them, O ye dry bones, hear the word of the LORD.

5 Thus saith the Lord GOD unto these bones; Behold, I will cause breath to enter into you, and ye shall live:

6 And I will lay sinews upon you, and will bring up flesh upon you, and cover you with skin, and put breath in you, and ye shall live; and ye shall know that I am the LORD.

7 So I prophesied as I was commanded: and as I prophesied, there was a noise, and behold a shaking, and the bones came together, bone to his bone.

8 And when I beheld, lo, the sinews and the flesh came up upon them, and the skin covered them above: but there was no breath in them.

9 Then said he unto me, Prophesy unto the wind, prophesy, son of man, and say to the wind, Thus saith the Lord GOD; Come from the four winds, O breath, and breathe upon these slain, that they may live.

10 So I prophesied as he commanded me, and the breath came into them, and they lived, and stood up upon their feet, an exceeding great army.

11 Then he said unto me, Son of man, these bones are the whole house of Israel: behold, they say, Our bones are dried, and our hope is lost: we are cut off for our parts.

12 Therefore prophesy and say unto them, Thus saith the Lord GOD; Behold, O my people, I will open your graves, and cause you to come up out of your graves, and bring you into the land of Israel.

13 And ye shall know that I am the LORD, when I have opened your graves, O my people, and brought you up out of your graves,

14 And shall put my Spirit in you, and ye shall live, and I shall place you in your own land: then shall ye know that I the LORD have spoken it, and performed it, saith the LORD.

GOLDEN TEXT: I will lay sinews upon you, and will bring up flesh upon you, and cover you with skin, and put breath in you, and ye shall live; and ye shall know that I am the LORD.—Ezekiel 37:6.

Christ and Creation
The Promise of New Life
Lessons 1–5

Lesson Aims

After participating in this lesson, each student will be able to:

1. Retell the story of Ezekiel's experience in the valley of the dry bones.

2. State some reasons a believer may feel spiritually dry—like the dry bones in Ezekiel's vision.

3. Write a prayer for personal spiritual renewal.

Lesson Outline

INTRODUCTION
    A. Dry Times
    B. Lesson Background
I. BONE-DRY SPIRIT (Ezekiel 37:1-3)
    A. The Valley of No Hope (vv. 1, 2)
        Culture Shock
    B. The Question of Hope (v. 3)
II. RECOVERING SPIRIT (Ezekiel 37:4-8)
    A. Preaching to the Dead (vv. 4-6)
    B. Reaction of the Dead (vv. 7, 8)
III. RENEWED SPIRIT (Ezekiel 37:9-14)
    A. Preaching to the Wind (v. 9)
    B. The Wind Giving Life (v. 10)
        Dem Dry Bones
    C. The House Without Hope (v. 11)
    D. Preaching to the Hopeless (vv. 12, 13)
    E. The Dead Live Again (v. 14)
CONCLUSION
    A. Negotiating Death Valley
    B. Prayer
    C. Thought to Remember

Introduction

A. Dry Times

The word *dry* means different things in different contexts. If we are told that something is "dry," that may refer to infrequent rain, to a certain type of humor, or to a prohibition against the sale of alcoholic beverages.

If we speak of going through a *dry time* spiritually, however, the meaning is quickly grasped. Who hasn't had such a period, a time of discouragement when one's relationship with God seems to have grown stale? This can be brief, or it can grow deeper into a "dark night of the soul" experience, a time of depression without relief. These are dry times.

David hinted at having such a time in Psalm 63. That psalm relates his emotions while hiding in a wilderness area to escape an enemy. David wrote of his hiding places as a "dry and thirsty land" (Psalm 63:1). His life was at risk, and he had been driven away from his home. He longed to be back in Jerusalem to worship God in the sanctuary. Yet he met this dry time with a response that can teach us much. He did not wallow in discouragement, but he recalled that God had never abandoned him, that he had been in the shadow of God's protective wings (Psalm 63:7).

B. Lesson Background

The book of Ezekiel is known for its fabulous visual descriptions of the prophet's unique experiences. The opening scene of the book is the incredible vision of the fiery four living creatures accompanied by the famous "wheel in the middle of a wheel." This has been interpreted variously as an ancient account of visitation by aliens in a flying saucer, a description of a gigantic, heavenly war chariot, even as a metaphor of the relationship between faith and grace ("big wheel run by faith, little wheel run by de grace of God"). The book ends with a colossal vision of the new temple (Ezekiel 40:2 and following). Many elements of the visions of Ezekiel reappear later in the Bible's final book, Revelation.

Ezekiel is also known for his experiences with the Spirit of God. At times, the Spirit seemed to possess him, causing him to stand and speak (see Ezekiel 2:2). At other times the Spirit transported Ezekiel to new locations. In one case the prophet experienced this as being lifted by the hair and flown cross-country from Babylon to Jerusalem (Ezekiel 8:3).

Whether Ezekiel experienced these things as physical events or through God-given mental imagery we do not know. But we can be sure that they were very real, authentic experiences for him. He was left with no doubt that God was dealing with him spectacularly and using him for an important ministry.

These profound visions and deep experiences of the Spirit intersect dramatically in chapter 37, the focus of today's lesson. Here, Ezekiel is transported (physically? spiritually?) to a place he has never been and does not recognize. It is a valley, but not a lush river valley of verdant pastures and crops. It is, rather, a valley characterized by an extreme lack of moisture and by death. It has no living residents, only piles of dry bones. This is the horrifying setting for one of the Bible's greatest one-chapter dramas: a vision that continues to give hope to those who find themselves "in a dry and thirsty" land (Ezekiel 19:13).

Today's lesson occurs in or after the year 586 BC, since Ezekiel and the exiles already had received the devastating news of Jerusalem's desolation (Ezekiel 33:21). In the aftermath of this emotional knockout blow, Ezekiel began to give prophesies of a more hopeful nature. He ended chapter 36 with a promise that the future land of Israel would be as fertile and green as "the garden of Eden" (Ezekiel 36:35). Then Ezekiel experienced a land as far from the ideal of that garden as could be imagined, a true Death Valley.

I. Bone-Dry Spirit
(Ezekiel 37:1-3)
A. The Valley of No Hope (vv. 1, 2)

1a. The hand of the LORD was upon me, and carried me out in the Spirit of the LORD.

Ezekiel uses the expression *the hand of the Lord was upon me* to convey the impression that God has taken complete control of him (compare Ezekiel 1:3; 3:14, 22; 33:22; 40:1). Whether he feels excitement or dread at these times, he does not say. He apparently offers no resistance, and another visionary experience is under way. This one includes being transported to a locale of God's choosing.

1b. And set me down in the midst of the valley which was full of bones.

The word used for *valley* here indicates a broad, flat river valley, not a steep canyon with a stream at the bottom. Such places are normally ideal for crop cultivation, for the river guarantees a regular water supply. It is for this reason that civilization first flourished in the Nile River valley and in Mesopotamia. The latter is the broad fertile plain that is the valley of the Tigris and Euphrates Rivers.

Mesopotamia is also the exile home for Ezekiel and his congregation. This part of the world generally has a year divided into a dry season and a rainy season. During the height of the dry season, some smaller rivers run dry, but larger rivers continue with a minimal flow.

What Ezekiel experiences, however, does not seem to be a normal valley. This one is *full of bones*; it is a picture of death. It is presented as the site of a long-ago catastrophe. It is like a battlefield where those left alive (if any) have fled from the area before burying the dead. As a result, the bodies have been left exposed to the elements and to wild animals. All the flesh is gone, and only the bones remain.

CULTURE SHOCK

Folks who live in the United States are not used to seeing piles of human bones. When we bury people, we expect them to stay buried, their mortal remains never to be seen again. When bones are discovered—whether by excavating for a building or even when a farmer plows up a field—there is great concern about identifying those bones and relocating them properly.

Other cultures in the world don't have such concerns. I have visited cemeteries in Europe where ancient graves are dug up, the bones all piled together in a central place, and the ground reused for new burials. The bone piles sometimes contain the bones of scores of people. In the town of Hallstatt, Austria, space is so limited that people are given only 12 years of peaceful slumber in their graves before they are removed. A chapel in Evora, Portugal, has the bones of thousands of monks on public display. Crypts in Palermo and Rome offer similar viewings.

Most Americans find this somewhat macabre, perhaps even indecent. But that may say more about American culture than about the cultures of others. We may wonder if it was a "cultural shock" for Ezekiel to see all those bones in that valley. None of us should be startled that God can bring them back to life. That's God's specialty!—J. B. N.

2. And caused me to pass by them round about: and, behold, there were very many in the open valley; and, lo, they were very dry.

The Spirit gives the prophet a panoramic view of the bones strewn across the broad *valley*. Ezekiel notes that there are *very many*, as if the piles of bones extend as far as his eyes can see.

Ezekiel does not say what kind of bones he views. Since the dead are described as "these slain" in 37:9, the picture may indeed be that of a battlefield. If so, the bones may be of both humans and animals, for horses, mules, and sometimes camels are used in war campaigns. Ezekiel's only

---

How to Say It

DEUTERONOMY. Due-ter-*ahn*-uh-me.
ECCLESIASTES. Ik-*leez*-ee-*as*-teez (strong accent on *as*).
EUPHRATES. You-*fray*-teez.
EZEKIEL. Ee-*zeek*-ee-ul or Ee-*zeek*-yul.
JERUSALEM. Juh-*roo*-suh-lem.
MACABRE. muh-*cob*.
MESOPOTAMIA. *Mes*-uh-puh-*tay*-me-uh (strong accent on *tay*).
TIGRIS. *Tie*-griss.
XYLOPHONES. *zye*-luh-fonz (o as in own).

specific observation about the qualitative nature of the bones is that they are *very dry.* They have been parched by an unrelenting sun. There is not a hint of life in them.

This is apparently a cursed land of no water and acres of unburied dead. Ezekiel must wonder why God would bring him to such a hopeless place.

B. The Question of Hope (v. 3)

3. And he said unto me, Son of man, can these bones live? And I answered, O Lord GOD, thou knowest.

The *Lord* offers no explanation for the cause of the bone valley, and Ezekiel does not ask for one. Instead, *God* puts a question to the prophet: *Can these bones live?* On the surface, this question is ridiculous. It is like asking "Any survivors?" to the police officer who is surveying the wreckage of a small car that has been hit and demolished by a freight train. Reason, intuition, and common sense all say *No!* without hesitation.

Ezekiel, however, already has been through some extraordinary experiences via the hand of God. He therefore does not exhibit any impulse to say "of course not." Rather, he lets the Lord proceed with the experience, for Ezekiel trusts God and knows that there is a lesson in this bonefield. [See question #1, page 256.]

Ezekiel's patience is rewarded, as God shows him that the situation isn't as hopeless as it looks. But before Ezekiel receives that revelation, he is asked to perform an act of faith (next verse).

II. Recovering Spirit
(Ezekiel 37:4-8)

A. Preaching to the Dead (vv. 4-6)

4. Again he said unto me, Prophesy upon these bones, and say unto them, O ye dry bones, hear the word of the LORD.

God's instructions must seem as strange as His question! From Ezekiel's point of reckoning, there is no one present within miles to listen to any prophecy. But God commands Ezekiel to get to his primary vocation: preaching.

Countless generations of preachers since Ezekiel have joked about preaching to unresponsive congregations. But Ezekiel truly is being directed to preach to lifeless *bones.* It is as if a solitary preacher were to hold an evangelistic meeting in a deserted graveyard. [See question #2, page 256.]

5, 6. Thus saith the Lord GOD unto these bones; Behold, I will cause breath to enter into you, and ye shall live: and I will lay sinews upon you, and will bring up flesh upon you, and cover you with skin, and put breath in you, and ye shall live; and ye shall know that I am the LORD.

The message is simple: the dead will *live.* This is pictured as a reversal of the process of decay. The *sinews* will be reconstituted on the framework of the dry *bones.* These are the tendons and cartilages of the body. Other than the bones, these are the parts that resist decay the longest. Next, the *flesh* is to return. This is comprised of the muscles and internal organs of the body. Following that, the body will be recovered with protective *skin.* As the outer layer of any corpse, the skin is the first part to be consumed by carnivorous animals.

This process of body rebuilding includes God's promise to restore the bodies' *breath,* or that which will bring each body back to life (see Genesis 2:7). This spark of life can be given only by God. Unless God enlivens the bodies in this way, they are still corpses as if just killed in battle.

B. Reaction of the Dead (vv. 7, 8)

7. So I prophesied as I was commanded: and as I prophesied, there was a noise, and behold a shaking, and the bones came together, bone to his bone.

We are prone to forget that biblical visions are not just "video." They often contain an "audio" track. At this point Ezekiel just watches and listens. He sees the scattered *bones* reorder themselves and come into alignment. They make an enormous clatter as they reassemble, perhaps like a thousand xylophones being played at once. The bones are not moving from some inner bone intelligence. It is obvious to the prophet that the hand of God is causing all this to happen.

8. And when I beheld, lo, the sinews and the flesh came up upon them, and the skin covered them above: but there was no breath in them.

Everything is reconstituted and the decay of the corpses is completely reversed, but there everything stops. There is still *no breath* of life *in them.* It may seem to Ezekiel as if the old, dry field of battle has become simply a fresh site of carnage and death with newly dead bodies lying everywhere, ready to begin decaying again. There is one more act in God's drama of restoration, but it again requires that Ezekiel act in faith to God's command.

III. Renewed Spirit
(Ezekiel 37:9-14)

A. Preaching to the Wind (v. 9)

9. Then said he unto me, Prophesy unto the wind, prophesy, son of man, and say to the wind, Thus saith the Lord GOD; Come from the four

winds, O breath, and breathe upon these slain, that they may live.

Ezekiel already has preached to a field of bones, with amazing results. Next, God commands him to speak to *the wind*. *The four winds* signify the universal wind as directed by God himself (see Jeremiah 49:36; Revelation 7:1). The missing ingredient to this point in the story is God's animating *breath*, and this is where the four winds come in. The corpses are ready to come back to life.

B. The Wind Giving Life (v. 10)

10. So I prophesied as he commanded me, and the breath came into them, and they lived, and stood up upon their feet, an exceeding great army.

Earlier, Ezekiel had experienced the Spirit entering him and setting him on his own feet (see Ezekiel 2:2; 3:24). Now Ezekiel witnesses the power of God to do this with a vast multitude. As a result, the purpose of the revivified bones becomes clear: they are an *army*, an uncountable host for war. [See question #3, page 256.]

DEM DRY BONES

There's an old Negro spiritual, which some attribute to James Weldon Johnson, called "Dem Dry Bones." It's a somewhat humorous recounting of Ezekiel's vision and the need to "hear de word of de Lord." The song has often been used to teach anatomy to children, although some of the references are not precise. But for the purposes of teaching children the basics of the human skeleton, they suffice.

Your toe bone connected to your foot bone,
Your foot bone connected to your ankle bone,
Your ankle bone connected to your leg bone,
Your leg bone connected to your knee bone,
Your knee bone connected to your thigh bone,
Your thigh bone connected to your hip bone,
Your hip bone connected to your back bone,
Your back bone connected to your shoulder bone,
Your shoulder bone connected to your neck bone,
Your neck bone connected to your head bone.

And then, of course, *Dem bones gonna walk aroun'!*

The great fact in that last line is empowered by Ezekiel's preaching the word of the Lord. It is not clear that the basic purpose of this old spiritual is to emphasize the power of preaching, but it fits the theme of the context quite well. Ezekiel preached and the dry bones came together. He preached, and sinews, flesh, and skin appeared as well. He preached, and a whole army of reconstituted bodies stood up on their feet. Now that's empowered preaching!   —J. B. N.

Visual for Lessons 3 & 4. *Point to this visual as you ask, "What else in nature reminds you of the reality of God?"*

C. The House Without Hope (v. 11)

11. Then he said unto me, Son of man, these bones are the whole house of Israel: behold, they say, Our bones are dried, and our hope is lost: we are cut off for our parts.

God explains this dramatic experience to Ezekiel in straightforward terms. The dry *bones* symbolize the state of being of *Israel* at this point in history. The Israelites were once a united body, but that body has been *cut* to pieces. Even the most optimistic among the Israelites has no rational basis for *hope*. [See question #4, page 256.] As a nation, Israel seems to be as good as dead.

D. Preaching to the Hopeless (vv. 12, 13)

12. Therefore prophesy and say unto them, Thus saith the Lord GOD; Behold, O my people, I will open your graves, and cause you to come up out of your graves, and bring you into the land of Israel.

Yet *Israel* is not dead or forgotten in God's eyes. He still has plans for the nation and intends that the nation be restored. Just as dry and scattered bones can be transformed back into living bodies, so the dismembered and dispirited nation will be given new hope through Ezekiel's vision. Israel will live again.

13. And ye shall know that I am the LORD, when I have opened your graves, O my people, and brought you up out of your graves.

God's continuing purpose in Ezekiel is to bring His people to a full awareness and knowledge of Him. God is not to be disobeyed or ignored. He is the God of the universe who has chosen the Israelites to be His special possession from all the peoples of the earth (Deuteronomy 7:6). Just as God had created humankind from the literal dust of the earth, so He will recreate His holy nation from the figurative dust of the grave. [See question #5, page 256.]

Our perspective allows us to know the outcome of this plan, including the eventual return of some exiles to Jerusalem and the rebuilding of the temple. But for anyone speculating about this at the time of Ezekiel, such an outcome would seem ludicrous. Israel has been wiped from the map. In every possible way from a political standpoint, Israel has ceased to exist. She is a nation seemingly consigned to the scrap heap of history. For Israel to live again will be nothing short of miraculous.

E. The Dead Live Again (v. 14)

14. And shall put my Spirit in you, and ye shall live, and I shall place you in your own land: then shall ye know that I the LORD have spoken it, and performed it, saith the LORD.

This verse pushes the reader to a future time to look back on what has happened. After Israel is restored as a people, reoccupying its promised land, how can anyone doubt that this was accomplished through God's mighty hand? How will anyone be able to question God's mercy or His power?

God is willing that the evidence of His actions be tested by any foolish skeptics. *The Lord* has *spoken it*, that is, said what He is going to do in the future. The Lord has *performed it*, that is, done what He promised (looking back in the future to an accomplished action). When all that happens, surely Israel will know God in a way that will leave no room for doubt. In the darkest hours of the history of the people of Israel, God refuses to abandon them.

Home Daily Bible Readings

Monday, Mar. 16—God Will Do Something New (Isaiah 43:14-21)

Tuesday, Mar. 17—A New Strength (Isaiah 40:25-31)

Wednesday, Mar. 18—A New Covenant (Luke 22:14-23)

Thursday, Mar. 19—A New Creation (2 Corinthians 5:16-21)

Friday, Mar. 20—New Mercies Every Day (Lamentations 3:19-31)

Saturday, Mar. 21—A New Song (Psalm 40: 1-5)

Sunday, Mar. 22—You Shall Live! (Ezekiel 37:1-14)

Conclusion
A. Negotiating Death Valley

Fannie Crosby began life with personal tragedy. At age six months she was made blind as a result of incompetent treatment for an eye infection. When just a year old, her father died and left her mother as a 21-year-old widow with four little children. Despite Fannie's disability and disadvantages, she grew to be a woman of strong faith. She excelled in music, learning to play several instruments and to sing. Yet tragedy continued to follow her. She married, but her only child died in infancy.

Fannie dedicated herself to writing songs and hymns that would praise God and touch lives. She wrote over 9,000 hymns in her lifetime, some of which are still sung in churches today. Yet we can imagine that there were dry times for this marvelous Christian woman too. Did she ever question why God had allowed her to lose her sight? Why had she been assigned the lot of poverty as a child? How could God let her only child die?

Fannie Crosby answers these sorts of questions many places in her songs. One such place is drawn from Exodus 33:22, but seems to fit the story of Ezekiel and the valley of dry bones too. In the song, "He Hideth My Soul," Fannie wrote, *He hideth my soul in the cleft of the rock, that shadows a dry, thirsty land*. In this context, to hide means to protect. Even in the scorching, arid deserts of our lives, we are protected by God.

There are people in our churches with many stories to tell of these desert experiences. How do we negotiate our way through the figurative valley of death? We do so only because we know that God is with us (Psalm 23:4). Otherwise, we are ultimately alone in the world, without hope of restoration (compare Ecclesiastes 12:1). When those days threaten, we can recall one of the greatest of Jesus' many promises to His followers: "lo, I am with you alway" (Matthew 28:20). He will never abandon us. He gives us hope day by day, a hope that brings life from death.

B. Prayer

O God, we are so often parched and dry. Our souls falter. Doubts creep in. It seems that evil is winning and our efforts to serve You are ineffective. Give us a new empowerment from Your Spirit, a spiritual downpour for the soul. May our doubt be transformed into faith. May we, like the dry bones, hear Your Word and be encouraged. We pray this in the name of Your Son, Jesus. Amen.

C. Thought to Remember

God defeats the dry times.

Learning by Doing

This page contains an alternative lesson plan emphasizing learning activities. Some of these activities are also found in the helpful student book, Adult Bible Class.

Into the Lesson

Provide paper and pencils. Tell your students that you are going to give them a 12-question pop quiz with easy answers. Then ask who or what is:

1. *the smallest of the United States in terms of land area;*
2. *the deceased rock and roll legend known as "the king";*
3. *a major musical composition for orchestras;*
4. *a radioactive element beginning with U;*
5. *the four transportation "properties" on the Monopoly board;*
6. *the world empire into which Jesus was born;*
7. *the continent including Italy and Germany;*
8. *the things the diet-conscious count;*
9. *a "pick up" vehicle some drive;*
10. *the U.S. government agency that collects federal income taxes;*
11. *the river that runs from Pittsburgh, Pennsylvania, to Cairo, Illinois;*
12. *the major television network that is not ABC, CBS, or Fox.*

Once finished, ask if any learner can establish a relationship between the answers and today's lesson. If no one notices, suggest they look at the initial letters of the answers Rhode Island, Elvis, symphony, uranium, railroads, Roman, Europe, calories, truck, I.R.S., Ohio, NBC. The word is *RESURRECTION*.

Say, "Ezekiel's vision is of resurrection, new life for old, dried bones, new bodies for old ones lost to death." Time allowing, consider having learners read aloud some of the key New Testament texts on resurrection, such as John 5:28, 29; 1 Corinthians 15:42-44, 49-52; Philippians 3:10-14; 1 Thessalonians 4:16, 17; Revelation 20:11-13. This can be saved until the end of the Into the Word segment.

Into the Word

On a handout have the sermon titles below, listed in a column. Give these directions: "Assume that a preacher has announced a sermon series on today's text. Which verse from Ezekiel 37 do you think he intends to emphasize in each of the following sermons? Write a verse number by each. Be prepared to explain your rationale."

Titles are given here in alphabetical order; verse numbers are shown here but should *not* be

included in copies to your learners. "Announcing Coming Additions" *(v. 5)*; "The Army of God" *(v. 10)*; "Bodies Without Spirits" *(v. 8)*; "Carried Away" *(v. 1)*; "Death Valley" *(v. 2)*; "Home Again" *(v. 12)*; "Hopelessness" *(v. 11)*; "The Power of the Four Winds" *(v. 9)*; "Proof Positive" *(v. 13)*; "Reversal of Fortunes" *(v. 6)*; "A Seemingly Silly Question" *(v. 3)*; "What Do I Hear?" *(v. 7)*; "Who Said It? Who Did It?" *(v. 14)*; "World's Worst (or Best) Audience" *(v. 4)*.

Give your learners several minutes, then call for responses. If some have differing choices, let each explain his or her reasoning. This can be a small-group discussion.

Once completed, ask your class to suggest additional sermon titles based on the text verses, singly or in combinations of verses. To get them started, say, "If I were preaching a sermon on verse one, I'd call it 'Handed Over,' because that's what Ezekiel did with himself in submission to the Lord." You may be surprised at the creativity and insight class members show.

Into Life

The lesson writer's Prayer at the end of the study can be an excellent vehicle for review and commitment. Consider asking the class to pray this prayer idea by idea as you lead. Read the phrases as follows and call for the class to repeat:

O God, we are so often parched and dry. / Our souls falter. Doubts creep in. / It seems that evil is winning and our efforts to serve You are ineffective. / Give us a new empowerment from Your Spirit, / a spiritual downpour for the soul. / May our doubt be transformed into faith. / May we, like the dry bones, hear Your Word and be encouraged. / We pray this in the name of Your Son Jesus, amen.

Tell the class you want them to use the word *RENEWAL* as a stimulus for their prayers this week, one letter per day, as they seek spiritual rejuvenation. Suggest that they can either start the prayer with the appropriate letter or can simply key on an important word or concept with that initial letter. For example, say, "On Monday, the *R* can be for *resurrection* and you can thank God for that hope we have in Christ, or it could begin a petition, 'Refresh me by your Spirit, Lord, when I am dry.'"

Let's Talk It Over

The questions on this page are designed to promote discussion of the lesson by the class and to encourage application of the lesson Scriptures. The answers provided are only discussion starters. Let your class talk it over from there.

1. In responding to God's question "can these bones live?" Ezekiel showed wisdom in allowing God to provide the answer. What can we learn from Ezekiel's example as we face life's (seemingly) hopeless situations?

Ezekiel believed in God's power to do whatever He pleases (Psalm 115:3), so he didn't jump to any conclusions. When we find ourselves discouraged with the way life is going, we should not automatically assume that we know how things will turn out. Instead, we can ask God for solutions to our problems, and He will give us the answers (James 1:5, 6). We remind ourselves that God can bring good out of the worst situations (Romans 8:28).

2. When was a time you felt the Lord leading you to do something that didn't make a lot of sense at the time? How did you react? How did things turn out?

Could any situation seem more ridiculous than being asked to prophesy to a valley filled with the bones of the dead? Yet, since God asked him to do it, Ezekiel obeyed without hesitation. God's Spirit may urge us to do something less "foolish" (examples: give more money than we can afford for a special offering; go on a short-term mission trip to a foreign country; invite a friend to church). Yet we may hesitate to act on it.

Of course, Ezekiel had the advantage in knowing for sure what God wanted him to do. Our difficulty comes when we are uncertain whether the urge is from the Lord or from our own selfish or imperfect desires. Until we've been able to work through this by praying for wisdom, studying God's Word, and/or seeking advice from wise Christians, we should probably delay the decision to act.

3. How much "life" is there in your congregation? If there is need for it, what could you do to help start a revival?

As exiles in Babylon, the Israelites learned that the temple had been destroyed and Jerusalem had been burned. The nation of Israel seemed to be dead and gone. But as lifeless as any particular congregation may seem, surely it's not in a situation as dire as that!

No matter how "dead" a congregation seems to be, the members should not give in to despair.

Instead, with fervent prayer, godly leaders, and a will to work together, they should put their trust in God's power to bring the dead to life again. Sometimes life-from-death comes about when a church courageously decides to close its doors, then use its assets to assist a church-planting organization in establishing a new congregation.

4. How can we reach out to help someone in the grips of depression? What spiritual resources can we rely on to keep ourselves strong during those times?

Times of depression come to all of us. Sometimes people experience a depth of hopelessness from which they can't seem to recover on their own. Educating ourselves to identify the symptoms of a serious depression is the first step. These symptoms include extreme sadness, inability to experience pleasure, oversleeping, insomnia, fatigue, self-loathing, etc. People who seem to be severely depressed should be encouraged first to get a medical evaluation to determine if there is a physical cause of the depression.

Whether the person agrees to this or not, he or she will need a friend who can listen and show loving concern. Such a friend will encourage him or her to take steps to regain equilibrium. Since being a friend to a depressed person can be a draining process, you will need to ensure that your own mental and spiritual well-being does not suffer in the process. Entrusting the person to God and allowing Him to be the healer will keep you from falling into a "rescuer" mind-set, taking on too much responsibility for another's mental health.

5. How has God acted in your life to help you know that He is the Lord?

The answers to this will be as individual as the students in your class. Most will respond with personal stories of such things as God helping them overcome temptation, solve difficult problems, heal their illnesses, and comfort their sorrows. Others may respond with evidence of God's power in creation and the victory over sin and death. Our worship experiences, both public and private, increase our willingness to say with Paul that "Jesus Christ is Lord, to the glory of God the Father" (Philippians 2:11).

A New Source of Life

DEVOTIONAL READING: John 4:7-15.

BACKGROUND SCRIPTURE: Ezekiel 47:1-12.

PRINTED TEXT: Ezekiel 47:1-12.

Ezekiel 47:1-12

1 Afterward he brought me again unto the door of the house; and, behold, waters issued out from under the threshold of the house eastward: for the forefront of the house stood toward the east, and the waters came down from under, from the right side of the house, at the south side of the altar.

2 Then brought he me out of the way of the gate northward, and led me about the way without unto the outer gate by the way that looketh eastward; and, behold, there ran out waters on the right side.

3 And when the man that had the line in his hand went forth eastward, he measured a thousand cubits, and he brought me through the waters; the waters were to the ankles.

4 Again he measured a thousand, and brought me through the waters; the waters were to the knees. Again he measured a thousand, and brought me through; the waters were to the loins.

5 Afterward he measured a thousand; and it was a river that I could not pass over: for the waters were risen, waters to swim in, a river that could not be passed over.

6 And he said unto me, Son of man, hast thou seen this? Then he brought me, and caused me to return to the brink of the river.

7 Now when I had returned, behold, at the bank of the river were very many trees on the one side and on the other.

8 Then said he unto me, These waters issue out toward the east country, and go down into the desert, and go into the sea: which being brought forth into the sea, the waters shall be healed.

9 And it shall come to pass, that every thing that liveth, which moveth, whithersoever the rivers shall come, shall live: and there shall be a very great multitude of fish, because these waters shall come thither: for they shall be healed; and every thing shall live whither the river cometh.

10 And it shall come to pass, that the fishers shall stand upon it from Engedi even unto En-eglaim; they shall be a place to spread forth nets; their fish shall be according to their kinds, as the fish of the great sea, exceeding many.

11 But the miry places thereof and the marshes thereof shall not be healed; they shall be given to salt.

12 And by the river upon the bank thereof, on this side and on that side, shall grow all trees for meat, whose leaf shall not fade, neither shall the fruit thereof be consumed: it shall bring forth new fruit according to his months, because their waters they issued out of the sanctuary: and the fruit thereof shall be for meat, and the leaf thereof for medicine.

GOLDEN TEXT: Every thing shall live whither the river cometh.—Ezekiel 47:9.

Christ and Creation
The Promise of New Life
Lessons 1–5

Lesson Aims

After participating in this lesson, each student will be able to:

1. Summarize Ezekiel's vision of a river.

2. Compare and contrast the life-bringing water in Ezekiel's vision with Jesus' image of living water in John 4.

3. Explain how he or she will bring (or work with others to bring) the water of life to someone this week.

Lesson Outline

INTRODUCTION
    A. Dead Sea(s)
    B. Lesson Background
 I. OVERWHELMING FLOOD (Ezekiel 47:1-5)
    A. Water's Direction (vv. 1, 2)
    B. Water's Rise (vv. 3-5)
II. LIVING RIVER (Ezekiel 47:6-12)
    A. Abundant Trees (vv. 6, 7)
    B. Reclaimed Sea (vv. 8-11)
      Evaluating Rivers
    C. Fruitful Trees (v. 12)
      That Which Heals
CONCLUSION
    A. Ezekiel's New Jerusalem
    B. Fresh Spiritual Water
    C. Prayer
    D. Thought to Remember

Introduction

A. Dead Sea(s)

The Dead Sea, on the border between modern Israel and Jordan, is a place featuring a couple of world records. It is the lowest spot on earth, about 1,350 feet below the level of the nearby Mediterranean Sea. It is also one of the saltiest natural bodies of water on earth, estimated to be between 5 and 10 times saltier than normal sea water.

The Dead Sea has no outlet, and its water level is maintained by evaporation—and the arid location of the Dead Sea allows a lot of evaporation. Its high concentration of salt and minerals does not permit plants or fish to live within it, thus its name *Dead Sea*.

Today's lesson looks prophetically at a vision in which a mighty freshwater stream flows out of the temple in Jerusalem eastward to the Dead Sea. The result is that a life-giving, tree-lined river is created that brings the Dead Sea to life and allows it to be teeming with fish.

Does the Dead Sea remind you of anything in your life? Do you have personal areas that are "dead zones," where all the life seems to have been sucked out? Maybe you have relationships that are toxic and joy-killing. Today's lesson is about spiritual refreshment and renewal. Our application is that Ezekiel's vision of a renewed Dead Sea can help us understand the renewal of our personal dead seas.

B. Lesson Background

Many Christians are not very familiar with the Old Testament prophets and the material in their books. This is particularly true of Ezekiel, partly because the New Testament authors rarely quote Ezekiel (2 Corinthians 6:16, 17 is the only place). Yet, as our lesson series leaves this book, we should appreciate the significant place it occupies in our larger understanding of the biblical history.

Ezekiel bridges the gap between the final days of the kingdom of Judah and the resettlement of its residents by the Babylonians (also known as the Chaldeans) in the Mesopotamian valley. Ezekiel tells this story from several perspectives. He gives the perspective of the exiles, both before and after the temple's destruction in 586 BC. He is also able to give the perspective of the people in Jerusalem up to the final battle; Ezekiel gives this perspective through visionary experiences and reports that he receives during those terrible days.

Most importantly, however, Ezekiel reveals the perspective of God in all of these events. We learn why God did not protect Jerusalem from the marauding Babylonian army. This was because it was the Lord himself who orchestrated these events and used the Babylonians as a tool to accomplish His ultimate plan (see Habakkuk 1:5, 6).

But Ezekiel revealed God's perspective far beyond the circumstances of Jerusalem's demise. God's purpose was to purify Israel from its long-standing religious unfaithfulness and from the general injustices found in its society (see Ezekiel 18:10-13). It was through this process that Israel would truly come to know God, because the nation would recognize the nature of His holy and righteous character.

Ezekiel also gives God's perspective on the future. God did not deal with His people so harshly out of a mere desire to see them punished. He initiated a corrective action so that His people could enjoy eternity with Him. Ezekiel's vision of the future came in several ways, and the previous lessons in this series have shown some of them. These included a Davidic Messiah, empowerment from God's Spirit, and a cleansed and productive Holy Land.

Beginning with chapter 40 and going through chapter 48, the end of the book, Ezekiel presents the future in the context of worship from the glorious, perfect temple of God. This description of the new temple represents about 20 percent of the entire book, so understanding it is crucial if we are to appreciate this great book fully. Ezekiel dates this vision "in the five and twentieth year of our captivity" (40:1). If that reference is to the exile that included Ezekiel himself, this puts the date at about 571 BC, or some 15 years after the destruction of the Jerusalem temple.

Ezekiel's vision of the new temple began with him at the top of "a very high mountain." There he could see the outline of the new city and temple (Ezekiel 40:2). He was then taken through the new temple by an angel guide and allowed to see all of its wonders.

The new temple was similar to the temple of Solomon, but built on a grander scale. It was oriented to face east. It was dedicated by God when His glory returned to occupy it (Ezekiel 43:2; 44:4). The new temple still had a central sanctuary building with a place like the Holy of Holies, where humans could not enter.

I. Overwhelming Flood (Ezekiel 47:1-5)

A. Water's Direction (vv. 1, 2)

1. Afterward he brought me again unto the door of the house; and, behold, waters issued out from under the threshold of the house eastward: for the forefront of the house stood toward the east, and the waters came down from under, from the right side of the house, at the south side of the altar.

The *he* is the heavenly guide of Ezekiel 40:1, 2. We think of a *threshold* as the small gap between a closed *door* and the floor. The imagery allows us to presume that Ezekiel sees that the door is closed while water runs out from this narrow crack. We are to assume that the glory of the Lord is behind the door and is the source of this gushing water (44:4).

For some reason that Ezekiel does not explain, the flow is much stronger on the *right side* of the threshold. This is from the perspective of one looking out the door, for the door faces *east*, and the right side is the *south side*.

2. Then brought he me out of the way of the gate northward, and led me about the way without unto the outer gate by the way that looketh eastward; and, behold, there ran out waters on the right side.

Ezekiel, still with his guide, leaves the main temple precincts by the north gate and circles around to the front. Here he can see the eastern *outer gate*. What Ezekiel sees is the eastern counterpart of the northern gate from which he has just left.

Here he observes the same phenomenon in that the flow of water favors the *right* (south) *side*. We begin to understand this detail: the destination of the stream of water is not straight east; it is southeast. Physical details of geography are not important here, but direction is. The flow of water is headed to the Dead Sea, but it will enter on the westward side, not from the Jordan River valley.

B. Water's Rise (vv. 3-5)

3. And when the man that had the line in his hand went forth eastward, he measured a thousand cubits, and he brought me through the waters; the waters were to the ankles.

A cubit is traditionally the distance from a man's elbow to the end of his longest finger. This should be understood as about 18 inches, or half a yard. So we can think of *a thousand cubits* as about 500 yards. Ezekiel's guide still has his measuring stick (Ezekiel 40:5), and he now uses it to determine a place in the new river about this distance from the eastern gate. The water is still shallow, only ankle deep, or about 6 inches.

4. Again he measured a thousand, and brought me through the waters; the waters were to the knees. Again he measured a thousand, and brought me through; the waters were to the loins.

How to Say It

BABYLONIANS. Bab-ih-*low*-nee-unz.
BOISE. *Boy*-zee.
CARIBBEAN. Ka-ruh-*bee*-un or Ka-*rih*-bee-un.
CHALDEANS. Kal-*dee*-unz.
EN-EGLAIM. En-*egg*-lay-im.
ENGEDI. En-*gee*-dye.
HABAKKUK. Huh-*back*-kuk.
JEBUSITES. *Jeb*-yuh-sites.
MEDITERRANEAN. *Med*-uh-tuh-*ray*-nee-un (strong accent on *ray*).
MELCHIZEDEK. Mel-*kiz*-eh-dek.
MESOPOTAMIAN. *Mes*-uh-puh-*tay*-me-un (strong accent on *tay*).
ORINOCO. Or-ee-*no*-ko.
VENEZUELA. Veh-neh-*zway*-luh.

The man measures a second *thousand* cubits. He compels Ezekiel to wade into the water to determine its depth. It is now at knee level, about 18 or 20 inches. This is done a third time, and the river is now up to *the loins,* waist level. This is about 3 feet.

5. Afterward he measured a thousand; and it was a river that I could not pass over: for the waters were risen, waters to swim in, a river that could not be passed over.

A fourth and final sounding is taken after another *thousand* cubits. This is a total of 4,000 cubits, which is about 2,000 yards or a little over a mile. Now the flow is a true *river.* When Ezekiel walks out to determine its depth relative to his body, he finds that it is over his head and can *not be passed over* without swimming.

We must understand this to be a supernatural river, then. The shallow flow that escapes from under a door of the sanctuary has grown into a mighty stream. Just as there is no natural explanation for the source of water behind the door, there is no explanation for the stream's increasing depth except that the power of God is escalating its volume. [See question #1, page 264.]

II. Living River
(Ezekiel 47:6-12)

A. Abundant Trees (vv. 6, 7)

6, 7. And he said unto me, Son of man, hast thou seen this? Then he brought me, and caused me to return to the brink of the river. Now when I had returned, behold, at the bank of the river were very many trees on the one side and on the other.

The city of Boise, Idaho, derives its name from French trappers who first saw the area after traveling many days across barren, sagebrush desert. They exclaimed *boisé,* the French word meaning "trees," for they had seen trees for the first time in many weeks. These were trees lining the Boise River as it made its way out of the mountains through this desert region.

Ezekiel has a similar experience. He knows that the region east of Jerusalem is dry and barren. Now, however, the wonderful temple *river* has brought *trees* to the area, a sure sign of abundant fresh water. This is a river bringing life to a dry, dead region.

B. Reclaimed Sea (vv. 8-11)

8. Then said he unto me, These waters issue out toward the east country, and go down into the desert, and go into the sea: which being brought forth into the sea, the waters shall be healed.

The sea that is the destination of the living river is the Dead Sea, also called *the salt sea* in the Bible (example: Genesis 14:3). As mentioned earlier, the Dead Sea is 5 to 10 times saltier than normal ocean water. This means that the river would need to pump in 5 to 10 times as much water as the sea originally contained just to bring its salt concentration down to that of the ocean.

But this is not what Ezekiel intends us to understand. The Dead Sea, the deadest body of water on the face of the earth, is being *healed* through the gracious power of God. There is no natural explanation for this, because it can be understood only as a miracle. [See question #2, page 264.]

9. And it shall come to pass, that every thing that liveth, which moveth, whithersoever the rivers shall come, shall live: and there shall be a very great multitude of fish, because these waters shall come thither: for they shall be healed; and every thing shall live whither the river cometh.

Another measure of the transformation of the Dead Sea is that Ezekiel experiences it as thriving with *fish.* The River of Life has created the Sea of Life. It has healed the entire region. Wherever this *river* goes, it brings life. Even ocean fish will die if their water is too salty or polluted. Fresh water will yield abundant life in the water and on the land that is near the water.

10. And it shall come to pass, that the fishers shall stand upon it from Engedi even unto Eneglaim; they shall be a place to spread forth nets; their fish shall be according to their kinds, as the fish of the great sea, exceeding many.

This part of the vision is outrageously wonderful for anyone who has direct knowledge of the Dead Sea. Ezekiel observes that a new fishing industry has sprung up. The *fish* are so plentiful that boats aren't even needed! The fishermen just throw nets while standing on the shore from *Engedi* to *En-eglaim.* That is roughly the middle third of the western shoreline.

The exact entry point of the new river is not given, but we may conjecture from this image that it is smack in the middle of the western side of the Dead Sea. The bumper crop of fish ensures a never-ending food supply for the new Jerusalem, the source of the River of Life. There will be many *kinds* of fish to provide a varied and interesting diet. [See question #3, page 264.]

EVALUATING RIVERS

Every schoolchild knows that "In fourteen hundred and ninety-two, Columbus sailed the ocean blue." Actually, Columbus sailed to the western hemisphere four times. His first two voyages led him to numerous islands in the Caribbean, but he was still convinced that he had located islands off the main Asian coast.

On his third voyage, in 1498, he came to a lower point in the Caribbean, arriving off Trinidad. Then he moved north. When he came to the mouth of the Orinoco River in what is now Venezuela, he was convinced that he had come to a major continent and not just an island.

He reached this conclusion by reasoning backward, from effect to cause. The flow of the river extended fresh water several miles into the Atlantic Ocean. Columbus was convinced that no island could have a river large enough to empty this much fresh water. Therefore, Columbus reasoned, this river must be a big one, and the land it traveled must be a continent rather than just an island. Columbus was correct: the Orinoco River, estimated at 1,300 miles, is one of the longest river systems in the world.

We can use the same logic to evaluate God's River of Life. When we see the effect of eternally changed lives, we cannot but conclude that the source is God himself.   —J. B. N.

11. But the miry places thereof and the marshes thereof shall not be healed; they shall be given to salt.

Below Engedi the sea will still have *marshes* (swamps) and *miry places* (mud flats). These areas will retain their salty character. The point is that one must be near the River of Life to gain its benefits. Without this miraculous flow of fresh water, the sea will remain its old, salty self.

C. Fruitful Trees (v. 12)

12a. And by the river upon the bank thereof, on this side and on that side, shall grow all trees for meat, whose leaf shall not fade, neither shall the fruit thereof be consumed.

Ezekiel's attention returns to the *river* itself and the *trees* lining it. There are *fruit* trees yielding *meat* (food). These are not ordinary trees. They have no dormant cycle since the leaves do *not fade.* Instead, the trees are always producing. They put forth an inexhaustible supply of fruit for the holy city on a year-round basis.

12b. It shall bring forth new fruit according to his months, because their waters they issued out of the sanctuary: and the fruit thereof shall be for meat, and the leaf thereof for medicine.

The productivity of these riverbank orchards is described in more detail. These trees are not on an annual cycle of dormancy to production and back again; rather, they are on a monthly cycle. This means that it will only take a month to go from blossom to full, ripe *fruit.*

Visual for Lesson 5. *Point to this visual as you challenge your students to name "dead seas" in their lives that God has made alive.*

The trees will also be ever green in the sense of never losing their leaves. There will be no piles of leaves to rake in the fall, because these trees keep their leaves. This is important, for some of these leaves have medicinal value and will always be available for their healing properties. (See Revelation 22:2, where the leaves are for the "healing of the nations.")

The exact genus of these healing trees is not mentioned. But even today we use the leaves of aloe vera plants and eucalyptus trees to produce health-related products. Herbalists use various leaves to create healing elixirs and balms. Such natural remedies are highly prized in Ezekiel's day, thus the imagery resonates profoundly with the original readers.

THAT WHICH HEALS

We who live in the Western world rely heavily on pills as medicine. I'm not opposed to that! Because of my medical conditions, I pop 10 pills per day.

But other areas of the world rely more on natural healing. Such is the case with traditional Chinese medicine, or TCM as it is referred to. Mulberries are highly prized, and that fruit is credited with healing the blood, benefiting the kidneys, and treating premature graying of one's hair as well as aiding tinnitus and dizziness. Papaya fruit is considered good for digestion and the heart. Guava is considered to be one of the most therapeutic plants in the Philippines.

"Natural" healing methods go back centuries. So when Ezekiel talks about trees bearing not only edible fruit, but also leaves that can be used for medical purposes, he is referring to situations familiar to his readers. But to take this as an endorsement of the natural healing methods of modern herbalists is to miss the point. This is an endorsement of *supernatural* healing—the kind available only from God himself.   —J. B. N.

Conclusion

A. Ezekiel's New Jerusalem

The book of Revelation has many parallels with Ezekiel. Both books include aspects of God's terrible judgments and of God's gracious restoration of His people. Both offer certain descriptions of the city of Jerusalem.

Jerusalem first appears in the Bible as the city of King Melchizedek in Genesis 14:18. There the city is simply called *Salem*, a name meaning "peace." This meaning is used by the author of Hebrews to show Jesus as the "King of peace" and the "King of righteousness" (see Hebrews 7:1, 2). This city was named *Jerusalem* long before David took it from the Jebusites and made it his capital city (2 Samuel 5:6, 7).

In the book of Revelation, we are given a picture of "new Jerusalem," the utterly holy city created by God. The purpose of the vision of new Jerusalem is to encourage believers concerning God's provisions and plans for the future, beyond any tribulation and pain they may be suffering at the time. [See question #4, page 264.]

This lesson has dealt with part of Ezekiel's vision of new Jerusalem. Our primary focus has been the wonderful River of Life that proceeds from the temple to the Dead Sea, causing flora and fauna to flourish in its path. Such a marvelous, gracious river is also part of the vision of Revelation (see Revelation 22:1). But Ezekiel includes

a prophecy that is not found in Revelation. At the very end of his book, Ezekiel tells us about Jerusalem's new name.

The name *Jerusalem* is very ancient and means "city of peace." In Ezekiel's vision, the new name will be *The Lord is there* (Ezekiel 48:35). Transliterated from Hebrew, this name is *Yaweh-shamah*, which sounds a lot like the Hebrew way of saying Jerusalem, which is *Yeru-shalem*. Jerusalem will truly become a city of peace and life, for God will be there and never leave the city again (Revelation 21:22).

B. Fresh Spiritual Water

The personal water bottle is everywhere today, carried by some people everywhere they go. It is even common to see water bottles in many worship services, either among the congregants or being sipped by worship leaders and others up front. Although some people carry water as more of a fashion accessory, this widespread phenomenon also reflects increased respect for health values of drinking plenty of pure water.

When He attended the Feast of Tabernacles in Jerusalem, Jesus proclaimed, "He that believeth on me, as the Scripture hath said, out of his belly shall flow rivers of living water" (John 7:38). [See question #5, page 264.] Jesus was not quoting a single, particular Old Testament passage, but the general message derived from several passages, including our lesson text for today. The apostle John goes on to explain, "But this spake he of the Spirit, which they that believe on him should receive" (John 7:39).

This means that we can enjoy right now the benefits of the spiritual refreshment that come from the Holy Spirit. He can right now break down the spiritual barriers that keep us from having complete fellowship with our creator. He can reverse all the life-killing areas of our selves, transforming us into the likeness of God's Son, Jesus Christ (2 Corinthians 3:18). The Holy Spirit brings joy, peace, and comfort to the most troubled soul.

C. Prayer

Lord God, we have a thirst for Your Spirit. We need our souls to be refreshed by Your sweet water of life. May the waters of Your living river flood us, cleanse us, and sustain us every day, even as we look forward to being in Your presence for all eternity. We pray in the name of the one who promised us living water, Jesus Christ. Amen.

D. Thought to Remember

Seek God's living water;
accept no substitutes.

Home Daily Bible Readings

Monday, Mar. 23—Wash Yourselves (Isaiah 1:12-17)

Tuesday, Mar. 24—The Water of Rebirth (Titus 3:1-7)

Wednesday, Mar. 25—Like Showers and Spring Rains (Hosea 6:1-6)

Thursday, Mar. 26—Planted by Streams of Water (Psalm 1)

Friday, Mar. 27—Give Me Living Water (John 4:7-15)

Saturday, Mar. 28—The Water of Life (Revelation 22:12-17)

Sunday, Mar. 29—Water from the Sanctuary (Ezekiel 47:1-12)

Learning by Doing

This page contains an alternative lesson plan emphasizing learning activities. Some of these activities are also found in the helpful student book, Adult Bible Class.

Into the Lesson

Give your learners copies of this word-find activity as each arrives. Use the heading *Water, Water, Everywhere.*

```
H W A T S G E R W A T
N A E R N M A E R T S
R W I I O R T I A W T
E E R L W E O E A E R
T P W A T V L T E L E
S R W A R I E D S L T
I I K E E R C E D W S
C E S R F W A A T U E
R E L A K E W I A T P
R E L R O C E A N W A
T L E G R E B E C I R
```

Direct students to find and mark all the sources of water they can find. The words run in all directions, including diagonals. These 18 words can be found: *cistern, creek, hail, iceberg, lake, oasis, ocean, puddle, rain, reservoir, river, sea, sleet, snow, spring, stream, waterfall, well.* Distributing the answers to be found will make the puzzle easier to solve; withholding the answers will make the puzzle much harder.

After a time of looking and discussion, say, "Today's study is all about water—flowing, life-enriching water."

Into the Word

For today's study, display a map showing the area eastward from Jerusalem to the Dead Sea. This is the geographic reference point for Ezekiel's vision.

Establish four discussion groups. Name them *Ankle Deep, Knee Deep, Waist Deep,* and *Over the Head,* based on the descriptions Ezekiel offers in chapter 47. Give each group this same note of direction:

"Decide what you would consider to be an idyllic place. What characterizes it? What is there? What is *not* there? Once your group has its 'Garden of Eden,' turn to Ezekiel 47:1-12 and decide what Ezekiel's place of bliss has that yours doesn't, and vice versa. In your group, decide whether Ezekiel's picture is one of Heaven or simply of a restored state of Israel."

Give the groups at least 10 minutes. At the end call for each group's conclusions. This will allow a close look at the text.

Say, "Jesus' teaching on living water, in John 4:7-14, is a beautiful picture echoing the refreshing message of Ezekiel 47 and the river that brings new life." Have one of your best oral readers stand and read that passage to the class. After the reading ask the following questions:

1. How are these two passages—Ezekiel 47 and John 4—similar in their reflection of God's love and grace?

2. Though God uses the image of life-giving water throughout His Word, what are the differences in the promises made in these two texts?

Anticipate such responses as the following. For question #1, "both come to those whose external circumstances are stressed and stressful"; "in both scenes God is willing to provide all that the hearer needs"; "in both contexts there are those who will be 'left standing on the bank'"; "though both use temporal and material imagery, their real significance is in spiritual truth."

For question #2, possible responses may be "the former is a national image, the latter is personal and individual"; "the first is given in the spirit, the latter is a face-to-face encounter"; "the former offers a prosperous future, the latter offers a thirst-free present"; "the former is restricted in geography and scope, the latter is universal and unrestricted."

Your class will see additional similarities and contrasts.

Into Life

Say, "One of the most challenging tasks the Christian has is to attract thirsty sinners to God's water of life. How do we get spiritually thirsty people to realize how to fill their need? What opportunities for presenting the water of life are you anticipating in the week ahead?"

If the means are available, give each learner a bottle of water you have relabeled prominently *Water of Life.* Add such key Bible references as Isaiah 55:1, 2; John 4:13; John 7:38; and/or Revelation 7:17. Challenge them to look up the passage(s) before drinking the water later on. If there is room on the label, you can print one or more of the passages in its (their) entirety.

Let's Talk It Over

The questions on this page are designed to promote discussion of the lesson by the class and to encourage application of the lesson Scriptures. The answers provided are only discussion starters. Let your class talk it over from there.

1. In what ways is this rapidly rising river an image of God's love for His people, both in Ezekiel's day and today?

Rising waters naturally cause alarm, but Ezekiel's vision involves a gentle, benevolent inundation. The trickle of water from the temple turns into a mighty deep river that has wonderful, life-giving powers.

For many people, the experience of God's love may be small at first; they may find it hard to believe that God could actually love sinners in general and them in particular. But once they understand that God loved them enough to send His Son to die for them on the cross, their awareness of His love begins to grow. They may begin to see God's love as a flood. As Christians we can all live secure in the reality of the "breadth, and length, and depth, and height" of Christ's love for us (Ephesians 3:18).

2. If God can heal "the deadest body of water on the face of the earth," what can He do to heal you? What has He already done? How can you be a source of healing to others?

Even after we become Christians and have our sins forgiven, we still have painful areas of our lives that need to be healed because of damage done. In some of these areas we have been the victims; in other areas we have been the perpetrators. Whether it's the long-term effects of childhood abuse, the pain of damaged relationships, or the consequences of our sins, we all need God's healing touch on our lives.

Remembering that God loves us unconditionally is a good beginning place. This knowledge gives us the courage to bring our problems to Him for His healing grace. Often, God provides healing help through the church in the form of support groups, counselors, and biblical teaching. By sharing how we have been healed, we can encourage others to believe that change is possible.

3. When was a time that God provided for your needs in an abundant way?

The abundance of fish in the once-dead sea is a picture of God's great bounty. Encourage your students to share their personal stories of experiencing God's bounty. In addition to material blessings,

we know that we are blessed "with all spiritual blessings in heavenly places in Christ" (Ephesians 1:3). Our sins are forgiven, we are new creatures in Christ, our daily needs are provided, and we have purpose for living. One may hope that responses to God's generosity will include increased faith, heartfelt gratitude, loving praise, good works, and evangelistic outreach.

4. Which of God's promises give you the most comfort and hope for the future? Why?

The people of Ezekiel's day were comforted with the promise that they would return home and see their nearly dead nation restored to life. These promises were fulfilled. Eventually, Jerusalem was restored and the temple was rebuilt.

The promises that comfort us most should involve more than the blessings we will receive in this life. Instead, we look for the fulfillment of John's vision in the book of Revelation. We find our comfort in the fact that we will live with the Lord in Heaven, where there will be "no more death, neither sorrow, nor crying, neither shall there be any more pain" (Revelation 21:4).

The river we are expecting is "a pure river of water of life" that will flow from God's throne in Heaven (Revelation 22:1). This makes it possible for us to live forever in God's presence.

5. What can we do to restart the water of life flowing through us and out to others?

While Jesus says that His followers will be a source of "rivers of living water," we occasionally may wonder how, if we feel that our lives are all dried up. Remember: the only way that living water can flow within us and outward from us is by being connected to the source, which is Jesus (John 4:10). The further we are from Him in our daily walk, the more likely we are to see the joy evaporate from our lives.

We can stay connected to Jesus by allowing His Holy Spirit, who indwells us, to have His way with us. When we shut ourselves off from the Holy Spirit by ignoring Bible study, neglecting prayer, and indulging in sinful behavior, we will begin to dry up spiritually. We need to seek the Spirit's help so we can enjoy life "more abundantly" (John 10:10).

Jesus Is Crucified

DEVOTIONAL READING: 1 Corinthians 15:1-11.

BACKGROUND SCRIPTURE: Luke 23.

PRINTED TEXT: Luke 23:32-47.

Luke 23:32-47

32 And there were also two others, malefactors, led with him to be put to death.

33 And when they were come to the place, which is called Calvary, there they crucified him, and the malefactors, one on the right hand, and the other on the left.

34 Then said Jesus, Father, forgive them; for they know not what they do. And they parted his raiment, and cast lots.

35 And the people stood beholding. And the rulers also with them derided him, saying, He saved others; let him save himself, if he be Christ, the chosen of God.

36 And the soldiers also mocked him, coming to him, and offering him vinegar,

37 And saying, If thou be the King of the Jews, save thyself.

38 And a superscription also was written over him in letters of Greek, and Latin, and Hebrew, THIS IS THE KING OF THE JEWS.

39 And one of the malefactors which were hanged railed on him, saying, If thou be Christ, save thyself and us.

40 But the other answering rebuked him, saying, Dost not thou fear God, seeing thou art in the same condemnation?

41 And we indeed justly; for we receive the due reward of our deeds: but this man hath done nothing amiss.

42 And he said unto Jesus, Lord, remember me when thou comest into thy kingdom.

43 And Jesus said unto him, Verily I say unto thee, Today shalt thou be with me in paradise.

44 And it was about the sixth hour, and there was a darkness over all the earth until the ninth hour.

45 And the sun was darkened, and the veil of the temple was rent in the midst.

46 And when Jesus had cried with a loud voice, he said, Father, into thy hands I commend my spirit: and having said thus, he gave up the ghost.

47 Now when the centurion saw what was done, he glorified God, saying, Certainly this was a righteous man.

GOLDEN TEXT: When Jesus had cried with a loud voice, he said, Father, into thy hands I commend my spirit: and having said thus, he gave up the ghost.—Luke 23:46.

Lesson Aims

After participating in this lesson, each student will be able to:

1. Retell Luke's account of Jesus' crucifixion.

2. Compare and contrast the reactions of those who witnessed Jesus' death with the reactions of people today.

3. Write a letter to a modern skeptic explaining how Jesus' death provides forgiveness for sin.

Lesson Outline

INTRODUCTION
    A. Power of the Cross
    B. Lesson Background
 I. ACTIONS AND ATTITUDES (Luke 23:32-38)
    A. Crucified with Criminals (vv. 32, 33)
    B. Reacts to Persecutors (v. 34a)
    C. Robbed of Clothing (v. 34b)
    D. Mocked by Onlookers (vv. 35-38)
      Unknown to Known . . . And Back Again?
 II. TAUNT AND REACTIONS (Luke 23:39-43)
    A. Attack (v. 39)
    B. Rebuke (vv. 40, 41)
    C. Request (v. 42)
    D. Promise (v. 43)
III. DEATH AND ACKNOWLEDGMENT (Luke 23:44-47)
    A. Cosmic Disruption (vv. 44, 45)
      Darkness
    B. Confident Death (v. 46)
    C. Thoughtful Centurion (v. 47)
CONCLUSION
    A. Carrying Our Cross
    B. Prayer
    C. Thought to Remember

Introduction

A. Power of the Cross

When we think of the power of the cross, we tend to think of how Jesus conquered our sins through His death so that we may stand blameless before God in the final judgment. This much is clear in 1 Peter 2:24, which explains how Jesus bore our sins on the cross so that we may live for righteousness. Colossians 2:14, 15 goes on to explain how Christ's cross triumphed over both the record that stands against us and the "principalities and powers" that seek to dominate us.

Do we sometimes focus on the forgiveness part at the expense of other meanings of the cross? We do if, for example, we continue to fear the "principalities and powers" as if Christ has not overcome them. In this lesson we will pay careful attention to how Christ's cross both abolished sin and demonstrated God's unique power to overcome evil.

B. Lesson Background

After more than three years of public ministry, Jesus returned once again to Jerusalem, but this time to die. After the Passover feast, Jesus departed to a quiet place to pray. That was interrupted when Judas, one of His close followers, betrayed Him.

Jesus was brought before a succession of authorities: the Jewish elders, Pilate, Herod, then Pilate again. Pilate was certain that Jesus was innocent. To satisfy the people, however, Pilate offered to flog and release Jesus. The chief priests, leaders, and people refused this verdict. Instead, they demanded that Pilate crucify Jesus and release Barabbas—a man charged with murder and revolt. The pressure was so intense that Pilate eventually relented and granted the request.

Jesus had every reason to be bitter. He stood abandoned by His closest friends, falsely accused by the people He came to save, and unjustly sentenced to death by Roman officials. If ever God's people deserved wrath, if ever the ruling powers deserved to be smitten, it was right then. But Jesus did not respond in kind. As we pay careful attention to His response, we learn the superior power of the cross.

I. Actions and Attitudes
(Luke 23:32-38)

A. Crucified with Criminals (vv. 32, 33)

32. And there were also two others, malefactors, led with him to be put to death.

The innocent, holy one of God is placed between *two* genuine criminals, as if He were one of them. This fulfills the prophecy of Isaiah, who said that God's suffering servant would be "numbered with the transgressors" (Isaiah 53:12). That prophecy can be taken in a general sense, as Jesus is treated as criminals are treated. In a particular sense, Jesus is placed right alongside criminals literally.

33. And when they were come to the place, which is called Calvary, there they crucified him, and the malefactors, one on the right hand, and the other on the left.

Criminals condemned to die are normally escorted outside of the city proper to be *crucified* in a prominent place. This may be at a crossroads so passersby can see what happens to those who defy Rome. *Calvary,* the place where Jesus is crucified, is called *Golgotha* in Aramaic, the other language of the area besides Greek (Mark 15:22). Despite a long history of pictures locating the crucifixion on top of a hill, there is no evidence for this in Scripture.

Luke does not describe the process of crucifixion; his original readers are familiar with it. For our part, we depend on nonbiblical accounts and archaeological evidence from Jesus' day in addition to the Gospels to grasp the full impact of crucifixion. One account depicts a man with forearms nailed to a crossbeam, with buttocks supported by a small shelf. He is turned sideways with knees bent so a large nail can be driven through both heels into the vertical beam.

B. Reacts to Persecutors (v. 34a)

34a. Then said Jesus, Father, forgive them; for they know not what they do.

Jesus doesn't command legions of angels to rescue Him from pending death (Matthew 26:53). He doesn't call on God to rain judgment down on His false accusers. He doesn't even plead His innocence before onlookers or vow to avenge himself. Instead, He asks God to *forgive.*

The text does not specify exactly who Jesus is requesting forgiveness for. It may be the Roman and/or Jewish leaders who sentenced Him to death, the mob who lobbied for His execution, or His close friends who denied and betrayed Him. Or perhaps it's all of them together.

The phrase *for they know not what they do* does not help much in determining whom Jesus has in mind. None of the above persons understands the

---

How to Say It

ARAMAIC. *Air*-uh-*may*-ik (strong accent on *may*).
BARABBAS. Buh-*rab*-us.
DEMOTIC. Deh-*mot*-ic.
GOLGOTHA. *Gahl*-guh-thuh.
HADES. *Hay*-deez.
HEROD. *Hair*-ud.
HIEROGLYPHICS. hi-ruh-*glih*-fix.
JUDAS. *Joo*-dus.
MALEFACTORS. *mal*-ih-fac-ters.
MESSIAH. Meh-*sigh*-uh.
NAPOLEON. Nuh-*pole*-yun.
NAZARETH. *Naz*-uh-reth.
PILATE. *Pie*-lut.
ROSETTA. Row-*zeh*-tuh.

---

significance of Christ's death, and each of them contributes to Jesus' suffering in some way, either by acts of commission or acts of omission. Luke appears intentionally to leave open the identity of those for whom Jesus requests forgiveness. That may signify that the request for forgiveness is open to the thieves, the betrayers, the deniers, the accusers, and the crucifiers. It remains open for us.

Jesus' request for the Father's forgiveness is certainly an expression of grace. Forgiveness is possible because Jesus is dying on a cross to pay sin's penalty. This is God's way of putting an end to the hostility between himself and humanity. Jesus is absorbing all the hostility that the powers of this world can throw at Him, but more importantly He is absorbing the wrath of God. [See question #1, page 272.]

In doing so, Jesus deprives human hatred and violence of their power. Hatred and violence thrive on bitterness and retaliation, but they wilt before nonretaliatory love and grace. This, of course, is what Jesus has been teaching throughout His ministry (Matthew 5:21, 22, 38-48; 18:21, 22; Mark 11:25; Luke 6:27-37; etc.). See Stephen's reaction on being stoned (Acts 7:60).

Jesus' request for the Father's forgiveness on "them" raises an important question: Did the Father honor Jesus' request and actually forgive "them"? We may answer with a confident *yes* if they repented. But that's a big *if* because God conditions His forgiveness on human repentance. Always.

C. Robbed of Clothing (v. 34b)

34b. And they parted his raiment, and cast lots.

Jesus' humiliation includes that of having his clothing stolen. This was predicted in Psalm 22:16-18. The value of Jesus' garments is seen in John 19:23, 24. The seamless nature of Jesus' tunic may be echoed in Exodus 28:32.

D. Mocked by Onlookers (vv. 35-38)

35. And the people stood beholding. And the rulers also with them derided him, saying, He saved others; let him save himself, if he be Christ, the chosen of God.

The people's response reinforces just how lost and clueless they are. Right in front of their eyes is God's Son hanging on a tree! As He asks that they be forgiven, they gamble for His clothes and mock Him. They argue that if Jesus is the *Christ,* then He will show it with impressive feats of strength and self-deliverance (see also Matthew 27:40-43; Mark 15:29-32). They do not comprehend the message that Jesus has been preaching: true power is not self-saving but self-giving.

36. And the soldiers also mocked him, coming to him, and offering him vinegar.

This verse reminds us that the taunting that Jesus receives is not only from Jews who reject Jesus, but also from representatives of the pagan Roman Empire. His rejection is wide-sweeping enough to include religious powers, political powers, common folk, and *soldiers*.

The word *vinegar* refers to a type of cheap wine that is common among Roman soldiers. The offer of this vinegar echoes Psalm 69:21: "in my thirst they gave me vinegar to drink." The psalm implies that the liquid that is offered only agitates a throat that is parched with thirst. This is not an act of kindness on the part of the soldiers.

37. And saying, If thou be the King of the Jews, save thyself.

From the soldiers' perspective, Jesus' most scandalous offense is His claim to be a *king*. They may not be familiar with the Jewish expectation of a Messiah (a Christ) who will restore the Jews and subject all nations under God's reign. But as servants of Rome, they find it amusing that a nobody from Podunkville (Nazareth) can entertain such delusions of grandeur.

38. And a superscription also was written over him in letters of Greek, and Latin, and Hebrew, THIS IS THE KING OF THE JEWS.

The Romans sometimes place a sign over the head of the crucified person to indicate the nature of the offense. John 19:19 makes clear that it is Pilate who authorizes this sign. It is published in multiple languages so travelers from various places can read it. This placard is obviously laced with sarcasm. Who can believe that this condemned man is a king whom God has sent to change the course of world history?

The inscription is also Pilate's jab at the Jewish leaders, as John 19:20, 21 makes clear. We may note that the phrase *in letters of Greek, and Latin, and Hebrew* does not appear in the earliest Greek manuscripts of Luke. But the idea is factual since it appears in those manuscripts of John 19:20.

UNKNOWN TO KNOWN . . . AND BACK AGAIN?

The hieroglyphic language of Egypt became a dead language at some point in ancient history. Even people in the Roman Empire thought it was only pictures, not a language.

All that began to change in 1798. That was the year Napoleon invaded Egypt. In the process of rebuilding some forts, some Frenchmen discovered a black basalt stone near the city of Rosetta.

This Rosetta stone (carved in 196 BC) is about four feet high, over two feet wide, and almost a foot thick. It has three specimens of writing on it:

hieroglyphics, an Egyptian script called Demotic, and Greek. Scholars could translate the Greek, but it took over 20 years of study for them to realize that the three texts were all the same. Ultimately they decoded the hieroglyphics as a language. The use of a known language became the means of translating the unknown.

Three languages were also used on the top of the cross where Jesus was crucified. Like the Rosetta stone, the message in all three languages was the same. But in this case, all three languages were known. The only "decoding" then necessary was for people to recognize Jesus not only as the King of the Jews, but also as the Messiah and Savior. This is the message the church must always preach, lest the gospel disappear into the mists of history, becoming unknown to future generations.
—J. B. N.

II. Taunt and Reactions
(Luke 23:39-43)

A. Attack (v. 39)

39. And one of the malefactors which were hanged railed on him, saying, If thou be Christ, save thyself and us.

One of the criminals, with nails through his own hands, also taunts Jesus. This criminal's challenge *If thou be Christ, save thyself and us* reflects that of the Jewish leaders in verse 35, above. Jesus' verbal response to this man is the same as His response to Herod: nothing. Of course, Jesus' nonverbal response is also the same: suffering crucifixion on their behalf.

B. Rebuke (vv. 40, 41)

40, 41. But the other answering rebuked him, saying, Dost not thou fear God, seeing thou art in the same condemnation? And we indeed justly; for we receive the due reward of our deeds: but this man hath done nothing amiss.

The *other* criminal cannot remain silent. He acknowledges his and the other man's guilt as well as Jesus' innocence. In so doing, he becomes an example to us. When the world mocks our Lord, we must correct the impious speech. We cannot force people to discipline their tongues, but we can expose the error of their speech and provide a truthful alternative. [See question #2, page 272.]

C. Request (v. 42)

42. And he said unto Jesus, Lord, remember me when thou comest into thy kingdom.

This same criminal then turns to *Jesus* and exhibits the first recorded expression of confidence in the power of Christ over death. Until the resurrected Jesus shows himself to the disciples, they fail to see how His death can be anything but the end of the *kingdom* He has been proclaiming.

But with great faith this humble criminal somehow sees Jesus' death as the doorway to the kingdom. Perhaps Jesus' serene acceptance of death and His startling request that God forgive His oppressors has transformed the criminal's heart.

D. Promise (v. 43)

43. And Jesus said unto him, Verily I say unto thee, Today shalt thou be with me in paradise.

Jesus honors the fledging faith of the contrite criminal. [See question #3, page 272.] Some students wonder, however, about the nature of the *paradise* that Jesus promises. Exactly what and where is this? Is it the same as Heaven?

One idea is that paradise is not Heaven, but is the temporary abode of the righteous dead. Many first-century Jews believe that that which lies beyond the grave is divided into two realms: one where the righteous wait peacefully and another where the wicked wait in a state of torment until the final judgment. Some students think that these correlate with the two realms of Abraham's bosom and Hades as depicted in the story of the Rich Man and Lazarus in Luke 16:19-31.

The danger here is in trying to draw a precise connection of "this equals that" when such a precise connection may not exist in the New Testament. A good place to start for drawing at least a tentative connection for the issue at hand is to examine other places in the Bible where the word *paradise* is used. There are only two: 2 Corinthians 12:4 and Revelation 2:7.

In 2 Corinthians 12, Paul relates the experience of "a man" (probably Paul himself) who was "caught up to the third heaven" (v. 2), which seems to be the same as being "caught up to paradise" (v. 4). Revelation 2:7, for its part, speaks of "the tree of life, which is in the midst of the paradise of God." The discussion of the tree of life appears again in Revelation 22:2, where it is found in the new Jerusalem, where God dwells. Thus it is likely that *paradise* means the same as *Heaven*.

III. Death and Acknowledgment (Luke 23:44-47)

A. Cosmic Disruption (vv. 44, 45)

44, 45. And it was about the sixth hour, and there was a darkness over all the earth until the ninth hour. And the sun was darkened, and the veil of the temple was rent in the midst.

The three hours of *darkness* is literal, as the reference to *the sun* makes clear. The physical dark-

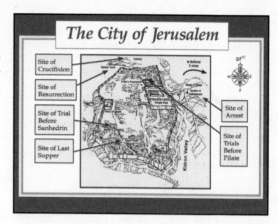

Visual for Lesson 6. *This map will refresh your students' memories about key locations in the Jerusalem of Jesus' day.*

ness undoubtedly points to the spiritual darkness that Jesus had noted earlier (Luke 22:53). This may be creation's way of participating in these earth-shattering events. There are other instances in Luke where creation will or can be involved in God's plan in unexpected ways (Luke 17:22-37; 19:40; 21:25-28; compare Matthew 27:51).

The *veil of the temple* is the curtain that separates the Holy Place from the Most Holy Place (see Exodus 26:31-35). The Most Holy Place is entered only once a year, by the high priest on the Day of Atonement (Leviticus 16:2, 29, 34). On this day, the sins of Israel are atoned for so that Israel can have a clean slate before God. The tearing of this curtain seems to indicate how Christ's death reconciles God and humans with the result that the temple no longer serves this purpose. Hebrews 9 and 10 supports this interpretation.

The torn curtain may also signify that that which separates Jew from Gentile is no more. This theory is supported by the fact that a major theme of Acts (which book is a sequel to Luke's gospel) is how Christ offers salvation to Gentiles, as in Acts 10. (See also Galatians 3:28; Ephesians 2:11-22.)

DARKNESS

How dark is "dark"? The answer varies with context. In a total solar eclipse (which is not what happened at Jesus' crucifixion), the sun is completely blocked out. But even in a total solar eclipse, it is not "midnight dark."

Eclipses aside, I have been in situations where midday storm clouds cut the sunlight to the point that it became dark enough to trigger sensors to turn on outside lights. I have walked through wooded areas on dark nights, and I had an uneasy feeling of vulnerability. On one occasion I was in a public restroom where there were no windows and the door fit snugly. Someone inadvertently turned off the lights, forgetting I was in there. That was dark! I literally could not see my hand in front of my face.

We are creatures of light, and darkness is confounding and uncomfortable. The exact theological implications of the darkness at Jesus' crucifixion are controversial, but it certainly got the attention of those who were there. We may safely say that it was a darkness like no other.   —J. B. N.

B. Confident Death (v. 46)

46. And when Jesus had cried with a loud voice, he said, Father, into thy hands I commend my spirit: and having said thus, he gave up the ghost.

Before dying, *Jesus* musters enough energy for one final cry that is surely heard by all nearby. On the surface it seems as if He is simply surrendering His life to God. But the words He cries come from Psalm 31:5.

The theme of this psalm is the confidence of the righteous and afflicted that salvation is in God's hands alone, that God delivers the righteous from their enemies, and that God will repay those who exalt themselves. So while surrendering His *spirit* to God, Jesus is simultaneously claiming the type of victory that accompanies such surrender. [See question #4, page 272.]

It is also worth noting that Jesus "gives up" His life. He doesn't try to fight off death, only to ultimately lose. He faces death and submits to it on His own terms. Death will serve Him in His plan. Jesus' early surrender also means that the Roman practice of dragging out the crucifixion as long as possible, as a statement of their power and author-

ity, will not work with Jesus. (We recall that Pilate is surprised at Jesus' relatively quick death; Mark 15:44). Rome does not take Jesus' life—He gives it.

C. Thoughtful Centurion (v. 47)

47. Now when the centurion saw what was done, he glorified God, saying, Certainly this was a righteous man.

Jesus' peaceful composure, forgiving spirit, submissive nature, and confidence before death are not lost on at least one Roman soldier. Like the contrite thief on the cross, he recognizes the *righteous* nature of Jesus. [See question #5, page 272.]

This particular soldier is a *centurion,* which is an officer in charge of 100 men. Other godly centurions are seen in Luke 7 and Acts 10. The centurion's faith in the verse before us demonstrates that the ground at the foot of the cross is truly level.

Conclusion

A. Carrying Our Cross

In dying on the cross, Jesus submitted to the will of the Father, overcame sin and death, and provided a model for us (Philippians 2:5-11). We will not change the course of world history the way Jesus did, but we may participate in the change He brought about. We will do so by imitating both the way He lived and the way He faced death.

Jesus beckoned His followers to take up their crosses and follow Him (Luke 9:23; 14:27). At that time they did not understand the full meaning of this invitation. It became clearer after Jesus was raised from the dead and showed himself to them. We can forgive one another numerous times because God gave His only Son in order to forgive us. We can accept the torturing of our bodies and the plundering of our possessions because this life and its treasures are not our ultimate hope. We can acknowledge with the apostle Paul in Galatians 6:14 that through Christ's cross the world has been crucified to us and we have been crucified to it.

B. Prayer

We thank You, God, for the cross. Give us the same mind as Jesus who emptied himself of heavenly glory, who humbly accepted death on a cross, and who has been exalted to the highest place of glory. Teach us to walk in His steps so that we may truly live both now and forevermore. In Jesus' name, amen.

C. Thought to Remember

Take up your cross and follow Him.

Home Daily Bible Readings

Monday, Mar. 30—The Message of the Cross (1 Corinthians 1:18-25)

Tuesday, Mar. 31—The Suffering Servant (Isaiah 53:1-9)

Wednesday, Apr. 1—A Ransom for Many (Mark 10:32-45)

Thursday, Apr. 2—A Sacrifice of Atonement (Romans 3:21-26)

Friday, Apr. 3—A Single Sacrifice for Sin (Hebrews 10:10-18)

Saturday, Apr. 4—Bought with a Price (1 Corinthians 6:12-20)

Sunday, Apr. 5—The Death of Jesus (Luke 23:32-47)

Learning by Doing

This page contains an alternative lesson plan emphasizing learning activities. Some of these activities are also found in the helpful student book, Adult Bible Class.

Into the Lesson

Ask class members what they would like to have said about them at their funerals and afterward. Allow the discussion to continue for a few minutes.

Then ask, "Did you find talking about death difficult? Many people find it difficult to think or talk about death. Yet the calmness with which Jesus faced His crucifixion and death is worth talking about. His demeanor showed that He was prepared for death. His talks with the disciples sometimes related to the inevitability of death and to His own death particularly."

Into the Word

Say, "People from a variety of backgrounds watched as Jesus died. Everyone there saw the same thing: a man being crucified. But each individual or group had a different perspective on the meaning of what happened."

Recruit class members to represent the following eyewitnesses to Jesus' crucifixion:

- *a Roman soldier*
- *the Roman centurion*
- *a Jewish leader*
- *a foreign visitor to Jerusalem*
- *an ordinary Jewish peasant*
- *a disciple*
- *the forgiven thief*
- *the unrepentant thief*

You may wish to do your recruiting a week in advance so that your "eyewitnesses" can practice their responses. This advance notice will also give your recruits a chance to procure apparel appropriate for their characters.

Interview each one in turn, asking what he or she saw and felt. Ask your interviewees in advance to make their responses match today's text; they should use their "sanctified imaginations" to fill in the gaps. Here are some general questions to ask:

"Why were you in Jerusalem?"

"What was the atmosphere in Jerusalem?"

"When did you first hear of Jesus?"

"What did you see at Calvary?"

"What were you thinking and feeling as you watched the crucifixion?"

"How was this crucifixion similar to and different from other crucifixions you have seen?"

"Later, did you experience any aftereffects from being a witness to this crucifixion?"

As the interviewer, be prepared to move from general questions to specific questions that fit the particular one being interviewed. This will involve quoting the words of the eyewitnesses back to them for clarification and explanation. For example, you can say to the repentant thief, "You said, 'We receive the due reward of our deeds: but this man hath done nothing amiss.' What did you mean by that statement?"

Note: Interviewing each one in turn may be overly time-consuming. You may choose, instead, to do a group interview, with all your interviewees seated around a table. If not dressed in period garb, each should wear a large sign indicating his or her identity. In a group interview (or what may be called a roundtable discussion), not all interviewees will answer each and every question, thus saving some time on this segment. Interactions among the interviewees will add an interesting element.

You can complete this portion of the lesson by asking the class to speculate how nonbelievers react when viewing realistic recreations of the crucifixion, such as in Mel Gibson's *The Passion of the Christ*. You can note that the gospel message, in whatever medium it is presented, often has a polarizing effect: those with soft hearts have their hearts softened further yet, while those with hard hearts are hardened all the more. This is nothing new (see Acts 13:48-50).

Into Life

Divide the class into smaller groups. Have each group member tell of a true story of reconciliation that they are familiar with personally. What caused the problem to begin with? What were the feelings before the people came together? How did the reconciliation come about? What was the result? Next, explore how God reconciled us to himself. How is that similar to and different from person-to-person reconciliations?

The resulting small-group discussion should include today's text. Also ask your groups to read 2 Corinthians 5:18 as they discuss their responsibilities to proclaim God's reconciliation. End with prayer within each group for those who were mentioned as needing to be in relationship with Jesus.

Let's Talk It Over

The questions on this page are designed to promote discussion of the lesson by the class and to encourage application of the lesson Scriptures. The answers provided are only discussion starters. Let your class talk it over from there.

1. What are some areas you have been wronged by others in which you should work toward forgiveness instead of revenge? How will you go about doing this?

Revenge is not an option for the Christian (see Romans 12:19). At the cross Jesus demonstrated that forgiveness is available to all. But we would often prefer to get even or to seethe in anger and bitterness.

Everyone has been injured by another in some way. It may be harsh words exchanged between spouses. It may be impatience demonstrated by parents to their children. Sometimes the hurts go much deeper. It may be that others have stolen from us, they might even have taken the life of a loved one. Having the attitude Jesus had is not easy, and it is not something we can do in our own strength. But the strength of the Holy Spirit is available.

2. In what ways have you been called on to defend the character and name of Christ? How can you do better in this regard?

The unchristian world takes various views about Christ. Some consider Him to be a good moral teacher, but little more. Others question whether the teaching of Scripture about Jesus is true in any way. And some are openly hostile to Jesus. We defend the name of Christ when we teach the truth of the person of Jesus; but this requires much study on our part in order to be able to do so. To those who attack the name of Christ, we exhibit the character of Christ; but this requires practice and consistency.

In all this, we imitate Christ's attitude: "When he was reviled, [He] reviled not again; when he suffered, he threatened not; but committed himself to him that judgeth righteously" (1 Peter 2:23). We also remember that "If ye be reproached for the name of Christ, happy are ye; for the Spirit of glory and of God resteth upon you" (1 Peter 4:14).

3. How will you live this day as you hear God's promise that one day you will be with Him for eternity?

Knowing the promise of God should lead to anticipation of the return of Christ. Knowing that this event will usher us into the very presence of

God in Heaven, it is a day to be longed for. This means that there are two extremes to avoid. One extreme is to get so focused on that day that we fail to live effective lives while here on earth. The other extreme is to float through our days with barely a thought that history is moving toward a glorious conclusion.

Holiness is what the Lord desires of His people while we wait for the return of Christ. Also, we are to be active in sharing our faith so that others will be able to wait with grateful anticipation for that day as well.

4. What should be our response to the irony of the death of Jesus?

Jesus died the death of the worst of sinners, even though He had not sinned; yet Scripture teaches us that Jesus is life (John 14:6). The fact that the creator and sustainer of life experienced death is thus paradoxical.

We have a bent toward sin, and Scripture teaches that we all have sinned (Romans 3:23). What Jesus did in dying, even though He is life, should compel us to die to sin, even though we are full of sin. "I am crucified with Christ: nevertheless I live; yet not I, but Christ liveth in me: and the life which I now live in the flesh I live by the faith of the Son of God, who loved me, and gave himself for me" (Galatians 2:20).

5. In what ways have you seen God working in this world, in your life, and in your church? How can you glorify Him because of the way He has worked in these ways?

God was working through the hearts of the repentant thief and the Roman centurion some 2,000 years ago. God still works through hearts today. He has not left this world, His church, or His people on their own.

There have been those whom we have thought to be so hardened in their sin that there apparently was no hope for them. But the God of grace worked a mighty work and brought about a complete change. When we see His working, we give Him the glory and praise His name. We never reach the conclusion that a particular person is beyond hope. We care for those whom He has saved and extend grace to them as God did.

He Is Risen!

DEVOTIONAL READING: 1 Corinthians 15: 12-26.

BACKGROUND SCRIPTURE: Luke 24:1-12.

PRINTED TEXT: Luke 24:1-12.

Luke 24:1-12

1 Now upon the first day of the week, very early in the morning, they came unto the sepulchre, bringing the spices which they had prepared, and certain others with them.

2 And they found the stone rolled away from the sepulchre.

3 And they entered in, and found not the body of the Lord Jesus.

4 And it came to pass, as they were much perplexed thereabout, behold, two men stood by them in shining garments:

5 And as they were afraid, and bowed down their faces to the earth, they said unto them, Why seek ye the living among the dead?

6 He is not here, but is risen: remember how he spake unto you when he was yet in Galilee,

7 Saying, The Son of man must be delivered into the hands of sinful men, and be crucified, and the third day rise again.

8 And they remembered his words,

9 And returned from the sepulchre, and told all these things unto the eleven, and to all the rest.

10 It was Mary Magdalene, and Joanna, and Mary the mother of James, and other women that were with them, which told these things unto the apostles.

11 And their words seemed to them as idle tales, and they believed them not.

12 Then arose Peter, and ran unto the sepulchre; and stooping down, he beheld the linen clothes laid by themselves, and departed, wondering in himself at that which was come to pass.

GOLDEN TEXT: Why seek ye the living among the dead?
He is not here, but is risen.—Luke 24:5, 6.

Christic and Creation
The Dawn of New Life
Lessons 6–9

Lesson Aims

After participating in this lesson, each student will be able to:

1. Retell Luke's account of the women's experience on resurrection morning.

2. Compare and contrast the various levels of belief of those first told of the resurrection with the varying levels of faith expressed.

3. Plan to discuss with an unbeliever the facts of Jesus' resurrection.

Lesson Outline

INTRODUCTION
    A. Remembering to Remember
    B. Lesson Background
  I. EMPTY TOMB (Luke 24:1-3)
    A. Routine Preparations (v. 1)
    B. Unexpected Findings (vv. 2, 3)
  II. HEAVENLY MESSENGERS (Luke 24:4-8)
    A. Angels Appear to the Women (vv. 4, 5)
      Cemeteries
    B. Angels Remind the Women (vv. 6-8)
 III. RELAYED MESSAGE (Luke 24:9-12)
    A. Women Tell the Apostles (vv. 9, 10)
    B. Apostles Doubt the Women (vv. 11, 12)
      Tall Tales
CONCLUSION
    A. Secondhand Testimony
    B. Prayer
    C. Thought to Remember

Introduction

A. Remembering to Remember

It is funny how the human mind remembers. Friends and family will sometimes tell us stories of events we participated in firsthand only a few years back, but we may have absolutely no recollection of them. Then we may hear an old song on the radio that we haven't heard in years and, instantly, every word of the lyrics comes back to mind. I imagine some of this has to do with the level at which the original context affected us.

Forgetfulness takes several forms. Some forgetfulness is harmless and some is harmful. Some is accidental and some is intentional. Does it surprise us that Jesus' followers all seemed to have forgotten that He foretold His suffering, death, and resurrection? How could they forget something so crucial? And what do we learn from the different ways they responded to the news of this life-changing event when reminded?

B. Lesson Background

In Luke 9:20, Peter was the first disciple to confess Jesus as Messiah (or Christ). Jesus responded by warning that He was to suffer, die, and rise on the third day. Shortly thereafter, following a crowd-dazzling healing display, Jesus impressed upon His followers that He would be betrayed. But they didn't grasp what He was saying (9:44, 45). Jesus later alluded to being killed in Jerusalem (13:33). He also told the disciples that He had to suffer and face rejection (17:25).

As the time of His death drew closer, Jesus repeated these predictions. He was to be handed over, mocked, beaten, and killed, but would rise on the third day (18:31-33). Still His disciples did not grasp what He was saying.

Jesus gave His disciples several opportunities to expect His death and recognize it for what it was: a temporary stop on the path to resurrection. But they did not comprehend. Indeed, they could not because it had been concealed from them (Luke 9:45; 18:34). In God's infinite wisdom, He planted a seed within them that was to bear fruit only after Christ's resurrection. Our text today records how Jesus' closest followers first responded to the news of that resurrection.

The events that transpired before it are familiar to long-time Christians. Jesus was betrayed by Judas and handed over to Jewish authorities. They subsequently handed Him over to Roman authorities. Pilate gave in to the crowd's wish that the innocent man Jesus be crucified. Since it was the day before the Sabbath, Jesus' body was removed quickly from the cross and placed in the tomb of Joseph of Arimathea. Then on the third day the unbelievable happened.

I. Empty Tomb
(Luke 24:1-3)

A. Routine Preparations (v. 1)

1. Now upon the first day of the week, very early in the morning, they came unto the sepulchre, bringing the spices which they had prepared, and certain others with them.

The first day of the week is of course Sunday. Jesus was crucified and died two days previously, on Friday. Since Saturday was the Sabbath, it would not have been appropriate to anoint

Christ's body with *spices* on that day. Pious Jews are careful to avoid all forms of work on the Sabbath (Luke 23:56). Coming into contact with a dead body, especially on a "high" Sabbath (John 19:31), creates problems of ceremonial uncleanness (Numbers 19:11).

So Friday evening the body had been taken off the cross and hastily placed in a tomb to await final burial preparations. Luke 23:54-56 tells us that the women who followed Jesus from Galilee (referred to as *they*) take it upon themselves to prepare the spices the day of Christ's death and then wait until the first day of the week, after the Sabbath, to administer them. [See question #1, page 280.]

The time of day *(very early in the morning)* shows us how eager the women are to complete this task. Psalm 30:5 says "weeping may endure for a night, but joy cometh in the morning." God is about to dry the tears of all Jesus' followers and change the course of world history.

B. Unexpected Findings (vv. 2, 3)

2. And they found the stone rolled away from the sepulchre.

Mark 16:3 tells us that the women wonder who will roll *the stone* away so they can gain entrance to *the sepulchre*. When they see that the stone is already moved, they may be both relieved and startled. Who has done this, and why? Perhaps the women think that Joseph of Arimathea has courteously spared them the burden of trying to roll back the heavy stone. After all, the grave site does belong to him, and he has taken a keen interest in providing for Jesus' burial (Luke 23:50-53).

One mental image of this gravestone is that of a giant sphere that rolls downhill into the cave mouth, thus securing it from intruders. This is one possibility, but there is at least one other. The stone may be a flat, round disc that rolls side to

---

How to Say It

ARIMATHEA. *Air*-uh-muh-*thee*-uh (*th* as in *thin*; strong accent on *thee*).
CLEOPHAS. *Klee*-o-fus.
CORINTHIANS. Ko-*rin*-thee-unz (*th* as in *thin*).
DEUTERONOMY. Due-ter-*ahn*-uh-me.
GALILEE. *Gal*-uh-lee.
JOSES. *Jo*-sez.
JUDAS. *Joo*-dus.
MAGDALA. *Mag*-duh-luh.
MAGDALENE. *Mag*-duh-leen or Mag-duh-*lee*-nee.
PILATE. *Pie*-lut.
SEPULCHRE. *sep*-ul-kur.

---

side in a track running in front of and parallel to the cave opening. Such stones may thus be *rolled* to the left or right to gain access to the interior.

3. And they entered in, and found not the body of the Lord Jesus.

If the women are not disturbed by the moved stone, the fact that the *body* is missing certainly alarms them! What thoughts flash through their minds? Have they come to the wrong tomb? Not a chance! These same women personally had followed Joseph to the grave and witnessed the location of Jesus' lifeless body (Luke 23:55).

Have Jesus' enemies stolen His body in order to subject it to further disgrace? One can only imagine the rush of mixed thoughts that come over the women. But they do not wonder for long. [See question #2, page 280.]

II. Heavenly Messengers
(Luke 24:4-8)

A. Angels Appear to the Women (vv. 4, 5)

4. And it came to pass, as they were much perplexed thereabout, behold, two men stood by them in shining garments.

God quickly supplies an answer through *two men* who are clad *in shining garments*. They are later identified as angels (Luke 24:23). This event parallels the appearance of two men to the disciples to interpret Jesus' ascension into Heaven (Acts 1:10). Perhaps God chooses two angelic messengers to satisfy the requirement that weighty claims be confirmed by two witnesses (Deuteronomy 17:6; 2 Corinthians 13:1; Hebrews 10:28; Revelation 11:3).

5. And as they were afraid, and bowed down their faces to the earth, they said unto them, Why seek ye the living among the dead?

Apparently the appearance of the angels is more startling than verse 4 would imply! The women respond to the awe-inspiring presence of angels as any of us would if approached by heavenly messengers: the women are terrified, bowing *their faces* to the ground in respect. The angels respond just as in Acts 1:11: they greet Jesus' followers with a question. In Acts, angels ask why His followers are staring up into Heaven; here, angels ask why these women are looking for their *living* Savior *among the dead*.

CEMETERIES

I have an abnormal interest in cemeteries. Perhaps it is because of my interest in history, but I find cemeteries fascinating. Sometimes I like to wander through old cemeteries just to see what I can find.

One day when I was in Baltimore, I was walking through a section near downtown and discovered an old church with a small cemetery. Included was the grave of Edgar Allan Poe. I have visited the grave sites of Washington, Lincoln, Robert Frost, and several other famous people. I have visited the cemetery in Salzburg, Austria, that was used for some of the footage near the end of the movie *The Sound of Music*.

In all these visits I was keenly aware that the graves held the mortal remains only of people who were dead. If a person is alive, we do not expect to find him or her in a cemetery except for brief visits. *The Wall Street Journal* of July 23, 2007 carried a front-page story entitled "Liberia's Tombs Shelter Much More Than the Dead." The story was about children, criminals, and poor people who live subsistence lives in a cemetery after being displaced by war. This grates against our sensibilities (compare Mark 5:3). The location of Jesus' tomb is irrelevant today precisely because we don't seek the living among the dead.   —J. B. N.

B. Angels Remind the Women (vv. 6-8)

6, 7. He is not here, but is risen: remember how he spake unto you when he was yet in Galilee, saying, The Son of man must be delivered into the hands of sinful men, and be crucified, and the third day rise again.

The prospect that Jesus could be alive is certainly inviting. But what do the messengers mean by their question in verse 5? Those words can be interpreted in more than one way. So the messengers quickly clarify. They remind the women of Christ's prediction of both His death and resurrection (Luke 9:22; 18:31-33).

Jesus had known all along what would take place, and He had told His followers as much. Yet His followers do not *remember.* It is as if God wanted Jesus' followers to hear the predictions for the purpose of later recollection as a testimony of God's control over these events.

It is also important to note the language the angels use to describe what happened to Jesus. *He . . . is risen* is the language of resurrection. The kind of resurrection at issue is not just any kind of postmortem existence. It certainly does not mean that Jesus' spirit mystically departed His body to take on a new bodiless form (Luke 24:39). It does not mean merely that the disciples will feel Jesus to be alive in their hearts. Rather, it means that God has raised Jesus bodily. [See question #3, page 280.]

8. And they remembered his words.

With the angel's words of clarification, it all begins to make sense. What the disciples had

never caught on to during Jesus' ministry, the women finally begin to grasp. Jesus' suffering and death have been intentional, as is His resurrection. These are deliberate parts of God's plan.

This passage teaches us an important lesson about instruction and memory. Words don't always hit home when first heard. They may be recalled and recognized as being true only after being fulfilled. Parents know this all too well! Although they are not divinely inspired prophets, parents know from experience how a certain course of action their child is about to take is bound to turn out. The parent warns the child, but the warning "goes in one ear and out the other." The child goes ahead, suffers, and then hears the parent say, "I told you that would happen. You should have listened."

But one cannot recall what one has not heard. So it is important that Christians continually proclaim the good news of Christ to the lost. They may not immediately respond favorably to our message, but as life deals its ups and downs they may be able to discern God's hand at work, if they have been told already of a God who loves them enough to work in their lives. For similar reasons, parents continue to raise even their most rebellious children in the Lord. They hope with tears that later in life their own prodigals will someday recognize and submit to the gospel truths that they heard long before.

III. Relayed Message
(Luke 24:9-12)

A. Women Tell the Apostles (vv. 9, 10)

9. And returned from the sepulchre, and told all these things unto the eleven, and to all the rest.

The eleven disciples are the first to hear the relayed news. There are only eleven because Judas has taken his own life (Matthew 27:3-10). In his Gospel, Luke does not tell us of Judas's suicide, but he alludes to it in Acts when the apostles select another to take his place (Acts 1:12-26).

The eleven are not alone. There are other followers *(the rest)* with them or very close by. One wonders what they are all doing together (see John 20:19). Are they trying to regroup, trying to figure out how to put their lives back in order, having previously turned them upside down to follow Jesus? Or are they praying to God for some bit of guidance about what to do next? Jesus' ministry has been too powerful among them simply to believe it could end just like that.

Whatever their thoughts and activities, one suspects that they should be the most receptive group to the women's testimony. Jesus had told the disciples personally that He was to die and rise again.

But like a good storyteller, Luke holds us in suspense before reporting their response. He does this by pausing to name the women who bring the good news.

10. It was Mary Magdalene, and Joanna, and Mary the mother of James, and other women that were with them, which told these things unto the apostles.

Here we are given the names of the first witnesses to Christ's resurrection. We don't know if they are simply in the right place at the right time or if God intentionally chooses to entrust the message of Christ's resurrection to *women* first. [See question #4, page 280.] The latter idea is in keeping with Luke's presentation of God's high regard for those whom the first-century world does not esteem highly. Women, children, foreigners, and social outcasts often play important roles in Luke's Gospel account.

Luke first introduced *Mary Magdalene* and *Joanna* back in 8:2, 3. We learn there that Jesus cured these women of various evil spirits and infirmities. They then began traveling with Him and providing for His financial needs. The word *Magdalene* is not a surname as we think of such today; rather, it refers to the fact that this particular Mary is the one who comes from Magdala, which is near the Sea of Galilee. An amazing thing about Joanna is that her husband is the manager of Herod's household.

Identifying *Mary the mother of James* is more difficult since there are several women named Mary in the New Testament. This particular Mary is also identified as the mother of Joses (Matthew 27:56, 61; 28:1), and we know that Jesus had brothers named James and Joses (Matthew 13:55). Thus one logical guess is that this Mary is Jesus' mother.

It would be odd, however, that Jesus' mother would not be called as such at this point rather than by two of His half-brothers. In Acts 1:14, Luke refers to Jesus' mother as "Mary the mother of Jesus," not the mother of James and Joses. So Luke has no problem identifying Jesus' mother in this way.

John's Gospel does not help us resolve this issue. He mentions only Mary Magdalene as discovering and relating the story of the empty tomb (John 20:1, 2). John locates three different women named Mary at Jesus' crucifixion: Mary Magdalene, Jesus' mother, and Mary the wife of Cleophas (John 19:25). This latter Mary could also possibly be the mother of men named James and Joses.

B. Apostles Doubt the Women (vv. 11, 12)

11. And their words seemed to them as idle tales, and they believed them not.

"In *Christ* shall all be made *alive*."
—1 Corinthians 15:22

Visual for
Lesson 7

Ask your class, "Why does the message on this visual bear continuous repeating?"

Firsthand testimony is what the angels have given to the women. Secondhand testimony is what the women pass along to the disciples, and this results in disbelief. Jesus had told the disciples firsthand of His impending death and resurrection, but they do not accept the women's secondhand testimony regarding fulfillment. They go so far in their disbelief as to think that the women have fabricated *tales*—pure nonsense!

We should not assume that the disciples reject this testimony because the witnesses are women. The resurrection is an extraordinary event that requires great faith to accept. Even when Jesus later reveals himself to disciples in person, they express doubt, wondering if He is a ghost (Luke 24:36-43). It is not until they touch Him with their hands that they truly believe. Even so, Jesus will pronounce blessing on all who believe reliable testimony about Him, although that testimony be secondhand (John 20:29).

TALL TALES

There is a genre in American literature called *the tall tale*. It consists of a "hero story," featuring a larger-than-life character. The character is bigger and stronger than most people, even if the story is based on an actual person. Exaggeration and hyperbole are major ingredients in these stories. The hero usually faces a particular task and then resolves it in an unusual and humorous way. Exaggerated details flesh out the story, adding to the humor and the novelty of the tale.

Well-known examples of tall tale are the ones told about Paul Bunyan and his Blue Ox, Pecos Bill, John Henry the Steel-Driving Man, and Johnny Appleseed. A typical exaggeration is the story of Paul Bunyan pulling a ship through the English Channel—a ship so large that it scraped the sides, thus creating the white cliffs of Dover. The tall tale format has been used in teaching creative writing to children; they imagine a scenario in which they can improvise on a normal situation but exaggerate it and develop it into a tall tale.

It is always presumed that listeners can tell the difference between a tall tale and a truthful account. But some tale-tellers can become very credible in their exaggerations, and some truthful accounts are hard to imagine. That's the dilemma faced by the apostles when they heard the women. Was it a tall tale? Or was truth stranger than fiction? The answer became clear to them, and so must it to us.   —J. B. N.

12. Then arose Peter, and ran unto the sepulchre; and stooping down, he beheld the linen clothes laid by themselves, and departed, wondering in himself at that which was come to pass.

The action of *Peter* represents another kind of response to secondhand testimony: investigation. [See question #5, page 280.] Peter will not accept the women's testimony blindly, nor does he merely reject it without testing it for himself. So he runs straightway to the tomb. Peter, whose last recorded deed to this point has been to weep over denying Jesus, is more than mildly interested in his master's possible return!

Peter's findings are inconclusive. The empty tomb and the pile of body wrappings do not contradict the women's testimony. But there is no angel sighting. Peter departs the cave *wondering* what has happened, wondering where his Lord may be, and likely wondering whether he will get a second chance to prove his love for Jesus.

Home Daily Bible Readings

Monday, Apr. 6—God Raised Him from the Dead (Acts 13:26-33)

Tuesday, Apr. 7—God's Power for Us (Ephesians 1:15-23)

Wednesday, Apr. 8—First Fruits of the Dead (1 Corinthians 15:12-26)

Thursday, Apr. 9—Buried and Raised with Christ (Colossians 2:6-15)

Friday, Apr. 10—Walk in Newness of Life (Romans 6:3-11)

Saturday, Apr. 11—Seek the Things Above (Colossians 3:1-11)

Sunday, Apr. 12—Christ Has Risen (Luke 24:1-12)

Peter will get all the proof he needs soon enough! Jesus' resurrection means a new start for us still today. There are many who have heard of God's offer of forgiveness and new life, but they are waiting on more evidence. They are looking at the lives of Christians and evaluating whether we truly possess the new life we claim is possible. Unfortunately, when they don't see it in us, they often assume it is not true. So God's people must not only talk of new life, we must diligently seek to embrace it fully and live it daily in the sight of nonbelievers.

Conclusion

A. Secondhand Testimony

Today's lesson reveals a critical time for "the eleven" because they, as we, were in a position of relying on secondhand testimony. Of course, they go on to see Jesus firsthand, which placed them in a different position from ours. During this brief but critical window—the time between getting secondhand and firsthand testimony—we see some variation in response to testimony of Christ's resurrection. Some thought others to be peddling tall tales. Some tested the claims. At least one believed after conducting a test without actually having seen the risen Jesus (John 20:8). Another absolutely refused to believe without firsthand evidence (John 20:25).

Despite the variety of initial responses, all of Jesus' followers ultimately believed His resurrection. Today, Jesus does not stand among us physically to invite us to touch His nail-scarred hands as He did with Thomas. But God has left us with plenty of other evidence to create belief.

So let us not be discouraged by the variety of responses we receive to the gospel message. Let us not give up persistently proclaiming Christ to all people regardless of how they initially respond to us. Equally important, let us live with integrity and joy the new life Christ's resurrection has made possible for us. For Christ is indeed risen!

B. Prayer

Father in Heaven, may we not keep Your plan to ourselves. May we offer it boldly to all whom we meet. Let us not be intimidated by appearances or status. Let us not be discouraged by rejection or ridicule. Forsaking worldly praise, let us do Your will, knowing that the Lord of resurrection life is also Lord of the harvest. Through Jesus Christ our risen Lord, amen.

C. Thought to Remember

Live and proclaim Christ's resurrection.

Learning by Doing

This page contains an alternative lesson plan emphasizing learning activities. Some of these activities are also found in the helpful student book, Adult Bible Class.

Into the Lesson

Lead into a discussion of burial rituals by saying, "Death has always been mysterious to us. Various explanations have surfaced throughout the centuries to explain what happens at the point of death and afterward. Humans naturally want to 'make sense' out of things. What are some of the different rituals and ceremonies surrounding death and burial that have been practiced by various civilizations? What customs do we observe today? How do these ceremonies help people make sense of, or at least cope with, the mystery of death?"

At some point in the discussion, have the class contrast the Christian view of death with a non-Christian view. What makes the difference? Be sure to point out that the resurrection of Jesus is the defining point of belief and hope for the follower of Christ.

Into the Word

Select class members to represent various characters in a skit about the story in Luke 24. These include Mary Magdalene, Joanna, the second Mary, two men (angels), Peter, and some other apostles. As either you or another narrator reads verses 1-12, have the characters act out the scenes. Read slowly, pausing long enough for each scene to be enacted.

When the skit is completed, divide the class into two groups. Alternate in asking each group the following questions. Ask them to answer from memory if they can, but allow them to use their Bibles if necessary.

Group 1: "What was the day and time when the women came to the sepulchre?" *(Very early Sunday morning.)*

Group 2: "What had the women brought with them, and for what purpose?" *(They brought spices they had prepared to place around Jesus' body.)*

Groups 1 and 2: "What surprised the women when they arrived?" *(The stone was rolled away, and Jesus' body was missing.)*

Group 1: "How did the women react to the angels?" *(Fear and bowing down.)*

Group 2: "What did the angels tell them had happened to Jesus?" *(He had risen from the dead.)*

Group 1: "What words of Jesus did the angels repeat?" *("The Son of man must be delivered into the hands of sinful men, and be crucified, and the third day rise again.")*

Group 2: "What did the women do after they heard the angels' message?" *(Returned and told what had happened to the apostles.)*

Group 1: "What were the names of some of the women who went to the sepulchre?" *(Mary Magdalene, Joanna, Mary the mother of James.)*

Group 2: "How did the apostles react to the women's report?" *(They didn't believe them.)*

Group 1: "What did Peter do?" *(He ran to the sepulchre to see for himself.)*

Group 2: "What did Peter find?" *(The burial clothes, but no body.)*

Conclude by saying, "The events in today's text caused a turning point for all the people involved and even for us today. Let's see how many things we can name that are different because of this day in history." Jot answers on the board. You can ask the two groups to alternate in answering.

Into Life

The application of these exercises is that Jesus' resurrection changes lives. Write the following words across the top of the board or on a poster: *Home, Work/School, Community,* and *World.* Have the students relate ways that Jesus' resurrection has affected them in each area of life listed. Write answers under each heading.

Then say, "At first even Jesus' closest friends did not believe that He had risen. They wanted proof. The same is true today. Many people do not believe in the resurrection at all. They reject Christ's resurrection." Ask someone in class to represent the point of view of a person who does not believe in the resurrection. (Arrange for this before class time so the person can be prepared.) Have students tell the "unbeliever" of Jesus' resurrection, trying to persuade him or her that it is true. Keep in mind that perhaps someone in the class is not fully convinced of the resurrection and will be listening for answers to his or her uncertainty.

Ask if some would be willing to tell of a time they doubted Jesus' resurrection. Why did they doubt? Do they doubt now? What changed their belief? Did another person's life have any effect on them, either causing doubt or causing faith? How do we as Christians appear to those who do not follow Christ? Discuss how our lives can be a hindrance or an encouragement to those seeking the truth.

Let's Talk It Over

The questions on this page are designed to promote discussion of the lesson by the class and to encourage application of the lesson Scriptures. The answers provided are only discussion starters. Let your class talk it over from there.

1. How do you prepare to honor Christ on the first day of each week?

Christians may think that the only ones who need to prepare for worship on Sunday are the preacher, musicians, and those who will lead in prayers and meditations. But all Christians have a responsibility to see that they are prepared to express worship to the risen Christ.

This preparation includes getting a good night of sleep so that drowsiness does not become a hindrance to worship. Rising early enough to allow adequate time for arriving for worship avoids frantic rushing around, which can impede effective worship. We can consider our offering ahead of time, having this ready. If the preacher has announced in advance his text for the sermon, a careful reading of this text is a proper way to prepare. We don't prepare burial spices as the women did; we prepare ourselves!

2. What was a time when you didn't find Christ as you expected to find Him? How do you remain open to admitting and adjusting your wrong expectations?

Many deserted Jesus during His earthly ministry because He was not the kind of Messiah they expected (John 6:66). The women expected to find the body of Jesus, and when they did not, they were confused. The apostles did not expect to find Jesus alive after the crucifixion, so they prepared for a life without Him. Today people create their own expectations about Jesus that don't match up with the Bible.

We may be guilty of trying to force Jesus into our ideas of what He should be doing in our lives or in the world. When He does not fit those expectations, too often He is forsaken. Yet His ways are not our ways. We naturally expect to find Him in our church gatherings, but surprisingly we also may find Him in our workplace as we have opportunities to live out our faith in everyday life.

3. What are some ways you can remind yourself of the fact of the resurrection? Why and when do you need this reminder?

The resurrection of Jesus is the capstone of Christian faith. Because of the resurrection we have hope of our own resurrection with Christ at His second coming (1 Corinthians 15:12-14). You can post the simple, two-word phrase *Jesus Lives!* in places where you will see it often. Digging deeper, you can remind yourself of the fact of the resurrection as you study the evidence in Holy Scripture.

4. What lessons do you learn from the first telling of the message of the resurrection?

The women could not keep silent—can we? These women were not the apostles, but they had a message nonetheless. It is imperative that the church not rely on an "elite few," such as those who are paid as ministers or evangelists, to be the only ones to take the good news. That is a task for all who have been touched by the message.

The women also went to those who would (or should) be receptive to the information. It can be a mistake to spend a lot of time trying to convince people who are very hardened against the message. Time may be better spent with those ready to hear. Jesus told both the Twelve and the Seventy to shake the dust from their feet if people were not receptive (Luke 9:5; 10:10, 11).

5. How does the testimony of your church cause others to come to it and check it out? What do (or should) they find when they arrive?

Just as Peter wanted to investigate the testimony he heard about Christ, so people today will want to check out the testimony of God's people if it is something that is shared with excitement and conviction. Jesus stated that one of the ways the testimony of Christians would be seen would be in their love for one another (John 13:35). If we share a testimony of the love of God with the unsaved, it is imperative that this be what they see when they attend a gathering of the church.

Sadly, in some churches the unbelievers find hypocrisy and legalism, which drives them further from Christ. The worship testimony that Christians present should focus on glorifying God. A polished worship service may accomplish this if sincerity and love are evident. If those are not evident, a polished worship service will be seen as so much superficial glitz. It is through relationships and not empty rituals that people will be drawn to Christ.

You Are Witnesses

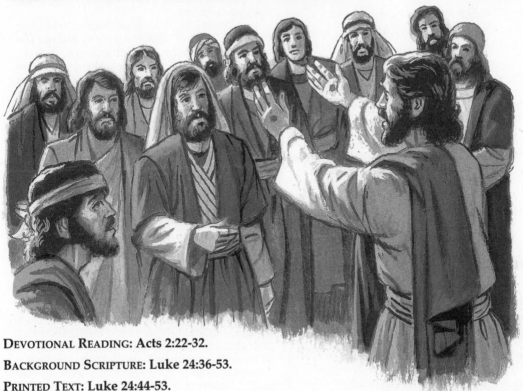

DEVOTIONAL READING: Acts 2:22-32.

BACKGROUND SCRIPTURE: Luke 24:36-53.

PRINTED TEXT: Luke 24:44-53.

Luke 24:44-53

44 And he said unto them, These are the words which I spake unto you, while I was yet with you, that all things must be fulfilled, which were written in the law of Moses, and in the prophets, and in the psalms, concerning me.

45 Then opened he their understanding, that they might understand the Scriptures,

46 And said unto them, Thus it is written, and thus it behooved Christ to suffer, and to rise from the dead the third day:

47 And that repentance and remission of sins should be preached in his name among all nations, beginning at Jerusalem.

48 And ye are witnesses of these things.

49 And, behold, I send the promise of my Father upon you: but tarry ye in the city of Jerusalem, until ye be endued with power from on high.

50 And he led them out as far as to Bethany, and he lifted up his hands, and blessed them.

51 And it came to pass, while he blessed them, he was parted from them, and carried up into heaven.

52 And they worshipped him, and returned to Jerusalem with great joy:

53 And were continually in the temple, praising and blessing God. Amen.

GOLDEN TEXT: Ye are witnesses of these things. And, behold, I send the promise of my Father upon you.—Luke 24:48, 49.

> *Christ and Creation*
> The Dawn of New Life
> Lessons 6–9

Lesson Aims

After participating in this lesson, each student will be able to:

1. List the evidences revealed in Luke's ascension account for believing in Jesus.

2. Explain how the combination of scriptural evidence and personal experience equips one to bear witness of Christ.

3. Write out a personal testimony that he or she can use to tell of Christ.

Lesson Outline

INTRODUCTION
    A. Acknowledging the Ascension
    B. Lesson Background
  I. ENLIGHTENED NOW (Luke 24:44-48)
    A. Remember Scripture (vv. 44, 45)
      Smarter, Younger, Sharper
    B. Remember Jesus (vv. 46, 47)
    C. Remember Responsibility (v. 48)
      Credible Witnesses
  II. EMPOWERED LATER (Luke 24:49-53)
    A. Promise and Instruction (v. 49)
    B. Blessing and Ascension (vv. 50, 51)
    C. Worship and Praise (vv. 52, 53)
CONCLUSION
    A. Celebrating Jesus' Ascension
    B. Prayer
    C. Thought to Remember

Introduction

A. Acknowledging the Ascension

Most churches faithfully celebrate Jesus' birth and resurrection. Christmas and Easter have become significant annual observances, and we have created many helpful traditions that keep these commemorations meaningful.

Less common, however, is celebration of Jesus' ascension. The reason for this cannot be that this event is not important in Scripture. There are at least as many references to the ascension as there are to Jesus' birth. Nor can it be that this event is not on anyone's Christian calendar like other notable days. Ascension Day on liturgical calendars is 40 days into the Easter Season and 10 days before Pentecost. Several Christian traditions acknowledge it on their calendars, even if they pay comparatively little attention to what the day commemorates.

In a sincere effort to avoid human traditions that have flooded Christianity and blurred the clear gospel message, some churches have deemphasized the idea of a Christian calendar. Yet there is an important difference between celebrating feast days that honor "saints" and recognizing key events in Jesus' life. Jesus' ascension was a pivotal point in world history, and what it signifies bears directly on the daily life of Christians and churches. In today's lesson we focus on the events leading up to Jesus' ascension and its abiding significance for both His followers and the world.

B. Lesson Background

After Jesus died, His body was removed from the cross, wrapped in linen, and placed in a borrowed tomb before the Sabbath could begin (Luke 23:50-56). After that particular Sabbath day was over, some women who followed Jesus went to His tomb with burial spices, but found His body gone. An angel told them He had risen as He had said (Luke 24:1-12).

When the women told the disciples, they doubted, although Peter ran to the tomb to test their claim. Jesus then appeared to two disciples on the road to Emmaus (Luke 24:13-35) and finally showed himself to the eleven. They were startled by His appearance and wondered if He were a ghost. But He demonstrated the truth of His resurrection by inviting them to inspect His wounds, touch His body, and watch Him eat food (Luke 24:36-43).

The disciples could see and feel the evidence, but it still made little sense to them. That's where today's lesson begins.

I. Enlightened Now
(Luke 24:44-48)

A. Remember Scripture (vv. 44, 45)

44. And he said unto them, These are the words which I spake unto you, while I was yet with you, that all things must be fulfilled, which were written in the law of Moses, and in the prophets, and in the psalms, concerning me.

When the angels appeared to the women earlier, they noted how Jesus had predicted the events of His passion (Luke 24:6). Luke records these predictions in 9:22-27; 43b-45; 13:33; 17:25; and 18:31-33. Jesus confirms this angel's testimony about Him and adds that these events are the fulfillment of the *law, prophets,* and *psalms.*

Jesus' statement here is one of our earliest witnesses to the Jewish canon of Scripture. The word *canon* (literally, "measuring rod") refers to the authoritative collection of sacred writings. The text of the Jewish canon is the same as our Old Testament, although it is organized differently. The Jewish canon has the three sections that Jesus mentions here. The designation *psalms* as used here is more inclusive than the book we know as Psalms; that third section refers to all the books that don't fit within the Law and the Prophets. Naturally, the book of Psalms itself constitutes a large portion of this segment. By contrast, today we arrange the Old Testament in a 5-12-5-5-12 format: 5 books of law, 12 books of history, 5 books of wisdom, 5 books by "major" prophets, and 12 books by "minor" prophets.

If Jesus is alluding to the entirety of the Jewish canon, then He is claiming boldly that what He has undergone is nothing less than the fulfillment of the entire Old Testament. The whole story, from Adam to the return from exile and beyond, points to and finds its fulfillment in Jesus' death, burial, and resurrection. In directing the disciples toward Scripture, Jesus may have specific passages in mind as well, as we shall see.

45. Then opened he their understanding, that they might understand the Scriptures.

Jesus has to open the disciples' *understanding*, not only because they are unable to connect the dots on their own, but also because these truths have been concealed from them, presumably by God (see Luke 9:45; 18:34). For reasons not entirely clear, the disciples to this point have not been able to grasp the reality and implications of Christ's passion. But the time is now right, so Jesus gives them eyes to see.

We are often like the disciples in this regard. The truth stands directly in front of us, but we

cannot grasp it. Sometimes we blind our own eyes, whether by sin or by lack of focus. God may blind us to what we are unable to handle, at least for the moment.

Yet God may help us to see what we are blind to. He sent us His Spirit to guide us into truth (John 16:13). The presence of the Spirit is not a guarantee that we will understand all things properly at all times. Some things the Lord will not reveal to us (Acts 1:7). But the Spirit helps overcome our weakness that we may see what God wills us to see. [See question #1, page 288.]

SMARTER, YOUNGER, SHARPER

Would you like to make your brain "smarter, younger, sharper," as one advocate of video games phrases it? The idea is that "mental workout games" can do just that for us. Neuroscience researchers and game designers are teaming up to create such mind-stimulating games as *Brain Trainer*, *BrainBuilder*, and *Vigorous Mind*. Many older adults experience forgetfulness and difficulty in learning new things, but electronic games offer some hope for slowing, even if not reversing, the process. And just to give some added veracity to the concept, AARP has added a page called "Games and Puzzles" to its Web site to help sharpen minds.

Stimulating the prefrontal cortex with problem-solving activity seems to help keep the brain "young." We need mental exercise, along with physical exercise and a balanced diet. Absolute scientific proof is lacking at this point, but the games are fun nevertheless.

In our drive to stay young mentally, we need to remember that healthy brain function is no guarantee of spiritual understanding. Today's text makes it obvious: Jesus' disciples were in the prime of their lives, but He still had to "open their understanding" so they could comprehend the meaning of Scripture. Regardless of our age, a proper spiritual perspective isn't the same as being "smarter, younger, sharper."   —C. R. B.

B. Remember Jesus (vv. 46, 47)

46. And said unto them, Thus it is written, and thus it behooved Christ to suffer, and to rise from the dead the third day.

Luke does not say which specific Old Testament passage(s) Jesus has in mind here, if any. Perhaps Luke is waiting to do this in Acts, his second book. For example, in Acts 2:25-28 Luke records Peter quoting David in Psalm 16:8-11, which says that God will not abandon Jesus in death nor let Him experience decay. See also Acts 4:11 quoting Psalms 118:22; Acts 4:25, 26 quoting Psalm 2:1, 2; Acts 8:32, 33 quoting Isaiah 53:7, 8; etc.

How to Say It

BARNABAS. *Bar*-nuh-bus.

DEUTERONOMY. Due-ter-*ahn*-uh-me.

ELIJAH. Ee-*lye*-juh.

EMMAUS. Em-*may*-us.

GENTILES. *Jen*-tiles.

ISAIAH. Eye-*zay*-uh.

JACOB. *Jay*-kub.

JERUSALEM. Juh-*roo*-suh-lem.

JUDEA. Joo-*dee*-uh.

MICAH. *My*-kuh.

MOSES. *Mo*-zes or *Mo*-zez.

PENTECOST. *Pent*-ih-kost.

SAMARIA. Suh-*mare*-ee-uh.

Another relevant passage is Luke 11:29, 30, where Jesus alludes to the sign of Jonah. As the fish spewed Jonah from its belly after three days, so the grave surrendered Jesus on *the third day*. Interestingly, Jonah refers to his time in the fish in terms that Jews associate with the grave (Jonah 2:2).

47. And that repentance and remission of sins should be preached in his name among all nations, beginning at Jerusalem.

Jesus announces a critical new phase in the life of His followers: the beginning of the mission to Gentiles. They had been proclaiming *repentance* and forgiveness *of sins* to Jews throughout their ministry (Matthew 10:5, 6). But now they must turn their attention to the *nations*, that is, the Gentiles. The disciples may not grasp this idea fully just yet, given Peter's surprise at being sent to Gentiles in Acts 10.

In Acts, Luke supplies Old Testament passages that anticipate the Gentile mission that Jesus may have had in mind. Luke records Paul and Barnabas quoting Isaiah 49:6, which states that Israel will be a light to the nations so God's salvation may reach the ends of the earth (Acts 13:47). Luke notes James quoting Amos 9:11, 12, which includes a reference to "all the Gentiles, upon whom my name is called" (Acts 15:15-18).

However, we must not miss the fact that this mission is intended to begin in *Jerusalem*. It is in Jerusalem that the disciples receive the Holy Spirit. They begin their mission first in Jerusalem, then move outward to Judea, Samaria, and the ends of the earth (Acts 1:8). It is important for the mission to begin with Jerusalem because of passages such as Isaiah 2:3 and Micah 4:1, 2. God fulfills these prophecies by gathering the disciples in Jerusalem, empowering them with His Spirit, and then sending them forth to the nations.

C. Remember Responsibility (v. 48)

48. And ye are witnesses of these things.

Those who follow Jesus during His earthly ministry are unique in world history for being eyewitnesses to God's saving work through Him. Others of that time period may have seen some things that Jesus did, but His apostles are taught how to interpret these events without error.

As firsthand *witnesses*, these particular disciples have important responsibilities. The apostle Paul also becomes a firsthand witness through extraordinary means (Acts 9:1-19; 1 Corinthians 15:1-10; etc.). The apostles are commissioned to take the gospel to the world and personally verify it. For this reason the apostolic testimony, as preserved in the New Testament, constitutes the reliable baseline for Christian faith.

We may confidently continue the first disciples' missionary witness as we pass on to others what we have received from them in Scripture. [See question #2, page 288.] What God says to us through the new covenant in Scripture is normative and binding on all churches and Christians everywhere. Scripture is the standard by which all Christian speech, practice, church order, and doctrine are to be judged.

CREDIBLE WITNESSES

You may have seen the video clip that made its way around the world a while back showing a commercial airliner making an emergency landing on the I-405 freeway in Los Angeles. The freeway had been cleared except for a hapless young man in a Jeep wagon and a little old lady in a sedan. The man sees the plane approaching in his rearview mirror and vainly tries to accelerate out of danger. The huge plane comes down on top of the Jeep and the two vehicles continue down the freeway. The woman is oblivious to what is happening, but fortunately the plane straddles her car so she is unharmed.

"Pictures don't lie," we used to say. However, with the arrival of digital technology, it is no longer so. This video was digitally contrived—just like many of the "unbelievable" pictures we receive by e-mail. The apparent eyewitness view of the incident is deceptive. In this case, "seeing is *not* believing."

With Jesus' disciples, it was entirely different. They were physically present to observe the events that comprise the essence of the gospel story. When they went out to fulfill Jesus' commission to preach the gospel to all the nations, they did so as uniquely qualified eyewitnesses. This makes their testimony superior to all the naysayers in ages since who have sought to discredit the story of Jesus.   —C. R. B.

II. Empowered Later
(Luke 24:49-53)

A. Promise and Instruction (v. 49)

49. And, behold, I send the promise of my Father upon you: but tarry ye in the city of Jerusalem, until ye be endued with power from on high.

Jesus' commission includes waiting. His followers need to remain in *Jerusalem* until God initiates the next step. Jesus does not convey that they will wait long, but it is imperative that they wait in Jerusalem. [See question #3, page 288.] Despite Jerusalem's track record of killing prophets and despite its unjust crucifixion of Jesus, God remains faithful to that city. He uses this unfaithful city for His purposes by making it His launching pad for global missions.

The promise of the *Father* and *power from on high* are one and the same. They refer to the Holy Spirit. The Spirit is God's empowering presence to enable His people to carry out His mission in the world. Jesus provides an extended discussion of this promise in John 16. But Luke mentions it here for the first time in his Gospel without specifying what it means. He alluded to it previously when recounting John the Baptist's teaching that Jesus would baptize with the Holy Spirit and with fire (3:16), but he develops it more fully in Acts 1:4-8.

These passages don't indicate, however, exactly in what sense this promise is fulfilled. This only becomes clear when the promise is fulfilled in Acts 2. On the Day of Pentecost, God pours out the Spirit on Jesus' disciples. When Peter explains what is going on (Acts 2:17-21), he quotes God's promise to pour the Spirit on His people (from Joel 2:28-32). We continue the apostles' mission by the strength of the Holy Spirit.

B. Blessing and Ascension (vv. 50, 51)

50. And he led them out as far as to Bethany, and he lifted up his hands, and blessed them.

In the footsteps of Jacob (Genesis 49) and Moses (Deuteronomy 33), Jesus gathers His people and blesses them before departing. We are not told the content of this blessing, but it likely concerns their well-being, safety, and faithfulness as they carry out His mission. Jesus' prayer recorded in John 17 may also reflect some of what He says at this time.

By leading His disciples out of the city, Jesus ensures peace and quiet. Perhaps He wants to avoid creating a big scene by the nature of His departure. *Bethany* is an important place to Jesus. It is the hometown of Mary, Martha, and Lazarus (John 11:1), and it is the place where Mary anointed Him with expensive perfume, unknowingly preparing for His burial (Mark 14:3-8; John 12:1-8). It is located on the southeastern slope of the Mount of Olives, about two miles outside of Jerusalem (John 11:18). Luke also locates the ascension in this area in Acts 1:12.

51. And it came to pass, while he blessed them, he was parted from them, and carried up into heaven.

Finally, what Luke is building up to comes to pass. At Jesus' transfiguration in Luke 9:31, Moses and Elijah speak with Jesus about His departure. Then in 9:51, Luke says the time for Jesus to be taken away is drawing near. This goal of ascension is reached only through the cross and resurrection, but that the ascension is Jesus' goal should not

Visual for Lesson 8. *Point to this visual as you ask question #2 on page 288: "How are you doing as a witness for Christ?"*

be overlooked. It marks the completion of Jesus' earthly pilgrimage. It isn't enough for Him to be born and to walk among people. It isn't enough to teach His followers about the kingdom and how to live. It isn't even enough for Him to die and rise again. Jesus' destiny is to sit at God's right hand in glory; that can happen only after the ascension.

It is not until He is crowned in glory that Jesus assumes His rightful position over the nations and powers to which He was temporarily and voluntarily subject. It is not until He is exalted on high that He will send His Spirit to empower His people to carry out their mission. It is not until He leaves this world that He will be with us everywhere and always as He promises in Matthew 28:20. Before His ascension people speak with Him, touch Him, and eat with Him. After His ascension they are stricken with awe and reverent fear at His presence (see Acts 9:3-6; Revelation 1:17).

The ascension is indeed a pivotal event in the life of Jesus and in world history. Jesus' ascension is discussed or assumed in numerous passages (see Matthew 26:64; Mark 16:19; Luke 9:31, 51; John 1:18; 3:13; 6:62; 14:2; 20:17; Acts 1:9; 2:33; 3:21; 5:31; 7:56; Ephesians 1:20; 4:8-10; Philippians 2:9; 1 Timothy 3:16; Hebrews 1:3; 4:14; 6:19, 20; 1 Peter 3:22; and Revelation 12:5). The fact of Jesus' ascension also is arguably a culminating point of Peter's Pentecost sermon in Acts 2. Listing all these passages (and there are more) is important because today's church sorely neglects this critical event in Jesus' life.

We celebrate Jesus' death because in it we receive forgiveness of sins. We celebrate His resurrection because in it we find hope for eternal life. Perhaps we should celebrate His exaltation because in it we learn submission to our sovereign Lord.

Yet submission is not all that we learn. In submitting we learn of power that only the exalted Christ can bestow on us (John 16:7). We learn confidence before enemies of the cross, because Christ has already triumphed over them and is subjecting them under His feet (1 Corinthians 15:25). We learn comfort in our weakness, because the ascended and exalted Jesus intercedes for us continually before the Father (Romans 8:34). [See question #4, page 288.]

C. Worship and Praise (vv. 52, 53)

52. And they worshipped him, and returned to Jerusalem with great joy.

The disciples had been stunned and broken after Jesus' death. After Jesus' resurrection they had been skeptical, confused, amazed, and joyous. Now, after Jesus' ascension, they are filled *with great joy* that overflows to worship. [See question #5, page 288.] Many godly people have died on behalf of others. A few have been raised back to life. But only Jesus dies, rises, and is taken up to be seated at God's right hand.

The ascension culminates and concludes Jesus' earthly ministry. It makes concretely visible to the disciples the power of the gospel they have been preaching. They have been preaching that the kingdom of God begins in Jesus, but they have been confused that their king refuses to be a political Messiah (John 6:15; Acts 1:6). Now their king is properly situated, not merely over *Jerusalem*, but over the entire cosmos. The disciples' expectations to this point have been too small!

The exalted Christ elicits worship. He doesn't have to request it or demand it from the disciples who are truly His. They offer worship freely out of the surplus of joy they find in serving Him. So it goes without saying that they will obey their master, return to Jerusalem, and wait. In this single verse the disciples demonstrate the proper threefold response of worship, obedience, and joy to Christ's death, resurrection, and ascension.

53. And were continually in the temple, praising and blessing God. Amen.

The disciples still think of themselves as Jews. So as they await the promised Spirit, they gather in *the temple* to praise God. This temple has been a den of robbers, a house of profiteering. This element undoubtedly is still present. But that doesn't deter these disciples. They peer through the spiritual darkness to see the temple as a house of praise.

It is important to note that the disciples are intentionally public about their faith. Even before the divine empowerment that comes on Pentecost, they can't help but radiate before others the joy of Christ. Should we not be able to be as joyous?

Conclusion

A. Celebrating Jesus' Ascension

The normal rhythm of society doesn't quite come to a grinding halt around Christmas and Easter, but it does slow down to varying degrees. Due to the influence of Christians, these have become recognized events on the secular calendar. Christians gather together and celebrate these events meaningfully. However, no such space is created for the ascension.

How sad! Jesus' ascension means that He now sits at the right hand of the Father in glory and that every ruler and authority is either being eliminated or subjected to Him (1 Corinthians 15:24-27). The birth of a baby may seem harmless. The resurrection of a man who no longer walks the earth is not seen as a threat. The placement of a ruler over all earthly realms, however, is shattering. We cannot allow our Christian calendars to be determined or shaped by national interests. We must proclaim, celebrate, and live according to the full story of Jesus, including His birth, death, resurrection, and ascension on high.

B. Prayer

Father in Heaven, one of our main enemies is busyness. Busyness keeps us distracted so we are not able to pause and think Your thoughts after you. Allow us to pause right now and marvel at what Jesus' ascension means. In His name, amen.

C. Thought to Remember

Bear witness to Christ's ascension.

Home Daily Bible Readings

Monday, Apr. 13—Women at the Tomb (Matthew 28:6-10)

Tuesday, Apr. 14—Mary Magdalene (John 20:11-18)

Wednesday, Apr. 15—On the Road to Emmaus (Luke 24:13-23, 28-31)

Thursday, Apr. 16—Thomas (John 20:24-29)

Friday, Apr. 17—Seven Disciples (John 21:1-14)

Saturday, Apr. 18—Witnesses of the Resurrection (1 Corinthians 15:1-8)

Sunday, Apr. 19—You Are Witnesses (Luke 24:44-53)

Learning by Doing

This page contains an alternative lesson plan emphasizing learning activities. Some of these activities are also found in the helpful student book, Adult Bible Class.

Into the Lesson

Ask a professional salesperson or fundraiser in your class or church to give an enthusiastic one-minute sales pitch for the product or organization he or she represents. After the presentation, ask students what emotions, passion, or enthusiasm they saw in the presentation. For a different approach, have an actor give a lackluster sales pitch for a product or service that the actor obviously doesn't have much enthusiasm for.

Remind the class that Jesus has asked that each Christian be a witness (salesperson) for Him. Ask, "What enthusiasm or conviction do others see in the average Christian for the gospel message?" The responses will serve as your transition to the Into the Word segment.

Into the Word

Say, "In order for your message to persuade, you have to be convinced about the subject. Christians must become impressed and excited anew about who Jesus is and what He did (and does) for them." Have a class member with dramatic reading ability read aloud Luke 24:44-53. At the end of the reading, ask what is exciting about this account. Ask students to compare and contrast the emotions of the people in this week's lesson with those of last week's lesson. Digging deeper, ask what facts and experiences led to those emotions.

After that discussion, reread verses 48 and 49. Ask the class, "After reading this account of some of Jesus' last words on earth, what do you see as your Christian purpose in life? How is our purpose the same as and different from the purpose of Jesus' original disciples?"

The "same as" thought that should emerge is that we all are to be witnesses for Christ. The "different from" thought that should emerge is that Jesus' instruction "tarry ye in the city of Jerusalem, until ye be endued with power from on high" was a one-time instruction to specific individuals. This distinction can lead to an interesting and useful discussion about how to tell the difference between instructions for all Christians and instructions meant only for some Christians.

Follow up by asking "What is it about today's text that helps you the most in fulfilling your purpose for Christian witness?" Responses will be highly personal.

Into Life

Remind the class that every believer has *a witness* to share with others. Quickly stress that you're using the word *witness* in the Merriam-Webster's dictionary senses of "attestation of a fact or event" and "public affirmation by word or example of . . . conviction." Write these two definitions on the board. Also stress that you are not using the word *witness* in the sense of "eyewitness," since none of us was present to see the resurrected Jesus personally or to watch Him ascend.

With these safeguards in place, ask, "What is the witness that all Christians have in common? What variations to this witness are allowable?" Answers to the first of these two questions should focus on the fact of Christ's resurrection. The variations may include personal stories of how the resurrected and ascended Christ has led one to reject a certain sinful lifestyle.

Finally, allow some silent time for each class member to write out a short version of his or her witness. Make sure that where you stand or sit does not block students' view of the definitions you wrote on the board; your learners will need to see those definitions as they write.

Say, "Most Christians have never taken time to put into written words their personal witness or testimonial, so this exercise can be a challenge. Public testimonials usually involve some dramatic life change such as a drug addict's becoming clean and now fighting against drug use. You may not have experienced this kind of life change and thus do not think you have a testimonial. But you do. Your testimonial is about two things: (1) you are convinced regarding the facts of Jesus' resurrection and ascension and (2) Jesus has made an impact on your life in profound ways."

After a few minutes, divide the class into groups of three or four and ask (but do not insist) that each one relate his or her testimonial to the small group. They may read it if they are too nervous, but actually just telling the things they have written is more effective. After students have finished, explain that what they have been doing with one another is witnessing for Christ. Ask, "Do you think you can do the same with nonbelievers?" Encourage your students to tell their testimony to at least two people this week. Close with prayer that asks God to open doors in this regard.

Let's Talk It Over

The questions on this page are designed to promote discussion of the lesson by the class and to encourage application of the lesson Scriptures. The answers provided are only discussion starters. Let your class talk it over from there.

1. Why do we sometimes fail to understand the teaching of Scripture? What roadblocks need removing in this regard? How do we do that?

At one level, understanding Scripture is like understanding anything: it takes time and effort to think through what is being said. Modern culture likes to communicate in easily digestible "sound bites." Some of Scripture is written that way, but much of it isn't.

Sometimes we fail to understand the Bible because we listen to teachers who are not strong in the Scriptures. Paul warns about those who would gather around teachers who would simply tell what itching ears want to hear (2 Timothy 4:3). To understand the truth of Scripture, we must take the attitude of Apollos and be open to people like Aquila and Priscilla to share the truth with us (see Acts 18:24-26).

2. How are you doing as a witness for Christ? How can you make your life a stronger testimony?

When we actively witness for the Lord, we demonstrate the impact that our faith is having in our lives. When our outward life reflects true faith, others are drawn to us and then to Christ. Our testimony is strengthened when we learn to walk with Christ daily in His Word and in prayer.

A person may be a Christian for 30 years, but end up being spiritually immature if the only spiritual nourishment he or she gets during all those years is Sunday morning worship and Sunday school. A regular, persistent private time of worship and devotion is necessary. This is how we learn more about Christ and grow in our love for Him. Those things that we love we naturally share with others.

3. Why do you think God requires us at times to wait? Why do we find this hard to do? What happens if we "jump the gun"?

We can imagine that when the disciples saw Jesus in His resurrected state, they wanted to begin immediately to take that message to others. But they had to wait. At times we too may want to rush ahead of the Lord's plan in advancing His kingdom. Abraham is an example of someone who jumped the gun in trying to improve on the Lord's timing (Genesis 16).

Waiting can be a tricky thing. Sometimes we wait because of laziness; sometimes we wait out of a desire that someone else will do the task of evangelism. But there are appropriate times for waiting. Maybe we have shared the gospel with another person, but he or she needs time to process what has been heard. Waiting allows the Holy Spirit time to work through our testimony to bring conviction.

Unfortunately, sometimes people have to "hit bottom" before they see the need for Christ. Waiting is essential though hard in these times. Our culture wants instant results. Godly waiting cuts against the grain of this cultural tendency.

4. In what ways has the ascended Lord blessed you? How can you use these blessings to bless others as you serve as His witness?

Many times we focus on those blessings from God that are merely "of the flesh." For example, we may think of health, finances, and family as being the major blessings we receive. Though Christ indeed has blessed us in these ways, the major focus should be on the spiritual blessings we have received.

When we realize that the greatest blessing given us is that of forgiveness of sin and salvation, we should want to share this blessing with others. A way to do this is to develop a personal (but not scripted) testimony to share with others with whom you come in contact. Extending forgiveness and grace to others as Christ has extended it to us is a way to be a blessing.

5. How is your joy in Christ? How well are you expressing that joy?

"The joy of the Lord is your strength" (Nehemiah 8:10). In a day when people seek fulfillment in so many things that in the end do not satisfy, it is vital that Christians find their joy in Christ. This joy can be present in the midst of struggles and hardships.

We must not confuse the joy of Jesus with the happiness the world pursues. Joy is based on the internal presence of the Spirit of Christ. This joy is expressed in praising God, who is the giver of all good gifts. Joy is evident in the expectation of the fulfillment of all things when Christ returns. A gloomy Christian is a contradiction in terms.

Help Those in Need

DEVOTIONAL READING: John 14:8-14.

BACKGROUND SCRIPTURE: Acts 9:32-43.

PRINTED TEXT: Acts 9:32-43.

Acts 9:32-43

32 And it came to pass, as Peter passed throughout all quarters, he came down also to the saints which dwelt at Lydda.

33 And there he found a certain man named Aeneas, which had kept his bed eight years, and was sick of the palsy.

34 And Peter said unto him, Aeneas, Jesus Christ maketh thee whole: arise, and make thy bed. And he arose immediately.

35 And all that dwelt at Lydda and Sharon saw him, and turned to the Lord.

36 Now there was at Joppa a certain disciple named Tabitha, which by interpretation is called Dorcas: this woman was full of good works and almsdeeds which she did.

37 And it came to pass in those days, that she was sick, and died: whom when they had washed, they laid her in an upper chamber.

38 And forasmuch as Lydda was nigh to Joppa, and the disciples had heard that Peter was there, they sent unto him two men, desiring him that he would not delay to come to them.

39 Then Peter arose and went with them. When he was come, they brought him into the upper chamber: and all the widows stood by him weeping, and showing the coats and garments which Dorcas made, while she was with them.

40 But Peter put them all forth, and kneeled down, and prayed; and turning him to the body said, Tabitha, arise. And she opened her eyes: and when she saw Peter, she sat up.

41 And he gave her his hand, and lifted her up; and when he had called the saints and widows, he presented her alive.

42 And it was known throughout all Joppa; and many believed in the Lord.

43 And it came to pass, that he tarried many days in Joppa with one Simon a tanner.

Apr 26

GOLDEN TEXT: Forasmuch as Lydda was nigh to Joppa, and the disciples had heard that Peter was there, they sent unto him two men, desiring him that he would not delay to come to them.—Acts 9:38.

Lesson Aims

After participating in this lesson, each student will be able to:

1. Tell how God used Peter to heal Aeneas and raise Tabitha.

2. Tell the importance of doing acts of kindness after the model of Peter (who could do miraculous acts) and Tabitha (who used more "ordinary" means).

3. Describe one act of benevolence he or she will perform in the week ahead.

Lesson Outline

INTRODUCTION
  A. Self-Help Mania
  B. Lesson Background
 I. PETER HEALS AENEAS (Acts 9:32-35)
  A. Setting #1 (v. 32)
  B. Miracle #1 (vv. 33, 34)
  C. Reaction #1 (v. 35)
   Good from Bad
II. PETER RAISES TABITHA (Acts 9:36-43)
  A. Setting #2 (vv. 36-38)
  B. Miracle #2 (vv. 39-41)
   Talking About the Dead
  C. Reaction #2 (vv. 42, 43)
CONCLUSION
  A. Giving and Receiving Help
  B. Prayer
  C. Thought to Remember

Introduction

A. Self-Help Mania

The Wall Street Journal of July 31, 2007 featured an article titled "Bibliotherapy: Reading Your Way to Mental Health." The idea is that "some self-help books can measurably improve mental health." An online search reveals that scores of self-help books have been published in recent years. Such books constitute "one of publishing's hottest categories."

Common topics include building one's self-esteem, overcoming past failures, and taking life by the horns. Skill-oriented books teach one how to cook, represent oneself in court, get rich, and even write one's own self-help book. Perhaps the most telling sign that self-help mania has secured a strong market share is the publication of a book that gathers 50 "classics" of self-help literature.

Christian writers have also joined the crusade. In addition to countless books identifying certain Bible passages or principles as the ultimate source of self-help, one may choose from a variety of self-help editions of the Bible. Christians are so deeply enmeshed in self-help philosophy that a bibliography has been compiled that briefly introduces 700 of the 5,000 Christian self-help books that were available during a mere 15-year period.

The common proverb "God helps those who help themselves" has apparently struck a chord. The astute Bible reader knows, however, that this influential proverb is not only absent from Scripture, but it rubs deeply against Scripture's grain. God has called His people to be both fully dependent on Him and heavily reliant on one another. This much is clear in 1 Corinthians 12, which reminds us that no part of Christ's body can claim it doesn't need the help of others.

Such interdependence does not mean that self-discipline and motivation have no place (see, for example, 2 Thessalonians 3:6-10). Rather, God's Word motivates all believers to use their gifts to help others. In today's reading from Acts 9, we see healthy interdependence in action.

B. Lesson Background

In Acts 1:8 Jesus told His disciples that after God poured His Holy Spirit on them, they were to be His witnesses in Jerusalem, Judea, Samaria, and the ends of the earth. That passage thus serves as something of a table of contents for the book of Acts. Chapters 2–7 show the spread of the gospel in Jerusalem and Judea. Chapter 8 demonstrates the church's beachhead in Samaria, and chapters 13–28 document the gospel's spread throughout the Mediterranean area. Chapters 9–12 offer us some important transition points in the gospel's progress. Before the good news could be taken afar, God had to teach Jewish Christians to embrace Gentile (non-Jewish) believers fully as Christian brothers and sisters.

Chapter 9 begins with the conversion of Saul, who would later become the foremost apostle to the Gentiles. Then in chapter 10 God graphically demonstrated to Peter that it was time to make Gentiles converts. Sandwiched between these pivotal conversions is today's text, namely Acts 9:32-43. In this passage Peter ministered on the fringes of Jewish society, in towns located away from the Jewish power structure of Jerusalem.

Out there God used Peter to help the needy, enlist helpers, and tap into the divine help necessary for catching the next wave of the Spirit's work into the world beyond Jerusalem.

I. Peter Heals Aeneas
(Acts 9:32-35)
A. Setting #1 (v. 32)

32. And it came to pass, as Peter passed throughout all quarters, he came down also to the saints which dwelt at Lydda.

Here we find the apostle *Peter* functioning as an itinerant preacher, traveling around Palestine. He spreads the gospel to the lost and encourages those who are saved. About 30 miles northwest of Jerusalem, he visits the believers of *Lydda*. This town is strategically located at the intersection of one road leading from Syria to Egypt and another road linking the Mediterranean coast with Jerusalem. Lydda is called *Lod* in the Old Testament (1 Chronicles 8:12; Ezra 2:33; Nehemiah 11:35).

We are not told when the gospel first reached this town. Perhaps some of its inhabitants were present in Jerusalem when Peter preached his famous Pentecost sermon. Or maybe the persecutions that rocked Jerusalem in Acts 8:1 dispersed certain believers to this strategic locale. Philip the evangelist may also have preached in this town on his way from Azotus to Caesarea (8:40).

Whether from Peter, Philip, or some unknown evangelist, the gospel is already present in Lydda. The believers are referred to as *saints* (literally, "holy ones"). This term is seldom used in Acts, but throughout the New Testament it always refers to groups of Christians, never to individual believers. The emphasis is not on the heroic faith of extraor-

dinary individuals, but on the "set apart status" of a group of people who order their lives according to the will of their holy God.

B. Miracle #1 (vv. 33, 34)

33. And there he found a certain man named Aeneas, which had kept his bed eight years, and was sick of the palsy.

We are not told if *Aeneas* is a believer. All we know is that he has been paralyzed for *eight years*. Though there are many believers in the town, this man has not encountered God's healing power. After eight years he may have given up hope. But the arrival of Peter, one of Jesus' closest followers, is one of the best scenarios possible!

34. And Peter said unto him, Aeneas, Jesus Christ maketh thee whole: arise, and make thy bed. And he arose immediately.

Like his master, *Peter* is moved with compassion to help. Speaking the words similar to those of Jesus when He healed the paralytic in Capernaum (Mark 2:11), Peter invites the man to get up and get moving. The man wastes no time.

Even though he is an apostle of Jesus' "inner circle," Peter claims no power for himself. Instead he tells the man, even before healing him, that *Jesus Christ* makes him whole. Peter is a gifted man— gifted as a healer and gifted as an apostle (Acts 3:1-10; 5:12-16). Yet he places emphasis neither on his personal gifting nor his unprecedented Christian experience. Instead, he acknowledges that whatever good may come of this encounter, Jesus Christ is its source.

C. Reaction #1 (v. 35)

35. And all that dwelt at Lydda and Sharon saw him, and turned to the Lord.

Not only does the news spread throughout the town of *Lydda,* but also through the whole region of *Sharon.* This is roughly a 50-mile stretch from Joppa to Mt. Carmel (see Old Testament references in 1 Chronicles 27:29 and Isaiah 35:2).

The result is that people turn *to the Lord.* Notice that it does not say that people are drawn to Peter (contrast Acts 14:8-13). We hear nothing of Peter's growing reputation. We are not told that people leave their jobs to follow him as he had left his job to follow Christ (Luke 18:28). Instead, the people turn to Christ and serve Him in their own ways in their local communities. [See question #1, page 296.]

GOOD FROM BAD

Kyle Maynard "stands" three feet tall. He was born in 1986 with a rare birth defect known as congenital amputation. Without elbows, knees, or

---

How to Say It

AENEAS. Ee-*nee*-us.
ARAMAIC. *Air*-uh-*may*-ik (strong accent on *may*).
AZOTUS. Uh-*zo*-tus.
CAESAREA. Sess-uh-*ree*-uh.
ELIJAH. Ee-*lye*-juh.
ELISHA. E-*lye*-shuh.
JONAH. *Jo*-nuh.
JOPPA. *Jop*-uh.
JUDEA. Joo-*dee*-uh.
LYDDA. *Lid*-uh.
MEDITERRANEAN. *Med*-uh-tuh-*ray*-nee-un (strong accent on *ray*).
PENTECOST. *Pent*-ih-kost.
SAMARIA. Suh-*mare*-ee-uh.
SYRIA. *Sear*-ee-uh.
TABITHA. *Tab*-ih-thuh.

the extremities that should attach to those joints, Kyle competed in the 2004 Georgia High School Wrestling Championships. He barely missed becoming an All-American. Kyle's coach, Cliff Ramos, invented new wrestling moves that used Kyle's low center of gravity and great strength as assets, even though Kyle does not use prosthetics (http://www.kmaynard.com).

In spite of his physical challenges, Kyle's outstanding characteristic is his attitude about life. Those who know him say he refuses to think about his limitations. Instead, he focuses on accomplishments, among which are eating with regular utensils and typing 50 words per minute. An important dimension to his attitude is his ready acknowledgment that family and friends have contributed to his success. His attitude has also been an inspiration to many.

That's the way "bad things" can turn out, particularly if God is directly involved. Luke tells us that Aeneas had been bedridden for eight years. It was that very fact that made the healing so astonishing. Think about it: if Peter had cured Aeneas of a mere blister, would anyone have been impressed? Would anyone have turned to the Lord? Before we moan and groan too much about our situations, we do well to remember that God may be preparing to work through that problem as a witness to others.   —C. R. B.

II. Peter Raises Tabitha
(Acts 9:36-43)

A. Setting #2 (vv. 36-38)

36. Now there was at Joppa a certain disciple named Tabitha, which by interpretation is called Dorcas: this woman was full of good works and almsdeeds which she did.

Joppa is a primary port city of Judea. It is from here that Jonah boarded a ship in order to flee from God (Jonah 1:3). Other Old Testament references are 2 Chronicles 2:16 and Ezra 3:7. In our own day Joppa goes by the name Jaffa.

Tabitha is the Aramaic version of a name as is likely used by the locals. In Greek, the language in which Luke writes, this name is *Dorcas*. In both languages her name means "doe" or "gazelle."

Unlike Aeneas, whose spiritual status we are not told, we know that Tabitha is a follower of Christ. And whereas Aeneas's disability had rendered him immobile for eight years, Tabitha has been quite active. Luke does not say that she has performed token good deeds here or there, but that her life is characterized by service to others. Loving her neighbor is not a rigid requirement but a joyous lifestyle. For this reason she remains an

important role model for us. Perhaps this is why God pays special attention to her. [See question #2, page 296.]

37. And it came to pass in those days, that she was sick, and died: whom when they had washed, they laid her in an upper chamber.

When Tabitha dies, her loved ones wash her body in the customary preparation for burial. Typically, those who die in first-century Palestine are buried on the same day (Acts 5:5-10), as is still the practice in parts of the world today. Bodies decompose quickly in the heat of the area, and the Israelites do not practice the elaborate embalming procedure of the Egyptians (Genesis 50:26).

But in Tabitha's case, the friends and family postpone her burial and store her body in an *upper* room. Her loved ones apparently have heard news of how Peter healed Aeneas. This perhaps gives them hope that Peter might raise Tabitha from the dead, especially given the stories they must have heard of Jesus doing similar miracles.

Their choice to store the body in an upper room may be a simple matter of convenience. Perhaps it is an out-of-the-way place with plenty of ventilation to minimize odor.

38. And forasmuch as Lydda was nigh to Joppa, and the disciples had heard that Peter was there, they sent unto him two men, desiring him that he would not delay to come to them.

When Tabitha dies, Peter is still in *Lydda*. That is located 10 to 12 miles southeast of *Joppa*. This is not a long trip. But given the limitations imposed by darkness and traveling by foot, there is only a small window of opportunity to get a message to get to Peter and for Peter to make the trip before dark. So the *two* messengers urge Peter to drop everything and return with them immediately. [See question #3, page 296.]

B. Miracle #2 (vv. 39-41)

39. Then Peter arose and went with them. When he was come, they brought him into the upper chamber: and all the widows stood by him weeping, and showing the coats and garments which Dorcas made, while she was with them.

Peter can respond to the request in various ways. He can stay in Lydda where God is working through him mightily. He can make excuses about needing more advance notice; after all, he is an apostle. He can opt out on the grounds that apostles mainly preach and perform healings, whereas Jesus raised only a few people and even these under exceptional circumstances. Peter also can tell Tabitha's friends that since Jesus died and arose, faithful believers like Tabitha will someday rise again anyway (compare John 11:24).

All of these replies can be justified as reasonable at some level. But Peter doesn't think in any of these ways. Instead of wracking his brain for answers to avoid having his current ministry interrupted, he remains open to God's leading in unexpected ways. So he answers the call and heads for Joppa immediately.

On arrival Peter soon catches a glimpse of what has made Tabitha so special. We do not read that he encounters the typical group of sorrowful close relatives or professional mourners (contrast Matthew 9:23-25); rather, he encounters a band of weeping *widows*. The fact that the poorest and most helpless sector of first-century society mourns Tabitha's death speaks volumes about the way she lived her life. James 1:27 teaches us that pure religion involves special concern for widows. Tabitha obviously took this duty seriously, and she is thus an important role model for us. At the least, it should cause us to wonder who will weep (and why) when we die. [See question #4, page 296.]

By drawing Peter's attention to the clothing made by Tabitha *(Dorcas)*, which the widows are likely wearing, the women reveal what kind of concrete service Tabitha has rendered. We hear nothing of her speaking ability, Bible knowledge, life experience, or profound wisdom. Instead we see everyday garments created with hours of labor and love.

Many Christians today assume they must do something impressive to be great in God's eyes. Tabitha probably wasn't trying to be great, but her life clearly reflects Jesus' view of greatness (see Mark 10:44).

Visual for Lesson 9. *Point to this visual as you ask question #2 on page 296: "What are some good works Christians can do in the world today?"*

TALKING ABOUT THE DEAD

Katie Falzone has an interesting job: she oversees online guest books at an obituary Web site. (Now *that's* a career that didn't exist until just a few years ago!) Falzone's job is to edit unflattering comments made by bloggers about recently deceased people. In that regard, she and 44 other screeners sift through 18,000 Weblog postings her company receives each day.

Some of those entries barely conceal their anger. For example, a disgruntled son wrote, "Reading the obit, he sounds like he was a great father." A client of an embezzling accountant said, "Everyone gets their due." A former employee wrote, "I sincerely hope the Lord has more mercy on him than he had on me during my years reporting to him." Family dysfunction showed in another posting that read, "She never took the time to meet me, but I understand she was a wonderful grandmother to her other grandchildren."

There are positive entries, of course, and they sound much like what Luke records regarding Tabitha. Praise for good deeds done, lessons taught, and lives changed through the influence of the departed make the screeners' jobs less odious. It is obvious from what Luke writes about Tabitha that she was a fine person and a blessing to those who knew her. Her death brought forth testimony to her gracious character. It's worth considering how we each shall be remembered. How will our "obit blogs" read?   —C. R. B.

40. But Peter put them all forth, and kneeled down, and prayed; and turning him to the body said, Tabitha, arise. And she opened her eyes: and when she saw Peter, she sat up.

Peter demonstrates his conviction that any miracle this woman receives will have to come from God. So he clears the room of any spectators who otherwise may be impressed by his own actions, and he falls on his knees before the only one having power over death.

His command that follows is similar to what we see on Jesus' lips in the parallels of Mark 5:41 and Luke 8:54. Peter was one of three eyewitnesses to Jesus' raising of the young girl in that case. It is as if Peter so believes that only Jesus can raise this woman that he does not improvise beyond Jesus' own procedure.

41. And he gave her his hand, and lifted her up; and when he had called the saints and widows, he presented her alive.

Both Elijah and Elisha had raised the dead long before (1 Kings 17:17-24; 2 Kings 4:32-37). Yet this does not render the miracle any less spectacular. God alone is the giver of life. When God grants a resurrection, He is making an important statement about the ministry of those whom He uses.

C. Reaction #2 (vv. 42, 43)

42. And it was known throughout all Joppa; and many believed in the Lord.

Many residents of *Joppa* respond in the same way as those who witnessed Aeneas's healing in Lydda: they place faith *in the Lord.* This makes perfect sense. The most pointed claim Christians make is that Jesus died, rose again, and ascended into Heaven. Now that a former fisherman who had followed Jesus is healing the lame and raising the dead, this claim does not seem so outrageous. Where can a man like Peter receive such power if not from God on high?

It is worth noting in passing that Luke says the people in Joppa *believed in the Lord,* whereas those from nearby Lydda "turned" to Him. Thus the two ideas mean the same thing. Believing in the Lord equals turning to Him. [See question #5, page 296.]

43. And it came to pass, that he tarried many days in Joppa with one Simon a tanner.

Peter does not head back to Lydda from whence he had come with so much haste. Apparently the Spirit convicts Peter to remain *in Joppa* and tend to developments that result from his work there. What is scandalous, however, is his choice to stay in the house of *a tanner.*

Tanners often conduct business near the coast because salt water is a key ingredient in the tanning process. This process involves transforming raw animal skins into useful leather by protecting the material from decay and adding color. Jews have a low view of tanners. This is evident in the later Jewish saying, "Woe to him who is a tanner by trade."

Peter's willingness to stay with Simon thus testifies to his open disposition toward the rejected.

Peter may be going through some mental turmoil regarding reaching out to others while attempting to remain ceremonially clean, as Acts 10 will make clear (compare Galatians 2:14). Peter is a Christian missionary who needs to remain open to whatever hospitality God provides. Peter has learned firsthand from Jesus that outcasts are not to be avoided, but embraced. The events of Acts 10, which immediately follow, will show God leading Peter from openness to Jewish outcasts to openness to all God's children.

Conclusion

A. Giving and Receiving Help

Peter and Tabitha teach us valuable lessons about helping others in Jesus' name. Peter does so as a high-profile traveling evangelist. Tabitha does so as a low-profile seamstress who probably seldom left town.

Peter demonstrated faithful service by spreading the gospel to new territory, strengthening believers, following the Spirit's lead when inconvenient, imitating the example of Jesus, giving all glory and credit to God, and accepting the hospitality of outcasts. Tabitha demonstrated faithfulness by using the practical skills God gave her to help others and by ministering consistently to an extremely needy segment of the population, a segment close to the Father's heart. Both lives were extraordinary in their impact. Both lives were blessed by God in significant ways.

Some spiritual gifts are high profile, others are not. No gift set is "more Christian" than another. We all need to find our niche of service in the body of Christ. We all need to serve faithfully, walking in the steps of the first-century examples, even as they walked in the steps of Jesus. Rather than learning that "God helps those who help themselves," today's passage has shown us that God blesses those who obey His call to be a blessing to others.

B. Prayer

You, O Lord, are our helper. You alone possess the resources we need. Yet You have chosen not to keep this work to yourself. You have chosen to use Your followers to meet our needs, and You have chosen us to meet theirs. We confess that we would rather deal directly with You or handle matters by ourselves. So teach us, O Lord, to receive help graciously and to offer it generously. In Jesus' name, amen.

C. Thought to Remember

Look for ways to serve.

Home Daily Bible Readings

Monday, Apr. 20—Father Is Glorified (John 14:8-14)

Tuesday, Apr. 21—The Promise of Healing (Isaiah 57:14-21)

Wednesday, Apr. 22—O Lord, Heal Me (Psalm 6)

Thursday, Apr. 23—Heal My Sin (Psalm 41)

Friday, Apr. 24—Return and Be Healed (Jeremiah 3:19-23)

Saturday, Apr. 25—Joy Comes with the Morning (Psalm 30:1-5)

Sunday, Apr. 26—God Healing Through Peter (Acts 9:32-43)

Learning by Doing

This page contains an alternative lesson plan emphasizing learning activities. Some of these activities are also found in the helpful student book, Adult Bible Class.

Into the Lesson

Invite guests from a local nonprofit Christian organization or a leader of a helping ministry within your church to tell about the work that is being done in that organization or ministry. Give the class an opportunity to ask questions.

If not many questions are forthcoming, here are some you can ask yourself: "What is the mission and the target population of your organization/ministry?" "What are some needs in our community that your group is meeting?" "What is your personal motivation for being involved in this work?" "Do you partner with churches in the community? If so, in what way?"

Ask your class to help you make a list of the Christian and secular helping ministries and agencies within your community. Write on the board the mission of each group as they perceive it. Start another list that details needs in the community that may not be addressed. These should include not only physical needs such as poverty and health issues, but also such things as emotional, relational, and spiritual needs. Say, "Let's leave this list on the board until later in the class period."

Into the Word

Read the lesson passage aloud, instructing the class to pay particular attention to the helping attitudes of the people involved. At the end of the reading, give four students the following questions on slips of paper, one each:

1. What was the motivation of the helper?
2. Who was helped?
3. What were their needs?
4. What instructions were given to those who were helped?

Then tell your class you're going to play a game of *Jeopardy*. Ask the four students holding the questions to verbalize answers to those questions without reading the questions. Then the class is to guess what the question is.

Note that the text discusses Tabitha's action in providing care for those in need. Peter utilized prayer to deal with the man who had palsy and with Tabitha's death. Ask, "Which is more important, prayer or action? Or can they be separated? Why, or why not? Today, what would be the result of prayer without action? What would be the result of action without prayer?" (Exodus 14:15; James 2:14-16; and 1 John 3:17, 18 will add depth to this discussion.)

Have class members relate a time when a specific situation or person was the intense focus of prayer. What was the final resolution of the matter? How do they think prayer affected the outcome?

Say, "From the beginning, God created people to depend on Him but also on each other." Divide the class into groups and have them read Mark 10:44 and James 1:27. Each group will discuss how these passages relate to the accounts just read from Acts. If time allows, have the groups read 1 Corinthians 12 and discuss how different gifts are involved in fulfilling the need to be in community and to help one another.

Into Life

In their same groups, have students tell what spiritual gifts they have to offer in service to the body of Christ. Some may be hesitant to discuss their gifts, and there should be no pressure to do so. People may be more forthcoming if you stress that we take no credit for spiritual gifts—they are from God.

As each person's gifts are identified, discuss how those abilities can work with others for the benefit of the class, church, and community. This should be an affirming exercise, not a guilt trip.

Refer back to the list on the board that your class created regarding unmet needs in your community. Come to a class consensus about a group project from that list. Spend some time talking about how this project can be done. Do you need to appoint a small committee to research and organize the effort? Try to ensure that the final plan involves every class member. Stress that prayer is part of the work.

Finally, select a Christian nonprofit agency in your region and make plans for the entire class to visit it. At the end of the visit, meet somewhere (a coffee shop, a member's home, a park, etc.) to discuss this visit. Evaluate the work being done and how it fits into God's plan of interdependency and service. What can you learn from the agency that would benefit the class project identified in the preceding paragraph? Your class may like to "adopt" this agency as its project.

Let's Talk It Over

The questions on this page are designed to promote discussion of the lesson by the class and to encourage application of the lesson Scriptures. The answers provided are only discussion starters. Let your class talk it over from there.

1. What responses do you see people make toward servants of God who do great things for God? What responses should we make?

There is a tendency to err in two directions as we witness the high-impact ministry of certain servants of God. One wrong response is to revere those servants in inappropriate ways (compare Acts 14:11-13). While it is proper to commend them for the work they do as a means of encouragement, it is wrong to lift them up as objects of adoration. In some cases, people begin to follow them instead of God. These followers are more likely to quote this leader than to quote the words of Jesus.

The other improper response is to try to find fault with them. This happens sometimes out of jealousy. Like those at Lydda, our response should always be to turn to the Lord. And if we are the one who is doing a mighty work for God, our goal is to be sure that we are turning people to the Lord.

2. What are some good works Christians can do in the world today? Which ones will you do?

Answers to these questions will be far-ranging, of course. But a good starting point is to read Matthew 25:37-40. There Jesus clarified how people would minister to Him. Doing our acts of service in Jesus' name sets them apart from secular works of service.

3. How does your faith compare with that of the disciples at Joppa? In what areas do you need to demonstrate stronger faith?

Faith can be a very fragile thing. We believe in the power of Christ and the Word of God, but somehow we also struggle with doubt. There is an opinion that tells us to do all we can do, then turn the rest over to God. But like the disciples in Joppa, the first place we must turn to is the Lord. It seems they saw in Peter the hope that God provides. Calling on other Christians to help us in these times that try our faith is important.

Trusting God in areas such as health and finances comes easier to some than to others. But there are many other areas where faith is required as well. Parents need to trust the raising of their children to God and be willing to release them to service to God. Trusting God in our workplace and remaining open to being used by Him there is an area where stronger faith is needed for many Christians.

4. How do you respond to the death of a great servant of God?

We know that death comes to all. We all have probably known of a great servant of the Lord who seemed to have passed from this life while still in his or her "prime." The death is questioned. We wonder why God would allow such a righteous and effective servant of His to die when there seems to be so much more that person could have done.

Psalm 116:15 tells that it is precious in the sight of God when one of His servants dies. Such a one is ushered into the presence of God. Instead of questioning the death, we can instead celebrate the person's life. We can honor those who die in the Lord by carrying on the work. Making memorial gifts in the person's name is good; following the person's example of service is better.

5. How is the power of the gospel being made known in your life? Is that power being reflected in people coming to the Lord? If not, why not?

In a world that often focuses on tasks and accomplishments, we can sometimes get things out of focus in the church. We may feel that the power of God is reflected in how many programs our church has, how large the budget is, or how many people are on our church's staff. We can draw the conclusion that the church that has the most activity going on is the church that is having the greatest impact in the community.

But we need to look a little deeper to see what that impact really is. This is an issue of focusing on *outcome* rather than *output*. The power of the gospel is evident through changed (redeemed and sanctified) lives. If our programs do not lead to people submitting themselves to Christ, the activity is in vain.

This calls for us to make a continuous evaluation regarding what we should and should not be doing. Sometimes tough decisions, such as dropping long-standing programs, may need to happen so that the true purpose of changing lives can be accomplished.

New Family in Christ

DEVOTIONAL READING: Exodus 19:1-8.

BACKGROUND SCRIPTURE: Ephesians 1:3-14.

PRINTED TEXT: Ephesians 1:3-14.

Ephesians 1:3-14

3 Blessed be the God and Father of our Lord Jesus Christ, who hath blessed us with all spiritual blessings in heavenly places in Christ:

4 According as he hath chosen us in him before the foundation of the world, that we should be holy and without blame before him in love:

5 Having predestinated us unto the adoption of children by Jesus Christ to himself, according to the good pleasure of his will,

6 To the praise of the glory of his grace, wherein he hath made us accepted in the beloved.

7 In whom we have redemption through his blood, the forgiveness of sins, according to the riches of his grace;

8 Wherein he hath abounded toward us in all wisdom and prudence;

9 Having made known unto us the mystery of his will, according to his good pleasure which he hath purposed in himself:

10 That in the dispensation of the fulness of times he might gather together in one all things in Christ, both which are in heaven, and which are on earth; even in him.

11 In whom also we have obtained an inheritance, being predestinated according to the purpose of him who worketh all things after the counsel of his own will:

12 That we should be to the praise of his glory, who first trusted in Christ.

13 In whom ye also trusted, after that ye heard the word of truth, the gospel of your salvation: in whom also, after that ye believed, ye were sealed with that Holy Spirit of promise,

14 Which is the earnest of our inheritance until the redemption of the purchased possession, unto the praise of his glory.

May
3

GOLDEN TEXT: [God] predestinated us unto the adoption of children by Jesus Christ to himself, according to the good pleasure of his will.—Ephesians 1:5.

Christ and Creation
The Fruits of New Life
Lessons 10–14

Lesson Aims

After participating in this lesson, each student will be able to:

1. Summarize Paul's description of predestination in Ephesians 1.

2. Contrast the biblical view of predestination with popular but unbiblical views.

3. Express confidence in his or her salvation because of God's "seal."

Lesson Outline

INTRODUCTION
  A. The Chosen Ones
  B. Lesson Background
I. BEING CHOSEN, PART 1 (Ephesians 1:3-10)
  A. God's Action (vv. 3-6)
    Adopted
  B. Our Status (vv. 7, 8)
  C. God's Plan (vv. 9, 10)
II. BEING CHOSEN, PART 2 (Ephesians 1:11-14)
  A. Plan (v. 11)
  B. Praise (v. 12)
  C. Promise (v. 13)
  D. Possession (v. 14)
    "Always"
CONCLUSION
  A. Down Payment
  B. Prayer
  C. Thought to Remember

Introduction

A. The Chosen Ones

A friend of ours once gave her adopted daughter a little plaque with the inscription, "You grew in my heart, not in my womb." This tender sentiment reflects the fact that couples who cannot have children biologically often pursue adoption. In our culture, raising children is perceived to be an important life experience and (in theory at least) a source of joy, thus the desirability of adoption.

The ancient Romans of the apostle Paul's time also practiced adoption, but usually for a very different reason. According to Roman law, a father's property could pass only to his legitimate heir, who was expected to continue the household and

the family name. Men who had no children would therefore often adopt a son, sometimes a liberated slave, to stand as their heirs. The adopted son may already have reached adulthood by the time of the adoption.

Those adopted for this purpose severed ties with their former families in order to be able to receive their new father's name and property upon his death. Of course, they were also expected to submit to their new father and live in a way that would honor him as repayment for his generosity. Being chosen to be an heir and elevated from slavery thus carried both privileges and responsibilities. In our passage today, Paul uses the legal principles behind the concepts of *adoption* and *redemption* to illustrate our experience of God's grace.

B. Lesson Background

Paul's letter to the church at Ephesus is known for its teachings on unity in the church (Ephesians 2:11-22; 4:1-6), spiritual gifts (4:7-16), Christian living (4:17–5:21), marriage and family relationships (5:22–6:9), and the armor of God (6:10-18). Many readers prefer to focus on these more practical passages, while avoiding the difficult and controversial teachings on grace, works, and predestination in the first two chapters.

Yet Paul's ethical instructions are based on the principle stated at 5:1: "Be ye therefore followers of God, as dear children." Christians, in other words, are to act a certain way *because* we have been adopted into God's household as His children; we must live in a way that protects the family name. Following this logic, Paul opens Ephesians with an extended theoretical discussion of our adoption as God's heirs. In so doing, Paul emphasizes God's grace and our need to respond to that grace through lives of service.

I. Being Chosen, Part 1 (Ephesians 1:3-10)

A. God's Action (vv. 3-6)

3. Blessed be the God and Father of our Lord Jesus Christ, who hath blessed us with all spiritual blessings in heavenly places in Christ.

In the original Greek text, Ephesians 1:3-14 is one long sentence, a series of phrases that are stacked up to emphasize the wonder of God's gracious love for His people. Because of this love, God is *blessed*. The idea here is the praise that is due to God because of His mercy and goodness.

Verse 3 is particularly important to the larger argument of Ephesians because it clarifies the concept that Christians are to be in this world but not of this world. Paul uses the term *heavenly places* elsewhere in this book to refer to the *spiritual* realm beyond our day-to-day, earthly experiences. Christ is seated at God's right hand "in the heavenly places" (1:20); these same heavenly or "high" places are the abode of angels and demons and the battleground for their spiritual warfare (3:10; 6:12). As Paul will stress at 2:6, Christians are raised up to this realm with Christ when God saves us from a life of sin.

Thus, we engage two worlds at once: the earthly realm of sin, darkness, and temptation, and the supernatural realm, where God and Christ abide eternally. Throughout this letter, Paul will seek to persuade us to act like citizens of the heavenly places while we live our lives in this fallen world. God has *blessed us* to do so.

4. According as he hath chosen us in him before the foundation of the world, that we should be holy and without blame before him in love.

The word translated *according* means "just as." As such, it connects the thought of these verses to the blessings mentioned in verse 3. The Christian's current citizenship in the heavenly places with God was, in fact, secured *before the foundation of the world.*

Paul borrows the notion of being *chosen* or "elect" from the story of faithful Abraham, who became the father of God's people. Before the coming of Christ, "election" into God's chosen people was grounded in physical descent from Abraham.

Now, however, we are chosen on the basis of faith in Christ, regardless of our ethnic or religious background (Galatians 3:28, 29). The phrase *before the foundation of the world* naturally makes us think of the time before Genesis 1:1; the general idea is that of "always." God always has planned for people to come to Him through Christ, a plan that the Ephesians (and we) have seen fulfilled personally. [See question #1, page 304.]

5. Having predestinated us unto the adoption of children by Jesus Christ to himself, according to the good pleasure of his will.

Of course, the Ephesian Christians, many of whom have come from a sinful, pagan background (see 2:2, 3), are well aware that they are not born into the family of faith. Paul therefore compares their experience with an *adoption.* An adopted son is not related physically to his father in the same way as a natural child, but according to Roman law adopted children enjoy the same legal rights and privileges as other members of the family. Similarly, anyone who accepts Christ becomes one of His elect children, regardless of background or previous lifestyle.

Verses 4, 5 raise two further points that will become important later in the letter. First, verse 4 emphasizes the implications of our new status as adopted children: we are to be holy and blameless, like our new heavenly Father. Our lifestyle must reflect the fact that we are now members of God's household.

Second, verse 5 indicates that God did not choose and adopt us because we deserved it, but rather because it pleased Him to do so. We cannot earn the right to become members of God's family. All the credit belongs to Him; indeed, the credit can fall only to God, since our salvation was worked out before the foundation of the world, long before we were even born. [See question #2, page 304.]

ADOPTED

Tinkerbell is a black and white cat with six babies in her litters. Yes, *litters.* You see, she has three kittens to which she gave birth, but she also has adopted three puppies whose mother rejected them. Two years earlier, the Mason family in Murrieta, California, had found Tinkerbell as a stray and adopted her. Then she did the same thing for the puppies.

We may wonder what inner drive makes a member of one species accept responsibility for the young of another. Apparently, Tinkerbell's action is not unique. Typing "mother cat adopts puppies" into an Internet search engine will result in several such stories in which cats have offered life to babies not their own (dogs do it too). As usual when browsing the Web, many of the stories are about the same cat, but video clips provide varying examples of this nurturing behavior.

As heartwarming as these stories are, we realize that these cats are responding unthinkingly to some maternal urge when presented with the orphaned puppies. By contrast, God's adoption of His children is highly intentional. Our lesson text speaks of His willing purpose in giving us an eternal inheritance—an inheritance given only to His children. As part of God's adopted family, our proper response is to praise Him for giving us life.   —C. R. B.

6. To the praise of the glory of his grace, wherein he hath made us accepted in the beloved.

How to Say It

ABRAHAM. *Ay*-bruh-ham.
DISPENSATION. dis-pen-*say*-shun.
EPHESUS. *Ef*-uh-sus.
GENTILES. *Jen*-tiles.
PREDESTINATED. pree-*des*-tuh-nay-ted.

The word *to* at the beginning of this verse indicates the result or, perhaps better, the intended purpose of our adoption. Ultimately, our salvation brings *praise* and *glory* to God; it does so because it demonstrates how very gracious He is.

For Paul, the word *grace* summarizes God's unmerited love for sinners, especially as revealed by Jesus' death on the cross. The phrase translated *made us accepted* is actually based on the verb form of the word for grace. The original Greek text literally says, "the glory of his grace with which he graced us." The last part of the verse stresses the source of this gracious blessing: Jesus Christ.

The phrase *accepted in the beloved* builds on the reference to adoption in verse 5. Jesus, as God's *beloved* Son, bears full rights to His father's estate. As the heir of all things, Jesus secures our relationship with God under the umbrella of His own rights and privileges.

B. Our Status (vv. 7, 8)

7. In whom we have redemption through his blood, the forgiveness of sins, according to the riches of his grace.

Paul has been using the idea of adoption into a family to illustrate our new relationship with God through Christ. Because trusted slaves in Paul's day are sometimes freed and adopted as heirs, Paul switches to the metaphor of *redemption*.

In the Greco-Roman world, *redemption* is an economic term, with similarities to the way we refer to redeeming stocks, bonds, or coupons today. Redemption is the process of making payment for the freedom of a slave; the cash paid is referred to as a *ransom*, similar to the way we refer to the ransom money that kidnappers require for the lives of their victims.

Before accepting Christ, the Ephesians were enslaved to sin. God, however, paid the price to set them free: the *blood* of Jesus. Paul uses another economic term to describe the benefits of this gracious act: *forgiveness*. Just as a creditor might forgive a debt, God does not require repayment for what Christ did on our behalf. Indeed, we could never pay Him back, even if we tried.

In many ways, this verse sums up Paul's thinking about salvation. Previously, we were slaves to sin, unable to free ourselves. God, however, paid the ransom for our liberty by giving His Son's life on the cross. But God does not demand that we pay Him back. He expects us neither to pay for our own sin debt nor to pay for the work Christ did to pay our sin debt. Rather, God forgave any debt we may owe Him. He adopts us into His family and makes us heirs of His wealth. Recognition of this fact should motivate us to trust His judgment and

to serve Him with all our strength. [See question #3, page 304.]

8. Wherein he hath abounded toward us in all wisdom and prudence.

Paul frequently uses words like *abound* and *abundance* when speaking of God's grace. These terms evoke the image of a bubbling fountain that overflows its basin and, building on verse 7, emphasizes that God has more than enough grace to cover our sins.

The terms *wisdom* and *prudence* probably refer not so much to the quality of God's actions as they do to the effect of His grace in our lives. Wisdom is spiritual insight, the new understanding of God that we gain when we experience His grace and come to know Him as our liberator and adopted Father.

If wisdom refers to the content of our knowledge of God, prudence means that God has given us the ability to put that information into practice. Thus, God's grace is not simply something we know about—not just a doctrine that can be described and discussed—but is rather a fact of our experience that should be evident in the way we live.

C. God's Plan (vv. 9, 10)

9. Having made known unto us the mystery of his will, according to his good pleasure which he hath purposed in himself.

Our wisdom comes from the fact that God has revealed *his will* and eternal plan to us. Paul often uses the word *mystery* to refer to the gospel, God's eternal plan for salvation (examples: Romans 11:25; Ephesians 6:19; Colossians 2:2). This plan was mysterious in the sense that it was hidden throughout the Old Testament period, when God's people expected to receive salvation by being born into the Jewish nation, keeping the Law of Moses, and offering animal sacrifices.

No one in that era could have predicted that God was planning all along to send His Son as the ultimate sacrifice. Now, however, the fullness of the story has been made public by the death of Jesus on the cross and by Paul's miraculous call to preach the gospel to Gentiles.

10. That in the dispensation of the fulness of times he might gather together in one all things in Christ, both which are in heaven, and which are on earth; even in him.

The word *dispensation* translates the Greek word for stewardship, what we today call "management." From a human point of view, God waited a very long time to reveal His plan for salvation in Christ. Paul stresses, however, that God has been "managing the time," meaning that everything is working out according to His master plan. [See question #4, page 304.]

Even now, however, that plan is not yet complete. One day God will bring *all things . . . which are in heaven, and which are on earth* under Christ's authority (1 Corinthians 15:25). He has already begun to do this by bringing us into God's family.

II. Being Chosen, Part 2 (Ephesians 1:11-14)

A. Plan (v. 11)

11. In whom also we have obtained an inheritance, being predestinated according to the purpose of him who worketh all things after the counsel of his own will.

Paul picks up the theme of our adoption again. As God brings all things under Christ's authority, at the same time He makes us heirs and beneficiaries of His estate. These benefits are certain. When we reflect on our sinfulness and the fact that we can do nothing to repay our debt to God, we may fear that He will give up on us and throw us out of the family. This verse offers two responses to that concern.

First, as noted earlier in this passage, God didn't choose us on the basis of our inherent goodness; He chose us when we were slaves to sin. His choosing is on the basis of a plan that He had worked out long before we were born—the word *predestinated* stresses that our inheritance is not, and never was, contingent on our own worthiness. Second, God doesn't make mistakes: He does what He does because it fits into His larger plan. We are not redeemed accidentally.

Of course, this emphasis on God's act and plan does not relieve us of responsibility. Although we are saved by His grace (as opposed to works; Ephesians 2:8, 9) and for His purposes, He expects us to live in a way that will honor Him. Paul will describe many significant aspects of that lifestyle through the remainder of this letter.

B. Praise (v. 12)

12. That we should be to the praise of his glory, who first trusted in Christ.

The word *we* refers to Jewish people who, like Paul, *first trusted in Christ.* These Jews first trusted in the sense that, historically, Jesus' disciples and the first Christians were Jewish. For example, Paul-the-Jew became a Christian before the Gentile Ephesians ("ye also" in v. 13, below) heard the gospel. In a more general sense, this verse reminds all believers that God sent His Son and offered us salvation to bring glory to himself. The focus is always on God.

Visual for
Lesson 10

Point to this visual as you ask, "How will we make room for the next person to accept Christ?"

C. Promise (v. 13)

13. In whom ye also trusted, after that ye heard the word of truth, the gospel of your salvation: in whom also after that ye believed, ye were sealed with that Holy Spirit of promise.

In Paul's time, the idea that Gentiles can be saved is a radical notion, one that many Jews do not accept. Even the Gentile Ephesians, who have been raised in a variety of pagan religions, may wonder at times whether they really are equal in God's eyes to Jewish Christians. A similar problem may plague Christians today who reflect on their past sinfulness: how can we know for certain that God has accepted us into His family?

Paul answers this question by using the image of a seal or signet ring. In the ancient world, official documents are signed by pressing into melted wax a ring that bears the family crest. This seal guarantees that the contents of the letter or contract are valid (see 1 Kings 21:8; Esther 8:8).

Of course, God doesn't literally write His name on people; instead, He gives them His *Holy Spirit*, proof positive that He accepts us as His own. Following the earlier theme of this passage, Paul may be thinking of a father's signature on the adoption papers that make a slave to be his legal son and heir. [See question #5, page 304.]

D. Possession (v. 14)

14. Which is the earnest of our inheritance until the redemption of the purchased possession, unto the praise of his glory.

In verse 13, Paul refers to the Holy Spirit as the "Spirit of promise." This could mean that we receive the Spirit when we become believers just as God promised we would (see Acts 2:38, 39).

Verse 14, however, suggests that Paul is thinking of the Spirit as a promise of better things to come.

Here we see two sets of images that Paul has used throughout the passage (adoption and redemption) come together. The word *earnest* means "down payment": our experience of the Holy Spirit is God's deposit on the eternal life we will enjoy. At the same time, we are God's *purchased possession*, paid for with the blood of His Son.

The timing of *redemption* may refer to our death or to the second coming of Christ; either way, Paul is thinking of the time when God's investment will pay off in eternal fellowship with His children. Meanwhile, we should prepare ourselves to be in His presence by living pure and holy lives that will bring *praise* to Him.

"ALWAYS"

In 1953, Roy Stern sent his Navy buddy Dick Rewalt a Christmas card. As a joke the following year, Rewalt sent the card back with his signature on it. Each year since then, Stern and Rewalt and their families have exchanged the card. On the front are four snowmen. Inside, the card reads, "Happy hearts and happy homes are filled with old-time cheer / And it's time for two grand wishes: Merry Christmas! Glad New Year." Surrounding those lines are signatures and dates the families have added through the years.

The card is wearing out. Now it is held together with tape on the creases, which have given way to time. However, the friendship has endured for more than 50 years, and the Stern and Rewalt families are probably thinking, "We've *always* sent this Christmas card back and forth between us."

Half-a-century is a long time, but for God it is nothing. His "Christmas card" to us is the incarnation. Our salvation that results from it had "always" been planned. The lifelong, loving relationships many of us have had with friends and family is only a shadow of the intentional and complete love and goodwill God has "always" had for the children He has chosen to save.   —C. R. B.

Conclusion

A. Down Payment

My wife and I met in high school. After dating for two years I decided to buy her a hope chest in anticipation of our engagement. After looking at several stores, I found one that I thought she would like. I wanted to get it for her for Christmas.

But back then I had only a part-time job, making less than four dollars an hour, so I had to put the chest on layaway. (This was before high schoolers had credit cards!) I made the initial deposit, then returned to the store every month with another payment until, come December, my investment was paid off. My initial deposit was, of course, a promise that more money would be forthcoming.

In another sense, the hope chest itself was a sort of down payment in anticipation of the engagement ring that my wife-to-be received a year later. Until the ring came, she could look at the hope chest any time she wanted reassurance of my commitment, just as the engagement ring would serve as a promise that the wedding day would come.

As Christians we know that we have experienced God's grace, and we also understand that He has brought us into His family. We also hope to live with Him in Heaven someday. But in the meantime, we face numerous temptations and go through periods of doubt. In such times the promise may seem very, very far away. For this reason, God gives us His Spirit both as proof that better things are coming and for the strength and confidence to finish the course. If we do, we will one day learn that our most profound spiritual experiences in this life were only a down payment on something much, much greater.

B. Prayer

God, help us remember two things: the price You paid for us and what You expect in return. We know that we can do nothing to save ourselves. Give us the strength to live as redeemed people. As You do this for us, please extend Your grace to others who do not know You, and help us to spread the message of Your love. In Jesus' name, amen.

C. Thought to Remember

Christians are God's children,
heirs to all that He owns.

Home Daily Bible Readings

Monday, Apr. 27—A Priestly Kingdom (Exodus 19:1-8)

Tuesday, Apr. 28—An Inheritance Promised (Galatians 3:15-18)

Wednesday, Apr. 29—Children of God Through Faith (Galatians 3:23-29)

Thursday, Apr. 30—Adoption as God's Children (Galatians 4:1-7)

Friday, May 1—Inheriting Eternal Life (Matthew 19:23-30)

Saturday, May 2—Guided by the Spirit (Galatians 5:16-25)

Sunday, May 3—God's Own People (Ephesians 1:3-14)

Learning by Doing

This page contains an alternative lesson plan emphasizing learning activities. Some of these activities are also found in the helpful student book, Adult Bible Class.

Into the Lesson

Begin with a brief interview of a class member or a guest who has adopted a child. If someone in your church is not available, use this opportunity to reach into the community. Tell that person that you will ask the three questions below. Remind the person to be brief, keeping the interview to about five minutes. Therefore, the questions will require some thought and preparation before class begins.

Begin the interview by introducing the guest. Then ask the following questions:

1. *Where and how did you locate the child you chose to adopt?*
2. *Each child in a home, whether born to it or adopted into it, has a unique place. What gives an adopted child uniqueness?*
3. *What are some of the joys and challenges of parenting an adopted child?*

After thanking your interviewee, make the transition to Bible study by telling the class that adoption can be a wonderful blessing to a child. Say, "God chose to use the concept of adoption as a picture of His grace and our relationship with Him. Today we will celebrate our adoption as God's children. However, before the celebration, we must also examine the implications of adoption for Christian living."

Into the Word

Before beginning the next activity, read today's printed text aloud. After reading it, tell the class that there are concepts and words in this text that you will look at in order to understand the new life a believer has as a child of God. Study groups will examine these words and concepts. Make four group-study assignments by distributing copies of the following instructions and photocopies of the appropriate passages from the lesson commentary.

Slaves and Servants: Your task is to give the class a snapshot of the practice and purpose of adoption in the Roman world. Also be ready to report the expectations that accompanied the adoption. The photocopies of the lesson's introduction and background will be helpful.

The Predestined: Your task is to define the concept of predestination as Paul applies it to being adopted as children of God. Be ready to share your definitions with the class. Focus on Ephesians 1:4-6, 10, 11. The photocopy of the lesson commentary will be helpful.

The Adoption Agency: Your task is to help the class understand the blessings and responsibilities that are ours as adopted children of God. Focus on Ephesians 1:7, 8. The photocopy of the lesson commentary will be helpful.

The Realtors: Paul uses two terms that realtors understand: *earnest* (v. 14) and *sealed* (v. 13). Read Ephesians 1:13, 14 and the photocopy of the lesson commentary. Then be ready to explain these concepts and applications to the rest of the class.

Into Life

Ask the following discussion questions:

1. *How does knowing you are adopted change your view of yourself?*
2. *What does the concept of adoption imply about your inheritance?*
3. *We may not naturally think of the Holy Spirit in terms of a "seal" or a "deposit." How does this snapshot of the Holy Spirit affect your view of your relationship with God?*

Now ask the participants to work in groups one more time and help make today's lesson personal. Describe (or distribute on a handout) the following situation and allow the groups to develop an answer to the young woman's questions.

Susan's situation: Susan had been a faithful Christian, active in her local church throughout her childhood and teenage years. However, after she left for college, she chose friends who were not Christian. They drew her into an unchristian lifestyle. As a result, she drifted away from the Lord and into unholy behaviors, behaviors that she knew would offend Him. Now Susan is dating a Christian man. She is wondering if God can still love and accept her. What are some ways this young man can respond to her by using the concepts of *adoption*, a *seal*, and an *earnest* or *deposit*?

If time is running short, the groups need not share their answers with the rest of the class. Conclude with a reminder and prayer thanking God for the possibility of becoming an adopted child of God. Ask for strength to live up to that obligation.

Let's Talk It Over

The questions on this page are designed to promote discussion of the lesson by the class and to encourage application of the lesson Scriptures. The answers provided are only discussion starters. Let your class talk it over from there.

1. What images spring to mind when you think of the terms *holy* and *without blame*? How do you pursue holiness?

Holiness is, among other things, a lifestyle choice. It is something to pursue, yet we realize that the only one who has ever been holy and without blame in an absolute sense is Jesus. At the same time, we also recall that God refers to Job as "a perfect and an upright man" (Job 1:8). Since all people have sinned, this declaration should be taken in a relative sense. That is, Job probably had no earthly peers when it came to being a model of holiness. His lifestyle was such that no legitimate accusation could be leveled against him. Can the same be said of us?

2. If you were adopted into a family, what did it feel like when you found out? If you were not adopted, how did you react to the idea of adoption when you first found out about it?

Adoptees, once they're old enough to think about it, may deal with two emotional issues. The first issue is that of the loss of the biological parents. This loss may be due to death. It may be due to the state taking the child away from an unfit parent. It may be due to rejection of the youngster if the biological parents simply did not want the responsibility of a child. The emotional reaction to each is highly individual.

The second issue is the acceptance by the adoptive parents. Adoptees can find a great deal of comfort in the fact that they were chosen and wanted. God was pleased to choose us by adoption through Jesus. There is a great need within people to be wanted, to have a sense of belonging. This need is fulfilled when we realize how much God desires us and to what lengths He was willing to go to get us.

3. Is being in debt monetarily a good thing, a bad thing, a "necessary evil," a morally neutral tool, or something else? Which label, if any, illustrates the idea of spiritual indebtedness? Why?

Most of us have experienced debt. Many seem to spend their lives working to pay off cars, homes, or student loans. What a wonderful sense of freedom comes when we finally pay off a debt!

Yet imagine a debt that you can never pay off, no matter how hard you work. Then one day someone else comes along and pays that debt for you! You are free by the grace of Christ. The result is, among other things, the creation of a new indebtedness: the obligation to love one another (Romans 13:8). This enduring debt is not a burden, but a joy.

4. What are some areas in life that are particularly sensitive to the "fulness of times" concept? Which of these, if any, can we use to illustrate Ephesians 1:10?

All of us are familiar with the expiration dates that we see on cartons of milk, etc. Those dates indicate fullness of times in a negative sense: the closer those dates approach, the more things deteriorate! On the other hand, there are many positive senses. We can think of maturity dates on certificates of deposit, the planned date for a wedding, the approach of an eighteenth birthday, etc. Good things happen when those dates arrive.

It was in the fullness of time that Christ came into the world (Galatians 4:4). God does not explain why that particular point in history was indeed the fullness of time for the advent of Christ. No human was able to predict when that event would happen. And unlike the fullness of times as they relate to maturity dates on certificates of deposit, etc., we cannot compute when Christ's second advent will be (Acts 1:6, 7). What God expects us to do is live in expectation of that advent. God often seems to work more slowly than we want Him to, but He always works in the fullness of time.

5. What are some modern ways of creating seals as the ancient signet rings did? Which of these methods, if any, can be used to illustrate the seal of the Holy Spirit on our lives?

Most of us are familiar with the idea of getting something *notarized*. Stronger than having a document notarized is to get a *signature guarantee*; typically this can be done by a bank officer.

We all like the security of guarantees! The presence of the Holy Spirit is a guarantee of God's promises, and this guarantee is freely given. God's faithfulness to His promises is also guaranteed by Scripture (see 2 Timothy 2:13). God has consistently kept His promises to His people, even when they have not kept theirs.

New Works in Grace

DEVOTIONAL READING: Psalm 86:1-13.

BACKGROUND SCRIPTURE: Ephesians 2:1-10.

PRINTED TEXT: Ephesians 2:1-10.

Ephesians 2:1-10

1 And you hath he quickened, who were dead in trespasses and sins;

2 Wherein in time past ye walked according to the course of this world, according to the prince of the power of the air, the spirit that now worketh in the children of disobedience:

3 Among whom also we all had our conversation in times past in the lusts of our flesh, fulfilling the desires of the flesh and of the mind; and were by nature the children of wrath, even as others.

4 But God, who is rich in mercy, for his great love wherewith he loved us,

5 Even when we were dead in sins, hath quickened us together with Christ, (by grace ye are saved;)

6 And hath raised us up together, and made us sit together in heavenly places in Christ Jesus:

7 That in the ages to come he might show the exceeding riches of his grace, in his kindness toward us, through Christ Jesus.

8 For by grace are ye saved through faith; and that not of yourselves: it is the gift of God:

9 Not of works, lest any man should boast.

10 For we are his workmanship, created in Christ Jesus unto good works, which God hath before ordained that we should walk in them.

GOLDEN TEXT: By grace are ye saved through faith; and that not of yourselves: it is the gift of God.—Ephesians 2:8.

Christct and Creation
The Fruits of New Life
Lessons 10–14

Lesson Aims

After participating in this lesson, each student will be able to:

1. Describe the nature of the sinful life.

2. Explain how good works can be "worthless" in terms of earning salvation and indispensable in terms of expressing it.

3. Describe one good work that Christ has prepared him or her to do.

Lesson Outline

INTRODUCTION
  A. "I Don't Need Your Charity"
  B. Lesson Background
 I. DEATH TO LIFE (Ephesians 2:1-3)
  A. Past and Present (v. 1)
  B. Course and Devil (v. 2)
  C. Lusts and Desires (v. 3)
II. LIFE FROM DEATH (Ephesians 2:4-10)
  A. Loved by God (vv. 4, 5)
  B. Raised with Him (v. 6)
  C. Blessed for Eternity (v. 7)
    Recognizing Worth
  D. Saved by Grace (vv. 8, 9)
  E. Prepared in Advance (v. 10)
    Principle vs. Application
CONCLUSION
  A. How Can I Be Sure?
  B. Prayer
  C. Thought to Remember

Introduction

A. "I Don't Need Your Charity"

I was brought up in a lower–middle class, blue-collar neighborhood where most people worked in trades or heavy industry. My grandfather was a construction worker who had grown up on a farm and left school after the eighth grade; he retired as vice president of a major company through sheer hard work and determination. My father worked two jobs, serving as a firefighter and running his own remodeling business on off days.

Many times I saw families in my neighborhood suffer because the parents refused to accept aid from anyone. Through this upbringing, I learned to take pride in hard work and, especially, to avoid taking charity or welfare. This attitude in many ways reflects the American definition of success: taking care of yourself and never admitting that you need help.

This same spirit of self-sufficiency and independence can be found in American religion. Many American Christians feel very little responsibility for fellow believers. They may also often feel (at least subconsciously) that they must prove their worth to God by doing good deeds. The apostle Paul characterized his own religious life similarly in Philippians 3:4-6, noting that he once took great pride in his Jewish heritage, membership in the sect of the Pharisees, and strict obedience to the Old Testament. Indeed, he asserted that he was "blameless" in keeping the Law of Moses.

But Paul's sudden and dramatic conversion experience on the road to Damascus (Acts 9:1-19) started him down a path of thinking differently. That new thinking eventually was written down in a series of letters. A key issue in those letters is Paul's conclusion that we cannot earn our salvation.

All people, even the most righteous, are saved only by God's grace. That means that He does what we cannot do so that we may be acceptable to Him. In our passage for today, Paul makes this point by noting that God did not save us when we were good people, but rather when we were sinners. Good works become possible only because of what He did for us. Recognizing this fact, we should respond to His mercy through loyal service.

B. Lesson Background

Ephesus was one of the best known cities in the ancient world. Its fame came not only from its size and commercial importance, but also and particularly from Ephesian religious culture. One of the largest temple complexes of the day—in fact, one of the so-called "seven wonders of the ancient world"—was located there. It was dedicated to Artemis, the goddess of the wilderness and fertility. Ephesus was also a world center of occult practices and black arts (compare Acts 19:19).

When Paul first arrived in Ephesus in about AD 54, he spent three months teaching in local synagogues, but was eventually expelled. So he established a school in the lecture hall of Tyrannus (Acts 19:8, 9). The Ephesian church eventually was threatened by pressures from local trade unions. They feared a loss of profit, since Paul's preaching against idolatry was so effective that it jeopardized sales of articles that bore the image of Artemis (Acts 19:23-27).

Thus the various elements of Ephesian culture presented special challenges and opportunities to the apostle Paul when he visited the city on his third missionary journey. In view of their deeply pagan background, Paul wanted the Ephesian Christians to understand two points clearly: (1) God had completely forgiven the sins of their previous lifestyle, and (2) God expected them to produce good works as expressions of redemption. Our passage for today covers both topics.

I. Death to Life
(Ephesians 2:1-3)
A. Past and Present (v. 1)

1. And you hath he quickened, who were dead in trespasses and sins.

Paul opens this section of Ephesians by equating life without Christ with spiritual death. This means that our conversion is a kind of resurrection. *Dead* probably refers here both to our alienation from God and to the actual physical consequences of our sin. This concept is developed more fully in Romans 6, where Paul stresses that "the wages of sin is death" (6:23; see also Colossians 2:13).

Yet the Christian has been *quickened*, meaning "made alive." While Christians expect to live eternally in Heaven after death, in a very real sense we are already experiencing eternal life through our relationship with God in this world right now.

B. Course and Devil (v. 2)

2. Wherein in time past ye walked according to the course of this world, according to the prince of the power of the air, the spirit that now worketh in the children of disobedience.

Paul has just described the Ephesians as having been dead in their sins. In verses 2, 3 he clarifies exactly what he means by offering a concise summary of their former, pagan lifestyle. The word *walk* can be used as a figure of speech for one's lifestyle. With this figure Paul suggests that nonbelievers are following the lead of two forces that continually steer them away from God.

How to Say It

ARCHIMEDES. Ar-kuh-*me*-deez.
ARTEMIS. *Ar*-teh-miss.
CANARD. kuh-*nard*.
DAMASCUS. Duh-*mass*-kus.
EPHESUS. *Ef*-uh-sus.
MOSES. *Mo*-zes or *Mo*-zez.
PHARISEES. *Fair*-ih-seez.
PHILIPPIANS. Fih-*lip*-ee-unz.
SYNAGOGUES. *sin*-uh-gogs.
TYRANNUS. Ty-*ran*-nus.

First, they follow *the course of this world*. While the biblical authors insist that God created the earth and everything in it, they also characterize the world as evil, materialistic, and hostile to Him (see John 1:10; Romans 12:2; 1 John 2:15). The world is evil because the entire human social system is focused on power, personal pleasure, and success at the expense of others. This is a self-centered, as opposed to God-centered, system.

Second, and more specifically, worldly people are driven along by *the prince of the power of the air*. This unusual title obviously refers to the devil, but scholars are divided on why Paul would refer to Satan as ruler of the air.

The most likely explanation is that Paul is referring to the pagan religious systems that the Ephesians formerly accepted. Today we generally think of God living above the earth while demons are trapped in Hell down below. But most ancient people believe that the earth is at the bottom of a cosmic ladder, with evil spirits and minor deities just above us and the more powerful gods on a higher plane yet. By calling Satan *prince of the air*, Paul thus acknowledges his influence, but also stresses that his authority is far below that of the true God, who dwells in the highest Heaven.

In any case, Paul is less concerned with Satan's domain than with his impact on people's lives. While many nonbelievers would not attribute their actions to any supernatural influence, Paul makes clear that their lives are heavily influenced by the devil. There are no innocent bystanders: one is either alive in faith or dead in sin, either a servant of God or a slave of the devil. [See question #1, page 312.]

C. Lusts and Desires (v. 3)

3. Among whom also we all had our conversation in times past in the lusts of our flesh, fulfilling the desires of the flesh and of the mind; and were by nature the children of wrath, even as others.

As in chapter 1, the word *we* probably refers to Jewish Christians such as Paul himself. It takes little effort to prove that pagans live lives *fulfilling the desires of the flesh and of the mind*. But Paul everywhere emphasizes that even "good" Jews are *children of wrath* before coming to Christ.

Of course, Jews believe in and worship the true God, not idols and demons. But this fact does not stop them from breaking God's law and pursuing self-gratification. The phrase *lusts of our flesh* refers to things that we do because they feel good to our bodies, even though we know that God disapproves of them: getting drunk, engaging in illicit sex, etc.

Paul also admits that he too was once enslaved to *the desires* of the *mind*, a likely reference to the more intellectual sins: covetousness, pride, etc. Those who do such things show that they are alienated from God and deserving of punishment. (Remember that the word *conversation* in the *King James Version* means "way of living.") [See question #2, page 312.]

II. Life from Death (Ephesians 2:4-10)

A. Loved by God (vv. 4, 5)

4, 5. But God, who is rich in mercy, for his great love wherewith he loved us, even when we were dead in sins, hath quickened us together with Christ, (by grace ye are saved;).

The story that begins in verses 2, 3 could have ended with the fire and brimstone of eternal damnation. Every person of every religious background is guilty of *sins* of the body and the mind. A righteous God is justified in repaying such rebelliousness with eternal death.

Genesis 7 ends with a worldwide flood that nearly wipes out the human race. But this time things work out differently: God decides to forgive us. Paul can offer only two explanations for this remarkable twist in the plot, and neither of them has anything to do with our efforts. First, God is *rich in mercy*, a phrase that stresses His willingness to forego the punishment we deserve. Second, God's mercy is driven by the simple fact that He loves us, even when we do not love Him.

Both the reason for and the expression of God's *love* are indicated in the phrase *with Christ*. Christ's death on the cross secures our salvation; His resurrection from the tomb also brings our spirits to life. Thus for the first time people are able to come to God fully forgiven after years of seeking fulfillment in false religions and pleasures of the flesh. It almost goes without saying by this point in Paul's argument that our salvation is the result of God's *grace*, not our own merit.

B. Raised with Him (v. 6)

6. And hath raised us up together, and made us sit together in heavenly places in Christ Jesus.

Raised us up extends the resurrection imagery in verse 5. At the end of chapter 1, Paul speaks of Christ's ascension to Heaven and exaltation after His resurrection. There He sat down at God's right hand to rule the universe (Ephesians 1:20-23; see Philippians 2:8-11). Now Paul says that Christ not only redeemed us and brought us back to life, He also raised us together so that we may share in His glorious reign. [See question #3, page 312.]

Notably, these words refer not only to our eternal reward in Heaven, but also to our status as believers now, at the present time. Not only has God forgiven us, He has also raised us up with and through His Son. See also Colossians 2:12 for other features associated with being "raised."

C. Blessed for Eternity (v. 7)

7. That in the ages to come he might show the exceeding riches of his grace, in his kindness toward us, through Christ Jesus.

Paul has just stressed that God's *grace* has already been revealed in an incredible way through our unmerited salvation. Now Paul says that these blessings will continue forever. While some have suggested that *in the ages to come* refers to future generations of humanity, the phrase more likely refers to eternity beyond the end of human time. At some point Christ will come and this world will pass away, but even then (or especially then) we will continue to enjoy the benefits of God's grace.

Further, God has done all this not only for our own benefit, but also and primarily so that He can demonstrate His graciousness to all creation. The fact of our salvation reveals His nature as a loving and merciful God.

RECOGNIZING WORTH

Archimedes was the ancient philosopher who discovered the principle of water displacement. The only known source for two of his treatises is a tenth-century copy on a goatskin. Because parchment was scarce, an anonymous scribe in the twelfth century AD eradicated the writing with a weak acid solution and rubbed the skin smooth so it could be used again, not realizing the value of what was being erased. He then wrote a prayer book on the skin.

Forgers in the twentieth century made the situation worse by painting religious images over four pages of the skin, hoping to make the prayer book more valuable. However, a few years ago scientists at Stanford University found that powerful X-rays would react with the iron-based ink that was used centuries earlier. With this technique, they were able to read the lost ancient text.

Neither the twelfth century scribe nor the twentieth century forgers appreciated the value of what they were destroying with their "improvements." Do we ever end up destroying what Paul calls "the exceeding riches of [God's] grace" with our own ideas or "improvements"?   —C. R. B.

D. Saved by Grace (vv. 8, 9)

8. For by grace are ye saved through faith; and that not of yourselves: it is the gift of God.

Up to this point in the chapter, Paul has used fairly grandiose language to describe God's love and our salvation. The Ephesians have lived out the ultimate "rags to riches" story, going from ignorant slaves to exalted children of God. But lest this lead to spiritual arrogance, Paul proceeds to stress two critical points.

First, our salvation is a product of God's *grace*, not of anything we have done or could do. It is, in fact, categorically impossible for any person to be saved by works (see v. 9, next). Second, salvation, being a gift, is not something we can take for granted. The fact that God did all the work to bring us back to life doesn't mean that we can kick back and relax. Quite the opposite! Verse 10 (below) stresses that we are saved for the purpose of works for Christ.

The phrase *through faith* indicates the premier means by which we are saved, the way that God's grace comes to us. (The parallel passage Colossians 2:12 adds the important dimension of baptism.) Jesus' death on the cross was a public act, a fact of history. But, sadly, not everyone receives forgiveness through His sacrifice. God's grace becomes relevant to us as we believe in Him. This means believing not only that God exists, as Paul believed when he was still a Jewish sinner (v. 3), but also believing to the point that we have faith in Christ as our only way of salvation. The gift to which Paul refers is the forgiveness that we enjoy once faith allows us to receive God's grace.

The phrase *that not of yourselves* is among the more controversial statements in the Bible. Paul is clearly using this clause to modify something he has just said, but the grammar makes us wonder whether Paul is referring to grace, faith, or something else. Exactly what is it that is not of ourselves?

Although not apparent in English, the words *grace* and *faith* are feminine in gender in the original language, while the word *that* is neuter in gender in this particular passage. Thus whatever it is that *is not of yourselves* must be something other than either faith or grace specifically since the genders of the words don't match. Paul probably means that it is the whole system of *grace . . . through faith* that is *not of yourselves*. This signifies that salvation through Christ as a covenant relationship originates entirely with God. This proposal gains strength in light of verse 9 (next). [See question #4, page 312.]

Our discussion of this single verse has been lengthy because Ephesians 2:8 is one of the most significant verses in the New Testament. Certainly this verse should be in anyone's "top ten" list! *Grace* refers to God's favor toward us—a vital

Visual for Lesson 11. *Use this visual to start a discussion as you introduce question #4 on page 312.*

topic. It could not be earned by our effort because, as Paul has just said, we were dead to God because of our sins and evil thoughts. Proof of God's goodwill may be found in the cross, which reveals the price God was willing to pay to restore our relationship with Him.

9. Not of works, lest any man should boast.

This verse completes and underscores the thought of verse 8. We do not receive grace because we have done good *works* (Romans 3:28; 2 Timothy 1:9; Titus 3:5). If salvation could come by works, then people could *boast* about their salvation. Of course, God would not be impressed by any such boasting (1 Corinthians 1:29).

Humility is important. We may be tempted to criticize the lifestyles of worldly friends and relatives, but let us not forget that we did nothing to merit God's favor ourselves. A proper understanding of who we were and what God has done should instead make us feel deep appreciation to Him and a deep sorrow for those who are lost.

E. Prepared in Advance (v. 10)

10. For we are his workmanship, created in Christ Jesus unto good works, which God hath before ordained that we should walk in them.

Once we are saved, *good works* are not optional. In chapter 1, Paul reassures the Ephesians of their salvation by stressing that God's grace is not contingent on human effort; rather, God has had us in His plans since "before the foundation of the world" (1:4). Now Paul extends that thought to stress that God also *ordained* long ago that we are to live in a way that reflects our status as His children. While we are not saved by means of good works, a faith that does not result in works is not a saving faith (see James 2:14-26). [See question #5, page 312.]

PRINCIPLE VS. APPLICATION

The aircraft design we are most familiar with features large wings toward the front of the plane and smaller "elevators" at the tail. The large wings provide aerodynamic lift while the small ones help change the elevation or altitude. Most airplanes are still built this way. However, after World War II experimental aircraft appeared that featured main wings toward the rear of the plane and smaller wings at the front. The design came to be known as a *canard* (from the French word for *duck* because of the similar appearance).

Certain military and civilian aircraft now use this design. The "backward" wing configuration may strike us as rather curious, exotic, and high tech. But at the same time it is also very "old school": the first airplane flown by Orville and Wilbur Wright was a canard design!

The canard design was abandoned for years because of stability issues; computer guidance now solves the stability problem. The canard design has come back into vogue because of a desire to achieve greater maneuverability and lower aerodynamic drag, not because the underlying aerodynamic principles of flight have changed. Those principles never change!

Similarly, God's grace through Christ is an unchanging principle of the Christian life. The fact that "we are his workmanship, created in Christ Jesus unto good works" is another unchanging principle. We may (and, at times, should) change the design of our worship services, music styles, outreach programs, etc., as we recognize better ways of doing things. But let us not confuse what can or should be changed with what never changes. Applications change; principles do not.

—C. R. B.

Conclusion

A. How Can I Be Sure?

Christians may be plagued with doubts about their salvation. "Trying hard, never sure" is the way such self-doubt has been described. When we reflect on our past lives and our ongoing sinfulness, we don't seem to be making the grade. Indeed, if God evaluated our performance in the same way that our employers do, we might have been cut a long time ago.

This approach to faith, which reflects the spirit and ethic of a Western marketplace, typically generates two responses, which often work together in something of a vicious cycle. First, we may try to do good deeds to prove that we are worthy of God's love and mercy; second, when we inevitably fail to be perfect, we feel guilty and ashamed. These feelings of guilt will lead us either to try even harder or to give up. This cycle of effort/failure/guilt leads to depression and burnout. It never leads to genuine biblical faith.

The apostle Paul had lived in a cycle something like this before becoming a Christian. Perhaps for this reason he stressed God's grace again and again. The work necessary for us to become members in God's family has been done on the cross; it has nothing to do with anything we have done or could do. Of course, God expects us to do what is right, but we do this as an expression of our salvation, not as merit points toward it.

So whenever we begin to feel guilty, insecure, or burned out, we need to pause and ask why. Are we focusing on our own (in)abilities? If so, the cure is to recall that God has called us to Him through His Son, not through our own efforts. The cross puts an end to self-doubt.

B. Prayer

Father, we understand that the Bible says You love us. Help us to know this love in our hearts. Please take away our feelings of guilt so that we can focus entirely on Your infinite grace.

Give us a real desire to serve You, not just because we have to but because we know that You have made us for this reason. Give us also compassion toward those who do not know You and opportunities to help them learn of the wonderful grace we have received.

C. Thought to Remember

Meditate on God's grace.

Home Daily Bible Readings

Monday, May 4—Full of Grace and Truth (John 1:14-18)

Tuesday, May 5—Wait for the Gracious Lord (Isaiah 30:15-21)

Wednesday, May 6—No Good Withheld (Psalm 84:8-12)

Thursday, May 7—The Throne of Grace (Hebrews 4:14–5:10)

Friday, May 8—Set Your Hope on Grace (1 Peter 1:10-16)

Saturday, May 9—The Blessing of Grace (Numbers 6:22-27)

Sunday, May 10—Saved by Grace Through Faith (Ephesians 2:1-10)

Learning by Doing

This page contains an alternative lesson plan emphasizing learning activities. Some of these activities are also found in the helpful student book, Adult Bible Class.

Into the Lesson

Prepare a two-sided handout to be used throughout the lesson. The content of the handout is described in each section of this lesson plan.

At the top of side #1 of the handout, print the question, "What are my chances of going to Heaven?" Then in a vertical column down the left side, write the following: *0%, 20%, 40%, 60%, 80%, 100%.* Keeping all this on the top half of the page, write these two questions to the right of those percentages:

1. What would keep me from going to Heaven?
2. What will enable me to go to Heaven?

Begin the lesson by asking, "If you died tonight, what would be your chance of going to Heaven? Circle the percentage that you think best reflects your situation today." After your students do so, ask them to jot a few notes to the two questions that are on the worksheet. Do not ask your learners to share these personal reflections and answers. (You may wish to assure them that you will not do so.)

Say the following as your transition to Bible study: "To biblically answer the question we just raised about our chances of going to Heaven, we need to understand the relationship of God's grace to our good works. Paul's teaching in Ephesians 2:1-10 holds the key."

Into the Word

Include a photocopy of today's printed text on the lower half of side #1 of the handout. Print the phrase *Dead or Alive?* at the top of this photocopy.

On the top of side #2 of the handout, print the following verse designations and phrases down the left side under the heading *Understanding the Text.* Leave a little space for class members to jot notes; use only the top half of the page:

Verse 1: Dead in trespasses and sins
Verse 2: Prince of the power of the air
Verse 3: By nature the children of wrath
Verse 5: Hath quickened us together with Christ
Verses 8, 9: And that not of yourselves
Verse 10: Unto good works

This segment of your Bible study will have three parts:

1. Three-Minute Introduction: Give (or ask a student to give) a very brief lecture on the Lesson Background from the lesson commentary.

2. Dead or Alive? Using the photocopy of the lesson text, ask students to underline all the words and phrases that emphasize what life was like when they were dead in Christ. Then ask them to circle the words that indicate the change to becoming alive in Him. You can divide your class into small groups for this task. Ask students or groups to report their discoveries; jot these on the board as they do.

3. Understanding the Text: Ask students to turn to side #2 of the handout. Ask the following questions about the words and phrases listed there. You may need to clarify your students' understanding by using the lesson commentary.

Verse 1: What does Paul imply by using the word *dead* in this verse?

Verse 2: Why do you think Paul used this unusual title for Satan?

Verse 3: Who is Paul talking about in this verse? What does he mean by the word *nature*?

Verse 5: What do the two words *with Christ* imply in this verse?

Verses 8, 9: What does this passage say about the relationship between our salvation and our behavior? What makes it possible for us to be saved?

Verse 10: What does this phrase tell us about *why* Christians do good works?

Display this statement that you have prepared on a poster board: "True or False? Good works are worthless in terms of earning salvation, but indispensable in terms of expressing it." Allow time for discussion.

Into Life

On the lower part of side #2 of the handout, print the heading *Next Step.* Under it print *Created in Christ Jesus unto Good Works.*

Remind the class that God expects us to do good works because we are saved. Say, "It is appropriate to evaluate our good works on Jesus' behalf occasionally. We should ask ourselves, 'What good work(s) has Christ prepared for me to do?'" Each person is to identify one good work he or she would like to develop in life for God's glory. Students should write that commitment next to the words *Next Step.*

Let's Talk It Over

The questions on this page are designed to promote discussion of the lesson by the class and to encourage application of the lesson Scriptures. The answers provided are only discussion starters. Let your class talk it over from there.

1. In what areas do you think that the "prince of the power of the air" is most effective in influencing lives against God? In which of these are you most vulnerable? How do you guard against this vulnerability?

Many Christians can point to times when God or godly people influenced their lives for the better. Satan certainly tries to influence people as well, but for their hurt. An eye-opening treatment in this regard is C. S. Lewis's book *The Screwtape Letters*. There, a novice demon is instructed by a more experienced demon on the tricks to lead a person toward destruction. Some of the methods are obvious, others are more subtle. All have the primary purpose to lead people as far from God as possible. Satan is a master at using "whatever works." To deny our vulnerability in any given area is the first step to falling in that particular area.

2. Which sins cause you the most trouble: those of the flesh or those of the mind? How have you grown spiritually in being able to triumph over these trouble spots?

Sin may be classified in various ways. Paul's two-sphere classification is foundational. Sins of the flesh are more obvious to ourselves and outsiders; these kinds of sins therefore are potentially easier for us to take action against. Sins of the mind do not always result in obvious visible behaviors. The mind is a place where others cannot see into (but God can). It is a place about which we often delude ourselves.

The two often interact, as sin in one area leads to sin in the other. For example, lustful thoughts (sin of the mind) can lead to adultery (sin of the flesh). Working the other way around, what a person gains through theft (sin of the flesh) can lead to even greater covetousness (sin of the mind). If we focus on triumphing over the sins of the mind first, then the sins of the flesh have the potential of disappearing entirely.

3. In what ways do we sit with Jesus even now?

Sitting together brings to mind the idea of *fellowship*. We sit with friends and family to enjoy the fellowship of meals, conversation, etc. Paul's thought indicates that Christians will be sitting together in eternity with Jesus.

Jesus described the kingdom of Heaven in terms of a wedding banquet (Matthew 22:1-14); the full advent of the kingdom of Heaven will feature a sit-down feast (Matthew 8:11). To be invited to participate proclaims that a relationship exists between those invited and the one doing the inviting. Because we have been raised up, we sit with Christ even now, though all the benefits of our relationship are yet to be fully realized.

4. How do you feel when you receive something as a gift as opposed to having worked for it? How do you feel when you see someone else receiving something as a gift as opposed to having worked for it? What adjustments to your attitude do you need to make, if any?

In Matthew 20:1-16, Jesus told a story of certain workers who were angry because their employer distributed equal pay for unequal work. They had a false sense of entitlement, and their anger showed itself in envy over the fact that their employer was more generous to others than to them. The generous way the employer treated those hired later in the day (and worked less) amounted to a gift.

The employer pointed out that if he wished to be generous, that was his prerogative. It was his money to do with as he chose. Under the concept of salvation by grace, God offers the same salvation as a gift to everyone. Those of us who have been Christians for a very long time should have no sense of "entitlement" above the worst of sinners who became a Christian just an hour ago.

5. What feelings are appropriate and inappropriate for accompanying our good works? How have you grown spiritually in this regard?

The Holy Spirit not only convicts us concerning sin, but also concerning righteousness (John 16:8). Conviction is an emotional response (compare Acts 2:37), thus we should not expect our good works to be accompanied by no feelings whatsoever. The good deeds of the first-century believers were accompanied by "gladness" (Acts 2:44-46) and "joy" (2 Corinthians 8:2).

Then as now, there was/is to be no feeling of "now this person owes me one." Also, failing to do what we know we ought to do should bring us feelings of guilt (compare James 4:17).

New Message from God

DEVOTIONAL READING: Isaiah 40:1-11.

BACKGROUND SCRIPTURE: Ephesians 3:1-13.

PRINTED TEXT: Ephesians 3:1-13.

Ephesians 3:1-13

1 For this cause I Paul, the prisoner of Jesus Christ for you Gentiles,

2 If ye have heard of the dispensation of the grace of God which is given me to you-ward:

3 How that by revelation he made known unto me the mystery; (as I wrote afore in few words;

4 Whereby, when ye read, ye may understand my knowledge in the mystery of Christ,)

5 Which in other ages was not made known unto the sons of men, as it is now revealed unto his holy apostles and prophets by the Spirit;

6 That the Gentiles should be fellow heirs, and of the same body, and partakers of his promise in Christ by the gospel.

7 Whereof I was made a minister, according to the gift of the grace of God given unto me by the effectual working of his power.

8 Unto me, who am less than the least of all saints, is this grace given, that I should preach among the Gentiles the unsearchable riches of Christ;

9 And to make all men see what is the fellowship of the mystery, which from the beginning of the world hath been hid in God, who created all things by Jesus Christ:

10 To the intent that now unto the principalities and powers in heavenly places might be known by the church the manifold wisdom of God,

11 According to the eternal purpose which he purposed in Christ Jesus our Lord:

12 In whom we have boldness and access with confidence by the faith of him.

13 Wherefore I desire that ye faint not at my tribulations for you, which is your glory.

GOLDEN TEXT: Unto me, who am less than the least of all saints, is this grace given, that I should preach among the Gentiles the unsearchable riches of Christ; and to make all men see what is the fellowship of the mystery, which from the beginning of the world hath been hid in God, who created all things by Jesus Christ.—Ephesians 3:8, 9.

Christer and Creation
The Fruits of New Life
Lessons 10–14

Lesson Aims

After participating in this lesson, each student will be able to:

1. Summarize the content of what Paul calls the *mystery* made known to him by revelation.

2. Identify how Paul uses the term *mystery*.

3. Plan a class activity that will demonstrate "one body" unity.

Lesson Outline

INTRODUCTION

  A. What's the Secret Password?

  B. Lesson Background

I. GOOD NEWS (Ephesians 3:1-6)

  A. Paul's Chains (v. 1)

  B. God's Grace (vv. 2, 3)

  C. Ephesians' Understanding (vv. 4, 5)

  D. Gentiles' Status (v. 6)

    A Divided House?

II. ETERNAL PURPOSE (Ephesians 3:7-13)

  A. Paul's Task (vv. 7-9)

  B. God's Intent (vv. 10, 11)

    Plans and Purposes

  C. Readers' Reaction (vv. 12, 13)

CONCLUSION

  A. Will You Tell the Secret?

  B. Prayer

  C. Thought to Remember

Introduction

A. What's the Secret Password?

When you hear the word *mystery,* what comes to mind? Sherlock Holmes? *Masterpiece Theater*? When biblical writers speak of mystery, they do not refer to a fictional story. Rather, they use the word *mystery* much the same way we would use the word *secret*. Thus when they speak of revealing a mystery, they intend to reveal a secret to you.

In New Testament times, the Greeks were known for their *mystery religions*. These were pagan cults that claimed to have secret knowledge of the spirit world. The initiation rites were bizarre. Like kids in a tree house saying, "You can't come in unless you tell us the secret password," members of the cult were those who had the secret

knowledge that (supposedly) gained a person the best kind of afterlife. In our passage today, Paul uses the terminology of those cults to highlight God's mystery—the revealed secret—that Paul was called to preach. But unlike those mystery religions, God's revealed secret is available to *all*, not just to a select few. Also unlike those mystery religions, mere possession of certain knowledge isn't enough; it has to be put into practice.

B. Lesson Background

We take for granted the fact that a person can become a Christian without converting to Judaism. But that fact wasn't always so clear. In the very earliest days of the church, most Christians were Jews first. The common thought in those earliest days was that Christianity was a variation of Judaism or was a Jewish sect (Acts 24:5, 14).

After all, didn't Jesus Christ come to be the Jewish Messiah, to save God's people from their sins? Jesus made it clear that His message was to go "to the ends of the earth," but many assumed that those wanting to become Christians would have to become Jews first, toeing the line with regard to the Law of Moses. To think of becoming a Christian without becoming a Jew was like someone wanting to become a Kentuckian without becoming an American citizen.

In a vision to Peter in Acts 10, God revealed that Gentiles were not to be considered "unclean." The gospel was open to the Gentiles *without* their having to convert to Judaism. But many in the early church objected to this radical idea. The issue was so hotly debated that the Jerusalem church held a special council just to resolve this issue (Acts 15; compare Galatians 2).

After a long discussion, the apostles confirmed that a Gentile did not have to become a Jew in order to become a Christian. The intervention of the Holy Spirit and the courage of the apostles to be obedient to God's call ensured that Christianity would not be a mere sect of Judaism.

By the time that Paul wrote his letter to the Ephesians (about AD 63), the famous Jerusalem Council was more than a decade in the past. The thinking of the church had matured on the issue discussed there. Even so, there was more yet to be said!

I. Good News
(Ephesians 3:1-6)

A. Paul's Chains (v. 1)

1. For this cause I Paul, the prisoner of Jesus Christ for you Gentiles.

Paul is in prison because of his commitment to take *Christ* to the *Gentiles*. The details of this imprisonment can be found beginning in Acts 21:27 through the end of that book. Acts 22:21, 22 especially reveals the ire of Paul's opponents regarding his mission to the Gentiles. Yet Paul calls himself a *prisoner of Jesus Christ.* Does Paul believe that his prison warden is Jesus? In essence, yes! (See also Ephesians 4:1.)

We might be more likely to see Paul's prison warden as the devil, not Jesus. But Paul consistently submits to the situations in his life as if God has put him there. Paul sees that even this "evil" of imprisonment can be used (and is being used) by God for good.

Perhaps Paul meditates on Joseph's imprisonment (Genesis 39, 40) and how that turned out. "God never wastes a hurt," someone has said. Paul's imprisonment means he must write letters to his churches since he cannot visit in person. Since we have those letters to study, Paul's jail time certainly has resulted in good things for us! [See question #1, page 320.]

B. God's Grace (vv. 2, 3)

2. If ye have heard of the dispensation of the grace of God which is given me to you-ward.

Dispensation is a word we don't use much in everyday speech. We may think of something being dispensed, administered, or managed. Paul is saying, "You know about this particular assignment that God, by His grace, gave me to manage." This thought can cause us to reflect on the things God has entrusted to our own stewardship. The word *things* may bring to mind material objects such as food, clothing, and money. But have you ever thought that you have *information* that God wants you to manage?

Mature Christians understand God's grace, God's truth, and God's promises in ways that others don't understand. God has given you that infor-

How to Say It

CORINTHIANS. Ko-*rin*-thee-unz (*th* as in *thin*).
DISPENSATION. dis-pen-*say*-shun.
EPHESIANS. Ee-*fee*-zhunz.
GENTILES. *Jen*-tiles.
HEBREWS. *Hee*-brews.
ISAIAH. Eye-*zay*-uh.
JUDAISM. *Joo*-duh-izz-um or *Joo*-day-izz-um.
MANOAH. Muh-*no*-uh.
MESSIAH. Meh-*sigh*-uh.
OMNISCIENT. ahm-*nish*-unt.
PHILIPPIANS. Fih-*lip*-ee-unz.
THESSALONIANS. *Thess*-uh-*lo*-nee-unz
(strong accent on *lo*; *th* as in *thin*).

mation not just for your own benefit but for the benefit of others: perhaps your children, your coworker, or your neighbor. We have information that has been revealed to us through God's Word, and God expects us to be good stewards of what we know.

For Paul, the *dispensation of the grace of God* is clear and dramatic. There is no question regarding what he is a steward of: it is that God's salvation is available to Gentile as well as Jew. [See question #2, page 320.]

3. How that by revelation he made known unto me the mystery; (as I wrote afore in few words).

Paul is about to tell more specifically what he has been given to administer. He refers to this as *the mystery.* He got this mystery *by revelation.*

God reveals himself to humanity in two ways: by general revelation and by special revelation. General revelation is knowledge about God that is available merely by looking around at creation (Psalm 19:1; Romans 1:20). Special revelation includes God's messages to the prophets, apostles, etc., that end up as written Scripture. What Paul is talking about is special revelation. Such messages come directly from God (see Acts 9:5-7; 22:21).

Paul notes that he has written about this in a *few words* already. This may refer to Ephesians 1:9, 10 or 2:11-22.

C. Ephesians' Understanding (vv. 4, 5)

4, 5. (Whereby, when ye read, ye may understand my knowledge in the mystery of Christ,) which in other ages was not made known unto the sons of men, as it is now revealed unto his holy apostles and prophets by the Spirit.

For the Ephesians to understand this *mystery of Christ* is Paul's goal. Part of this understanding includes the realization that the mystery has not been revealed only to Paul, but *it is now revealed unto his holy apostles and prophets by the Spirit.* We may review Acts 10:9-20, where God first reveals the secret of the inclusion of the Gentiles to Peter. Paul repeats his argument in Colossians 1:25-27.

D. Gentiles' Status (v. 6)

6. That the Gentiles should be fellow heirs, and of the same body, and partakers of his promise in Christ by the gospel.

The revealed mystery is that through the gospel the *Gentiles* can be equal with Jews. The two can be united together to make up the church. Gentiles are *fellow heirs,* members of *the same body,* and *partakers* of the same *promise*—without having to become Jews first! Everything available to Jews in Christ is available to Gentiles too. The Gentiles are not second-class citizens of the church. Jews and

Gentiles should be treating one another as brothers and sisters in Christ (see Galatians 3:26-29).

To recognize that we are all one in Christ is vital. This does not mean that we promote tolerance to the point of accepting sinful behavior. Being one in Christ means, rather, that distinctions with regard to race, culture, and economic status are irrelevant. The church should be leading the charge in genuine racial reconciliation in the way she models the interactions of her members. Christians are all one in Christ.

Are you seeking to love members of the body of Christ no matter what their racial background? Consider the language that you use in describing those of another race: Do you stereotype or demean others by your labels? Look at a list of your friends: Does it include people from other races and socioeconomic backgrounds?

A DIVIDED HOUSE?

Chana and Simon Taub shared the same $1 million house for 18 years. Then something went wrong in their 21-year marriage. The result was called "one of New York's strangest divorce battles." Each accused the other of exaggerated lies to bolster his or her case.

Feelings were so intense that neither would give up the house, so the judge ordered interior walls to be built, dividing the house. Chana got possession of the garage, front door, three bathrooms, four bedrooms, the second-floor kitchen, the third-floor nursery, and a spiral staircase to reach them. Simon got a side entrance, the living room and bathroom on the first floor, and the dining room on the second floor.

Some in the first-century church were in danger of dividing "the house of God" in a way equally ridiculous. But Paul reminded his readers that *both* Jewish and Gentile Christians were equally entitled to inherit the blessings of the gospel of Christ. When we see how the twenty-first century church has divided and segregated herself, Paul's words should come to mind.   —C. R. B.

II. Eternal Purpose (Ephesians 3:7-13)

A. Paul's Task (vv. 7-9)

7. Whereof I was made a minister, according to the gift of the grace of God given unto me by the effectual working of his power.

Our use of the English language in the twenty-first century often causes us to think of a *minister* as a preacher—someone who leads a church. But the idea behind *minister* in the original language is "servant."

Paul thus says he is a servant of the now-revealed gospel secret: both Jews and Gentiles have equal parts in the body of Christ and are one in Him. Paul feels privileged that this is what he's been commanded by God to do. Paul is a servant, but he is glad to be one.

Notice how Paul became a servant of the gospel: it was by God's *grace*. He knows he doesn't deserve it, especially given his track record of persecuting the church (1 Corinthians 15:9). The very fact that he is the primary preacher to the Gentiles is an illustration of God's grace.

Paul notes that he has received *the gift* through the *working* of God's *power*. Have you ever been asked to do something and thought, "Why in the world did they ask me, of all people? I'm the least likely person to be able to do this!" It is the realization of our inadequacies that forces us to trust that God will empower us to do what He has called us to do. Think about all that Paul endured! (See 2 Corinthians 11:23-28.) Yet he trusts in God's power to carry him through. He considers himself blessed to be called by God to do this job. [See question #3, page 320.]

8. Unto me, who am less than the least of all saints, is this grace given, that I should preach among the Gentiles the unsearchable riches of Christ.

In 1 Corinthians 15:9, just noted above, Paul calls himself "the least of the apostles." In 1 Timothy 1:15, he refers to himself as chief of sinners. Here he creates a superlative, saying he's *less than the least of all saints* (meaning all Christians). You can't get much lower than that!

Again, Paul is emphasizing how unlikely he is to be the one chosen to carry this message to the Gentiles. Consider some of the reasons he may think this way. First of all, he is a Jew—a "Hebrew of the Hebrews" (Philippians 3:5)—not a Gentile. Second, he had persecuted Christians, even to their deaths. Third, he had been legalistic, not one naturally to understand *grace*.

But Paul now has the assignment to preach to the Gentiles *the unsearchable riches of Christ*. What a startling phrase! *Unsearchable* conveys the idea of "untraceable" or "unmeasurable." In other words, you can't measure how abundant the riches of God are. An economics professor may tell you that the idea of an abundant commodity to be valuable beyond measure is a contradiction in terms, because what usually makes something valuable is its rarity. For example, a flawless diamond is difficult to find and thus is very valuable. If the world had as many flawless diamonds as grains of sand on the seashore, then diamonds would not be valuable.

But God's gifts have great value not because they are rare but because of the way they meet our deepest needs. God's riches are eternal love, joy, grace, inner peace, and so on. And He never runs out of these. He can give you more and more of these blessings, and in Heaven they will be in abundance even though they will be the most treasured of all possessions.

9. And to make all men see what is the fellowship of the mystery, which from the beginning of the world hath been hid in God, who created all things by Jesus Christ.

Not only is Paul to preach these things to the Gentiles, Paul also has been sent to explain to Jew and Gentile alike that we are all one in Christ. That's the idea of *all men.* Even though Paul is the preeminent messenger to the Gentiles, he also speaks to Jews as often as he can. Even while writing to the Gentile believers back in Ephesus, Paul speaks to Jews about Christ during his imprisonment in Rome (Acts 28:17-31).

B. God's Intent (vv. 10, 11)

10. To the intent that now unto the principalities and powers in heavenly places might be known by the church the manifold wisdom of God.

The phrase *principalities and powers in heavenly places* refers to the angelic hierarchy. Evidence for the existence of a hierarchy among angels is seen in the term *archangel* in 1 Thessalonians 4:16 and Jude 9. The fact that angels now have information that they did not have before indicates that angels are not all-knowing (omniscient).

This mystery—that the Gentiles are to have equal access to the eternal God—has been kept hidden even from the angels. When the secret was revealed, the angels learned something about God's *manifold wisdom.* The angels already knew of God's power and beauty: they had seen God create the universe (Job 38:4-7). They knew of God's intelligence and character: they have watched Him create people and deal with those stiffnecked humans for thousands of years. But they had not understood this part of the extent of His wisdom until His plan of grace and redemption unfolded (see Romans 11:33).

11. According to the eternal purpose which he purposed in Christ Jesus our Lord.

God has had this plan from the beginning of time—it has been an *eternal purpose.* Some have claimed that the church is a sort of "parentheses" in God's salvation-history timeline. Under this idea, the church became God's Plan B, since Jesus was rejected during His first coming. The truth is that God has had this plan from the begin-

Visual for
Lesson 12

Point to this visual as you ask, "What hinders your message's signal strength?"

ning. It is the way that God chooses to make His glory known and understood. This story of God's grace gives us the greatest possible glimpse into the character of God.

PLANS AND PURPOSES

A few years ago, Sunroad Enterprises built a 180-foot tall office tower near Montgomery Field in San Diego. It was so near, in fact, that it violated Federal Aviation Administration (FAA) rules that limit buildings within a certain distance of airports to 160 feet in height. Even though warned of the violation by the FAA, the developer finished the superstructure, claiming the right to build according to the architect's plans because the city had approved those plans.

City officials got into a name-calling political battle over the matter. The city filed suit against Sunroad; the developer filed a countersuit for $40 million. Finally, on June 26, 2007, an "unrepentant" Sunroad (as the San Diego newspaper called the firm) agreed to lower the building to legal height, even while proceeding at full speed with the lawsuit. "The city approved the plans" was the company's reasoning as to why it resisted for months the calls to conform its plans to FAA regulations.

Human plans can be illegal, selfish, foolish, changeable, and contradictory to other human plans. However, God's plans are never self-contradictory. The question is, do our plans match His plans? If there's a mismatch, guess whose plans need to be changed!

—C. R. B.

C. Readers' Reaction (vv. 12, 13)

12. In whom we have boldness and access with confidence by the faith of him.

The revealed mystery means that God's plan is to make peace with all humanity, Jew and Gentile alike. We no longer need fear His judgment. Because of our faith in Christ, we can approach God boldly, *with confidence* (Romans 5:2; Hebrews 4:16; 10:19).

This confidence to approach God should not result in undue familiarity, however. People have been heard to say, "I can't wait to get to Heaven and give Jesus a big hug!" But according to the Bible, what really will happen when we get to Heaven is that "every knee [will] bow" (Philippians 2:10). Think about how people in the Bible react when they realize they are in the presence of God. Manoah says, "We shall surely die because we have seen God" (Judges 13:22); Isaiah says, "Woe is me! for I am undone" (Isaiah 6:5); Peter says, "Depart from me; for I'm a sinful man, O Lord" (Luke 5:8).

Nevertheless, Paul says that those who have faith in Jesus Christ can approach God with *boldness* and *confidence.* How different would our prayer lives be if we really believed this? [See question #4, page 320.]

13. Wherefore I desire that ye faint not at my tribulations for you, which is your glory.

If the Ephesian Christians are discouraged about Paul's situation, they should not be. His trials and *tribulations* are for their *glory.* What a great perspective on suffering! Paul is not bitter or angry about all the pain he is enduring. The fact that he is willing to undergo his persecutions shows the Ephesians how much he believes what he preaches.

We humans will try to avoid even brief periods of minor irritation. Suffering often surprises us. We take pills to try to wipe out pain as quickly

as possible. When we can't see any point to our pain, we get angry.

Yet Paul embraces his suffering as glorious because he trusts God to make good out of it—not necessarily for Paul, but for others. If we adopt the values of a self-absorbed culture, we may ignore the benefits to others or glory to God that our suffering can bring. When you understand what God is calling you to do and are submissive to it, you can withstand great suffering. You can see the glory in it even when it doesn't seem to benefit you personally.

God called Paul to suffer greatly (Acts 9:16). God may not call us to suffer in just the same way Paul did, but we do have our crosses to bear (Mark 8:34). Suffering for Christ will come to each of us in some way. Paul's suffering is for the *glory* of his beloved Ephesians. When that happens, God ultimately is the one glorified. When we understand our calling, we can withstand great suffering and see the glory in it—not for ourselves, but for those we try to reach and ultimately for God himself. [See question #5, page 320.]

Conclusion

A. Will You Tell the Secret?

Paul was willing to go to great lengths—even endure great suffering—so that as many people as possible could be told the secret: God's grace is available to everyone. It doesn't matter what country you were born in, what race you are, how poor you are, whether you are tall or short, fat or skinny, male or female. The God of the universe sent His Son, Jesus Christ, to die for your sins, and He wants to have a relationship with you. Are you willing to do what may be awkward or uncomfortable, to suffer a little or a lot, in order to communicate to those who may be different from you that Jesus loves them?

B. Prayer

Father, we confess that at times we have been proud. Sometimes we have considered our fellow human beings who are created in Your image as less valuable because of various reasons. Please forgive us and remind us to love others as You have loved us. We pray for the opportunity and courage to express Your love to others and to tell them of the free gift of Your grace that is available to all people who will put their faith in Your Son Jesus Christ. In His name we pray. Amen.

C. Thought to Remember

Make sure God's revealed secret remains revealed.

Home Daily Bible Readings

Monday, May 11—God's Dominion over All (Job 12:13-25)

Tuesday, May 12—Mysteries of the Kingdom (Matthew 13:10-17)

Wednesday, May 13—God Reveals Mysteries (Daniel 2:25-30)

Thursday, May 14—God's Secret Revealed (Amos 3:1-8)

Friday, May 15—The Son Reveals the Father (Matthew 11:25-30)

Saturday, May 16—Stewards of God's Mysteries (1 Corinthians 4:1-5)

Sunday, May 17—Sharing the Promise in Christ (Ephesians 3:1-13)

Learning by Doing

This page contains an alternative lesson plan emphasizing learning activities. Some of these activities are also found in the helpful student book, Adult Bible Class.

Into the Lesson

Option #1: Play a word-association game. Ask students to jot down the very first thing that comes to their minds as you recite the following three words: *secret, password, mystery.* Allow a few moments of silence for students to write, then have them share some of their responses. Make the transition to Bible study by saying, "The word *mystery* is often used to imply a surprise ending to a great story. Buried in the story is a secret that will be revealed at the end. Paul uses the word *mystery* to reveal Jesus in a wonderful way. Let's investigate this mystery in our study today."

Option #2: Have one student write down five activities he or she enjoys or would enjoy doing. At the same time, have all the other class members write down five activities that they *think* this student enjoys or would enjoy. Then have the first student read his or her list aloud so that everyone else can see what they did and didn't get right.

Make the transition to Bible study by saying, "For most of you, this was a guessing game based on partial knowledge of [person's name]. Only one of you knew the whole truth about [person's name]'s preferences for activities. This is a bit of a snapshot of today's study about a great mystery hidden for centuries, hinted at, but finally revealed to all."

Into the Word

Start with a brief lecture consisting of a summary of the Lesson Background. This will give your students a perspective on the first-century use of the word *mystery.*

Then divide the class into seven study teams of two or three students each. A smaller class may either double up on the assignments or make assignments to individuals rather than teams. The task of the teams is to examine, interpret, and apply words and phrases that come from today's printed text. Give each team a photocopy of the lesson commentary for their assignments as needed.

Display the following prepared instructions on the board or (better) on handouts: "Your tasks are to (1) give the background or interpretation of your assigned word or phrase, (2) draw out the implications for the Ephesians, and (3) set forth the implications for us today.

The seven assignments are

1. "the prisoner of Jesus Christ" (v. 1)
2. "the dispensation of the grace of God" (v. 2)
3. "mystery" (vv. 3-6)
4. "minister" and "less than the least" (vv. 7, 8)
5. "unsearchable riches" (v. 8)
6. "principalities and powers in heavenly places" (v. 10)
7. "eternal purpose" (v. 11)

Allow each team to report its findings.

Into Life

Activity #1: Central Theme. Ask the study teams to define the central theme they think arises from today's text, writing it into one sentence or phrase. Allow each team to report its conclusions. Make the transition to the next activity by saying, "The commentary writer says an important lesson from this text is that 'we are all one in Christ.' Our challenge is applying that principle to everyday life in our community. How will we do that?"

Activity #2: Brainstorming! Prepare two posters. One poster's heading should read *People Groups in Our Community.* The other poster's heading is *Strategies and Ideas.* Display the first poster. Ask students to identify different people groups in the community. People groups may refer to ethnic backgrounds, educational or social status, youth subcultures, etc. List these on the poster board.

Then say, "Let's evaluate our effectiveness in reaching these groups with the gospel." After discussion, check mark each group that is being touched by your church. Put a circle around the groups that are not being reached satisfactorily by your church.

Say, "Churches are usually not effective in reaching every people group in the community. However, most churches can improve their outreach." Ask the class to discuss ideas and strategies to reach different groups on the list. Jot the ideas on the second poster. Discuss which people group may be your church's greatest opportunity to reach. Finally, appoint a team to continue to explore this outreach and develop a plan. The team will make a recommendation for action at an appropriate time in the future.

Let's Talk It Over

The questions on this page are designed to promote discussion of the lesson by the class and to encourage application of the lesson Scriptures. The answers provided are only discussion starters. Let your class talk it over from there.

1. How can Paul's understanding of being a prisoner of Christ Jesus be lived out today?

Paul certainly knew all about prison life, having been imprisoned on various occasions on account of the gospel. But here he may be using *prisoner* in more than just a literal bars-and-chains way. Paul is in subjection to the authority of Jesus Christ. While we can understand what it is to submit to an employer or a parent, there are few relationships in which a person must submit to an authority figure so completely that one thinks of self as a prisoner to the one in charge. Yet this is the kind of attitude that Paul had toward his Savior. It was a joy for Paul to see himself in this light.

2. What information in the Bible do you believe you are especially responsible for sharing with others?

We may find it useful to divide the Bible's contents into two broad categories: information that's most appropriate for believers and information that's most appropriate for nonbelievers. Good stewards of Bible information recognize this distinction and apply it.

For example, John 3:16 and Acts 2:38 are two of the premier evangelistic passages in the Bible. Nonbelievers need to hear these. But does a Sunday school teacher need to quote those two passages every time he or she teaches a class of longtime Christians? Hebrews 5:12-14 answers *no*. That passage challenges us to move from milk to meat. This is an important part of our "information management" obligation.

3. In what ways do you consider yourself to be an unlikely servant of the gospel? How does this speak of God's grace toward you?

Paul certainly understood the unusual nature of his ministry of the gospel! The irony of a former murderer of Christians being engaged in making more followers of Christ was not lost on him.

Yet God has often used unlikely people to bring about His purposes. He used a man with halting speech to lead a nation (Moses; Exodus 4:10). He used the eighth-born son of a shepherd to fell a giant and rule a kingdom (David; 1 Samuel 16:8-12). He used unschooled men to articulate gospel truth (Peter and John; Acts 4:13). Paul correctly

understood that "it wasn't about him." Rather, it was about God's power to accomplish His will through whomever He chose.

4. What benefits do we enjoy in being able to boldly draw near to God? What responsibilities are there?

Because of the work of Jesus, fear and guilt at the realization God's presence (like what Isaiah felt in Isaiah 6) have been done away with. The wrath of God has been taken away; it was spent at Calvary many years ago. Since we have direct access to God, we can be certain that He hears us. There are many more benefits that could be listed, but consider just the benefit of being able to approach God yourself, not having to go through someone else as people had to do in Old Testament times.

This possibility of approaching God directly creates the responsibility to do so. But so many don't bother. Daily life to some is an endless sequence of work and entertainment. To those stuck in this cycle, a daily quiet time before God is a pointless concept. How sad!

5. In what ways have you personally benefited from suffering?

More than one person has said, "I would not choose to go through that particular valley of suffering ever again, but I wouldn't trade the experience at having done so for anything." Suffering always changes us, in one way or another. We will allow suffering either to push us away from God or to draw us closer to Him.

On the surface of things, one would not typically think that there is any benefit to suffering—that suffering is something to be avoided, not embraced. But Paul certainly had a different perspective as he viewed his suffering to be for the Ephesians' glory. Others would become bolder in their witness for the gospel due to Paul's witness in suffering. The pages of history speak of the courage of Christian martyrs. These witnesses strengthen our faith. James 1 speaks of how trials and tribulations can produce in us endurance, an endurance that we may need when even bigger trials come upon us. Suffering reminds us that we are not the ones in control.

New Life in the Home

DEVOTIONAL READING: 1 Corinthians 1:4-17.

BACKGROUND SCRIPTURE: Ephesians 5:1–6:4.

PRINTED TEXT: Ephesians 5:21–6:4.

Ephesians 5:21-33

21 Submitting yourselves one to another in the fear of God.

22 Wives, submit yourselves unto your own husbands, as unto the Lord.

23 For the husband is the head of the wife, even as Christ is the head of the church: and he is the saviour of the body.

24 Therefore as the church is subject unto Christ, so let the wives be to their own husbands in every thing.

25 Husbands, love your wives, even as Christ also loved the church, and gave himself for it;

26 That he might sanctify and cleanse it with the washing of water by the word,

27 That he might present it to himself a glorious church, not having spot, or wrinkle, or any such thing; but that it should be holy and without blemish.

28 So ought men to love their wives as their own bodies. He that loveth his wife loveth himself.

29 For no man ever yet hated his own flesh; but nourisheth and cherisheth it, even as the Lord the church:

30 For we are members of his body, of his flesh, and of his bones.

31 For this cause shall a man leave his father and mother, and shall be joined unto his wife, and they two shall be one flesh.

32 This is a great mystery: but I speak concerning Christ and the church.

33 Nevertheless let every one of you in particular so love his wife even as himself; and the wife see that she reverence her husband.

Ephesians 6:1-4

1 Children, obey your parents in the Lord: for this is right.

2 Honor thy father and mother; which is the first commandment with promise;

3 That it may be well with thee, and thou mayest live long on the earth.

4 And, ye fathers, provoke not your children to wrath: but bring them up in the nurture and admonition of the Lord.

GOLDEN TEXT: Submitting yourselves one to another in the fear of God.
—Ephesians 5:21.

Christy and Creation
The Fruits of New Life
Lessons 10–14

Lesson Aims

After participating in this lesson, each student will be able to:

1. List Paul's commands for wives, husbands, children, and fathers.

2. Evaluate his or her family relationships in light of Paul's commands.

3. State one change to make to align his or her family with God's Word.

Lesson Outline

INTRODUCTION
  A. Serious Problem
  B. Lesson Background
  I. TRANSITION (Ephesians 5:21)
 II. FOR WIVES (Ephesians 5:22-24)
    A. Instruction (v. 22)
    B. Hierarchy (vv. 23, 24)
III. FOR HUSBANDS (Ephesians 5:25-33)
    A. Command (v. 25a)
    B. Extent (vv. 25b-27)
      Perceptions and Corrections
    C. Parallel (vv. 28-30)
    D. Genesis (v. 31)
    E. Mystery (v. 32)
    F. Mutuality (v. 33)
IV. FOR CHILDREN (Ephesians 6:1-3)
    A. What to Do (v. 1)
    B. Why to Do It (vv. 2, 3)
 V. FOR FATHERS (Ephesians 6:4)
    A. Negative Command (v. 4a)
    B. Positive Command (v. 4b)
      That Which Is Noticed
CONCLUSION
  A. Your Discipleship Group
  B. Prayer
  C. Thought to Remember

Introduction

A. Serious Problem

"I hate divorce." Do you ever hear anyone say that? Children of divorced parents may say it with their actions, if not literally with their words. People who have been divorced may say it with their misery. So do their friends and loved ones who

watch the misery unfold. Ministers and counselors who help clean up the mess are certainly no fans of divorce. God himself hates divorce (see Malachi 2:16, where it is called "putting away").

As painful as divorce is, many families who stay together don't do much better at modeling God's love for one another as the Scriptures command. As a result, children may reject their parents' values after experiencing such dysfunction. For the sake of our children and the future of the church, we need to make sure our family relationships conform to Scripture rather than to cultural norms.

Note: Some in your class may be single and/ or childless, either voluntarily or involuntarily. Be sensitive to these as you teach today's lesson. However, don't shy away from the topics at hand because of oversensitivity. Remember that the apostle Paul, author of today's Scripture text, was himself almost certainly both single and childless.

B. Lesson Background

Paul knew the families of the Ephesian church well. After all, he had spent about three years among them (Acts 20:31). It was the Ephesian elders who had given him such an emotional farewell as he set sail for Jerusalem (Acts 20:13-38).

That farewell was about five years in the past when Paul wrote to his beloved Ephesians. The families of that church were under pressure (compare Revelation 2:1-7). Parents had to bring up their children in the shadow of the great pagan temple to Artemis. Much of the economy of the city revolved around that edifice (Acts 19:23-41). The temptation of "to get along, you have to go along" is not new to the twenty-first century.

I. Transition
(Ephesians 5:21)

21. Submitting yourselves one to another in the fear of God.

The *King James Version*, as other versions, organizes the flow of the text in paragraphs. Paragraphs help us identify units of thought and transitions to new thoughts. In this regard, the verse before us isn't really the opening line of Ephesians 5:22 and following. Rather, verse 21 sums up some of Paul's thoughts leading to Ephesians 5:20. Those thoughts include the need for Christians to avoid certain things (example: drunkenness, v. 18) while embracing various holy practices (example: singing to the Lord, v. 19).

Christian harmony in these areas requires *submitting yourselves one to another in the fear of God*. While Paul is on the topic of submission, he decides to dig deeper. [See question #1, page 328.]

II. For Wives
(Ephesians 5:22-24)
A. Instruction (v. 22)

22. Wives, submit yourselves unto your own husbands, as unto the Lord.

The meaning of this verse has been hotly debated. That word *submit* strikes a raw nerve in many. Genesis 3:16 reminds us that Paul is not coming up with something new. And 1 Peter 3:1 is similar. The reason for the instruction we see here is the subject of the next verse.

B. Hierarchy (vv. 23, 24)

23. For the husband is the head of the wife, even as Christ is the head of the church: and he is the saviour of the body.

Why should *the wife* submit? Because *the husband is the head of the wife*. The word *head* is often symbolic in the Bible for authority (examples: 2 Samuel 22:44; Ephesians 1:22). Even today we talk about someone being "head cheerleader" or "heading up a project." Back in the 1980s and 1990s, some scholars proposed that *head* should be understood not as "authority," but as "source." However, that idea was never supported by evidence. In a biblical home, the husband is the head.

Some say this is degrading to women. Yet are we demeaned if we submit to other authorities such as the police, church elders, or the boss at work? Paul discusses this hierarchy also in 1 Corinthians 11:3.

24. Therefore as the church is subject unto Christ, so let the wives be to their own husbands in every thing.

We would never question whether *the church* should follow the leadership of Jesus *Christ*. In the same way, the Bible indicates that God expects the wife to follow the lead of her husband, although it may seem old-fashioned or "out of touch" in today's culture.

How to Say It

ABSALOM. *Ab*-suh-lum.
ARTEMIS. *Ar*-teh-miss.
BABYLON. *Bab*-uh-lun.
COLOSSIANS. Kuh-*losh*-unz.
CORINTHIANS. Ko-*rin*-thee-unz (*th* as in *thin*).
DEUTERONOMY. Due-ter-*ahn*-uh-me.
EPHESIANS. Ee-*fee*-zhunz.
EZEKIEL. Ee-*zeek*-ee-ul or Ee-*zeek*-yul.
MALACHI. *Mal*-uh-kye.
SADDUCEES. *Sad*-you-seez.
TITUS. *Ty*-tus.

Notice the Bible does not command a woman to submit to each and every man; if she is married, she is to submit to the one man to whom she has vowed to be faithful. A woman who chooses to marry is to be devoted to following her husband as *unto Christ* himself.

It is indeed a high and difficult calling for wives to be subject *to their own husbands in every thing*. Scripture is clear that there are limits to obedience to authority when a violation of God's law is at stake (Acts 4:19; 5:29). If a woman has a husband who asks or tries to force her to do something that contradicts God's Word, she must obey God.

II. For Husbands
(Ephesians 5:25-33)
A. Command (v. 25a)

25a. Husbands, love your wives.

Paul now turns his attention to the *husbands*. The command *love your wives* could be taken in different senses if the thought ended right there. But Paul quickly follows by listing a model.

B. Extent (vv. 25b-27)

25b. Even as Christ also loved the church, and gave himself for it.

For husbands to love their wives *even as Christ also loved the church, and gave himself for it* is no small command! As hard as it may be for the wife to submit to her husband, the command for a husband to love his wife in this way may be the more difficult one to follow. [See question #2, page 328.]

PERCEPTIONS AND CORRECTIONS

Mary Winkler was known as "the perfect mother, the perfect wife." But in March 2006, this minister's wife killed her husband with a shotgun. After her arrest, she claimed the shooting was an accident, but also hinted at years of abuse by her husband. Her father later spoke of the abuse he believed to have triggered the crime: "[It was] physical, mental, verbal. . . . I saw bad bruises. The heaviest of makeup covering facial bruises."

As the case was nearing trial, someone self-identified as "Shannon" wrote a blog saying, "The [church Winkler attended] is very degrading to women. Has anyone looked into that[?] They are not allowed to do anything in church services and are made to feel lesser than their husbands." One analysis claimed, "Statistics indicate that beneath the smiling, steadfast veneer of a pastor's wife, there often lies a deeply isolated woman who . . . frequently feels neglected and left without a support system of her own."

"Shannon" voices a common (mis)perception of how the church applies today's text. How can that perception be corrected? Are some ministers-as-husbands guilty of ignoring the spirit of what Paul is saying? If so, what can the church do to correct this problem?   —C. R. B.

26. That he might sanctify and cleanse it with the washing of water by the word.

According to the standard of Jesus, the test of one's success as a husband is whether or not his wife is growing in holiness. Some wives we asked suggested several practical ways to do this: praying with and for her; guarding her from temptation; taking her to church every week; and taking the initiative to be the spiritual leader in your home by praying at meals are just a few ideas. [See question #3, page 328.]

The Word of God has the central place in anyone's growth in holiness. The description of *washing* recalls Titus 3:5.

27. That he might present it to himself a glorious church, not having spot, or wrinkle, or any such thing; but that it should be holy and without blemish.

God declares the church to be *holy and without blemish* because the blood of Christ has forgiven our sins. The church's beauty in holiness grows as a result of her faithfulness. Jesus looks to no bride other than His church (compare Revelation 21:2). She looks to no bridegroom other than Jesus (contrast Ezekiel 23).

Husbands and wives will have eyes only for each other. Men are known to be more "visually oriented" than women when it comes to interacting with the opposite sex. Perhaps this is why Paul draws on the visual cues of *spot, wrinkle*, and *blemish* in illustrating a husband's responsibility. These refer, of course, to spiritual issues, not physical ones. God calls husbands to see their wives as beautiful and attractive for all the right reasons (Proverbs 31:30). [See question #4, page 328.]

C. Parallel (vv. 28-30)

28. So ought men to love their wives as their own bodies. He that loveth his wife loveth himself.

The next three verses bring to mind the "one body" illustrations that Paul uses elsewhere. In Romans 12:4, 5 and 1 Corinthians 12:12-31, the "body" is the church, with a stress on the fact that the individual members form a unit. Here, that idea is delayed until verses 29, 30 (below). The verse at hand stresses a certain logic that finds overtones in the "one flesh" concept of Genesis 2:24 (more on this below). Husband and wife form a unit. Thus *he that loveth his wife loveth himself.*

This fact has implications that are more profound than first meets the eye. At various times in history (and even in some cultures today), women have been treated as property. Paul will have none of this! Men today may love their cars, tools, and lawn tractors in a certain "pride of ownership" sense, but men are not to love their wives in that way. Rather, they are *to love their wives as their own bodies.*

29. For no man ever yet hated his own flesh; but nourisheth and cherisheth it, even as the Lord the church.

Think about how difficult it is to find anyone who hates *his own flesh.* There are a few who do, but that is very often due to some kind of mental illness. And there are a few religious people who hate their own flesh because of a misguided doctrinal conviction that the human body is inherently evil (but see Genesis 1:31). These are not the situations that Paul expects.

30. For we are members of his body, of his flesh, and of his bones.

This verse completes the parallel drawn between husband-and-wife as a unit and Christ's body as a unit. The Christian married couple thus enjoys a kind of double unity: between themselves and within the church.

D. Genesis (v. 31)

31. For this cause shall a man leave his father and mother, and shall be joined unto his wife, and they two shall be one flesh.

We mentioned Genesis 2:24 earlier, and this is the specific reference. After God performed the first wedding, He gave this summary of the purpose of marriage. Jesus quoted this same passage when He defended the purpose of marriage before the Sadducees (Matthew 19:5). Here is the ultimate test of a husband's love: Is his wife the primary human relationship in his life?

E. Mystery (v. 32)

32. This is a great mystery: but I speak concerning Christ and the church.

Marriage is an illustration of *Christ and the church.* Paul says it is a *mystery* how this all works. But when a Christian couple truly loves one another on the biblical model, they are showing the world the love, in some sense, that Christ has for His bride, the church.

F. Mutuality (v. 33)

33. Nevertheless, let every one of you in particular so love his wife even as himself; and the wife see that she reverence her husband.

Perhaps you have admired the skill of a couple performing a waltz in a motion picture. The man leads confidently and lovingly; the woman follows gracefully and beautifully. Jesus Christ wants to take our marriages and turn them into a beautiful dance that illustrates His love for His bride. When Christian husbands and wives love each other, the world says, "Look at that beautiful couple!" And God gets the glory. [See question #5, page 328.]

IV. For Children (Ephesians 6:1-3)

A. What to Do (v. 1)

1. Children, obey your parents in the Lord: for this is right.

This command is certainly most difficult for the child whose *parents* do not know God or who are not exhibiting the fruit of the Spirit. So many excuses seem legitimate: my father is a jerk; my mother's demands are unrealistic; he's not even a Christian; she drinks; he's a hypocrite; she's not even my real mom; they don't care about me.

Even so, children are to obey their parents. The *in the Lord* qualifier perhaps brings back the idea we discussed earlier that we are not to obey people ahead of God (again, Acts 4:19; 5:29). If parents command a child to steal, lie, etc., then the child is to trust God and disobey the command. But that seldom happens. Usually it is stubborn, rebellious hearts that lead children to disobey.

B. Why to Do It (vv. 2, 3)

2. Honor thy father and mother; which is the first commandment with promise.

Paul, still addressing children, quotes the Fifth Commandment. This is found in Exodus 20:12 and Deuteronomy 5:16. While "children, obey" speaks to the outward actions, *honor* speaks to the motivation of the heart.

This command applies at all stages of life. Christians are to provide for their parents and grandparents in their old age (1 Timothy 5:4-8). Jesus had words of condemnation for those who refused to do this (Mark 7:9-13). This commandment is *the first* of the Ten Commandments that comes with a *promise*. See the next verse.

3. That it may be well with thee, and thou mayest live long on the earth.

The promise is twofold: it will go *well* with you, and you will *live long on the earth*. If we compare Exodus 20:12 with Deuteronomy 5:16, we see that the one in Deuteronomy is the longer version. That is the one Paul is using.

Does it not go well with children when they obey their parents, and does it not go poorly with them when they disobey? Consider a teenager who comes to his parents requesting permission

Visual for Lesson 13. *Point to this visual as you ask, "How does the text you see here tie in with today's lesson text?"*

to go out with his friends that evening. If he has been sour, complaining, even outright disobedient throughout the day, he is less likely to be granted his request. If on the other hand he has been pleasant, obedient, and industrious, his parents are more likely to trust him with privileges.

The promise *thou mayest live long on the earth* should be seen in the original light as given to the nation of Israel. If the Israelites were a people who respected and obeyed their parents, then their days "in the land" would not be cut short. Ezekiel 22:7 reveals that a refusal to honor parents was one reason the people of Judah were exiled to Babylon, cutting short the nation's life. We reap what we sow (Galatians 6:7). Those who are rebellious and violent invite the same in return. Absalom is a good example (2 Samuel 15–18).

V. For Fathers (Ephesians 6:4)

A. Negative Command (v. 4a)

4a. And, ye fathers, provoke not your children to wrath.

Fathers will give account before God for how they handled (or didn't handle) their parental duties. The father's responsibility is summed up with two commands, one negative and one positive.

The negative command is to *provoke not your children to wrath*. Have you ever seen a child embittered toward his or her father? This tragedy does not usually happen overnight. It happens when a series of emotional wounds go unattended, and the wounds fester until they become an infected pool of emotions. Consider some of the ways a father can embitter his children: belittling them; disciplining too strictly; setting unrealistic expectations; breaking promises; being uninvolved at home—the list goes on.

B. Positive Command (v. 4b)

4b. But bring them up in the nurture and admonition of the Lord.

Paul moves on to the positive command: *bring them up in the nurture and admonition of the Lord.* The word translated "bring them up" is translated "nourisheth" in Ephesians 5:29. Fathers are to nourish their children, but this is talking about spiritual rather than physical nourishment.

The two words translated *nurture* and *admonition* have to do with loving discipline and correction. They are used in similar contexts in Hebrews 12:5 and Titus 3:10, respectively. What a wonderful balance Paul provides! Fathers are to be involved in their children's lives, with the goal that their children will be brought up under the discipline of God's Word. However, they are to do this lovingly, not harshly lest they embitter their children (compare Deuteronomy 6:7; Colossians 3:21).

THAT WHICH IS NOTICED

A certain Ohio couple seemed to be kind, caring, and noble. The evidence for this was that they had done something few other parents would do: they had adopted *11* special needs children.

The picture changed when authorities removed all the children from the home, charging the parents with cruelty. Witnesses in the case—including some of the children—testified that the children were forced to sleep in filthy wood-and-wire cages. The parents claimed the children were put in the cages for protection, not punishment. They also blamed social services personnel for not helping

Home Daily Bible Readings

Monday, May 18—Trained by God's Grace (Titus 2:1-13)
Tuesday, May 19—Partnership in Marriage (Genesis 2:18-25)
Wednesday, May 20—Interpreting Traditions (Exodus 12:21-28)
Thursday, May 21—Parental Advice (Proverbs 4:1-9)
Friday, May 22—Spiritual Guidance for Families (Colossians 3:12-24)
Saturday, May 23—Providing for Family Members (1 Timothy 5:1-8)
Sunday, May 24—Christian Family Relationships (Ephesians 5:21–6:4)

them with the destructive behavior of some of the children. The parents were sentenced to prison.

Child-rearing is a significant, divine responsibility. It involves providing both nurture and correction in a godly manner. The extremes and the criminal behavior need to be dealt with, of course. But in so doing, let us not let godly parenting go unnoticed. —C. R. B.

Conclusion

A. Your Discipleship Group

Imagine that the elders of your church came to you and said, "We are beginning a new discipleship program, and we believe you are the perfect candidate to lead a small group of people in this new program. We want you to prayerfully consider investing a significant portion of your time into three disciples we are going to assign to you."

Later, you tell your spouse what the elders have asked of you. "I have thought and prayed about this all day," you say. "I'm thinking that perhaps God is leading me to say yes to this opportunity. It will mean I will have to make some sacrifices. I will need to cut out some activities so that I can have time to spend with these three people. I'll have to get my own spiritual habits in order so that I can be an example. We'll have to let them come into our home so they can witness a godly marriage. It's a little frightening to think of this kind of responsibility, but I really think we can do it. Imagine what it would be like to really make a difference in the lives of these three individuals!"

Perhaps the elders have not come to you asking you to lead a discipleship group. But if you are a husband/wife and/or father/mother, Jesus Christ has commissioned you to "love your wife as Christ loved the church" or "respect your husband" and "bring your children up in the nurture and admonition of the Lord." You have your marching orders. Will you make the sacrifices necessary to succeed?

B. Prayer

Father, thank You for creating the family. We pray for our marriages. Forgive us when we are a poor illustration to the world of Christ's love for the church. Empower us with Your Spirit that we will love one another with the sacrificial love that You demonstrated when You were on this earth. Help us to live in such a way that our children will want to follow our Lord Jesus. In His name we pray. Amen.

C. Thought to Remember

Illustrate Christ's love by loving one another.

Learning by Doing

This page contains an alternative lesson plan emphasizing learning activities. Some of these activities are also found in the helpful student book, Adult Bible Class.

Into the Lesson

Ask your class to form small groups of two or three. Encourage members of couples to go into different groups. Then distribute all the following questions to each group and ask them to give each person a chance to answer them, if he or she wishes. Tell them they have 10 minutes to work through the questions.

1. "What was the atmosphere in your home like when you were growing up? How well did everyone get along?"

2. "What kind of marriage did your parents have? If there was divorce in your family, what was that situation like?"

3. "What impact does your parents' marriage have on your family life today?"

Conclude the discussion time by remarking, "Your parents' approach to their marriage probably had a significant effect on your family life while you were growing up. Today's Scripture will give us some very helpful information on how to improve our own marriages and families."

Into the Word

Read today's printed text aloud. Say, "Successful relationships in the home are built on the principles in verse 21. The first step, beyond submitting ourselves to God the Father, is for all Christians to have a spirit of submission toward one another."

Use the discussion groups created in the first activity to complete one of the following three tasks each. (If your class is large, assign duplicate tasks; if your class is small, double up on tasks.) Give each team a written copy of their task, a photocopy of the lesson commentary on the appropriate passage of Scripture, a piece of poster board, and a marker.

Task #1, Instructions for Wives: State practical conclusions about wives' relationships with their husbands. Begin by reading Ephesians 5:22-24, 33. Then use the lesson commentary to help you answer the following questions: 1. What foundational principle is Paul teaching about the wife's responsibility in the marriage relationship? 2. What reasons are given for wives submitting to their husbands? 3. What are some practical ways to apply the emotionally charged issue of submission? Be ready to share your conclusions with the class.

Task #2, Instructions for Husbands: State practical conclusions about husbands' relationships with their wives. Begin by reading Ephesians 5:25-33. Then use the lesson commentary to help you answer the following questions: 1. What foundational principle is Paul teaching about the husband's responsibility in the marriage relationship? 2. In what ways is the marriage relationship to be like Christ's relationship to the church? 3. How can husbands demonstrate their love for their wives? Be ready to share your conclusions with the class.

Task #3, Instructions for Children and Fathers: State practical conclusions about children's relationships with parents. Begin by reading Ephesians 6:1-4. Then use the lesson commentary to help you answer the following questions: 1. What principles are being taught about a child's relationship to parents? 2. What reasons are given for children obeying and honoring their parents? 3. How can adults continue to honor their parents? 4. Why do you think Paul zeroes in on fathers in verse 4? Be ready to share your conclusions with the class.

This can be a time-intensive activity, so you may not have time to have more than one of the teams report its findings. If teams have used poster boards to write out their answers, you can display them. If you have several teams working on each task and want to give them all a chance to report, each team can report its findings on just one of the questions.

Into Life

Say, "People may blame their parents' bad example for their own failures as spouses or as parents. How valid is that excuse?" Allow several class members to share their thoughts.

Then say, "A certain author has said, 'The family you come from isn't as important as the family you're going to have.' Do you agree with that statement? Why, or why not?"

Conclude with, "If we don't want to be stuck in bad habits that we learned from our families of origin, then we need to take seriously the teachings of Scripture about how to be good wives, good husbands, and good parents. What one change will you make to align your family with God's Word?" Close with a prayer for the members of your class to be filled with God's wisdom and strength to make godly decisions within their families.

Let's Talk It Over

The questions on this page are designed to promote discussion of the lesson by the class and to encourage application of the lesson Scriptures. The answers provided are only discussion starters. Let your class talk it over from there.

1. How has the fear of God played a role in your submission to fellow believers?

The fear of the Lord is (or should be) the beginning point for all our thoughts and deeds. It is the beginning of wisdom (Psalm 111:10; Proverbs 9:10). It is God to whom we first submit; this was the case back in the Garden of Eden and is (or should be) the case today.

The fear of God serves as a wonderful check on submission relationships, for this fear should prevent anyone from exercising tyrannical authority over anyone else. All parties know (or should know) that they are under God's authority. This authority is based in the fact that He is the creator.

2. In which areas of life is it easiest and hardest for you to love and submit? Why?

Interpersonal relationships always have their difficult places. It is hard to love when the spouse is unkind or just plain neglectful. It is difficult to submit when in your heart you believe your spouse is making a foolish decision.

This is probably the reason why Paul phrases both statements as commands; if these were mere suggestions, we might not do either of these when difficulties arise. Yet it is often the times when it is hardest to submit and hardest to love that the most personal growth occurs. Pray and work on those difficult places, for the rewards of doing so are very great. Remembering that God is in charge is vital.

3. What are some additional ways in which a husband can nurture his wife spiritually?

There are dozens of good answers! We should realize at the start that there is no denying that cultivating a good spiritual life for oneself is difficult, but to be responsible for aiding another's is a great responsibility and challenge. Being actively involved in church together is a good start, but is not sufficient in and of itself. The husband is to be a teacher for his wife (1 Corinthians 14:35), and therefore he must develop an excellent spiritual life for her sake as well as his.

One area where husbands can help is in increasing their awareness of their wives' need for substantive relationships with other women. Women gain emotional and spiritual support from other women in ways that men can find difficult to comprehend. Men speak to other men primarily to exchange information, but often that's not what a wife needs from her husband. A family must be intentional about its spiritual growth, even setting aside part of the family budget for such concerns.

4. What are some ways a husband and wife can continue to see one another as attractive as the years take their toll?

Although physical appearance may attract our attention initially, the decision to marry will (or should) depend on a variety of factors. Finding someone with a strong commitment to the Lord, someone whose personality is compatible with ours, and who shares similar interests will be important factors in choosing a life mate. These enduring qualities will allow husband and wife to continue to find one another fascinating.

Physical beauty, like flowers, fades with time. A marriage that is based solely on the physical element won't last more than about two years. Time needs to be spent learning about the inner person that your spouse is and coming to appreciate his or her God-created uniqueness.

5. What relationships or potential relationships can become a threat to the primacy of the husband-wife relationship?

This question may strike some raw nerves, so use with care. Threatening relationships can be put into two categories: personal and impersonal. Regarding the former, we know that work relationships can threaten a marriage when coworkers become attracted to each other. Regarding impersonal relationships, we have all heard sad tales about people who were "married to their jobs." How many ministers have sacrificed their marriages by being overcommitted to working for their churches?

It almost goes without saying that certain kinds of relationships with parents can cause problems in a marriage; parental interference makes for hilarious sitcoms, but miserable marriages in real life. When relationships with children become more important than the relationship with the spouse, danger looms. The #1 relationship is between a person and God. The #2 relationship is between a husband and wife. No other family relationship should be allowed to take over that #2 spot.

New Armor for Battle

DEVOTIONAL READING: Luke 11:14-23.

BACKGROUND SCRIPTURE: Ephesians 6:10-18.

PRINTED TEXT: Ephesians 6:10-18.

Ephesians 6:10-18

10 Finally, my brethren, be strong in the Lord, and in the power of his might.

11 Put on the whole armor of God, that ye may be able to stand against the wiles of the devil.

12 For we wrestle not against flesh and blood, but against principalities, against powers, against the rulers of the darkness of this world, against spiritual wickedness in high places.

13 Wherefore take unto you the whole armor of God, that ye may be able to with-stand in the evil day, and having done all, to stand.

14 Stand therefore, having your loins girt about with truth, and having on the breast-plate of righteousness;

15 And your feet shod with the prepara-tion of the gospel of peace;

16 Above all, taking the shield of faith, wherewith ye shall be able to quench all the fiery darts of the wicked.

17 And take the helmet of salvation, and the sword of the Spirit, which is the word of God:

18 Praying always with all prayer and sup-plication in the Spirit, and watching there-unto with all perseverance and supplication for all saints.

GOLDEN TEXT: Take unto you the whole armor of God, that ye may be able to withstand in the evil day, and having done all, to stand.—Ephesians 6:13.

Christy and Creation
The Fruits of New Life
Lessons 10–14

Lesson Aims

After participating in this lesson, each student will be able to:

1. List the elements of the armor of God.
2. Explain the need for each piece of "armor" in more literal terminology.
3. Identify one element of the armor of God that he or she needs to don and make a plan to do so.

Lesson Outline

INTRODUCTION
  A. Dressing for Battle
  B. Lesson Background
 I. THE PERIL OF BELIEVERS (Ephesians 6:10-13)
  A. Spiritual Resources (v. 10)
  B. Spiritual Wrestling (vv. 11, 12)
    Spiritual Warfare
  C. Spiritual Victory (v. 13)
II. THE PROTECTION OF BELIEVERS (Ephesians 6: 14-18)
  A. Battle Dress (vv. 14-17)
    What Doesn't Change
  B. Battle Communication (v. 18)
CONCLUSION
  A. Spiritual Combat
  B. Prayer
  C. Thought to Remember

Introduction

A. Dressing for Battle

One of the most popular spectator sports of the twenty-first century is American-style football. Although it is somewhat obscure outside the United States and Canada, this is one of the highest revenue-generating sports on the planet. High school football teams have rabid fans. The fans of football teams of major universities are no less passionate. The "identity" of a large city can be tied to its professional football franchise.

At its core, football is a type of mock warfare. Points are scored by pushing the battle line into the opponent's end zone. Brutal, hand-to-hand combat occurs *in the trenches*, the line of scrimmage. The key player, the quarterback, is often referred to as the *field general* who directs his

troops. Players with experience are *veterans*. A long pass is called *a bomb*.

As the game of football has developed, there have been many improvements in equipment. A fully dressed football player wears many items to protect himself from the physical pounding of the game. All players wear helmets with face masks. Each player wears a custom mouth guard to protect his teeth. Very prominent are the pads that allow players to use their shoulders like battering rams. Some players wear flak jackets to protect their ribs. Football pants are equipped with hip pads, thigh pads, and knee pads to guard those body parts. Some players even use shoes with steel toes to protect their feet.

While there are many injuries in football, this system of body armor is amazingly effective, given the speed of the game and the intensity of the hits. We can imagine how quickly a person wearing only a soccer player's gear would be injured on the full-contact football field.

When we look at a depiction of a Roman soldier of Paul's day, the soldier may appear to us to have used strange equipment. But he was armed and armored using the finest equipment available at the time. If his armor kept him from becoming a casualty, he could fight the next battle too.

The apostle Paul never served in the Roman army. But he had seen Roman soldiers up close on more than one occasion. Paul knew that there was a far more consequential war being waged outside the realm of earthly armies. Paul understood and taught that all believers would be called upon to engage in warfare against spiritual powers that would seek to destroy their faith. Their commander was not sending them into battle unarmored, though. God has provided spiritual armor for each believer.

B. Lesson Background

In writing Ephesians, Paul revealed a special concern for spiritual realities. He was acutely aware that there is a spiritual realm, unseen to us, where important things take place that affect us. Paul referred to this realm as the "heavenly places."

This realm is the source of our spiritual blessings (Ephesians 1:3). Yet this realm is also the habitation of "principalities and powers," meaning the evil spiritual forces that seek to enslave humanity (Ephesians 3:10). The New Testament teaches that all spiritual powers eventually will be brought to submission (1 Corinthians 15:24; Philippians 2:10; 1 Peter 3:22), but that time has not yet come (Hebrews 2:8).

There are two extremes to be avoided when considering the nature of the spiritual realm or the spirit world. *Animism*, on the one hand, is the belief that almost everything in nature has a spirit associated with it. There is a river god, a tree god, a monkey god, a mountain god, a storm god, etc. In this worldview, life is a matter of tiptoeing through the spheres of these little gods, pleasing and appeasing each as necessary.

On the other end of the spectrum, *secular materialism* is based on the idea that there are no spiritual realities at all. In this worldview, gods and angels are no different from elves and leprechauns. At the end of the day, if there is no tooth fairy, then there are no gods, either. There are no hidden spiritual powers, good or bad, and humans are called to make their way boldly in a godless world.

Paul taught neither the chaotic and fearful world of the animists nor the lonely and even scarier world of the materialists. He personally had experienced the spiritual world in dramatic, convincing ways (see 2 Corinthians 12:1-4). Yet he understood that this realm was not a playground for competing deities of varying powers. Paul knew that there is one God. The spiritual world is delineated between those forces aligned with God and those forces in rebellion against God.

We do not understand why the all-powerful God continues to allow these evil spiritual forces to exist (nor did Paul). However, for as long as the spiritual realm is populated with these rebellious powers, they will seek to bring men and woman under their thrall as co-rebels against God.

This, then, is cosmic warfare of the most deadly type. Paul knew that Christians must constantly be on guard against spiritual attacks, for their hearts and minds are the battleground. Paul also knew that God had not left believers without defenses. Such is the focus of this week's lesson.

I. The Peril of Believers (Ephesians 6:10-13)

A. Spiritual Resources (v. 10)

10. Finally, my brethren, be strong in the Lord, and in the power of his might.

Paul begins the final section of the letter by urging his readers to *be strong*. This has the sense of empowerment, of the unleashing of latent strength.

The source of this strength is nothing physical, however. It is not a matter of weight training or nutritional supplements. It does not come from an injection of steroids. Instead, spiritual strength comes from our relationship with God, from being *in the Lord*.

Paul uses an unusual phrase to describe God's strength: *the power of his might*. This is similar to a common Bible description of God as the *Almighty*. There are no holes in God's power. He is strong everywhere.

A repeated mistake for most Christians is to fall into the trap of trusting in their own inner strength in times of trial. If we spurn the spiritual assistance and power of God, we will become casualties in life's battles. As Paul explains it elsewhere, when we understand our weakness and rely on God, then we are truly strong (2 Corinthians 12:10).

B. Spiritual Wrestling (vv. 11, 12)

11. Put on the whole armor of God, that ye may be able to stand against the wiles of the devil.

Paul admonishes us to dress ourselves in the protective *armor* provided by *God*. The emphasis is on using the entirety of our gear, for none of it is optional. Paul's purpose for this is clear: to allow us to withstand the devil's attacks.

The Greek word translated *wiles* is the term from which we get our English word *methods*. One commentator noted that the most dangerous thing about Satan is his inconsistency. Satan will attack any weakness when least expected. (Ironically, we may say that he is very consistent in this regard!) His craftiness and trickery are a constant threat. We can neither predict nor anticipate these assaults, and thus we must be fully protected and on guard in order to resist him.

12. For we wrestle not against flesh and blood, but against principalities, against powers, against the rulers of the darkness of this world, against spiritual wickedness in high places.

The nature of our spiritual struggle against evil is presented as a cosmic wrestling match. The object of a wrestling competition in the athletic games of the ancient world is to toss one's opponent to the ground and hold him down. Satan seeks to trip us up and to keep us from recovering.

How to Say It

ANIMISM. *a*-nuh-mi-zum (*a* as in *mat*).

APOCALYPTIC. uh-pock-uh-*lip*-tik.

CORINTHIANS. Ko-*rin*-thee-unz (*th* as in *thin*).

EPHESIANS. Ee-*fee*-zhunz.

EPISTLE. ee-*pis*-ul.

ISAIAH. Eye-*zay*-uh.

LEGIONNAIRES. Lee-juh-*nairs*.

MEDIEVAL. mee-*dee*-vul.

PHILIPPIANS. Fih-*lip*-ee-unz.

THESSALONIANS. *Thess*-uh-*lo*-nee-unz (strong accent on *lo*; *th* as in *thin*).

We sometimes are prone to think that the fight for righteousness, goodness, and holiness is a test of human wills and different philosophies. It is true that our fallen world produces some unimaginably evil and depraved human beings. But Paul knows that this is but an outcome produced by the spiritual warfare that is constantly being waged.

Men and women *(flesh and blood)* are not our ultimate enemies. They are the fallen children of God. [See question #1, page 336.] Our true adversaries are *rulers of the darkness* and *spiritual wickedness in high places.* This is not a cryptic reference to world governments or conspiracy theories. It is a description of very real evil spiritual beings who are in league with Satan.

SPIRITUAL WARFARE

Various doctrinal points of view divide today's Christians. One such divide concerns Christian pacifists and what might be called Christian militarists.

Some with a pacifist bent believe we need to get rid of the war imagery when we talk about the faith. For example, the words of Sabine Baring-Gould's 1864 hymn are deeply troubling to some: "Onward, Christian soldiers, marching as to war . . . forward into battle . . . like a mighty army moves the church of God," etc. After all, isn't Jesus the Prince of Peace? Didn't He command us to "turn the other cheek"? Then how can we use the imagery of warfare when praising Him?

Other Christians see all of life as a continuous, "every incident" cosmic and/or physical battle against the forces of evil. Armies from supposedly Christian nations went on religious "crusades" in centuries past. Not many propose a return to that line of thinking. Yet some Christians see demons behind each and every incident that seems to be even the slightest bit troubling.

To the former group we may ask, have you ever read Ephesians 6? To the latter group we can say that implements of war are not the only images Scripture uses to describe the Christian life. With study and prayer we can find between these two perspectives the biblical view of the nature of our struggles.   —C. R. B.

C. Spiritual Victory (v. 13)

13. Wherefore take unto you the whole armor of God, that ye may be able to withstand in the evil day, and having done all, to stand.

The *evil day* that Paul foresees is not necessarily a time of apocalyptic distress for all humanity. It is, rather, the day that each believer faces, the day when faith itself is sorely tested. It is the day when our trials wear us down, and we are

tempted to forsake our Savior for the life of sin and despair. This day may be repeated many times in our lives.

Paul's image here is of a soldier who is still standing when the battle is done. If the fight is over and we are standing, then we are not casualties. We have not been thrown down and dominated in the spiritual wrestling match. As Paul says elsewhere, we are victors in the battle, "more than conquerors" (Romans 8:37).

This survival will not be from our own resources, but from the protective *whole armor* provided by God for our safety. God does not save us one day only to lose us later. He wants us to be safe, even on the most evil of days.

II. The Protection of Believers (Ephesians 6:14-18)

A. Battle Dress (vv. 14-17)

14a. Stand therefore, having your loins girt about with truth.

The *loins* is the area from waist to knees. This area is lightly armored for the Roman soldier so that he can maintain his maneuverability. Depictions of Roman soldiers show that they favor a short, skirt-like contraption made of broad strips of leather hanging from a heavy leather belt. Underneath could be a brightly colored cloth garment extending to the knees.

Paul uses the image of a belt to describe the protective function of truth for the believer. To "gird up one's loins" is a common expression in Paul's day that means "prepare for a fight" (see 1 Peter 1:13). The belt is tightened to the ready position when the battle is about to begin.

Undermining or twisting the *truth* is one of Satan's favorite strategies (example: Matthew 4:1-11). Yet truth can be an impenetrable defense. If we always tell the truth, we will not be caught in a tangle of our own lies. Lies—whether ones we tell or false philosophies we accept—bog us down. Truth keeps us mobile and active because relying on God's truth means that the devil won't be able to draw us into his quagmire of deceit. [See question #2, page 336.]

14b. And having on the breastplate of righteousness.

The Roman *breastplate* is made of leather covered with bronze. It is "muscled" to make the warrior look strong and fearsome. This armor protects only the front of the soldier, for he is expected to face the battle. There is no protection for the back, no armor for the one who turns and runs.

Protection of the torso is critical, for this part of the body houses many vital organs. If a spear or arrow is not deflected by the breastplate, death can follow quickly.

Righteous behavior is a protection from attacks on one's personal integrity. When a believer falls publicly, the entire church is damaged and its witness is compromised. This is why Paul calls for leaders who are "blameless" (Titus 1:6, 7) and have a "good report" in the community (1 Timothy 3:7).

Ultimately, our righteousness is brought about through the atoning sacrifice of Christ. But our daily manifestation of this through right living is a protection against being ensnared in hidden sins and hypocrisy (compare Isaiah 59:17; 1 Thessalonians 5:8).

15. And your feet shod with the preparation of the gospel of peace.

The Roman soldier's footwear is a half-sandal, half-boot apparatus with thick leather soles. It is not designed to protect the upper foot from sword slashes or arrows. Rather, its purpose is to guard the foot from rugged terrain so that the soldier can march and advance into battle without worrying about stepping on a sharp rock or a splintered piece of wood.

Paul presents an image here of the gospel preacher who acts in order to proclaim the *gospel of peace*. The emphasis on *peace* would seem inconsistent with Paul's warrior analogy, but peace between Jews and Gentiles has been a major point of this epistle (see Ephesians 2:14). The gospel of peace is the proclamation that the war between God and humanity is over; the two are now reconciled (2 Corinthians 5:18-20). In Romans, Paul uses this same image to emphasize the "beautiful feet" of the gospel preacher, the one who announces peace (Romans 10:15, quoting Isaiah 52:7).

16. Above all, taking the shield of faith, wherewith ye shall be able to quench all the fiery darts of the wicked.

The *shield* is the most important defensive implement in the Roman soldier's armor. Legionnaires use a rectangular shield that resembles a half cylinder. This curved surface causes arrows and spears to hit a glancing blow because of the angle. These shields are made of wood, with various types of leather and metal trim.

The shields used by the foot soldiers of the legion are large, four feet in height. This allows a squadron of soldiers to take a formation in which the shields are placed together on all sides and above, making a movable fortification structure that protects advancing troops from arrows, spears, or other missiles. This formation is known as *the tortoise* and is a key tactic that leads to the success of the Roman legions in battle.

The Old Testament often pictures God as a shield for the faithful (example: Genesis 15:1; Psalm 28:7; Proverbs 30:5). Thus Paul's analogy of a *shield of faith* is an apt one. When Satan is waging an all-out assault upon us, we may have no resources left except our faith. We can absorb tremendous hits if we believe that God loves us, that Christ died for us, and that our future in Heaven is secure. Satan's greatest tool is doubt. Our most effective defense is faith.

17a. And take the helmet of salvation.

The Roman soldier's *helmet* serves as both a protective device and an identifier. It is designed to protect the head and neck, particularly from blows that come from hand-to-hand combat. Most helmets have a head-covering bowl, an extended neck guard, side flashings to protect the cheeks and ears, and (sometimes) a metal face mask. Helmets also may hold a large, colorful crest on the top, undoubtedly the most eye-catching part of the soldier's dress.

The helmet is not normally worn by the soldier unless battle is pending. No prudent Roman soldier neglects to don his helmet as he prepares for warfare, for a blow to the unprotected head is likely to be fatal. Likewise, our *salvation* is that which protects us from the threat of eternal death. Salvation is God's gracious gift, and we are foolish to neglect it (see Hebrews 2:3).

17b. And the sword of the Spirit, which is the word of God.

The final part of Paul's "whole armor" is the only offensive weapon in the list: *the sword of the Spirit* (compare Hebrews 4:12). When do we stage a counterattack against the devil? We do so whenever we proclaim *the Word of God*, when we

BE STRONG IN THE LORD
Ephesians 6:10

Visual for
Lesson 14

Point to this visual as you ask, "What was a time when the helmet of salvation helped you the most?"

communicate the truths of the Bible. We bring light to the darkness, and our active resistance to Satan causes him to flee (James 4:7).

The spiritual battle is not a matter of holding our position. It is our assault on the strongholds of Satan (see 2 Corinthians 10:4). To make this assault requires an offensive weapon. [See question #3, page 336.]

WHAT DOESN'T CHANGE

A soldier's defensive body armor has not always been a top priority in wartime. Its use has waxed and waned over the centuries. In the Roman army, body armor was important. Such armor became even more important by medieval times, when chain mail and suits of armor were common. However, these were so heavy and cumbersome that they eventually were dispensed with (compare 1 Samuel 17:38, 39). The advent of gunpowder hastened their demise. Soldiers in the American Revolution and the American Civil War had virtually no body armor.

The twentieth century saw an interest in flak jackets develop. In the twenty-first century, this has evolved into advanced personal armor. *Interceptor* body armor became standard issue during the Iraq War. A newer type, called *Dragon Skin®*, takes its cue from medieval chain mail. At about 18 pounds, the weight problem has been solved.

Yet one thing has never changed throughout the history of warfare: the need for an offensive weapon. If a soldier has all the best defensive armor available, but no offensive weapon, we may rightly ask, "What good is that soldier?"—C. R. B.

B. Battle Communication (v. 18)

18. Praying always with all prayer and supplication in the Spirit, and watching thereunto with all perseverance and supplication for all saints.

Spiritual warfare is not waged in the streets or on the high seas. Rather, it is fought in the hearts and minds of men and women. This is why *prayer* is so important in this context. We will win the battle through prayer. This includes both prayers for ourselves and our prayers *for all* the *saints*. [See question #4, page 336.] By *saints*, Paul means our fellow believers, our Christian brothers and sisters in battle. We will win these battles if we pray with *perseverance*, with the dogged persistence that will not accept defeat.

Conclusion

A. Spiritual Combat

In real warfare, soldiers have long recognized the value of protective body armor. Although this can be expensive, military strategists know that shielding a soldier from the enemy's attack allows that soldier to fight another day. No army has ever had an inexhaustible supply of troops, so wise commanders always have sought to protect the ones they had.

The truth is that many churches are littered with spiritual casualties. This problem is traceable to a failure to put on the full armor of God. We have let the cares of our materialistic world grow strong and choke us (Mark 4:19). We have not equipped ourselves with the many spiritual resources that God has provided for our protection. [See question #5, page 336.]

The first step to spiritual victory is to recognize the dangerous reality of the battle: Satan is real, and he wants to destroy us. The second step is to unite with other believers in resistance to Satan's methods and tricks. An army must fight as a team. "An army of one" is a contradiction in terms.

The third step is to attack our adversary with the truths of the gospel, with the love of the fellowship, with our prayers for the saints. May we be vigilant and bold in this battle!

B. Prayer

God, our shield and protector, You are our rock, our strong tower, our mighty fortress. You are our armory. It is You who have provided all the equipment we need to prevail.

May we be wary of Satan and his schemes. But help us keep that wariness from becoming fear. We gain this victory when we focus on You and the power of Your strength. We pray these things through the mighty name of Jesus, amen.

C. Thought to Remember

God provides all the spiritual armor we need.

Home Daily Bible Readings

Monday, May 25—Truth (Psalm 25:1-5)
Tuesday, May 26—Righteousness (Proverbs 11:1-10)
Wednesday, May 27—The Good News of Peace (Isaiah 52:7-12)
Thursday, May 28—Faith (Hebrews 10:35–11:3)
Friday, May 29—Salvation (Isaiah 12:1-6)
Saturday, May 30—The Word of God (Psalm 119:105-112)
Sunday, May 31—The Whole Armor of God (Ephesians 6:10-18)

Learning by Doing

This page contains an alternative lesson plan emphasizing learning activities. Some of these activities are also found in the helpful student book, Adult Bible Class.

Into the Lesson

Display or pass around pictures of modern battle gear as used by the individual soldier. (This means pictures of helmets, etc., not pictures of tanks and airplanes. Such pictures are easy to find on the Internet.) Use the pictures to start a discussion about the specific purpose of each item.

Make the transition to Bible study by saying, "Good equipment is important for any battle, whether it is fighting enemy soldiers, fighting crime, or fighting fires. Good equipment is also important for Christians as we battle the evil one. Unfortunately, Christians often do not give their gear the attention or care that a good soldier should. Let's explore our gear and its use."

Into the Word

Explain that Paul's illustration of our battle gear comes from his knowledge of the Roman soldier's gear. After reading today's printed text from Ephesians 6:10-18, assign the following tasks to study squads. (Call them *squads* to keep with the nature of the lesson.) Give each squad a poster board and a marker.

Alpha Squad: Your task is to identify who the Christian's enemy is and isn't. Read the printed text, then list the terminology that describes the enemy. Be ready to explain the significance of each descriptive phrase or word.

Bravo Squad: Your task is to identify modern expressions of Satan's work in today's culture. One of our other squads is doing a study of today's printed text to identify the enemy. However, you will try to identify current works of Satan. How is he attacking us through our values, thought processes, technology, etc.? Remember, if we are to win the battle, we need to identify the enemy's strategies. List your thoughts on the poster board.

Charlie Squad: Your task is to identify the battle dress or spiritual gear available to believers for this battle. Make a stick drawing of the battle armor mentioned in our printed text. Then label each piece with the metaphorical application to spiritual gear available to the Christian. Be ready to explain the significance of each piece of offensive and defensive gear for spiritual warfare. Do *not* include verse 18 in your discussion.

Delta Squad: Your task is to identify the gear for battle communication and the importance of such to Christians (v. 18). Answer the following questions. Then be ready to read those questions and your conclusions to the rest of the class.

1. What gear is available for the Christian's battle communication?

2. With whom must we communicate . . . and what must we communicate?

3. How well do Christians communicate with the commander?

4. What suggestions would you give to Christian warriors about battle communication?

After each squad reports its findings and conclusions, tell the class that it is exam time. Hand out a drawing of a Roman soldier in battle gear and ask each person to try to label from memory each piece of equipment with the appropriate metaphorical application to Christian armor.

Into Life

Ask class members to examine their personal spiritual battles. Say, "What are you wrestling with in your spiritual life? biblical literacy? communication with your commander? disconnection from the rest of your team? temptations? faithfulness or desertion? perfectionism? failure to accept responsibilities?"

Then ask the class members to identify the piece of equipment on the picture of armor that will best help in his or her spiritual battle. Circle that piece of equipment. Within their original squads, have students brainstorm with one another about ways that each can make greater use of the piece of equipment most neglected or lacking.

Close the lesson by distributing the following prayer. Ask the class to read it in unison.

Mighty God, our shield and protector! You are our rock, our strong tower, our mighty fortress. Help us to remember that Satan is always scheming to attack our relationship with You. But we do not fear because of the power of Your strength.

Help us, O God, to be strong when attacked. Help us to be faithful when challenged by ungodly philosophies and worldviews. Lord, help us to stand together as Your people, relying and giving strength to each other.

You are our strength. We place our trust in You, our mighty fortress. Through our redeemer's name we pray. Amen.

Let's Talk It Over

The questions on this page are designed to promote discussion of the lesson by the class and to encourage application of the lesson Scriptures. The answers provided are only discussion starters. Let your class talk it over from there.

1. When we realize that the true conflict is with evil spiritual forces, how will this change our dealings with nonbelievers? How well are you doing in this regard?

Different tactics are called for when we realize that the battle is not against the flesh and blood person, but against the spiritual forces of evil. Our focus will not be to defeat or put down the misguided person standing in front of us. The focus, rather, will be against the wicked impulses that control him or her.

Part of Paul's strategy when dealing with sinful people was to do a kindness for them (see Romans 12:14, 17, 20, 21). As a result, evil is overcome with good. Jesus instructed us to pray for those who persecute us (Matthew 5:44). Even if this does not result in a change in the other person, it definitely will change us.

2. Why do you think Paul picks *truth* to list first as a piece of the armor of God?

Truth is vital. When truth is absent, all that is left is falsehood. Without bedrock truth, society stumbles along the shifting sands of relativism, trying to figure out "what works."

Jesus referred to himself as being the truth (see John 14:6). The truth makes us free (see John 8:32). If we wish to worship God, then we must do so in spirit and in truth (John 4:24). Satan is the father of lies (John 8:44). The first sin committed by humans resulted from a lie of Satan (Genesis 3:4, 5). It is truth that exposes the wiles of the evil one. Without a concern for truth as a first order of business, none of the other aspects of the armor of God will matter much.

3. What does good swordsmanship look like in a spiritual sense?

Soldiers do not win wars by remaining strictly on defense. Using a sword merely to parry the attacks of an opponent will not win the battle. Soldiers must go on the offense to defeat the enemy and cause him to flee. James tells us that if we submit to God, the devil will flee from us (see James 4:7). We submit to God by developing skill in handling our sword—the Word of God.

Jesus used this sword to send the devil packing during the temptation in the wilderness (Matthew 4:1-11). During that battle, the devil attempted to use the Word of God for his own purposes. But Jesus' greater skill won the day. This is a valuable lesson for us: we must develop good skills in using this sword (compare 2 Timothy 2:15). Like most weapons, improper use of this sword can end up hurting us. Many of us have firsthand knowledge of individuals whose spiritual wounds were self-inflicted due to their own faulty use and application of the Word (compare Acts 19:13-16).

We should recall as well that this piece of spiritual equipment is a sword, not a club. Its use is to penetrate a person's innermost being, to lead him or her to repent (Hebrews 4:12). It is not a club we use to beat people over the head.

4. Practically speaking, how do we go about praying "for all saints"?

Obviously, it's not practical to make a prayer list of thousands of names of Christians, then pray for each one individually every day! And we may rightly wonder how much good it really does to pray a generic prayer for God to "bless all Christians everywhere."

A solution starts with the general recognition that fellow Christians need our prayers (as we need theirs). This realization will help create a mind-set to pray for others. If your church is small (as the church at Ephesus in her early days probably was), it may indeed be practical to pray for each Christian there by name on a regular basis.

Beyond that, some churches have developed creative ways to make sure that everyone is prayed for. For example, a larger church may distribute monthly prayer calendars on which are listed member names on a rotating basis. This means that each person's name or each family comes up for prayer before everyone in the congregation at least once a year.

5. Which aspect of the armor of God are you most lacking right now? How will you correct this problem?

Answers will be, of course, highly personal. This could be a good question to address in small groups or study pairs. Have the groups or pairs include a brief time of prayer for each individual who mentions a need in this area.

Summer Quarter 2009

Call Sealed with Promise

(Exodus, Leviticus, Numbers, Deuteronomy)

About These Lessons

We see *calls* and *promises* all the time. For example, TV commercials call us to buy something, while promising certain benefits if we do. We hear so many of these that we get numb to them. God's calls and promises do the opposite: they refresh our spirit. That's what will happen as we study these lessons.

Jun 7

Jun 14

Jun 21

Jun 28

Jul 5

Jul 12

Jul 19

Jul 26

Aug 2

Aug 9

Aug 16

Aug 23

Aug 30

Quarterly Quiz

The questions on this page may be used in several ways: as a pretest at the beginning of the quarter; as a review at the end of the quarter; or as a review after each lesson. The questions are based on the Scripture text of each lesson (King James Version). ***The answers are on page 340.***

Lesson 1

1. What was the name of the mountain of God? (Tabor, Carmel, Horeb?) *Exodus 3:1*

2. Moses was amazed by the burning bush because there was no apparent reason why a bush in the desert should be on fire. T/F. *Exodus 3:2, 3*

Lesson 2

1. Moses protested that he should not be God's spokesman because he was not an eloquent speaker. T/F. *Exodus 4:10*

2. What did the Israelites do when they realized that God was acting to take away their affliction? (wept, worshiped, celebrated?) *Exodus 4:31*

Lesson 3

1. Initially, Moses and Aaron asked Pharaoh to let the people of Israel go so that they could hold a _____ in the desert. *Exodus 5:1*

2. To punish the Israelites, Pharaoh ordered that they no longer be provided what for making bricks? (straw, water, wooden molds?) *Exodus 5:7*

Lesson 4

1. A wind from God blew all night in order to divide the Red Sea and dry out the ground for the passage of the people of Israel. T/F. *Exodus 14:21*

2. The Egyptians bogged down in the middle of the Red Sea because of locusts. T/F. *Exodus 14:25*

Lesson 5

1. Moses told the Israelites that God gave them His laws so they might learn them, keep them, and _____ them. *Deuteronomy 5:1*

2. Moses said that God made His covenant with the current people of Israel, not with their fathers. T/F. *Deuteronomy 5:3*

Lesson 6

1. The people of Israel left Egypt in the early morning. T/F. *Deuteronomy 16:1*

2. Moses referred to the bread of Passover as the bread of affliction. T/F. *Deuteronomy 16:3*

Lesson 7

1. The breastplate of the high priest included two special stones called the Urim and Thummim. T/F. *Leviticus 8:8*

2. What fixture of the tabernacle did Moses sprinkle with oil seven times? (ark of the covenant, altar, candle holder?) *Leviticus 8:11*

Lesson 8

1. In the Year of Jubilee, the people of Israel were told to proclaim _____ throughout the land. *Leviticus 25:10*

2. The law of jubilee said that land could not be sold permanently. T/F. *Leviticus 25:23*

Lesson 9

1. What was one of the foods of Egypt that the people of Israel claimed to miss greatly? (apples, radishes, cucumbers?) *Numbers 11:5*

2. The food that the people of Israel grew tired of was _____. *Numbers 11:6*

Lesson 10

1. While in the wilderness, the thing the people of Israel feared the most was that they might be forced to return to Egypt. T/F. *Numbers 14:3, 4*

2. God was so angry with Israel that he threatened to begin a new nation with _____ as its father. *Numbers 14:11, 12*

Lesson 11

1. Who died when the people of Israel came to Kadesh? (Miriam, Aaron, Jethro?) *Numbers 20:1*

2. When they arrived at Kadesh, the people were upset because there was no _____. *Numbers 20:2*

Lesson 12

1. The people of Israel were told that they did not need to fear the Lord as long as they were faithful in keeping His commandments. T/F. *Deuteronomy 6:2*

2. Where did Moses command the people of Israel to bind the words of the Lord? (ankles, hands, necks?) *Deuteronomy 6:8*

Lesson 13

1. God would circumcise the hearts of the people of Israel so that they might _____. *Deuteronomy 30:6*

2. The return and obedience of the people of Israel would cause the Lord to do what? (rejoice, reward, forgive?) *Deuteronomy 30:8, 9*

Obeying God's Calls

by Walter D. Zorn

PETER WROTE "Wherefore the rather, brethren, give diligence to make your calling and election sure: for if ye do these things, ye shall never fall" (2 Peter 1:10). The implications of this thought are twofold: first, being called as God's people requires obedience as a response to God's grace; second, the possibility of falling away from God's purposes presents itself when rebellion and disobedience start to infect God's people.

Our lessons for summer 2009 concentrate on how God's call was sealed with a promise for the ancient Israelites. Essentially, the promise said that God would be faithful to His people. God makes a similar promise today to the church. We can learn much by observing the interactions of God's call and the responses of His Old Testament covenant community.

Unit 1: June
Called Out of Egypt

Lesson 1 examines God's call to Moses to lead His people out of Egypt. God had prepared Moses for this call by his first 40 years of life in Egypt and then through 40 years in the desert (Midian) leading sheep. At 80 years of age, however, Moses was reluctant to accept the task. God promised to be with Moses during this ordeal. With the call of Moses, God was fulfilling His promises to the patriarchs. God's concern for His people who were suffering from oppression and slavery shows us God's mercy.

Lesson 2 looks closely at Moses' reluctance to say *yes* to God's call. He resisted with several excuses. He had to be shown miracles in order to be convinced of his call, and even then he continued to try to avoid the call. God then promised that Moses would have the help of Aaron in the task of delivering the people from Egyptian bondage. Moses finally accepted the call.

Lesson 3 is about recognizing God's authority. Moses, Aaron, and Pharaoh had to learn this lesson. Moses and Aaron questioned God's way of doing things because of the increasing hardship imposed by Pharaoh on the people. Pharaoh himself questioned the Lord's authority because he refused to "know" Him. Like Pharaoh, many people today fail (or refuse) to recognize authority outside of themselves. When Pharaoh refused to obey God's command to release the Israelites, God promised to force obedience with a mighty hand.

Moses and Aaron struggled to recognize God's strategy. Things didn't seem to be happening as fast as the two brothers would have liked. We still struggle in this regard today.

A picture of redemption is found in **Lesson 4**. Here we observe how God protected the Israelites by parting the waters, leading them out of slavery, and destroying their enemies. The triumph of the power of God over the power of Pharaoh, Egypt, and Egypt's supposed gods could hardly have been more dramatic. Israel's faith was tested to the fullest as the Egyptian army came within striking distance. Yet God was faithful to His promise; Israelites lived, Egyptians died.

Unit 2: July
Called to Be God's People

While a covenant creates a relationship with God, obedience to His laws maintains that relationship. **Lesson 5** explores the importance of accepting God's rules for life.

The Ten Commandments begin by recognizing God as the source of life and the source of the law. When these laws are obeyed, they create a just and merciful community. They also create a deeper relationship with the lawgiver. Understanding the original purposes of the Ten Commandments helps Christians see how the laws relate to them in the New Testament era of grace.

Lesson 6 recounts the institution of the Passover festival. God designed this annual observance to help Israel remember and celebrate the exodus from Egyptian bondage. The celebration of Passover was to bind the past with the present, thus unifying the people with a common heritage and memory. This celebration was a command, not a social development.

Christians understand that the Passover was a type of Christ, pointing forward to the deliverance from sin He would provide by becoming the ultimate sacrificial lamb. It was during a Passover meal that Jesus took the bread and the cup and instituted the Lord's Supper. Christians remember and celebrate the Lord's death whenever they observe the Lord's Supper (Communion).

Sometimes God calls individuals for special types of service. **Lesson 7** reveals how God commanded Aaron and his sons to be set apart for priestly functions. The people needed go-betweens or mediators to represent them to God and to represent God to them. That was a function of the priesthood. So important was this concept that God gave very exacting instructions regarding Aaron's clothing.

Lesson 8 teaches us that God's call to be God's people brings with it issues of economic justice. The accumulation of property in the hands of a few people means that some would be permanently wealthy while others would have little or no chance to escape poverty. As a result, God's jubilee laws were designed to prevent potential land barons from accumulating vast amounts of property and inflicting economic slavery on those who had been compelled to sell the property. Jubilee promised the destitute a new start.

Jesus projected His ministry as a "spiritual jubilee" (see Isaiah 61:1, 2; Luke 4:18, 19). Concern for the poor and destitute is still to be a hallmark of God's people.

Unit 3: August
Called to Obey

Lesson 9 gives us a negative example of disobedience and its consequences. The Israelites were not far into the wilderness when they began to grumble and complain. While God provided their needs with manna and water, the people wanted more. There was talk of returning to Egypt. Even Moses became discouraged by the complaints. He felt the full burden of the people as he attempted to lead them to the promised land. The grumbling and complaining caused some to suffer the fiery wrath of God. But none of us ever grumble and complain about our situations, do we?

Lesson 10 continues the negative theme of rebellion. The discouraging report of the 10 faithless spies sent a terrifying fear among the people, causing them to reject the call of God to conquer the promised land.

Joshua and Caleb had a different spirit. They fully expected God to lead them to victory over the Canaanites. Joshua and Caleb saw Canaan as an opportunity for success while the other 10 spies saw it as a threat of annihilation. God judged the people by prolonging their stay in the wilderness until a whole generation perished. Only Joshua and Caleb experienced God's promise and blessing of entering the promised land. But none of us have ever been as faithless as the 10 spies, have we?

The constant grumbling and complaining of the people finally had its effect on Moses, their leader. **Lesson 11** delves into the disobedience of Moses as he twice struck a rock, rather than speak to it, in order to cause water to gush out. That happened at Kadesh, the very place where the people had rebelled and chosen not to enter Canaan some 38 years previous. Thus Moses and Aaron forfeited their hopes of entering the promised land. While we may be sympathetic toward Moses and his burden, God holds leaders to a high standard. A leader's disobedience has dire consequences.

Lesson 12 teaches us about the *Shema* ("hear") and the Great Commandment ("Love the Lord thy God with all thine heart"). To love God is to obey God. Because the love we are to have for God can be commanded, it is not primarily a feeling (which cannot be commanded). Rather, it is a willingness to revere God that takes the form of obedience. The commandments of God are to be taught by word and lifestyle to children. Blessings will result.

Lesson 13 draws the quarter's lessons to a conclusion with one of the greatest chapters in the Old Testament: Deuteronomy 30. It is an invitation to obey God's call to be His people, set against the backdrop of the curses and blessings in Deuteronomy 28. Only a "circumcised heart" can love, and only a loving heart will obey. Israel had to decide. So must we.

Calls of God's People

The calls of God's people are always sealed with the promise "I will be with you!" The great rescue from Egypt began a covenant community. This redemption was celebrated every Passover festival. Obedience to law, the intercessory work of a priesthood, and proper stewardship of the land by the ideal of jubilee were some of the hallmarks of this community. Today as then, God is faithful to His promises. He stands ready to restore the blessings of His wayward people. We must choose. "Therefore choose life" (Deuteronomy 30:19).

Answers to Quarterly Quiz
on page 338

Lesson 1—1. Horeb. 2. false, he was amazed because the burning bush was not consumed. **Lesson 2**—1. true. 2. worshiped. **Lesson 3**—1. feast. 2. straw. **Lesson 4**—1. true. 2. false. **Lesson 5**—1. do (or obey). 2. true. **Lesson 6**—1. false, they left at night. 2. true. **Lesson 7**—1. true. 2. the altar. **Lesson 8**—1. liberty. 2. true. **Lesson 9**—1. cucumbers. 2. manna. **Lesson 10**—1. false, they wanted to return to Egypt. 2. Moses. **Lesson 11**—1. Miriam. 2. water. **Lesson 12**—1. false, keeping the commandments showed they feared the Lord. 2. hands. **Lesson 13**—1. live. 2. rejoice.

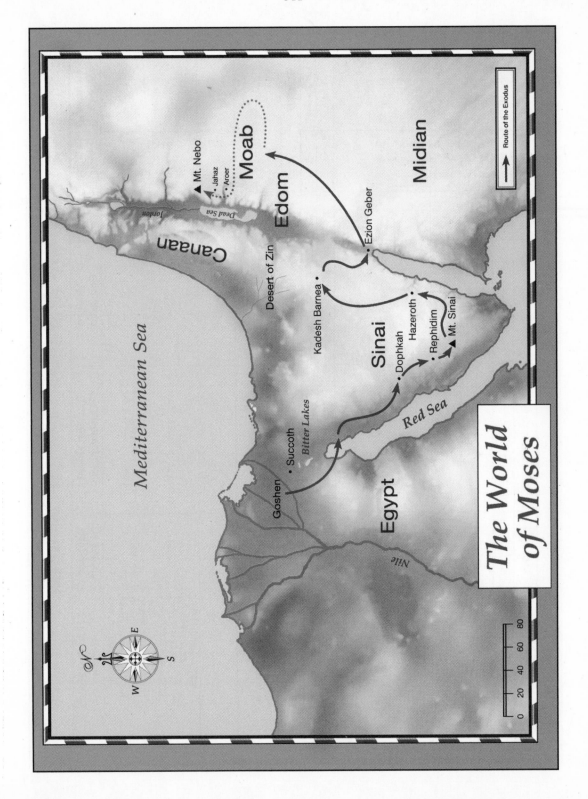

The Old Testament Jewish Calendar

Hebrew Month	Religious Year	Civil Year	Modern Equivalent	Old Testament Observances	Day(s) of the Month	Old Testament Reference
Nisan (or Abib)	1	7	March—April	Passover Feast of Unleavened Bread	14 15-21	Exodus 12:6, 43-49 Leviticus 23:5 Numbers 28:16 Deuteronomy 16:1, 2 Exodus 12:15-20 Leviticus 23:6 Numbers 28:17 Deuteronomy 16:3, 4
Iyyar (or Ziv)	2	8	April—May			
Sivan	3	9	May—June	Pentecost (or Feast of Weeks)	6	Leviticus 23:15-21 Numbers 28:26-31 Deuteronomy 16:9-12
Tammuz	4	10	June—July			
Ab	5	11	July—August			
Elul	6	12	August—September			
Tishri (or Ethanim)	7	1	September—October	Feast of Trumpets Day of Atonement Feast of Tabernacles (or Booths, or Ingathering)	1 10 15-21	Leviticus 23:23-25 Numbers 29:1-6 Leviticus 23:26-32 Numbers 29:7-11 Leviticus 23:33-43 Numbers 29:12-38 Deuteronomy 16:13-15
Marchesvan (or Bul)	8	2	October—November			
Kislev	9	3	November—December			
Tebet	10	4	December—January			
Shebat	11	5	January—February			
Adar	12	6	February—March	Feast of Purim	14-15	Esther 9:18-28

Reaching Every Learner

One Size Doesn't Fit All

by Wendy Guthrie

ANYONE WHO is a parent or who has taught children can testify to the fact that what works for one will not necessarily work for another. And what works today may not work tomorrow.

If these truths are enduring (as I believe they are), then I wonder why they get lost along the way. And believe me, they do get lost! Walk into the average adult Sunday school class and you will find a group of adults sitting in chairs (usually three or four rows deep) listening to a lecturer. Now this is not necessarily a bad thing, but it does assume that every member of that class learns in the same way—which just isn't true.

The apostle Paul reminds us of each member's uniqueness when he uses the analogy of "many members in one body" (Romans 12:4). Paul was referring specifically to the giftedness of each member and his or her place in service to the church. By extension, we can apply the "many" idea to the learning styles of the students who sit in your Sunday school class. Students take in and process information in different ways. Marilee B. Sprenger proposes that there are four types of learners.

Four Types of Learners

The imaginative learner is people-oriented. She learns through emotions; she trusts her perceptions. This learner needs dialogue in order to process information and is most interested in how the content of the lesson applies to her personal life. She wants to know the value of the lesson, so her favorite question is "Why?"

The analytic learner is knowledge-oriented. He needs information, and lots of it. This learner thrives in the lecture format. He is a sponge that soaks up the information and then needs time to process it and reflect on it. This learner thinks logically and analyzes content before he is ready to do anything with it; his favorite question is "What?"

The common-sense learner is solution-oriented. She needs to put her knowledge into action. This learner is a pragmatist who wants "just the facts, ma'am." She doesn't need much time to think through material, and she processes information better if it is hands-on. This learner is most interested in the usefulness of the lesson material, so her favorite question is "How?"

The dynamic learner is discovery-oriented. He sees the world differently from most; he is the visionary. This learner takes in information through all of his senses and processes it through his actions. He likes to "think outside the box" and try things that "have never been done that way." This learner is most interested in what the lesson content could become, so his favorite question is "What if?"

As you read through the characteristics, I'm sure you found the one that best describes you. However, I'm also sure you said "Well, that could be me" about at least two other learning styles. Thus the four styles are not "air tight." In His infinite wisdom, God has placed aspects of these various learning styles within each of us. That means we all need lessons that meet the criteria above if we are going to be the disciples Christ has called us to be.

The Learning Cycle

Right about now you may be tempted to throw your hands up in surrender and say "I have only 45 minutes for a lesson; how can I possibly address everyone's learning needs in that amount of time?" Let me assure you it's not as hard as it seems. By following a learning cycle called *4MAT* developed by Bernice McCarthy, any teacher can meet the needs of every learning style in the class.

The cycle has distinct phases. First, you must connect the lesson to students in some way that makes them want to learn. When you have done this, students will attend to the specifics of the lesson in order to derive value from it. At this point, students are ready for the underlying theories and are able to imagine or conceptualize them.

Then comes the time to inform students of the facts of the lesson. (This is the part of the cycle with which teachers feel most comfortable.) After students know what the lesson says, they're ready to practice or master that information.

But the lesson cannot stop there. Students also need to know how to extend the information outside of the classroom. They will need to refine it so it fits the needs of the community. Finally, they need to perform or put it into action so it makes a difference in someone's life.

The best way to make sure your lessons reach students in each of these phases is to ask yourself the following questions:

- How will your students connect with the lesson? *(connect)*
- How do you plan to deliver the lesson content? *(inform)*
- How do you plan for your students to practice the content? *(practice)*
- How will they examine or reflect on their experience? *(attend)*
- How will your students apply this lesson to their lives? *(extend)*
- In what ways will your students need to critique and modify the lesson for application? *(refine)*
- How can your students share what they have developed with others? *(perform)*
- How well do your students understand everything that has happened in the lesson? *(imagine)*

Creating the Lesson

Once you've wrestled with these questions, you're ready to turn the answers into a lesson. Here's how you could develop Lesson 7 of the summer quarter using the 4MAT system:

1. Retell the details of the dedication of Aaron's family for special service to God and the community; help learners understand the principle of being dedicated for service; encourage individuals to accept roles of special service and to recognize persons called for service.

2. Summarize the details of Leviticus 8:1-13 and write them on strips of poster board (one concept per strip). Have students read the passage to themselves and then work as a group to put the strips in the correct order.

3. Have students work in small groups to plan a Sunday school teacher dedication service. Make sure the groups translate the principles from the Scripture text into their services.

4. Ask students to recap a dedication or installation service they attended.

5. Have students reflect on what made the service in #4 so special. Connect their remarks with the principles from the lesson text.

6. Have one or more groups volunteer to work with the Sunday school superintendent (or other leader) to plan a teacher dedication service prior to the fall quarter.

7. Have students brainstorm ideas about having dedication or installation services for those who perform other tasks in the church.

8. Have students take a spiritual gifts inventory to determine their spiritual strengths. Then have each student identify at least two areas of service they could perform within the church that would enable them to use their spiritual gifts.

9. Have students identify some guiding principles from the lesson text that could apply to ceremonies within the church today. (This activity will need to follow the one in #2 above.)

Once you establish the various activities that can be used in the lesson, the next step is to organize them into a plausible order for the lesson. The nice thing about the 4MAT system is that you don't have to organize the lesson in the same way every Sunday. Some days you may want to start with the text, while other Sundays you may want to start by having students connect with the lesson topic.

One possible order for this lesson is to begin by having students recap a dedication service they attended (#4), then explain what made it special (#5). From that point you can move right into the Scripture by having students arrange the lesson events in the correct order (#2), then formulate overriding principles from the text (#9).

This naturally leads into the application phase of the lesson by asking students to prepare a "mock" dedication service using the principles from the previous activity (#3). Extend that activity by asking students to brainstorm similar services they could design (#7).

It's important to make sure that applications that begin in the class make it to the other side of the door. Having students volunteer to organize a teacher (or other worker) dedication service based on the class activity (#6) is a good way to accomplish this. The cycle is completed by suggesting that students complete a spiritual gifts inventory on a Web site such as www.churchgrowth.org; they can use the results to commit themselves to greater service within the local body (#8).

Conclusion

If you decide to use the 4MAT system to meet the lesson objectives, be prepared for students to take notice. The *imaginative learners* will now be able to engage in conversation that relates to the lesson rather than conversation that distracts others. The *common-sense learners* will be motivated to put hands and feet to their faith; they will find a new motivation to attend Sunday school. The *dynamic learners* will no longer feel like misfits because your class will encourage them to cast the vision for everyone else. The *analytic learners* will still be sitting on the front row taking in every word. But now they'll have to get to class a lot earlier if they want to get those choice seats.

The important thing to remember is that learners are more in tune when the lesson is relevant. The best way to make a lesson relevant is for you to stay in tune with the learning styles of your students.

Hearing God's Call

June 7
Lesson 1

DEVOTIONAL READING: Hebrews 3:1-13.

BACKGROUND SCRIPTURE: Exodus 2:23–3:12.

PRINTED TEXT: Exodus 3:1-12.

Exodus 3:1-12

1 Now Moses kept the flock of Jethro his father-in-law, the priest of Midian: and he led the flock to the back side of the desert, and came to the mountain of God, even to Horeb.

2 And the angel of the LORD appeared unto him in a flame of fire out of the midst of a bush: and he looked, and, behold, the bush burned with fire, and the bush was not consumed.

3 And Moses said, I will now turn aside, and see this great sight, why the bush is not burnt.

4 And when the LORD saw that he turned aside to see, God called unto him out of the midst of the bush, and said, Moses, Moses. And he said, Here am I.

5 And he said, Draw not nigh hither: put off thy shoes from off thy feet; for the place whereon thou standest is holy ground.

6 Moreover he said, I am the God of thy father, the God of Abraham, the God of Isaac, and the God of Jacob. And Moses hid his face; for he was afraid to look upon God.

7 And the LORD said, I have surely seen the affliction of my people which are in Egypt, and have heard their cry by reason of their taskmasters; for I know their sorrows;

8 And I am come down to deliver them out of the hand of the Egyptians, and to bring them up out of that land unto a good land and a large, unto a land flowing with milk and honey; unto the place of the Canaanites, and the Hittites, and the Amorites, and the Perizzites, and the Hivites, and the Jebusites.

9 Now therefore, behold, the cry of the children of Israel is come unto me: and I have also seen the oppression wherewith the Egyptians oppress them.

10 Come now therefore, and I will send thee unto Pharaoh, that thou mayest bring forth my people the children of Israel out of Egypt.

11 And Moses said unto God, Who am I, that I should go unto Pharaoh, and that I should bring forth the children of Israel out of Egypt?

12 And he said, Certainly I will be with thee; and this shall be a token unto thee, that I have sent thee: When thou hast brought forth the people out of Egypt, ye shall serve God upon this mountain.

GOLDEN TEXT: Come now therefore, and I will send thee unto Pharaoh, that thou mayest bring forth my people the children of Israel out of Egypt.—Exodus 3:10.

Lesson Aims

After participating in this lesson, each student will be able to:

1. Recount the sequence of events that led to God's call of Moses.

2. Compare and contrast the call of Moses with calls to ministry today.

3. Explain how he or she will evaluate a perceived call of God on his or her life.

Lesson Outline

INTRODUCTION
  A. Answering God's Call
  B. Lesson Background
 I. GOD APPEARS TO MOSES (Exodus 3:1-6)
  A. God Gets Moses' Attention (vv. 1-3)
    That Which Never Goes Out
  B. God Gains Moses' Respect (vv. 4-6)
II. GOD OBSERVES ISRAEL (Exodus 3:7-9)
  A. God Knows Israel's Plight (v. 7)
  B. God Predicts Israel's Deliverance (vv. 8, 9)
    Rescue from Slavery
III. GOD COMMISSIONS MOSES (Exodus 3:10-12)
  A. God Calls a Deliverer (v. 10)
  B. God Counters Insecurities (vv. 11, 12)
CONCLUSION
  A. Embracing God's Call
  B. Prayer
  C. Thought to Remember

Introduction

A. Answering God's Call

"You can't be serious, God! My family situation just isn't what it should be." "Not me, Lord. I'm from a family of nobodies, and I'm least among even them." "I'm not worthy; I am a lowly sinner." "I just can't do it; I'm too young, and I have no public-speaking skills."

When God calls us to challenging tasks, we have little trouble manufacturing reasons why God couldn't possibly use us. Perhaps you've hidden behind excuses like those above. If so, you're in good company. When God promised to make Abraham a mighty nation, Abraham claimed that his childless status was a problem (Genesis 15:1-

3). When God called Gideon to deliver the Israelites from their enemies, he declared himself the nobody of nobodies (Judges 6:14, 15). Isaiah was overwhelmed with a sense of sinfulness (Isaiah 6:5). Jeremiah was insecure about his youth and speaking ability (Jeremiah 1:4-6).

Fortunately for us, God has a great deal of experience working with less-than-perfectly-capable people! He seems to delight in turning the world's misfits into giants of faith. In today's lesson we will see how God recruited a career fugitive and began shaping him into one of the most significant figures in human history.

B. Lesson Background

It had been some 400 years since Israel settled in northern Egypt in order to survive a terrible drought. What began as gracious divine provision in Joseph's day (about 1877 BC) eventually led to harsh Egyptian oppression in Moses' time. In Exodus 2:23, however, we learn of a change in power in Egypt. Would the new Egyptian regime ease the burden? Perhaps Israel's God would personally see to it. So the Israelites cried out for help and God took notice (Exodus 2:24, 25).

God had never forgotten His people. Instead, He had been preparing a leader to deliver them. He was shaping Moses to be familiar with both the intrigues of Egypt and the pilgrim nature of Israel's heritage.

The events of this shaping are recorded in Exodus 1 and 2, as well as in Stephen's speech to the Sanhedrin in Acts 7:20-38. Having been brought up in Pharaoh's household for the first 40 years of his life, Moses undoubtedly received the best education royalty could afford. Yet Moses later fled Egyptian security as an outlaw and wandered as a shepherd for an additional 40 years. He thus could identify also with the enslaved Israelites and the nomadic lifestyle they were to face.

At age 80 (Exodus 7:7), however, Moses probably was completely unaware of God's plans for him. Having left both the Egyptians and the Israelites behind, he had found refuge and acceptance among the tents of a hospitable Midianite family. Moses likely thought he would die in peace among these foreigners. But God had other ideas!

I. God Appears to Moses (Exodus 3:1-6)

A. God Gets Moses' Attention (vv. 1-3)

1. Now Moses kept the flock of Jethro his father-in-law, the priest of Midian: and he led the flock to the back side of the desert, and came to the mountain of God, even to Horeb.

After killing an Egyptian and agitating the Israelites, *Moses* had fled eastward (Exodus 2:11-15); Moses was age 40 at the time (Acts 7:23). This flight took him beyond the Red Sea. Eventually, he encountered a friendly tribe that welcomed him (Exodus 2:16-22). Moses soon picked up shepherding, the trade of his Israelite forefathers.

At a certain time, Moses' shepherding work leads him in the direction of Egypt. The *back side of the desert* means westward. Since the sun rises in the east during the "front" side of the day and sets in the west during the "back" side of the day, these terms take on directional meanings.

The word *desert*, here and elsewhere, does not always refer to a vast stretch of sand-filled land. Often it signifies uninhabited and unirrigated pastureland. It is sometimes translated *wilderness*, but this too leads to misunderstandings for those who associate wilderness with thick, tree-filled forests. Here the word *desert* refers to the mountainous terrain of the Sinai Peninsula. This area is fertile enough to graze flocks temporarily, but not fertile enough to sustain a permanent dwelling.

It is thus fitting that *Horeb* means "drought" or "desert." Horeb may stand for the wider area within which Mount Sinai and the Sinai wilderness are located. Before God claims this territory for His special purposes, it is marginally useful. Afterward, it is honored with the designation *mountain of God.* Today, people travel thousands of miles to visit this area.

Yet Moses does not think he is heading toward sacred turf. Encountering God is likely the furthest thing from Moses' mind! God is about to meet with Moses at an unexpected time (Moses is now age 80) in an unlikely place. [See question #1, page 352.]

2, 3. And the angel of the LORD appeared unto him in a flame of fire out of the midst of a bush:

How to Say It

ABRAHAM. *Ay*-bruh-ham.
ABRAM. *Ay*-brum.
AMORITES. *Am*-uh-rites.
CANAANITES. *Kay*-nun-ites.
EGYPTIANS. Ee-*jip*-shuns.
HITTITES. *Hit*-ites or *Hit*-tites.
HIVITES. *Hi*-vites.
JEBUSITES. *Jeb*-yuh-sites.
MIDIANITE. *Mid*-ee-un-ite.
PERIZZITES. *Pair*-ih-zites.
PHARAOH. *Fair*-o or *Fay*-roe.
SANHEDRIN. *San*-huh-drun or San-*heed*-run.
SINAI. *Sigh*-nye or *Sigh*-nay-eye.

and he looked, and, behold, the bush burned with fire, and the bush was not consumed. And Moses said, I will now turn aside, and see this great sight, why the bush is not burnt.

From Moses' first-glance perspective, a *bush* is burning without being *consumed.* This apparent suspension of natural laws stops him in his tracks. The sight is intriguing enough to make him want to take a closer look.

We wonder about the identity of this *angel* who appears *in a flame of fire* in the *midst* of the bush. We hear no more about an angel in this narrative, and God himself does all the talking. There are at least two options. This could be an angelic messenger who does the speaking and acting on God's behalf, or it could be God manifesting himself to Moses in a guarded form so Moses will not be consumed by His awe-inspiring presence (compare Exodus 33:20). The latter interpretation seems to be favored by Deuteronomy 33:16, which refers to God as one who "dwelt in the bush."

Little may be learned about this event by analyzing the potential scientific conditions necessary for a bush to burn without being incinerated. Israel's God, who will later reveal himself again by way of fire (see Exodus 13:21, 22; 19:18), is performing a miracle. Although the text never tells us, God may be choosing a fiery bush to reveal something about himself to Moses. If that is the case, it may stand for God's self-generating and self-sustaining nature. It may also reflect the nature of His judgment. [See question #2, page 352.]

THAT WHICH NEVER GOES OUT

One dark night when we were all in bed,
Mrs. O'Leary left her lantern in the shed.
Well, the cow kicked it over,
    and this is what they said,
"There'll be a hot time in the old town tonight."

In a bygone era, this ditty expressed the popular sentiment about the origin of the Great Chicago Fire. That popular expression is fiction, but the fire itself wasn't. It began around 9 PM on October 8, 1871. When it was over, the fire had killed between 200 and 300 people, leaving 90,000 of the city's 300,000 homeless. Property loss exceeded $200 million (several billion dollars in today's money) as more than 17,000 structures were lost.

In 1971, the city of Chicago held a centennial commemoration of the event. This featured a parade as well as a massive fireworks display over Lake Michigan. It seems that we humans are forever fascinated with fire, whether it is meant for entertainment or results in disaster.

A similar fascination drew Moses to the burning bush, especially since the bush was not being consumed. From that fire, the Lord spoke. The message of God still speaks to us, a never extinguished flame of truth. Perhaps the question we each need to ask is, "Do God's words hold the same fascination for me as that bush did for Moses?" —C. R. B.

B. God Gains Moses' Respect (vv. 4-6)

4. And when the LORD saw that he turned aside to see, God called unto him out of the midst of the bush, and said, Moses, Moses. And he said, Here am I.

Now that *God* has Moses' undivided attention, He calls Moses' name twice. God frequently repeats someone's name when demanding immediate attention (see Genesis 22:11; 46:2; 1 Samuel 3:10).

Also noteworthy is Moses' response: *Here am I.* When God calls one by name, one does not respond glibly or halfheartedly. One responds decisively and submissively. This is why Abraham, Jacob, and Samuel respond to God the same way as Moses. In responding "Here am I," these godly people are not telling God something He doesn't already know about their location. Instead, they are at attention, waiting to hear and obey whatever God may say.

God may convict us to act through various means. These include preaching, teaching, or Bible reading. When that conviction comes, we must respond as Moses does. Hebrews 12:18-29 reminds Christians that even though God does not speak to us from a fearsome, flaming mountain, we must not refuse Him who calls us.

5. And he said, Draw not nigh hither: put off thy shoes from off thy feet; for the place whereon thou standest is holy ground.

Genesis 2:3 sets the Sabbath day apart as a *holy* period of time, and the verse before us is the first mention of a holy *place*. It is not holy by virtue of its natural properties or ideal location. It is holy because God chooses to inhabit it for Moses' calling and for Israel's later worship and instruction (Exodus 3:12, below). When Joshua, Moses' suc-

cessor, enters the promised land in order to take it, he encounters the commander of the Lord's army, who also calls him to remove his footwear for similar reasons (Joshua 5:13-15).

This kind of holiness is a temporary characteristic. The fact that God indwells a particular place at a particular time does not make it and those around permanently immune to harm or corruption. Centuries later, the Israelites will assume wrongly that no harm can befall them since God's holy temple stands in their midst (Jeremiah 7:4).

6. Moreover he said, I am the God of thy father, the God of Abraham, the God of Isaac, and the God of Jacob. And Moses hid his face; for he was afraid to look upon God.

Moses learns that *God* is not simply the God of this mountain. He is the God of Moses' ancestors. He is the God who called *Abraham* out of his home country and who provided for *Isaac* and *Jacob* as they wandered about the area we now call Palestine. Unlike the fictitious gods of the nations, Israel's God is not restricted to certain plots of land. He stands high above the cosmos and graciously identifies with humble Israelites who are willing to bear His name and submit to His lordship. He is their God, wherever they live. Through Christ He is also our God, wherever we may serve Him. He is God of all creation, whether His creatures worship Him or not.

God's cosmic reign should serve as an important warning to those in our own day who would identify God as the deity of this or that nation where they happen to live. Since Christians wish God to be worshiped properly in every land, we rightly desire Him to be worshiped where we live too. But we must be careful not to assume that because He was formerly extolled in a given land that that particular land is somehow forever tied to God in a special or unique way.

God did not spread His global mission outward from Jerusalem only to be co-opted by particular cities or countries elsewhere. Rather, God has formed a transterritorial kingdom. Its capital city is the new Jerusalem in Heaven. Its citizens live on every continent (Philippians 3:20). Jesus' prayer for this scattered people is that they would be one as He and the Father are one (John 17:20-23). That unity is threatened, however, when God's children mistakenly identify God with their preferred nation, as if God cares less for other nations.

When Moses hears his ancestors' God speaking to him, he rightly fears. Even sinless heavenly creatures that are made to worship God in His very presence are equipped with a second set of wings in order to shield themselves from God's glory (Isaiah 6:1-3). [See question #3, page 352.]

VISUALS FOR THESE LESSONS

The visual pictured in each lesson (example: page 349) is a small reproduction of a large, full-color poster included in the *Adult Resources* packet for the Summer Quarter. That packet also contains the very useful *Presentation Helps* on a CD for teacher use. The packet is available from your supplier. Order No. 492.

II. God Observes Israel
(Exodus 3:7-9)

A. God Knows Israel's Plight (v. 7)

7. And the LORD said, I have surely seen the affliction of my people which are in Egypt, and have heard their cry by reason of their taskmasters; for I know their sorrows.

God reveals the purpose for His visit: He sees and hears how badly the Israelites are being treated *in Egypt.* Their oppression is spelled out in Exodus 1:11-14. There we read that these taskmasters conscript Israelites to bear the burden of Pharaoh's numerous building projects. The taskmasters work the Israelites into the ground in response to the growth of their population. Slavery is the only word for this.

None of this catches God by surprise. Back in Genesis 15:13, 14, God had told Abraham that his descendants would be mistreated for 400 years. This had to happen because the sin of those inhabiting the promised land had not yet reached full measure (Genesis 15:16). We may take this to mean that God so loved those inhabiting Canaan that He refused to bring judgment on them until they deserved it. A collateral result is that God's chosen people end up in slavery. [See question #4, page 352.] However, this turn of events allows God to display His power in unmistakable ways.

B. God Predicts Israel's Deliverance (vv. 8, 9)

8. And I am come down to deliver them out of the hand of the Egyptians, and to bring them up out of that land unto a good land and a large, unto a land flowing with milk and honey; unto the place of the Canaanites, and the Hittites, and the Amorites, and the Perizzites, and the Hivites, and the Jebusites.

Israel's patient God is now poised to deliver on the promise He first made to Abraham (as Abram) back in Genesis 12:1-3. The description of *milk and honey* is a broad reference to agricultural abundance. It is important to note that God does not simply deliver His people "out of" something; He also leads them "into" something else. As Jesus teaches, deliverance from a bad situation that does not include replacing the bad with something better only sets one up for a potentially worse future (Matthew 12:43-45).

The most comprehensive list of the promised land's inhabitants is provided in Genesis 15:19-21. The presence of these competing people groups in an area about the size of the state of Vermont highlights both the instability of the area and the challenge the Israelites have ahead of them. Yet if Israel's God is powerful enough to free them from

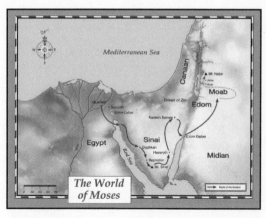

Visual for Lesson 1. *Keep this map posted throughout the quarter. This will help your students keep a geographical perspective.*

an imperial powerhouse like Egypt, these comparatively miniscule clans will be no problem.

9. Now therefore, behold, the cry of the children of Israel is come unto me: and I have also seen the oppression wherewith the Egyptians oppress them.

We are told again of Israel's *cry.* We should not think of this cry as an infantile whimper. Rather, this verse expresses moral outrage and soul-stirring passion. It is the anguished cry of the oppressed and the agonizing plea of helpless victims.

RESCUE FROM SLAVERY

"As unimaginable as it seems, slavery and bondage still persist in the early twenty-first century. Millions of people around the world still suffer in silence in slave-like situations of forced labor and commercial sexual exploitation from which they cannot free themselves. Trafficking in persons is one of the greatest human rights challenges of our time." So says the U.S. State Department *Trafficking in Persons Report* of June 2003.

The names of the offending countries are familiar to us: Sudan, North Korea, and Burma (Myanmar) are just a few. Many nations in the Middle East are on the list. The type of slavery varies from political to economic to sexual. Some countries are infamous for their "sex tourist trade." The toll in human dignity is enormous. Americans pride themselves on having outlawed slavery over a century ago. Nevertheless, one occasionally still hears about the "sweat shop" garment factories in America where illegal immigrants labor in virtual slavery as payment for a ticket to live there.

Only God could rescue the ancient Hebrews. Modern slaves also may feel that God is their only hope. Shouldn't Christians be God's agents in trying to end these abuses? What means do we have for assisting those who are treated as if the image of God were not in them? And then there is still slavery to sin! What can we do about that? —C. R. B.

III. God Commissions Moses (Exodus 3:10-12)

A. God Calls a Deliverer (v. 10)

10. Come now therefore, and I will send thee unto Pharaoh, that thou mayest bring forth my people the children of Israel out of Egypt.

Up to this point, Moses has been receptive to what God has to say. Moses is more than willing to remove his footwear and hear God's concern for Israel. But Moses' receptivity is about to change as God gets personal. God calls Moses to do the seemingly impossible: to approach the powerful *Pharaoh* and ask him to set free his cheap labor force.

B. God Counters Insecurities (vv. 11, 12)

11. And Moses said unto God, Who am I, that I should go unto Pharaoh, and that I should bring forth the children of Israel out of Egypt?

Moses' last words up to this point were "Here am I"; his next words are *Who am I?* This is Moses' first attempt to avoid the job God has for him. In Exodus 4:1 Moses expresses concern that the people will reject him. In 4:10 he claims to be tongue-tied. In 4:13 he flatly requests that God send someone else. But God is not fazed by human excuses. Instead, He shows great patience. He listens to Moses' objections, takes them seriously, and offers support. [See question #5, page 352.]

12. And he said, Certainly I will be with thee; and this shall be a token unto thee, that I have sent thee: When thou hast brought forth the people out of Egypt, ye shall serve God upon this mountain.

God knows Moses' track record. According to Exodus 2:10, Moses grew up in Pharaoh's household and thus received the finest education. Moses also has spent 40 years exiled in Midian; he may thus sympathize with Israel's "outsider" status. Finally, Moses possesses courage, as evident when he risked his life to avenge an Israelite and when he boldly confronted two feuding Hebrew men (2:11-13). Yet Moses' impressive pedigree is not his greatest asset. It is God's presence that will be the decisive factor.

God predicts a sign as a demonstration of His assurance of victory: those currently enslaved will soon freely *serve God* on the very *mountain* of Moses' calling. This reminds us of the sign of the rainbow that God gave Noah (Genesis 9:12-17). It is a sign of remembrance that is to recall a past event and an associated promise. As the rainbow reminded Noah of God's prior promise never again to flood the earth, Israel's later worship on Mount Sinai will remind them of Moses' call to deliver them from *Egypt*.

Conclusion

A. Embracing God's Call

Abraham discovered that his family situation was no limitation for the ancient of days. Gideon learned that *nobodies* are *somebodies* when God goes with them. Isaiah received a holiness from God that far exceeded what the most righteous saint could achieve on his or her own. Jeremiah found that God's Word and presence surpass the rhetoric and "wisdom" of learned foes.

Thus Moses stood within a long line of underdogs who were made to be overachievers by the mighty arm of God. It makes perfect sense therefore that those of us with all the "wrong" credentials can find ourselves at God's disposal to accomplish what only He can do through us.

B. Prayer

God of Moses, we stand in awe of You. You call us to tasks that we cannot complete without You. You call us to live like Jesus. You send us into a world that dismisses Your wisdom as foolishness. You call each of us to great works that You have prepared in advance for us. May we never hide behind our excuses. As You did with Moses, push through those excuses until we see Your promises unfold before our eyes. In Jesus' name. Amen.

C. Thought to Remember

Embrace God's call with confidence.

Home Daily Bible Readings

Monday, June 1—Moses' Birth (Exodus 2:1-10)

Tuesday, June 2—Moses Flees (Exodus 2:11-22)

Wednesday, June 3—Moses' Purpose Misunderstood (Acts 7:23-29)

Thursday, June 4—Moses' Call (Acts 7:30-34)

Friday, June 5—Moses' Death Foretold (Deuteronomy 32:48-52)

Saturday, June 6—Moses' Uniqueness (Deuteronomy 34)

Sunday, June 7—Come, I Will Send You (Exodus 3:1-12)

Learning by Doing

This page contains an alternative lesson plan emphasizing learning activities. Some of these activities are also found in the helpful student book, Adult Bible Class.

Into the Lesson

Open your class with a "hearing test." Prior to class, locate three portable stereos ("boom boxes") and music CDs (music with lyrics is helpful, but not absolutely necessary). Set the portable stereos around the classroom in different locations. Additionally, bring a copy of your church's most recent newsletter.

As students take their seats, simply begin reading the announcements from the church newsletter. After you are finished, ask, "How many of you can recall just one of the announcements?" Take a few responses from the participants, noting, "We could all hear the announcements read, so we are able to recall them fairly well."

Arrange for several individuals to turn on the three stereos simultaneously to a volume level that drowns out your voice. (Be careful not to have them so loud that other classes are disturbed.) Begin reading another item, such as the minister's newsletter article. When you have completed the reading of the article, turn the stereos off.

Now ask students to recall anything about what you just read. Very few, if any, should be able to answer. Ask why they could recall the information from the first reading, but not from the second (although the reason is obvious). To move into the Bible study, say, "We sometimes cannot hear the voice of God because of other stuff that we allow to drown out His voice. God has to get our attention for us to hear His call."

Into the Word

Form groups of four or five; each group must have at least one Bible. Write *Exodus 3:1-12* on the board. Ask the groups to read the passage and answer the following questions. The questions may be written on the board, projected on a screen, or reproduced onto a handout. Reproduce only the questions, not the italicized answers. Each group will have the same set of questions. Smaller classes will adjust group sizes accordingly.

1. Where was Moses when he received his call? What was he doing? *(near Mount Horeb, tending his father-in-law's sheep; verse 1)*

2. How did God get Moses' attention? *(burning bush that wasn't consumed; verses 2, 3)*

3. Why the burning bush? Why didn't God just tell Moses immediately what to do? *(perhaps wanted to impress Moses with the importance of the task; verse 4)*

4. How did Moses react to God's presence? *(hid his face, feared God; verses 5, 6)*

5. Who did God say was going to free the Israelites from their Egyptian bondage? *(God would free Israel; verses 7-9)*

6. Who was going to be God's agent in bringing about freedom from bondage? *(Moses; verse 10)*

7. How did Moses respond to the awe-inspiring opportunity to serve God? *(questioned his ability to fulfill God's call; verse 11)*

8. How did God respond to Moses' question? *(Moses would not be alone—God would be with him; verse 12)*

After giving ample time for the groups to work through the questions, go through the answers as a class. To make the transition to the application say, "We too have been called by God to serve among His people, the church."

Into Life

Have class members stay in their groups. Ask them to share with one another the following items about their lives, if applicable to them. (You may find it useful to write these questions on the board, distribute them on a handout, use PowerPoint®, etc.)

• When was a time you sensed God calling you to serve Him in a certain way?
• How did God get your attention? What was your burning bush?
• How did you respond to God's call? If you hesitated, why?

After the time of small-group discussion, say, "There are two mistakes we may make with regard to God's calls. One is to turn a deaf ear to a genuine call of God; the other is to think God is calling us to do something when He really isn't." Ask the participants to identify what call they believe God has given them, how they evaluate the validity of that supposed call, and if they are currently engaged in fulfilling that call.

You may wish to share with the class a personal story of a time when you made one of those two mistakes. Ask for volunteers to explain how they guard themselves from distractions that hinder them from hearing God more clearly.

Let's Talk It Over

The questions on this page are designed to promote discussion of the lesson by the class and to encourage application of the lesson Scriptures. The answers provided are only discussion starters. Let your class talk it over from there.

1. What can the case of Moses tell us about God's plan to use people of various ages in His service today?

Some people may be tempted to think that they are too old or too young to be active in a leadership role for God. Yet Moses was 80 years old when he was called! At the other end of the spectrum, Timothy started leading when he was young (1 Timothy 4:12). These cases should instill in us a sense of caution about drawing conclusions regarding whom we think God will or will not use to lead His people.

Leadership can take various forms: some leaders serve in the spotlight, others make sure that behind-the-scenes details are handled, etc. With that fact in mind, ask the class to list areas in which Christians of various ages and life situations can lead. For example, an elderly shut-in may be a great leader for an e-mail prayer-chain ministry.

2. In what ways today does God let people know that He wants them to serve or to lead a ministry? Should we expect burning bushes? Why, or why not?

God's manner for contacting Moses proves that God can use various methods to nudge (or shove) someone into His service. Today, the Holy Spirit may lay a burden or conviction on a person's heart through a magazine article, a news report, a passage of Scripture, etc. One individual may find the perfect place of service only after aiding a friend who needed a helper.

A person's means of earning a living may become so unsatisfying that "divine discontent" sets in. As a result, the person ends up using his or her skills in a more challenging place—perhaps even on a mission field. Discerning friends may repeatedly tell a person to consider using God-given abilities in certain ways. The most important thing is for Christians to be listening when God calls, no matter the means He chooses to use to make that call.

3. What is the difference, if any, between being afraid of God and having a reverence for Him? How does this difference influence the way you live?

There are a variety of appropriate reactions to God. At times, we can be overwhelmed with the full majesty of God, become fearful when seeing the fullness of the power of God, and show respect and reverence when sensing the love and compassion of God. While fearing the Lord is wise and biblical, we also are encouraged to come with confidence to God's throne of grace (Hebrews 4:14-16).

4. How do you react to the news of fellow believers suffering injury, imprisonment, or death for their faith? How should you react?

Many Christians face minimal, if any, persecution. If we could listen in on their prayers, we might conclude that most of them are interested only in what God can do for them. Praying for oneself is natural and appropriate. However, the fact that we have access to information about places where fellow Christians are threatened or oppressed creates an obligation and a privilege to pray for them.

In addition to praying for their deliverance, we can pray for their daily walk with God, their patience during persecution, their spiritual and physical stamina during the toughest times, etc. We cannot be sure how or when God may bring deliverance, but we are sure that God is faithful in providing for daily needs (Matthew 7:7-12).

5. What is the connection, if any, between personality type and the way individuals respond to God's leading? How is this important to the way you react to God's leading and to the way you lead others?

Some people just seem to be natural leaders, being eager and capable for that role. They may be good at inspiring people and making sure they feel good about what is going on. Others, like Moses, may be reluctant to be leaders, but may end up being very good in that role given proper encouragement. Still others have personalities for being selfless followers; some of these folks are excellent at taking care of the smallest details.

God calls individuals to work within their areas of spiritual giftedness (see Romans 12:4-8), although the relationship between spiritual giftedness and personality type is not always clear-cut. Leaders will be wise to help folks choose their paths of service in ways that are consistent with their personalities and spiritual gifts.

Accepting Responsibility

June 14
Lesson 2

DEVOTIONAL READING: Proverbs 1:20-33.

BACKGROUND SCRIPTURE: Exodus 4.

PRINTED TEXT: Exodus 4:10-16, 27-31.

Exodus 4:10-16, 27-31

10 And Moses said unto the LORD, O my Lord, I am not eloquent, neither heretofore, nor since thou hast spoken unto thy servant; but I am slow of speech, and of a slow tongue.

11 And the LORD said unto him, Who hath made man's mouth? or who maketh the dumb, or deaf, or the seeing, or the blind? have not I the LORD?

12 Now therefore go, and I will be with thy mouth, and teach thee what thou shalt say.

13 And he said, O my Lord, send, I pray thee, by the hand of him whom thou wilt send.

14 And the anger of the LORD was kindled against Moses, and he said, Is not Aaron the Levite thy brother? I know that he can speak well. And also, behold, he cometh forth to meet thee: and when he seeth thee, he will be glad in his heart.

15 And thou shalt speak unto him, and put words in his mouth: and I will be with thy mouth, and with his mouth, and will teach you what ye shall do.

16 And he shall be thy spokesman unto the people: and he shall be, even he shall be to thee instead of a mouth, and thou shalt be to him instead of God.

. . . .

27 And the LORD said to Aaron, Go into the wilderness to meet Moses. And he went, and met him in the mount of God, and kissed him.

28 And Moses told Aaron all the words of the LORD who had sent him, and all the signs which he had commanded him.

29 And Moses and Aaron went and gathered together all the elders of the children of Israel:

30 And Aaron spake all the words which the LORD had spoken unto Moses, and did the signs in the sight of the people.

31 And the people believed: and when they heard that the LORD had visited the children of Israel, and that he had looked upon their affliction, then they bowed their heads and worshipped.

GOLDEN TEXT: Aaron spake all the words which the LORD had spoken unto Moses, and did the signs in the sight of the people.—Exodus 4:30.

Call Sealed with Promise
Unit 1: Called Out of Egypt
(Lessons 1–4)

Lesson Aims

After participating in this lesson, each student will be able to:

1. Describe Moses' hesitancy to accept God's call and tell how God supplied a solution.

2. Give a contemporary example of someone's overcoming an apparent obstacle to ministry.

3. Confess one area of hesitancy to accept a responsibility in God's service and express faith in God's power to supply what is needed to carry out that responsibility.

Lesson Outline

INTRODUCTION
  A. God of the Impossible
  B. Lesson Background
 I. MOSES' HESITATION (Exodus 4:10-16)
  A. Excuse Given (v. 10)
  B. Excuse Overcome (vv. 11, 12)
    Empowered to Communicate
  C. Moses' Plea (v. 13)
  D. God's Anger (vv. 14-16)
II. BROTHERS' UNITY (Exodus 4:27-31)
  A. Assignment (v. 27)
    Following Fallible Leaders
  B. Explanations (vv. 28-31)
CONCLUSION
  A. Not About Our Limitations
  B. Prayer
  C. Thought to Remember

Introduction

A. God of the Impossible

A humble woman runs a modest ministry center for homeless children in the Ukraine. Her church recently took possession of a large vacated building that was completely gutted of anything of value. It stands as little more than an enormous concrete shell. It will take hundreds of thousands of dollars to make it functional.

This building is surrounded by a vast stretch of fertile, government-owned land. This woman dreams of transforming this building into a Christian orphanage and acquiring the surrounding land in order to develop it into a work center for these youngsters. They can both live in the building and learn valuable farming skills in order to sustain themselves in their adult years.

When I first heard these ideas, I was tempted to write them off as mere pipe dreams. This woman lacked both the funding and staffing for such a large project. In addition, the center she already operated was hardly thriving. There was no way she could pull this off. But as I listened to her pray, I was deeply convicted. Both her demeanor and her words demonstrated the conviction that her God is Lord of the cosmos. With Him no project is too big. Though well aware of her own limitations, she worships a God of unlimited possibilities. When He is behind it, nothing is impossible.

Moses also faced a seemingly impossible task: God called him to liberate an enslaved people from one of the most powerful empires in the Ancient Near East. Moses did not have to wonder whether God was behind this project. Yet Moses still doubted.

Fortunately, God is not deterred by human doubt. He taught Moses that projects God authorizes are projects God underwrites. We who worship the same God must pay close attention to Moses' story. Inspired stories like his still create and sustain faith in the God of unlimited possibilities.

B. Lesson Background

In Exodus 3, God called Moses to be His messenger. Moses was to proclaim to the Israelites and to Pharaoh that God intended to free the Israelites from bondage (last week's lesson). Moses' initial response was self-doubt: "Who am I?" (3:11). Moses then received the assurance of God's presence. Moses' ability was not the main issue.

Moses then asked what he should call God. After revealing the divine name and nature, God gave Moses specific details about his mission (3:13-21). Moses responded with doubt that the Israelites would believe him (4:1). God answered by empowering Moses to perform three signs (4:2-9). That was about the year 1446 BC.

I. Moses' Hesitation (Exodus 4:10-16)

Up until this point it is not clear whether Moses is being humble and simply covering all his bases or whether he is trying to negotiate his way out of a mission that terrifies him. In today's passage, Moses' dialogue with God continues.

A. Excuse Given (v. 10)

10. And Moses said unto the LORD, O my Lord, I am not eloquent, neither heretofore, nor since

thou hast spoken unto thy servant; but I am slow of speech, and of a slow tongue.

Fear of public speaking is known as *glossophobia*. It is a common fear today. This fear can be so paralyzing that some people may face death with more confidence than they do the task of speaking before a large crowd. Moses apparently is in this camp, although there seems to be more behind Moses' reservations.

Scholars are divided over the exact cause of Moses' concern. Does he have a *speech* impediment? Does he lack powers of persuasion? Is he worried about knowing what to say? Or has Moses lost fluency of speech after being separated from both the Egyptians and Israelites for 40 years (Acts 7:29, 30)?

In Acts 7:22, Stephen suggests that Moses grew powerful in wisdom and speech at a young age. This casts doubt upon the speech impediment theory. Moses' failure to convince fellow Israelites to stop fighting may support claims that Moses is not very persuasive (Exodus 2:13, 14). On the other hand, God's response in Exodus 4:12 (below) seems to focus on the content of Moses' speech. So it is difficult to know for sure what Moses has in mind. It may be a combination of two or more issues. [See question #1, page 360.]

B. Excuse Overcome (vv. 11, 12)

11. And the LORD said unto him, Who hath made man's mouth? or who maketh the dumb, or deaf, or the seeing, or the blind? have not I the LORD?

God is aware of Moses' speaking ability or lack thereof. Yet God-as-Creator has power over all human abilities and senses. He opens and shuts mouths, ears, and eyes. In fact, Moses would not even exist had God not opened the wombs of Moses' foremothers Sarah and Rebekah. Surely Moses' speaking problem is not an obstacle to the almighty Creator!

How to Say It

AARON. *Air*-un.
GLOSSOPHOBIA. gloss-uh-*foe*-bee-uh.
GUYANA. Guy-*a*-nuh (*a* as in map).
JACOB. *Jay*-kub.
JETHRO. *Jeth*-ro.
LEVI. *Lee*-vye.
LEVITICAL. leh-*vit*-ih-kul.
MOSES. *Mo*-zes or *Mo*-zez.
REBEKAH. Reh-*bek*-uh.
UKRAINE. You-*crane*.
VENTRILOQUISM. ven-*trih*-luh-kwi-zum.

Shockingly, it is as though Moses has forgotten to whom He is speaking. The bush continues to burn without being consumed (Exodus 3:2), and Moses stands barefoot with shielded face out of reverence for God's awe-inspiring presence (3:5, 6). Yet somehow Moses forgets whom He is dealing with or, more appropriately, who is dealing with him.

Such forgetfulness is all too common in the church today. "We can't pioneer this ministry; it will cost too much." "We can't witness in that part of the city; it's not safe there." "We can't give X percent; we wouldn't be able to make ends meet." "Our kids can't do that in school; what would their teachers and classmates think?" We may be tempted to think that excuses like these stem from a humble assessment of our own (in)abilities and limitations. But is that really the issue?

God teaches us in this verse that such excuses are the result of focusing on self rather than God. To know the God of Moses is to know a power who knows no bounds. As we cannot serve both God and money, so also we cannot fear both God and Pharaoh. Moses has to make a choice, and so do we.

EMPOWERED TO COMMUNICATE

The vital nature of communication leads society to try to make continual improvements in this area. One creative attempt is called FasTrack Signing, part of a program called FasTracKids. This involves teaching sign language to babies who are too young to use much spoken language.

More than 20 years of research have shown that children who are 6 months old can learn sign-language skills in 8 weeks. At age 12 months, the typical child in the program is said to be able to use 25 signs and 16 spoken words, compared with 1 to 3 spoken words for children in a control group. Not surprisingly, one mom says the sign that her 18-month-old son uses most is the one for *more*. The child had been empowered to communicate something that the parent does not necessarily look forward to hearing!

God's spoken instructions to Moses were quite clear to him. However, this was not a message Moses wanted to hear, as evidenced by the fact that he immediately tried to maneuver out of his daunting assignment. At times we may feel overwhelmed by the task that Jesus sets before us in Matthew 28:19, 20. When we are tempted to say "Let so-and-so do it; he's more persuasive than I am," may God's words to Moses ring in our ears: "Who hath made man's mouth? or who maketh the dumb, or deaf, or the seeing, or the blind? have not I the Lord?"

—C. R. B.

12. Now therefore go, and I will be with thy mouth, and teach thee what thou shalt say.

If Moses possesses some kind of speech impediment, God makes no promise to heal it. God reveals no intention of "fixing" Moses to make him better. Instead He promises to go with Moses and *teach* him what to *say*. God doesn't need the perfect spokesman who can present His message flawlessly without divine help. God wants humble servants who will allow God to work in their lives despite their imperfections.

Notice also that God does not simply take over Moses' mouth. God rejects the path of divine ventriloquism. To go this route would reduce Moses to the status of puppet. God has respect for His creatures. He has made us in His image and wants us to grow spiritually in that regard. So God promises to teach Moses what to say. God is not merely conveying a message, but is forming a leader through whom He will later form other leaders.

Churches today have much to learn from God's way of working with Moses. Though we may never experience it quite as Moses did, God wants to work with us. God's Spirit does not overpower Christians in ways that eclipse our unique identities. He works in and through us in such ways that we grow up in our salvation (1 Peter 2:2).

Since this is how God works with us, then we ought to do likewise with others. For churches to truly honor the priesthood of all believers (1 Peter 2:4-9; Revelation 1:6), then church leaders must find healthy ways to encourage the formation of every member. This means giving "undeserving" people sufficient power and opportunities both to succeed and to fail. When we relinquish attempts to control absolutely, others may grow as our heavenly Father desires them to.

C. Moses' Plea (v. 13)

13. And he said, O my Lord, send, I pray thee, by the hand of him whom thou wilt send.

We arrive at an important clue for interpreting Moses' previous objections. Having run out of excuses, Moses finally implores God to *send* someone else. Moses is not simply being humble, although he is known for humility (Numbers 12:3). At this point, Moses flat out rejects his calling. He is trying his best to weasel out.

God has known Moses' mind-set all along, but God denies him an easy way out. A veil of clever excuses is clearly seen as just that since the fact that the excuses didn't "work" now results in a last gasp "pick someone else" plea. Moses has not been able to manipulate God into choosing someone else, so Moses is reduced to asking God to do so forthrightly.

D. God's Anger (vv. 14-16)

14. And the anger of the LORD was kindled against Moses, and he said, Is not Aaron the Levite thy brother? I know that he can speak well. And also, behold, he cometh forth to meet thee: and when he seeth thee, he will be glad in his heart.

God has been patient with Moses, but God's patience has limits. It is one thing to express initial insecurity; it is another to trifle with God. In showing Moses *anger*, God indicates that the haggling is over. [See questions #2 and #3, page 360.]

Even so, God provides one more source of aid. Moses' articulate brother, *Aaron*, will be arriving shortly, and God will appoint him as the spokesman. We presume that Aaron still lives in Egypt. As such, Aaron probably is both fluent in the languages and trusted by the Israelites.

Aaron is a descendant of Jacob's son Levi. We know little about the nature of this tribe as it exists in Moses' day. We do know, however, that Jacob had prophesied that Levi's descendants were to be dispersed among Israel's tribes (Genesis 49:5-7). Moses, as Aaron's brother, also descends from this tribe (Exodus 2:1, 2), but one wonders why this detail is given about Aaron here.

One possible explanation is that Aaron later becomes the father of the levitical priesthood (Leviticus 8). Perhaps Aaron's willingness to play an important role in the exodus contributes to God's desire to set apart his descendants for such a sacred purpose. The fact that the Levites are to be scattered among the Israelites in fulfillment of Jacob's prophecy promotes their priestly function.

15, 16. And thou shalt speak unto him, and put words in his mouth: and I will be with thy mouth, and with his mouth, and will teach you what ye shall do. And he shall be thy spokesman unto the people: and he shall be, even he shall be to thee instead of a mouth, and thou shalt be to him instead of God.

Though *God* will use Aaron, God will not replace Moses with Aaron. Instead, God clearly states that He will continue to work directly with Moses. In turn, Moses will work with Aaron, and Aaron will speak to the people. [See question #4, page 360.] In this sense—and only this sense—does Aaron function as Moses' *mouth* and Moses as Aaron's God. Moses does not function for Aaron in this way because of anything "godlike" in Moses. He does so because God makes His will so abundantly clear to Moses that to listen to Moses is to hear God. This is why Moses is later considered Israel's greatest prophet (Deuteronomy 34:10).

But God will not work with Moses alone. He will also guide Aaron's mouth. This brings up a natural question: Why not bypass Moses and use only Aaron? Scripture does not tell us directly, but we see a certain pattern in how God works throughout Scripture. God is not a replacing God, but a restoring God. He works with fallen humans despite their deficiencies rather than replacing such humans with others less deficient.

This fact is demonstrated in God's promise to Noah and all creation after the flood. When God committed not to "smite any more every thing living" (Genesis 8:21), He committed himself to finding a way to work through us. He places the burden on himself to bring about His will through sinful creatures rather than wipe us out and replace us each time we sin. God's love is such that He would rather help the unsuccessful succeed than work with only those most likely to succeed. God is not opposed to using a talented person like Aaron to help Moses, but God refuses to reinforce the faulty notion that He can use only those with extraordinary ability.

Moses' silence to God's proposal signals assent. God's decision to break the cycle of excuses is exactly what Moses needs. Godly discipleship today will do the same. We must not, however, skip the beginning of this process. We must not rush a decision before giving people time to think through the repercussions. Jesus encourages His followers to count the costs before committing (Luke 14:25-33) even as He draws a line and demands a firm decision (Luke 9:57-62).

II. Brothers' Unity
(Exodus 4:27-31)

After Moses accepts God's plan, he returns to Jethro's household to announce his departure and gather his family (Exodus 4:18-23). Moses then survives a mysterious and dangerous encounter with God en route to Egypt (4:24-26). Afterward, Moses meets Aaron in the Sinai region.

A. Assignment (v. 27)

27. And the LORD said to Aaron, Go into the wilderness to meet Moses. And he went, and met him in the mount of God, and kissed him.

The fact that God commissions *Aaron* to *meet Moses* clarifies the meaning of verse 14, where God tells Moses that Aaron is on the way. Aaron is not simply visiting his brother; rather, he is obeying a specific calling from God.

By the time Moses returns from gathering his family, Aaron has traveled as far as Sinai. So the brothers meet on the mountain where God called Moses. The kiss is a standard greeting among close relatives (Genesis 27:26; 31:28).

Visual for Lesson 2. *Point to this visual as you ask, "Why is it not wise to engage in a tug-of-war with God?"*

FOLLOWING FALLIBLE LEADERS

The sad saga of Peoples Temple remains as a testimony to the danger of giving over one's life to fallible leaders. In the mid-1970s, that church was a thriving countercultural congregation in California. Jim Jones was its charismatic leader. The church grew rapidly, in part because of its reputation for helping the down-and-out.

When news media began doing exposés on the cultlike aspects of the church, Jones moved his flock to a "promised land" in Jonestown, Guyana. Horror stories began coming out of there. Parents of young people involved in the cult urged U.S. government intervention. A member of Congress led a fact-finding party to the compound in 1978. While preparing to return, the congressman and members of his party were shot to death. Soon the world learned that 913 of the cult members had committed mass suicide, either willingly or under duress, by drinking cyanide.

Moses and Aaron were God's choices to lead the Israelites to their promised land. As time would tell, they would be fallible leaders. But their fallibility was counterbalanced by an accountability to the God who chose them. Jim Jones, by contrast, apparently saw himself as accountable to no one but himself. How is leadership accountability handled in your church? —C. R. B.

B. Explanations (vv. 28-31)

28. And Moses told Aaron all the words of the LORD who had sent him, and all the signs which he had commanded him.

Apparently, God has given *Aaron* only sparse details about what has happened, so *Moses* fills him in on the rest. Moses also explains about *the signs* God has given to validate the message. These signs include turning a staff into a snake and inflicting leprosy. Aaron's silence implies that he fully submits to God's will; note Aaron's silence in Leviticus 10:3. [See question #5, page 360.]

29, 30. And Moses and Aaron went and gathered together all the elders of the children of Israel: and Aaron spake all the words which the LORD had spoken unto Moses, and did the signs in the sight of the people.

Moses and Aaron gather Israel's leaders as directed (Exodus 3:16) and perform *the signs* God has specified. It is interesting to note that even though the Israelites are enslaved in a foreign land, they take the initiative to develop their own leaders. This helps Israel maintain her identity on foreign soil.

This is the first reference in the Bible to the leaders of the Israelites as *elders*. We may safely presume that they are the leaders of whatever clans exist at this time. The word *elders* is used dozens of times in the Old Testament in this regard. The New Testament, for its part, uses this important word to describe certain church leaders, but definitely not in a "heads of clans" kind of way.

31. And the people believed: and when they heard that the LORD had visited the children of Israel, and that he had looked upon their affliction, then they bowed their heads and worshipped.

As God foretold in Exodus 3:18, *the people* believe. Not only has God been preparing Moses to lead Israel, but God has prepared Israel to receive his leadership. These are the same people who have cried out to God in anguish (2:23). They have cried in faith that God will act. Now Moses and Aaron return performing signs and declaring God's intent to deliver them.

The people respond by bowing to God with gratitude and worship. Moses had feared that the people would focus on him and find him to be lacking. Instead, they focus on God and find Him to be more than sufficient. God is again teaching Moses that this mission is not about Moses. Rather, it is about God.

Leaders today must learn from Moses. It's not about us either. It never is and never will be. One might object that in real life experience it is often very much about the human leader. There are some churches in which members hang on the preacher's every word; the preacher responds by striving to cultivate an impressive public persona and seeking to deliver dazzling sermons that keep people returning. Godly leaders, however, will direct attention away from themselves and toward God. They will exhort the people to adore God, not His messengers (see 1 Corinthians 1:12, 13; 3:21-23).

Conclusion

A. Not About Our Limitations

It must have been extremely liberating for Moses to discover that God's mission was not about Moses. The God who resolved to free Israel took full responsibility for convicting Israel to leave, for forcing Pharaoh to release them, and for empowering Israel to march out. Moses was God's instrument. It is interesting to watch how the rest of the narrative unfolds. At first, Moses leans heavily on Aaron. But as the story progresses, Aaron recedes to the background, and Moses begins fulfilling the role God originally intended for him.

Likewise, God's mission for the church is not about our limitations. Though God uniquely equips each believer to play an integral part in His mission (1 Corinthians 12), we do so only by God's power. Ephesians 1:18-23 teaches us that the same power that raised Jesus from the dead and seated Him at the Father's right hand, far above all earthly powers, is at work in those who believe. Jesus reminds His disciples that all things are possible for God (Mark 10:27).

B. Prayer

Powerful God, please increase our faith. Teach us to esteem You so highly that we do not underestimate what You can do with us. Give us such big dreams for Your kingdom that we are not paralyzed by the smallness of our own abilities. In Jesus' name. Amen.

C. Thought to Remember

Worship and obey the God of the impossible.

Home Daily Bible Readings

Monday, June 8—The God Who Calls (Exodus 3:13-18)

Tuesday, June 9—The God Who Equips (Exodus 4:1-9)

Wednesday, June 10—The God Who Sends Back (Exodus 4:18-23)

Thursday, June 11—Do Not Be Afraid (Zechariah 8:11-17)

Friday, June 12—God Will Help You (Isaiah 41:8-13)

Saturday, June 13—Refusing God's Call (Proverbs 1:20-33)

Sunday, June 14—A Team of Two (Exodus 4:10-16, 27-31)

Learning by Doing

This page contains an alternative lesson plan emphasizing learning activities. Some of these activities are also found in the helpful student book, Adult Bible Class.

Into the Lesson

During your lesson preparation prior to class, reflect on a time in your life when you were challenged to accept a responsibility for which you felt somewhat or entirely unsuited. Be ready to share that story with the class. Reflect on why you felt so unsuited or unsuitable: was it the nature of the task itself? personal shortcomings? unique circumstances? the timing of the event? The more humorous the account, the more open your learners will be to share similar stories.

To begin class, write *Unsuited for the Task* on the board. Share your story of when you felt unsuited for a task; remember to keep it lighthearted, even humorous.

Next, form the class into groups of no more than five. Ask each student to share (within the group) a time when he or she was faced with an "unsuitable moment." Encourage everyone to share a story, but give permission to "pass" in the event someone is new or uncomfortable with doing so. You may wish to announce ahead of time (via your class's e-mail list, etc.) that you will be doing this. That will allow each student a time of thoughtful reflection in advance.

After this time of intragroup sharing, write these two phrases on the board: *Right Task, Wrong Person* and *Right Person, Wrong Timing*. Explain that when God challenges us with a task, we may find ourselves confronted with one or both of these doubts.

Say, "Being the wrong person means you don't feel your skills, knowledge, or personality are a good match for what God is asking of you, even though you can see that the task needs to be done (this was Moses' issue). On the other hand, you may feel that you are the right person for the job, but the timing doesn't seem to be right for that particular task (compare Haggai 1:2)."

As students make comments or share parts of their stories, note their insights on the board. Make a transition to Bible study by noting that God doesn't make wrong choices.

Into the Word

Divide the class into three groups; if your class is small, use pairs. Write *Exodus 4:10-16* on the board. Provide each group with paper and pencil. Instruct the groups to read the passage and discuss why Moses' felt that he was unsuited for God's call. Ask groups to note especially those comments that would indicate that Moses felt he was the wrong person for a task that was indeed worthy.

After a few minutes, asks students to share thoughts. You will need to decide whether it is best to open the floor to any and all thoughts that students want to share, or if you have time only for thoughts from spokespersons of the groups. Use the Lesson Background and commentary to add insights.

Next, write *Exodus 4:27-31* on the board. Read that text to the class. Say, "In spite of Moses' reluctance to accept God's call, what was the result of doing what the Lord called him and Aaron to do?" Allow the class to give answers. Make the observation that Moses served God in spite of his initial reluctance, and God brought about the deliverance of His people from slavery as a result.

You may wish to consider using a film clip from such movies as *The Ten Commandments*, *Moses*, or the animated film *The Prince of Egypt* in addition to reading the text. The clip can introduce the Bible portion of the lesson, or it can be used after the discussion.

Into Life

Explain that some of us have had figurative "burning bush" experiences already; these were times when God's call was very evident. Some readily accept the call; some hesitate and resist; and some downright refuse. There are also cases of people who readily accepted at first, but later on began to doubt their abilities or the validity of the call.

Ask your students to give reasons they have ever heard (or used) for questioning a call to serve God in a certain way. Write responses on the board. Then ask students to form pairs so they can share personal concerns in this area and pray for one another regarding an excuse for not fulfilling God's call. (*Option*: Ask couples to pair with others.)

Provide students with a list of ministry opportunities within your church. (Prepare this ahead of time as a handout.) Allow time to reflect on the list to see if any of the tasks create a burden on anyone's heart. If time is short, this can be a take-home exercise.

Let's Talk It Over

The questions on this page are designed to promote discussion of the lesson by the class and to encourage application of the lesson Scriptures. The answers provided are only discussion starters. Let your class talk it over from there.

1. What is the difference between giving an excuse and raising a legitimate concern when asked to do something? How do we keep from fooling ourselves in thinking our concern is legitimate when it's not?

At any point in time, we may need more information before deciding if saying *yes* is a good idea. Also, we may not be able to see how our contribution will help a project be successful. Wise individuals will express appropriate issues of concern while also keeping their minds open to future courses of action. Those who give excuses usually know that they could do the work, but just do not want to enlist. For others, the excuse is a way to avoid evaluating their strengths as well as the possibilities of becoming involved.

God can tell the difference between a legitimate concern and an excuse. He works patiently with us when we need encouragement, information, or direction. It is also true that God can become angry with us when we will not attempt to visualize the opportunities and blessings that He already sees. (Compare the excuses and the anger in Luke 14:15-24.)

2. How would you respond to someone who asks, "Since God was very capable of engineering the release of the Israelites without using human leadership, why didn't He just do it himself to save a lot of aggravation?"

God seems to have a preference for accomplishing and communicating His work of salvation through human intermediaries. But when He is unable to find a suitable person through whom to work, He is quite capable of bringing about the appropriate result on His own (as in Ezekiel 22:30, 31). When we allow ourselves to be intermediaries for God, we learn something about faith that can be learned in no other way.

We note that in the New Testament era Jesus came in the form of a human in order to accomplish the work of salvation. In the process, He recruited fallible humans to launch and oversee His church. For those who respond to His call, God blesses these individuals as they serve faithfully. It is also true that God receives the honor due Him as He shows His power through the dedication of His servants.

3. What are some ways that people react when an authority figure shows anger toward them? How did God's anger toward Moses demonstrate confidence in that man?

Some may conclude that when an authority figure shows anger toward them that the authority figure has already judged them to be incompetent and worthless. The result can be withdrawal, shame, and a loss of self-confidence.

But everyone, including God, is capable of having more than one reaction at the same time. Parents often become angry with their children while continuing to believe in and support those children. The anger may arise because of the parent's belief that the child is capable of much more than is being exhibited at the moment. We are thankful that God does not become as angry with us as we may deserve. See Numbers 14:18; Nehemiah 9:17; Psalm 86:15; 103:8; Jonah 4:2.

4. In what ways have you served as a "spokesman unto the people"? What more can you do in this regard?

We can take the concerns of our fellow believers to God on their behalf when we pray. Looking at being a spokesperson in the other direction, we take on the role of God's mouthpiece when we inform both believers and unbelievers of God's expectations as revealed in His Word.

To serve in either role is a privilege. The books of Jeremiah, Acts, etc., also reveal, however, that to become God's mouthpiece can involve a lot of work, much responsibility, and even danger. Further, we may discover that God wants us to meet the needs that we express in the prayers that we pray on behalf of others.

5. Recall the time when it took you the longest to say *yes* when God asked you to serve. Why did it take you that long?

Ask class members what their initial response was to God, how they debated with themselves as they agonized over the decision, and how they finally came to an answer. Ask if anyone sensed pressure or anger either from God or from the person doing the recruiting. Compare the answers from the class with the conversation between Moses and God (Exodus 3:4-17).

Recognizing Authority

DEVOTIONAL READING: Psalm 10:1-14.

BACKGROUND SCRIPTURE: Exodus 5:1–6:1.

PRINTED TEXT: Exodus 5:1-9, 22–6:1.

Exodus 5:1-9, 22, 23

1 And afterward Moses and Aaron went in, and told Pharaoh, Thus saith the LORD God of Israel, Let my people go, that they may hold a feast unto me in the wilderness.

2 And Pharaoh said, Who is the LORD, that I should obey his voice to let Israel go? I know not the LORD, neither will I let Israel go.

3 And they said, The God of the Hebrews hath met with us: let us go, we pray thee, three days' journey into the desert, and sacrifice unto the LORD our God; lest he fall upon us with pestilence, or with the sword.

4 And the king of Egypt said unto them, Wherefore do ye, Moses and Aaron, let the people from their works? get you unto your burdens.

5 And Pharaoh said, Behold, the people of the land now are many, and ye make them rest from their burdens.

6 And Pharaoh commanded the same day the taskmasters of the people, and their officers, saying,

7 Ye shall no more give the people straw to make brick, as heretofore: let them go and gather straw for themselves.

8 And the tale of the bricks, which they did make heretofore, ye shall lay upon them; ye shall not diminish ought thereof: for they be idle; therefore they cry, saying, Let us go and sacrifice to our God.

9 Let there more work be laid upon the men, that they may labor therein; and let them not regard vain words.

. . . .

22 And Moses returned unto the LORD, and said, Lord, wherefore hast thou so evil entreated this people? why is it that thou hast sent me?

23 For since I came to Pharaoh to speak in thy name, he hath done evil to this people; neither hast thou delivered thy people at all.

Exodus 6:1

1 Then the LORD said unto Moses, Now shalt thou see what I will do to Pharaoh: for with a strong hand shall he let them go, and with a strong hand shall he drive them out of his land.

GOLDEN TEXT: Afterward Moses and Aaron went in, and told Pharaoh, Thus saith the LORD God of Israel, Let my people go, that they may hold a feast unto me in the wilderness.—Exodus 5:1.

Call Sealed with Promise
Unit 1: Called Out of Egypt
(Lessons 1–4)

Lesson Aims

After participating in this lesson, each student will be able to:

1. Tell what happened when Moses first delivered God's message to Pharaoh and the people complained about it.

2. Compare and contrast Pharaoh's response with the response of unbelievers today when they hear God's message.

3. Determine a means of entering into dialogue with an unbeliever so that he or she may be led to recognize God's authority.

Lesson Outline

INTRODUCTION
  A. The Powers That Be
  B. Lesson Background
I. CONFRONTATION (Exodus 5:1-5)
  A. Inquiry and Response, Part 1 (vv. 1, 2)
     Selective Agnosticism
  B. Inquiry and Response, Part 2 (vv. 3-5)
II. RETALIATION (Exodus 5:6-9)
  A. Fewer Resources (vv. 6, 7)
  B. Same Quota (vv. 8, 9)
III. EXPLANATION (Exodus 5:22–6:1)
  A. Moses' Complaint (vv. 22, 23)
     Power Struggle
  B. God's Response (6:1)
CONCLUSION
  A. Facing (Down) the Powers
  B. Prayer
  C. Thought to Remember

Introduction

A. The Powers That Be

Since 1988, novels written by Frank Peretti have shaped how many Christians think about spiritual warfare. Books such as *This Present Darkness* depict a fictional world where large armies of angelic hosts and demonic forces constantly battle one another for human souls. The more fervently Christians pray, the better the angels fare, as well as the humans they defend. Peretti thus has influenced popular Christian thinking about the "principalities and powers" discussed in Scripture. This

has been a positive development insofar as it has encouraged Christians to take seriously the power of prayer for winning spiritual battles.

But evil influences are nothing new, of course. The apostle Paul acknowledged such influences (see Lesson 14 for spring). In Exodus 5–14, Moses encountered "principalities and powers" as he faced down demonic elements of Egyptian magic. The political powers of the Pharaoh cult and the economic powers of slavery and oppression found a comfortable home alongside this demonic magic. Such powers beset the Israelites on all sides.

Evil powers still exert influence. Sometimes we feel helpless to do anything about them. The experience of Moses can help us to distinguish between godly and ungodly power structures.

B. Lesson Background

In Exodus 3 and 4, God called Moses to the seemingly impossible task of freeing the Israelites from Egyptian bondage. [See question #1, page 368.] God used miracles to overcome Moses' anxieties about his mission. God empowered him with words to speak, signs to perform, and support from his brother. The Israelites' initial response was favorable (4:29-31). Then came time to confront Pharaoh.

I. Confrontation
(Exodus 5:1-5)

It is important to read the following verse in light of Exodus 3:18, where God tells Moses exactly how he is to confront Pharaoh. Moses is to go with the elders of Israel and to tell Pharaoh that the Lord, the God of the Hebrews, has met with them. In that context they are to beseech Pharaoh to allow them to take a three-day journey to the wilderness to offer sacrifices.

A. Inquiry and Response, Part 1 (vv. 1, 2)

1. And afterward Moses and Aaron went in, and told Pharaoh, Thus saith the LORD God of Israel, Let my people go, that they may hold a feast unto me in the wilderness.

Moses does indeed appear before *Pharaoh*, but only *Aaron* is noted as accompanying Moses. There are no elders mentioned. Perhaps the elders have come along, but only Moses and Aaron are admitted into the king's presence.

We also note that Moses calls God the *God of Israel* here rather than "God of the Hebrews" as in Exodus 3:18; 5:3; etc. The distinction is subtle. The word *Israel* names a distinct, cohesive tribal group or political entity, whereas *Hebrews* is more of a general indication of ethnicity. Of these two, the designation *Hebrews* should be much less threatening to Pharaoh.

Moses' demand is straightforward: Pharaoh is to free God's people so they may *hold a feast* for God. We should not make too much of the distinction between *feast* (here) and sacrifice (in 3:18). These terms go hand in hand in Israelite worship because sacrifices provide the meal for the feasts.

2. And Pharaoh said, Who is the LORD, that I should obey his voice to let Israel go? I know not the LORD, neither will I let Israel go.

Pharaoh receives Moses' request as a religious threat. The mere mention of another deity who claims jurisdiction over Pharaoh's slaves is enough to perturb him. Ancient Egyptians vest at least semi-divinity in their pharaohs. Moses and Aaron's acknowledgement of Israel's God is thus a serious challenge to Pharaoh's political authority and religious status.

Pharaoh's claim not to *know* the *Lord* (Yahweh) means two things. First, since Pharaoh thinks he possesses divine knowledge, the fact that he does not know Yahweh means that Yahweh is nobody from Pharaoh's perspective. Second, to *know* an authority figure implies recognizing or submitting to that authority. Pharaoh is unwilling to do so. So Pharaoh's response is clear and decisive. Since he recognizes neither Moses' God nor His authority, Pharaoh refuses to grant the request.

SELECTIVE AGNOSTICISM

The Washington Monthly ranked the Massachusetts Institute of Technology (MIT) number one in its 2006 list of American universities. Were Christians to draw up a ranking of "best" universities, MIT might not make the list at all due to the presence of student organizations such as the Massachusetts Institute of Technology Atheists, Agnostics, and Humanists (MITAAH).

Of course, we shouldn't condemn an entire university because we disapprove of one of its student organizations. But the presence of organizations such as MITAAH puts us on guard concerning the mind-set that seems to dominate the secular campus.

We are to be on guard against creeping secularism (see Colossians 2:8). This danger presents itself, in part, via agnostics (who neither affirm nor deny the existence of God) and their first cousin the atheists (who claim with self-assurance that God does not exist). Interestingly, Pharaoh doesn't really fit into either of those two categories, although he said "Who is the Lord? . . . I know not the Lord." Since the land of Egypt featured widespread worship of various gods, we may pronounce Pharaoh guilty of "selective agnosticism." He indeed knows of many gods, but he claims ignorance of the only God that counts—*the Lord*.

Those who claim to be agnostics and atheists today live as gods of their own lives. Practically speaking, they too are guilty of selective agnosticism, since something is always sitting on the throne of a person's heart, ruling behaviors and thoughts. The question is, who or what will it be? Our task as Christians is to take the offensive and show the world that faith in the one true God is practical, reasonable, and necessary.   —C. R. B.

B. Inquiry and Response, Part 2 (vv. 3-5)

3a. And they said, The God of the Hebrews hath met with us: let us go, we pray thee, three days' journey into the desert.

Rather than apologize for insulting Pharaoh and quickly retreating, Moses and Aaron hold their ground and reword their request. This time they cite nearly verbatim the words God originally gave Moses in Exodus 3:18. Do they think their initial request failed because they did not use the right words? Is there something inherently powerful in the exact phrasing God gave them?

The rewording of the request to line up with 3:18 should soften the appeal, making it more acceptable to Pharaoh. God is now introduced as *the God of the Hebrews*; perhaps Pharaoh will accept the existence of what he may view as a more limited deity of a specific group. Second, Moses now highlights the temporary nature of this trip. The people will be gone only *three days*. A short trip should be more appealing to Pharaoh.

3b. And sacrifice unto the LORD our God; lest he fall upon us with pestilence, or with the sword.

A third softening presents itself. Moses and Aaron clarify that the purpose of their trip is to make sacrifices of appeasement (this is an addition to 3:18). If the Hebrews do not make these sacrifices, God may afflict *us*. But who is included in that word *us*? If Moses and Aaron are referring

---

How to Say It

AGNOSTICISM. ag-*noss*-tuh-sih-zum.
ASSYRIANS. Uh-*sear*-e-unz.
BABYLONIAN. Bab-ih-*low*-nee-un.
EGYPTIAN. Ee-*jip*-shun.
HABAKKUK. Huh-*back*-kuk.
ISRAELITES. *Iz*-ray-el-ites.
MOSES. *Mo*-zes or *Mo*-zez.
PERSIAN. *Per*-zhuhn.
PHARAOH. *Fair*-o or *Fay*-roe.
POLYGAMY. puh-*lih*-guh-mee.
YAHWEH *(Hebrew)*. *Yah*-weh.

only to the Hebrews, the appeal is for Pharaoh not to take a chance on having his precious workforce depleted. Should the Israelites perish, Pharaoh himself will lose out.

On the other hand, the *us* of the affliction may be broad enough to include Pharaoh and the Egyptians. Given the overall softer tone of this second attempt, the threat implied by this idea seems less likely.

4. And the king of Egypt said unto them, Wherefore do ye, Moses and Aaron, let the people from their works? get you unto your burdens.

Pharaoh does not budge an inch. Instead, he puts his own spin on the request of *Moses and Aaron*. According to Pharaoh, the two standing in front of him are rebels trying to unsettle Pharaoh's smooth economic machine. So he sends them back to work.

5. And Pharaoh said, Behold, the people of the land now are many, and ye make them rest from their burdens.

Pharaoh's observation that the Israelites are numerous can be taken in two ways. From an economic perspective, he may be concerned about the loss of productivity. From a national-defense perspective, he may be worried about rebellion. Either way, we have no record that Moses and Aaron are allowed time for rebuttal. Pharaoh has the last word (so he thinks). The question is whether or not Moses and Aaron will accept Pharaoh's spin.

II. Retaliation
(Exodus 5:6-9)

No one challenges Pharaoh's authority and then escapes with only a verbal rebuke! If that were the only consequence, then Pharaoh would soon be flooded with trivial complaints from "nobodies." His failure to retaliate would be perceived as weakness, and his oppressive grip over the people would be diminished.

A. Fewer Resources (vv. 6, 7)

6. And Pharaoh commanded the same day the taskmasters of the people, and their officers, saying,

Pharaoh knows that slaves must not be allowed to have hope. This is why Pharaoh acts *the same day* to crush any rebellion before it can grow.

7. Ye shall no more give the people straw to make brick, as heretofore: let them go and gather straw for themselves.

Pharaoh devises a scheme. He knows that one of the best ways to punish Moses and Aaron is to alienate them from their own people. So Pharaoh gathers those in charge of the Israelites; this includes

both the Egyptian supervisors and the Israelite foremen who serve under them (see also Exodus 5:10). He commissions them to institute a new policy: the Jews must *gather straw* for themselves rather than have it provided. That will teach those Israelites not to trust people like Moses and Aaron!

Straw is a bonding agent that helps hold bricks together. Thus straw is an essential ingredient for making bricks. The Egyptians mix straw and other stubble with Nile River mud, shape it all into molds, and leave the resulting bricks to dry in the sun.

B. Same Quota (vv. 8, 9)

8, 9. And the tale of the bricks, which they did make heretofore, ye shall lay upon them; ye shall not diminish ought thereof: for they be idle; therefore they cry, saying, Let us go and sacrifice to our God. Let there more work be laid upon the men, that they may labor therein; and let them not regard vain words.

This additional task for the Hebrews to gather their own straw might not be so bad as long as Pharaoh does not demand the same quota of *bricks*. But like many tyrants, Pharaoh responds to challenges by tightening his grip and depleting his servants' energy for further resistance.

Pharaoh also continues to put his own spin on these events. The official message he publishes is that the Israelites are lazy. This is why they want to get away and *sacrifice to* their *God*. Pharaoh is determined that everyone will view Moses and Aaron not as liberators, but as deceivers.

Such false recasting is a critical tool for oppressive powers in every age. Tyrants must keep the oppressed believing that they shouldn't mess with the system. They shouldn't imagine that things can be better. Their survival (if not prosperity) lies only in the goodwill of their oppressors. Those who try to liberate them are their worst enemies. [See question #2, page 368.]

III. Explanation
(Exodus 5:22–6:1)

Exodus 5:10-21 (not in today's text) describes the aftershocks of Pharaoh's decision. The people scramble unsuccessfully to meet the new demands. Their taskmasters respond by beating them. This causes dissension among the Israelites. Their immediate supervisors, fellow Hebrews, are receiving flak for the decreased productivity. So they must then come down on their own people. This sets the Israelites against one another.

Pharaoh's false accusations regarding who is to blame begin to take hold. The Israelites despise

Moses for bringing Pharaoh's scorn on them. They doubt Moses' claim that God has sent him and instead call on God to judge Moses for deceiving them (v. 21). Far from being their deliverer, Moses has become the bane of their existence. The support of Exodus 4:31 has vanished as Pharaoh's sinister edict is enforced. Pharaoh can sit back with a smile because he has single-handedly turned this whole scenario on its head.

A. Moses' Complaint (vv. 22, 23)

22. And Moses returned unto the LORD, and said, Lord, wherefore hast thou so evil entreated this people? why is it that thou hast sent me?

Moses is definitely "feeling the heat." Pharaoh has Israelite and Egyptian alike believing that Moses suffers delusions of grandeur and that Moses is guilty of sowing seeds of laziness and ingratitude among the Israelites. Moses knows for certain that God has spoken to him. But the pressure is so great that Moses now questions that calling. [See question #3, page 368.]

POWER STRUGGLE

Colorado City and Hildale are twin towns on the Arizona–Utah border. This area is infamous for the practice of polygamy. The Fundamentalist Church of Jesus Christ of Latter-day Saints has long exerted strong influence in the area.

Warren Jeffs succeeded his father as the church's leader after the latter's death in 2002. Jeffs solidified his power when he excommunicated two rivals in the church some time later. Jeffs used his position to "reassign" the wives and children of excommunicated men to others. In effect, Jeffs became the church's absolute ruler.

Jeffs ended up on the FBI's *Ten Most Wanted* list in 2006. After his capture, he was tried and convicted in 2007 as an accomplice to rape for performing in 2001 what the church called "a celestial marriage" between a 14-year-old girl and her 19-year-old cousin. Jeffs' role in that "marriage" was part of the power struggle.

Pharaoh also was a man willing to do evil to protect his position of power. He could not tolerate Moses' threat to his position, so he tried to "excommunicate" Moses from his position as leader of the Hebrews. This lesson about human nature is still with us after all these centuries: those in power who perceive a threat to their position may go to great lengths to eliminate the threat.

—C. R. B.

23. For since I came to Pharaoh to speak in thy name, he hath done evil to this people; neither hast thou delivered thy people at all.

Visual for Lesson 3

Start a discussion by asking, "Under what circumstances does this question apply? Why?"

We may find it difficult to blame Moses at this point. He has done what God asked him, and the end result is the opposite of what Moses expects. The *people* are still enslaved, and things have gotten worse. So Moses rightly seeks God and asks Him to make sense of this scandalous turn of events. He is wrong, however, to blame God for Israel's misfortunes. It is one thing to question what is happening and why; it is another to claim that one already knows the answer and that God is lacking.

Moses commits Job's error. Job was right that God was somehow connected with the miseries that befell him and his household. Job went too far, however, when he assumed that God caused it all. Job prided himself in being immune to all charges concerning the situation (Job 40:8). So God rebuked Job for speaking out of ignorance (Job 38).

Christians today tend to toggle between two extremes in bringing their concerns to God. Some read passages such as Job 38 and conclude that it is never appropriate to question God about what they are experiencing. Others speak presumptuously to God, as Moses and Job did.

Biblical books such as Job, Psalms, Lamentations, and Habakkuk help us chart a better path. They teach us that it is appropriate to voice our concerns to God. But they also show us that we must do so as ones who know we do not see the big picture. We must trust that God will work all things for the good of those who love him (Romans 8:28). [See question #4, page 368.]

B. God's Response (6:1)

1. Then the LORD said unto Moses, Now shalt thou see what I will do to Pharaoh: for with a

strong hand shall he let them go, and with a strong hand shall he drive them out of his land.

God does not chide Moses for his complaint. Moses' concerns are valid from the perspective of someone in the midst of a crisis who does not see the end. God has indeed allowed *Pharaoh* to do everything he has done. God does, however, set the record straight. Pharaoh certainly will *let* the people *go.* In fact, Pharaoh himself will *drive* the Israelites *out of his land.*

Notice the emphasis God places on His own action. When Pharaoh releases the Israelites, it will be God's work. If Pharaoh thinks this is a contest of divine authority, he is right! In the end, Pharaoh will experience the authority and power of Yahweh.

We must not think of this contest as a mere battle of egos. God is not as concerned with teaching Pharaoh a lesson as He is with instructing Israel. God is creating Israel to be a priestly nation to mediate the glory of His reign. For the Israelites to succeed in this mission, they must learn firsthand that none can compare with Him. God will demonstrate His power over Pharaoh so that Israel may not be tempted to defer unduly to other human rulers later on, whether they be Egyptian, Assyrian, Babylonian, Persian, Greek, Roman, or even Israelite.

Furthermore, God is teaching His people that they are to depend fully on Him for their deliverance. If the first attempt at softening Pharaoh's heart had convinced him to release the Israelites, they may be tempted to think of Moses and Aaron as the source of deliverance. Instead, God hardens Pharaoh's heart (see Exodus 4:21) to the point that God will have to intervene with signs and wonders that one may attribute only to the Lord of all creation. [See question #5, page 368.]

Home Daily Bible Readings

Monday, June 15—Making Bricks Without Straw (Exodus 5:10-21)

Tuesday, June 16—The Voice of the Lord (Psalm 29)

Wednesday, June 17—Return to God and Heed Him (Deuteronomy 4:25-31)

Thursday, June 18—God's Plan to Strengthen (Zechariah 10:6-12)

Friday, June 19—The Lord's Deliverance (Psalm 18:13-19)

Saturday, June 20—All Nations Shall Worship God (Zechariah 14:12-19)

Sunday, June 21—Moses' Complaint (Exodus 5:1-9, 22, 23; 6:1)

Conclusion

A. Facing (Down) the Powers

In Egypt, the Israelites found themselves confronted by powers that were far beyond their control. They struggled against a hierarchy of self-serving political powers, from local foremen to Pharaoh himself. They struggled against oppressive economic powers fueled by Pharaoh's insatiable desire to build architectural monuments. They struggled against ideological powers of manipulators who twisted reality and spread powerful lies that pitted victims against one another.

However, God taught Moses that such powers remained wholly subservient to the God who allowed them to have power only temporarily. When the right moment came, God turned His eternal might against them.

Christians today also face powerful authority structures that seek to exert undue influence over their lives. In many parts of the world, political powers persecute Christians for their faith. In other parts, Christians face economic powers whose persecution is subtler but no less real. We are often called to work all hours of the day and all days of the week, since the economic machine cannot rest. We lose standing and compensation at work for refusing to compromise our faith for the good of the business.

In various parts of the world, Christians appear to be losing a lopsided battle in the war against false ideologies. Those endowed with the power to dispense information routinely misrepresent Christ and His bride (the church) by highlighting the church's failings and ignoring the church's positive contributions. Thus they flood the world with faulty views of reality.

Yet Christ reigns at God's right hand. In that position, Christ has dominion over all power and authority. He will indeed reign until all modern pharaohs are subjugated under His feet (1 Corinthians 15:24, 25). May we recognize daily that He alone is our ultimate authority.

B. Prayer

Lord, we confess to You that we, like Moses, sometimes lose sight of Your power. The powers that we face are so real and immediate that we often forget that they are temporary. Remind us continually that You alone reign supreme. Guard us against the lies of this world and keep us in Your Word and truth. We pray this in Jesus' name. Amen.

C. Thought to Remember

God's power and authority are final.

Learning by Doing

This page contains an alternative lesson plan emphasizing learning activities. Some of these activities are also found in the helpful student book, Adult Bible Class.

Into the Lesson

In preparation for class, collect recent newspapers and magazines. Place all the newspapers and magazines on a table in the room just prior to class. Write the word *Obey* on the board; underneath that word write these questions:

1. Whom did the subject of the story disobey?
2. What was their reason for disobeying?
3. What was the result of the disobedience?

As class begins, form students into small groups. Ask each group to send a representative to grab a few of the newspapers and magazines. Instruct the groups to scan through the material and find instances of individuals who did *not* obey. For example, crime reports would be excellent. Also good would be stories about trouble that children got themselves into that resulted from disobedience to parents. Injury due to a failure to follow safety procedures or label instructions is a third possibility.

After a few minutes, ask for groups to summarize one or two of their news stories. After this, have students stay in their groups and recount a time when they disobeyed someone, answering the same three questions. After a few minutes, ask volunteers to share their personal stories of disobedience. Make a transition by saying, "We all disobey, and sometimes even feel justified in doing so; but what about when we disobey God?"

Into the Word

Begin with a dramatic reading of the printed text of Exodus 5:1-9, 22, 23; 6:1. Ask for five volunteers to read the following four parts: *narrator* (who reads all nonspeaking parts of the text), *Moses and Aaron* (who will read in unison), *Pharaoh*, and *God*. To make sure that the reading goes smoothly, ask all participants to use the same version of the Bible.

After the reading, form the class into small groups again. Distribute to each group a handout that asks the following questions.

1. Did God make it clear to Pharaoh what He expected him to do? Defend your answer.
2. What specific request did Moses and Aaron make?
3. Why did Pharaoh react so harshly to such a simple request?

4. In what way did Moses and Aaron's request make things worse for the Israelites?
5. How did Moses respond to this turn of events? What do his words to God teach us about how to handle (or not handle) our times of frustration?
6. In what way did Pharaoh's response play into God's plan for delivering the Israelites?

After an appropriate amount of time, ask groups to share their insights. You can do this by moving down through the questions in sequence, or you can use a generalized opener such as "What jumped out at you as you reviewed these questions?" Make a transition to the life application portion of the lesson by observing, "It is easy to see when others are disobeying God, but what about ourselves?"

Option: As with last week, you may wish to consider using a film clip from movies such as *The Ten Commandments, Moses,* or the animated film *The Prince of Egypt* in addition to reading the text. The clip can introduce the Bible portion of the lesson or it could be used after the discussion.

Into Life

Provide two or three index cards to each participant. (If you have a large class, distribute only two each; if you have a smaller class, distribute three each.) Ask students to provide a reason that either they or someone they know has used to justify disobedience to God. Each reason should be on a separate card. After a few minutes, ask the participants to give the reasons. (If the reason was heard from another, that person's name should not be mentioned.)

As each response is given, write it on the board and ask, "Does anyone else have this reason?" Tally the number of occurrences for each. Make a note of the three most frequent reasons (excuses).

Next, have groups discuss the best ways to respond to these justifications for disobedience. (If your class is smaller, this can be a whole-class discussion.) Ask, "How could we safeguard ourselves from disobeying God? How can we help someone not use these three common justifications for disobedience?"

After sufficient time, ask the groups to share their insights. If your class likes a more philosophical approach, ask, "Why is disobedience to God another way of saying 'I know better than God'?"

Let's Talk It Over

The questions on this page are designed to promote discussion of the lesson by the class and to encourage application of the lesson Scriptures. The answers provided are only discussion starters. Let your class talk it over from there.

1. Why do you think God allowed several generations of His people to suffer in Egypt before coming to their rescue? Why didn't He do it sooner?

We may not be able to formulate a coherent answer to this question because of the many unknowns. We do not know when the Israelites were forced to make the transition from being resident aliens to being slaves. We have limited knowledge of the intensity or frequency of prayers for deliverance (Exodus 2:23, 24). We know little of the history of the Jews' faithfulness to God during the time in Egypt.

While we cannot know fully how God thinks, we can be sure that God always waits for the optimal time to move His plan ahead (see Galatians 4:4). We remind ourselves that God also suffers. For example, God's distress is almost palpable in Jeremiah 45:4 as He describes the judgment He is about to inflict. God's distress is evident when His Son is dying (Luke 23:45). God understands what it means to suffer! We may be sure that He took no pleasure in punishing the Egyptians.

2. What strategies can Christian leaders use to stand strong during a smear campaign from enemies?

Pharaoh was the master of the strategy of *divide and conquer*. He knew that if the people mistrusted their leaders, they would lose confidence in their dream. Unfortunately, people do not always evaluate carefully the reason for misfortune. It is easy to blame God or one's leaders. Proactively, leaders can talk with their followers about contingency steps if an ideal time line does not unfold as expected. Those leaders can equip the people in advance with various responses to the claims of critics. Above all, everyone can commit to praying for God's leading, discernment, patience, and daily strength for every person involved.

3. How can Christians protect against feeling disappointed with God when His response does not match expectations?

Unrealistic or unwarranted expectations can create a certain vulnerability. It is very possible that the Israelites jumped to the conclusion that the arrival of Moses and Aaron meant their plight in Egypt would be resolved immediately. When their condition worsened instead, they turned against their new leaders.

We can review the successes and apparent setbacks in the Bible as these reveal God's character. As we face an unpleasant situation, we can position ourselves for God to act either slowly or quickly. In this way we prepare to grow spiritually in the midst of difficulties. We develop perseverance if God takes longer than anticipated (see Galatians 6:9, 10; James 1:2-4).

4. What are some things that prevent the average Christian from praying appropriately when he or she feels God is not following through on His promises? How do we guard against these?

Some Christians believe that following God faithfully means never questioning God about anything, that any hint of doubt equals a moral failure. But our text reveals that God did not get angry at Moses' reaction. God simply told him what would happen in the end. (See Psalm 10 for an example of David's complaining to God.) Christians can seek to understand why God is responding (or not responding) in a particular way without blaming God or calling His justice into question.

Sometimes a heartfelt inquiry is a first step in building a stronger faith. In the Garden of Gethsemane, Jesus' "talked straight" with the Father. This provides something of an example for us to follow, although the work Jesus was doing at the time was a one-time, one-person thing. As we review that example, we will be cautious about using the term "unanswered prayer," since *no* is an answer.

5. Why would it not be a good idea for Christians to live in the midst of perpetual miracles?

The motives for becoming a Christian would change, as many would confess Christ just to live in a perceived utopia. God would become a cosmic vending machine, where anyone could put in a request for God to provide. No one would learn to walk by faith. Interest in what the next miracle would "do for me" would eclipse interest in Bible study; every day would be spent dreaming up the next miracle. We recall that during the Exodus the Israelites lived with the perpetual miracles of the pillars of cloud and fire (Exodus 13:21, 22), but those miracles didn't seem to increase their faith!

Finding Protection

DEVOTIONAL READING: Exodus 15:1-13.

BACKGROUND SCRIPTURE: Exodus 13:17–14:30.

PRINTED TEXT: Exodus 14:15-25, 30a.

Exodus 14:15-25, 30a

15 And the LORD said unto Moses, Wherefore criest thou unto me? speak unto the children of Israel, that they go forward:

16 But lift thou up thy rod, and stretch out thine hand over the sea, and divide it: and the children of Israel shall go on dry ground through the midst of the sea.

17 And I, behold, I will harden the hearts of the Egyptians, and they shall follow them: and I will get me honor upon Pharaoh, and upon all his host, upon his chariots, and upon his horsemen.

18 And the Egyptians shall know that I am the LORD, when I have gotten me honor upon Pharaoh, upon his chariots, and upon his horsemen.

19 And the angel of God, which went before the camp of Israel, removed and went behind them; and the pillar of the cloud went from before their face, and stood behind them:

20 And it came between the camp of the Egyptians and the camp of Israel; and it was a cloud and darkness to them, but it gave light by night to these: so that the one came not near the other all the night.

21 And Moses stretched out his hand over the sea; and the LORD caused the sea to go back by a strong east wind all that night, and made the sea dry land, and the waters were divided.

22 And the children of Israel went into the midst of the sea upon the dry ground: and the waters were a wall unto them on their right hand, and on their left.

23 And the Egyptians pursued, and went in after them to the midst of the sea, even all Pharaoh's horses, his chariots, and his horsemen.

24 And it came to pass, that in the morning watch the LORD looked unto the host of the Egyptians through the pillar of fire and of the cloud, and troubled the host of the Egyptians,

25 And took off their chariot wheels, that they drave them heavily: so that the Egyptians said, Let us flee from the face of Israel; for the LORD fighteth for them against the Egyptians.

. . . .

30a Thus the LORD saved Israel that day out of the hand of the Egyptians.

GOLDEN TEXT: Thus the LORD saved Israel that day out of the hand
of the Egyptians.—Exodus 14:30.

Call Sealed with Promise
Unit 1: Called Out of Egypt
(Lessons 1–4)

Lesson Aims

After participating in this lesson, each student will be able to:

1. Tell how God saved Israel at the Red Sea.
2. Draw a parallel between the deliverance at the Red Sea and how God delivers today.
3. Write a poem or song praising God for His protection.

Lesson Outline

INTRODUCTION
   A. Trapped?
   B. Lesson Background
 I. GOD DIRECTS (Exodus 14:15-18)
   A. What Moses Is Told to Do (vv. 15, 16)
      Panic Attack
   B. What God Will Do (vv. 17, 18)
II. GOD DELIVERS (Exodus 14:19-22)
   A. Protection from Egypt (vv. 19, 20)
   B. Pathway for Israel (vv. 21, 22)
III. GOD DEFEATS (Exodus 14:23-25, 30a)
   A. Egyptian Pursuit (vv. 23-25)
   B. Israelite Salvation (v. 30a)
      The Fall of Empires
CONCLUSION
   A. Enslaved
   B. Prayer
   C. Thought to Remember

Introduction

A. Trapped?

Quicksand is not the dangerous natural threat that Hollywood makes it out to be. It simply is a mixture of a certain ratio of water to sand, possible anywhere in the world. Quicksand seldom accumulates more than a few feet deep. In extreme situations, like those caused by earthquakes or underground streams, quicksand may be deep enough to engulf an adult's body. However, since the human body can float in water, it floats even more easily amidst a mixture of water and sand, which is far denser. The key to survival is not panicking. One must relax, maintain composure, and allow the body to rise to the surface through small subtle movements.

Christians face many quicksands throughout life. These are moments when we feel helplessly trapped with no discernible end in sight. In a flash we imagine the worst. So we panic.

Panic may result in rash decisions, like throwing money we do not have at a problem in order to buy our way out of it. The result also may be excessive worrying, complaining, or even gossiping if we think someone else is to blame. We suppose that if we scramble fast enough we can reverse the problem, make it disappear entirely, or at least minimize the damage.

In such instances it is easy to forget that God is in control. We may forget that no problem we face is too big for Him. We may forget that He never calls His people to make rash or unholy decisions to right a perceived wrong. He calls us, instead, to be still, wait on Him, and trust that He will deliver us.

In today's lesson, the Israelites saw themselves to be sinking fast. They were trapped between Pharaoh's army and a large body of water, with no discernible way out. Their instinct was to panic. But God beckoned them to be still and to watch His promised deliverance.

B. Lesson Background

By the time of today's lesson, God had showed His power over the mighty Egyptian empire in a sequence of stunning plagues. As a result, Pharaoh practically begged Moses to take the Israelites and leave (Exodus 12:31, 32). On top of this, the Egyptians themselves blessed the Israelites with parting gifts of clothing and precious metals (12:35, 36).

Though God triumphed decisively, He was not finished teaching a lesson to both Israel and Egypt. As the people approached the Red Sea, God called them to turn back a bit in order to provoke Pharaoh to pursue them (Exodus 14:1-4). That is exactly what happened. The Israelites turned, Pharaoh assumed they were confused and vulnerable, and he gathered his army to march after them. This was all part of the plan God disclosed to the Israelites.

But as the Egyptians drew near, the Israelites panicked. They cried out to Moses and God that it would have been better to remain slaves in Egypt than to be killed in the desert (Exodus 14:10-12). Moses tried to encourage the people, apparently to no avail.

So God intervened. The idea was both to assure the Israelites of His protection and to prove to them (again) that He alone could deliver them. It did not matter how deeply they thought themselves sinking in the quicksand of adversity; God was on their side.

I. God Directs
(Exodus 14:15-18)

A. What Moses Is to Do (vv. 15, 16)

15. And the LORD said unto Moses, Wherefore criest thou unto me? speak unto the children of Israel, that they go forward.

God hears Israel's desperate pleas, but with little sympathy. What more does He have to do to show them that Pharaoh is no match for Him? He has squashed Egyptian power through dramatic signs and plagues. He has led the Israelites out of Egypt with a supernatural flame and cloud (Exodus 13:21, 22). He has just used them to lure Pharaoh into a trap. But as the trap begins to work, the Israelites still doubt and panic.

The fact that God asks Moses *Wherefore criest thou unto me?* may indicate that Moses shares in the doubt and panic. God has the cure: *go forward.* There is a time to pray and a time for action. Knowing the right time for each is important. It's now time for Moses and the Israelites to stop crying out to God. It's time to get moving! [See question #1, page 376.]

16. But lift thou up thy rod, and stretch out thine hand over the sea, and divide it: and the children of Israel shall go on dry ground through the midst of the sea.

In previous encounters with Pharaoh, God caused the staff of Aaron to become a serpent (Exodus 7:10); turned water into blood (7:20); drew frogs out of various waters (8:5, 6); made lice of the earth's dust (8:17); brought thunder, hail, and fire from Heaven (9:23); and called on the east wind to blow in a horde of locusts (10:13). Now God calls on Moses with his staff *(rod)* to work one of the most memorable miracles in Israel's history: the parting of the Red Sea. [See question #2, page 376.]

The identity of this *sea* is not given in this verse, but it is clearly stated in Exodus 15:4 as the Red Sea. In the original (Hebrew) language, however, the sea is identified as *Yam Suf,* which means Sea of Reeds. It is not until the third century BC that a Greek version of the Old Testament translates this as Red Sea.

This leads some students to speculate that it is not the Red Sea as we know it today that is parted. However, Acts 7:36 and Hebrews 11:29 follow the Greek translation and identify this body of water as the Red Sea. Furthermore, the details of two walls of water in Exodus 14:22 (below) hardly fit any body of water in the area other than the Red Sea. Therefore the Red Sea is the same as the Sea of Reeds.

PANIC ATTACK

Caffeine is the most widely used psychoactive drug in the world. This drug is found not only naturally in coffee, but also artificially in many soft drinks and so-called "energy" beverages.

But caffeine use can cause problems. Some studies show a connection between caffeine use and the occurrence of panic attacks in certain people. Genetic factors may predispose them to strong reactions to large amounts of caffeine. Giving up caffeine is not that easy, however. *Coffee jitters* is what happens when coffee drinkers experience caffeine withdrawal symptoms. The short-term cure, of course, is to have a cup of coffee!

Israel's panic attack was not a case of coffee jitters. But they were indeed experiencing withdrawal symptoms—withdrawal from "the known" of Egypt into "the unknown" of a journey ahead. That fact combined with the sight of Pharaoh's hordes coming after them was a recipe for panic. God's prescription for their panic is good advice for us. In times of stress, God still says "Believe in me and move in the direction I'm leading you."
—C. R. B.

B. What God Will Do (vv. 17, 18)

17. And I, behold, I will harden the hearts of the Egyptians, and they shall follow them: and I will get me honor upon Pharaoh, and upon all his host, upon his chariots, and upon his horsemen.

Christians have long wrestled with the fact that God hardened *the hearts* of *Pharaoh* and the Egyptians against the Israelites. Some say such hardening demonstrates that God fully controls all human action; the result of this proposal is that humans lack genuine free will (meaning the power of opposite choice). Others who are committed to the principle of free will may try to "explain away" these verses so that the human will is never overridden by God.

As a result, passages like this have become fodder for a doctrinal debate. We cannot resolve that debate here. But three factors should be kept in mind if we are to read this passage in context.

How to Say It

AARON. *Air*-un.
EGYPT. *Ee*-jipt.
EGYPTIANS. Ee-*jip*-shuns.
ISRAELITES. *Iz*-ray-el-ites.
MOSES. *Mo*-zes or *Mo*-zez.
PHARAOH. *Fair*-o or *Fay*-roe.
SINAI. *Sigh*-nye or *Sigh*-nay-eye.

First, this is not the only passage in Exodus to discuss God's hardening of the hearts of Pharaoh and the Egyptians (compare Exodus 4:21; 7:3; 9:12; 10:1, 20, 27; 11:10; 14:4, 8). Second, other passages in Exodus discuss Pharaoh hardening his own heart (8:15, 32; 9:34). Third, what God does in one particular situation does not prove what God "must" do in another situation or with most humans in most places.

With these facts in mind, a proper reading of this narrative may be attempted. Going back to Exodus 4, the text depicts a scenario in which Pharaoh genuinely and freely desires to deny Israelite release from captivity and to punish them for even asking. Though God announces in advance His plan to *harden* Pharaoh (Exodus 4:21; 7:3), Pharaoh hardens his own heart twice (8:15, 32) before God does so for the first time (9:12). This is why Pharaoh and the Egyptians serve as negative examples in 1 Samuel 6:6 of those who harden their own hearts.

Thus when God finally joins the hardening process, He is not forcing the Egyptians to do something that is uncharacteristic of them. They have made their intentions clear, and God uses their existing stubbornness to advance His glory. What we may safely infer from this narrative is that at a critical time in Israel's development God strengthened an enemy's resolve to pursue His people. The reason why is the subject of the next verse.

18. And the Egyptians shall know that I am the Lord, when I have gotten me honor upon Pharaoh, upon his chariots, and upon his horsemen.

God's purpose for hardening the Egyptians' hearts is not to provide fodder for doctrinal debates, but to *honor* himself in the sight of His people and their foes. Pharaoh dishonored God by denying His existence (Exodus 5:2) and ruthlessly oppressing His people (5:6-9). God is about to set the record straight. Not only does the *Lord* exist, but He also is sovereign over all creation. He will not be mocked without consequences.

II. God Delivers
(Exodus 14:19-22)

A. Protection from Egypt (vv. 19, 20)

19. And the angel of God, which went before the camp of Israel, removed and went behind them; and the pillar of the cloud went from before their face, and stood behind them.

We are told in Exodus 13:21 that God leads the Israelites with a *pillar* of *cloud* by day and a pillar of fire by night. These supernatural manifestations assure them of God's presence, show them where to go, and enable them to travel at any time.

In the verse before us we also learn that *the angel of God* leads the people. It is not clear whether this angel travels in the cloud, before the cloud, or behind it. But this angel now relocates behind the Israelites, and the cloud follows.

20. And it came between the camp of the Egyptians and the camp of Israel; and it was a cloud and darkness to them, but it gave light by night to these: so that the one came not near the other all the night.

In this new location, the cloud takes on a new purpose: protection. *The Egyptians* are gaining ground on the Israelites. The relocated pillar provides light for the Israelites while at the same time covering the Egyptians with *a cloud* of *darkness*. Night-vision goggles do not exist at this time! The ancient military commander does not launch attacks when darkness prevents his troops from seeing the enemy, let alone being unable to see one another. We can assume that the darkness is this severe.

B. Pathway for Israel (vv. 21, 22)

21. And Moses stretched out his hand over the sea; and the Lord caused the sea to go back by a strong east wind all that night, and made the sea dry land, and the waters were divided.

With the Egyptians contained behind the cloud, it is time for God to act and Israel to move. Moses raises his *hand* and staff according to God's instructions in verse 16, and God summons the *east wind* once more to do His bidding. This time the wind does not bring locusts as in Exodus 10:13, but divides the *sea*. The result is a *dry* passageway from one side to the other.

It is worth noting here that there are three agents in this miracle: God, Moses, and the wind. God didn't have to use Moses, nor did He need the wind. Like day three of creation (Genesis 1:9), God simply can command the waters to gather together, causing dry land to appear. Yet when working on behalf of His people, God often chooses not to work alone. He may involve His creation and creatures in His mighty acts of deliverance. Though God is primary, He may choose to work through secondary agents.

Similarly, Jesus is no Lone Ranger. In His time on earth, He does much of His work through disciples (Luke 9:1-6; 10:1-17). After completing His unique work on the cross, Jesus sends them (and us) into the world to continue His mission.

God has a purpose for the Israelites. For them to carry it out, they need to learn to follow Moses' leadership. [See question #3, page 376.] God does not want them to depend solely on miracles for their security. God ultimately hopes to wean them off of the extraordinary in order that they may function in the context of the small—but extremely important—everyday acts of ordinary faithfulness.

22. And the children of Israel went into the midst of the sea upon the dry ground: and the waters were a wall unto them on their right hand, and on their left.

Israel has just cried out helplessly to God. The people seemingly were trapped, with no way out. They have scolded Moses for leading them out of Egypt, stating a preference for Egyptian slavery to divine freedom (Exodus 14:11, 12). Now they are doing the impossible: walking through *the sea* on *dry ground*!

We can wonder what goes through their minds during this faith walk. Perhaps their thoughts go something like this: "We should have trusted God! How foolish we are to doubt His promises. Nothing is impossible for God. How did we lose sight of this after all He did for us in Egypt? We'll never make that mistake again!"

Of course, Israel does repeat this sad mistake. They grumble several times shortly after the Red Sea deliverance, and they upbraid Moses for liberating them (Exodus 15:24; 16:2, 3; 17:3). We may be tempted to belittle them for such lack of faith. How can they be so fickle? But we do the same whenever we worry about job security, healthcare coverage, or retirement packages.

Jesus tells us not to worry about such things. He tells us that pagans worry about them, but God's children have nothing to worry about, since their heavenly Father looks after them (Matthew 6:25-34). This is not a license for idleness and irresponsibility (2 Thessalonians 3:6-13). But it should remind us to discipline our thoughts and speech as we enter periods of change and instability that have no end in sight. It is during such times of testing that the genuineness of our faith is revealed (James 1:2-4).

III. God Defeats
(Exodus 14:23-25, 30a)

A. Egyptian Pursuit (vv. 23-25)

23. And the Egyptians pursued, and went in after them to the midst of the sea, even all Pharaoh's horses, his chariots, and his horsemen.

The Egyptians recklessly pursue the Israelites. [See question #4, page 376.] At this point, it is shocking to see how clouded the vision of the Egyptian leadership has become. Israel's God has defeated the Egyptians soundly with spectacular plagues, and now He parts the Red Sea before their very eyes. Yet still they believe that human

might and horse-drawn *chariots* can defeat the Israelites! What faith Pharaoh places in his army! Yet it won't be long before Pharaoh finds out how terribly misplaced this faith is. [See question #5, page 376.]

24. And it came to pass, that in the morning watch the LORD looked unto the host of the Egyptians through the pillar of fire and of the cloud, and troubled the host of the Egyptians.

The morning watch spans the time between two and six AM. Since the Egyptians likely wait until the light of dawn is available, this means that they make their move in the latter part of that time frame.

25. And took off their chariot wheels, that they drave them heavily: so that the Egyptians said, Let us flee from the face of Israel; for the LORD fighteth for them against the Egyptians.

At just the right time, God moves against the source of Egypt's strength: the impressive horse-drawn chariots. *Wheels* pop off, chariots topple, and horses struggle vainly to pull their loads.

The Egyptians do not write off their collective misfortune to fate or to the military skill of the Israelites. They confess, at last, that Israel's God is fighting *for them*, just as Moses said He would (Exodus 14:14). They acknowledge God's existence, recognize His authority, and fear His power. Their only recourse is to attempt to *flee*.

B. Israelite Salvation (v. 30a)

30a. Thus the LORD saved Israel that day out of the hand of the Egyptians.

It is too late to escape. Verses 26-28 (not in today's text) record that Moses once again stretches out his hand, and the waters collapse over the

Visual for
Lesson 4

Point to this visual as you ask, "What other images of God's protection come to mind?"

Egyptians. All drown. Though the Egyptians' fate had been sealed previously at Mount Sinai and during the plagues on Egyptian soil, the conflict ends decisively in the midst of the Red Sea.

The difference between God's victories on Egyptian soil and in the Red Sea may be compared with two key moments in World War II. On June 6, 1944, the Western Allies' D-Day invasion delivered the fatal blow to the enemy; this made the ultimate victory certain. Even so, the war was not over. Axis powers continued fighting for many months before finally surrendering.

God's two-stage victory for Israel is also analogous to the victory Christ won on our behalf. Jesus' death, resurrection, and ascension are the defining moments in establishing God's kingdom. Yet defeated opponents endure. They will continue to do so until Christ returns to vanquish His enemies and finalize His reign.

Our God continues fighting for us as He did for the Israelites, and He will finish His war. We must be patient during the turbulent times between now and the completion of His victory. We must not, like the Israelites, lose heart before the final day. God's victory is certain! [See question #6, page 376.]

THE FALL OF EMPIRES

Soon after the end of World War II, it became apparent that America's Soviet friends had been on the side of the Allied powers only because they shared a common enemy. With Nazi Germany out of the way, the Soviet government's true colors began to show. Thus the Cold War and a nuclear arms race began.

By the time the Soviet Union collapsed in 1991, both sides had a nuclear deterrent capable of destroying each other many times over. Even so, Soviet military might could not prevent the erosion of the Communist bloc from within. The West offered its citizens freedom and an amazing array of consumer goods. By contrast, citizens of East Germany had to have government-issued coupons just to buy a pair of socks. Repression was the only means the Communist governments had for keeping their subjects in line.

We can safely say that God allowed the collapse of the Soviet Union. But can we say that He caused it to fall? We cannot, because God has not told us as much. But the pages of Scripture are clear that God can do with world empires as He pleases (see Isaiah 13, among many similar passages). All who seek to flaunt power should take note!

—C. R. B.

Conclusion

A. Enslaved

We sometimes find ourselves helplessly enslaved by terrible situations, don't we? Our enslavement may not be like the physical slavery of the Israelites. Many are bound, instead, by life-sapping addictions such as substance abuse, gambling, and Internet pornography.

Other folks are held in captivity by less acknowledged but equally destructive habits such as gossiping, overeating, or manipulating others into getting one's own way. Still others are hemmed in by oppressive people who make life miserable. These can be overbearing bosses, greedy landlords, devious coworkers, or controlling parents.

In some cases it is appropriate to stop and cry out to God. There may also be "Red Sea moments" when God wants us to go forward in faith. The one thing we must not do is try to go forward only in our own strength.

Whether or not we experience earthly deliverance in any given situation, we know that eternal deliverance is certain. We must follow Israel's example (the good parts, that is) and walk forward in faith down that path.

B. Prayer

Mighty God, who delivered Israel from Egypt and who raised Jesus from the dead, we call on You to increase our faith. We believe in Your power, but we often convince ourselves to rely only on our own strength. Teach us to trust You always and to trust in You alone. We pray this in Jesus' name. Amen.

C. Thought to Remember

Trust God to deliver you.

Home Daily Bible Readings

Monday, June 22—Led to Freedom by God (Exodus 13:17-22)

Tuesday, June 23—Pursued by the Enemy (Exodus 14:1-9)

Wednesday, June 24—Overtaken by Fear (Exodus 14:10-14)

Thursday, June 25—God Is Our Refuge (Psalm 46)

Friday, June 26—Trust in the Lord (Proverbs 3:3-10)

Saturday, June 27—Celebrating Deliverance (Exodus 15:1-13)

Sunday, June 28—Saved from the Enemy (Exodus 14:15-25, 30)

Learning by Doing

This page contains an alternative lesson plan emphasizing learning activities. Some of these activities are also found in the helpful student book, Adult Bible Class.

Into the Lesson

Find stories on the Internet of people making seemingly impossible escapes. These can include survival of car accidents, building collapses, or weather-related catastrophes (do not include "escapes" as are found in the shows of magicians). These kinds of stories also can be found in magazines such as *Guideposts* and *Reader's Digest*. Print out the stories for use in class. (In all cases, make sure not to violate copyright restrictions.)

To begin class, form small groups and give a story to each group. Ask students to read the stories within their groups. You will need to make sure that the stories are short—just a couple of paragraphs at most (create your own summaries if need be). Students are to answer these questions (write them on the board):

1. What was the nature of the danger, threat, or conflict?
2. What factors made the escape or survival so amazing?

After a few minutes, have groups share with the whole class the contents of their stories and their responses to the questions. Then ask volunteers to share within their groups stories of situations when they felt "between a rock and a hard place," that is, when they were faced with the proverbial "no-win situation."

Option: If your classroom has Internet access, you can show video clips of such stories from television news reports, etc. In this case, keep the class in one large group as you show a succession of clips. Ask the same questions as above after all the clips have been shown. This will require some advance preparation of bookmarking in your web browser the stories you wish to show.

Make a transition by saying, "Tight situations are nothing new. The ancient Israelites also found themselves in a tight situation, with the Red Sea in front of them and the Egyptian army coming up from behind."

Into the Word

Ask the groups to read Exodus 14:15-25 and the first line of verse 30 (end with "of the Egyptians"). Write on the board the following questions or provide them on a handout. Ask the groups to reflect on today's passage as they respond to the questions:

1. Describe the difficult circumstances Israel was facing.
2. In this situation, what reasons might the Israelites have had for questioning their faith in God? for questioning if they were going to survive?
3. What was God's plan for rescuing the Israelites and gaining glory over the Egyptians?
4. How did the angel of God and the pillar of cloud provide help and support to the Israelites' escape?
5. Once the Egyptians were in the middle of the sea, what slowed down their escape? How complete was their destruction?
6. How should the Red Sea events have changed the Israelites' attitude toward God and His ability to help them?
7. What if God had not intervened? Could the Israelites have saved themselves?
8. Create your own question for #8. Write it down and pass it to the next group clockwise for it to answer.

Allow at least 10 minutes for small-group discussion. Then have the class as a whole discuss the answers. Ask what the students found to be most troubling or controversial.

Make a transition to life application by saying, "God is faithful to His people. How has God intervened in your life situations?"

Into Life

Ask the class to reflect on the needs of the community in which your church is located. What needs are most evident? Write their responses on the board, leaving space between each item.

After at least three responses, ask, "How can our congregation be God's deliverance in these circumstances? What can we do to be God's agents in the community?" Write responses underneath the need in question.

Next, say, "Let's discuss how the church is to help meet needs in comparison with secular helping agencies such as the Red Cross. What's the difference? How can we provide help in Jesus' name in ways that secular agencies cannot?"

Ask the class to form into small groups once again. Request that each student share within the group one way in which he or she can help address these needs personally. Close with a few minutes of prayer for mutual support in doing so.

Let's Talk It Over

The questions on this page are designed to promote discussion of the lesson by the class and to encourage application of the lesson Scriptures. The answers provided are only discussion starters. Let your class talk it over from there.

1. How do we wisely pray for missionaries working in situations where they may be attacked or imprisoned? How do we discern that it's time to put our prayers into personal action?

Praying specific prayers for missionaries by name is undoubtedly the best way to pray. Many of them long for prayers for strength and patience in hard times, for wisdom in decision-making, and for faithfulness among the people they have led to Christ. Part of the action we can take is to make sure they know about the prayers. They want to hear from those Christians who are standing behind them. Your class may want to contact several missionaries to ask what they need and how your class can support them.

2. What resources are available to Christians when circumstances start to turn bad or when the situation seems impossible?

We do not have a magic rod to take obstacles out of our way—and neither did Moses! What we have is the power of God. We draw on this power through prayer, relying on strength from the Holy Spirit, finding support from fellow Christians, visualizing how this struggle can lead to spiritual strength and/or an effective witness, sharing in the suffering of Christ, and remembering the final goal—Heaven.

When we do not use these assets, there is a danger that disappointment will turn to disillusionment. Despair can then follow. Discuss with the students how they have found their spiritual resources helpful during difficult times.

3. In today's text, Moses seemed more "settled" than many of the other Israelites. What is it about serving on the front line that may give leaders an advantage in their confidence in God? What can the average Christian do to gain this perspective?

Serving on the front line allows a person repeated experiences of how God acts in various situations. Once a leader is convinced of the wisdom and faithfulness of God, it is much easier to have a confident faith during the tough times. The voice of experience seems to speak with more authority at those times when it is necessary to exhort other followers to trust God.

When we hold back from service, we rob ourselves of this close walk with God as well as practice in "firming up" for future times of trial. Ask each class member to share how this has been true for him or her. Challenge each to step up to the next level, toward the front line of service.

4. What do God's responses to the differing reactions of Pharaoh and Moses reveal about how He may respond to us today?

God is not befuddled when individuals do not respond immediately to His call. God knows the difference between caution and defiance. We serve a God who is reasonable and wise in understanding human tendencies (see Genesis 18:23-33; Jonah 4). Lead the class in discussing the differences in the characteristics between reluctance and defiance.

5. Thinking about one of your darkest hours of doubt and confusion, what role did God play? How did you grow spiritually from that experience?

Ask for volunteers to share the *Reader's Digest* (condensed) version of a very difficult experience. (You may want to contact a few class members early in the week so they can be prepared.) Be sure to put the three parts above (the nature of the doubt, the role of God, your growth) on the board to give structure to each testimony. Ask the class to draw conclusions after some have shared.

6. If you were to write a single-stanza hymn telling of God's feats in Lessons 1–4, what would you include? Would you focus on specific events or on broader issues such as timing and empowerment? Why? What would be gained from singing this hymn over and over?

The use of repetition has been a part of the worship patterns of God's people throughout the Bible as well as the history of the church. A hymn celebrating what God accomplished during the deliverance of Israel might include God's timing, His ability to call and empower leaders, His impact on the faith of the Israelites, His power through miracles, His loving care, and His wisdom. Being reminded of the majesty and power of the God we serve is one of the ways to increase one's faith.

Accepting God's Rules

July 5
Lesson 5

DEVOTIONAL READING: Matthew 22:34-40.

BACKGROUND SCRIPTURE: Deuteronomy 5:1-27.

PRINTED TEXT: Deuteronomy 5:1-9a, 11-13, 16-21.

Deuteronomy 5:1-9a, 11-13, 16-21

1 And Moses called all Israel, and said unto them, Hear, O Israel, the statutes and judgments which I speak in your ears this day, that ye may learn them, and keep and do them.

2 The LORD our God made a covenant with us in Horeb.

3 The LORD made not this covenant with our fathers, but with us, even us, who are all of us here alive this day.

4 The LORD talked with you face to face in the mount out of the midst of the fire,

5 (I stood between the LORD and you at that time, to show you the word of the LORD: for ye were afraid by reason of the fire, and went not up into the mount,) saying,

6 I am the LORD thy God, which brought thee out of the land of Egypt, from the house of bondage.

7 Thou shalt have none other gods before me.

8 Thou shalt not make thee any graven image, or any likeness of any thing that is in heaven above, or that is in the earth beneath, or that is in the waters beneath the earth:

9a Thou shalt not bow down thyself unto them, nor serve them.

. . . .

11 Thou shalt not take the name of the LORD thy God in vain: for the LORD will not hold him guiltless that taketh his name in vain.

12 Keep the sabbath day to sanctify it, as the LORD thy God hath commanded thee.

13 Six days thou shalt labor, and do all thy work.

. . . .

16 Honor thy father and thy mother, as the LORD thy God hath commanded thee; that thy days may be prolonged, and that it may go well with thee, in the land which the LORD thy God giveth thee.

17 Thou shalt not kill.

18 Neither shalt thou commit adultery.

19 Neither shalt thou steal.

20 Neither shalt thou bear false witness against thy neighbor.

21 Neither shalt thou desire thy neighbor's wife, neither shalt thou covet thy neighbor's house, his field, or his manservant, or his maidservant, his ox, or his ass, or any thing that is thy neighbor's.

GOLDEN TEXT: Hear, O Israel, the statutes and judgments which I speak in your ears this day, that ye may learn them, and keep and do them.—Deuteronomy 5:1.

Call Sealed with Promise
Unit 2: Called to Be God's People
(Lessons 5–8)

Lesson Aims

1. Recite the Ten Commandments from memory.
2. Explain the relationship between the Ten Commandments and the new covenant in Jesus.
3. Identify one of the Ten Commandments that he or she has the most trouble keeping and make a plan for change.

Lesson Outline

INTRODUCTION
 A. Keeping the Rules
 B. Lesson Background
I. COVENANT RECALLED (Deuteronomy 5:1-6)
 A. Summons (v. 1)
 B. History (v. 2)
  CC&Rs
 C. Audience (vv. 3, 4)
 D. Mediator (v. 5)
 E. Basis (v. 6)
II. LAWS REPEATED (Deuteronomy 5:7-9a, 11-13, 16-21)
 A. No Other Gods (v. 7)
 B. No Graven Image (vv. 8, 9a)
 C. No Misuse of the Name (v. 11)
 D. Keep the Sabbath Day Holy (vv. 12, 13)
 E. Honor Parents (v. 16)
 F. Do Not Murder (v. 17)
 G. Do Not Commit Adultery (v. 18)
 H. Do Not Steal (v. 19)
 I. Do Not Give False Testimony (v. 20)
 J. Do Not Covet (v. 21)
  Intent
CONCLUSION
 A. Relevance of the Ten Commandments
 B. Prayer
 C. Thought to Remember

Introduction

A. Keeping the Rules

Have you ever received a speeding ticket? It's irritating. I could justify myself very easily, for I had been following a slow-moving car for about 3 miles. The speed limit was 55 mph; the other car was doing 50 mph, and I couldn't pass. Finally, I saw my opportunity to pass and did so. Then I saw the flashing lights of the town police. At first I was puzzled, but then I realized he was after me, not the slow driver!

He said I was doing 65 mph in a 55 mph zone. "But officer, I had to reach that speed to get around this slow driver," who was still slow-poking his way down the road. "Sir, I thought I was being safe by getting around the car as quickly as I could so that I could get back on the right side of the road." His response? "You really were doing over 65, but I'll write the ticket for only 10 mph over the limit, which will cost you $175."

Did I think I deserved the ticket? Nooooo! Did I learn my lesson about the law? Yes: break the law and pay the consequences. Obey the law and everyone is safer.

God gave rules of conduct by which Israel was to live. There were hundreds of rules, but the most familiar expression of these is the Ten Commandments. Paul stresses that today we are not under law, but under grace (Romans 6:14). This does not mean that rules of conduct are thrown out the window—quite the contrary. The church has been given rules in a new format by Jesus (see Matthew 22:34-40). Commandments that are expressions of the nature of God are unchanging since God himself does not change (Malachi 3:6). We ignore the Old Testament origin of such commands at our peril.

B. Lesson Background

The book of Deuteronomy is a covenant renewal treaty, delivered by Moses in a series of speeches (Deuteronomy 1:1–4:43; 4:44–28:68; etc.). The recipients were the Israelites of a new generation who were about to enter the promised land. Moses was about to die on Mount Nebo, located in Moab (Deuteronomy 34).

Deuteronomy 5–11 is the high point of the book. Here the Ten Commandments are recounted (Deuteronomy 5; compare Exodus 20:1-17 and Deuteronomy 4:13; 10:4). This is followed by an exposition of how to love and obey the one true God (Deuteronomy 6–11).

There are different ways to categorize the laws in the Bible. One helpful way is to distinguish between laws that are *conditional* and those that are *unconditional*. The first kind has a conditional clause (beginning with "if" or "when," either expressed or implied), followed by a declarative judgment (beginning with "then," either expressed or implied; examples: Exodus 21:28; 22:26, 27). Unconditional laws are what we have with the Ten Commandments. They are foundation principles for Israel's covenant relationship. Covenant creates a relationship, and the rules maintain the relationship.

The setting for today's lesson is "on [the east] side [of the] Jordan, in the valley over against Beth-peor, in the land of Sihon king of the Amorites" (Deuteronomy 4:46). The year is about 1406 BC.

I. Covenant Recalled (Deuteronomy 5:1-6)

A. Summons (v. 1)

1. And Moses called all Israel, and said unto them, Hear, O Israel, the statutes and judgments which I speak in your ears this day, that ye may learn them, and keep and do them.

All Israel must *hear* and obey these laws. No one is exempt, because all are part of the covenant community. *Hear, O Israel* is a special phrase in Deuteronomy (compare Deuteronomy 4:1; 6:3, 4; 9:1; 20:3; 27:9). "To hear" includes the idea of obedience. Moses emphasizes obedience by using the additional words *learn them, and keep and do them.* [See question #1, page 384.]

B. History (v. 2)

2. The LORD our God made a covenant with us in Horeb.

Horeb refers at least to Mount Sinai (Exodus 3:1; 33:6; Deuteronomy 1:6; etc.) and perhaps some of the surrounding area. The *covenant* that *God made* with His people there is recorded in Exodus 19 and following. But as Moses speaks now, the 40 years of wilderness wanderings are at an end (Deuteronomy 1:3). Thus, this is Moses' exhortation to a new generation.

CC&Rs

Many people now live in communities governed by CC&Rs—covenants, conditions, and restrictions. CC&Rs cover issues involving setbacks, lot lines, easements, fees for road and commons areas, pets, landscaping, fencing, placement of basketball goals, and even allowable paint colors.

What would make a person agree to the stringent stipulations of CC&Rs? The answer is that the restrictions provide a means of maintaining property values and the quality of life for the residents. They maintain a consistent, predictable ambiance in the neighborhood.

The covenant that God announced at Horeb had the intended purpose of helping Israel maintain a proper spiritual ambiance within their newly forming nation. If Israel would keep the covenant, spiritual decline would not take place. The Israelites would find their lives blessed. The new covenant we have through Christ will accomplish this too, but only if we keep it. Like Israel, we have to honor the covenant to enjoy its blessings.   —C. R. B.

C. Audience (vv. 3, 4)

3. The LORD made not this covenant with our fathers, but with us, even us, who are all of us here alive this day.

The phrase *The Lord made not this covenant with our fathers* has drawn more than one interpretation. It is possible that *our fathers* refers to the patriarchs (forefathers) Abraham, Isaac, and Jacob—long dead by Moses' day (see Deuteronomy 1:8; 4:31, 37; 7:8, 12; 8:18; 9:5). If that is the case, then a contrast is being made between the promise of land and blessing to the patriarchs and the Sinai covenant for the nation of Israel.

Another suggestion is that *our fathers* refers to those immediate ancestors who died during the 40 years of wilderness wanderings. Under this idea, God had tried to include them in the covenant, but they rejected the covenant because of rebellion (Deuteronomy 1:26-46). Either way, we do not want to lose sight of the fact that Moses is emphasizing the relevance of the Sinai covenant for the generation standing before him. It is this generation that is soon to conquer Canaan.

4. The LORD talked with you face to face in the mount out of the midst of the fire.

The event this verse refers to is found in Exodus 19:16-25. At first glance, the verse before us seems like a contradiction to what actually happened, for the people themselves never really talked with Yahweh *face to face.* But verse 5 (next) clears up the matter.

D. Mediator (v. 5)

5. (I stood between the LORD and you at that time, to show you the word of the LORD: for ye were afraid by reason of the fire, and went not up into the mount,) saying.

How to Say It

ABRAHAM. *Ay*-bruh-ham.
ADONAI *(Hebrew)*. Ad-owe-*nye.*
AMORITES. *Am*-uh-rites.
BETH-PEOR. Beth-*pea*-or.
CANAAN. *Kay*-nun.
ISAAC. *Eye*-zuk.
JACOB. *Jay*-kub.
JERICHO. *Jair*-ih-co.
MOAB. *Mo*-ab.
MOSES. *Mo*-zes or *Mo*-zez.
NEBO. *Nee*-bo.
PATRIARCHS. *pay*-tree-arks.
SIHON. *Sigh*-hun.
YAHWEH *(Hebrew)*. Yah-weh.

This verse restates the mediating position of Moses. Indeed, the people had been *afraid* of *the fire* (see Exodus 19:16-19), and they had trembled. On the mountain, Moses had represented Israel before God (Deuteronomy 5:23-31). It is in that sense that the people had talked with the Lord face to face. [See question #2, page 384.]

E. Basis (v. 6)

6. I am the LORD thy God, which brought thee out of the land of Egypt, from the house of bondage.

The nation of Israel certainly didn't bring itself *out of the land of Egypt*! It was none other than *the Lord thy God* who did that. This is important to stress at this point in light of what immediately follows: a restating of the Ten Commandments. The fact that it is the Lord who provided the deliverance is a vital part of the basis for obedience to Him.

II. Laws Repeated
(Deuteronomy 5:7-9a, 11-13, 16-21)

A. No Other Gods (v. 7)

7. Thou shalt have none other gods before me.

This is an exclusive statement, since the people are commanded to exclude *other gods* from thoughts, actions, and worship. The pluralistic society we live in today doesn't like such statements. But it is just as valid today as it was in Moses' day.

The fertility gods of Canaan will be a great temptation to Israel when she enters the promised land, as time will tell. Yet it is Yahweh who has "married" Israel (compare Ezekiel 16:8). This covenant relationship is to be exclusive, as the marriage of one man and one woman should be. This ideal is foundational to all the other rules of God. It cuts very much against the cultural practices of Israel's day. [See question #3, page 384.]

B. No Graven Image (vv. 8, 9a)

8, 9a. Thou shalt not make thee any graven image, or any likeness of any thing that is in heaven above, or that is in the earth beneath, or that is in the waters beneath the earth: thou shalt not bow down thyself unto them, nor serve them.

This, the Second Commandment, is a summary of what has already been rehearsed in the historical prologue of Deuteronomy. There Moses warns the people against the idolatrous worship that is so prevalent in Egypt and Canaan (see 4:9-24). The prohibition we see here includes attempts to present Yahweh God in the *likeness* of anything created.

At some point in life, everyone becomes curious about what God "looks like." The answer is that the Creator doesn't look like anything that He has created. Cartoons often portray God as a kindly, white-haired old man. Such depictions violate this commandment. Although we are created in the image of God, that doesn't mean we know what God looks like when we glance at a mirror.

C. No Misuse of the Name (v. 11)

11. Thou shalt not take the name of the LORD thy God in vain: for the LORD will not hold him guiltless that taketh his name in vain.

This commandment is usually thought of in the context of the use of God's *name* in cursing. But the implications are much deeper in the original historical and cultural context. The Law of Moses forbids using God's name for personal gain in terms of magical arts or divination (see Numbers 22–24). To swear an oath by God's name is not forbidden in and of itself (see Deuteronomy 6:13; 10:20), but the Israelites must not make false oaths in Yahweh's name (see Leviticus 19:12).

Today, we are sadly aware of cases where televangelists have traded on the name of God to enrich themselves. This is a violation of this commandment. The ancient Hebrews became fearful to the point that they used the designation *Adonai* ("Lord") as a substitute for Yahweh's name, thinking that this would avoid the misuse of God's name. This practice did not solve the problem.

D. Keep the Sabbath Day Holy (vv. 12, 13)

12, 13. Keep the sabbath day to sanctify it, as the LORD thy God hath commanded thee. Six days thou shalt labor, and do all thy work.

The word *sabbath* means "ceasing." *The sabbath day* has to be observed on the seventh day of every week in imitation of God's ceasing His labors from creating (see Exodus 20:11). While Exodus says to remember this day for reasons tied to God's original work in creation, Deuteronomy adds the idea of keeping the Sabbath because of the deliverance of Israel from slavery. This is creation in terms of forming the people of God (Deuteronomy 5:15, not in today's text).

These two reasons complement one another and give full force to the importance of using one day a week for worship and rest. This commandment puts the brakes on unending economic competition (compare Nehemiah 13:15-22). Observing this day of rest will provide needed respite to people, beasts, and equipment.

Some modern businesses run by Christians practice this rule by not opening for business on Sunday, the Christian worship day. A day of rest is still a good idea, but to insist that Sunday is a kind of "Christian Sabbath" for all believers would violate freedom in Christ (Romans 14:5; Colossians 2:16). [See question #4, page 384.]

Before moving on, we should observe that nine of the Ten Commandments always apply because they are based on the unchanging nature of God. One of the Ten Commandments—the one we are looking at here—is based on the work of God. In the New Testament era, our focus is on God's work of a new creation in Christ (2 Corinthians 5:17; Galatians 6:15). Thus Sabbath-keeping is not in force for us. Our concern is not primarily with the seventh day of the week, but with the first (Acts 20:7); this is the Lord's Day (Revelation 1:10).

E. Honor Parents (v. 16)

16. Honor thy father and thy mother, as the LORD thy God hath commanded thee; that thy days may be prolonged, and that it may go well with thee, in the land which the LORD thy God giveth thee.

This commandment is vital to the continuity of the covenant. Children are to honor their parents by heeding their teaching and looking after them in old age. The apostle Paul notes that this is the first commandment that has a promise attached to it—the promise that *thy days may be prolonged* (see Ephesians 6:2).

So important is this rule to the social, economic, and spiritual strength of Israelite society that rebellious children in ancient Israel are to be put to death (see Deuteronomy 21:18-21)! Today, we should take seriously our obligation to take care of aging parents (Mark 7:9-13; 1 Timothy 5:4). Practice of this rule will strengthen the fabric of the family, society, and the church. [See question #5, page 384.]

F. Do Not Murder (v. 17)

17. Thou shalt not kill.

Murder is what is being prohibited here. This prohibition is based on the fact that we are created in God's image (see Genesis 1:26, 27; 9:6). Murder is considered to be a capital crime in ancient Israel, meaning that it is punishable by death (see Exodus 21:12; Leviticus 24:17; Numbers 35:30, 31). Manslaughter has its own law (Deuteronomy 19:4-6). Some students believe that support for capital punishment may be found in the New Testament in Acts 25:11 and Romans 13:4.

G. Do Not Commit Adultery (v. 18)

18. Neither shalt thou commit adultery.

Adultery is sexual relations between two adults where at least one is married to someone else. Adultery strikes at the heart of the covenant relationship between man and wife, and it is con-

Visual for Lessons 5 & 12. *Be sure to have this visual displayed as you begin the* Into the Word *segment on page 383.*

sidered a great sin in Israel. Since adultery is so disruptive to the foundation of family, it is considered a capital crime (Leviticus 20:10; Deuteronomy 22:23-27). The seriousness of adultery is seen in how this word is used figuratively to describe Israel's unfaithfulness to God (Jeremiah 3:6-9; Ezekiel 23).

The prohibition against adultery continues in the New Testament (compare Matthew 5:27-30). The sad commentary on modern Western society is how often this rule is violated. The evil consequences have a ripple effect, as we know.

H. Do Not Steal (v. 19)

19. Neither shalt thou steal.

Land and property in ancient Israel are to be considered God-given. To *steal* is to violate the owner as well as God who grants the property. Even kings are prohibited from misappropriating personal property (1 Kings 21). If someone is caught stealing, restitution and a severe penalty are to be exacted (see Exodus 22:1-13). Once again, the fabric of society rests on this rule. Today, there seems to be no end to the imagination of those who steal. The problem involves not just property and possessions, but identities as well. Identity theft can ruin reputations, credit ratings, etc.

I. Do Not Give False Testimony (v. 20)

20. Neither shalt thou bear false witness against thy neighbor.

All societies must depend on the truthfulness of testimony for justice to be done in the courtroom. The penalty for lying under oath (perjury) is severe: the perjurer is to suffer the punishment of the crime involved (see Deuteronomy 19:16-21).

At least two witnesses are required to establish the truth (19:15). When justice is perverted in the courtroom, the result is a corrupt society.

J. Do Not Covet (v. 21)

21. Neither shalt thou desire thy neighbor's wife, neither shalt thou covet thy neighbor's house, his field, or his manservant, or his maidservant, his ox, or his ass, or any thing that is thy neighbor's.

Coveting is the unnatural and excessive desire for something. We could say that the Tenth Commandment treats the real cause for the violation of all God's rules. By coveting another man's wife, King David illustrates how that one sin can lead to adultery and murder (2 Samuel 11, 12). Although not discussed in this commandment, it is even possible to covet one's own possessions; by Jesus' day this led some people to dishonor their parents via the Corban procedure, a way of skirting the Fifth Commandment (see Mark 7:8-13).

We are to be content with what we have (Luke 3:14; 1 Timothy 6:8; Hebrews 13:5). Covetousness is a sin of the mind that will lead to sins of the flesh if left unchecked.

INTENT

The latter portion of the Ten Commandments deals with human relationships. We are all aware of how the Jews by Jesus' time had devised all sorts of ways to violate the spirit of God's instructions while still seeming to keep the letter of the law (Matthew 23). It is easy enough to condemn those who did so, although the same thing happens today, sometimes in very innovative ways.

Consider stealing for instance. One of the ways to appear to do good for our neighbors is to donate a used vehicle to charity. In one such case, a 1990

Mercury was donated to charity, and its owner claimed its value was $2,915 for the tax write-off. The car brought $30 at auction. By the time the auctioneer was paid and other costs were taken care of, the charity actually lost $130! The U.S. government's General Accounting Office has discovered numerous cases in which owners valued their cars at many times over the auction price.

This was an attempt to defraud the government via an unjustified deduction (compare Matthew 22:21; Romans 13:7). We may try to rationalize our behavior just as the Jews in ancient times did. But God knows the motives of the heart.   —C. R. B.

Conclusion

A. Relevance of the Ten Commandments

Any society that adheres to the principles of the Ten Commandments will experience stability in various ways. Christians believe that these rules came from God himself to the people of God. Christ said, "Think not that I am come to destroy the law, or the prophets: I am not come to destroy, but to fulfil" (Matthew 5:17). We must not substitute human traditions for God's good commands (Mark 7:8, 9).

The apostle Paul stresses that we are under the system of grace, not the system of law, for salvation (Romans 6:14). But Paul also applies the Fifth Commandment to all Christian parents and children (Ephesians 6:2, 3). He proclaims boldly in Romans 13:10 that "love is the fulfilling of the law"; this statement follows his quotation of four of the Ten Commandments in Romans 13:9. Paul advises in Romans 7:7 that the law has made us knowledgeable about sin; as an example, he quotes the Tenth Commandment. Thus the Ten Commandments are by no means obsolete!

God has entered into a new covenant with His people through Jesus Christ. Since Christ is the "end" (culmination) of the law (Romans 10:4), we now continue the new covenant relationship with God by keeping the law of Christ. This is a committed love for God and our neighbor (see Galatians 6:2). By living in the power of the Holy Spirit, Christians fulfill the "righteousness of the law"; the Ten Commandments help us to "walk not after the flesh" (Romans 8:4).

B. Prayer

Father, may our look to Israel's past help guide our Christian future. May Your Ten Commandments teach us most of all about You. In Christ's name. Amen.

C. Thought to Remember

Obeying God's rules pleases Him.

Home Daily Bible Readings

Monday, June 29—A Covenant by Sacrifice (Psalm 50:1-6)

Tuesday, June 30—Listening to the Prophet (Acts 3:17-25)

Wednesday, July 1—A Covenant of Obedience (Psalm 132:11-18)

Thursday, July 2—Mediator of a Better Covenant (Hebrews 8:6-12)

Friday, July 3—A Covenant of Mercy (Romans 11:25-32)

Saturday, July 4—The Greatest Commandment (Matthew 22:34-40)

Sunday, July 5—God Makes a Covenant (Deuteronomy 5:1-9, 11-13, 16-21)

Learning by Doing

This page contains an alternative lesson plan emphasizing learning activities. Some of these activities are also found in the helpful student book, Adult Bible Class.

Into the Lesson

Say, "Fireworks are used in many nations as a form of celebration, just as they were used this week in the U.S. Independence Day observances. However, there are rules one must follow in using fireworks. What are some of those rules?" Jot responses on the board. Then ask, "What are some possible consequences of breaking those rules?" Write these responses on the board as well.

Make the transition to Bible study by saying, "Rules are made for our protection and for the good of society. It was God's concern for the well-being of His people that He issued the most famous set of rules in history."

Alternative introduction: Arrange classroom chairs in close rows with an aisle down the center; have four chairs in each row, with two chairs on either side of the aisle. The idea is to simulate a bus. As students are seated, ask them to imagine they are riding in a bus traveling to visit the state capital. However, the bus must pass through a dangerous part of the city. Ask, "What are some terrible things that might happen on this tour?" Write answers on the board. Ask what law or rule has been made to help protect us from each of the dangers mentioned. Make the transition to Bible study by stating, "Laws or rules are usually made for our protection and security. A concern for protection and security prompted God to issue the most famous set of laws recorded in history."

Into the Word

Read Deuteronomy 5:1-6 aloud. Give a very brief lecture from the Lesson Background that explains why the Ten Commandments were being repeated at that particular point in history.

Divide the class into 6 study teams of 2 to 4 people each. For Teams #1 through #5, make the following Scripture assignments: Team #1, verses 7-9a; Team #2, verses 11-13; Team #3, verses 16, 17; Team #4, verses 18, 19; and Team #5, verses 20, 21. Give each team a photocopy of the page of the lesson commentary that applies to their verses. Note: for smaller classes, use fewer teams and assign more than two commandments to each team.

Write on the board (or list on handouts) the following tasks:

1. Read the Scriptures assigned and the lesson commentary on those verses.

2. Explain and clarify the commandments for the class.

3. Give examples of how the commandments you are studying may be broken in Christian lives in 2009.

4. Remembering that rules are usually made for personal and societal benefit, explain how the commandments you are studying bless God's people in today's world.

As the teacher, make personal notes about the responses to the third task. You will need these notes later in the lesson.

Give Team #6 a photocopy of the Conclusion in the commentary along with the following assignment: Your task is to read the printed text and the copy of the lesson conclusion from the lesson commentary. Be ready to explain briefly the relationship between the Ten Commandments and the new covenant in Jesus.

As Teams #1 through #5 make their reports, write the commandments on the board using abbreviated headings similar to those used in the lesson commentary outline (example: "Honor Parents"). Then allow Team #6 to make its report.

Into Life

Memorization Activity: Tell the class that many believers cannot list more than about five of the Ten Commandments. We would like to do better! Say, "The first four commandments address our relationship with God. The last six focus on our relationship with each other."

Read through the list together as you refer to the abbreviated headings you wrote on the board. As you work through the list, erase all but the first letter of a key word in each commandment. Have your class recite the Ten Commandments by using these letters as clues; then give each student a handout with those 10 letters listed down the left edge. Ask each student to try to write the Ten Commandments using these clues.

Personal Application: Remind the class of the ways these commandments may be broken in today's world. Use your notes from the third task of the study teams to shape this reminder. Say, "Most of us need some improvement in our thinking to comply with these rules." Ask each class member to circle the commandment he or she would most like (need) to work on to honor God's will.

Let's Talk It Over

The questions on this page are designed to promote discussion of the lesson by the class and to encourage application of the lesson Scriptures. The answers provided are only discussion starters. Let your class talk it over from there.

1. Why does hearing often not result in obeying? How do we counteract this tendency?

Today there are many messages bombarding us that compete for our "hearing." Advertising exhortations abound, trying to get us to "obey" by buying certain products. This information overload causes us to become very selective in translating what we hear into what we do—and that's a good thing with regard to "things of the flesh."

However, this can be a bad thing when it extends to the church. Many Christians hear the Word of God preached every week, but they allow it to have little impact on their patterns of behavior. Obedience requires taking positive action on those things we have heard. See James 1:22.

2. How can we talk to God and know that He is listening? How can we make sure we hear what God is saying to us? How do we counteract interference in each direction of communication?

Moses had direct encounters with God; in that light, he served as a mediator for the people. Today, Christ is our mediator to God (1 Timothy 2:5). Even so, Moses and the other authors of Scripture still have a mediating function of sorts, for they reveal God's will for our lives through His Word. It is through the Word that God communicates with us most specifically. We assure ourselves that we have heard God when we obey Him.

We talk to God by means of a deep, sincere prayer life. Our study of Scripture and fellowship with other praying believers adds fuel to our prayer lives. When it seems as if our access to God is blocked, we should examine our hearts to see if personal or corporate issues of sin or lack of repentance may be hindering our prayer life (examples: Lamentations 3:8, 44; 1 Peter 3:7).

3. What are some "other gods" that exist in society today? in our own lives? How do we counteract these?

The Ten Commandments disallow any other gods from taking the place of the Lord God; yet our society is very diverse in its religions. People who may be our neighbors openly worship the earth, Buddha, or (in effect) themselves. But Christians often allow material things and concerns to squeeze God out of their lives. Sometimes we

allow relationships with nonbelievers to compromise our faith and diminish our obedience.

We can evaluate this by looking at how we spend our time and money. If we are too busy to spend time in God's Word or attend church services but have lots of time to watch television or attend sporting events, our priorities are out of whack. We can examine our passion index too. If we have no sincere love for God and for serving Him, it is time to rekindle that passion.

4. In what ways have you applied to your life the Old Testament principle of regular, scheduled periods of rest?

Many Christians do not know quite what to do with the commandment to keep the Sabbath. This can be a controversial issue. Observance of the Sabbath had special significance as it represented God's pattern of creation. But as with other commands, by Jesus' day the Jewish leaders had adopted improper views toward Sabbath-keeping (Mark 2:23-28).

The principle of taking time to slow down in order to rest and reflect is still of great value today (compare Exodus 23:12). The psalmist advises, "Be still, and know that I am God" (Psalm 46:10). We are not of much use to God if we are exhausted. Christians are wise to have a deliberate practice of taking sufficient time to relax and be refreshed. Parents will teach their children in this area much more by example than by words.

5. What are some practical ways we can honor our parents? How does (or should) the way we honor our parents change as the years pass?

Many middle-aged adults feel caught between the responsibilities of launching their children into adulthood and assisting parents who are in their golden years. This can cause severe strains on time and money. The role reversal of an adult son or daughter becoming the primary caregiver and/or decision-maker for an elderly parent may be especially difficult to experience. But when we fulfill this responsibility to the best of our ability, we reinforce an important pattern on which stable society depends. If we take care of our parents, our children are more likely to take care of us when we need them.

Remembering and Celebrating

DEVOTIONAL READING: 1 Corinthians 5:1-8.

BACKGROUND SCRIPTURE: Deuteronomy 16:1-8.

PRINTED TEXT: Deuteronomy 16:1-8.

Deuteronomy 16:1-8

1 Observe the month of Abib, and keep the passover unto the LORD thy God: for in the month of Abib the LORD thy God brought thee forth out of Egypt by night.

2 Thou shalt therefore sacrifice the passover unto the LORD thy God, of the flock and the herd, in the place which the LORD shall choose to place his name there.

3 Thou shalt eat no leavened bread with it; seven days shalt thou eat unleavened bread therewith, even the bread of affliction; for thou camest forth out of the land of Egypt in haste: that thou mayest remember the day when thou camest forth out of the land of Egypt all the days of thy life.

4 And there shall be no leavened bread seen with thee in all thy coast seven days; neither shall there any thing of the flesh, which thou sacrificedst the first day at even, remain all night until the morning.

5 Thou mayest not sacrifice the passover within any of thy gates, which the LORD thy God giveth thee:

6 But at the place which the LORD thy God shall choose to place his name in, there thou shalt sacrifice the passover at even, at the going down of the sun, at the season that thou camest forth out of Egypt.

7 And thou shalt roast and eat it in the place which the LORD thy God shall choose: and thou shalt turn in the morning, and go unto thy tents.

8 Six days thou shalt eat unleavened bread: and on the seventh day shall be a solemn assembly to the LORD thy God: thou shalt do no work therein.

GOLDEN TEXT: Observe the month of Abib, and keep the passover unto the LORD thy God: for in the month of Abib the LORD thy God brought thee forth out of Egypt by night.—Deuteronomy 16:1.

Call Sealed with Promise
Unit 2: Called to Be God's People
(Lessons 5–8)

Lesson Aims

After participating in this lesson, each student will be able to:

1. Describe how the Passover was to be celebrated in Israel.

2. Tell what the Passover celebrated and how Christians today can celebrate similar things.

3. Plan a worship service of celebration for God's grace.

Lesson Outline

INTRODUCTION
  A. Celebrating a Jewish Passover
  B. Lesson Background
I. WHAT TO CELEBRATE (Deuteronomy 16:1)
  A. Special Time (v. 1a)
  B. Special Reason (v. 1b)
    Remembering
II. HOW TO CELEBRATE (Deuteronomy 16:2-4)
  A. Special Sacrifice (v. 2)
  B. Special Bread (vv. 3, 4a)
  C. Special Absence (v. 4b)
III. WHERE TO CELEBRATE (Deuteronomy 16:5-7)
  A. Special Place (vv. 5, 6)
  B. Special Continuation (v. 7)
IV. HOW LONG TO CELEBRATE (Deuteronomy 16:8)
  A. Special Week (v. 8a)
  B. Special Assembly (v. 8b)
    Celebrations
CONCLUSION
  A. Passover in the Old Testament
  B. Passover Superseded
  C. Prayer
  D. Thought to Remember

Introduction

A. Celebrating a Jewish Passover

I used to lead a group of Christian college students to work in the New York City area every year the week before Easter. One year our host couple had made friends with another couple who lived in an upscale apartment on Bay Ridge. Of that second couple, the husband was Jewish and the wife was a Protestant Christian. They were rearing their two daughters in the Jewish faith and heritage.

My host couple and I were invited to that Bay Ridge apartment to help that family celebrate the Jewish Passover. This was a special opportunity for witnessing, for we, being Gentile and Christian, should not have been there.

The modern Jewish Passover observance is an elaborate ceremony that has been developed over the centuries. It involves the children in the telling of the story of Israel's exodus from Egypt. All leaven is "looked for" and put in the trash. The meal is blessed, and the first of four cups of wine ("the cup of sanctification") is served.

Greens are dipped in salt water and eaten. Three unleavened loaves of bread are presented—the middle one broken, with a larger piece hidden for the children to find later for a treat. The second cup of wine is blessed and consumed. Then comes the recounting of the story of the exodus from a certain booklet.

At this point in our meal the Jewish father became frustrated because he was not familiar enough with the procedure to keep us all on track. As he was fumbling with the booklet, his wife turned to me and asked if I would explain how a Christian viewed the Jewish Passover.

What an opportunity! With the husband's permission, I carefully and humbly proceeded to explain the original Passover meal—its simplicity of roasted lamb or goat, unleavened bread, and bitter herbs. Then I mentioned the additions of the four cups, greens dipped in salt water, a sweet-apple dish, and a roasted egg (to commemorate the destruction of the temple in AD 70).

Then I said that the retrieving of the hidden piece of bread by the children signified payment of ransom. I explained the ransom the Messiah paid when he was broken, buried, and brought back to life. I noted that Jesus said "Take, eat; this is my body" when breaking the bread.

I then asked the two daughters to go to the door and open it to see if "Elijah" would come and take his seat at the table where "Elijah's cup" was set. I explained that Christians understand John the Baptist to have been the one who came in the spirit and power of Elijah (Matthew 11:10-15; 17:10-13) in preparing the way for Messiah Jesus.

As part of the wrap-up, we sang a hymn; I suggested that Jesus' disciples may have sung Psalms 113, 114 at the beginning of the last supper and Psalm 115–118 at the close. In conclusion I noted that Christ is our Passover Lamb, and we celebrate this "new Passover" whenever we meet around the Lord's Table (1 Corinthians 5:7, 8; 11:23-26).

To my knowledge, no one became a believer in Christ that evening. But I think I did what the wife and mother of the household wanted me to do.

More importantly, I think I did what Jesus wanted me to do. It was a great privilege and opportunity. [See question #1, page 392.]

B. Lesson Background

As today's lesson opens, the 40 years of wilderness wandering were over, and the Israelites were ready to enter the promised land. But first, Moses (age 120) had many important reminders to offer. One of those reminders involved the issue of the Passover celebration.

The historical basis of the Passover celebration is the last plague on Pharaoh and the land of Egypt. That involved the death of the firstborn, both human and animal, in about 1446 BC (Exodus 11). To protect themselves from the plague, the Israelites had to slaughter either sheep or goats and smear a portion of the blood on the sides and tops of the doorposts where they lived. When Yahweh struck down every firstborn in Egypt, He *passed over* (and thereby did not harm) the households where the blood protected the doorway.

The original Passover feast is described in Exodus 12. The Feast of Unleavened Bread occurred right alongside the Passover (Exodus 13:3-10; 23:15; Leviticus 23:4-8; Numbers 28:16-25; Mark 14:1). Our lesson text for today is a general overview of these two feasts.

I. What to Celebrate (Deuteronomy 16:1)

A. Special Time (v. 1a)

1a. Observe the month of Abib, and keep the passover unto the LORD thy God.

Abib, which means "ears of grain," is the old Hebrew name from an agricultural calendar. Much later, the name of this particular *month* will be changed to *Nisan* due to the influence of the Babylonian calendar (see Esther 3:7; Nehemiah 2:1).

This month is designated as Israel's first month of the religious year (Exodus 12:2); eventually it becomes the seventh month of Israel's civil year. It equates to late March and early April. The *passover* observance is to begin on the evening of the fourteenth day of this month, as established by God (Exodus 12:6, 18). [See question #2, page 392.]

B. Special Reason (v. 1b)

1b. For in the month of Abib the LORD thy God brought thee forth out of Egypt by night.

Darkness had become a plague for the Egyptians (Exodus 10:21, 22). In the middle of the *night* God had begun the deliverance of his "firstborn" (Israel) by killing all the firstborn of Egypt (Exodus 11). The contrast thus is between the grief of the Egyptians because their firstborn died and the celebration by the Hebrews because their firstborn were protected by the blood of lambs. All subsequent generations of Old Testament Israelites are to observe this festival. A continual emphasis throughout the exodus story is that deliverance comes about at *night* (see Exodus 11:4; 12:6, 8, 12, 22, 29, 30, 31, 42).

REMEMBERING

Every nation has its memorials. America's great memorials can be found in various places around the country. They may be the sites of historic battles, such as Gettysburg. Some are located where singular acts of human depravity were committed, such as the sixth-floor museum at the former Texas School Book Depository, from which President Kennedy was shot. Others are at the sites of significant triumphs of the human spirit, such as the Wright Brothers National Memorial at Kitty Hawk, North Carolina.

America's monuments primarily honor people who made important contributions to the progress of the nation. America's greatest collection of such monuments is to be found in Washington, D.C. There one can find the Washington Monument, the Lincoln Memorial, the Jefferson Memorial, and memorials to those who died fighting in World War II, Korea, and Vietnam. (The list goes on.)

Passover was ancient Israel's unique memorial. But it was not a sign at the side of a road that called to mind the life of some outstanding political leader or the place where a horrendous battle was fought. Rather, it commemorated the time when God acted to save a nation. That memorial— a meal rather than a stone monument or historic

The Old Testament Jewish Calendar

Hebrew Month	Religious Year	Civil Year	Modern Equivalent	Old Testament Observances	Day(s) of the Month	Old Testament Reference
Nisan (or Abib)	1	7	March–April	Passover	14	Exodus 12:6, 43-49 / Leviticus 23:5 / Numbers 28:16 / Deuteronomy 16:1, 2
				Feast of Unleavened Bread	15-21	Exodus 12:15-20 / Leviticus 23:6 / Numbers 28:17 / Deuteronomy 16:3, 4
Iyyar (or Ziv)	2	8	April–May			
Sivan	3	9	May–June	Pentecost (or Feast of Weeks)	6	Leviticus 23:15-21 / Numbers 28:26-31 / Deuteronomy 16:9-12
Tammuz	4	10	June–July			
Ab	5	11	July–August			
Elul	6	12	August–September			
Tishri (or Ethanim)	7	1	September–October	Feast of Trumpets	1	Leviticus 23:23-25 / Numbers 29:1-6
				Day of Atonement	10	Leviticus 23:26-32 / Numbers 29:7-11
				Feast of Tabernacles (or Booths, or ingathering)	15-21	Leviticus 23:33-43 / Numbers 29:12-38 / Deuteronomy 16:13-15
Marcheshvan (or Bul)	8	2	October–November			
Kislev	9	3	November–December			
Tebet	10	4	December–January			
Shebat	11	5	January–February			
Adar	12	6	February–March	Feast of Purim	14-15	Esther 9:18-28

Visual for Lesson 6. *You can use this poster whenever you teach a lesson that deals with one of the Jewish feasts of the Old Testament.*

site—was the point of departure for another memorial that Christians have kept for two millennia: the Lord's Supper. May we keep that memorial until Christ returns.   —C. R. B.

II. How to Celebrate
(Deuteronomy 16:2-4)

A. Special Sacrifice (v. 2)

2. Thou shalt therefore sacrifice the passover unto the LORD thy God, of the flock and the herd, in the place which the LORD shall choose to place his name there.

This verse takes for granted all the details of Exodus 12:3-11 concerning the *passover sacrifice*. Each family is to select a lamb (the Hebrew refers to either a young sheep or goat) on the tenth day of the first month. Guests are to be invited in order that the lamb may be eaten completely.

The instructions are clear. The lamb must be a year old, without defect; it is to be slaughtered at twilight on the fourteenth of Nisan (Abib). The blood is to be smeared on the lintel and doorposts. The meat is to be roasted over a fire, not boiled. It is to be eaten along with unleavened bread and bitter herbs. No meat is to remain; leftovers are to be burned before dawn. The people are to eat hastily. Their sandals are to be on their feet, clothing tucked into belts, and staffs in their hand. Thus, everyone has the appearance of being ready to leave at a moment's notice.

The Gospels present Jesus' death as coinciding with the Feast of Passover (Luke 22:13-15; John 13:1; etc.). The fact that John 19:36 refers to Psalm 34:20 ("He keepeth all his bones: not one of them is broken") indicates that Jesus becomes the world's Passover Lamb when we compare Exodus 12:46 and Numbers 9:12. See also 1 Corinthians 5:7.

How to Say It

DEUTERONOMY. Due-ter-*ahn*-uh-me.
EGYPT. *Ee*-jipt.
EZRA. *Ez*-ruh.
GILGAL. *Gil*-gal (G as in *get*).
HEZEKIAH. Hez-ih-*kye*-uh.
JERUSALEM. Juh-*roo*-suh-lem.
JOSHUA. *Josh*-yew-uh.
JOSIAH. Jo-*sigh*-uh.
MARDI GRAS. *Mar*-dee Grah.
PENTECOST. *Pent*-ih-kost.
PHARAOH. *Fair*-o or *Fay*-roe.
SHILOH. *Shy*-low.
YAHWEH *(Hebrew)*. *Yah*-weh.

B. Special Bread (vv. 3, 4a)

3, 4a. Thou shalt eat no leavened bread with it; seven days shalt thou eat unleavened bread therewith, even the bread of affliction; for thou camest forth out of the land of Egypt in haste: that thou mayest remember the day when thou camest forth out of the land of Egypt all the days of thy life. And there shall be no leavened bread seen with thee in all thy coast seven days.

The *seven days* at issue here occur between the fourteenth and twenty-first days of the month (Exodus 12:18). The only kind of bread that may be eaten for that week is bread made without leaven (yeast). This kind of bread serves to remind the people of their haste to leave Egypt (Exodus 12:11) as well as their slavery in Egypt; thus it is *bread of affliction* (see Exodus 3:7, 17; 4:31). [See question #3, page 392.]

The word *leaven* is used here in its natural, literal sense. In time this word comes to mean figuratively "things that influence, whether for good or bad." Using this idea in a negative sense, Jesus cautions His disciples to "Take heed and beware of the leaven of the Pharisees and of the Sadducees" (Matthew 16:6; compare 1 Corinthians 5:6-8; Galatians 5:7-9). The disciples misunderstand, but after further teaching by Jesus, they comprehend that Jesus is talking about "the doctrine of the Pharisees and of the Sadducees" (Matthew 16:12). Evil teaching corrupts the mind and heart persistently and thoroughly, just as leaven permeates dough.

In a positive sense, Jesus said "The kingdom of heaven is like unto leaven, which a woman took, and hid in three measures of meal, till the whole was leavened" (Matthew 13:33). The principle of permeation is the imagery of leaven. But permeation takes time—and that's exactly what the Israelites preparing to leave Egypt didn't have much of. They were to be prepared to leave in haste (Exodus 12:11).

The phrase *there shall be no leavened bread seen with thee in all thy coast seven days* stresses the special care that must be taken with regard to leaven. Removal is to be done prior to eating the Passover meal (Exodus 12:15, 19; 13:7). The modern Jewish Passover ceremony ties the removal of leaven to the necessity of ridding the home of any corruption or evil. But the biblical text simply says, "This is done because of that which the Lord did unto me when I came forth out of Egypt. And it shall be for a sign unto thee upon thine hand, and for a memorial between thine eyes, that the Lord's law may be in thy mouth: for with a strong hand hath the Lord brought thee out of Egypt" (Exodus 13:8, 9).

Unleavened bread is a key element in our observance of the Lord's Supper. This element connects directly with the special bread of the Passover.

C. Special Absence (v. 4b)

4b. Neither shall there any thing of the flesh, which thou sacrificedst the first day at even, remain all night until the morning.

Also, all leftover meat must be ceremonially burned up (Exodus 12:10). Nothing from the sacrificial meat is to be kept past morning. Once the purpose of the meat is accomplished, nothing can remain. To honor this instruction requires a certain strength of faith. It's a human tendency to try to preserve unused food "just in case." We may compare the Israelites' disobedience in trying to save manna in Exodus 16:20.

III. Where to Celebrate (Deuteronomy 16:5-7)

A. Special Place (vv. 5, 6)

5, 6. Thou mayest not sacrifice the passover within any of thy gates, which the LORD thy God giveth thee: but at the place which the LORD thy God shall choose to place his name in, there thou shalt sacrifice the passover at even, at the going down of the sun, at the season that thou camest forth out of Egypt.

Remember that Deuteronomy is a covenant renewal treaty given by Moses to the people just before they enter the promised land. [See question #4, page 392.] That fact means that no permanent location has yet been designated as *the place* for the ark of the covenant and a central place for worship. Yet it is only in the presence of God that *the Passover* lamb can be sacrificed, not just in any location *(gates)* of the Israelites.

After the crossing of the Jordan and the circumcision of all the males, the people will celebrate the Feasts of Passover and Unleavened Bread at Gilgal where, of course, the ark of the covenant also will be (Joshua 5:1-10). Shiloh is the chosen place during the period of the Judges (Joshua 18:1; 1 Samuel 4:3, 4). Much later, King David moves the ark to Jerusalem (2 Samuel 6). That will be the final place God chooses for His *name* to dwell in Old Testament Israel (1 Kings 8:29; Psalm 132).

B. Special Continuation (v. 7)

7. And thou shalt roast and eat it in the place which the LORD thy God shall choose: and thou shalt turn in the morning, and go unto thy tents.

Years later, the population of Jerusalem will swell manyfold during the time of the annual Passover celebration. This logically means that many visitors to Jerusalem will have to stay in tents as temporary housing for that week. Does the phrase *go unto thy tents* refer to this? Or perhaps is the reference to the nomadic existence at the time of the writing of Deuteronomy?

It may be best to understand the phrase *go unto thy tents* as an idiom meaning "go home" (see 2 Samuel 20:1; 1 Kings 12:16). The main idea is that the lambs are to be sacrificed in God's presence (where the tabernacle or temple is located) and the Passover celebrated somewhere near God's chosen place for worship (which eventually will be Jerusalem). *In the morning* following the observance of the night before, all the people are to return to their own abodes to continue the celebration of the Feast of Unleavened Bread for a week.

IV. How Long to Celebrate (Deuteronomy 16:8)

A. Special Week (v. 8a)

8a. Six days thou shalt eat unleavened bread.

The *six days* does not include the day of the Passover observance itself. When we add that day in, the total is seven days of eating unleavened bread (see v. 3, above; Numbers 28:16-24). A full week of sacrifices, special rituals of grain and drink offerings, and eating unleavened bread makes this a special time in the life of the ancient Israelite. No Israelite, young or old, can (or should) forget the great salvation God has given to them. The Lord's Supper, which supersedes the Passover, is also a memory device (1 Corinthians 11:24, 25).

B. Special Assembly (v. 8b)

8b. And on the seventh day shall be a solemn assembly to the LORD thy God: thou shalt do no work therein.

The combination Passover and Unleavened Bread celebration begins and ends with *solemn* (or sacred) days of no work. (Numbers 28:25 uses the phrase "holy convocation.") This involves the cessation of all normal activity (except food preparation). It is to be a time of worship and reflection. [See question #5, page 392.] What more can God do to impress on the minds of every Israelite generation that God had defeated the "gods" of Egypt and had delivered Israel from a mighty Egyptian army? Only the one true God could have won such a contest. Israel is to remember and live by that fact.

CELEBRATIONS

The most famous celebration of the year in New Orleans is *Mardi Gras*, which means "fat Tuesday." This week of raunchy goings-on precedes the period of fasting and discipline of Lent, as much of the Christian world knows it.

Ironic, isn't it? The idea seems to be something like, "Since we're going to have to behave ourselves for many days, we'd better have a really good time before that long period of self-denial!" The idea of enforced self-discipline flies in the face of the Western world's attitude of "I want what I want when I want it."

The Jewish Passover week was the exact opposite of Mardi Gras in many ways. A time of solemn assembly before the Lord was included. When Christians gather to observe the Lord's Supper, when we remember the sacrifice of our Passover Lamb, it too can be solemn. But it can also be joyous. Slavery to sin and death has been conquered by our living Lord! Whatever it is that is being celebrated at Mardi Gras is less than trivial compared with this.
—C. R. B.

Conclusion

A. Passover in the Old Testament

Celebrations of the Passover (and the Feast of Unleavened Bread that go along with it) are rarely recorded in the narrative of the Old Testament. Perhaps that is because its observance is taken for granted. But the few records of the celebrations are instructive and interesting: Joshua 5:10-12 (second generation of the exodus just before the conquest of the promised land, about 1406 BC); 2 Chronicles 30 (Hezekiah's reform, about 727 BC); 2 Kings 23:21-23 as paralleled in 2 Chronicles 35:1-19 (Josiah's reform, about 622 BC); and Ezra 6:19-22 (Ezra's reform after the exile, about 515 BC).

It seems that when great reform swept over the people, they celebrated the Passover extravagantly.

Home Daily Bible Readings

Monday, July 6—Remember and Rejoice (Ecclesiastes 11:7–12:1)

Tuesday, July 7—Remember the Lord's Deeds (Psalm 77:3-15)

Wednesday, July 8—Remember and Give Thanks (Psalm 105:1-11)

Thursday, July 9—Keeping the Covenant (2 Kings 23:1-3, 21-23)

Friday, July 10—Preparing for the Passover (Luke 22:7-13)

Saturday, July 11—Christ, Our Passover Lamb (1 Corinthians 5:1-8)

Sunday, July 12—The Passover Observance (Deuteronomy 16:1-8)

The Passover became the most important celebration for the Israelites, for it commemorated their origin as a people in God's great deliverance from slavery. The exodus event becomes the model for the idea of salvation throughout the Bible.

B. Passover Superseded

The church today should continue to remember and celebrate deliverance from the bondage of sin no less than the ancient Israelites celebrated deliverance from their bondage of the flesh. Certainly Christmas is a great time to celebrate the birth of our Lord—the Word become flesh (John 1:14). The greatest gift ever given is Jesus (John 3:16), and that is worthy to celebrate. Gift exchanges can enhance the celebration as long as Christians avoid the crass materialism and secularism of the season as practiced in America and many other places in the world.

The church often celebrates the resurrection of Jesus in a nobler manner than His birth. Resurrection Day (Easter) recognizes the Sunday morning when death was swallowed up in victory! The resurrection is at the very heart of the Christian faith; it must not be forgotten in the collective mind of the church. Remembering the resurrection means that Christians celebrate salvation from sin.

The Day of Pentecost (the Jewish Festival of Weeks) is a time for the church to remember her birth through the outpouring of the Holy Spirit (Acts 2). Yet there seems to be no consistency in remembering and celebrating this birth in the church-at-large today. More needs to be done. There is no reason why we should allow such a day to pass without even a mention.

Those three are annual observances. Much more frequent should be celebrations of the Lord's Supper. Each time we celebrate we recall Christ's victory over sin. "For as often as ye eat this bread, and drink this cup, ye do show the Lord's death till he come" (1 Corinthians 11:26). If we allow it to do so, the Lord's Supper can bind us together, keeping us close to God and one another.

C. Prayer

Our Father, bind us together as we remember and celebrate the occasions of Your great salvation for us. Help us as individuals and corporately as the church to recall Your actions of mercy, justice, and love for all people. May we be wise as we pass our faith on to the next generation and the generation beyond that. In Jesus name. Amen.

D. Thought to Remember

Remember to celebrate.
Celebrate to remember.

Learning by Doing

This page contains an alternative lesson plan emphasizing learning activities. Some of these activities are also found in the helpful student book, Adult Bible Class.

Into the Lesson

Begin the lesson by saying, "Many celebrations and holidays are designed to help people remember specific events. For example, adoptive parents may have a celebration to remember the day the child came to the parents' home." Ask students to help you fill out an acrostic with special days they celebrate. National holidays may be included.

Create the acrostic using the letters of the word *CELEBRATION* vertically on the board. At the letter *O*, write the word *adOption* across the word *celebration* as an example. If you need another example, you may use the phrase *spiritual birthday* on any matching letter. Some families observe this as a day of remembrance of a person's baptism or conversion.

Make the transition to Bible study by saying, "Holiday celebrations have value for the persons involved and for our culture. God gave a very special celebration to the Jewish people that forms a vital part of Christianity's background. Today's text unfolds that observance."

Into the Word

Read today's printed text regarding celebrating the Feast of the Passover. Then say, "We need to explore *what* was being celebrated, *how* the feast was to be celebrated, *where* it was to be celebrated, and *how long* the people were to celebrate. We will use four research teams to answer these questions." Give each team a photocopy of the lesson commentary that is appropriate for the verses to be researched plus the following instructions. Team #1 will also need a copy of the Lesson Background.

Team #1: Your task is to explore and report on *what* was being celebrated. Read Deuteronomy 16:1 and the lesson commentary for your answers. Verse 1a tells about the special time and verse 1b tells about the special event. The copy of the Lesson Background will be helpful in preparing your remarks about the reason for this event.

Team #2: Your task is to explore and report on *how* the celebration was to take place. Read Deuteronomy 16:2-4 and the lesson commentary for your answers. Be sure to report on the special sacrifice, special bread, and special ceremony.

Team #3: Your task is to explore and report on *where* the celebration was to take place. Read Deuteronomy 16:5-7 and the lesson commentary for your answers. Be sure to report on the special place and the special conclusion to the ceremony.

Team #4: Your task is to explore and report on *how long* the Passover was to be celebrated. Read Deuteronomy 16:8 and the lesson commentary for your answers. Be sure to report on the special week and the solemn assembly.

As teams report, list abbreviated answers on the board. Finish by making this observation: "A newspaper reporter typically wants to know *who, what, where, when, why,* and *how.*" Write those six words on the board as you speak them. Then ask, "Have we left any of those out?" This will promote an extended discussion of the text. If your class is small, a whole-class discussion will work. If your class is large, small-group discussions will allow more people to participate.

Into Life

Do both of the following activities if your time permits. Do only the second activity if your time is limited.

Activity #1: Remind the class that there are several opportunities for celebrations that teach and remind of Christian events. Four of them are Christmas, Resurrection Sunday (Easter), Pentecost, and the Lord's Supper. For each of these celebrations it is appropriate to ask, "What do we do well?" and "How can we improve the celebrations?" Assign one of the four observances mentioned above to each of the four study teams; have them discuss the two questions.

Activity #2: Say, "One of the great gifts of God that Christians should celebrate is His grace." Ask the class to design a worship service that helps both to celebrate God's grace and teach about that grace. Team #1 will plan the music for the service. Team #2 will select appropriate Scripture passages and decide how they will be presented. The Scripture presentations should include what will be said in the offering and Communion meditations. Team #3 will decide the major points or concepts the sermon should address. Team #4 will discuss special activities to include in the service. These may include drama, choral readings, children's presentations, testimonials, etc.

Conclude the class by singing one of the songs Team #1 selected.

Let's Talk It Over

The questions on this page are designed to promote discussion of the lesson by the class and to encourage application of the lesson Scriptures. The answers provided are only discussion starters. Let your class talk it over from there.

1. Should Christians hold Passover celebrations or participate in modern Jewish celebrations of Passover? Why, or why not?

Some Christians avoid Passover celebrations entirely, believing that such observances detract from the finality of the Lord's Supper. The lesson writer participated in a Passover observance for the purpose of witnessing for Christ, who is the ultimate Passover lamb. Such witnessing should be the goal of Christians who decide to participate, although harm can be done if those hosting the observance end up feeling "ambushed" by a Christian witness that was not expected.

Some Jewish-Christian groups offer opportunities for churches to experience a narrated Passover celebration. These can help Christians better understand the Last Supper and the symbolism involved. Passover reenactments may help us better appreciate the Jewishness of Jesus and His disciples.

2. The pain of being *passed over* in a negative way—as in being passed over for a job, a promotion, or a deserved honor—can be very real. What was a time when you were *passed over* in a positive way? How did you see God's hand in this?

Many of us have experienced a sense of injustice when we were not selected for something we thought we deserved or for which we were most qualified. It can sting when someone else is chosen over us. Yet as time goes by, we may come to see that what we thought to be a negative pass over was actually a positive thing.

For example, a certain man needed to change jobs, so he interviewed for a position that seemed ideal for him. Things were lining up just right. But at the last minute, one of the decision makers gave a thumbs-down. The man was stunned to have been rejected. But later a job that fit the man even better became available, and he took it. Had he been accepted for the first job he would not have been available to take the second, better job. What he initially thought was a negative pass over turned out to be positive. True story.

We also experience positive pass overs in those times when we know we deserve to be punished or penalized but are shown mercy instead. Such was the experience of the people of Israel time after time.

3. What were the circumstances surrounding your personal day of salvation, your deliverance from the bondage of sin? How does remembering those circumstances strengthen your faith?

Many believers are able to mark a specific day, event, or set of circumstances that brought them to faith. For some, this may involve a sequence of events over a period of time. We especially remember the people who played an important role in our decision for Christ. Remembering this milestone of our spiritual journey is important for both ourselves and our witness to others.

4. What aspects of your own "spiritual Egypt" hinder your full enjoyment of the promised land of Christ? How will you correct this situation?

Many adults are overly satisfied with their current situation and thus resistant to change; that resistance ends up being a "spiritual Egypt." The busyness of life can crowd out our relationship with God, leaving us unable to hear His call. Unresolved sin issues make us unprepared to undertake new ventures that God might offer to us. The Israelites were to be in a high state of readiness as the time of their exodus approached. Jesus directs us to be in a state of constant readiness (see Mark 13:37). A lazy satisfaction with being in a "spiritual Egypt" works against this.

5. How much time are you willing to devote to worshiping and remembering God? How do you deal with limits on your time commitment?

Ancient Israel held annual worship and remembrance celebrations that lasted for an entire week in addition to weekly Sabbath observances. Today, many Christians struggle to attend a weekly worship service for even one hour. The lure of family activities, sporting events, etc., can crowd out our commitment to God and His people. We can correct this by anticipating specific events that will build our spiritual commitment.

For example, it's not a good idea to wait until December 10 to ask, "Now what day is the church's Christmas play?" A proactive approach will ask that question on, say, November 1 in order to make definite plans both to attend and to bring a neighbor. Spending extended time with God's people helps us grow in the Lord.

Commissioning for Service

DEVOTIONAL READING: Romans 11:33–12:2.

BACKGROUND SCRIPTURE: Leviticus 8:1-13.

PRINTED TEXT: Leviticus 8:1-13.

Leviticus 8:1-13

1 And the LORD spake unto Moses, saying,

2 Take Aaron and his sons with him, and the garments, and the anointing oil, and a bullock for the sin offering, and two rams, and a basket of unleavened bread;

3 And gather thou all the congregation together unto the door of the tabernacle of the congregation.

4 And Moses did as the LORD commanded him; and the assembly was gathered together unto the door of the tabernacle of the congregation.

5 And Moses said unto the congregation, This is the thing which the LORD commanded to be done.

6 And Moses brought Aaron and his sons, and washed them with water.

7 And he put upon him the coat, and girded him with the girdle, and clothed him with the robe, and put the ephod upon him, and he girded him with the curious girdle of the ephod, and bound it unto him therewith.

8 And he put the breastplate upon him: also he put in the breastplate the Urim and the Thummim.

9 And he put the mitre upon his head; also upon the mitre, even upon his forefront, did he put the golden plate, the holy crown; as the LORD commanded Moses.

10 And Moses took the anointing oil, and anointed the tabernacle and all that was therein, and sanctified them.

11 And he sprinkled thereof upon the altar seven times, and anointed the altar and all his vessels, both the laver and his foot, to sanctify them.

12 And he poured of the anointing oil upon Aaron's head, and anointed him, to sanctify him.

13 And Moses brought Aaron's sons, and put coats upon them, and girded them with girdles, and put bonnets upon them; as the LORD commanded Moses.

GOLDEN TEXT: [Moses] poured of the anointing oil upon Aaron's head, and anointed him, to sanctify him.—Leviticus 8:12.

Call Sealed with Promise
Unit 2: Called to Be God's People
(Lessons 5–8)

Lesson Aims

After participating in this lesson, each student will be able to:

1. Tell how and why Aaron and his sons were commissioned for special service.

2. Explain the significance of the idea of being commissioned or set apart as it relates to his or her own service for the Lord.

3. Write a note of encouragement to someone who is serving the Lord.

Lesson Outline

INTRODUCTION
    A. Ordained for a Lifetime
    B. Lesson Background
 I. GOD'S INSTRUCTIONS (Leviticus 8:1-3)
    A. Everything Needed (vv. 1, 2)
    B. Everyone to Gather (v. 3)
II. MOSES' ACTIONS (Leviticus 8:4-13)
    A. Gathering (v. 4)
    B. Instructing (v. 5)
    C. Washing (v. 6)
    D. Robing (v. 7)
       How Should Ministers Dress?
    E. Breastplate (v. 8)
    F. Turban (v. 9)
    G. Tabernacle (v. 10)
    H. Altar (v. 11)
    I. Aaron (v. 12)
       Aromatherapy Not Needed
    J. Aaron's Sons (v. 13)
CONCLUSION
    A. Commissioning for Service
    B. Prayer
    C. Thought to Remember

Introduction

A. Ordained for a Lifetime

I was ordained into Christian ministry on August 23, 1964. I remember it as if it were yesterday. Why? It was one of the most important events in my life! I felt it was like a marriage covenant; it was supposed to last for a lifetime. It continues to control my life and my decisions as I march toward the twilight of my Christian ministry.

As I sit in my office and look at my ordination certificate hanging on the wall, I reminisce about that day. I was dressed in my best suit, white shirt, and a skinny tie. I was only 21 years old, and I was entering my senior year at Bible college. I recently had accepted a youth ministry position at a church in LaGrange, Georgia.

Several close friends participated in the service at a church in Bainbridge, Georgia. The minister signed the certificate. All the elders signed too; these men had faithfully provided financial support toward my college expenses for four years. What an encouragement to my preparation for ministry! The whole congregation celebrated with me with a decorated cake and punch. I have always felt obligated to that little church for my ministry, because the Christians there were the ones who set me apart for special service to the Lord.

Most of the people who were influential in directing my life into full-time Christian ministry are now gone. But their influence is still there. The echoes of the ordination service still ring in my heart. The obligation of commitment and responsibility still rests on my shoulders. I can still feel the hands of the elders on my head. My knees ached as several prayers were spoken to God on my behalf while I knelt before the congregation. The mood was serious. The moment has lasted a lifetime.

I think God still invites His people to gather to recognize and celebrate a person's call to specialized service. It should never be lightly planned or executed. A call to full-time, specialized ministry is by God's grace, and the church is obligated to support and affirm the call.

B. Lesson Background

The institution of the priesthood in Leviticus 8:1–10:20 continues the historical narrative woven through Exodus 25–40. Of those 16 chapters, Exodus 28 and 29 form the primary background to Leviticus 8 for today.

We may be amazed that Yahweh God allowed Aaron to be the high priest for the people after his participation in the incident of the golden calf of Exodus 32! Aaron's lame excuse (Exodus 32:22-24) did nothing for his character. But because God is "merciful and gracious, long-suffering, and abundant in goodness and truth" (Exodus 34:6), Aaron was allowed to be Israel's high priest to God.

Instructions for making priestly garments are given in Exodus 28 and then carried out in Exodus 39. Elaborate instructions for the consecration of Aaron and his sons are found in Exodus 29, while a summary of this same ceremony is given in Exodus 40:12-16. All of these instructions and making of the sacred garments are presupposed by the narrative of Leviticus 8:1–10:20.

Thus, Leviticus 8–10 recounts how the priesthood was instituted and how the first sacrifices were offered. The fact that two of Aaron's sons died at the Lord's hand when they offered "strange fire" (Leviticus 10:1, 2) emphasized the need for strict obedience and holiness by the priests. So this ordination service for Aaron and his sons was elaborate, serious, and holy. The purpose for all these ceremonies was for God to dwell in the midst of the Israelites (Exodus 29:43-46).

I. God's Instructions
(Leviticus 8:1-3)

A. Everything Needed (vv. 1, 2)

1, 2. And the LORD spake unto Moses, saying, Take Aaron and his sons with him, and the garments, and the anointing oil, and a bullock for the sin offering, and two rams, and a basket of unleavened bread.

God begins to speak to *Moses* in order to give him specific instructions concerning the ordination of *Aaron and his sons*. Leviticus 8 is a general account based on the more detailed instructions in Exodus 28, 29; for example, the nature of *the garments* is detailed in Exodus 28:4-43 (noted below). The actual making of the garments is recorded in Exodus 39:1-31. We remember that Aaron is Moses' older brother.

The anointing oil that Moses is to use is described in detail in Exodus 30:22-33 (compare 25:6). The oil is a unique combination of myrrh (balsam sap), cinnamon (bark of the cinnamon tree, a species of laurel), calamus (pith from the root of a reed plant), cassia (from the cinnamon tree), and olive oil. Everything and everyone who is to be anointed is to be anointed with this oil. It is not to be reproduced or used for any other purpose (Exodus 30:31-33).

The sacrificial animals are to be "without blemish," according to Exodus 29:1. The details as to

how the animals are to be sacrificed, the blood administered, and the meat used is given in both Exodus 29:10-37 and Leviticus 8:14-36.

These sacrifices are to be repeated over a seven-day period (Exodus 29:35-37; Leviticus 8:33-35). This is the length of time for the full ordination of Aaron and his sons and the sanctifying of everything connected with the tabernacle and the priestly service. The nature of the *basket of unleavened bread* is spelled out in more detail in Exodus 29:2, 3.

B. Everyone to Gather (v. 3)

3. And gather thou all the congregation together unto the door of the tabernacle of the congregation.

It is obvious that the phrase *all the congregation* is not intended to signify the absolute entirety of the Israelite people. That would be several hundred thousand individuals all trying to *gather* at *the door of the tabernacle*!

Instead, it is a group of elders representing the congregation that is to come together. Such representation is implied on several occasions: (1) gifts to build the tabernacle in Exodus 35:4-9, (2) the census of Numbers 1:18, (3) the dedication of Levites in Numbers 8:9, and (4) an instance of water from a rock in Numbers 20:8. Naturally, such representation may be expanded or reduced according to the circumstances.

II. Moses' Actions
(Leviticus 8:4-13)

A. Gathering (v. 4)

4. And Moses did as the LORD commanded him; and the assembly was gathered together unto the door of the tabernacle of the congregation.

Moses is a key figure throughout this narrative. He is unique, for God speaks to Moses "mouth to mouth" (Numbers 12:8). No other person has that privilege. Moses acts as a priest before the priesthood is established with Aaron and his sons. Therefore, it is imperative for Moses to obey the Lord's commands to the letter (contrast Leviticus 10:1, 2).

B. Instructing (v. 5)

5. And Moses said unto the congregation, This is the thing which the LORD commanded to be done.

Today's lesson text is punctuated four times by the phrase "as the Lord commanded Moses" or very close to it (here and vv. 4, 9, 13). The vital importance of this phrase is further revealed when we see it occur at least 16 times in Leviticus 8–10.

How to Say It

AARON. *Air*-un.
CALAMUS. *ka*-luh-mus.
CASSIA. *ka*-shuh.
LEVITICUS. Leh-*vit*-ih-kus.
MYRRH. mur.
POMEGRANATES. *pom*-ih-gran-its.
THUMMIM. *Thum*-im (*th* as in *thin*).
URIM. *You*-rim.
YAHWEH *(Hebrew)*. *Yah*-weh.

This assures the reader that all that is being done with regard to Aaron and his sons is by divine authority. [See question #1, page 400.]

C. Washing (v. 6)

6. And Moses brought Aaron and his sons, and washed them with water.

The word *brought* may carry the idea of a presentation of an offering before God. Thus *Moses may be seen as presenting Aaron and his sons* before the congregation as if they are "offerings" for God. And they are. One is reminded what the apostle Paul wrote concerning all Christians: "I beseech you therefore, brethren, by the mercies of God, that ye present your bodies a living sacrifice, holy, acceptable unto God, which is your reasonable service" (Romans 12:1).

Exodus 30:17-21 describes a laver of brass that is filled with *water* for the regular, ritual washings of Aaron and his sons. They have to become clean before anything else can be done (Exodus 29:4; 40:12). This is a matter of life and death: "So they shall wash their hands and their feet, that they die not" (Exodus 30:21). [See question #2, page 400.]

It is likely that the initial washing is a complete immersion rather than simply the hands and feet as on other, "normal" occasions (Exodus 30:19-21). For the Day of Atonement the high priest has to be immersed entirely (Leviticus 16:4, 24).

The washing of Aaron and his sons has its counterpart in the washing of the parts of the animals for sacrifice (see Exodus 29:17; Leviticus 1:9, 13; 8:21; 9:14). The author of Hebrews uses this idea for Christian baptism: "Let us draw near with a true heart in full assurance of faith, having our hearts sprinkled from an evil conscience, and our bodies washed with pure water" (Hebrews 10:22).

Home Daily Bible Readings

Monday, July 13—We Are God's (Psalm 100)

Tuesday, July 14—Sanctify the Congregation (Joel 2:12-16)

Wednesday, July 15—The Ministry of Generosity (2 Corinthians 9:6-12)

Thursday, July 16—Doing the Father's Will (Matthew 21:28-32)

Friday, July 17—Present Your Bodies (Romans 11:33—12:2)

Saturday, July 18—The Example Christ Left (Romans 15:1-6)

Sunday, July 19—Consecrated for Service (Leviticus 8:1-13)

D. Robing (v. 7)

7. And he put upon him the coat, and girded him with the girdle, and clothed him with the robe, and put the ephod upon him, and he girded him with the curious girdle of the ephod, and bound it unto him therewith.

The way the high priest dresses is a symbol of his high position before God and the people. That is the reason his attire is described in such detail in Exodus 28 and 39. Combining those texts with the text before us reveals that the high priest's clothing consists of breeches, *coat, girdle,* bonnet, *robe, ephod,* breastplate, and mitre (turban). The details are interesting.

The breeches, not mentioned here in Leviticus 8:7, are short drawers made of fine twined linen (Exodus 39:28). This article of clothing reaches from the loins to the thighs. They are to cover the priest's nakedness (Exodus 28:42).

The coat is made of fine linen, all in one piece in the loom; it has sleeves, and it reaches from the neck to the feet. The English translation *embroider* of Exodus 28:39 attempts to capture the idea that it is woven in squares or checker work. This gives it a dazzling look in pure white.

The girdle is something like a sash. Finely made by the weavers, it also is of white linen, but includes blue, purple, and scarlet thread as well (Exodus 39:29). It is wrapped around the waist several times to bind the loose garments to the body. The loose end hangs down to the ankles. When at work, the priest can throw the end over his shoulder to keep it out of the way. If the priest is walking or running, he can use it to hold up the skirts of his garments, hence the phrase "gird up the loins" (1 Peter 1:13).

The bonnet, not mentioned here in Leviticus 8:7, is the last of the pure white garments (Exodus 39:28). It is a solid piece of cloth wrapped several times to resemble a crown, sewn so as not to lose its shape.

The robe reaches from the neck to a little below the knees. This allows the white checkered coat to be seen at the feet. The robe, blue in color, has no sleeves, just an opening for the head (Exodus 39:22-26; compare Numbers 15:37-40). All around the hem of this blue coat is an ornamental fringe of golden bells alternating with pomegranates (Exodus 28:33-35). The bells make a sound as the high priest enters the Holy Place and the Holy of Holies once a year, perhaps giving God notice that the only authorized person is about to enter His presence.

The ephod is a richly colored vestment that reaches from the shoulders to a little above the knees. Shoulderpieces bind back and front together. The ephod is made of beautiful cloth that features the colors gold, blue, purple, and scarlet. On the shoulderpieces are set 2 onyx stones. Engraved on them are the names of the 12 tribes (Exodus 28:6-12).

There is a girdle made of the same material to hold the ephod close to the body. In the antique English of the *King James Version*, the phrase *curious girdle* signifies something like "waistband." [See question #3, page 400.] We will discuss the breastplate and mitre (turban) below.

HOW SHOULD MINISTERS DRESS?

When many of us were growing up, ministers had a "uniform"; it consisted of white shirt, tie, dark suit, and hat. A Bible under the arm when one was to be seen in public was also not a bad idea. A minister who drove a sporty coupe or convertible indicated someone who did not take either his life or his calling seriously. Even driving a sedan in a color other than black, dark blue, or green was a no-no.

One evangelist was holding a revival meeting back in the 1950s and was lodging in the home of a local minister. He arrived at his host's breakfast table in dress pants and a tieless dress shirt. The (older) minister who was his host sat down wearing both tie and suit coat. The guest asked, "Do you have a funeral this morning?" The host's wife said, "No. In our many years of married life, he has never appeared at breakfast less than fully dressed."

Such a standard seems quaint and unimaginable today. Ministers appear on Main Street wearing jeans; they drive red convertibles; some even (gasp) ride motorcycles! Reflecting a less formal culture, it is not uncommon to see leaders of contemporary worship services dressed in khakis and sport shirts. Clothing styles change with the times. But what should not change is the leader's character. That is the message of both Old and New Testaments for those who would lead the people of God. —C. R. B.

E. Breastplate (v. 8)

8. And he put the breastplate upon him: also he put in the breastplate the Urim and the Thummim.

Details about *the breastplate* are found in Exodus 28:15-30, with a parallel in Exodus 39:8-21. The first of these two descriptions is God's instructions; the second description relates how the instructions for making the breastplate are carried out.

The breastplate is square, about 9 inches long and broad (Exodus 28:16). The cloth is doubled, being made of the same material as the ephod (28:15). It has to be strong enough to hold 12 precious stones. The precious stones represent the 12 tribes of Israel (28:17-20).

The breastplate is connected to the ephod by means of gold rings and chains (Exodus 28:27, 28). Within the breastplate is placed *the Urim and the Thummim* (28:30). The names of these two stones probably mean "light" and "perfection," but scholars still debate their meaning and how they are to be used. They are a means of getting a negative or positive answer from God on any given question or concern of the people (see Numbers 27:21; Deuteronomy 33:8; 1 Samuel 28:6; Ezra 2:63; and Nehemiah 7:65).

F. Turban (v. 9)

9. And he put the mitre upon his head; also upon the mitre, even upon his forefront, did he put the golden plate, the holy crown; as the LORD commanded Moses.

Those not familiar with the word *mitre* should think in terms of a turban. We have already discussed the high priest's "bonnet" previously, but the mitre is different in that it has a *plate* of pure gold attached to the front by means of a blue ribbon (Exodus 28:36-38).

On the gold plate is inscribed the phrase HOLINESS TO THE LORD (again, Exodus 28:36-38). The high priest, representing all of Israel, is to live a life of holiness before Yahweh God. Only then can the sacrifices be acceptable before God.

G. Tabernacle (v. 10)

10. And Moses took the anointing oil, and anointed the tabernacle and all that was therein, and sanctified them.

Everything connected with worship at *the tabernacle* is now *anointed* with the special *oil* that we described earlier. The anointing sanctifies the furniture and thus reserves it for sacred use only. The furnishings of the tabernacle are described in Exodus 30:26-28 (compare 40:9-11). [See question #4, page 400.]

H. Altar (v. 11)

11. And he sprinkled thereof upon the altar seven times, and anointed the altar and all his vessels, both the laver and his foot, to sanctify them.

The brazen *altar* used for animal sacrifices is sanctified by sprinkling oil on it *seven times*. Compared with the anointing of the other furniture, this shows the importance of this altar. This altar and *the laver* are the two "outside" pieces of tabernacle furniture—one for sacrifice and one for washings.

I. Aaron (v. 12)

12. And he poured of the anointing oil upon Aaron's head, and anointed him, to sanctify him.

Now Aaron himself is *anointed*. As kings will later be anointed to symbolize the empowering by the Spirit of God (see 1 Samuel 16:3, 13), so also are priests and prophets. The scene of Aaron's ordination is marked so indelibly in the Israelite consciousness that King David can use it as a figure of speech for unity some 400 years later per Psalm 133. Only the Spirit can give unity and blessing. [See question #5, page 400.]

AROMATHERAPY NOT NEEDED

Anointing with oil has become a big business since the arrival of the New Age era. For example, a Web site for "chakra therapy" capitalizes on the sacred implications of the word *anoint* by calling itself just that. This site states, "Your Chakras store, filter, and regulate the flow of energy in and out of the body." We are further advised that negative spiritual and emotional vibrations can interfere with good chakras, and thus we need aromatherapy since "such vibrations that can be found in sounds, colour, nature, gemstones, [and] spiritual healing."

This supposed wisdom has been gleaned from "Indian seers [and] wise men." The Christian worldview that once undergirded Western society is decaying. Now, gullible Western minds are replacing a righteous God's moral claims on sinful humanity with a mix of Eastern mysticism and other philosophies.

As the worship system of ancient Israel was being firmed up, tabernacle, altar, and priests were sanctified by being anointed with oil. The difference between this anointing and modern,

Visual for Lesson 7. *Point to this visual as you ask, "In what capacity do you think God has called you to serve? How did you reach this conclusion?"*

eclectic practices is to be found in the concept of *sanctification*, as things and people were *set apart* for God's service. When the New Testament calls Christians priests and saints, it is making the same statement about what our lifestyles should be. We are to live as God wants us to, trusting Christ, not the "magic" of Eastern mysticism! —C. R. B.

J. Aaron's Sons (v. 13)

13. And Moses brought Aaron's sons, and put coats upon them, and girded them with girdles, and put bonnets upon them; as the LORD commanded Moses.

The *sons* wear the simple white clothing that the high priest has on underneath the ephod, breastplate, and blue robe (Exodus 39:27, 28). Nothing in this passage says anything about the sons' anointing, but Exodus 28:41; 30:30; 40:14, 15; Leviticus 7:35, 36; 10:7; and Numbers 3:3 establish that they are indeed anointed.

Conclusion

A. Commissioning for Service

Today, we have a high priest far greater than Aaron (Hebrews 4:14). Jesus ever lives to intercede on our behalf and save us completely (Hebrews 7:23-25). At the outset, I talked about my ordination, but remember that all who follow Christ are called priests (1 Peter 2:5; Revelation 1:6). In fact, the church as a whole is a "royal priesthood" (1 Peter 2:9; compare Exodus 19:6). Thus every Christian is commissioned for service as a priest. As priests, we can offer intercessory prayer (Hebrews 13:18; etc.). We pray for healing for the sick (James 5:14, 15) as part of this priestly duty and privilege.

We recognize God's special call on a person's life by honoring that person by public recognition and celebration. This is well and good. But we may also think of a person's conversion to Christ as an ordination to priesthood. May God increase our royal priesthood!

B. Prayer

Our Father, we recognize persons of special skills and abilities that You are calling into specialized ministry. But may we also remember that You have called each and every one of us to Your royal priesthood. May we never forget that priesthood requires holiness. In the name of our great high priest, Jesus the Christ. Amen.

C. Thought to Remember

Strive toward holiness
in your priestly service.

Learning by Doing

This page contains an alternative lesson plan emphasizing learning activities. Some of these activities are also found in the helpful student book, Adult Bible Class.

Into the Lesson

Option #1: Invite a minister to describe an ordination ceremony. The presentation should last five to eight minutes. The guest should briefly tell of the purpose of an ordination, some fond memories of ordinations performed (or of being ordained), and some things that can or should happen in an ordination ceremony. A photocopy of the lesson's Introduction may help this guest shape the presentation. If the minister cannot appear in person, ask if a video presentation can be prepared.

Make the transition to Bible study by saying, "Today's ordination services have a history. In the Old Testament, we find that God used commissioning ceremonies to set apart people to special tasks. Let's look at one of the most important."

Option #2: Use a copy of the *Christian Minister's Manual* (Standard Publishing) to introduce the concept of ordinations. Your minister may have a copy to lend you. Mention the types of ordination (of ministers, elders and other officers, teachers) that are described in the manual. Tell of the common elements of the services that are suggested for these ordination services. Ask what other types of commissioning services are found in our culture. Use the same transition mentioned in Option #1.

Into the Word

Early in the week, ask a class member to assist with the Bible-study portion of the lesson by portraying Moses. Give him a photocopy of today's lesson commentary. Also, give him a copy of the list of questions below so he can think about responses in advance. Further, give him a Bible dictionary with articles on the priesthood and Aaron marked. If you can locate a depiction of the high priest's garment, include it as well. Also provide some props such as a robe, staff, and/or beard.

Begin the Bible study with a reading of the printed text. You can have class members take turns reading two or three verses each. Say, "This ceremony of ordination was elaborate and purposeful. However, there are details about it that we may overlook if we're not careful. I have invited a guest to help us understand this grand ceremony that was commanded by God." Introduce "Moses," saying you have asked him for a brief interview about this ordination event. Ask the following interview questions:

1. "Moses, apparently the ordination of Aaron and his sons was not your idea. It was a 'God thing.' Why do you suppose God wanted a priesthood and a high priest? Why do you think He chose Aaron?"
2. "I'm curious about the elaborate garments designed by the Lord for the priests. Give us a brief description of the garments and your impression of why God thought these were important."
3. "Apparently, the actual ceremony of setting apart these men was very impressive. Describe it for us as best you can remember. Feel free to mention the significance of some of these ceremonial activities."
4. "What values do you see for the average Christian to witness a setting-apart ceremony to unique leadership and service roles in today's church?"
5. "One more question before you leave. All Christians have a high priest far greater than Aaron was in his day. Identify this high priest and tell us what He does for us."

Express gratitude to "Moses" as he leaves. Say to the class, "God has not only given today's believer a high priest in Jesus, but He actually calls every believer a priest. All Christians are commissioned for service as priests."

Into Life

Read 1 Peter 2:4-10. Ask the following two discussion questions. 1. What was your reaction when you first realized that you were part of a royal priesthood? 2. Knowing you have been commissioned as a priest, what are you responsible for doing and thinking? (This can be a small-group discussion for larger classes.)

Say, "Special ceremonies were used not only for commissioning the priesthood, but also in setting apart prophets and kings. In today's church, we still value ceremonies that set leaders apart for service. Ordination or commissioning services are common for ministers and elders. Some churches even have them for teachers."

Ask the class to design a commissioning service for teachers. Four teams can do one each of the following: (1) select songs, (2) select Scriptures, (3) jot ideas about the "charge" or challenge to be read to the teachers, and (4) write a statement for the congregation to make when accepting and commissioning the teachers.

Let's Talk It Over

The questions on this page are designed to promote discussion of the lesson by the class and to encourage application of the lesson Scriptures. The answers provided are only discussion starters. Let your class talk it over from there.

1. How do we know if we are doing what "the Lord commanded to be done"? How do we keep from fooling ourselves in this regard?

Israel could rely on Moses, a man with whom God spoke "mouth to mouth." We too have reliable mouthpieces available to us in the form of the writers of the Bible (who include Moses). It is important for us to measure our actions by the standard of God's Word.

However, the Bible does not provide precise instructions for each and every situation we may encounter. In some instances, we are wise to seek the advice of spiritually mature people, who can keep us from talking ourselves into things that we should not. We do have the privilege of speaking to God directly, so decisions should be bathed in prayer for an appropriate period of time. Ultimately, we must trust God to guide us in the right ways by yielding our hearts and wills to Him.

2. What things disqualify us from holding positions of leadership in ministry, either temporarily or permanently? How do we guard ourselves against such things?

Today's lesson is about Aaron being set apart as the high priest of Israel; God did this despite Aaron's role in the notorious golden calf incident of Exodus 32. While we do not want to entrust ministry positions to novices or charlatans, we all have a history of failings. As with Aaron, we can be consecrated anew and find important ways of serving Christ and His church. Remember that Peter was reinstated after denying Christ (John 21:15-19).

This is not to sidestep or minimize the sexual, financial, and integrity scandals that have rocked Christianity in the last few decades. We must hold ourselves to high standards if we are to be useful and effective in ministry leadership roles.

3. Does the nature of Aaron's clothing say anything about what we should wear to church? Why, or why not?

When clothed in all his finery, Aaron must have presented a spectacular appearance! By contrast, the trend in many churches today is to "dress down," even among those who lead worship services. Many attend church in clothing that is more casual than what is expected at their workplaces.

Dress standards will be different in various countries and regions, but we should consider carefully why God wanted Aaron to be dressed as he was. No one would suggest that we wear ephods, but does casualness in dress indicate casualness in our attitude toward worship? Going in the other direction, will our attempts to "dress up" cause us to stand out and thus draw attention to ourselves and away from Christ? It should go without saying that modesty is to prevail always.

4. Are there places or things within modern church buildings that should be considered holy? Why, or why not?

Moses anointed the tabernacle and its furniture with special oil that served to sanctify those things for God's purposes. The New Testament teaches us that God does not dwell in places that are made with human hands (Acts 7:48). But this does not necessarily mean that there are no holy spaces or dedicated furniture. The table that is used for serving the Lord's Supper is ultimately just a piece of wood, yet we would not wish to see it used as a workbench during a church clean-up day.

A good practice is to view the church building and its distinctive furnishings as tools that are to be reserved for ministry use. Nondistinctive furnishings can be used for nonministry purposes without raising questions of conscience; an example would be lending out some of the church's folding tables for a family reunion.

5. Do you feel like you are a priest? How do we acknowledge and practice this role in our lives as believers?

It is a mistake to view the issue of being a priest as something that is to be restricted to the Old Testament. The New Testament teaches us that we are part of a royal priesthood (1 Peter 2:5, 9), and we should understand what this means. We can offer intercessory prayer. Priests offer sacrifices, and we can all offer a sacrifice of praise to the Lord (Hebrews 13:15). Being part of a community of priests means that we can minister freely to one another. We should not expect someone on the ministerial staff of the church to be the only one performing such functions. We can care for one another as we have opportunity and ability.

Providing a Fresh Start

DEVOTIONAL READING: Matthew 18:21-35.

BACKGROUND SCRIPTURE: Leviticus 25:1-31.

PRINTED TEXT: Leviticus 25:8-21, 23, 24.

Leviticus 25:8-21, 23, 24

8 And thou shalt number seven sabbaths of years unto thee, seven times seven years; and the space of the seven sabbaths of years shall be unto thee forty and nine years.

9 Then shalt thou cause the trumpet of the jubilee to sound on the tenth day of the seventh month, in the day of atonement shall ye make the trumpet sound throughout all your land.

10 And ye shall hallow the fiftieth year, and proclaim liberty throughout all the land unto all the inhabitants thereof: it shall be a jubilee unto you; and ye shall return every man unto his possession, and ye shall return every man unto his family.

11 A jubilee shall that fiftieth year be unto you: ye shall not sow, neither reap that which groweth of itself in it, nor gather the grapes in it of thy vine undressed.

12 For it is the jubilee; it shall be holy unto you: ye shall eat the increase thereof out of the field.

13 In the year of this jubilee ye shall return every man unto his possession.

14 And if thou sell aught unto thy neighbor, or buyest aught of thy neighbor's hand, ye shall not oppress one another:

15 According to the number of years after the jubilee thou shalt buy of thy neighbor, and according unto the number of years of the fruits he shall sell unto thee:

16 According to the multitude of years thou shalt increase the price thereof, and

according to the fewness of years thou shalt diminish the price of it: for according to the number of the years of the fruits doth he sell unto thee.

17 Ye shall not therefore oppress one another; but thou shalt fear thy God: for I am the LORD your God.

18 Wherefore ye shall do my statutes, and keep my judgments, and do them; and ye shall dwell in the land in safety.

19 And the land shall yield her fruit, and ye shall eat your fill, and dwell therein in safety.

20 And if ye shall say, What shall we eat the seventh year? behold, we shall not sow, nor gather in our increase:

21 Then I will command my blessing upon you in the sixth year, and it shall bring forth fruit for three years.

. . . .

23 The land shall not be sold for ever: for the land is mine; for ye are strangers and sojourners with me.

24 And in all the land of your possession ye shall grant a redemption for the land.

GOLDEN TEXT: Ye shall hallow the fiftieth year, and proclaim liberty throughout all the land unto all the inhabitants thereof: it shall be a jubilee unto you; and ye shall return every man unto his possession, and ye shall return every man unto his family.—Leviticus 25:10.

Call Sealed with Promise
Unit 2: Called to Be God's People
(Lessons 5–8)

Lesson Aims

After participating in this lesson, each student will be able to:

1. Summarize the features of the year of jubilee.
2. Tell how the principles of the jubilee year can be expressed in the church.
3. State one way he or she can grant jubilee-like freedom to a brother or sister in Christ.

Lesson Outline

INTRODUCTION
    A. Announcing Jubilee
    B. Lesson Background
I. CONCEPT OF JUBILEE (Leviticus 25:8-12)
    A. Calculation (v. 8)
    B. Proclamation (v. 9)
      Trumpeted Celebration
    C. Consecration (v. 10)
    D. Restriction (vv. 11, 12)
II. RETURN DURING JUBILEE (Leviticus 25:13-17)
    A. Reclaim Family Property (v. 13)
    B. Restrict Undue Advantage (vv. 14-17)
III. OBEDIENCE TO GOD (Leviticus 25:18-21)
    A. Mandate and Benefit (vv. 18, 19)
    B. Question and Answer (vv. 20, 21)
IV. PROVISION OF REDEMPTION (Leviticus 25:23, 24)
    A. What Not to Do (v. 23)
      Land Ownership
    B. What to Do (v. 24)
CONCLUSION
    A. The Jubilee Ideal and Practice
    B. New Testament Jubilee
    C. Prayer
    D. Thought to Remember

Introduction

A. Announcing Jubilee

At a certain point very early in Jesus' ministry, He returned to His hometown of Nazareth (Luke 4:14-30). Luke reports that He went there "in the power of the Spirit," and He went into the synagogue "as his custom was." Isaiah the prophet was the reading for that particular Sabbath.

Jesus, considered to be a special guest, unrolled the scroll to the place we know as Isaiah 61:1, 2.

There He read "The Spirit of the Lord is upon me, because he hath anointed me to preach the gospel to the poor; he hath sent me to heal the brokenhearted, to preach deliverance to the captives, and recovering of sight to the blind, to set at liberty them that are bruised, to preach the acceptable year of the Lord" (Luke 4:18, 19).

After giving the scroll back to the attendant, Jesus sat down to teach about this text. The congregation was startled to hear Him say "This day is this Scripture fulfilled in your ears."

Jesus had just announced a kind of "jubilee" with the beginning of His preaching, teaching, and healing ministry. In essence, He had claimed to be the Messiah, for the rabbis anticipated such a jubilee when the Messiah would come. Those gathered couldn't believe it! "Is not this Joseph's son?" they asked rhetorically. Jesus pushed back by saying "Ye will surely say unto me this proverb, Physician, heal thyself" and "No prophet is accepted in his own country."

Jesus went on to apply His announcement of jubilee by mentioning God's concern for Gentiles, such as the Sidonian widow (1 Kings 17:7-24) and Naaman, the Syrian leper (2 Kings 5). In other words, the genuine Messiah's jubilee would be for the whole world, including Gentiles.

This enraged the congregation to the point that they acted as an angry mob. They attempted (but failed) to cast Him down from the brow of the Nazareth hill. How could Jesus' hometown move so quickly from treating Him as a special guest to seeing Him only as "Joseph's son" and then to having a willingness to murder Him as a false prophet? Perhaps today's study on *jubilee* will shed light on this question.

B. Lesson Background

The concept of *Sabbath* (which means "ceasing") is built into the fabric of the story of creation (Genesis 2:1-3; see Leviticus 23:3). In six days God created the world and everything in it. On the seventh day God halted His labors and declared it a "cease day." When God "created" Israel by delivering the nation from bondage, He provided in the wilderness a Sabbath-manna (Exodus 16). On the sixth day of the week, the people collected twice their daily need. If they went out on the Sabbath, they would find none. The people had to exercise faith with regard to the Sabbath day.

In addition to the Sabbath day was the Sabbath year, described in Exodus 23:10, 11; Leviticus 25:1-7 (just prior to today's text); and Deuteronomy 15:1-18. Every seventh year was a Sabbath year, during which all debts had to be canceled (Deuteronomy 15:1, 2). The Year of Jubilee, what may be called "a Sabbath of the Sabbath year," was an extension of this concept. This is where today's lesson picks up.

I. Concept of Jubilee (Leviticus 25:8-12)

A. Calculation (v. 8)

8. And thou shalt number seven sabbaths of years unto thee, seven times seven years; and the space of the seven sabbaths of years shall be unto thee forty and nine years.

A special Sabbath year must be observed every 50 years. This is known as *the Year of Jubilee,* as we shall see below. Its design is such that every Israelite who lives a normal lifetime will experience this special year at least once. The calculation *seven times seven* is obviously simple. But alongside this simplicity is the elegance of the number *seven* as part and parcel of the concept of Sabbath (see the Lesson Background).

B. Proclamation (v. 9)

9. Then shalt thou cause the trumpet of the jubilee to sound on the tenth day of the seventh month, in the day of atonement shall ye make the trumpet sound throughout all your land.

Some scholars think that the meaning of the word *jubilee* is literally "ram's horn." This makes a certain sense, due to the fact that a ram's horn is what is to be blown to announce the jubilee. (We should not think of a *trumpet* here in terms of the modern brass musical instrument!)

The seventh month, in which *the day of atonement* occurs, is late September and early October to us. The designation *seventh month* is in reference to the cycle of the Israelite religious year, although this particular month eventually becomes the first month of the Jewish civil year. A full explanation of the Day of Atonement is found

How to Say It

GENTILES. *Jen*-tiles.
LEVITICUS. Leh-*vit*-ih-kus.
MOSES. *Mo*-zes or *Mo*-zez.
NAAMAN. *Nay*-uh-mun.
NABOTH. *Nay*-bawth.
NAZARETH. *Naz*-uh-reth.
PEONAGE. *pea*-uh-nij.
SIDONIAN. Sigh-*doe*-nee-un.
SYNAGOGUE. *sin*-uh-gog.
SYRIAN. *Sear*-ee-un.
YAHWEH *(Hebrew).* *Yah*-weh.
ZELOPHEHAD. Zeh-*low*-feh-had.

in Leviticus 16:29-34; see also 23:26-32. The greatest of releases in ancient Hebrew experience is to be the annual release of sins on this day. The tabernacle (or temple) is to be sanctified once again, and the people are to have their collective sins atoned for by means of the high priest's sprinkling of goat blood on top of the ark covering. What better time, then, to begin the Year of Jubilee in signaling, in part, the release from debts?

TRUMPETED CELEBRATION

Trumpets are ancient instruments, having been used for a variety of purposes. Apparently, early human tribes formed shells, bamboo, or animal horns into trumpets in order to communicate with each other. Before the invention of the radio, army generals had to figure out how to communicate with their troops on the battlefield. Trumpets served this purpose (compare 1 Corinthians 14:8). Evidence suggests that trumpets were used in religious services as early as 2000 BC. Moses had two trumpets of silver made for communicating with the Israelites (Numbers 10:2).

Many of these ancient instruments were straight tubes with curved bells. Modern trumpets are "folded" instruments, consisting of several feet of tubing. Valves, developed in the early nineteenth century, divert air into side chambers, allowing precise changes in pitch. Valves greatly improve trumpets' usefulness as musical instruments.

But even in ancient times, before trumpets had valves, trumpets were used on happy occasions of celebration. One such occasion was the Day of Atonement in the Year of Jubilee. The most joyous celebration that a trumpet will ever introduce, however, will be the return of Jesus (1 Corinthians 15:52; 1 Thessalonians 4:16). Expect it! —J. B. N.

C. Consecration (v. 10)

10. And ye shall hallow the fiftieth year, and proclaim liberty throughout all the land unto all the inhabitants thereof: it shall be a jubilee unto you; and ye shall return every man unto his possession, and ye shall return every man unto his family.

The Israelite nation is built on three tiers: the household, the clan, and the tribe (see Numbers 26; Judges 6:15). Jubilee is designed to protect the household's right to a particular piece of land (see the distribution of land in Numbers 26 and Joshua 13–21; compare Judges 21:24 and 1 Kings 21:1-3). Jubilee, *the fiftieth year,* is the year in which all debts are to be rescinded. Further, all Israelites who have indentured themselves into debt-slavery are to be released so they can return to their own possessions and household (extended *family*).

What a joy! The concepts of freedom and restoration come over into the New Testament era in profound, eternal ways through Jesus (see the lesson's Introduction). [See question #1, page 408.]

D. Restriction (vv. 11, 12)

11, 12. A jubilee shall that fiftieth year be unto you: ye shall not sow, neither reap that which groweth of itself in it, nor gather the grapes in it of thy vine undressed. For it is the jubilee; it shall be holy unto you: ye shall eat the increase thereof out of the field.

In addition to release from debt and the return of land, the land must lie fallow for *the jubilee*. It is to be a holy year, devoted to genuine rest for humans, animals, and land. No sowing is allowed, but one and all can certainly *eat* from the *field*, meaning the open country. [See question #2, page 408.]

II. Return During Jubilee (Leviticus 25:13-17)

A. Reclaim Family Property (v. 13)

13. In the year of this jubilee ye shall return every man unto his possession.

This is a repeat of part of verse 10. The purpose of repeating this statement is to emphasize the nature of land in Israel. No one owns the land (see v. 23, below); only the use of the land, in terms of harvests, is sold (v. 16, below). So any "sale" of land is really a form of leasing. Fuller explanation follows. [See question #3, page 408.]

B. Restrict Undue Advantage (vv. 14-17)

14. And if thou sell aught unto thy neighbor, or buyest aught of thy neighbor's hand, ye shall not oppress one another.

The command not to *oppress one another* is repeated in verse 17. Thus this repeated command serves as bookends for what is said in verses 15, 16.

15, 16. According to the number of years after the jubilee thou shalt buy of thy neighbor, and according unto the number of years of the fruits he shall sell unto thee: according to the multitude of years thou shalt increase the price thereof, and according to the fewness of years thou shalt diminish the price of it: for according to the number of the years of the fruits doth he sell unto thee.

Sale of land is to be regulated according to the *number of years* until a *jubilee* is proclaimed. The cost is calculated according to how many harvests remain before the jubilee, when the land is to be restored to ancestral ownership. The one who "buys" the land thus is leasing rather than purchasing.

The importance of family property is seen in the inquiry of Zelophehad's five daughters in Numbers 27:1-11. Since their father died without leaving any sons, they feared their father's name would disappear from the clan. An allowance of property to the daughters would ensure that the family name could continue.

A follow-up inquiry in Numbers 36 clarifies further still what is (and is not) to happen. Thus the jubilee procedure we see spelled out here is tied closely to household, clan, and tribal identities.

17. Ye shall not therefore oppress one another; but thou shalt fear thy God: for I am the LORD your God.

The exhortation not to *oppress one another* is repeated from verse 14. This exhortation is based on the *fear* of *God* that the people are to have. Thus we get the idea that economic oppression is carried out by those who do not fear God (see Proverbs 1:7).

The very fact that Yahweh is their God should cause the Israelites to value their relationships with each other by not oppressing one another economically. The sad story of Naboth and his vineyard reveals that even an Israelite king is not to force a fellow Hebrew to sell the family property (1 Kings 21, especially v. 3). What happened to Naboth is an example of the arrogance of power.

III. Obedience to God (Leviticus 25:18-21)

A. Mandate and Benefit (vv. 18, 19)

18. Wherefore ye shall do my statutes, and keep my judgments, and do them; and ye shall dwell in the land in safety.

We sometimes sing the old hymn "Trust and Obey." The Israelites are first to obey the Lord and then trust that He will provide the resources for them to live *in the land in safety*. This is the essential message of the book of Deuteronomy (see 28:1-14 for the blessings of obedience). To disobey is to be thrust from the land (29:25-28). [See question #4, page 408.]

19. And the land shall yield her fruit, and ye shall eat your fill, and dwell therein in safety.

When God's people obey the Lord in terms of jubilee, He blesses them beyond their imagination. To practice jubilee takes faith and even courage. "Can we survive by letting *the land* lie fallow?" the people may ask themselves. The Lord knows such a question will pop up, so He answers it in the next verse.

B. Question and Answer (vv. 20, 21)

20, 21. And if ye shall say, What shall we eat the seventh year? behold, we shall not sow, nor gather in our increase: then I will command my

blessing upon you in the sixth year, and it shall bring forth fruit for three years.

A good salesperson anticipates objections before they come up. God, the master salesman, does just that. He knows the people will hesitate to let the land lie fallow out of a concern for having enough to *eat*. This anxiety is not just about the jubilee year, but also concerns the Sabbath-years of Leviticus 25:1-7.

God gives a promise, and the people must trust! He fed them during all those years in the wilderness, didn't He? As He promises food during the fallow Sabbath-years (again 25:1-7), so He promises food during the Year of Jubilee.

IV. Provision of Redemption (Leviticus 25:23, 24)

A. What Not to Do (v. 23)

23. The land shall not be sold for ever: for the land is mine; for ye are strangers and sojourners with me.

Although the *land* is an inheritance to the Israelites (Leviticus 20:24), it ultimately belongs to God. Thus the Israelites should think of themselves as tenants. Since God is the owner, the land can only be leased, with the price being set by the number of harvests until the next jubilee.

To the phrase *strangers and sojourners* we may compare the phrase "strangers and pilgrims" in 1 Peter 2:11. These phrases speak to the mind-set that God's people are to have. (Contrast the use of the word *entitlement* that is thrown around so much today.) The strangers-and-sojourners outlook is to keep the ancient Israelites from having a wrong perspective. God is the real owner of the land. Under His protection and care, the people can experience the good of the land. These facts set the standard by which they are to treat one another. Treatment of the poor and those who have had to sell themselves into debt-slavery is of special concern (see Leviticus 25:35-43, 47-53).

For our part, we must remind ourselves continually that an attachment to the things of this world is deadly. The world itself is good (Genesis 1:31), but we do not own it. The principles of this world are bad, and we are to reject them (Colossians 2:8). Either way, we should be strangers to that which passes away (1 Corinthians 7:31). [See question #5, page 408.]

LAND OWNERSHIP

As settlers from Europe began to arrive in the new world, one of the most distressing points of contention to emerge between them and the American Indians was the issue of land owner-

Visual for Lesson 8. *Point to this visual as you ask, "What biblical safeguards do we have to help us not take advantage of others?"*

ship. Many explorers representing European royalty claimed land in the name of their sovereign. In the process, these explorers ignored the native peoples already established in the land.

Sometimes settlers purchased land from the Indians; think of the (in)famous purchase of Manhattan Island for about $24 worth of trade goods. On occasion, Indian leaders protested the whole idea of buying and selling land. In the early nineteenth century, Chief Tecumseh reacted, "Why not sell the air, the clouds, the great sea?" Many Indians could not understand the concept of "owning" land. Certain tribes might have hunting rights, agricultural investment, or occupation of the land, but how could anyone *own* the land?

God had given the promised land to the Israelites. They had possessed it, dividing it among the 12 tribes. But God said that ownership of land could not be transferred "for the land is mine." We would do well to apply that outlook to our own property today. Sure, we hold titles of ownership to our houses, cars, etc. And we're free to buy and sell such things as we see fit. But it all really belongs to God; we are the stewards. —J. B. N.

B. What to Do (v. 24)

24. And in all the land of your possession ye shall grant a redemption for the land.

Leviticus 25:23-38 discusses the details concerning the law of *redemption for the land* (compare Ruth 4; Jeremiah 32:6-8). Over several decades, an astute person can accumulate much land and become very wealthy. Rich landowners will have free reign with those caught in the spiral of poverty that can lead to permanent debt-slavery (the modern term for this is *peonage*). After selling land to pay off a debt, a person in economic distress loses the primary means of earning a living.

Jubilee prevents the land from being sold permanently (vv. 23-38) and keeps the debt-slaves from being in that condition indefinitely (vv. 39-55). In jubilee, land "ownership" reverts back and the slaves are set free. These are not rules to be sprung unfairly on someone who, unaware of jubilee provisions, has already paid for some land.

Conclusion

A. The Jubilee Ideal and Practice

Jubilee was to be the year in which (1) liberty was proclaimed for all Israelites who were enslaved for debt; (2) the remission of debt occurred; (3) land was restored to families who had been compelled to sell it in the previous 49 years; and (4) the land had to lie fallow. This is described fully in Leviticus 25:8-55 and referred to in Leviticus 27:16-25 and Numbers 36:4.

Jubilee thus was in large part God's loudspeaker of care for the poor. God has always been concerned for the poor. This is why the farmer was commanded not to glean the corners of his field (Leviticus 19:9, 10; 23:22; Ruth 2:2). The harvest in such areas was to be left for the poor. Jubilee was God's gift to the destitute and despairing, providing them a fresh start. Can this practice teach us something today?

We also may wonder if Israel ever practiced jubilee as a nation. We don't really have any firm evidence that they did (Isaiah 37:30 is a possible reference to jubilee ideas). We know that the generation that followed Moses rebelled against God and His laws (Judges 2:10-13). The lack of reference to jubilee in the historical narratives of the Old Testament does not mean that jubilee was not practiced. That would be an argument from silence. We simply do not know.

After Solomon's reign, the kingdoms of Israel and Judah were ruled by many kings who would not have welcomed the practice of jubilee. Other ancient Near Eastern kingdoms did practice the remission of debts at the accession of a new king, but nothing exactly like jubilee. Despite its possible disuse, the prophets appeal to the jubilee ideal metaphorically as part of the coming kingdom of God (example: Isaiah 61:1-3).

B. New Testament Jubilee

The "servant" of Isaiah has a jubilee-like ministry to restore Israel to the "land" (see Isaiah 35, 42, 58, 61). Jesus saw himself as that servant when He announced His jubilee ministry to those of His hometown (see the lesson's Introduction). But they rejected Him. Even so, Jesus inaugurated His ministry with the concept of jubilee in mind; forgiveness of the sin debt and restoration of relationship to God were key features of the proclamation of the kingdom. The first-century church proclaimed Jesus' idea of a kingdom characterized by a jubilee spirit (see Acts 4:32-37). The thought of "restoring" was jubilee vocabulary (Acts 1:6; 3:21).

As the church proclaims the eternal jubilee available in Christ, she needs to discern if she is practicing an earthly jubilee ideal as Jesus would have us do. Yet as we engage in prayer and soul searching in this regard, we will be careful not to "read into" the New Testament an Old Testament law that was operative only for ancient Israel.

The jubilee principle as stated by Paul to the Corinthians is this: "By an equality, that now at this time your abundance may be a supply for their want, that their abundance also may be a supply for your want: that there may be equality: as it is written, He that had gathered much had nothing over; and he that had gathered little had no lack" (2 Corinthians 8:14, 15). Practicing this ideal will be easier when we come to grips with the fact that we are "strangers and pilgrims" here (again, 1 Peter 2:11).

C. Prayer

Our Father, teach us to forgive as we have been forgiven, to give as we have been given to, and to love as we have been loved. In the comfort of Your sovereign provisions and the name of our Savior Jesus Christ. Amen.

D. Thought to Remember

Practice both the eternal and earthly ideals of jubilee in Christ.

Home Daily Bible Readings

Monday, July 20—Jesus' Vision of Ministry (Luke 4:14-19)

Tuesday, July 21—Forgiveness and Mercy (Matthew 18:21-35)

Wednesday, July 22—Compassion and Mercy (Luke 10:25-37)

Thursday, July 23—Compassion for the Helpless (Matthew 9:35-38)

Friday, July 24—Compassion for the Bereaved (Luke 7:11-17)

Saturday, July 25—Ministry to the Needy (Matthew 25:31-40)

Sunday, July 26—The Year of Jubilee (Leviticus 25:8-21, 23, 24)

Learning by Doing

This page contains an alternative lesson plan emphasizing learning activities. Some of these activities are also found in the helpful student book, Adult Bible Class.

Into the Lesson

Display the phrase *Fresh Start* on the board. Say, "There are many areas of life where people may long for a fresh start. What are some of those areas?"

Jot responses on the board. Some ideas include money management, marriage, spiritual disciplines, relationships with children, relationships with parents, relationships with the Lord, education, and career. Be ready to stimulate class thinking by offering examples.

Make the transition to Bible study by saying, "The concept of a fresh start is very appealing to those in trouble. God had a wonderful plan for a periodic fresh start for the Old Testament Israelites. From the Old Testament principle of jubilee, I believe we'll find great lessons for the church today."

Into the Word

Early in the week, ask a class member to prepare a brief lecture (about five minutes) on the Lesson Background. Give this person a photocopy of the Lesson Background from the commentary. Also give this person three strips of poster board on which you've written (one phrase each) these three words/phrases: *Sabbath Day, Sabbath Year,* and *Jubilee.* Ask your guest speaker to affix these small posters to the wall as each concept is defined in succession.

After the presentation, thank the speaker and say, "Wouldn't you find it a real joy to discover that all your debts are released? What a fresh start that would be! Let's read to see how the jubilee concept was to work."

Distribute a handout of today's printed text from Leviticus 25. You will need to create this handout so students can write on it. Then lead the class through the following sequence:

1. Read verses 8-10. Use the lesson commentary to explain to the class the concept of *atonement.* Also, note the three-tier structure of Old Testament Israel.

2. Ask your students to underline on their handouts everything the Israelites were to *do* during jubilee and circle everything they were *not* to do. Ask two class members to serve as "scribes" to list the *do* and *not do* answers on the board as findings are shared.

3. Ask the following three discussion questions. Use the lesson commentary to assist you in guiding responses:

a. What do verses 10, 13 mean when they state "ye shall return every man unto his possession"?

b. As you read verses 11, 12, what are some reasons you could suggest for God requiring His people to celebrate jubilee? What are some of the values you see to this program?

c. If the land were to lie fallow for a year, how would the people eat? (see vv. 20, 21)

4. Ask class members to paraphrase verses 14-17, 23, making the meaning as clear as possible. They may write their paraphrases on the bottom of the handouts you distributed. Ask two students to read their paraphrases. Follow that with a brief explanation of how land costs were to be calculated in relation to the Year of Jubilee.

5. Reread verse 23. Say, "This verse sounds like a worldview statement. What does this verse say about how we view our role in this world?"

6. Use your lesson commentary to summarize verse 24, emphasizing the fresh start given to people. Then summarize the practice of jubilee as given in the lesson's Conclusion.

Into Life

Create four think-tank teams. If you are short on time, ask only the question posed to Team #2.

Team #1: Discover reasons why a literal following of the jubilee law is not required of Christians today.

Team #2: What jubilee principles should still pervade Christianity? You may find Matthew 6:12 and 2 Corinthians 8:13-15 helpful.

Team #3: Forgiveness and restoration are key benefits of being a Christian. Review today's printed text and discover hints or shadows of these blessings that will come for today's Christian.

Team #4: List ways a Christian can grant a jubilee freedom to a brother or sister in Christ.

Allow each team to report. Conclude with two prayers. The first student to pray will thank God for grace and the fresh start we have in Jesus. The second to pray will ask God to help us develop an attitude of mercy, forgiveness, and generosity toward those in our Christian family.

Let's Talk It Over

The questions on this page are designed to promote discussion of the lesson by the class and to encourage application of the lesson Scriptures. The answers provided are only discussion starters. Let your class talk it over from there.

1. What was a time when you longed for a fresh start? How did things turn out?

We are surrounded by people who have seen us at our best and at our worst. Sometimes we are embarrassed by our past mistakes. Middle-aged adults may look at their lives and feel a lack of accomplishment. We live with regret and may think that if we had another chance, we would do better. We would make better friends, make better career choices, and spend our money and time more wisely. The idea of "fresh start" to many folks primarily conjures up the idea of declaring bankruptcy to get out of a financial mess.

From the Christian perspective, we have a fresh start every day, for our relationship with the Lord is ever new. We also know that while the past is less than perfect, we can be forgiven completely. We can receive constant renewal and revival through the Holy Spirit.

2. How are the Passover and Year of Jubilee observances different from one another in concept? How are they similar? How do those differences and similarities speak to us today?

The Year of Jubilee observance did not commemorate "something that happened" in history as Passover did. In this light, we may compare the American celebrations of Labor Day and the Fourth of July. The latter commemorates something that happened on a specific date in history: the signing of the Declaration of Independence on July 4, 1776. By contrast, Labor Day does not commemorate any specific historical occurrence, but is a general observance of the labor movement in the U.S.

Passover and the Year of Jubilee share the common ideal of focusing attention on God. Each observance was instituted by God. Passover reminded participants that God is the deliverer; the Year of Jubilee reminded participants that God is the ultimate owner. God is still our deliverer; He also still owns everything.

3. What does today's text teach us about the use of debt, if anything?

In many countries today, credit is easy to obtain. Easily available credit promotes increased personal debt. Many individuals and families are burdened by debt. One source notes the average credit card debt in U.S. households having at least one credit card to be over $9,000.

The Bible does not say that being in debt is a sin, but the Bible definitely discourages being in debt (see Proverbs 22:7). Debt can be crushing and worrisome. Some churches offer seminars to teach biblical principles for living without debt. Living debt-free requires hard work and self-discipline, but it's worth the struggle. "Owe no man any thing, but to love one another" (Romans 13:8).

4. Which is your usual pattern in your relationship with God: "trust, then obey," or "obey, then trust"? What's the difference?

The first approach can have the sense of "I won't obey until I know that God can be trusted." This may put us in the position of rationing our obedience. It lets us stay in control of the terms of service. The second attitude means that we will do what God asks us to do, then trust Him with the outcome. This way doesn't wait for confirmations or up-front assurances.

What we really need is a blending of trust and obedience. We trust in order to obey, and our obedience is offered with a sense of reliance on the trustworthiness of God. This makes obedience itself more important than any reward we might receive for obedience. A gratification-based society may rebel against this approach. We want to know the payoff before we make the investment. But obedience to God should never be conditional.

5. How does (or should) our perspective change when we remember that God owns all the land?

We are taught routinely that buying land is a good idea since, as the old saying goes, "they're not making any more of it." Yet this lesson gives us the larger perspective that all land is ultimately the Lord's (also Psalm 24:1). We are merely stewards of it. We realize that all of our land holdings will pass to others at our deaths.

The concepts of Sabbath year and jubilee year, when the land was to lie fallow, should have given the Israelites the same outlook. To obey those traditions was to release an individual's control over a field, returning it to God. We adopt this mind-set when we refuse to engage in undue worry about our needs (Luke 12:22-34).

Grumbling and Complaining

August 2
Lesson 9

DEVOTIONAL READING: **Psalm 142.**

BACKGROUND SCRIPTURE: **Numbers 11.**

PRINTED TEXT: **Numbers 11:1-6, 10-15.**

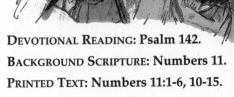

Numbers 11:1-6, 10-15

1 And when the people complained, it displeased the LORD: and the LORD heard it; and his anger was kindled; and the fire of the LORD burnt among them, and consumed them that were in the uttermost parts of the camp.

2 And the people cried unto Moses; and when Moses prayed unto the LORD, the fire was quenched.

3 And he called the name of the place Taberah: because the fire of the LORD burnt among them.

4 And the mixed multitude that was among them fell a lusting: and the children of Israel also wept again, and said, Who shall give us flesh to eat?

5 We remember the fish, which we did eat in Egypt freely; the cucumbers, and the melons, and the leeks, and the onions, and the garlic:

6 But now our soul is dried away: there is nothing at all, besides this manna, before our eyes.

· · · · · · · · · · · · ·

10 Then Moses heard the people weep throughout their families, every man in the door of his tent: and the anger of the LORD was kindled greatly; Moses also was displeased.

11 And Moses said unto the LORD, Wherefore hast thou afflicted thy servant? and wherefore have I not found favor in thy sight, that thou layest the burden of all this people upon me?

12 Have I conceived all this people? have I begotten them, that thou shouldest say unto me, Carry them in thy bosom, as a nursing father beareth the sucking child, unto the land which thou swarest unto their fathers?

13 Whence should I have flesh to give unto all this people? for they weep unto me, saying, Give us flesh, that we may eat.

14 I am not able to bear all this people alone, because it is too heavy for me.

15 And if thou deal thus with me, kill me, I pray thee, out of hand, if I have found favor in thy sight; and let me not see my wretchedness.

**Aug
2**

GOLDEN TEXT: The mixed multitude that was among them fell a lusting: and the
children of Israel also wept again, and said, Who shall give us flesh to eat?
We remember the fish, which we did eat in Egypt freely; the cucumbers,
and the melons, and the leeks, and the onions, and the garlic: but now
our soul is dried away: there is nothing at all, besides this manna,
before our eyes.—Numbers 11:4-6.

Call Sealed with Promise
Unit 3: Called to Obey
(Lessons 9–13)

Lesson Aims

After participating in this lesson, each student will be able to:

1. Tell why the Israelites complained and why Moses complained to the Lord about them.

2. Give a modern example of people who complain as they are greatly blessed.

3. Make a list of recent complaints and commit to seeing God's blessing in each situation that has produced a complaint.

Lesson Outline

INTRODUCTION
    A. Complaint Department
    B. Lesson Background
 I. COMPLAINERS (Numbers 11:1-3)
    A. Fire of the Lord Burns (v. 1)
      Some Things Never Change
    B. Prayer of Moses Saves (vv. 2, 3)
 II. GRUMBLERS (Numbers 11:4-6)
    A. Meat Eaters (v. 4)
    B. Egyptian-Cuisine Lovers (v. 5)
      The Good Old Days?
    C. Manna Haters (v. 6)
III. MOSES GRUMBLES AND COMPLAINS (Numbers 11:10-15)
    A. Griping Wave Reaches Moses (v. 10)
    B. Complaining Includes Moses (vv. 11-13)
    C. Moses Breaks Down (vv. 14, 15)
CONCLUSION
    A. Complaining
    B. Counting Blessings
    C. Prayer
    D. Thought to Remember

Introduction

A. Complaint Department

Does your church have a complaint department? Unfortunately, most churches do have such a department, which is staffed by one person: the preacher.

The preacher hears it all. The music is too loud. The church is cold; the church is hot. The sermon was too long. There is a misspelled word in the bulletin. There's no toilet paper in the men's rest-room. Someone left a light on downstairs. The new carpet is a dreadful color. And on and on and on.

People sure seem to find plenty to complain about! Traffic, coworkers, weather—you name it, and there is someone ready to grumble. This complaining occurs in the most technologically advanced, prosperous, and safest society that has ever existed in the history of the world!

Complaining has a long and extensive history. The Bible itself is full of complainers and gripers. One of the more startling examples, though, is found in the history of Israel during God's transplanting of the nation from Egyptian bondage to the promised land. The Israelites were promised a place that flowed with milk and honey. But when we read the book of Numbers, we are tempted to conclude that the Israelites spent most of the time griping and grumbling on the way there. This lesson will look at one such incident. By examining it, we will better understand God's perspective on our complaining.

B. Lesson Background

The book of Numbers takes up the story of Israel a little more than a year after the departure from Egypt (Numbers 1:1), or about 1445 BC. The nation was still encamped in the "wilderness of Sinai," meaning the area around Mount Sinai where Moses received the tablets of stone from the Lord (Exodus 24:12; 31:18).

The book of Numbers derives its name from the lengthy census data that occupies the first few chapters. Yet there is much more to the book than lists of numbers and names. It has a great deal of narrative, telling the story of the various adventures of Israel while in the wilderness period. Moses was clearly the leader of the nation, although his leadership was challenged from time to time (as in today's lesson).

Within a few weeks of the beginning of the book of Numbers, the Israelites left the area around Sinai and relocated to the "wilderness of Paran" (Numbers 10:11, 12). Eventually, they seemed to settle in the "desert of Zin" at a place named Kadesh (Numbers 20:1, compare Deuteronomy 1:46). This exact location is unknown today, but it would have been somewhere in the southern extremity of modern Israel, perhaps in the vicinity of the town of Beersheba.

Israel at this time was a very large group of people, with traditional estimates placing their number at more than two million. To camp in such an isolated place created enormous logistical problems in meeting daily needs for food and water. The food needs were met through a miraculous provision of God called *manna*. This was a bread-like substance that appeared in the camp in sufficient quantities to feed everyone.

Manna was white and had a honey-like flavor (Exodus 16:31). It was processed in various ways and seemed to have had oil within it (see Number 11:8). This was Israel's primary diet for the 40 years in the wilderness before entry into the promised land (Exodus 16:35). God also made miraculous provision at various times for the people to have water while in the wilderness (example: Exodus 17:1-7).

We can imagine that this was a terribly frustrating period for many Israelites. True, they had been rescued from being a nation of slaves and had witnessed mighty acts of God in their deliverance. But few people play the waiting game very well. The Israelites found themselves parked in the middle of nowhere (literally) without a clear understanding of their future. Their focus quickly shifted away from God and His mighty works to their own plight. This is the backdrop for today's lesson, where the focus of grumbling was the marvelous manna itself.

I. Complainers
(Numbers 11:1-3)
A. Fire of the Lord Burns (v. 1)

1. And when the people complained, it displeased the LORD: and the LORD heard it; and his anger was kindled; and the fire of the LORD burnt among them, and consumed them that were in the uttermost parts of the camp.

The exact nature of this particular complaint is not stated. But it probably is directly critical of God, for it causes His *anger* to be *kindled*. God's anger is manifested as a supernatural *fire* on the fringes of the *camp;* the fire is of such a nature as to kill some of the Israelites. It is among these "fringe dwellers" that the criticism is probably the deepest, so that is where God directs His anger.

The primary purpose of God's actions, however, is not to dispense justice. Rather, the main intent

---

How to Say It

ABRAHAM. *Ay*-bruh-ham.
BEERSHEBA. Beer-*she*-buh.
EGYPT. *Ee*-jipt.
ISRAELITES. *Iz*-ray-el-ites.
KADESH. *kay*-desh.
MOSES. *Mo*-zes or *Mo*-zez.
PARAN. *Pair*-un.
SINAI. *Sigh*-nye or *Sigh*-nay-eye.
TABERAH. *Tab*-eh-ruh.

---

is to get the attention of the people concerning a serious problem that needs to be corrected.

SOME THINGS NEVER CHANGE

My brother-in-law was a minister in rural and small-town churches in Iowa and Illinois. Members of these congregations often included farmers. As a result, my brother-in-law became acquainted with various farming attitudes. One man in particular often was given to complaining. If the rains did not come, he complained about the drought. When the rains did come, he complained about the humidity. If the corn crop was good, the farmer complained about the beans. If the beans were good, he complained about the wheat.

One year, however, everything was about perfect. All his crops yielded bumper harvests, and the prices for his livestock held up. Talking with this farmer near the end of the growing season, my brother-in-law remarked that things apparently had gone well. But the farmer complained, "A year like this sure takes a lot out of the soil."

Unfortunately, this farmer is not the only one with this kind of mind-set! I serve as an evaluator for an association that accredits universities and colleges. In the visits I have made to different schools, students always complain about the cafeteria. They complain about the quality of the food. (I have eaten in most of these cafeterias, and my experience does not match their complaints.) They complain about the lack of variety. They complain about the seats or the shape of the tables (round, rectangular, oval, or whatever). Some things never change; the ancient Israelites would find many kindred spirits in our world today! —J. B. N.

B. Prayer of Moses Saves (vv. 2, 3)

2. And the people cried unto Moses; and when Moses prayed unto the LORD, the fire was quenched.

The spirit of complaining is transformed into a desperate cry for help. The people do not cry to God, however, but to *Moses*. Moses has to intercede for them with God. His prayer is effective, and the *fire* threat passes.

3. And he called the name of the place Taberah: because the fire of the LORD burnt among them.

As happens at other times, this *place* is given a symbolic name: *Taberah*, which means "burning place." This and other places are remembered as the sites of Israel's disobedience and rebellion, where the nation provoked the wrath of the Lord (see Deuteronomy 9:22). Many centuries later, the apostle Paul will use some of these incidents as warnings to the Corinthians to stop their grumbling (see 1 Corinthians 10:10, 11).

II. Grumblers
(Numbers 11:4-6)

A. Meat Eaters (v. 4)

4. And the mixed multitude that was among them fell a lusting: and the children of Israel also wept again, and said, Who shall give us flesh to eat?

As dramatic and traumatic as the Taberah incident must be, it is quickly followed by another complaint. It is easy for us to condemn Israel for folly in this matter. Yet we should not think ourselves above falling into similar patterns of ingratitude.

The new round of grumbling is a *lusting*, but this has nothing to do with sexual desire. It is the lust for favorite foods. In particular, the people *of Israel* want a diet that includes meat. They are apparently unwilling to eat any of the livestock that remains from when they left Egypt (Exodus 17:3). Thus their only source of nourishment is the daily provision of manna.

These cravings for a steak or lamb chop are so strong that the people actually weep. Their behavior has passed the boundaries of rationality and moved to childishness. [See question #1, page 416.]

B. Egyptian-Cuisine Lovers (v. 5)

5. We remember the fish, which we did eat in Egypt freely; the cucumbers, and the melons, and the leeks, and the onions, and the garlic.

The list of cherished foods includes many items that apparently had been common to them, even as slaves, in Egypt. Assuming that they are not viewing the past through rose-colored glasses in

Visual for
Lesson 9

Point to this visual as you ask, "Under what circumstances are you most likely to grumble?"

this regard, they remember having had plenty of *fish*, for the Nile produced fish in abundance. They also had grown juicy vegetables and fruits in their gardens. Some of the produce of Egypt could be cooked into stews to provide savory flavors. [See question #2, page 416.]

It is doubtful that the people of Israel loved these foods so dearly while in Egypt. They are like American travelers of today who may spend an extended time in an isolated country, and then long for a cheeseburger. It is not that the cheeseburger is such fine food; it is just familiar.

The underlying problem here is a spiritual problem. The people of Israel are deeply dissatisfied with the way God is treating them, and they use their lack of diet options to express discontent and, ultimately, lack of faith.

THE GOOD OLD DAYS?

I am now old enough that I can join the refrain about remembering "the good old days." I was a teenager through most of the 1950s, and I can remember the good times that that decade represented. The blue-collar community where I grew up was part of a major industrial area, and work in the factories was good. Our local schools were integrated, and there were no racial tensions. I was not aware of any illegal drugs. Churches thrived. I can identify with the positive, idealized presentation of 1950s life as depicted in the TV series *Happy Days*.

But the 1950s also had its problems. My dad was a carpenter who worked outdoors in house construction; when the weather got bad in the winter, he didn't work and thus wasn't paid. I remember suppers of thin potato soup because that was all we had. I remember wearing shoes with holes in the soles because we couldn't afford new ones. I remember girls who dropped out of high school because of pregnancy. I remember gang fights. The decade of the 1950s was not ideal.

The Israelites idealized their past life in Egypt. They remembered (or thought they remembered) so many good things, but they forgot the slavery. They remembered the vegetables, but they forgot the whips. Human tendency toward having a selective memory hasn't changed much over the centuries, has it?
—J. B. N.

C. Manna Haters (v. 6)

6. But now our soul is dried away: there is nothing at all, beside this manna, before our eyes.

What if a restaurant today were able to offer authentic *manna* on its menu? The sky would be the limit as to what could be charged. Who would not want a bite of the miraculous, tasty bread from

Heaven? Yet the people of Israel, who had this perfect food in inexhaustible quantities for free, become bored with it.

At one time, lobster was considered to be the food of poor people. When the first European immigrants arrived in New England, they found that lobsters sometimes washed up on the beaches in such quantities that they were taken for granted. Lobsters were even cut up and used for fish bait. The lobster, after all, was seen as a type of sea insect—to be shunned by polite society. Today, however, lobster is among the most prized of foods. Its subtle and delicious flavor is appreciated by gourmets all over the world.

Tastes in food may change, but there is no excuse for being ungrateful for God's provision. For people to become distressed to the point that their souls are *dried away* over a repetitive diet is not acceptable. [See question #3, page 416.]

III. Moses Grumbles and Complains (Numbers 11:10-15)

A. Griping Wave Reaches Moses (v. 10)

10. Then Moses heard the people weep throughout their families, every man in the door of his tent: and the anger of the LORD was kindled greatly; Moses also was displeased.

Despite the recent incident at Taberah, *the people* of Israel persist in their petty complaining. The complaint is universal, being expressed by *every man*. They are tired of manna! From our perspective, this all seems to be quite silly and childish. They are even shedding tears over this!

Yet, again, we must remember that at its core this is not a problem with diet. It is a spiritual problem, a lack of faith in Moses' leadership and therefore in God. The Lord has a plan to create a people for himself. He will allow the Israelites to populate the land He had promised to Abraham, but the plan seems to be going awry because of the people's attitude and behavior. This causes God's wrath to be *kindled* anew.

We don't know how Moses himself feels about eating manna every day, but he seems to have no complaints about it. His displeasure is the complaint of leadership, of having to appease his grumbling nation. See the next verse.

B. Complaining Includes Moses (vv. 11-13)

11. And Moses said unto the LORD, Wherefore hast thou afflicted thy servant? and wherefore have I not found favor in thy sight, that thou layest the burden of all this people upon me?

The endless wave of complaining overwhelms *Moses*. Thus he joins the ranks of the complainers.

Moses takes his complaint directly to God, asking why *the Lord* has saddled him with a nation of grumblers.

Moses understands this to be a personal matter. He believes that Israel's dissatisfaction is a sign that he, Moses, has fallen out of *favor* with God. The experience is so negative that Moses sees leadership as a *burden* rather than a privilege and a responsibility. [See question #4, page 416.]

12. Have I conceived all this people? have I begotten them, that thou shouldest say unto me, Carry them in thy bosom, as a nursing father beareth the sucking child, unto the land which thou swarest unto their fathers?

Moses' litany of complaints grows deeper as he lays bare all of his frustrations before the Lord. In effect, he is saying, "This is not what I signed up for." That's the attitude behind the questions *Have I conceived all this people? have I begotten them?* All this is as if to ask, "Am I their *father*?"

The answer to this question obviously is *no*, he is not their father. The only one who fits the role of father is God himself. Moses is tired of babysitting these whiners. So he too gives in to the spirit of complaining. [See question #5, page 416.]

13. Whence should I have flesh to give unto all this people? for they weep unto me, saying, Give us flesh, that we may eat.

Moses then confronts God on the practical level. He knows the people are clamoring for *flesh* (meat) in their diet, but he has no solution. He cannot seem to quell their grumbling, and he has no resources to meet their requests.

While we may criticize Moses' attitude at this point, we should appreciate that his impulse to turn to God is a step in the right direction. In church leadership roles, it is tempting to turn first to our own skills; it is easy to think that we have all the answers, that we should be able to fix all conflicts in short order. Or we simply turn a deaf ear to complaints and hope they will go away.

Moses does neither of those. Instead, he takes the concerns seriously, turning to God for help. As with Paul, Moses understands his personal limitations, knowing that solutions can come only from God (compare 2 Corinthians 12:10).

C. Moses Breaks Down (vv. 14, 15)

14, 15. I am not able to bear all this people alone, because it is too heavy for me. And if thou deal thus with me, kill me, I pray thee, out of hand, if I have found favor in thy sight; and let me not see my wretchedness.

Leadership can be thankless, isolating, and lonely. When it gets to this point, any leader will say *it is too heavy for me*. And that leader will be correct. No one is able to survive the pressures of leadership without help. In this case, the pressure has crushed Moses to the point that he longs for death. Again, he reminds us of Paul, who admits that in his circumstances he "despaired even of life" (2 Corinthians 1:8); Paul ultimately learns that "we should not trust in ourselves, but in God" (1:9).

If we read beyond today's lesson text, we learn that the Lord directs Moses to create a leadership council of 70 elders to help him deal with the people (Numbers 11:16). God's intention is that this group of men will "bear the burden of the people with thee, that thou bear it not thyself alone" (11:17). It is never God's intention to abandon those who are leading His people.

What about the grumblers? God takes care of them too. The rest of this chapter reveals that God causes a miraculous deluge of quail to fall on the camp so that the tasty birds are three feet deep (Numbers 11:31). Israel's enjoyment of the meat is short-lived, though. Very soon—while the meat is "yet between their teeth"—God brings a "very great plague" on the people and many die (11:33, 34).

Conclusion

A. Complaining

Don't we have a right to complain? Don't we have an obligation to complain? We all know people who have refined their complaining skills to a very high level. Such individuals seem to enjoy complaining simply for the sake of complaining. There are limits to this, though, as the people of Israel found out while in the wilderness.

God does not reward ungrateful complaining. Yet we should never hesitate to express our discouragements and hurts to the Lord, for He truly

cares (1 Peter 5:7). It is difficult, however, to have much joy in our lives if we focus on our complaints. There is no more effective joy stealer than griping and grumbling. On the other hand, if we pause to reflect, then we will better appreciate the many ways God has blessed us and is blessing us.

B. Counting Blessings

The hymn writer Johnson Oatman, Jr. (1859–1922) advised Christians to "count your blessings, name them one by one." Oatman knew that we would find blessings "wealth can never buy."

Our materialistic world tends to equate blessings with wealth. We think we are blessed if we have abundant possessions. Yet this is not what the Bible teaches. Jesus teaches that material possessions are fleeting and perishable (Matthew 6:19-21). Jesus knows that we can become enslaved by possessions (6:24). The desire for money can become insatiable.

If we go through the exercise of counting our blessings, we may list some very mundane things. We have clothes to wear. We have homes to live in. We have food to eat. But our most precious blessings are nonmaterial. In God's economy, we are truly wealthy if we are rich in relationships. We should never take for granted the blessing of family and friends. We should never minimize the power of loving others and being loved by them.

Even more important are the mighty spiritual blessings we have been given by the grace of God. He has bought our salvation through the blood of His Son, Jesus. God has given His Holy Spirit to comfort us in times of distress. He has given us His Word to guide us and help us understand His will for us. He loves us deeply. These are blessings that wealth cannot buy. When we tire, we are tempted to go into complaint mode. But we are better served and more acceptable to God if we resist this temptation and thank God for the many blessings He has showered into our lives.

C. Prayer

God, from whom all blessings flow, we are too often guilty of letting life's disappointments steal our joy. We become grumblers, never satisfied. May we be content with Your care. May You remove the spirit of grumbling from us. Keep us from falling into the sin of the Israelites in the wilderness, who were not satisfied with Your miraculous manna. We pray this in the name of the true living bread from Heaven, Jesus. Amen.

D. Thought to Remember

Focus on your blessings, not your lack.

Home Daily Bible Readings

Monday, July 27—Give Heed to My Cry (Psalm 142)

Tuesday, July 28—A Test of Obedience (Exodus 16:1-12)

Wednesday, July 29—Living Bread (John 6:41-51)

Thursday, July 30—Complaining and Turning Back (John 6:60-68)

Friday, July 31—An Example to Instruct Us (1 Corinthians 10:1-11)

Saturday, Aug. 1—Faith, Love, and Mercy (Jude 14-23)

Sunday, Aug. 2—Complaining About Hardships (Numbers 11:1-6, 10-15)

Learning by Doing

This page contains an alternative lesson plan emphasizing learning activities. Some of these activities are also found in the helpful student book, Adult Bible Class.

Into the Lesson

To introduce the next three lessons, prepare seven pieces of poster board with the letters *N, U, M, B, E, R, S* on the front side, at least four inches in height, one letter per card. On the back of the *N* have a *G*; on the back of the *S* have an *L*.

Affix to the board or wall the seven cards to read *NUMBERS*; use small pieces of masking tape. Then move the letters around as follows: move the *U* under the *M* position; move the *M* under the *B*; move the *B* under the *E*; move the *E* under the *S*; move the *R* underneath the position that was first held by the *U* (that is, it will be to the left of where the *U* now is). Only the *N* and the *S* will remain in the top row.

Say, "Behind the *N* and the *S* are different letters. When we flip them and move them to different locations, we will have a sad theme of the Book of Numbers." See who can identify the letters. When the *G* and *L* are identified, flip the *N* to a *G* and place it to the left of where the *R* now is. Flip the *S* to an *L* and place it between the *B* and the *E*. The new word, of course, is *GRUMBLE*.

Say, "When one reads the book of Numbers, one is tempted to conclude that the ancient Israelites spent most of their time griping and grumbling on their way to the promised land."

Into the Word

Prepare on 13 strips of paper the following observations about complaining, one per strip. Give one to each learner. If you have more than 13 learners, repeat some of the strips; if you have fewer than 13 learners, double up some of the assignments.

Tell your learners you want them to relate the observation on each slip to a verse or idea in today's text of Numbers 11:1-6, 10-15. Verse numbers are suggested in italics with the observations given here, but do not include those verse numbers on your handouts. Shuffle the strips before handing them out.

Complaining reaches God's ears *(v. 1)*
Complaining makes God angry *(v. 1)*
Complaining to human leaders may be no better than complaining to God *(v. 2)*
Complaining can lead to destruction *(v. 3)*
Complaining may arise from physical wants *(v. 4)*

Complaining is often tied to "the good old days" *(v. 5)*
Complaining can ignore the good things that are present *(v. 6)*
Complaining may affect whole families *(v. 10)*
Complaining often infects leaders as well as followers *(v. 11)*
Complaining can deteriorate into self-pity *(v. 11)*
Complaining may arise from feelings of being overwhelmed *(v. 12)*
Complaining may arise from feelings of personal and faith inadequacy *(v. 13)*
Complaining can lead to self-deprecation, even despair *(vv. 14, 15)*

Read (or have read) the whole lesson text aloud. Then ask learners at random to read their complaint statements, identify the verse(s) associated, and relate how they see the same phenomenon at work in their own lives and/or in society.

As your learners relate current occasions that elicit complaints, ask them to consider if there ultimately was a "hidden blessing" in each occasion that was met with a complaint. Use this discussion as a transition to the Into Life segment.

Into Life

Suggest that each learner prepare a personal Complaint Box. This is the manner of construction: (1) cut a slot in the lid of an empty margarine tub; (2) write the word *Complaints* on the top of the lid; (3) write *God's Blessings* on the underneath side of the lid; (4) place the lid on the tub with the word *Complaints* showing.

Learners are to keep a small notepad handy throughout the week. They will use the notepad for writing down complaints that come to mind. After writing a complaint, they deposit it in the tub when they get home.

At the end of the week, your learners should remove the slips. As they look at them one by one, they are to ponder how each was "hiding" a blessing of God. They are then to flip the lid over so that the phrase *God's Blessings* shows. Next, they reinsert those same slips through the slot. Once the complaints and grumbles are thus deposited the second time, your learners are ready to pray with a different attitude over their concerns!

Let's Talk It Over

The questions on this page are designed to promote discussion of the lesson by the class and to encourage application of the lesson Scriptures. The answers provided are only discussion starters. Let your class talk it over from there.

1. Under what circumstances, if any, is it proper to complain to God?

Attitude is everything! Humble, heartfelt expressions of need are fine; "give us this day our daily bread" is an example. That doesn't really fit the idea of complaining. But expressions of need that come across as bellyaching are out of line.

Taking time daily to say *thank you* to God from the heart is the best way to refocus. We will find ourselves greatly blessed as we develop grateful hearts. The apostle Paul found himself under severe conditions time after time, yet he considered himself blessed. Since very few of us will ever face the stress and deprivations that he did, should we be any less grateful than he was?

2. What are your "top five" words to describe the attitudes of the children of Israel as they listed all the foods they used to enjoy in Egypt? How can we overcome our own tendencies to glory in memories of "the good old days"?

Many words come to mind. *Shortsighted* is just one. The Israelites probably salivated over what they had back in Egypt because they mentally dwelled on the idea of going back there.

Too often we do likewise: we pine for a previous life situation as we focus on what we don't have, on opportunities missed, or on relationships lost. Just as the Israelites remembered the food in Egypt without considering the misery of their slavery, we also may remember only the good in the past while overlooking the bad. Sometimes we may be in denial about the natural movement of the stages of life as time moves on. Making an effort to live in the present and see each new day as a gift from God can help us overcome such tendencies.

3. How do we recognize people who (1) are genuinely grateful and thankful, (2) put on a false front of gratitude and thankfulness, and (3) are outright ungrateful? How can you make sure you are in the first of these three categories?

We see genuine gratitude in the poor widow of Mark 12:41-44. People who know they have been blessed will try to be a blessing to others in sacrificial ways. Thankful people often praise God for His mercy and grace, both in public and in private. They are pleasant people to be around.

We see a false front of gratitude in the Pharisee of Luke 18:9-12. The "thankfulness" he expresses is for his own efforts at being better than others. Such folks may be condescending toward those who don't fit their mold.

We see downright ungratefulness in today's lesson. Ungrateful people tend to complain aloud; they tend to display a negative attitude. They may try to line up support for their position as they attempt to enlist others in their cause (examples: Numbers 14:4; 16:1-4). They are often unpleasant to be around.

4. How can complaining by church members affect church leaders? What corrective action is appropriate?

Relentless complaining can discourage church leaders, as it did Moses. Hebrews 13:17 offers at least a partial solution: "Obey them that have the rule over you, and submit yourselves: for they watch for your souls, as they that must give account, that they may do it with joy, and not with grief: for that is unprofitable for you." That word *unprofitable* should warn chronic complainers that causing grief in church leaders may make things worse, not better.

5. How should parents react when their children complain?

Parents normally have a great love for and a deep commitment to their children. It's normal for parents to make major sacrifices for their children at every age. In view of this, we would expect children to be more grateful to their parents than they frequently are.

When parents encounter ingratitude and lack of respect, they may slow down in blessing their children in extra ways. Parents will be more reluctant to respond positively to requests from their children as they would if the children exhibited more gratitude in words, attitudes, and actions. However, some of the blame for children's ingratitude can be the parents' fault for not modeling a grateful attitude themselves.

Being a proper role model is important. If you are a parent, do your children perceive a grateful attitude when they hear you discuss your job, your church, etc.?

Doubting and Rebelling

DEVOTIONAL READING: Psalm 78:5-17.

BACKGROUND SCRIPTURE: Numbers 14:1-25.

PRINTED TEXT: Numbers 14:1-12.

Numbers 14:1-12

1 And all the congregation lifted up their voice, and cried; and the people wept that night.

2 And all the children of Israel murmured against Moses and against Aaron: and the whole congregation said unto them, Would God that we had died in the land of Egypt! or would God we had died in this wilderness!

3 And wherefore hath the LORD brought us unto this land, to fall by the sword, that our wives and our children should be a prey? were it not better for us to return into Egypt?

4 And they said one to another, Let us make a captain, and let us return into Egypt.

5 Then Moses and Aaron fell on their faces before all the assembly of the congregation of the children of Israel.

6 And Joshua the son of Nun, and Caleb the son of Jephunneh, which were of them that searched the land, rent their clothes:

7 And they spake unto all the company of the children of Israel, saying, The land, which we passed through to search it, is an exceeding good land.

8 If the LORD delight in us, then he will bring us into this land, and give it us; a land which floweth with milk and honey.

9 Only rebel not ye against the LORD, neither fear ye the people of the land; for they are bread for us: their defense is departed from them, and the LORD is with us: fear them not.

10 But all the congregation bade stone them with stones. And the glory of the LORD appeared in the tabernacle of the congregation before all the children of Israel.

11 And the LORD said unto Moses, How long will this people provoke me? and how long will it be ere they believe me, for all the signs which I have showed among them?

12 I will smite them with the pestilence, and disinherit them, and will make of thee a greater nation and mightier than they.

**Aug
9**

GOLDEN TEXT: Wherefore hath the LORD brought us unto this land, to fall by the sword, that our wives and our children should be a prey? were it not better for us to return into Egypt?—Numbers 14:3.

Call Sealed with Promise
Unit 3: Called to Obey
(Lessons 9–13)

Lesson Aims

After participating in this lesson, each student will be able to:

1. Summarize the people of Israel's complaint as they rebelled against Moses and Aaron and refused to enter the promised land.

2. Tell how doubt leads people today to reject God's promises and His will for their lives.

3. Write a devotional thought that encourages faith in the face of rebellion.

Lesson Outline

INTRODUCTION
   A. Long Journeys
   B. Lesson Background
I. ANXIETY & REVOLT (Numbers 14:1-4)
   A. Despair of Fear (v. 1)
   B. Misery of Doubt (vv. 2, 3)
   C. Rashness of Rebellion (v. 4)
II. TRUSTING & BLESSING (Numbers 14:5-9)
   A. Reaction to Rebellion (vv. 5, 6)
   B. Challenge to Trust (vv. 7, 8)
   C. Freedom from Fear (v. 9)
     Piece of Cake
III. REBELLION & PUNISHMENT (Numbers 14:10-12)
   A. God Appears (v. 10)
   B. God Questions (v. 11)
     Signs
   C. God Threatens (v. 12)
CONCLUSION
   A. Do We Repeat the Problem?
   B. Will We Recognize the Promised Land?
   B. Prayer
   C. Thought to Remember

Introduction

A. Long Journeys

A friend recently described a transoceanic, 8,000-mile flight he had experienced (endured?). His description of being confined inside the tight quarters of a Boeing 747 with hundreds of other people for many hours made it sound like an experience that no sane person would ever agree to. Yet a century ago, this journey would have been by ship and would have taken weeks, even months. A

millennium ago this trip would have been unimaginable. I took my friend's complaints with a grain of salt, for I knew that he had been warm, fed, and safe, having gone halfway around the world in less than 24 hours.

The book of Numbers tells the crucial story of Israel's odyssey from the bondage of Egypt to the freedom of the promised land of Canaan. It was not an easy journey. There were no hotels along the way, no 747s to whisk people about. It was a move that required utter trust in the Lord and in His appointed leader, Moses.

Today's lesson focuses on a tragic turn of events in this story. It shows that Israel let the hardships and uncertainty of its situation turn into doubt and rebellion. The result was the delay of entry into the promised land for a generation and an unnecessary sojourn in the wilderness for 40 years.

B. Lesson Background

The first five books of the Bible (sometimes called *the Pentateuch*) tell the story of God's plan to create a people for himself (Exodus 6:7). This plan included the selection of Abram (later renamed Abraham) as the man of faith to be the father of this nation (Genesis 15:6). Abraham's descendants multiplied greatly, but ended up in Egypt as a nation of slaves under the bondage of the Pharaoh. God's plan was far from complete—His chosen people were hardly a nation, and they were in the wrong place (Egypt). God had promised Abraham that they would inherit the land of Canaan (Genesis 15:18).

The Exodus story is the account of God's miraculous liberation of an entire people-group from the slavery imposed by the Egyptians. The Egyptian threat was finally put to rest by Israel's experience at the Red Sea. While in the Sinai Peninsula, the people received revelations from God that were intended to form them into His holy people. They were to be controlled by His law, worshiping at His holy tabernacle. We might say that most of the process of nation-building had then been accomplished. The identity of Israel was clear: a holy people whose God was the Lord.

The book of Numbers shows that God intended a three-part plan for His people: rescue from Egypt, reception of the law, and movement to a new homeland. Israelite spies indeed saw the richness of the land before them, describing it as flowing "with milk and honey" (Numbers 13:27). They brought back a cluster of grapes so large that it required two men to carry it (13:23).

While the report of the spies verified the richness of this land, the majority of the spies also reported that the residents were too formidable.

The result was that the Israelites were terrified as they concentrated on the report of opposing armies rather than the report of a land with overflowing abundance.

There was a minority report as well. It came from 2 of the 12 spies. They were of the opinion that the time was ripe to sweep in and claim the land that God had promised them. Unfortunately, this minority opinion was drowned out by the fearful cries of the Israelite people in general. They believed that they had been led to a dead end and would be destroyed. We should remember that these were the same people who had watched God destroy the great army of the Egyptians in the waters of the Red Sea.

The prize was within their grasp, and yet they let fear overcome faith. They listened to the opinion of 10 cowards rather than claim a spirit of boldness. This is the immediate background of today's lesson.

I. Anxiety & Revolt (Numbers 14:1-4)

A. Despair of Fear (v. 1)

1. And all the congregation lifted up their voice, and cried; and the people wept that night.

The spies' report leads to mass hysteria and despair. The Israelites wallow together in this despondent response as they vent their frustrations and fears. The detail that they weep *that night* probably signifies that no one gets much, if any, sleep.

Many of us have had crises so intense that we were unable to sleep. This can become a vicious cycle, for lack of sleep wears us down and makes us even more susceptible to despair. The despair of the Israelites is brought on by a lack of faith in God and in their leaders. [See question #1, page 424.]

B. Misery of Doubt (vv. 2, 3)

2. And all the children of Israel murmured against Moses and against Aaron: and the whole congregation said unto them, Would God that we had died in the land of Egypt! or would God we had died in this wilderness!

A common component of the despair that comes from doubt is the desire to blame someone else for the situation. In this case, the blame is directed toward the two-brother leadership team of *Moses* and *Aaron*. This is more than simple griping about minor inconvenience. Shockingly, the people express the belief that they would be better off dead than being in their current situation! To their minds, this despair has gone beyond any hope of remedy.

3. And wherefore hath the LORD brought us unto this land, to fall by the sword, that our wives and our children should be a prey? were it not better for us to return into Egypt?

Think of what the phrase *return into Egypt* really implies: in Egypt, the people of Israel were slaves under brutal taskmasters. The Israelites are not now reminiscing about "the good old days." Their base fear is that their men will be killed in battle in the current situation, leaving their families as *prey* for their victorious enemies. Thus a return to Egypt is seen as the lesser of two evils.

C. Rashness of Rebellion (v. 4)

4. And they said one to another, Let us make a captain, and let us return into Egypt.

The result of the community's gripe session is that they propose taking matters into their own hands. Surely they must remember the awe-inspiring power of God displayed through Moses in the plagues and during the Red Sea experience! But yesterday's leader is not good enough for today. Earlier the Israelites had been willing to believe that God had provided Moses to be their leader. They had trusted Moses through frightening events (see Exodus 14:31). Now they are ready to cast him aside and choose their own man to lead them back to *Egypt*.

II. Trusting & Blessing (Numbers 14:5-9)

A. Reaction to Rebellion (vv. 5, 6)

5. Then Moses and Aaron fell on their faces before all the assembly of the congregation of the children of Israel.

Moses and Aaron display an instinctive reaction to this popular uprising: they fall facedown before the people. They don't seem to know what else to do. Symbolically at least, they have given

---

How to Say It

AARON. *Air*-un.
ABRAHAM. *Ay*-bruh-ham.
ABRAM. *Ay*-brum.
CALEB. *Kay*-leb.
CANAAN. *Kay*-nun.
EGYPT. *Ee*-jipt.
JEPHUNNEH. Jih-*fun*-eh.
JOSHUA. *Josh*-yew-uh.
MOSES. *Mo*-zes or *Mo*-zez.
PENTATEUCH. *Pen*-ta-teuk.
PHARAOH. *Fair*-o or *Fay*-roe.
SINAI. *Sigh*-nye or *Sigh*-nay-eye.

up. They have done their best and their best has been rejected. This is a dangerous situation, and some students think that these two are begging for their lives. If the nation chooses a new captain, the people may want to dispose of the old leaders. [See question #2, page 424.]

6. And Joshua the son of Nun, and Caleb the son of Jephunneh, which were of them that searched the land, rent their clothes.

Moses and Aaron are not the only champions for God's plan. There is also *Joshua the son of Nun* and *Caleb the son of Jephunneh.* These are men of credibility, having been chosen as 2 of the 12 spies (see Numbers 13:3, where the spies are identified as "heads" of the Israelites). They see this situation spiraling out of control, toward disaster. They respond publicly in a way that draws attention to themselves. To rend (tear) one's *clothes* shows extreme agitation. This is a demonstration of great sorrow (see Genesis 37:34).

B. Challenge to Trust (vv. 7, 8)

7. And they spake unto all the company of the children of Israel, saying, The land, which we passed through to search it, is an exceeding good land.

The people have drawn a line that leaves them with two choices. They can reject Moses (and the Lord) and attempt to appoint a new leader to take them back to Egypt; or they can continue to accept Moses (and the Lord) and prepare to enter the land of Canaan despite their great fears.

Joshua and Caleb give them two reasons to follow Moses. First, they remind the people that the *land* before them is *exceeding good.* They had seen the grape cluster so heavy it had to be carried on a pole between two men (again, Numbers 13:23). This is a prize worth fighting for. Canaan is "the glory of all lands" (Ezekiel 20:15). The second reason follows.

8. If the LORD delight in us, then he will bring us into this land, and give it us; a land which floweth with milk and honey.

Joshua and Caleb's second reason is that *the Lord* is on their side. God has promised *this land* to them. God's gifts are never inferior or defective. This is a land flowing with *milk and honey.* This is much more than a land of cows and bees, which produce those two things; this is, rather, a figure of speech for agricultural wealth. It is a land of abundance, purposed by God to be the land of the nation of Israel.

C. Freedom from Fear (v. 9)

9. Only rebel not ye against the LORD, neither fear ye the people of the land; for they are bread for us: their defense is departed from them, and the LORD is with us: fear them not.

Joshua and Caleb equate the Israelites' *fear* of the *people* of Canaan with rebellion against God himself. If the assistance of God is spurned, then the people should be afraid. These two spies know that this does not need to be the case. The adversaries of Israel are as *bread* for them. The territory and influence of those in Canaan is ready to be eaten up and claimed by the people of Israel. Those inhabitants will not be able to stand against the power of the Lord, so there is no reason to fear. [See question #3, page 424.]

PIECE OF CAKE

Piece of Cake was a novel written in 1983 by Derek Robinson. It tells the story of a Royal Air Force fighter squadron based in France during the early days of World War II. During the lackadaisical days of what was called the Phony War— the period of time when Germany had not yet unleashed its armies against the Western powers— the pilots of Hornet Squadron had a good life.

But when the real fighting started in April 1940, their lot changed. The easy times were over. The jolly young pilots had had heaps of fun to that point, but now they were being killed regularly. First in France, then later during the Battle of Britain, Hornet Squadron took heavy casualties. Most of its pilots were killed in action. The surviving commanding officer had to instill discipline to get his men to learn that being one of "the good guys" did not automatically lead to victory in aerial combat.

The phrase *piece of cake* is meant to describe something that is easy or pleasant to accomplish. What the pilots first thought would be a piece of cake turned into a difficult, deadly confrontation. The Israelites went in the other direction. They thought conquest of Canaan to be an impossible task; Joshua and Caleb said it would be a piece of cake ("they are bread for us"). If the Lord is on your side, hard tasks can indeed become a piece of cake.   —J. B. N.

III. Rebellion & Punishment (Numbers 14:10-12)

A. God Appears (v. 10)

10a. But all the congregation bade stone them with stones.

The *them* of this verse is Moses, Aaron, Joshua, and Caleb. The emotion of the people is so strong that they turn into a murderous mob, ready to kill those who oppose their will. [See question #4, page 424.]

10b. And the glory of the LORD appeared in the tabernacle of the congregation before all the children of Israel.

The four are saved by the Lord's miraculous intervention: the mob is stopped cold by an appearance of the *glory of the Lord.* This takes place at *the tabernacle,* which was probably the site of the earlier confrontation too. God's glory does not shine way off in the distance, but right in the middle of the people. The witnesses to this glory include *all the children of Israel.*

B. God Questions (v. 11)

11. And the LORD said unto Moses, How long will this people provoke me? and how long will it be ere they believe me, for all the signs which I have showed among them?

God does not address the nation as a whole, but speaks directly to *Moses.* It is possible, however, that the *people* also can hear God's voice. At any rate, they understand that God has responded to their act of rebellion in a dramatic way. They are not going to get away with their schemes.

God brings two charges against Israel. First, they have provoked Him, meaning they have called forth His wrath. Second, they have stubbornly refused to *believe* Him, to trust Him. [See question #5, page 424.] God has given them ample evidence of His power through many *signs,* but their unbelief persists. God rhetorically asks Moses *how long* He should put up with these acts of rebellion. This situation cannot continue.

Just because God is "long-suffering" (Numbers 14:18) does not mean that He overlooks rebellion. God is patient, but rebellion against Him is futile for He eventually will punish it.

SIGNS

When I was but a mere lad (many years ago!), I joined the local Boy Scouts troop. It was not an exceptionally good experience because of poor leadership, but it was a learning experience nonetheless. One incident I well remember was an overnight camping venture into a forested area about an hour's drive from town. We did a variety of things out in the woods, and at one point we had a lesson in following signs.

A couple of the older boys went off into the woods and were to leave various "signs" behind for us to follow. When the rest of us started out, we were looking for those signs (this was long before the days of handheld Global Positioning System devices!). At one location we found etched in the pathway an arrow pointing straight ahead, so we followed. At a fork in the path there was a branch broken to indicate the direction we should take.

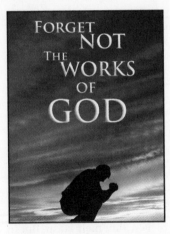

Visual for Lesson 10

Point to this visual as you ask, "What are some ways to make this idea a reality?"

Other signs led us on, and eventually we found the older boys waiting for us.

Think about it: if we had come across a clear, unmistakable sign, it would have been pretty silly to say "I think we made a mistake; let's backtrack and start over in a different direction." God's signs are unmistakable, particularly those found within His written Word. Understandably, there can be concern when we go a while without apparent reaffirmation, but each new sign confirms all the previous ones. The ancient Israelites reacted to God's signs in a less than faithful way. Will we repeat their mistakes?   —J. B. N.

C. God Threatens (v. 12)

12. I will smite them with the pestilence, and disinherit them, and will make of thee a greater nation and mightier than they.

God proposes a new plan to Moses: He will destroy Israel and take away their inheritance of the land of Canaan. He will abandon them in the wilderness to suffer and die. This does not mean that God will abandon His promise to Abraham, though. God proposes that He will raise up a new *nation* from the descendants of Moses himself, and thereby continue His promise.

Just as not all of the sons of Abraham shared in God's promise, neither will all the sons of Jacob. The way things are looking at this point, God intends the 12 tribes to be no more. Instead, God proposes that there is to be a new nation built on a new father. That person will be God's faithful servant Moses.

It may seem incredible to us, but Moses rejects this offer from the Lord. The rest of Numbers 14 relates that Moses asks God to forgive the people, and God agrees. Yet God does impose a punishment: this generation of the nation of Israel will not be allowed to enter Canaan. They will spend 40 years in the wilderness before the promised land becomes available again to their descendants (Numbers 14:22, 23).

Conclusion

A. Do We Repeat the Problem?

I recently watched a basketball game in which a talented team suffered a devastating loss. This losing team actually led most of the game, sometimes by double digits. It was clear to anyone watching that the losing team had superior players when it came to basketball skills.

Victory seemed to be within their grasp. But in the end, when they needed to trust each other and their coach, they crumbled. They began to bicker. They quit listening. The result was a humiliating, embarrassing, and avoidable defeat.

Today's lesson relates a similar defeat for the nation of Israel. The Lord had used Moses and Aaron to lead them to the edge of the land of Canaan, the territory that had been promised to them through their ancestor, Abraham. Yet when they were on the cusp of a mighty victory, they gave in to fear and doubt and suffered a national defeat that took 40 years to overcome.

B. Will We Recognize the Promised Land?

John Steinbeck's gritty novel *Of Mice and Men* tells the story of two transient farm workers in the 1920s. Their dream is to be able to buy a little farm of their own and then "live off the fatta the lan'." To live off the fat of the land means having a life where there is rich abundance with very little

effort. Such an existence is the goal of many people today. To win the lottery, to find out that the painting in the garage is worth $4 million, scoring the big jackpot on *Deal or No Deal*—these would bring us into the promised land of the easy life.

The story of Israel in this lesson shows us another side of the promised land quest. Is it possible that we, like Israel, won't recognize the promised land even when it stares us in the face? Are we forever trapped in a cycle of distrust and despair, leading to a desire to denounce God and the church and go our own way? Or is it possible that we are in the promised land right now but it doesn't seem like it because life is not as easy as we thought it would be?

Truly trusting God is very difficult at times. There is a central human desire to be in control of our situation, to call our own shots. Israel, in the bleak wilderness and facing strong adversaries, yielded to this desire and proposed moving away from God and making its own way. Israel had lost sight of the biblical principle that trust in God brings blessing.

All of us have experienced periods of doubt in our lives. We know firsthand the dilemmas of uncertainty, the perils of a lack of confidence. The Bible teaches that doubt is the enemy of faith (see John 20:27). The sorry history of Israel in today's lesson shows how doubt led to a direct challenge of God, with disastrous results.

Being a faithful follower of Jesus allows us to claim His promises. It does not allow us to expect that our lives will be devoid of hardship or frustration. The book of Joshua shows that Israel had to wage war in order to claim the promised land of Canaan. But they waged that war with God on their side, and eventually the land was theirs. Our lives may seem to be battlegrounds, but God fights for us too. We, the church, are heirs to the promise (Galatians 3:29). May we not despise the promised land that God has given us today (Psalm 106:24).

B. Prayer

Holy Father, we believe that You have prepared a place for us, a marvelous land of promise flowing with milk and honey. Yet our vision of these blessings is dimmed by the daily challenges that test our faith. May our doubts never progress to rebellion. May we always rest with assurance in Your promises and Your love for us. We pray this in the name of Your greatest blessing, Jesus Christ, Your only Son. Amen.

C. Thought to Remember

Never rebel against God.
Always trust Him.

Home Daily Bible Readings

Monday, Aug. 3—Rebelling Against God (Psalm 78:5-17)

Tuesday, Aug. 4—Reaping the Whirlwind (Hosea 8:1-10)

Wednesday, Aug. 5—An Offering for Transgression? (Micah 6:1-8)

Thursday, Aug. 6—Mourning for Our Rebellion (Lamentations 1:16-21)

Friday, Aug. 7—Return to the Lord (Lamentations 3:39-50)

Saturday, Aug. 8—A Compassionate God (Micah 7:14-20)

Sunday, Aug. 9—Go Back to Egypt? (Numbers 14:1-12)

Learning by Doing

This page contains an alternative lesson plan emphasizing learning activities. Some of these activities are also found in the helpful student book, Adult Bible Class.

Into the Lesson

Open your study with some humorous "good news/bad news" scenarios. Either devise your own or say the following.

"I've got good news: the stock market just set a new one-day record. The bad news? The stock market's record was the greatest single-day drop in history."

"I've got good news: your favorite baseball team held the other team scoreless for nine innings. The bad news? The other team scored five unanswered runs in the tenth inning."

"I've got good news: a new government study says coffee is good for your health. The bad news? Coffee prices just doubled."

"I've got good news: our community has a new business coming that will employ five hundred people. The bad news? It's a distillery for whiskey."

Option: just say the good news part, then ask your students to create their own bad news.

Make a transition by saying, "Today's study features both good news and bad news. A certain report by spies had some really good news. The reaction was really bad."

Into the Word

Give each learner a sheet with the two column headings *GOOD* and *BAD* in bold. Tell your learners that you want them to look at each verse in today's text (Numbers 14:1-12) and see if they can find something that is good (or has the potential of being good) and something that is bad in each.

Here are possible responses:

Verse 1: It can be a good thing to show unity of opinion; it is bad when that unity results in crying in fear all night.

Verse 2: It is good to take one's concerns to the delegated leaders; it is bad when trust in God is lacking.

Verse 3: It is good that the men express concern for their wives and children; it is bad to blame God for anything.

Verse 4: It is good to realize that the right leader is necessary for a contemplated action; it is bad to second-guess God regarding whom that leader and action should be.

Verse 5: It is good for leaders to respond to their followers; a bad situation may be indicated when it becomes necessary for leaders to humiliate themselves before their followers.

Verse 6: It is good that leaders are attentive to what others say; it is bad when such leaders must show signs of deep grief over wrong attitudes.

Verse 7: It is good that there is a favorable report made to the assembly; it is bad to have to offer good news from a minority position.

Verse 8: It is good that God is ready to give a blessing; it is bad when the people contemplate doing something that displeases God.

Verse 9: It is good that God is on the side of the Israelites; it is bad that God's people are afraid of the wicked.

Verse 10: It is good that God's glory makes a miraculous appearance to the assembled nation; it is bad that mob action is what calls it forth.

Verse 11: It is good that God reveals himself in miracles and signs; it is bad that disbelief lingers and contempt arises.

Verse 12: It is good that God has the power and will to continue His kingdom plans even if some reject them; it is bad that God must consider destroying the special people He has called and nurtured.

Conclude by observing that some folks never seem to be able to embrace good news because of the presence or possibility of bad news. Remind the class that with God's blessing, "We know that all things work together for good to them that love God" (Romans 8:28).

Into Life

Distribute handouts that each have this list of phrases: *A Tear-Filled Night; The Lesser of Two Evils; Think About the Wives and Children; Falling on Your Face; Tearing One's Clothes; If the Lord Delights in Us; That Which Causes Fear; Stones Hurt; When Glory Appears; All the Signs; Smitten and Disinherited;* and *A Greater, Mightier Nation.*

Note that all these ideas are part of today's lesson. Challenge your students with this assignment: "Select from these ideas to prepare your own devotional notes in your personal times this week. If any of you want to bring your devotional back to class next week, we will welcome your reading it."

Let's Talk It Over

The questions on this page are designed to promote discussion of the lesson by the class and to encourage application of the lesson Scriptures. The answers provided are only discussion starters. Let your class talk it over from there.

1. In what circumstances does our fear mirror that of the Israelites? How do we correct this?

Peter was able to walk on the water at first, but then fear and doubt took hold. As a result, he began to sink (Matthew 14:28-31). When we focus on Jesus, faith can prevail; when we focus on negative circumstances, fear takes over. Perhaps our fear means that we don't know Jesus as well as we should. The Israelites' extreme fear may indicate that they did not truly know God.

Too often we fear the worst in a difficult situation and then take action based on a perceived very-worst-case scenario. The result is an overly defensive mind-set. When that happens, we do not move forward spiritually. The Israelites would have moved forward in faith had they paused to reflect on how God had delivered them to that point (the plagues, the parting of the Red Sea, etc.). We are to use those very examples of deliverance to step out on faith yet today (1 Corinthians 10:1-13).

2. Why do you think Moses and Aaron—the very top leaders—fell on their faces before the assembly of the Israelites? What circumstances in life could (or should) cause us to do the same, at least figuratively?

Secular models of leadership are about power and authority. Such models would not predict or advise leaders to fall on their faces before those whom they lead! Yet we know that Moses was a very humble man (Numbers 12:3); falling face-down is characteristic of humility. When a crisis in life occurs, the first reaction should be to humble oneself in prayer before God. The arrogance of power says "I can handle it." The humility of powerlessness says "God must be involved."

3. What actions and attitudes of Joshua and Caleb can we live by today?

Joshua and Caleb demonstrated a strong faith in God's power to lead them into the promised land and to help them conquer enemies. They did not see their spying task in terms of answering the question "Can it be done?" but rather "How will we do it?" That's a lesson for today. When God says *do it,* the depth of unfaithfulness is to ask "Can it be done?"

God expects us not only to show faith in Him, but also to demonstrate courage before those whom we lead. Numbers 14:10 shows us the mob was ready to kill Joshua and Caleb. These two undoubtedly were aware of that hostile climate even before they spoke out. Yet they spoke out anyway. These two were radically committed to trusting and following God. May we be as well.

4. Have you ever experienced a time when church members strongly opposed their leaders? How was the situation resolved?

Use this question with caution if your church has had problems here! We all know that those in leadership may face fierce opposition to their proposals. When leaders make a decision that people don't like, some may react strongly.

Keep in mind that a *strong* reaction is not necessarily an *unholy* or *ungodly* reaction. Improper or underdeveloped plans should be challenged. The key is to do this in a biblical way. Some passages (among many) that teach us how to handle conflict in appropriate ways are Acts 6:1-6; 15:1-21, 36-41; and Galatians 2:14-21.

In all cases of church conflict, we should remember the distinction between *matters of doctrine* and *matters of expediency*. Baptism, for example, is a matter of doctrine, while the places where baptisms may be performed (rivers, swimming pools, church baptisteries, etc.) is a matter of expediency. Sometimes a person who is fearful about losing a favorite practice or tradition may try to give his or her concern more force by casting it as a matter of doctrine when it is not. In any case, angry denunciation of godly leaders should never be tolerated.

5. How do you trust God at those times when it seems hardest to do so?

What is "hardest" to one person may not be so to another. However, most would agree that one of the very hardest situations is that of a parent whose child suffers from a fatal disease or condition. Experience tells us that God does not always allow (or cause) healing. Trust during such times always should involve the acknowledgment that the God who gives the breath of life in the first place is the one who maintains control of life.

Dishonoring God

DEVOTIONAL READING: **Psalm 95.**

BACKGROUND SCRIPTURE: **Numbers 20:1-13.**

PRINTED TEXT: **Numbers 20:1-13.**

Numbers 20:1-13

1 Then came the children of Israel, even the whole congregation, into the desert of Zin in the first month: and the people abode in Kadesh; and Miriam died there, and was buried there.

2 And there was no water for the congregation: and they gathered themselves together against Moses and against Aaron.

3 And the people chode with Moses, and spake, saying, Would God that we had died when our brethren died before the LORD!

4 And why have ye brought up the congregation of the LORD into this wilderness, that we and our cattle should die there?

5 And wherefore have ye made us to come up out of Egypt, to bring us in unto this evil place? it is no place of seed, or of figs, or of vines, or of pomegranates; neither is there any water to drink.

6 And Moses and Aaron went from the presence of the assembly unto the door of the tabernacle of the congregation, and they fell upon their faces: and the glory of the LORD appeared unto them.

7 And the LORD spake unto Moses, saying,

8 Take the rod, and gather thou the assembly together, thou and Aaron thy brother, and speak ye unto the rock before their eyes; and it shall give forth his water, and thou shalt bring forth to them water out of the rock: so thou shalt give the congregation and their beasts drink.

9 And Moses took the rod from before the LORD, as he commanded him.

10 And Moses and Aaron gathered the congregation together before the rock, and he said unto them, Hear now, ye rebels; must we fetch you water out of this rock?

11 And Moses lifted up his hand, and with his rod he smote the rock twice: and the water came out abundantly, and the congregation drank, and their beasts also.

12 And the LORD spake unto Moses and Aaron, Because ye believed me not, to sanctify me in the eyes of the children of Israel, therefore ye shall not bring this congregation into the land which I have given them.

13 This is the water of Meribah; because the children of Israel strove with the LORD, and he was sanctified in them.

GOLDEN TEXT: The LORD spake unto Moses and Aaron, Because ye believed me not, to sanctify me in the eyes of the children of Israel, therefore ye shall not bring this congregation into the land which I have given them.
—Numbers 20:12.

Call Sealed with Promise
Unit 3: Called to Obey
(Lessons 9–13)

Lesson Aims

After participating in this lesson, each student will be able to:

1. Tell what happened at the site that came to be called *Meribah* and the sad consequences.

2. Explain how frustration or other emotional stress can lead one to dishonor God today.

3. Recruit an accountability partner for mutual growth in an area where both need to honor God more.

Lesson Outline

INTRODUCTION
- A. "Yes, Your Honor"
- B. Lesson Background

I. FRUSTRATION & COMPLAINING (Numbers 20:1-5)
- A. Thirsty in the Desert (vv. 1, 2)
- B. Longing for Egypt (vv. 3-5)
  - *Bad Places*

II. COMPLAINING & DISOBEDIENCE (Numbers 20: 6-11)
- A. God's Will Sought (v. 6)
- B. God's Instructions Received (vv. 7, 8)
  - *Instruments*
- C. God's Instructions Violated (vv. 9-11)

III. DISOBEDIENCE & PUNISHMENT (Numbers 20: 12, 13)
- A. God Condemns the Actions (v. 12)
- B. God's Sanctity Is Upheld (v. 13)

CONCLUSION
- A. Honor, Glory, and Holiness
- B. Prayer
- C. Thought to Remember

Introduction

A. "Yes, Your Honor"

Anyone who has ever appeared before a judge knows that proper courtesy and respect are necessary. If we want the judge to treat us favorably, we must do nothing to turn him or her against us.

A central part of this courtesy is our language. Courtroom protocol expects us to address the judge with respect, using the title "your honor." This does not mean we are honoring the judge on a personal-lifestyle level, for we may know noth-

ing about this. It means we are honoring the judge as a representative of the legal system that forms the backbone of our society.

Moreover, when we say "your honor," we are expressing an expectation that the judge will act in an honorable manner. It is disheartening to learn that a judge has taken a bribe, favored a crony, acted carelessly, or done other things that bring dishonor on the court.

Honor must be central in our relationship with the ultimate judge: the Lord our God. Since we live in an increasingly careless society, it has become more common to act disrespectfully toward God, the opposite of honoring him. Yet the Lord has promised that those "that honor me I will honor" (1 Samuel 2:30).

God's honor is not dependent on us. The psalmist wrote that God is "clothed with honor and majesty" (Psalm 104:1). This does nothing to relieve us of the responsibility of honoring God, however. Paul even goes so far as to imply that the failure to honor God is a type of voluntary insanity, a futility of mental processes (Romans 1:21). We as God's creatures not only have an obligation to honor God, we have a need to do so. Honoring God must be more than lip service. It must come from the heart (see Isaiah 29:13).

B. Lesson Background

Numbers 13 tells the story of a group of Israelite men who were sent into the land of Canaan as spies to evaluate the region. They returned with glowing reports of the land's bounty. But most of the men gave fearful reports of the military strength of the residents. This caused the nation to cry out for a return to Egypt, and even to make plans for replacing Moses as their leader. This story was the topic of last week's lesson.

The result of this lack of faith was for God to forbid the adults of the nation to enter the promised land. They would die in the wilderness, for anyone age 20 or over would be included in this death toll (Numbers 14:29). The only exceptions were to be the 2 spies who encouraged the nation not to fear and to go and possess the land (14:30). The other Israelites were told that they had to wander in the wilderness for 40 years until the adult population of the time had passed away (14:33).

The people of Israel did not take this news well. Therefore, they decided to try to force their way into Canaan in spite of the Lord's decision. This expedition was a disaster, and the Israelite force was soundly defeated by the Amalekites and Canaanites of the region (Numbers 14:45).

In today's lesson, the nation has returned to the site of this earlier rebellion, namely Kadesh

(Numbers 13:26; 20:1). While the exact location of Kadesh is a matter of conjecture today, it was a site about 50 miles south of Beersheba. Beersheba marked the southern border of Canaan. The land is increasingly arid and barren south from there. This is described as the "wilderness [and desert] of Zin" (13:21; 20:1). It is the northern part of the larger "wilderness of Paran," which includes most of the central area of the Sinai Peninsula (see 13:3, 26).

In these references, the word *wilderness* has the primary idea of "uninhabitable" because the conditions were so harsh. The water miracle in today's story means that Kadesh became an oasis in this wilderness. Today's lesson occurs at the end of the 40-year period of wilderness wandering (about 1406 BC). This is just prior to the campaigns and maneuvers that take Israel into the promised land of Canaan.

I. Frustration & Complaining (Numbers 20:1-5)

A. Thirsty in the Desert (vv. 1, 2)

1. Then came the children of Israel, even the whole congregation, into the desert of Zin in the first month: and the people abode in Kadesh; and Miriam died there, and was buried there.

The first month is the month of Abib in the Hebrew calendar (later called Nisan), as we learned in Lesson 6 of this quarter. Since the ancient Israelites use a lunar calendar system in contrast with our solar calendar system, Abib does not correspond precisely to any of our modern months. The use of a lunar calendar system means that Abib (as other months) "moves around" a bit year to year. But it roughly equates to late March and early

April. It is the month in which the Passover is celebrated (Exodus 12).

Few of the generation that was prohibited from entry into the promised land remain for the episode we are about to see unfold. The death of *Miriam*, one of the last of that older generation, is recorded here. She was the sister of Moses and Aaron (Numbers 26:59; 1 Chronicles 6:3; compare Exodus 2:4). Those three formed something of a family triumvirate of leadership during the wilderness period (see Micah 6:4).

Miriam had been a prophetess and had leadership skills (Exodus 15:20, 21). But she and Aaron also conspired against Moses at one point (Numbers 12). Thus the great Miriam had her problems too. Along with her two brothers, she does not enter the promised land.

Kadesh (also known as Kadesh-barnea) means "holy place." This was God's original launching point for the final push into the promised land some 40 years earlier (Numbers 13:26). But that plan had been thwarted by the rebellion and fear of the people of Israel.

2. And there was no water for the congregation: and they gathered themselves together against Moses and against Aaron.

Any water supply at Kadesh of some 40 years previous has dried up by now. We do not know the exact population of *the congregation* of Israel at this point, but a later count puts the number of men at 601,730 (Numbers 26:51). Adding in women and children makes the number much larger. This number of people requires an enormous supply of fresh water every day. The frustration of *no water* leads the people to turn against their leaders.

B. Longing for Egypt (vv. 3-5)

3. And the people chode with Moses, and spake, saying, Would God that we had died when our brethren died before the LORD!

Chode is the past tense of *chide,* and here means "to argue or dispute." The mass of *people* yapping at *Moses* probably is led by the remaining few from the rebellion at Kadesh some 40 years earlier, for they refer to the deaths of their *brethren.* Consider that God has provided for these people faithfully through 4 decades of nomadic life. Moses later will point out that even their clothes did not wear out during this 40-year period (Deuteronomy 8:4). Yet they still complain! [See question #1, page 432.]

4. And why have ye brought up the congregation of the LORD into this wilderness, that we and our cattle should die there?

Without water the people will quickly *die,* along with their livestock. The word *ye* indicates that

---

How to Say It

AARON. *Air*-un.

ABIB. *A*-bib.

AMALEKITES. *Am*-uh-leh-kites or Uh-*mal*-ih-kites.

BEERSHEBA. Beer-*she*-buh.

CANAAN. *Kay*-nun.

CANAANITES. *Kay*-nun-ites.

EGYPT. *Ee*-jipt.

ISRAELITES. *Iz*-ray-el-ites.

KADESH-BARNEA. *Kay*-desh-*bar*-nee-uh (strong accent on *bar*).

KORAH. *Ko*-rah.

MERIBAH. *Mehr*-ih-buh.

NISAN. *Nye*-san.

PARAN. *Pair*-un.

SINAI. *Sigh*-nye or *Sigh*-nay-eye.

they are again blaming Moses for this situation. The complainers assume that Moses has failed them, that he is no longer receiving directions from God. Thus the arrival in this desolate place. From Moses' perspective, the unfairness of this complaint is magnified when one considers that the complainers are (apparently) not even giving him a chance to mourn the death of his sister.

5. And wherefore have ye made us to come up out of Egypt, to bring us in unto this evil place? it is no place of seed, or of figs, or of vines, or of pomegranates; neither is there any water to drink.

Again, we see the "good old days" syndrome. It is highly active among the people of Israel. This is the attitude that perceives the better situation of the past. The Israelites seem to be idealizing *Egypt* as a place of plenty of water and lots of food. By contrast, they see Kadesh as a place of no water and no food.

As we analyze what the people "should" remember, we remind ourselves that most of the people at this time have had no experience of Egypt as adults. The memories are either dim from childhood or secondhand from others. Thus, it may be somewhat excusable that they fail to remember Egypt as a place of slavery and brutal work conditions. But dimness of memory also makes us wonder why the complainers presume to think that conditions back in Egypt were (and are) so much better than the current state of affairs.

Complaining comes easily for us, doesn't it? Dissatisfaction as a component of our personalities can be helpful in leading us to improvement. Complaints against God and His commands will have the opposite effect, though. If we try to "improve" on what God has ordained, we will be disobedient. This story before us presents an interesting twist on this process. In this case, the complaints of the people of Israel do indeed lead to disobedience. But it is not the people who disobey this time. It is Moses.

BAD PLACES

California's Death Valley is considered one of the most inhospitable places on earth, as attested by its name. Covering about 3,000 square miles, it has the reputation of being the hottest, driest place in North America. The temperatures often exceed 120 degrees in summer. With an average annual rainfall of about 2 inches, it is also quite dry.

But Death Valley also has surprising resources. Gold and silver mining took place in the 1850s. For a long time, borax mines were a constant of the local economy; the borax mule train of the 1880s was famous. After the winter rains come, flowers blossom and belie the valley's designation

as a desert. Tourism is a growing industry, and the National Park there remains popular.

If a place like Death Valley has these things to recommend it, could Kadesh have been all that bad? Yet the Israelites labeled it an "evil place" in their rabid desire to return to Egypt; we see irony in that the name of this "evil place" Kadesh means "holy place." As we ponder their attitude, let us recall that it is not natural resources or climate that ultimately determines whether any given place is *good* or *bad*. The main issue is the presence or absence of God (compare Ezekiel 48:35).

—J. B. N.

II. Complaining & Disobedience (Numbers 20:6-11)

A. God's Will Sought (v. 6)

6. And Moses and Aaron went from the presence of the assembly unto the door of the tabernacle of the congregation, and they fell upon their faces: and the glory of the LORD appeared unto them.

Moses apparently gives no answer to the people. Instead, he and *Aaron* go directly to seek the presence of God in *the tabernacle.* [See question #2, page 432.] If Moses and Aaron ask God any specific questions, we are not told what they are. At any rate, Moses and Aaron bow appropriately, and God appears to them.

B. God's Instructions Received (vv. 7, 8)

7, 8. And the LORD spake unto Moses, saying, Take the rod, and gather thou the assembly together, thou and Aaron thy brother, and speak ye unto the rock before their eyes; and it shall give forth his water, and thou shalt bring forth to them water out of the rock: so thou shalt give the congregation and their beasts drink.

The rod mentioned here is a stout wooden staff, the kind used by shepherds. For Moses and Aaron, their rods are signs of their authority and are used in their miraculous works.

After the revolt of Korah (Numbers 16), Israel was punished with a death plague. Aaron's actions had been the key to stopping the plague (Numbers 16:46-48); Aaron's authority then was vindicated when his rod miraculously sprouted blossoms and ripe almonds overnight. For this reason, Moses placed Aaron's rod before the ark of the covenant as a warning to rebels (Numbers 17:8-10; see Hebrews 9:4). It is likely, then, that the rod used in this story is Aaron's staff.

In today's text, Israel is near the end of the wilderness sojourn. Moses is told to reenact a scene from the beginning of the Sinai period that involved striking a *rock* with a rod to have it produce water miraculously (see Exodus 17:1-7). [See question #3, page 432.] Only this time Moses is to *speak* to the rock instead of striking it. This seemingly simple request of the Lord is played out in a way that leads to disaster.

INSTRUMENTS

I come from a musical family (although the music genes mostly have bypassed me). My mother and her sister both played the piano. Both of my grandmothers were pianists, with my dad's mother serving as a church organist for over 30 years. My dad received professional training as a vocalist. My wife was a vocal music major in college; she has a marvelously sweet soprano voice. Both of my daughters are musically gifted, one of them now teaching music at a Christian college.

As a result, I love piano music, both classical and religious (honky-tonk is not my style!). But I have learned through the years that the piano is just an instrument. Beautiful music comes from a piano when skilled performers apply their gifts to its keys.

The same applies to other "instruments." My dad was a carpenter, and in his hands various tools could create functional things like cabinets, toys, and houses. In my hands those same tools are worthless. Doctors use surgical instruments for healing purposes. Without their abilities and skills, those same instruments can inflict great damage on the human body.

Moses used a staff or rod as an instrument of power. Yet the power was not in the staff. (It is probably a good thing that this staff no longer exists, lest it be venerated.) The staff was merely an instrument to demonstrate God's power. May the same be said of us in our efforts to serve God. May we glorify Him and no other.   —J. B. N.

C. God's Instructions Violated (vv. 9-11)

9. And Moses took the rod from before the LORD, as he commanded him.

Moses starts well, taking the *rod* as *the Lord* commands. Rather than proceed with his simple task, however, Moses takes the opportunity to give a little speech. This speech contains two troubling elements.

10. And Moses and Aaron gathered the congregation together before the rock, and he said unto them, Hear now, ye rebels; must we fetch you water out of this rock?

Moses first chastises the people of Israel as *rebels*, although God has not told him to do so. God's response in Numbers 20:8 shows no impatience or exasperation with the people. In a later recounting

of this incident, the psalmist will write that Moses spoke "unadvisedly with his lips" (Psalm 106:33).

Second, Moses' question *Must we fetch you water?* seems to take personal credit (along with Aaron) for the miracle about to happen. Does Moses fail to recall that he is no more than God's instrument?

11. And Moses lifted up his hand, and with his rod he smote the rock twice: and the water came out abundantly, and the congregation drank, and their beasts also.

Moses disobeys the Lord by striking *the rock* instead of speaking to it. The fact that he strikes it *twice* may remind us of the impatient pedestrian at a crosswalk who pushes the button for the "walk" light several times when it does not change quickly enough. Moses is angry and impatient with the people. He lets this attitude distract him from the nature of God's miracle. We imagine that the *rod* must be sturdy, or else Moses' angry blows would shatter it.

III. Disobedience & Punishment (Numbers 20:12, 13)

A. God Condemns the Actions (v. 12)

12. And the LORD spake unto Moses and Aaron, Because ye believed me not, to sanctify me in the eyes of the children of Israel, therefore ye shall not bring this congregation into the land which I have given them.

The wilderness experience of Israel includes examples of God's forgiveness (compare Numbers 14:18). In this case, however, the disobedience of *Moses and Aaron* is to be punished. This is to be so even though Moses has been God's key man to this point in creating the nation of Israel. [See question #4, page 432.]

God brings two charges. The first charge is that the brothers have shown a lack of faith. This results in disobedience. They do not trust God enough to carry out His instructions in humility, but give in to anger. Second, the pair does not *sanctify* God, meaning that they do not respect God's holiness. What could be an occasion of reverence and celebration for the people of God turns into a joyless expression of Moses' anger and frustration.

These actions of Moses and Aaron are later lumped into the general category of "rebellion" (see Numbers 20:24; 27:14). Ironically, this casts Moses into the villainous rebel role of which he accuses the people (20:10, above).

There is a connection here that may not usually occur to us. Rebellion is easily understood as an action that is contrary to honoring. But rebellion also stands in opposition to God's holiness. We cannot sanctify God and oppose Him at the same time. We are called to yield to God's will in obedience. When we do this, we honor God. To fail to do so is to deny God's holiness.

B. God's Sanctity Is Upheld (v. 13)

13. This is the water of Meribah; because the children of Israel strove with the LORD, and he was sanctified in them.

There is an ironic clash of words here. The word *Meribah* means "place of contention"; Israel is to remember this as a place of contention with God and recall the grievous results. The place is also *Kadesh*, the "holy place." [See question #5, page 432.] God's purity and holiness cannot be thwarted by the human sin of contending with Him. Despite the whining of the people and the disobedience of the leaders, God's holiness prevails.

Visual for Lesson 11. *Turn this imperative into a question as you ask your students to name ways they will honor God in the week ahead.*

Conclusion

A. Honor, Glory, and Holiness

The complexities of our lives can lead to frustrations both big and small. We seem just to get on top of our finances when a big, unexpected expense comes our way. We are let down by people we depend on. A careless driver bumps our car. People reach breaking points as frustrations begin to pile up. By the time Israel returned to Kadesh, they had been through a lot. But at that place they were confronted with a situation that pushed their frustration tolerance past its limits.

The frustration of the people infected Moses. Forty years in the desert apparently took its toll on that elderly leader. He began well, standing up to Pharaoh's every threat and roadblock to free the people of Israel from Egypt. He followed God's directions, even though the commands must have seemed curious at times. No one expects to escape across a sea without boats or military protection. But Moses trusted God and performed the seemingly futile act of raising his rod over the sea, seeing it part to reveal a dry path of escape. In celebrating this victory, Moses sang that the Lord is "glorious in holiness" (Exodus 15:11).

The New Testament contains a reprise of the Song of Moses from Exodus 15 in Revelation 15:3, 4. In this brief passage, we gain the perspective that worship is a matter of fearing God, of glorifying God, and of respecting God's holiness. To worship God requires that we show Him honor in every possible way.

This is more than a Sunday morning task. As Moses learned the hard way, we can honor or dishonor God even in a seemingly straightforward job. Violating God's holiness is much more than disrespecting items or spaces in our church buildings. We violate God's holiness every time we rebel against Him and act in defiance to His will. This is because disobedience betrays our lack of fear for God and causes our praise of His glory to ring hollow. We respect God's holiness when we love Him and fear Him enough to obey Him.

B. Prayer

Holy God, may we honor You in all we say and in all we do. May we never despise Your provisions for us. May we sanctify You in our congregation. When complaints against You rise to our lips, may we have the wisdom to swallow them and sing Your praises instead. We pray these things through the name of our Savior Jesus. Amen.

C. Thought to Remember

Respect God's holiness by obeying Him.

Learning by Doing

This page contains an alternative lesson plan emphasizing learning activities. Some of these activities are also found in the helpful student book, Adult Bible Class.

Into the Lesson

Divide the class into three sections where they are seated. Give each person in the first group a slip of paper on which is written the word *grumble*. Each person in the second group is to be given a slip with the word *mumble*. Each in the third group is to have a slip with the word *murmur*.

Say, "On my signal—which will be the word *Israel*—say your word aloud over and over. Increase and decrease both speed and volume randomly until you hear me say *stop*. Ready? *Israel!*" After 10 seconds, say *stop*.

Then say, "When such noise reaches God's ears, He is both saddened and angered. Turn to Numbers 20 and listen to the complaints in the following *Israelites at Meribah* series of monologues."

Into the Word

Before class, recruit learners for a series of very brief monologues as follows. Direct the class to read through the text (or have it read aloud). Then present the monologues. After each monologue, ask the class to identify how today's text relates in some fashion.

Monologue #1: "Occasionally, I think our church leaders don't care a thing about those of us who like things as they are. They always want to start some *new* program!"

Monologue #2: "To be honest, sometimes I think about going back to my pre-Christian lifestyle. Call them slave masters if you want, but I certainly had more fun doing the old things!"

Monologue #3: "Well, if I should die 'at an inconvenient time,' I don't believe anyone would stop to grieve my passing. As they drive out of the cemetery, I suppose they'll forget all that I did for the church."

Monologue #4: "It often seems as if everything depends on me. Well, if I'm going to get the blame, I'm going to get the credit too."

Monologue #5: "It's just not fair. After all I had put into this endeavor, one little mistake and I'm excluded from the good times of accomplishment ahead."

Though your class may see other connections with the events of the text, here are some possibilities: (1) Israelite grumbling about water and food, forgetting the ultimate goal: safety and freedom in the promised land. (2) The people of Israel considering going back to Egyptian slavery. (3) Miriam being buried (apparently) without fanfare or an extended period of mourning despite her leadership role alongside Moses and Aaron. (4) Moses disobeying God regarding his action toward the rock, seemingly taking personal credit for God's miracle. (5) Moses and Aaron not being allowed to enter the promised land.

Say, "The supply of food and water for the large Israelite congregation in the wilderness was a matter of miraculous provision. When the water supply was inadequate at Kadesh, it was a matter of faith that God would provide. The complaining was a matter, then, not simply of thirst but of inadequate faith and patience."

Ask your class to discuss these questions:

1. In what sense does grumbling and complaining equal an attack on God's grace and love?

2. In what sense do occasions of complaining represent the impatience that shows a lack of the fruit of the Spirit in one's life?

Because this lesson deals with the sin of one of God's children who was considered a holy leader (Moses), ask the class to identify other biblical leaders who demonstrated sin in their lives. The task should be simple (David, Peter, etc.). After a brief listing, make the point that no human is above sin, but God is. He forgives sin when He sees true repentance. Have someone read 1 John 1:8-10.

Into Life

If your budget allows, purchase a bottle of water for each learner. If your budget does not allow for this, photocopy a picture of a bottle of water for each learner. As you pass out the bottles (or pictures), give this admonition: "Place this bottle (or picture) where you will see it each day this week as a reminder of today's study and as a deterrent to grumbling and complaining. At the end of the week, give thanks to God for providing for your daily needs."

Wrap up by saying, "Most of us could use an accountability partner at one time or another. With such a partner we can discuss and evaluate mutual growth in honoring God. Has anyone had a good experience with an accountability partner that you would like to discuss?" Close with an encouragement to seek out an accountability partner.

Let's Talk It Over

The questions on this page are designed to promote discussion of the lesson by the class and to encourage application of the lesson Scriptures. The answers provided are only discussion starters. Let your class talk it over from there.

1. How could the Israelites have presented their concerns in a positive way? What can we learn from their bad example about how to express our own concerns to those in leadership positions?

The people could have presented their need for water with an attitude that Moses and God would act in their best interests. The way things unfolded, however, offers the impression that the people viewed God as either lacking in power, as totally absent, or as a devious being who likes to torture people. When we see things that need to be done or problems that need to be dealt with in our congregation, we can approach our leaders not only with a clear presentation of the problem, but also with a proposed solution that involves our willingness to help.

One minister said that whenever someone comes to him with a complaint, he (the minister) immediately proposes a solution that involves the complainer as the key person to take the lead in fixing the problem. After about a year of using that procedure, that minister saw the number of complaints go way down!

2. Under what circumstances do you find it necessary to get away from other people to go before the Lord as opposed to staying with those people for group prayer?

When pressure builds and when the pace of events speeds up, a leader may feel that it's especially important to get away to a quiet place to pray. This allows the leader to slow the thought processes, setting a personal pace for the prayer; this is more difficult in a group setting. It may not be productive to pray in a group setting if the group is hostile toward the leader, as was the case in today's text.

Leaders, including those in the spiritual, political, and family spheres, all need to know that prayer is a critical ingredient in gaining the wisdom to make right decisions that will affect those they serve. Failure to pray means that the leader is deciding to try to solve things personally, without inviting God's involvement.

3. What are some of the ways that the Lord responds to our complaints today? How have you grown spiritually as a result?

We must be careful! Complaining can lead to a difficult situation becoming worse. Complaining can open the door wider for the devil to bring destruction into a given situation. When we honestly assess the effects of complaining, we may realize that complaining often magnifies problems rather than solving them.

We can grow spiritually as we recognize the negative effects of complaining; this will motivate us to stop doing it. We then can replace the complaining with deliberate thanksgiving and praise. The very short chapter Jeremiah 45 should be read by all complainers. There God responds to Baruch's complaint with a complaint of His own! God's final answer to Baruch is that that man will escape with his life. Be very cautious about complaining to God!

4. How have you discovered that disobedience to God always leads to loss in some way? How have you grown through such experiences?

Moses' disobedience resulted in not being allowed to lead the people into the promised land. When a believer disobeys, something is always lost. Sometimes the loss is large, sometimes it's small. Sometimes the loss is immediate, sometimes the consequences are delayed. But there is always loss. God will forgive when a person repents. But even with forgiveness, some consequences of the disobedience remain. The sordid episode of David and Bathsheba is an example.

5. Which is the more accurate description of your home: *place of contention* or *holy place*? How can you make it more of the latter?

Answers will be highly personal, of course. Some may view their homes as places of contention because they think, for example, in terms of the frequent arguments about what to watch on TV; they may suppose that the solution to reducing the number of arguments is to have several TVs. But the question should be taken in more of a spiritual sense. Is your prayer life at home primarily one of fussing with God about meeting the lacks that you perceive in your life? Or is your prayer life at home primarily characterized as holy conversations with God, with expressions of gratitude and thankfulness sprinkled liberally throughout?

Obeying the Commands

DEVOTIONAL READING: Proverbs 2:1-11.

BACKGROUND SCRIPTURE: Deuteronomy 6.

PRINTED TEXT: Deuteronomy 6:1-9, 20-24.

Deuteronomy 6:1-9, 20-24

1 Now these are the commandments, the statutes, and the judgments, which the LORD your God commanded to teach you, that ye might do them in the land whither ye go to possess it:

2 That thou mightest fear the LORD thy God, to keep all his statutes and his commandments, which I command thee, thou, and thy son, and thy son's son, all the days of thy life; and that thy days may be prolonged.

3 Hear therefore, O Israel, and observe to do it; that it may be well with thee, and that ye may increase mightily, as the LORD God of thy fathers hath promised thee, in the land that floweth with milk and honey.

4 Hear, O Israel: The LORD our God is one LORD:

5 And thou shalt love the LORD thy God with all thine heart, and with all thy soul, and with all thy might.

6 And these words, which I command thee this day, shall be in thine heart:

7 And thou shalt teach them diligently unto thy children, and shalt talk of them when thou sittest in thine house, and when thou walkest by the way, and when thou liest down, and when thou risest up.

8 And thou shalt bind them for a sign upon thine hand, and they shall be as frontlets between thine eyes.

9 And thou shalt write them upon the posts of thy house, and on thy gates.

. . . .

20 And when thy son asketh thee in time to come, saying, What mean the testimonies, and the statutes, and the judgments, which the LORD our God hath commanded you?

21 Then thou shalt say unto thy son, We were Pharaoh's bondmen in Egypt; and the LORD brought us out of Egypt with a mighty hand:

22 And the LORD showed signs and wonders, great and sore, upon Egypt, upon Pharaoh, and upon all his household, before our eyes:

23 And he brought us out from thence, that he might bring us in, to give us the land which he sware unto our fathers.

24 And the LORD commanded us to do all these statutes, to fear the LORD our God, for our good always, that he might preserve us alive, as it is at this day.

GOLDEN TEXT: Hear, O Israel: The LORD our God is one LORD: And thou shalt love the LORD thy God with all thine heart, and with all thy soul, and with all thy might. And these words, which I command thee this day, shall be in thine heart.
—Deuteronomy 6:4-6.

Call Sealed with Promise
Unit 3: Called to Obey
(Lessons 9–13)

Lesson Aims

After participating in this lesson, each student will be able to:

1. Tell how Israel was commanded to remember and keep the law and to pass it on to following generations.

2. Tell how Deuteronomy 6:4, 5 summarizes the intent of the whole law.

3. Explain to one other person the value of obeying God's law.

Lesson Outline

INTRODUCTION
  A. Refusing to Listen
  B. Lesson Background
 I. IMPORTANT BLESSINGS (Deuteronomy 6:1-3)
  A. Where (v. 1)
  B. Why (vv. 2, 3)
    Hear! Hear!
 II. PRIMARY COMMANDS (Deuteronomy 6:4, 5)
  A. Knowledge (v. 4)
  B. Love (v. 5)
III. FULL IMMERSION (Deuteronomy 6:6-9)
  A. Anchor Them (v. 6)
  B. Teach Them (v. 7)
  C. Bind Them (vv. 8, 9)
    Reminders
IV. FUTURE ANSWERS (Deuteronomy 6:20-24)
  A. Son's Question (v. 20)
  B. Parent's Response (vv. 21-24)
CONCLUSION
  A. Free to Obey
  B. Prayer
  C. Thought to Remember

Introduction

A. Refusing to Listen

Years ago, a letter appeared in a *Dear Abby* column to voice a complaint against the "selective hearing" of an elderly parent. It seems that the adult daughter who was writing the letter could communicate with her mother only to the point where the mother disagreed with something. When that point was reached, the mother would turn her hearing aid off, refusing to listen any further!

Needless to say, this tactic was extremely frustrating to the daughter. The daughter's frustration may make us wonder how exasperated God may become at the "selective hearing" that His people frequently display yet today.

B. Lesson Background

To gain the most understanding from today's lesson, we should come to grips with how the book of Deuteronomy functions within the Bible. Moses' speeches in this book were part of the formal covenant treaty between God and Israel. In the Ancient Near East, virtually all important agreements were sworn in oaths. Oaths that resulted in treaties and covenants were written down. This was especially true of treaties designed to set policy for many generations.

That's what Deuteronomy does as it outlines and regulates a conditional relationship between God and the people of Israel. God claimed absolute right of sovereignty, and He required total loyalty. In return, God pledged protection for His people.

The word *Deuteronomy* means "the second law." This can be a little misleading since the idea of a "second" law can be taken to mean "a different, additional" law. But the idea is really more along the lines of "a repetition of the law," referring to the law given on Mount Sinai (Exodus 19–31).

Deuteronomy's expression of the covenant can be outlined this way: (1) the preamble (1:1-5), which identifies some geographical and chronological information; (2) the historical prologue (1:6–3:29), where the relationship between the parties is reviewed; (3) the general covenant stipulations (chapters 4–11) and specific covenant stipulations (chapters 12–27); (4) the blessings and cursings section (chapter 28); (5) some summarization (chapters 29, 30); and (6) the witness section (chapter 31). The book wraps up with some facts about how Moses' life and ministry draw to a close.

If the Israelites were to be God's covenant people, then they were expected to keep the covenant stipulations (that is, the law). The laws of the covenant reflect something of the nature of God. By extension, when the Israelites kept the law they reflected God's nature to the world.

I. Important Blessings (Deuteronomy 6:1-3)
A. Where (v. 1)

1. Now these are the commandments, the statutes, and the judgments, which the LORD your God commanded to teach you, that ye might do them in the land whither ye go to possess it.

Deuteronomy 6:1-3 introduces what is called *the shema*, which we will study beginning in verse 4 (below). Just prior to Deuteronomy 6, Moses restates the Ten Commandments (5:7-21). Along with that restatement comes a brief reminder of Israel's experience at Sinai, some 40 years in the past at this point (5:22-33; compare Exodus 20:18-26).

All this is important to note because it helps us see that the word *these* here in verse 1 refers collectively to all *the commandments, the statutes, and the judgments* that Moses has been commanded to teach as the mediator of the covenant (Deuteronomy 5:31). [See question #1, page 440.] The phrase *in the land whither ye go to possess it* reminds us once again that the Israelites are right on the verge of crossing the Jordan River to enter the promised land, about 1406 BC.

B. Why (vv. 2, 3)

2. That thou mightest fear the LORD thy God, to keep all his statutes and his commandments, which I command thee, thou, and thy son, and thy son's son, all the days of thy life; and that thy days may be prolonged.

The Israelites have already experienced the *fear* of God at various times. A primary example was the Mount Sinai experience (Exodus 20:18, 19; Deuteronomy 5:5). But the fear recommended here is not the automatic reaction of terror caused by meeting a powerful being. This fear, rather, is a learned response, as we see in Deuteronomy 31:12, 13. It is the attitude and mind-set that God expects toward Him.

The Lord is the creator of the universe. As such He maintains justice on the earth and avenges the oppressed (Deuteronomy 32:35; Psalm 94; Nahum 1:2-6). There should be no doubt that He will bless those who both fear Him and honor their part of the covenant (Deuteronomy 28). The fear of God is to culminate in keeping and doing all His commandments (28:1). In the context of the covenant, one of the benefits of keeping all His commandments is the gift of *prolonged days*.

3. Hear therefore, O Israel, and observe to do it; that it may be well with thee, and that ye may increase mightily, as the LORD God of thy fathers hath promised thee, in the land that floweth with milk and honey.

Fearing God and keeping His commandments brings covenant blessings. To *increase mightily* speaks to the flourishing of the Israelite nation. This certainly includes the prolonged days of verse 2, just mentioned. It also includes the fact that the promised land will be rich in produce (Deuteronomy 28:3-5, 11, 12).

Variations of the phrase *land that floweth with milk and honey* occur 20 times in the Old Testament. We all know that milk is the product of cows and goats, while bees produce honey. But to take the phrase *milk and honey* to refer narrowly to just those two ideas is too restrictive. The broader idea is that the fertility of the land is beyond question.

HEAR! HEAR!

The simple verb *hear* has had an interesting pilgrimage in the English language over the centuries. Originally, it simply meant "to listen, to receive auditory impulses through the ear." According to the *Oxford English Dictionary*, this meaning can be documented as early as AD 950.

When the word is doubled as *Hear! Hear!* it carries greater meaning. Now the idea is that a speaker's words are significant and deserve approval. In this sense, the usage can be traced back to 1689, and this form is often used in Great Britain's Parliament. By this device, listeners indicate their support for the words of the speaker.

Perhaps you remember the phrase *Hear ye, Hear ye* from a movie or book. That phrase was used in centuries past by heralds who carried announcements of major import. The idea is that the words that follow carry great significance, and the listener ought to give undivided attention to them. That phrase is still used in modern courts of law to introduce the beginning of a court session; as such, the phrase announces the importance of the proceedings, the judge, and the decisions that are to be made there.

Thus in both English and ancient Hebrew forms, the word *hear* can call attention to the importance of a message and its weighty impact. If God is

Visual for Lessons 5 & 12. *Point to this visual as you ask, "How is loving God related to hearing Him and obeying Him?"*

about to speak (through Moses) His instructions, what more important directive can there be than "Hear therefore, O Israel"? The requirement to listen to God has never gone away.   —J. B. N.

II. Primary Commands (Deuteronomy 6:4, 5)

A. Knowledge (v. 4)

4. Hear, O Israel: The LORD our God is one LORD.

This verse begins what is known as *the shema*. The Hebrew word *shema* means "hear," which is the very first word in the verse. Thus the name.

The importance of this verse and the one that follows is seen in Mark 12:28, 29. When asked "Which is the first commandment of all?" by a scribe, Jesus replies by quoting Deuteronomy 6:4, 5. Verse 4 means that Israel's God is the only God there is. True, the Bible speaks of other gods at times (see Exodus 12:12; 15:11; 18:11; etc.). But that does not imply that other gods really exist (see Jeremiah 2:11); such gods are no more than images of carved wood, chiseled stone, and figments of the imagination. There is *one Lord*—Israel's Lord.

Israel needs to be very aware of this fact as the people prepare to enter a land that already has been cultivated successfully by other people groups. Israel is liable to worship the pagan agricultural deities of the area (which, sadly, is what ends up happening). This cannot be stressed enough: Israel's God is her only Lord. This is because He is the only true God (see also Deuteronomy 4:35, 39; 5:7; 32:39; Zechariah 14:9). The New Testament doctrine of the Trinity supports the fact that God is one even as He manifests himself in three persons (Mark 12:29; John 10:30; Romans 8:9-11; etc.).

How to Say It

ABRAHAM. *Ay*-bruh-ham.
AMON-RE. *Ay*-mun-Ree.
DEUTERONOMY. Due-ter-*ahn*-uh-me.
EGYPT. *Ee*-jipt.
ISRAELITES. *Iz*-ray-el-ites.
MACCABEES. *Mack*-uh-bees.
MERISM. *meh*-rizum.
MEZUZAH. meh-*zoo*-zuh.
MOSAIC. Mo-*zay*-ik.
PHYLACTERIES. fih-*lak*-ter-eez.
SHEMA *(Hebrew).* shih-*mah*.
SOVEREIGNTY. *saw*-vren-tee.
ZECHARIAH. *Zek*-uh-*rye*-uh (strong accent on *rye*).

B. Love (v. 5)

5. And thou shalt love the LORD thy God with all thine heart, and with all thy soul, and with all thy might.

This command is the language of covenant loyalty. God loves His people (see Deuteronomy 4:37; 7:7, 8; etc.), and the people are to *love* God (10:12; 11:13, 22; etc.).

This love is to result in faithful obedience (Deuteronomy 5:10; 7:9; 10:12, 13; 11:1; 13:3, 4; 30:16). But this "greatest commandment in the law" (Matthew 22:36, 37) is not exhausted by the behavior required by the covenant. It goes beyond the behavior that is required by the law to the innermost strength of a person's thought life. It involves the total commitment of the whole person.

The *heart* is the seat of the intellect, emotions, intentions, and will. Note that when the New Testament quotes this command, Jesus adds the word *mind* in order to make the idea as strong as possible (Matthew 22:37; Mark 12:30; Luke 10:27).

Finally, it is significant that this inclusive commandment of love immediately follows the Ten Commandments in the book of Deuteronomy. To love God is to be dedicated to Him and His designs and purposes for His people. To love God is to keep the Ten Commandments and all His law (see v. 1, above).

III. Full Immersion (Deuteronomy 6:6-9)

A. Anchor Them (v. 6)

6. And these words, which I command thee this day, shall be in thine heart.

There's an old story about a little girl who was standing up in the front seat of the car as her father drove along (this was in the days before child safety seats were required). Her father instructed her several times to sit down. She did so only when he threatened her with punishment. But after she was seated, the father heard her words of defiance: "Daddy, I'm still standing up on the inside."

The little girl's obedience was external only—her heart was still disobedient. That is not to be the godly person's stance toward God and His law. The law of God is to be internalized, to be deepseated in the source of one's intentions (see also Deuteronomy 32:46). The law can lead us best when it is anchored in the heart. There it can be called up readily to inform our decisions and conscience.

B. Teach Them (v. 7)

7. And thou shalt teach them diligently unto thy children, and shalt talk of them when thou

sittest in thine house, and when thou walkest by the way, and when thou liest down, and when thou risest up.

Teaching the commandments to one's *children* will maintain the covenant through the generations. The Israelites' responsibility and commitment to the teaching of their children is reflected in Psalm 34:11; 78:4-8; 132:12; Proverbs 4:1-4; 6:20-22; 7:24; 8:32, 33. [See question #2, page 440.]

Rather than offering a long list of specific times and places for teaching children, this verse uses a figure of speech known as a *merism*. A merism consists of contrasting pairs to represent the whole. For example, "young and old" is a merism that signifies "everyone." This verse uses the double merism *sittest . . . walkest* and *liest down . . . risest up* to emphasize that one should recount the law wherever one is and make it part of the fabric of one's life and conversation. This requires being alert for those "teachable moments." [See question #3, page 440.]

C. Bind Them (vv. 8, 9)

8. And thou shalt bind them for a sign upon thine hand, and they shall be as frontlets between thine eyes.

The question for the Bible student here is whether the binding in this verse is to be taken literally, figuratively, or both. By the time of Jesus, at least some Jews were applying this command literally through the wearing of phylacteries (Matthew 23:5). Phylacteries are special little boxes worn as *frontlets* between the eyes and/or on the left arm. These little boxes contain the four passages of Exodus 13:1-10, 11-16; Deuteronomy 6:4-9; 11:13-21. The third of these includes today's text; the other three are included because of similar wording.

However, the figurative idea is stronger than the literal! The figurative idea is something like "keep the law before you always and well in mind, no matter what you set your hands to do." This is how the law best functions as *a sign upon* the *hand* of the ancient Jew. The most important point is that the law is to be informing one's life and practice continually. If a literal binding of a phylactery on the body promotes this, then well and good. But it's easy for a literal, physical law-binding to become a holier-than-thou show. Such hypocrisy is exactly what Jesus condemns in Matthew 23:5.

9. And thou shalt write them upon the posts of thy house, and on thy gates.

Jews who take this verse literally attach a *mezuzah* to their door facings. Although the word *mezuzah* itself means "doorpost," in this context it signifies a small container for holding selected passages of Scripture to be attached to a doorpost

(Deuteronomy 6:4-9; 11:13-21). No one knows how far back this practice goes, but it dates from at least the first century BC. The bigger point must not be missed: it is not just the individual who is to be characterized by obedience to the law (v. 8, above); home and community are to be so as well.

The city gate is where court often is conducted in ancient Israel (example: Ruth 4:1-12). Court is to be conducted according to the justice of the Mosaic law.

Reminders

Some time ago, I heard a story about a peculiar habit of a certain bank employee. It seems that this person would unlock his desk every morning, peer into the middle drawer, close the drawer, lock it, and then go about his daily business. He did this for decades, much to the curiosity of the other people in the office.

When the man died, his coworkers were very interested in seeing what he had looked at every working day for most of his life. So they gathered around his desk when it came time to clean it out. Inside that middle drawer was a simple note that said "The debit side is on the left." When I told that story to the bookkeeper at a college where I used to teach, she laughed and said, "Only a bookkeeper would appreciate the humor of that."

Actually, there are several versions of that story floating around. One involves a naval officer who each day looked at a note that said "port, left; starboard, right." We may snicker at the need of those folks to remind themselves daily of the simplest fundamentals of their professions. But such "over-reminding" is the surest way to prevent forgetting. What will you do today to ensure that you do not forget the essentials of the Christian faith?—J. B. N.

IV. Future Answers (Deuteronomy 6:20-24)

A. Son's Question (v. 20)

20. And when thy son asketh thee in time to come, saying, What mean the testimonies, and the statutes, and the judgments, which the Lord our God hath commanded you?

As teachers of their children, the ancient Jews are responsible to understand the meaning of *the testimonies, and the statutes, and the judgments* so they can explain things intelligently to the youngsters. There is to be none of those superficial "because that's the way we've always done it" answers! Practicing the law without understanding it can degenerate to blind legalism. The meaning of the law that is to be passed along is given next. [See question #4, page 440.]

B. Parent's Response (vv. 21-24)

21. Then thou shalt say unto thy son, We were Pharaoh's bondmen in Egypt; and the LORD brought us out of Egypt with a mighty hand.

The parent's reply to the *son* is to be grounded in certain facts of history. God was the one who took the initiative to bring Israel *out of Egypt* and slavery (Exodus 3). God did this at His appointed time in order to fulfill His promise to Abraham to give his descendants the land that the Israelites are on the brink of occupying (Genesis 12:1, 2; 15:13, 14; Exodus 3:6, 8).

22. And the LORD showed signs and wonders, great and sore, upon Egypt, upon Pharaoh, and upon all his household, before our eyes.

The *signs and wonders, great and sore,* refer to the plagues visited *upon Egypt.* As signs and wonders, they demonstrated God's power to Egypt in general, to *Pharaoh* in particular, and to the Israelites themselves *(before our eyes).* The supernatural was clearly evident in the timing and intensity of the plagues, as well as in the specificity in who would and would not suffer them.

The plagues mocked, humiliated, and dethroned Egypt's fictitious gods. For example, the plague of blood dethroned the fertility god(s) of the Nile (Exodus 7:14-24). The plague on the livestock mocked the gods and goddesses of that realm (Exodus 9:1-7). The plague of darkness proved the Egyptian sun god Amon-Re (Egypt's king of gods) to be powerless (Exodus 10:21-23; compare Jeremiah 46:25); this plague was all the more striking given that Amon-Re was also considered to be Pharaoh's divine father. The plague against the firstborn targeted, among others, the heir to Egypt's throne (Exodus 11:5). None of Egypt's so-called gods could protect her from the Lord God.

Home Daily Bible Readings

Monday, Aug. 17—Rewards of Obedience (Leviticus 26:3-13)

Tuesday, Aug. 18—Penalties of Disobedience (Leviticus 26:14-26)

Wednesday, Aug. 19—Consequences of Disobedience (1 Samuel 15:17-26)

Thursday, Aug. 20—Disobeying the Son (John 3:31-36)

Friday, Aug. 21—Listening and Obeying (Psalm 81:11-16)

Saturday, Aug. 22—Treasure God's Commands (Proverbs 2:1-11)

Sunday, Aug. 23—Diligently Observing God's Law (Deuteronomy 6:1-9, 20-24)

23, 24. And he brought us out from thence, that he might bring us in, to give us the land which he sware unto our fathers. And the LORD commanded us to do all these statutes, to fear the LORD our God, for our good always, that he might preserve us alive, as it is at this day.

When children ask "What mean the testimonies, and the statutes, and the judgments?" (v. 20, above), the parents can reply truthfully "Because God said so." But the Lord requires the parents to give a deeper explanation. The ancient promise had granted land to the *fathers* and their descendants (Genesis 12:1-3; 17:8). The Mosaic covenant makes actual possession of land and its consequent blessings dependent on Israel's faithfulness. [See question #5, page 440.]

Conclusion

A. Free to Obey

The ancient Israelites were to understand that God's law was to be both heard and obeyed. One can readily see this in passages such as Deuteronomy 4:1, 5, 6, 13, 14. Centuries later, the non-biblical 1 Maccabees 2:67 offers this instruction: "You shall rally around you all who observe the law. . . . Obey the commands of the law." This requirement is no less important in the New Testament era: "But be ye doers of the word, and not hearers only" (James 1:22). At issue in this passage is obedience to "the perfect law of liberty" that we have in Christ (v. 25).

God brought ancient Israel out of a physical bondage. This was part of His longer-term plan to usher in the Messiah, who would make it possible for all to be redeemed out of spiritual slavery to sin. Committing our lives to Him should include daily obedience to His commandments so that sin may not regain a foothold in our lives. We also remember that Jesus said "If ye love me, keep my commandments" (John 14:15).

B. Prayer

Lord God, some people are neither hearers nor doers. Others hear but do not do. Others, out of misguided zeal, attempt to be doers without really being hearers first. But we need to be both hearers and doers!

We ask for the strength of Your Holy Spirit to be both. Help us to comprehend Your Word as we hear it. Give us courage to implement Your requirements. As we do, may we reap a harvest of souls for eternity. In Jesus' name. Amen.

C. Thought to Remember

Be both a hearer and a doer.

Learning by Doing

This page contains an alternative lesson plan emphasizing learning activities. Some of these activities are also found in the helpful student book, Adult Bible Class.

Into the Lesson

Place a small but noticeable box at the entrance to your classroom; have *OBEY!* written in bold on it. Put a small box on your forehead; you can attach it to a sweatband so it will stay in place. On that box have written the word *HEAR!* (If you desire, you can substitute for *HEAR!* the English transliteration *SHEMA*.)

Begin class by saying, "Few words are more necessary than these two." (Point to them.) Continue: "These two words can be tangible reminders that we must hear the Word of God and not forget it. These are key ideas that God wanted Moses to emphasize to His people. God still wants these ideas emphasized today."

Into the Word

Give each learner a slip of paper that is about 2" by 8½" in size. Say, "Look at today's text to discover important statements of doctrine or ethical truth. On your slip, write one grand doctrinal truth or ethical statement. It should be one you believe is critical to be taught to succeeding generations. In a few minutes, I'm going to collect the slips and read them aloud. Do not put your name on the slip."

If you want to give an example, use verse 1: "God has the authority to command." Anticipate ideas such as "God expects obedience to His commands"; "the laws of God are intended to permeate the lifestyle of the child of God"; and "the history of God's dealing with His people is worth being studied by every generation."

Collect the statements after a few minutes. Read each one aloud and allow time for discussion. Ask questions such as "Why is this one significant?" and "How can we emphasize such an idea to ourselves and to others, such as our children and youth?"

Since the slips will be anonymous, you can correct weak or wrong ideas without causing embarrassment. If your class is large, you can use small groups to discuss the proposals on the slips.

After your discussion winds down, say, "In the week ahead, I will put all these ideas on a single sheet of paper. I will bring copies next Sunday for everyone here. You can take your copy home and put it in a 'remember box.' From there you will be able to take it out for use at family meals, devo-

tional times, etc., for a week or two as a discussion or reflection tool." (Don't forget to do so.)

Have two people read aloud Mark 12:28-31 and Luke 10:25-28, one each. Note that Jesus uses parts of today's text on two different occasions in those texts. Ask the class to look at the contexts to discover differences and similarities. One difference, for example, is how Jesus is questioned.

Note that the responses of the Savior reflect the importance of today's text within the broader picture of Old Testament revelation. Note also that Jesus adds the word *mind*, further emphasizing the total life commitment to the truths here. (The parallel passage to Mark 12:28-31 is Matthew 22:34-40.)

Into Life

Say, "Every day each of us comes in contact with those who are disobeying God's law. What are some examples?" Let the class respond with a few examples, but don't let it drag out. Next, say, "As the Spirit affirms by John, 'Sin is the transgression of the law' (1 John 3:4). How can we interject into conversations this week the thought that there is value in obeying God's law?"

Next, make some observations on the twenty-first century tendency to make more and more laws to control human behavior. Ask how this tendency is like and is unlike the way God works when He creates laws. Make sure your students grapple with the motives that society has for creating laws as compared with the motives God has for doing the same. This can lead to a discussion on how Christians can help society improve its law-making process (you should be careful not to allow the discussion to end up promoting a certain political party, etc.).

Finally, tell your learners that you are going to have "a 7-3-4-7 exercise." Give each a sheet of paper with the word *HEAR* written vertically down the left-hand side. Say, "From the *H*, go forward 7 letters in the alphabet and write the new letter beside the *H*; from the *E*, go back 3 letters; from the *A*, go forward 4 letters; from the *R*, go forward 7 letters."

As the new letters are written down, learners will see the word change from *HEAR* to *OBEY*. Note that the idea is not just the aural reception of a truth, but its application as well.

Let's Talk It Over

The questions on this page are designed to promote discussion of the lesson by the class and to encourage application of the lesson Scriptures. The answers provided are only discussion starters. Let your class talk it over from there.

1. Since we live under the new covenant, why bother studying the Old Testament "commandments, . . . statutes, and . . . judgments"? After all, wasn't the old law nailed to the cross (Colossians 2:14)?

To be sure, many Old Testament laws were intended strictly for the culture of ancient Israel. The New Testament sets these aside, and they are not binding on Christians (examples: Mark 7:19; Acts 15:1-35; Colossians 2:16).

However, the fact that many Old Testament laws are quoted in the New Testament stops us from dismissing all Old Testament laws out of hand. We can propose as a rule of thumb that those Old Testament commandments that deal with the nature of God still apply since God himself never changes in His essence. Thus, "thou shalt have none other gods before me" (Deuteronomy 5:7) is still vital.

To teach and apply such commandments should be a high priority today. Modern culture seems to become ever darker as people drift further from the God who established the moral absolutes that are to frame our world. Success in teaching moral absolutes begins with reacquainting people with the God who first spoke them.

2. What are some spiritual disciplines or habits we can teach our children to help them fill their hearts and minds with God's Word?

The culture of our day is toxic—degradation, destruction, and disobedience can be seen in popular TV shows, advertisements, the Internet, video games, etc. Three important spiritual disciplines or habits we can teach children and youth are summarized with the acronym *PRO*. This stands for Pray daily, Read the Word of God daily, and Obey the Word daily. Teaching children to follow these three disciplines habitually can do much to help them to grow strong in their faith.

3. What are some things in our culture that are competing with the church for the attention of our youth? How do we counteract these?

We may immediately think of TV, music, video games, and the Internet as in question #2, above. But before we launch into a blanket condemnation of these, we should make a careful distinction between *form* and *content*. TV sets, portable mp3 music players, video game consoles, and the Internet are morally neutral forms in and of themselves. They become tools for evil when they are used to communicate unholy content.

The church can counteract cultural influences by using modern forms of communication to promote holiness in youth. You will find DVD-based curriculum, etc., at www.standardpub.com to help you do just that.

4. What are things adult believers can do to encourage youth to take an interest in their spiritual heritage? Why is it important to do so?

Many folks—both youth and adult—have a "that was then, this is now" outlook. We cannot expect youth to appreciate their spiritual heritage if the adults themselves do not. Thus, the solution begins with the adults setting the example in honoring their spiritual heritage.

The importance of spiritual heritage can be established by asking a question: "Would I be able to function today if I could remember nothing about my past to this point?" The obvious answer is *no*. And just as individual people would not be able to function without memory of their pasts, so also the church would not be able to function without memory of her past. Recalling spiritual heritage, either one's own or that of the church, allows us to build on past successes while avoiding the repeat of past mistakes.

5. Why is it important to teach, guide, and train people in the ways of the Lord while they are young?

Several years ago, Barna research made a sobering discovery: the percentage of people who accept Christ drops very sharply when crossing from the preteen into the teenage years. Children go through developmental stages, both mentally and physically. This means that children change their outlook on life as they grow (compare 1 Corinthians 13:11). By the time they become adults, certain thinking patterns have a tendency to become "set," for good or for ill. The existence of developmental stages means that thinking patterns are much more easily shaped and molded in the younger years. It is not manipulative or unethical to recognize that fact and use it to teach godliness.

Deciding to Follow

DEVOTIONAL READING: Joshua 24:14-24.

BACKGROUND SCRIPTURE: Deuteronomy 30.

PRINTED TEXT: Deuteronomy 30:1-10.

Deuteronomy 30:1-10

1 And it shall come to pass, when all these things are come upon thee, the blessing and the curse, which I have set before thee, and thou shalt call them to mind among all the nations, whither the LORD thy God hath driven thee,

2 And shalt return unto the LORD thy God, and shalt obey his voice according to all that I command thee this day, thou and thy children, with all thine heart, and with all thy soul;

3 That then the LORD thy God will turn thy captivity, and have compassion upon thee, and will return and gather thee from all the nations, whither the LORD thy God hath scattered thee.

4 If any of thine be driven out unto the outmost parts of heaven, from thence will the LORD thy God gather thee, and from thence will he fetch thee:

5 And the LORD thy God will bring thee into the land which thy fathers possessed, and thou shalt possess it; and he will do thee good, and multiply thee above thy fathers.

6 And the LORD thy God will circumcise thine heart, and the heart of thy seed, to love the LORD thy God with all thine heart, and with all thy soul, that thou mayest live.

7 And the LORD thy God will put all these curses upon thine enemies, and on them that hate thee, which persecuted thee.

8 And thou shalt return and obey the voice of the LORD, and do all his commandments which I command thee this day.

9 And the LORD thy God will make thee plenteous in every work of thine hand, in the fruit of thy body, and in the fruit of thy cattle, and in the fruit of thy land, for good: for the LORD will again rejoice over thee for good, as he rejoiced over thy fathers:

10 If thou shalt hearken unto the voice of the LORD thy God, to keep his commandments and his statutes which are written in this book of the law, and if thou turn unto the LORD thy God with all thine heart, and with all thy soul.

GOLDEN TEXT: The LORD thy God will circumcise thine heart, and the heart of thy seed, to love the LORD thy God with all thine heart, and with all thy soul, that thou mayest live.—Deuteronomy 30:6.

Call Sealed with Promise
Unit 3: Called to Obey
(Lessons 9–13)

Lesson Aims

After participating in this lesson, each student will be able to:

1. List some blessings promised to the Israelites for turning to the Lord.

2. Explain the connection between obedience to God and circumcision of the heart.

3. Write a prayer of thanksgiving to God for the blessings that he or she enjoys as a result of living in covenant with God.

Lesson Outline

Introduction

A. "God Bless You"

There are many legends about how the phrase "God bless you" originated as a response to sneezing. One theory involves the bubonic plague ("the black death") of the fourteenth century. Sneezing was thought to be associated with the plague, and so when someone sneezed they were immediately blessed in order to maintain health.

Whether or not this is the source of the practice is unknown. However, this theory does at least reflect a view that has been minimized today: one ultimately must reach out to God for blessing.

B. Lesson Background

The history of ancient Israel reveals a pattern of apostasy and rebellion, with sporadic repentance and reform woven in. Apostasy eventually led to the exiles of 722 and 586 BC. But all that is many centuries in the future from the standpoint of today's lesson (about 1406 BC).

By the time apostasy and rebellion come in those centuries of the distant future, it will be "nothing new." The Israelites of Moses' day have already proven their eagerness in that regard (compare Exodus 32; Numbers 14, 16). They are indeed "a stiffnecked people" (Exodus 32:9). Yet God knows how forgiveness and restoration will happen, even many centuries before those exiles occur.

I. Restoration
(Deuteronomy 30:1-5)

A. Action (vv. 1, 2)

1. And it shall come to pass, when all these things are come upon thee, the blessing and the curse, which I have set before thee, and thou shalt call them to mind among all the nations, whither the LORD thy God hath driven thee.

Moses is addressing the Israelites on the plains of Moab, just before their entry into the promised land (Deuteronomy 1:5; 29:1). This address continues Moses' third speech of this covenant renewal book. Moses is turning his attention to a future time when Israel will have been driven from the promised land. Moses uses this prediction to encourage his audience to obedience in the present (28:63-67; 29:28).

Moses has already set before the Israelites the alternatives of curses for disobedience to the covenant commands (Deuteronomy 28:15-68) and blessings for faithfulness and obedience to them (28:1-14; see also 11:26-28; 30:15, 19). The subsequent history of Israel reflects that the sad outcome for disobedience does indeed come to pass. The prediction of exile means that the harsh curses will (or should) bear on every sphere of Israel's existence. After swearing an oath to keep God's covenant, Israel will forsake it by chasing after fictitious gods and breaking the commandments.

But it does not have to be this way! There can be both present and future blessing instead of disaster. It is the reality of blessings that Israel is to call to mind as encouragement to keep the law. Sadly, the law will be "lost and found" as time moves on (2 Kings 22).

The reality of exile will bring a renewed desire to know and keep the law. This will be evident as Jews return to the promised land from exile (see Nehemiah 8). The desire for blessing is a natural human longing. Unfortunately, the desire to want blessings on our own terms seems equally natural. [See question #1, page 448.]

Blessings to ancient peoples come mainly in the form of agricultural bounty. Since about 98 percent of people live on farms, this is the natural way for them to think. As such, agricultural abundance is one of the leading images of divine blessing in the Bible. Such blessings include favorable weather and readily available water that result in bountiful crops and prolific livestock (Deuteronomy 7:13; 8:7; 28:12; Nehemiah 9:25; Psalm 65:9, 10). [See question #2, page 448.]

God is the one who gives and withholds the rain in its proper measure and time, not the pagan fertility gods (see Jeremiah 10:11-13; 14:22; Amos 5:8; 9:6). Drought comes as God's punishment (Deuteronomy 11:16, 17). The way to ensure adequate rain is not to solicit the favor of pagan gods, but to stay true to the God of Israel. A disinterest in the things of God results in agricultural disaster (Haggai 1:1-11). This is a lesson the Israelites have to learn and relearn, even after return from exile. [See question #3, page 448.]

Moving beyond crops and livestock, the Bible speaks also of other material blessings for the Israelites. These include the ready availability of useful metals. All this taken together adds up to wealth, the source of which is God (Deuteronomy 8:9, 18; Ecclesiastes 5:19).

The Bible speaks of spiritual blessings in addition to material ones. The law itself is seen as a blessing because it directs one's paths (Psalm 119). Blessing in the New Testament is the spiritual state of those who belong to Christ and His kingdom. In His beatitudes, Jesus has quite a bit to say about the nature of true blessings (Matthew 5:1-12). The ultimate blessing for humanity is the arrival of Christ, the promised Messiah (Galatians 3:8, 14).

2. And shalt return unto the LORD thy God, and shalt obey his voice according to all that I com-

---

How to Say It

ASHERAH. Uh-*she*-ruh.
ASSYRIAN. Uh-*sear*-e-un.
BAAL. *Bay*-ul.
BABYLONIAN. Bab-ih-*low*-nee-un.
CANAANITE. *Kay*-nun-ite.
CHAUCER. *Chaw*-sir.
ISRAELITES. *Iz*-ray-el-ites.
JUDAH. *Joo*-duh.
MEDIEVAL. me-*dee*-vul.
MOAB. *Mo*-ab.
PATRIARCHS. *pay*-tree-arks.

---

mand thee this day, thou and thy children, with all thine heart, and with all thy soul.

For violating the covenant, those of the (future) southern kingdom of Judah will be exiled to Babylon. That will happen about 820 years after Moses speaks these words. The Israelites will *return unto the Lord* only after God "gets their attention" through this tragedy. The return from exile will not be merely a physical return to the promised land, but also a spiritual return to God. Indeed, a spiritual return is a condition of the physical return.

The primary way the Israelites will *obey* the *voice* of God in exile will be to renounce idolatry permanently. Even though Israel will be tempted to adopt new gods via Greek and Roman expansions, idolatry will never again be a prominent feature of Israelite practice after the Babylonian exile.

B. Result (vv. 3-5)

3. That then the LORD thy God will turn thy captivity, and have compassion upon thee, and will return and gather thee from all the nations, whither the Lord thy God hath scattered thee.

The Israelites will need God's help to get back to their land because in exile they will be under the thumb of a foreign power. God's help will come only after the people seek Him (Deuteronomy 4:29). God's decision to *turn thy captivity* will be a response to, and consequence of, Israel's return to Him. The word *then* in this verse follows after the actions of verses 1 and 2. God indeed will grant forgiveness and restoration. But first Israel will have to call back to mind the words of the covenant.

Deuteronomy 30:1-10 thus functions as a forgiveness clause in the covenant. It offers a second chance after the covenant is violated. God's *compassion* is seen in His readiness to forgive sin, to replace judgment with grace (Deuteronomy 13:17; 2 Kings 13:23; Isaiah 14:1). Part of God's motivation for forgiveness is His promises to the patriarchs (Deuteronomy 4:31; 7:12; Micah 7:18-20). Repentance and recommitment to the covenant can result in restoration because of God's character (Jeremiah 31:20).

4. If any of thine be driven out unto the outmost parts of heaven, from thence will the LORD thy God gather thee, and from thence will he fetch thee.

Captivity and exile will occur in the context of the rise of hostile neighbors. The mighty empire of Assyria will dominate the northern kingdom of Israel (2 Kings 17). The southern kingdom of Judah will barely escape Assyrian captivity (2 Kings 18, 19). But the powerful Babylonian empire, which will overthrow Assyria, will be another story. This empire will thoroughly dominate Judah and carry her people into exile. This is what it means to *be driven out unto the outmost parts of heaven*.

Even so, verse 3 above makes clear that it is the Lord who ultimately scatters the Israelites among the nations. This happens because of sin. Assyria and Babylon will be tools in the Lord's hands to bring corrective punishment (Isaiah 8:7, 8; etc.). Even a Babylonian commander will recognize this fact (Jeremiah 40:1-3).

We stress that this will be *corrective* punishment. This is seen in the fact that God promises to *gather* His people again. The verse before us encourages the Israelites to believe that no nation is so powerful and no distance is so great as to cause God to overlook them or prevent their return. Although the hostile kingdoms may be at "the end of heaven" (Isaiah 13:5) or "the end of the earth" (Deuteronomy 28:49), that is not so far as to be outside the Lord's jurisdiction. [See question #4, page 448.]

5. And the LORD thy God will bring thee into the land which thy fathers possessed, and thou shalt possess it; and he will do thee good, and multiply thee above thy fathers.

The verb tenses here are interesting. As Moses speaks, the nation of Israel has not yet crossed the Jordan River to take possession of the promised land. Yet the about-to-happen possession of the land is such "a given" that the Lord can talk about the land being possessed yet again after the promised restoration.

Thus, the phrase *thy fathers possessed* is past tense for something that has not yet happened—the first possession of the land. The forefathers

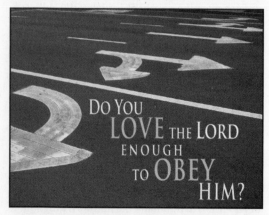

Visual for Lesson 13. *Point to this visual as you ask, "Do we love because we obey, or do we obey because we love? Why?"*

Abraham, Isaac, and Jacob had lived in this land hundreds of years before, but they never "possessed" it in the fullest sense of that word. Now the Israelites are about to do so. Eventually, they will do so a second time as well.

II. Circumcision
(Deuteronomy 30:6, 7)
A. Action (v. 6a)

6a. And the Lord thy God will circumcise thine heart, and the heart of thy seed.

Physical circumcision was instituted as a covenant sign (Genesis 17:1-14; compare Acts 7:8). For ancient Israelites to be circumcised physically is to be recognized as being part of God's covenant people. This sign is tied to the possibility of receiving the blessings promised in the covenant.

However, the fact that circumcision identifies God's people of the covenant can lead to a false confidence. This confidence is unfounded because God's physically circumcised people still have to honor God in their inmost being. This is referred to as circumcision of the *heart*—a spiritual circumcision, if you will (Deuteronomy 10:16; Jeremiah 4:4; 9:25, 26; Romans 2:25-29; Colossians 2:11). Being physically circumcised is not sufficient in and of itself to retain God's covenant blessings.

To have one's heart circumcised includes putting away stubbornness toward God (Leviticus 26:41, 42). The state of uncircumcision in the Old Testament is a figure of speech for the wicked and godless (1 Samuel 14:6; 31:4; 2 Samuel 1:20; Isaiah 52:1; Ezekiel 32:17-32; compare Acts 7:51). After the exile demonstrates that God's people need help in keeping God's laws, it is God himself who *will circumcise thine heart*.

This promise implies that God will strip from their hearts the impediments that make them dull and unresponsive to His commands. Thus God is committing himself to do what Israel herself has been called to do (Deuteronomy 10:16). The language before us resembles the later language of Jeremiah and Ezekiel, two of the exilic prophets. The language anticipates the new covenant (see Hebrews 8:8-10, quoting Jeremiah 31:31-33). God's promise to remove the impediments to obedience provides encouragement that the pattern of sin and punishment can be counteracted.

THE GRINCH

How the Grinch Stole Christmas was a 2000 movie based on the 1957 children's book of the same title. The Grinch is a resident of Whoville. Disgusted by the happiness that Christmas brings the residents of the town, the Grinch decides to "steal" the holiday from them. So he sneaks into town and makes away with all the presents and decorations connected with Christmas. Why is he so mean? As the narrator explains, perhaps it is because his heart is two sizes too small.

Cindy Lou Who then leads the villagers in recapturing the spirit of Christmas in spite of the missing presents. Ultimately, her kind spirit even melts the unfeeling heart of the Grinch. He undergoes a mysterious transformation of his undersized heart, which grows three sizes. The Grinch returns all the Christmas trappings, and the town celebrates once again.

This playful fiction can illustrate the message that Moses spoke to the Israelites when he described how they needed to circumcise their hearts. We all have a self-centered Grinch inside. We all need an operation on our hearts with regard to responding to God's love and devotion. With circumcised hearts, we can all then be more loyal to God's wishes for our lives.   —J. B. N.

B. Result (vv. 6b, 7)

6b. To love the LORD thy God with all thine heart, and with all thy soul, that thou mayest live.

When asked which commandment was the greatest, Jesus replied "Thou shalt love the Lord thy God with all thy heart, and with all thy soul, and with all thy mind" (Matthew 22:36, 37). That reference to Deuteronomy 6:5 looks very much like what we see here in 30:6b.

7. And the LORD thy God will put all these curses upon thine enemies, and on them that hate thee, which persecuted thee.

God had battled victoriously for Israel at the exodus. He will fight for Israel through the conquest period and beyond. But God eventually fights against Israel (Deuteronomy 28:63; Lamentations 2:5). The other nations' victories over Israel will not be because of God's inability. Rather, God will use other nations as "weapons of his indignation" in order to judge Israel (Isaiah 13:4, 5; see also Deuteronomy 28:25, 48; Isaiah 10:5).

But in the future time of Israel's restoration, God will again become the enemy of Israel's enemy. God will allow these other nations to serve His larger purposes. But eventually such nations are to be judged because of their own evil motivations (Isaiah 10:7; Jeremiah 25:12-14). Judgment oracles against foreign nations and against foreign capitals announce their defeat (Isaiah 13:1–23:18; Jeremiah 46–51; Ezekiel 25–32; Amos 1–2:3; Nahum). This will free Israel from future threat, assuring her security. These curses ensure that Israel's enemies won't be able to rise to become oppressive once again.

III. Obedience
(Deuteronomy 30:8-10)
A. Action (v. 8)

8. And thou shalt return and obey the voice of the LORD, and do all his commandments which I command thee this day.

Israel is to be judged harshly with exile because she will break the *commandments* of God. The Israelites have proven their susceptibility to lawbreaking at the incident of the golden calf (Exodus 32). Shockingly, this incident will be repeated (1 Kings 12:28-30).

The worship of gods such as Baal and Asherah round out the idolatry (Judges 3:6, 7; 1 Kings 18:19, 22). Canaanite texts depict them as violent gods who engage in crude sexual behavior, etc. They inspire neither proper worship nor moral behavior in their followers. The worship of Asherah and the planting of Asherah poles and groves probably even includes "sacred" prostitution (1 Kings 14:23, 24; 2 Kings 13:6; 17:16; 21:3, 7; 2 Chronicles 15:16).

Besides worshiping other gods, Israel will fail to keep the moral commandments of the covenant. This also leads to the enactment of curses, captivity, and exile (Amos 2:6-8; 5:10-12, 27; etc.).

To *obey the voice of the Lord, and do all his commandments* requires vigilance. To inform the people of the requirements only once or twice and assume that it will "take" is wishful thinking. After the Babylonian exile, Nehemiah will discover to his dismay that the people are susceptible to backsliding (Nehemiah 13). This speaks all the more to a need for a circumcised heart. Such a heart will enable and further encourage the Israelites to keep all the commandments of the Lord's covenant.

B. Result (v. 9)

9. And the LORD thy God will make thee plenteous in every work of thine hand, in the fruit of thy body, and in the fruit of thy cattle, and in the fruit of thy land, for good: for the LORD will again rejoice over thee for good, as he rejoiced over thy fathers.

Earlier in his speech to the Israelites, Moses set before the people first the blessings that God will give them if they obey His covenant (Deuteronomy 28:1-14). Then he noted the curses that will ensue if they do not obey (28:15-68). Many of the general curses in that chapter are a reversal of the general blessings of that same chapter.

The verse before us recalls these general blessings by reiterating the threefold fruitful bounty and fertility with respect to one's body, livestock, and land (compare 28:4, 11). God will once again *rejoice over* His people. He will once again seek their well-being. This reverses the curse of 28:63 as well. Blessing finally can predominate.

MADE PLENTEOUS

Cultures often fantasize collectively about things that are precious to them. For example, modern Americans may fantasize about money and fame. But cultures of different eras have fantasized about different things. For example, Chaucer, the English writer of the fourteenth century, often rhapsodized about food. It was a commodity not often available in quantity in medieval households.

In his famous *Canterbury Tales,* Chaucer talks about food as a key to understanding the personalities of various pilgrims on their way to Canterbury. The Prioress ate only the daintiest of foods and fed her dogs white bread, while peasants were often hard-pressed to have even brown bread. The Franklin (a land-owning freeman, but not of noble birth) was known for his abundance of foods. It "snowed" meat and drink in his house, and his table never lacked meat pies, fish, and partridges. By contrast, Chaucer also speaks of a poor widow who had no spiced sauces and drank no wine. She subsisted only on white milk, dark bread, broiled bacon, and an occasional egg.

Since abundant food is characteristic of most tables in Western democracies today, we may find it difficult to grasp the full impact of Moses' comments about the abundance of livestock and fruit. "Give us this day our daily bread" is not a heartfelt plea for many of us. Is it so with you?   —J. B. N.

C. Condition (v. 10)

10. If thou shalt hearken unto the voice of the LORD thy God, to keep his commandments and

---

Home Daily Bible Readings

Monday, Aug. 24—Observe God's Laws (Psalm 105:37-45)

Tuesday, Aug. 25—Obey Christ's Commands (Matthew 28:16-20)

Wednesday, Aug. 26—A Gracious and Merciful God (Nehemiah 9:16-20)

Thursday, Aug. 27—A Pledge of Obedience (Joshua 24:14-24)

Friday, Aug. 28—To Love God Is to Obey (1 John 5:1-5)

Saturday, Aug. 29—I Love You, O Lord (Psalm 18:1-6)

Sunday, Aug. 30—Turn to the Lord Your God (Deuteronomy 30:1-10)

---

his statutes which are written in this book of the law, and if thou turn unto the LORD thy God with all thine heart, and with all thy soul.

Although blessings can once again predominate, the first word *if* of this verse makes it clear that these future blessings are contingent on faithful obedience. One must still hear and obey *(hearken unto)* the Word of God and keep His commandments.

The connection between loving God and keeping His commandments is vital (see Deuteronomy 6:5; 1 John 5:3). Grudging obedience is not good enough. The qualifier *with all thine heart, and with all thy soul* calls for sincerity. True and consistent obedience to God's commandments flows from the dedicated heart and soul.

Conclusion

A. Decide for Blessing

The same choice that confronted Israel confronts us today. Will we wholeheartedly commit ourselves to obey God's commandments to yield the hope of blessing, or will we ignore His voice and invite His wrath? If we commit ourselves in obedience to Him, we know that He has enabled us in Christ Jesus to be faithful.

We have an advantage: we have the record of history to warn us. Various kings instituted idolatry in northern Israel (1 Kings 12:28-30; 16:30-33; 2 Chronicles 11:14, 15; etc.). For these sins the northern kingdom was sent into exile; thousands of her citizens were deported into captivity. Likewise, kings of southern Judah practiced idolatry and broke the commandments (2 Kings 8:16-18; 21:1-18; 2 Chronicles 21:5-7; etc.). The southern kingdom too was sent into exile. This happened in three distinct stages, but the people didn't allow themselves to be taught the lessons of stages one and two. [See question #5, page 448.]

"Now these things were our examples, to the intent we should not lust after evil things, as they also lusted" (1 Corinthians 10:6). To shun God invites being shunned by God in return. When we decide for God, we decide for blessing.

B. Prayer

Heavenly Father, we are surrounded by so many distractions! These cause us to walk by sight rather than by faith. But You are there. You always are, and You always will be. Lift our vision to You today so that we can hear Your voice and obey Your commandments. In Jesus' name. Amen.

C. Thought to Remember

Choose God all over again.

Learning by Doing

This page contains an alternative lesson plan emphasizing learning activities. Some of these activities are also found in the helpful student book, Adult Bible Class.

Into the Lesson

Put on display the sentence *To _be_ or not to _be_—that is the question* in large letters. Include the spaces as shown, but leave out the underlining of the spaces.

Refer to Shakespeare's presentation of that choice dilemma in Hamlet's famous monologue. Say, "Well, of course, that is *not* the question. Hamlet was contemplating suicide; that is never the godly choice for attempting to escape the consequences of sin and disaster. Each person does have a choice to make, but it is this." Add an *O* before and a *Y* after the two occurrences of *be* in your original display.

Say, "To obey or not to obey—that *is* the question. We have a choice to make. Will we choose righteousness and enjoy God's blessing, or will we choose sin and incur God's wrath?"

Into the Word

Continue, "I want you to look at the text as I suggest alternatives in each verse, what we may call polar opposites. I will suggest one choice, and I want you to suggest the other."

In the following list, a possibility for the students' choice is given in brackets; however, do not read these. Let students decide their own alternative words or phrases. Write these on the board as you go. To save time, you may wish to prepare these on handouts in advance, especially if you choose to make this an exercise of small groups. Again, do not include the bracketed words.

Verse 1: To be blessed or to be [cursed].
Verse 1: To forget or [call them to mind or remember].
Verse 2: To be separated or to [return].
Verse 2: To obey or to [disobey].
Verse 2: To be wholehearted or to be [halfhearted].
Verse 3: To be scattered or to be [gathered].
Verse 3: To be captive or to be [free].
Verse 4: To be there or to be [here].
Verse 4: To be driven out or to be [gathered].
Verse 5: To be inheritors or to be [dispossessed].
Verse 6: To be dead or to be [alive].
Verse 6: To be hard-hearted or to be [softhearted].
Verse 7: To be vindicated or to be [hated].

Verse 8: To be submissive or to be [disobedient].
Verse 9: To be fruitful or to be [unfruitful].
Verse 9: To be a joy or to be a [sorrow].
Verse 10: To be hearers or to [refuse to listen].
Verse 10: To learn or to be [ignorant].

After you or your small groups finish working through the list, say, "With the choices so clear, why do people disobey God?" Let learners suggest reasons, but also ask them to consider how to confront illogical, unspiritual thinking of those who disobey. Note that bad, sinful choices find their beginnings in selfishness, worldliness, etc.

Display on the board this excerpt from Deuteronomy 30:9, 10: "the Lord will again rejoice over thee for good, as he rejoiced over thy fathers. If thou shalt hearken unto the voice of the Lord thy God, . . . if thou turn unto the Lord thy God with all thine heart, and with all thy soul."

To help your class memorize this excerpt, use the technique from children's education of reading the whole together, erasing a few key words, and repeating the reading. Then erase a few more words and read it again. Repeat the procedure until the class has the thought well in mind. If you think this passage is too lengthy for your class, shorten it as appropriate.

Into Life

Give each learner a paper heart. (These are available at school supply stores, but you can also cut them out of construction paper.) On these hearts have drawn in advance an outline about one-quarter inch from the edge all the way around.

Give these directions: "In the small area around the edge of your heart, write in some of the sins that continue to 'clog' your spiritual heart. Sometime this week, consider letting God 'trim the sin' to make your heart spiritually healthy." Stress to your class that such "circumcision of the heart" is an essential element of obedience to God.

Alternative: distribute handouts with the heading *The Lord will delight in you and make you prosperous.* Ask each learner to prepare a list of personal blessings that result from being committed to living in covenant with Christ. Recommend that students use the list as a prayer stimulus for the week ahead. Their prayers will emphasize personal thanksgiving for blessing in the Lord.

Let's Talk It Over

The questions on this page are designed to promote discussion of the lesson by the class and to encourage application of the lesson Scriptures. The answers provided are only discussion starters. Let your class talk it over from there.

1. How do we recognize that we are starting to expect blessings on our own terms? How do we guard ourselves against this danger?

As Job and his friends found out, not every benefit and detriment that comes our way can be explained in an earthly cause-and-effect manner. Causes may be known only to God, and He may not allow us to discover them through our own reasoning processes. Danger looms when we begin to anticipate that such-and-such outcomes "must" occur because we are (or think we are) on God's side. If we fail to recognize that danger, we may find ourselves sitting in judgment of God when outcomes do not conform to our expectations.

2. How are God's blessings today similar to and different from God's blessings on ancient Israel?

The answers will vary widely according to one's personal situation. For the modern farmer reading this text, the blessings may not be much different from what the ancient Israelites desired: good weather for bountiful crops, etc. Others will think in terms of stable employment situations.

But we are to keep in mind that the most important blessings are spiritual in nature. There are devout Christians who may appear to be downright cursed because of severe problems of health, finances, and family issues. But the fact that they are Christians is itself the greatest blessing possible (compare Habakkuk 3:17, 18). They have the blessing of eternal life. Today we easily can purchase a copy of God's Word at low cost in print and electronic formats; that's a blessing the ancient Israelite did not have. To read, hear, and keep the Word of God is a profound blessing in any era (Revelation 1:3).

3. Which should be the more important motivator in serving God: the desire to have a blessing or the desire to avoid being cursed? Why?

The choices "to have" and "to avoid" look to the future. But the best way to approach this question is to start with a look at the past: we already *have* been blessed! The blessing of Christ came into the world long before any of us were born. None of us served God in order that He might grant that blessing.

Becoming a Christian means having the promise of eternal life—there is no greater blessing than

this. We serve God in gratitude for this accomplished fact. Concerning earthly blessings, we acknowledge that God "maketh his sun to rise on the evil and on the good, and sendeth rain on the just and on the unjust" (Matthew 5:45).

4. What kinds of exiles, if any, do people end up in today as a result of disobeying the Lord? Do you think such exiles are directly caused by God, or are they more along the lines of natural consequences? Why?

King David was one who found himself in various kinds of exile during his life. Before David became king, Saul tried to hunt him down and kill him. David had to hide in caves and deserted areas to remain alive (1 Samuel 19–26). Psalms 52, 54, 57, 59, etc., reveal David's emotions during those times. David had done nothing wrong, yet he found himself pursued.

Later, David found himself in an exile of his own making as a result of his sordid affair with Bathsheba. Because of the emotional relief we read in Psalm 51, we may conclude that those were months of personal misery for him, even though he was physically still in his palace. Even later, David found himself back in a physical exile as a result of Absalom's conspiracy (2 Samuel 15–19).

Today, some may find themselves ostracized (in emotional exile) by unbelieving family, etc., because of a stand for Christ. The title *My Prison Without Bars* of Pete Rose's 2004 book suggests a self-inflicted exile; this exile was due to the (finally admitted) gambling that resulted in a lifetime ban from Major League Baseball. Thus, not all forms of exile are direct punishments from God. But we are to obey Jesus no matter what.

5. What was a time when you felt as if the Lord brought you out of an exile? What happened?

Returning to Psalm 51, which we just mentioned with question #4 above, David felt a great burden lifted when he confessed his sin. Unconfessed sin is cancerous to the spirit. Many self-made exiles can be corrected simply by taking our repentance to the Lord. Some exiles of this life, however, may not end. In certain cases, a person may be permanently shunned by family members because he or she has accepted Christ (see Mark 10:29, 30).